Blackstone's Statutes on

EVIDENCE

Blackstone's Statutes on
EVIDENCE

Sixth Edition

Edited by

Phil Huxley LLB, LLM
Principal Lecturer in Law, The Nottingham Trent University

and

Michael O'Connell BL, M Phil
(King's Inns, Dublin), Barrister, of the Midland & Oxford Circuit

 Blackstone Press

Published by
Blackstone Press Limited
Aldine Place
London
W12 8AA
United Kingdom

Sales enquiries and orders
Telephone + 44-(0)-20-8740-2277
Facsimile + 44-(0)-20-8743-2922
e-mail: sales@ blackstone.demon.co.uk
website: www.blackstonepress.com

ISBN: 1 84174 214 7
© Phil Huxley and Michael O'Connell, 2001
First edition, 1991
Second edition, 1993
Reprinted, 1995
Third edition, 1995
Fourth edition, 1997
Fifth edition, 1999
Sixth edition, 2001

British Library Cataloguing in Publication Data
A CIP catalogue record for this book is available from the British Library

Typeset in 9/10pt Plantin by
Montage Studios Limited, Tonbridge Kent
Printed and bound in Great Britain by Ashford Colour Press Ltd,
Gosport, Hampshire

CONTENTS

EDITORS' PREFACE

This sixth edition of *Blackstone's Statutes on Evidence* follows within two years of the last. In the preface in September 1999 we expressed our view that legislation affecting the law of evidence, especially in criminal cases, would not diminish with the advent of the new millennium. Events may have proved that view to be fairly accurate, although much parliamentary time has been taken up with change and modifications to legal aid in criminal cases, which of course are outside the scope of this book, but of deep concern to criminal practitioners.

The Terrorism Act 2000 is a wide sweeping and highly important piece of legislation but most of its provisions are not yet in force, and a Code of Practice under that Act is still awaited, so we have accordingly decided to retain the Prevention of Terrorism (Temporary Provisions) Act 1989 in the text, in the knowledge that that Act will be wholly repealed when the 2000 Act comes fully into effect. The International Criminal Court Act 2001 received the Royal Assent on 11 May 2001 and although it contains some important evidential provisions we have decided not to include these since no section of that Act has yet been brought into law. The changes made to the Police and Criminal Evidence Act 1984 by the Criminal Justice and Police Act 2001 have been included, although that latter Statute is not yet in force.

We have been unable to resolve the difficulty created by Section 80(4) of the Criminal Justice and Police Act 2001 which attempts to amend Section 63 of PACE 1984 by the insertion of a new Section 9A. According to the current edition of *Archbold*, Section 9A of that Act already exists.

We thank colleagues who have kindly made suggestions on material they would like to see included in the text, and we thank especially Tessa Williamson, Course Leader on the Bar Vocational Course at Nottingham Law School for her view that we should include, *inter alia*, material from the Civil Procedure Rules 1998 and this we have done.

Phil Huxley
Michael O'Connell
July 2001

PART A   CRIMINAL STATUTES

CRIMINAL PROCEDURE ACT 1865
(1865, c. 18)

3.   How far witnesses may be discredited by the party producing

A party producing a witness shall not be allowed to impeach his credit by general evidence of bad character; but he may, in case the witness shall in the opinion of the judge prove adverse, contradict him by other evidence, or, by leave of the judge, prove that he has made at other times a statement inconsistent with his present testimony; but before such last-mentioned proof can be given the circumstances of the supposed statement, sufficient to designate the particular occasion, must be mentioned to the witness, and he must be asked whether or not he has made such statement.

4.   As to proof of contradictory statements of adverse witness

If a witness, upon cross-examination as to a former statement made by him relative to the subject matter of the indictment or proceeding, and inconsistent with his present testimony, does not distinctly admit that he has made such statement, proof may be given that he did in fact make it; but before such proof can be given the circumstances of the supposed statement, sufficient to designate the particular occasion, must be mentioned to the witness, and he must be asked whether or not he has made such statement.

5.   Cross-examinations as to previous statements in writing

A witness may be cross-examined as to previous statements made by him in writing, or reduced into writing, relative to the subject matter of the indictment or proceeding, without such writing being shown to him; but if it is intended to contradict such witness by the writing, his attention must, before such contradictory proof can be given, be called to those parts of the writing which are to be used for the purpose of so contradicting him: Provided always, that it shall be competent for the judge, at any time during the trial, to require the production of the writing for his inspection, and he may thereupon make such use of it for the purposes of the trial as he may think fit.

BANKER'S BOOKS EVIDENCE ACT 1879
(1879, c. 11)

3.   Mode of proof of entries in bankers' books

Subject to the provisions of this Act, a copy of any entry in a banker's book shall in all legal proceedings be received as prima facie evidence of such entry, and of the matters, transactions, and accounts therein recorded.

4. Proof that book is a banker's book

A copy of an entry in a banker's book shall not be received in evidence under this Act unless it be first proved that the book was at the time of the making of the entry one of the ordinary books of the bank, and that the entry was made in the usual and ordinary course of business, and that the book is in the custody or control of the bank.

Such proof may be given by a partner or officer of the bank, and may be given orally or by an affidavit sworn before any commissioner or person authorised to take affidavits.

Where the proceedings concerned are proceedings before a magistrates' court inquiring into an offence as examining justices, this section shall have effect with the omission of the words 'orally or'.

5. Verification of copy

A copy of an entry in a banker's book shall not be received in evidence under this Act unless it be further proved that the copy has been examined with the original entry and is correct.

Such proof shall be given by some person who has examined the copy with the original entry, and may be given either orally or by an affidavit sworn before any commissioner or person authorised to take affidavits.

Where the proceedings concerned are proceedings before a magistrates' court inquiring into an offence as examining justices, this section shall have effect with the omission of the words 'orally or'.

6. Case in which banker, etc., not compellable to produce book, etc.

A banker or officer of a bank shall not, in any legal proceeding to which the bank is not a party, be compellable to produce any banker's book the contents of which can be proved under this Act, or to appear as a witness to prove the matters, transactions, and accounts therein recorded, unless by order of a judge made for special cause.

7. Court or judge may order inspection, etc.

On the application of any party to a legal proceeding a court or judge may order that such party be at liberty to inspect and take copies of any entries in a banker's book for any of the purposes of such proceedings. An order under this section may be made either with or without summoning the bank or any other party, and shall be served on the bank three clear days before the same is to be obeyed, unless the court or judge otherwise directs.

9. Interpretation of 'bank', 'banker', and 'bankers' books'

    [(1)   In this Act the expressions 'bank' and 'banker' mean—
        (a)   an institution recognised under the Banking Act 1987 or a municipal bank within the meaning of that Act;
        (aa) a building society within the meaning of the Building Societies Act 1986;
        (b)   *a trustee savings bank within the meaning* [*the Trustee Savings Banks Act 1981*];
        (c)   the National Savings Bank; and
        (d)   the Post Office, in the exercise of its powers to provide banking services.
    (2)   Expressions in this Act relating to 'bankers' books' include ledgers, day books, cash books, account books and other records used in the ordinary business of the bank, whether those records are in written form or are kept on microfilm, magnetic tape or any other form of mechanical or electronic data retrieval mechanism.]

11. Computation of time

Sunday, Christmas Day, Good Friday, and any bank holiday shall be excluded from the computation of time under this Act.

CRIMINAL EVIDENCE ACT 1898
(1898, c. 36)

1. Competency of witnesses in criminal cases

(1) A person charged in criminal proceedings shall not be called as a witness in the proceedings except upon his own application.

(2) A person charged in criminal proceedings who is called as a witness in the proceedings may be asked any question in cross-examination notwithstanding that it would tend to criminate him as to any offence with which he is charged in the proceedings.

(3) A person charged in criminal proceedings who is called as a witness in the proceedings shall not be asked, and if asked shall not be required to answer, any question tending to show that he has committed or been convicted of or been charged with any offence other than one with which he is then charged, or is of bad character, unless—

(a) the proof that he has committed or been convicted of such other offence is admissible evidence to show that he is guilty of an offence with which he is then charged; or

(b) he has personally or by his advocate asked questions of the witnesses for the prosecution with a view to establish his own good character, or has given evidence of his good character, or the nature or conduct of the defence is such as to involve imputations on the character of the prosecutor or the witnesses for the prosecution or the deceased victim of the alleged crime; or

(c) he has given evidence against any other person charged in the same proceedings.

(4) Every person charged in criminal proceedings who is called as a witness in the proceedings shall, unless otherwise ordered by the court, give his evidence from the witness box or other place from which the other witnesses give their evidence.

2. Evidence of person charged

Where the only witness to the facts of the case called by the defence is the person charged, he shall be called as a witness immediately after the close of the evidence for the prosecution.

3. Right of reply

The fact that the person charged has been called as a witness shall not of itself confer on the prosecution the right of reply.

PERJURY ACT 1911
(1911, c. 6)

13. Corroboration

A person shall not be liable to be convicted of any offence against this Act, or of any offence declared by any other Act to be perjury or subornation of perjury, or to be punishable as perjury or subornation of perjury, solely upon the evidence of one witness as to the falsity of any statement alleged to be false.

14. Proof of certain proceedings on which perjury is assigned

On a prosecution—

(a) for perjury alleged to have been committed on the trial of an indictment . . .; or

(b) for procuring or suborning the commission of perjury on any such trial,

the fact of the former trial shall be sufficiently proved by the production of a certificate containing the substance and effect (omitting the formal parts) of the indictment and trial purporting to be signed by the clerk of the court, or other person having the custody of the records of the court where the indictment was tried, or by the deputy of that clerk or other person, without proof of the signature or official character of the clerk or person appearing to have signed the certificate.

INDICTMENTS ACT 1915
(1915, c. 90)

5. Orders for amendment of indictment, separate trial, and postponement of trial

(1) Where, before trial, or at any stage of a trial, it appears to the court that the indictment is defective, the court shall make such order for the amendment of the indictment as the court thinks necessary to meet the circumstances of the case, unless, having regard to the merits of the case, the required amendments cannot be made without injustice, . . .

(2) Where an indictment is so amended, a note of the order for amendment shall be endorsed on the indictment, and the indictment shall be treated for the purposes of the trial and for the purposes of all proceedings in connection therewith as having been found by the grand jury in the amended form.

(3) Where, before trial, or at any stage of a trial, the court is of opinion that a person accused may be prejudiced or embarrassed in his defence by reason of being charged with more than one offence in the same indictment, or that for any other reason it is desirable to direct that the person should be tried separately for any one or more offences charged in an indictment, the court may order a separate trial of any count or counts of such indictment.

(4) Where, before trial, or at any stage of a trial, the court is of opinion that the postponement of the trial of a person accused is expedient as a consequence of the exercise of any power of the court under this Act to amend an indictment or to order a separate trial of a count, the court shall make such order as to the postponement of the trial as appears necessary.

(5) Where an order of the court is made under this section for a separate trial or for the postponement of a trial—

(a) if such an order is made during a trial the court may order that the jury are to be discharged from giving a verdict on the count or counts the trial of which is postponed or on the indictment, as the case may be; and

(b) the procedure on the separate trial of a count shall be the same in all respects as if the count had been found in a separate indictment, and the procedure on the postponed trial shall be the same in all respects (if the jury has been discharged) as if the trial had not commenced; and

(c) the court may make such order . . . as to [granting the accused person bail] and as to the enlargement of recognizances and otherwise as the court thinks fit.

(6) Any power of the court under this section shall be in addition to and not in derogation of any other power of the court for the same or similar purposes.

PREVENTION OF CORRUPTION ACT 1916
(1916, c. 64)

2. Presumption of corruption in certain cases

Where in any proceedings against a person for an offence under the Prevention of Corruption Act 1906, or the Public Bodies Corrupt Practices Act 1889, it is proved that any money, gift, or other consideration has been paid or given to or received by a person in the employment of Her Majesty or any Government Department or a public body by or from a person, or agent of a person, holding or seeking to obtain a contract from His Majesty or any Government Department or public body, the money, gift, or consideration shall be deemed to have been paid or given and received corruptly as such inducement or reward as is mentioned in such Act unless the contrary is proved.

CHILDREN AND YOUNG PERSONS ACT 1933
(1933, c. 12)

42.   Extension of power to take deposition of child or young person
(1)   Where a justice of the peace is satisfied by the evidence of a duly qualified medical practitioner that the attendance before the court of any child or young person in respect of whom any of the offences mentioned in the First Schedule to this Act is alleged to have been committed would involve serious danger to his life or health, the justice may take in writing the deposition of the child or young person on oath, and shall thereupon subscribe the deposition and add thereto a statement of his reason for taking it and of the day when and place where it was taken, and of the names of the person (if any) present at the taking thereof.
(2)   The justice taking any such deposition shall transmit it with his statement—
(a)   if the deposition relates to an offence for which any accused person is already committed for trial, to the proper officer of the court for trial at which the accused person has been committed; and
(b)   in any other case, to the proper officer of the court before which proceedings are pending in respect of the offence.

43.   Admission of deposition of child or young person in evidence
Where, in any proceedings in respect of any of the offences mentioned in the First Schedule to this Act, the court is satisfied by the evidence of a duly qualified medical practitioner that the attendance before the court of any child or young person in respect of whom the offence is alleged to have been committed would involve serious danger to his life or health, any deposition of the child or young person taken under the Indictable Offences Act 1848, or this Part of this Act, shall be admissible in evidence either for or against the accused person without further proof thereof if it purports to be signed by the justice by or before whom it purports to be taken:
Provided that the deposition shall not be admissible in evidence against the accused person unless it is proved that reasonable notice of the intention to take the deposition has been served upon him and that he or his counsel or solicitor had, or might have had if he had chosen to be present, an opportunity of cross-examining the child or young person making the deposition.

50.   Age of criminal responsibility
It shall be conclusively presumed that no child under the age of [ten] years can be guilty of any offence.

PREVENTION OF CRIME ACT 1953
(1953, c. 14)

1.   Prohibition of the carrying of offensive weapons without lawful authority or reasonable excuse
(1)   Any person who without lawful authority or reasonable excuse, the proof whereof shall lie on him, has with him in any public place any offensive weapon shall be guilty of an offence, and shall be liable—
(a)   on summary conviction, to imprisonment for a term not exceeding [six months] or a fine not exceeding the prescribed sum or both;
(b)   on conviction on indictment, to imprisonment for a term not exceeding [four] years or a fine ... or both.

(2) Where any person is convicted of an offence under subsection (1) of this section the court may make an order for the forfeiture or disposal of any weapon in respect of which the offence was committed.

(3) ...

(4) In this section 'public place' includes any highway and any other premises or place to which at the material time the public have or are permitted to have access, whether on payment or otherwise; and 'offensive weapon' means any article made or adapted for use for causing injury to the person, or intended by the person having it with him for such use by him or by some other person.

SEXUAL OFFENCES ACT 1956
(1956, c. 69)

30. Man living on earnings of prostitution

(1) It is an offence for a man knowingly to live wholly or in part on the earnings of prostitution.

(2) For the purposes of this section a man who lives with or is habitually in the company of a prostitute, or who exercises control, direction or influence over a prostitute's movements in a way which shows he is aiding, abetting or compelling her prostitution with others, shall be presumed to be knowingly living on the earnings of prostitution, unless he proves the contrary.

HOMICIDE ACT 1957
(1957, c. 11)

2. Persons suffering from diminished responsibility

(1) Where a person kills or is a party to the killing of another, he shall not be convicted of murder if he was suffering from such abnormality of mind (whether arising from a condition of arrested or retarded development of mind or any inherent causes or induced by disease or injury) as substantially impaired his mental responsibility for his acts and omissions in doing or being a party to the killing.

(2) On a charge of murder, it shall be for the defence to prove that the person charged is by virtue of this section not liable to be convicted of murder.

(3) A person who but for this section would be liable, whether as principal or as accessory, to be convicted of murder shall be liable instead to be convicted of manslaughter.

(4) The fact that one party to a killing is by virtue of this section not liable to be convicted of murder shall not affect the question whether the killing amounted to murder in the case of any other party to it.

3. Provocation

Where on a charge of murder there is evidence on which the jury can find that the person charged was provoked (whether by things done or by things said or by both together) to lose his self-control, the question whether the provocation was enough to make a reasonable man do as he did shall be left to be determined by the jury; and in determining that question the jury shall take into account everything both done and said according to the effect which, in their opinion, it would have on a reasonable man.

CRIMINAL PROCEDURE (RIGHT OF REPLY) ACT 1964
(1964, c. 34)

1. Right of reply at trials on indictment

(1) Upon the trial of any person on indictment—

(a)   the prosecution shall not be entitled to the right of reply on the ground only that the Attorney General or the Solicitor General appears for the Crown at the trial; and

(b)   the time at which the prosecution is entitled to exercise that right shall, notwithstanding anything in section 2 of the Criminal Procedure Act, 1865, be after the close of the evidence for the defence and before the closing speech (if any) by or on behalf of the accused.

CRIMINAL JUSTICE ACT 1967
(1967, c. 80)

9.   Proof by written statement

(1)   In any criminal proceedings, other than committal proceedings, a written statement by any person shall, if such of the conditions mentioned in the next following subsection as are applicable are satisfied, be admissible as evidence to the like extent as oral evidence to the like effect by that person.

(2)   The said conditions are—

(a)   the statement purports to be signed by the person who made it;

(b)   the statement contains a declaration by the person to the effect that it is true to the best of his knowledge and belief and that he made the statement knowing that, if it were tendered in evidence, he would be liable to prosecution if he wilfully stated in it anything which he knew to be false or did not believe to be true;

(c)   before the hearing at which the statement is tendered in evidence, a copy of the statement is served, by or on behalf of the party proposing to tender it, on each of the other parties to the proceedings; and

(d)   none of the other parties or their solicitors, within seven days from the service of the copy of the statement, serves a notice on the party so proposing objecting to the statement being tendered in evidence under this section:

Provided that the conditions mentioned in paragraphs (c) and (d) of this subsection shall not apply if the parties agree before or during the hearing that the statement shall be so tendered.

(3)   The following provisions shall also have effect in relation to any written statement tendered in evidence under this section, that is to say—

(a)   if the statement is made by a person under the age of eighteen, it shall give his age;

(b)   if it is made by a person who cannot read it, it shall be read to him before he signs it and shall be accompanied by a declaration by the person who so read the statement to the effect that it was so read; and

(c)   if it refers to any other document as an exhibit, the copy served on any other party to the proceedings under paragraph (c) of the last foregoing subsection shall be accompanied by a copy of that document or by such information as may be necessary in order to enable the party on whom it is served to inspect that document or a copy thereof.

(3A)   In the case of a statement which indicates in pursuance of subsection (3)(a) of this section that the person making it has not attained the age of 14, subsection (2)(b) of this section shall have effect as if for the words from 'made' onwards there were substituted the words 'understands the importance of telling the truth in it'.

(4)   Notwithstanding that a written statement made by any person may be admissible as evidence by virtue of this section—

(a)   the party by whom or on whose behalf a copy of the statement was served may call that person to give evidence; and

(b)   the court may, of its own motion or on the application of any party to the proceedings, require that person to attend before the court and give evidence.

(5)   An application under paragraph (b) of the last foregoing subsection to a court other than a magistrates' court may be made before the hearing and on any such

application the powers of the court shall be exercisable [by a puisne judge of the High Court, a Circuit judge or Recorder sitting alone].

(6)   So much of any statement as is admitted in evidence by virtue of this section shall, unless the court otherwise directs, be read aloud at the hearing and where the court so directs an account shall be given orally of so much of any statement as is not read aloud.

(7)   Any document or object referred to as an exhibit and identified in a written statement tendered in evidence under this section shall be treated as if it had been produced as an exhibit and identified in court by the maker of the statement.

(8)   A document required by this section to be served on any person may be served—

(a)   by delivering it to him or to his solicitor; or

(b)   by addressing it to him and leaving it at his usual or last known place of abode or place of business or by addressing it to his solicitor and leaving it at his office; or

(c)   by sending it in a registered letter or by the recorded delivery service addressed to him at his usual or last known place of abode or place of business or addressed to his solicitor at his office; or

(d)   in the case of a body corporate, by delivering it to the secretary or clerk of the body at its registered or principal office or sending it in a registered letter or by the recorded delivery service addressed to the secretary or clerk of that body at that office.

10.   Proof by formal admission

(1)   Subject to the provisions of this section, any fact of which oral evidence may be given in any criminal proceedings may be admitted for the purpose of those proceedings by or on behalf of the prosecutor or defendant, and the admission by any party of any such fact under this section shall as against that party be conclusive evidence in those proceedings of the fact admitted.

(2)   An admission under this section—

(a)   may be made before or at the proceedings;

(b)   if made otherwise than in court, shall be in writing;

(c)   if made in writing by an individual, shall purport to be signed by the person making it and, if so made by a body corporate, shall purport to be signed by a director or manager, or the secretary or clerk, or some other similar officer of the body corporate;

(d)   if made on behalf of a defendant who is an individual, shall be made by his counsel or solicitor;

(e)   if made at any stage before the trial by a defendant who is an individual, must be approved by his counsel or solicitor (whether at the time it was made or subsequently) before or at the proceedings in question.

(3)   An admission under this section for the purpose of proceedings relating to any matter shall be treated as an admission for the purpose of any subsequent criminal proceedings relating to that matter (including any appeal or retrial).

(4)   An admission under this section may with the leave of the court be withdrawn in the proceedings for the purpose of which it is made or any subsequent criminal proceedings relating to the same matter.

CRIMINAL APPEAL ACT 1968
(1968, c. 19)

PART I
APPEAL TO COURT OF APPEAL IN CRIMINAL CASES

Appeal against conviction on indictment

1.   Right of appeal

(1)   [Subject to subsection (3) below] a person convicted of an offence on indictment may appeal to the Court of Appeal against his conviction.

[(2) An appeal under this section lies only—

(a) with the leave of the Court of Appeal; or

(b) if the judge of the court of trial grants a certificate that the case is fit for appeal.]

[(3) Where a person is convicted before the Crown Court of a scheduled offence it shall not be open to him to appeal to the Court of Appeal against the conviction on the ground that the decision of the court which committed him for trial as to the value involved was mistaken.

(4) In subsection (3) above 'scheduled offence' and 'the value involved' have the same meanings as they have in section 22 of the Magistrates' Courts Act 1980 (certain offences against property to be tried summarily if value of property or damage is small).]

2. Grounds for allowing an appeal under s. 1

[(1) Subject to the provisions of this act, the Court of Appeal—

(a) shall allow an appeal against conviction if they think the conviction is unsafe; and

(b) shall dismiss such an appeal in any other case.]

(2) In the case of an appeal against conviction the Court shall, if they allow the appeal, quash the conviction.

(3) An order of the Court of Appeal quashing a conviction shall, except when under section 7 below the appellant is ordered to be retried, operate as a direction to the court of trial to enter, instead of the record of conviction, a judgment and verdict of acquittal.

3. Power to substitute conviction of alternative offence

(1) This section applies on an appeal against conviction, where the appellant has been convicted of an offence and the jury could on the indictment have found him guilty of some other offence, and on the finding of the jury it appears to the Court of Appeal that the jury must have been satisfied of facts which proved him guilty of the other offence.

(2) The Court may, instead of allowing or dismissing the appeal, substitute for the verdict found by the jury a verdict of guilty of the other offence, and pass such sentence in substitution for the sentence passed at the trial as may be authorised by law for the other offence, not being a sentence of greater severity.

4. Sentence when appeal allowed on part of an indictment

(1) This section applies where, on an appeal against conviction on an indictment containing two or more counts, the Court of Appeal allow the appeal in respect of part of the indictment.

(2) Except as provided by subsection (3) below the Court may in respect of any count on which the appellant remains convicted pass such sentence, in substitution for any sentence passed thereon at the trial, as they think proper and is authorised by law for the offence of which he remains convicted on the count.

(3) The Court shall not under this section pass any sentence such that the appellant's sentence on the indictment as a whole will, in consequence of the appeal, be of greater severity than the sentence (taken as a whole) which was passed at the trial for all offences of which he was convicted on the indictment.

5. Disposal of appeal against conviction on special verdict

(1) This section applies on an appeal against conviction [in a case where] the jury have found a special verdict.

(2) If the Court of Appeal consider that a wrong conclusion has been arrived at by the court of trial on the effect of the jury's verdict they may, instead of allowing the appeal, order such conclusion to be recorded as appears to them to be in law required by the verdict, and pass such sentence in substitution for the sentence passed at the trial as may be authorised by law.

[6. Substitution of finding of insanity or findings of unfitness to plead etc.

(1) This section applies where, on an appeal against conviction, the Court of Appeal, on the written or oral evidence of two or more registered medical practitioners at least one of whom is duly approved, are of opinion—

(a) that the proper verdict would have been one of not guilty by reason of insanity; or

(b) that the case is not one where there should have been a verdict of acquittal, but that there should have been findings that the accused was under a disability and that he did the act or made the omission charged against him.

(2) Subject to subsection (3) below, the Court of Appeal shall either—

(a) make an order that the appellant be admitted, in accordance with the provisions of Schedule 1 to the Criminal Procedure (Insanity and Unfitness to Plead) Act 1991, to such hospital as may be specified by the Secretary of State; or

(b) where they have the power to do so by virtue of section 5 of that Act, make in respect of the appellant such one of the following orders as they think most suitable in all the circumstances of the case, namely—

(i) a guardianship order within the meaning of the Mental Health Act 1983;

(ii) a supervision and treatment order within the meaning of Schedule 2 to the said Act of 1991; and

(iii) an order for his absolute discharge.

(3) Paragraph (b) of subsection (2) above shall not apply where the offence to which the appeal relates is an offence the sentence for which is fixed by law.]

7. Power to order retrial

(1) Where the Court of Appeal allow an appeal against conviction . . . and it appears to the Court that the interests of justice so require, they may order the appellant to be retried.

(2) A person shall not under this section be ordered to be retried for any offence other than—

(a) the offence of which he was convicted at the original trial and in respect of which his appeal is allowed as mentioned in subsection (1) above;

(b) an offence of which he could have been convicted at the original trial on an indictment for the first-mentioned offence; or

(c) an offence charged in an alternative count of the indictment in respect of which the jury were discharged from giving a verdict in consequence of convicting him of the first-mentioned offence.

8. Supplementary provisions as to retrial

(1) A person who is to be retried for an offence in pursuance of an order under section 7 of this Act shall be tried on a fresh indictment preferred by direction of the Court of Appeal, . . . [but after the end of two months from the date of the order for his retrial he may not be arraigned on an indictment preferred in pursuance of such a direction unless the Court of Appeal give leave.]

[(1A) Where a person has been ordered to be retried but may not be arraigned without leave, he may apply to the Court of Appeal to set aside the order for retrial and to direct the court of trial to enter a judgment and verdict of acquittal of the offence for which he was ordered to be retried.

(1B) On an application under subsection (1) or (1A) above the Court of Appeal shall have power—

(a) to grant leave to arraign; or

(b) to set aside the order for retrial and direct the entry of a judgment and verdict of acquittal, but shall not give leave to arraign unless they are satisfied—

(i) that the prosecution has acted with all due expedition; and

(ii) that there is a good and sufficient cause for a retrial in spite of the lapse of time since the order under section 7 of the Act was made.]

(2)   The Court of Appeal may, on ordering a retrial, make such orders as appear to them to be necessary or expedient—

(a)   for the custody or subject to section 25 of Criminal Justice and Public Order Act 1994 release on bail of the person ordered to be retried pending his retrial; or

(b)   for the retention pending the retrial of any property or money forfeited, restored or paid by virtue of the original conviction or any order made on that conviction.

(3)   If the person ordered to be retried was, immediately before the determination of his appeal, liable to be detained in pursuance of an order or direction under Part V of the Mental Health Act 1959 [or under Part III of the Mental Health Act 1983 (other than under section 35, 36 or 38 of that Act)],—

(a)   that order or direction shall continue in force pending the retrial as if the appeal had not been allowed; and

(b)   any order made by the Court of Appeal under this section for his custody or release on bail shall have effect subject to the said order or direction.

[(3A)   If the person ordered to be retried was, immediately before the determination of his appeal, liable to be detained in pursuance of a remand under section 36 of the Mental Health Act 1983 or an interim hospital order under section 38 of that Act, the Court of Appeal may, if they think fit, order that he shall continue to be detained in a hospital or mental nursing home, and in that event Part III of that Act shall apply as if he had been ordered under this section to be kept in custody pending his retrial and was detained in pursuance of a transfer direction together with a restriction direction.]

(4)   Schedule 2 to this Act has effect with respect to the procedure in the case of a person ordered to be retried, the sentence which may be passed if the retrial results in his conviction and the order for costs which may be made if he is acquitted.

9.   Appeal against sentence following conviction on indictment

[(1)]   A person who has been convicted of an offence on indictment may appeal to the Court of Appeal against any sentence (not being a sentence fixed by law) passed on him for the offence, whether passed on his conviction or in subsequent proceedings.

[(2)   A person who on conviction on indictment has also been convicted of a summary offence under section 41 of the Criminal Justice Act 1988 (power of Crown Court to deal with summary offence where person committed for either way offence) or paragraph 6 of Schedule 3 to the Crime & Disorder Act 1998 (power of Crown Court to deal with summary offences where person sent for trial for indictable-only offence) may appeal to the Court of Appeal against any sentence passed on him for the summary offence (whether on his conviction or in subsequent proceedings) under subsection (7) of that section or sub-paragraph (4) of that paragraph.]

10.   Appeal against sentence in other cases dealt with at the Crown Court

(1)   This section has effect for providing rights of appeal against sentence when a person is dealt with by the Crown Court (otherwise than on appeal from a magistrates' court) for an offence of which he was not convicted on indictment.

(2)   The proceedings from which an appeal against sentence lies under this section are those where an offender convicted of an offence by a magistrates' court—

(a)   is committed by the court to be dealt with for his offence at the Crown Court, or

[(b)   having been made the subject of an order for conditional discharge, or a community order within the meaning of the Powers of Criminal Courts (Sentencing) Act 2000 or given a suspended sentence, appears or is brought before the Crown Court to be further dealt with for his offence.]

(3)   An offender dealt with for an offence at the Crown Court in a proceeding to which subsection (2) of this section applies may appeal to the Court of Appeal against sentence in any of the following cases:—

(a)   where either for that offence alone or for that offence and other offences for which sentence is passed in the same proceeding, he is sentenced to imprisonment [or to [detention in a young offender institution]] for a term of six months or more; or

(b)   where the sentence is one which the court convicting him had not power to pass; or

(c)   where the court in dealing with him for the offence makes in respect of him—

(i)   a recommendation for deportation; or

(ii)   an order disqualifying him from holding or obtaining a licence to drive a motor vehicle under Part II of the Road Traffic Offenders Act 1988; or

(iii)   an order under section 119 of the Powers of Criminal Courts (Sentencing) Act 2000 (orders as to existing suspended sentence when person subject to the sentence is again convicted);

(iv)   a banning order under section 14A of the Football Spectators Act 1989;] [or

(v)   a declaration of relevance under the Football Spectators Act 1989;] [or

(cc)   where the court makes such an order with regard to him as is mentioned in section 116(2) or (4) of the Powers of Criminal Courts (Sentencing) Act 2000.

(d)   ...].

(4)   For purposes of subsection (3)(a) of this section [and section 11], any two or more sentences are to be treated as passed in the same proceeding if—

(a)   they are passed on the same day; or

(b)   they are passed on different days but the court in passing any one of them states that it is treating that one together with the other or others as substantially one sentence;

and consecutive terms of imprisonment and terms which are wholly or partly concurrent are to be treated as a single term.

11.   Supplementary provisions as to appeal against sentence

(1)   [Subject to subsection (1A) below, an] appeal against sentence, whether under section 9 or under section 10 of this Act, lies only with the leave of the Court of Appeal.

[(1A)   If the judge who passed the sentence grants a certificate that the case is fit for appeal under section 9 or 10 of this Act, an appeal lies under this section without the leave of the Court of Appeal.]

(2)   Where [the Crown Court], in dealing with an offender either on his conviction on indictment or in a proceeding to which section 10(2) of this Act applies, has passed on him two or more sentences in the same proceeding (which expression has the same meaning in this subsection as it has for the purposes of section 10), being sentences against which an appeal lies under section 9[(1)] or section 10, an appeal or application for leave to appeal against any one of those sentences shall be treated as an appeal or application in respect of both or all of them.

[(2A)   Where following conviction on indictment a person has been convicted under section 41 of the Criminal Justice Act 1988 of a summary offence an appeal or application for leave to appeal against any sentence for the offence triable either way shall be treated also as an appeal or application in respect of any sentence for the summary offence and an appeal or application for leave to appeal against any sentence for the summary offence shall be treated also as an appeal or application in respect of the offence triable either way.

(2B)   If the appellant or applicant was convicted on indictment of two or more offences triable either way, the references to the offence triable either way in subsection (2A) above are to be construed, in relation to any summary offence of which he was convicted under section 41 of the Criminal Justice Act 1988 following the conviction on indictment, as references to the offence triable either way specified in the notice relating to that summary offence which was given under subsection (2) of that section.]

(3)   On an appeal against sentence the Court of Appeal, if they consider that the appellant should be sentenced differently for an offence for which he was dealt with by the court below may—

(a)   quash any sentence or order which is the subject of the appeal; and

(b)   in place of it pass such sentence or make such order as they think appropriate for the case and as the court below had power to pass or make when dealing with him for the offence;

but the Court shall so exercise their powers under this subsection that, taking the case as a whole, the appellant is not more severely dealt with on appeal than he was dealt with by the court below.

(4)   The power of the Court of Appeal under subsection (3) of this section to pass a sentence which the court below had power to pass for an offence shall, notwithstanding that the court below made no order under section 23(1) of the Powers of Criminal Courts Act 1973 or section 119 of the Powers of Criminal Courts (Sentencing) Act 2000 in respect of a suspended sentence previously passed on the appellant for another offence include power to deal with him in respect of that sentence where the court below made no order in respect of it.]

[(5)   The fact that an appeal is pending against an interim hospital order under [the Mental Health Act 1983] shall not affect the power of the court below to renew or terminate the order or to deal with the appellant on its termination; and where the Court of Appeal quash such an order but do not pass any sentence or make any other order in its place the Court may subject to section 25 of the Criminal Justice and Public Order Act 1994 direct the appellant to be kept in custody or released on bail pending his being dealt with by the court below.

(6)   Where the Court of Appeal make an interim hospital order by virtue of subsection (3) of this section—

(a)   the power of renewing or terminating it and of dealing with the appellant on its termination shall be exercisable by the court below and not by the Court of Appeal; and

(b)   the court below shall be treated for the purposes of [section 38(7) of the said Act of 1983] (absconding offenders) as the court that made the order.]

12.   Appeal against verdict of not guilty by reason of insanity

A person in whose case there is returned a verdict of not guilty by reason of insanity may appeal to the Court of Appeal against the verdict—

(a)   with the leave of the Court of Appeal; or

(b)   if the judge of the court of trial grants a certificate that the case is fit for appeal.

13.   Disposal of appeal under s. 12

(1)   Subject to the provisions of this section, the Court of Appeal—

(a)   shall allow an appeal under section 12 of this Act if they think that the conviction is unsafe; and

(b)   shall dismiss such an appeal in any other case.

(2)   ...

(3)   Where apart from this subsection—

(a)   an appeal under section 12 of this Act would fall to be allowed; and

(b)   none of the grounds for allowing it relates to the question of the insanity of the accused,

the Court of Appeal may dismiss the appeal if they are of opinion that, but for the insanity of the accused, the proper verdict would have been that he was guilty of an offence other than the offence charged.

(4)   Where an appeal under section 12 of this Act is allowed, the following provisions apply:—

(a)   If the ground, or one of the grounds, for allowing the appeal is that the finding of the jury as to the insanity of the accused ought not to stand and the Court of Appeal are of opinion that the proper verdict would have been that he was guilty of an offence (whether the offence charged or any other offence of which the jury could have found him guilty), the Court—

    (i)   shall substitute for the verdict of not guilty by reason of insanity a verdict of guilty of that offence; and

    (ii)   shall, subject to subsection (5) below, have the like powers of punishing or otherwise dealing with the appellant, and other powers, as the court of trial would have had if the jury had come to the substituted verdict; and

(b)   in any other case, the Court of Appeal shall substitute for the verdict of the jury a verdict of acquittal.

(5)   The Court of Appeal shall not by virtue of subsection (4)(a) above sentence any person to death; but where under that paragraph they substitute a verdict of guilty of an offence for which apart from this subsection they would be required to sentence the appellant to death, their sentence shall (whatever the circumstances) be one of imprisonment for life.

(6)   An order of the Court of Appeal allowing an appeal in accordance with this section shall operate as a direction to the court of trial to amend the record to conform with the order.

[14.   Substitution of findings of unfitness to plead etc.

(1)   This section applies where, on an appeal under section 12 of this Act, the Court of Appeal, on the written or oral evidence of two or more registered medical practitioners at least one of whom is duly approved, are of opinion that—

(a)   the case is not one where there should have been a verdict of acquittal; but

(b)   there should have been findings that the accused was under a disability and that he did the act or made the omission charged against him.

(2)   Subject to subsection (3) below, the Court of Appeal shall either—

(a)   make an order that the appellant be admitted, in accordance with the provisions of Schedule 1 to the Criminal Procedure (Insanity and Unfitness to Plead) Act 1991, to such hospital as may be specified by the Secretary of State; or

(b)   where they have the power to do so by virtue of section 5 of that Act, make in respect of the appellant such one of the following orders as they think most suitable in all the circumstances of the case, namely—

    (i)   a guardianship order within the meaning of the Mental Health Act 1983;

    (ii)   a supervision and treatment order within the meaning of Schedule 2 to the said Act of 1991; and

    (iii)   an order for his absolute discharge.

(3)   Paragraph (b) of subsection (2) above shall not apply where the offence to which the appeal relates is an offence the sentence for which is fixed by law.

14A.   Substitution of verdict of acquittal

(1)   This section applies where, in accordance with section 13(4)(b) of this Act, the Court of Appeal substitute a verdict of acquittal and the Court, on the written or oral evidence of two or more registered medical practitioners at least one of whom is duly approved, are of opinion—

(a)   that the appellant is suffering from mental disorder of a nature or degree which warrants his detention in a hospital for assessment (or for assessment followed by medical treatment) for at least a limited period; and

(b)   that he ought to be so detained in the interests of his own health or safety or with a view to the protection of other persons.

(2)   The Court of Appeal shall make an order that the appellant be admitted for assessment, in accordance with the provisions of Schedule 1 to the Criminal Procedure

(Insanity and Unfitness to Plead) Act 1991, to such hospital as may be specified by the Secretary of State.]

15. Right of appeal against finding of disability

(1) Where there has been a determination under section 4 of the Criminal Procedure (Insanity) Act 1964 of the question of a person's fitness to be tried, and the jury has returned [findings that he is under a disability and that he did the act or made the omission charged against him, the person may appeal to the Court of Appeal against either or both of those findings].

[(2) An appeal under this section lies only—
(a) with the leave of the Court of Appeal; or
(b) if the judge of the court of trial grants a certificate that the case is fit for appeal.]

16. Disposal of appeal under s. 15

(1) The Court of Appeal—
(a) shall allow an appeal under section 15 of this Act against a finding if they think that the finding is unsafe; and
(b) shall dismiss such an appeal in any other case.
(2) ...

[(3) Where the Court of Appeal allow an appeal under section 15 of this Act against a finding that the appellant is under a disability—
(a) the appellant may be tried accordingly for the offence with which he was charged; and
(b) the Court may make such orders as appear to them necessary or expedient pending any such trial for his custody, release on bail or continued detention under the Mental Health Act 1983;
and Schedule 3 to this Act has effect for applying provisions in Part III of that Act to persons in whose case an order is made by the Court under this subsection.

(4) Where, otherwise than in a case falling within subsection (3) above, the Court of Appeal allow an appeal under section 15 of this Act against a finding that the appellant did the act or made the omission charged against him, the Court shall, in addition to quashing the verdict, direct a verdict of acquittal to be recorded (but not a verdict of not guilty by reason of insanity).]

17. Repealed

18. Initiating procedure

(1) A person who wishes to appeal under this Part of this Act to the Court of Appeal, or to obtain the leave of that court to appeal, shall give notice of appeal or, as the case may be, notice of application for leave to appeal, in such manner as may be directed by rules of court.

(2) Notice of appeal, or of application for leave to appeal, shall be given within twenty-eight days from the date of the conviction, verdict or finding appealed against, or in the case of appeal against sentence, from the date on which sentence was passed or, in the case of an order made or treated as made on conviction, from the date of the making of the order.

(3) The time for giving notice under this section may be extended, either before or after it expires, by the Court of Appeal.

18A. Appeals in cases of contempt of court

(1) A person who wishes to appeal under section 13 of the Administration of Justice Act 1960 from any order or decision of the Crown Court in the exercise of jurisdiction to punish for contempt of court shall give notice of appeal in such manner as may be directed by rules of court.

(2)   Notice of appeal shall be given within twenty-eight days from the date of the order or decision appealed against.

(3)   The time for giving notice under this section may be extended, either before or after its expiry, by the Court of Appeal.

19.   Bail

(1)   The Court of Appeal may, subject to section 25 of the Criminal Justice and Public Order Act 1994 if they think fit,—

(a)   grant an appellant bail pending the determination of his appeal; or

(b)   revoke bail granted to an appellant by the Crown Court under paragraph (f) of section 81(1) of the Supreme Court Act 1981 [or paragraph (a) above]; or

(c)   vary the conditions of bail granted to an appellant in the exercise of the power conferred by [either of those paragraphs].

(2)   The powers conferred by subsection (1) above may be exercised—

(a)   on the application of an appellant; or

(b)   if it appears to the registrar of criminal appeals of the Court of Appeal (hereafter referred to as 'the registrar') that any of them ought to be exercised, on a reference to the court by him.

20.   Disposal of groundless appeal or application for leave to appeal

If it appears to the registrar that a notice of appeal or application for leave to appeal does not show any substantial ground of appeal, he may refer the appeal or application for leave to the Court for summary determination; and where the case is so referred the Court may, if they consider that the appeal or application for leave is frivolous or vexatious, and can be determined without adjourning it for a full hearing, dismiss the appeal or application for leave summarily, without calling on anyone to attend the hearing or to appear for the Crown thereon.

21.   Preparation of case for hearing

(1)   The registrar shall—

(a)   take all necessary steps for obtaining a hearing of any appeal or application of which notice is given to him and which is not referred and dismissed summarily under the foregoing section; and

(b)   obtain and lay before the Court of Appeal in proper form all documents, exhibits and other things which appear necessary for the proper determination of the appeal or application.

(2)   Rules of court may enable an appellant to obtain from the registrar any documents or things, including copies or reproductions of documents, required for his appeal and may authorise the registrar to make charges for them in accordance with scales and rates fixed from time to time by the Treasury.

22.   Right of appellant to be present

(1)   Except as provided by this section, an appellant shall be entitled to be present, if he wishes it, on the hearing of his appeal, although he may be in custody.

(2)   A person in custody shall not be entitled to be present—

(a)   where his appeal is on some ground involving a question of law alone; or

(b)   on an application by him for leave to appeal; or

(c)   on any proceedings preliminary or incidental to an appeal; or

(d)   where he is in custody in consequence of a verdict of not guilty by reason of insanity or of a finding of disability,

unless the Court of Appeal give him leave to be present.

(3)   The power of the Court of Appeal to pass sentence on a person may be exercised although he is for any reason not present.

23. Evidence

(1)   For the purposes of an appeal under this Part of this Act the Court of Appeal may, if they think it necessary or expedient in the interests of justice—

(a)   order the production of any document, exhibit or other thing connected with the proceedings, the production of which appears to them necessary for the determination of the case;

(b)   order any witness who would have been a compellable witness in the proceedings from which the appeal lies to attend for examination and be examined before the Court, whether or not he was called in those proceeedings; and

[(c)   receive any evidence which was not adduced in the proceedings from which the appeal lies.]

[(2)   The Court of Appeal shall, in considering whether to receive any evidence, have regard in particular to—

(a)   whether the evidence appears to the Court to be capable of belief;

(b)   whether it appears to the Court that the evidence may afford any ground for allowing the appeal;

(c)   whether the evidence would have been admissible in the proceedings from which the appeal lies on an issue which is the subject of the appeal; and

(d)   whether there is a reasonable explanation for the failure to adduce the evidence in those proceedings.]

(3)   Subsection (1)(c) above applies to [evidence of a] witness (including the appellant) who is competent but not compellable.

(4)   For [the purposes of an appeal under] this Part of this Act, the Court of Appeal may, if they think it necessary or expedient in the interests of justice, order the examination of any witness whose attendance might be required under subsection (1)(b) above to be conducted, in manner provided by rules of court, before any judge or officer of the Court or other person appointed by the Court for the purpose, and allow the admission of any depositions so taken as evidence before the Court.

23A.   Power to order investigations

(1)   On an appeal against conviction the Court of Appeal may direct the Criminal Cases Review Commission to investigate and report to the Court on any matter if it appears to the Court that—

(a)   the matter is relevant to the determination of the case and ought, if possible, to be resolved before the case is determined;

(b)   an investigation of the matter by the Commission is likely to result in the Court being able to resolve it; and

(c)   the matter cannot be resolved by the Court without an investigation by the Commission.

(2)   A direction by the Court of Appeal under subsection (1) above shall be given in writing and shall specify the matter to be investigated.

(3)   Copies of such a direction shall be made available to the appellant and the respondent.

(4)   Where the Commission have reported to the Court of Appeal on any matter which they have been directed under subsection (1) above to investigate, the Court—

(a)   shall notify the appellant and the respondent that the Commission have reported; and

(b)   may make available to the appellant and the respondent the report of the Commission and any statements, opinions and reports which accompanied it.

24–28   Repealed

29. Effect of appeal on sentence

(1)   The time during which an appellant is in custody pending the determination of his appeal shall, subject to any direction which the Court of Appeal may give to the contrary, be reckoned as part of the term of any sentence to which he is for the time being subject.

(2)   Where the Court of Appeal give a contrary direction under subsection (1) above, they shall state their reasons for doing so; and they shall not give any such direction where—

(a)   leave to appeal has been granted; or

(b)   a certificate has been given by the judge of the court of trial under—

(i)   section 1 or 11(1A) of this Act; or

(ii)   section 81(1B) of the Supreme Court Act 1981; or

(c)   the case has been referred to them [under section 9 of the Criminal Appeal Act 1995.]

(3)   When an appellant is [granted] bail under section 19 of this Act, the time during which he is [released on bail] shall be disregarded in computing the term of any sentence to which he is for the time being subject.

(4)   The term of any sentence passed by the Court of Appeal under section 3, 4, 5, 11 or 13(4) of this Act shall, unless the Court otherwise direct, begin to run from the time when it would have begun to run if passed in the proceedings from which the appeal lies.

30. Restitution of property

(1)   The operation of an order for the restitution of property to a person made by the Crown Court shall, unless the Court direct to the contrary in any case in which, in their opinion, the title to the property is not in dispute, be suspended until (disregarding any power of a court to grant leave to appeal out of time) there is no further possibility of an appeal on which the order could be varied or set aside, and provision may be made by rules of court for the custody of any property in the meantime.

(2)   The Court of Appeal may by order annul or vary any order made by the court of trial for the restitution of property to any person, although the conviction is not quashed; and the order, if annulled, shall not take effect and, if varied, shall take effect as so varied.

(3)   Where the House of Lords restores a conviction, it may make any order for the restitution of property which the court of trial could have made.

31. Powers of Court under Part I which are exercisable by single judge

(1)   There may be exercised by a single judge in the same manner as by the Court of Appeal and subject to the same provisions—

(a)   the powers of the Court of Appeal under this Part of this Act specified in subsection (2) below;

(b)   the power to give directions under section 3(4) of the Sexual Offences (Amendment) Act 1992; and

(c)   the powers to make orders for the payment of costs under sections 16 to 18 of the Prosecution of Offences Act 1985 in proceedings under this Part of this Act.

(2)   The powers mentioned in subsection (1)(a) above are the following:—

(a)   to give leave to appeal;

(b)   to extend the time within which notice of appeal or of application for leave to appeal may be given;

(c)   to allow an appellant to be present at any proceedings;

(d)   to order a witness to attend for examination;

(e)   to exercise the powers conferred by section 19 of this Act;

(f)   to make orders under section 8(2) of this Act and discharge or vary such orders;

    (g) ...
    (h)   to give directions under section 29(1) of this Act.

    (2A)   The power of the Court of Appeal to suspend a person's disqualification under [section 40(2) of the Road Traffic Offenders Act 1988] may be exercised by a single judge in the same manner as it may be exercised by the Court.

    (2B)   The power of the Court of Appeal to grant leave to appeal under section 159 of the Criminal Justice Act 1988 may be exercised by a single judge in the same manner as it may be exercised by the Court.

    (3)   If the single judge refuses an application on the part of an appellant to exercise in his favour any of the powers above specified, the appellant shall be entitled to have the application determined by the Court of Appeal.

31A.   Powers of Court under Part I which are exercisable by registrar

    (1)   The powers of the Court of Appeal under this Part of this Act which are specified in subsection (2) below may be exercised by the registrar.

    (2)   The powers mentioned in subsection (1) above are the following—

    (a)   to extend the time within which notice of appeal or of application for leave to appeal may be given;

    (b)   to order a witness to attend for examination; and

    (c)   to vary the conditions of bail granted to an appellant by the Court of Appeal or the Crown Court.

    (3)   No variation of the conditions of bail granted to an appellant may be made by the registrar unless he is satisfied that the respondent does not object to the variation; but, subject to that, the powers specified in that subsection are to be exercised by the registrar in the same manner as by the Court of Appeal and subject to the same provisions.

    (4)   If the registrar refuses an application on the part of an appellant to exercise in his favour any of the powers specified in subsection (2) above, the appellant shall be entitled to have the application determined by a single judge.

32.   Transcripts

    (1)   Rules of court may provide—

    (a)   for the making of a record (whether by means of shorthand notes, by mechanical means or otherwise) of any proceedings in respect of which an appeal lies (with or without leave) to the Court of Appeal; and

    (b)   for the making and verification of a transcript of any such record and for supplying the transcript (on payment of such charge, if any, as may be fixed for the time being by the Treasury) to the registrar for the use of the Court of Appeal or any judge exercising the powers of a judge of the Court, and to such other person and in such circumstances as may be prescribed by the rules.

    (2)   Without prejudice to subsection (1) above, the Secretary of State may, if he thinks fit, in any case direct that a transcript shall be made of any such record made in pursuance of the rules and be supplied to him.

    (3)   The cost—

    (a)   of making any such record in pursuance of the rules; and

    (b)   of making and supplying in pursuance of this section any transcript ordered to be supplied to the registrar or the Secretary of State,

shall be defrayed, in accordance with scales of payment fixed for the time being by the Treasury, out of moneys provided by Parliament; and the cost of providing and installing at a court any equipment required for the purpose of making such a record or transcript shall also be defrayed out of moneys so provided.

PART II
APPEAL TO HOUSE OF LORDS FROM COURT OF APPEAL (CRIMINAL DIVISION)

33. Right of appeal to House of Lords

(1)   An appeal lies to the House of Lords, at the instance of the defendant or the prosecutor, from any decision of the Court of Appeal on an appeal to that court under Part I of this Act [or section 9 (preparatory hearings) of the Criminal Justice Act 1987] or section 35 of the Criminal Procedure and Investigations Act 1996.

(2)   The appeal lies only with the leave of the Court of Appeal or the House of Lords; and leave shall not be granted unless it is certified by the Court of Appeal that a point of law of general public importance is involved in the decision and it appears to the Court of Appeal or the House of Lords (as the case may be) that the point is one which ought to be considered by the House.

[(3)   Except as provided by this Part of this Act and section 13 of the Administration of Justice Act 1960 (appeal in cases of contempt of court), no appeal shall lie from any decision of the criminal division of the Court of Appeal.]

34. Application for leave to appeal

(1)   An application to the Court of Appeal for leave to appeal to the House of Lords shall be made within the period of fourteen days beginning with the date of the decision of the Court; and an application to the House of Lords for leave shall be made within the period of fourteen days beginning with the date on which the application for leave is refused by the Court of Appeal.

(2)   The House of Lords or the Court of Appeal may, upon application made at any time by the defendant, extend the time within which an application may be made by him to that House or the Court under subsection (1) above.

(3)   An appeal to the House of Lords shall be treated as pending until any application for leave to appeal is disposed of and, if leave to appeal is granted, until the appeal is disposed of; and for purposes of this Part of this Act an application for leave to appeal shall be treated as disposed of at the expiration of the time within which it may be made, if it is not made within that time.

35. Hearing and disposal of appeal

(1)   An appeal under this Part of this Act shall not be heard and determined by the House of Lords unless there are present at least three of the persons designated Lords of Appeal by section 5 of the Appellate Jurisdiction Act 1876.

(2)   Any order of the House of Lords which provides for the hearing of applications for leave to appeal by a committee constituted in accordance with section 5 of the said Act of 1876 may direct that the decision of that committee shall be taken on behalf of the House.

(3)   For the purpose of disposing of an appeal, the House of Lords may exercise any powers of the Court of Appeal or may remit the case to the Court.

36. Bail on appeal by defendant

The Court of Appeal may, subject to section 25 of the Criminal Justice and Public Order Act 1994, if it seems fit, on the application of a person appealing or applying for leave to appeal to the House of Lords, [other than a person appealing or applying for leave to appeal from a decision on an appeal under section 9(11) of the Criminal Justice Act 1987 or section 35 of the Criminal Procedure and Investigations Act 1996 (appeals against orders and rulings at preparatory hearings) grant him bail pending the determination of his appeal.

37.   Detention of defendant on appeal by the Crown

(1)   The following provisions apply where, immediately after a decision of the Court of Appeal from which an appeal lies to the House of Lords, the prosecutor is granted or gives notice that he intends to apply for, leave to appeal.

(2)   If, but for the decision of the Court of Appeal, the defendant would be liable to be detained, the Court of Appeal may make an order providing for his detention, or directing that he shall not be released except on bail (which may be granted by the Court as under section 36 above), so long as an appeal to the House of Lords is pending.

(3)   An order under this section shall (unless the appeal has previously been disposed of) cease to have effect at the expiration of the period for which the defendant would have been liable to be detained but for the decision of the Court of Appeal.

(4)   Where an order is made under this section in the case of a defendant who, but for the decision of the Court of Appeal, would be liable to be detained in pursuance of—

(a)   an order or direction under [Part III of the Mental Health Act 1983 (otherwise than under section 35, 36 or 38 of that Act)] (admission to hospital of persons convicted by criminal courts); or

(b)   an order under section 5(1) of the Criminal Procedure (Insanity) Act 1964 (admission to hospital following verdict of insanity or unfitness to stand trial),

the order under this section shall be one authorising his continued detention in pursuance of the order or direction referred to in paragraph (a) or (b) of this subsection; and the provisions of [the Mental Health Act 1983] with respect to persons liable to be detained as mentioned in this subsection (including provisions as to the renewal of authority for detention and the removal or discharge of patients) shall apply accordingly.

[(4A)   Where an order is made under this section in the case of a defendant who, but for the decision of the Court of Appeal, would be liable to be detained in pursuance of a remand under [section 36 of the Mental Health Act 1983] or an interim hospital order under [section 38] of that Act, the order may, if the Court of Appeal thinks fit, be one authorising his continued detention in a hospital or mental nursing home and in that event—

(a)   subsection (3) of this section shall not apply to the order;

(b)   [Part III of the said Act of 1983] shall apply to him as if he had been ordered under this section to be detained in custody so long as an appeal to the House of Lords is pending and were detained in pursuance of a transfer direction together with a restriction direction; and

(c)   if the defendant, having been subject to an interim hospital order, is detained by virtue of this subsection and the appeal by the prosecutor succeeds, subsection (2) of the said [section 38] (power of court to make hospital order in the absence of an offender who is subject to an interim hospital order) shall apply as if the defendant were still subject to an interim hospital order.]

(5)   Where the Court of Appeal have power to make an order under this section, and either no such order is made or the defendant is released or discharged, by virtue of [subsection (3), (4) or (4A)] of this section, before the appeal is disposed of, the defendant shall not be liable to be again detained as the result of the decision of the House of Lords on the appeal.

38.   Presence of defendant at hearing

A defendant who has been convicted of an offence and who is detained pending an appeal to the House of Lords shall not be entitled to be present on the hearing of the appeal or of any proceedings preliminary or incidental thereto, except where an order of the House of Lords authorises him to be present, or where the House or the Court of Appeal, as the case may be, give him leave to be present.

39-42   Repealed

43. Effect of appeal on sentence

(1)   Where a person subject to a sentence is [granted] bail under section 36 or 37 of this Act, the time during which he is [released on bail] shall be disregarded in computing the term of his sentence.

(2)   Subject to the foregoing subsection, any sentence passed on an appeal to the House of Lords in substitution for another sentence shall, unless that House or the Court of Appeal otherwise direct, begin to run from the time when the other sentence would have begun to run.

44. Powers of Court of Appeal under Part II which are exercisable by single judge

[(1)]   [There may be exercised by a single judge—

(a)   the powers of the Court of Appeal under this Part of this Act—

(i)   to extend the time for making an application for leave to appeal;

(ii)   to make an order for or in relation to bail; and

(iii)   to give leave for a person to be present at the hearing of any proceedings preliminary or incidental to an appeal; and

(b)   their powers to make orders for the payment of costs under sections 16 and 17 of the Prosecution of Offences Act 1985 in proceedings under this Part of this Act],
but where the judge refuses an application to exercise any of the said powers the applicant shall be entitled to have the application determined by the Court of Appeal.

(2)   The power of the Court of Appeal to suspend a person's disqualification under section 40(3) of the Road Traffic Offenders Act 1988 may be exercised by a single judge, but where the judge refuses an application to exercise that power the applicant shall be entitled to have the application determined by the Court of Appeal.

PART III
MISCELLANEOUS AND GENERAL

44A.   Appeals in cases of death

(1)   Where a person has died—

(a)   any relevant appeal which might have been begun by him had he remained alive may be begun by a person approved by the Court of Appeal; and

(b)   where any relevant appeal was begun by him while he was alive or is begun in relation to his case by virtue of paragraph (a) above or by a reference by the Criminal Cases Review Commission, any further step which might have been taken by him in connection with the appeal if he were alive may be taken by a person so approved.

(2)   In this section 'relevant appeal' means—

(a)   an appeal under section 1, 9, 12 or 15 of this Act; or

(b)   an appeal under section 33 of this Act from any decision of the Court of Appeal on an appeal under any of those sections.

(3)   Approval for the purposes of this section may only be given to—

(a)   the widow or widower of the dead person;

(b)   a person who is the personal representative (within the meaning of section 55(1)(xi) of the Administration of Estates Act 1925) of the dead person; or

(c)   any other person appearing to the Court of Appeal to have, by reason of a family or similar relationship with the dead person, a substantial financial or other interest in the determination of a relevant appeal relating to him.

(4)   Except in the case of an appeal begun by a reference by the Criminal Cases Review Commission, an application for such approval may not be made after the end of the period of one year beginning with the date of death.

(5)   Where this section applies, any reference in this Act to the appellant shall, where appropriate, be construed as being or including a reference to the person approved under this section.

(6)   The power of the Court of Appeal to approve a person under this section may be exercised by a single judge in the same manner as by the Court of Appeal and subject to the same provisions; but if the single judge refuses the application, the applicant shall be entitled to have the application determined by the Court of Appeal.

45.   Construction of references in Parts I and II to Court of Appeal and a single judge

[(1)   References in Parts I and II [and section 44A] of this Act to the Court of Appeal shall be construed as references to the criminal division of the Court.]

(2)   The references in sections 31[, 31A, 44 and 44A] of this Act to a single judge are to any judge of the Court of Appeal or . . . of the High Court.

48.   Appeal in capital cases

Schedule 4 to this Act shall have effect so as to modify and supplement certain provisions in Parts I and II of this Act in relation to cases involving sentence of death.

49.   Saving for prerogative of mercy

Nothing in this Act is to be taken as affecting Her Majesty's prerogative of mercy.

50.   Meaning of 'sentence'

[(1)   In this Act 'sentence', in relation to an offence, includes any order made by a court when dealing with an offender including, in particular—

(a)   a hospital order under Part III of the Mental Health Act 1983, with or without a restriction order;

(b)   an interim hospital order under that Part;

(c)   a recommendation for deportation;

(d)   a confiscation order under the Drug Trafficking Offences Act 1986 other than one made by the High Court;

(e)   a confiscation order under Part VI of the Criminal Justice Act 1988;

(f)   an order varying a confiscation order of a kind which is included by virtue of paragraph (d) or (e) above;

(g)   an order made by the Crown Court varying a confiscation order which was made by the High Court by virtue of section 4A of the Act of 1986; and

(h)   a declaration of relevance under the Football Spectators Act 1989.]

[(1A)   Section 14 of the Powers of Criminal Courts (Sentencing) Act 2000 (under which a conviction of an offence for which . . . an order for conditional or absolute discharge is made is deemed not to be a conviction except for certain purposes) shall not prevent an appeal under this Act, whether against conviction or otherwise.]

(2)   Any power of the criminal division of the Court of Appeal to pass a sentence includes a power to make a recommendation for deportation in cases where the court from which the appeal lies had power to make such a recommendation.

(3)   An order under section 17 of the Access to Justice Act 1999 is not a sentence for the purposes of this Act.

51.   Interpretation

(1)   In this Act, except where the context otherwise requires—

'appeal', where used in Part I or II of this Act, means appeal under that Part, and 'appellant' has a corresponding meaning and in Part I includes a person who has given notice of application for leave to appeal;

'the court of trial', in relation to an appeal, means the court from which the appeal lies;

'the defendant', in Part II of this Act, means, in relation to an appeal, the person who was the appellant before the criminal division of the Court of Appeal, and references to the prosecutor shall be construed accordingly;

'duly approved', in relation to a registered medical practitioner, means approved
for the purposes of section 12 of the Mental Health Act 1983 by the Secretary of
State as having special experience in the diagnosis or treatment of mental disorder;
'the judge of the court of trial' means, where the Crown Court comprises justices
of the peace, the judge presiding;
['registered medical practitioner' means a fully registered person within the
meaning of the Medical Act 1983;]
'under disability' has the meaning assigned to it by section 4 of the Criminal
Procedure (Insanity) Act 1964 (unfitness to plead); and
. . .

(2)   Any expression used in this Act which is defined in [section 145(1) and (1AA)
of the Mental Health Act 1983] has the same meaning in this Act as in that Act.

[(2A)   Subsections (2) and (3) of section 54 of the Mental Health Act 1983 shall
have effect with respect to proof of the appellant's medical condition for the purposes of
section 6, 14 or 14A of this Act as they have effect with respect to proof of an offender's
mental condition for the purposes of section 37(2)(a) of that Act.]

(3)   . . .

COURTS-MARTIAL (APPEALS) ACT 1968
(1968, c. 20)

28.   Evidence

(1)   The Appeal Court may—

(a)   order the production of any document, exhibit or other thing connected with
the proceedings the production of which appears to them necessary for the determination of the case;

(b)   order any witness who would have been a compellable witness at the trial to
attend for examination and be examined before the Court, whether or not he was called
at the trial; and

(c)   receive [any evidence which was not adduced at the trial].

[(2)   The Appeal Court shall, in considering whether to receive any evidence, have
regard in particular to—

(a)   whether the evidence appears to the Court to be capable of belief;

(b)   whether it appears to the Court that the evidence may afford any ground for
allowing the appeal;

(c)   whether the evidence would have been admissible at the trial on an issue
which is the subject of the appeal; and

(d)   whether there is a reasonable explanation for the failure to adduce the
evidence at the trial.]

(3)   Subsection (1)(c) above applies to [evidence of a] witness (including the
appellant) who is competent but not compellable. . . .

(4)   The Appeal Court may order the examination of any witness whose attendance
may be required under subsection (1)(b) of this section to be conducted in the
prescribed manner before any judge of the Court or before any other person appointed
by the Court for that purpose, and allow the admission of any depositions so taken as
evidence before the Court.

THEFT ACT 1968
(1968, c. 60)

22.   Handling stolen goods

(1)   A person handles stolen goods if (otherwise than in the course of the stealing)
knowing or believing them to be stolen goods he dishonestly receives the goods, or
dishonestly undertakes or assists in their retention, removal, disposal or realisation by or
for the benefit of another person, or if he arranges to do so.

(2)   A person guilty of handling stolen goods shall on conviction on indictment be liable to imprisonment for a term not exceeding fourteen years.

25.   Going equipped for stealing, etc.

(1)   A person shall be guilty of an offence if, when not at his place of abode, he has with him any article for use in the course of or in connection with any burglary, theft or cheat.

(2)   A person guilty of an offence under this section shall on conviction on indictment be liable to imprisonment for a term not exceeding three years.

(3)   Where a person is charged with an offence under this section, proof that he had with him any article made or adapted for use in committing a burglary, theft or cheat shall be evidence that he had it with him for such use.

(4)   Any person may arrest without warrant anyone who is, or whom he, with reasonable cause, suspects to be, committing an offence under this section.

(5)   For purposes of this section an offence under section 12(1) of this Act of taking a conveyance shall be treated as theft, and 'cheat' means an offence under section 15 of this Act.

27.   Evidence and procedure on charge of theft or handling stolen goods

(1)   Any number of persons may be charged in one indictment, with reference to the same theft, with having at different times or at the same time handled all or any of the stolen goods, and the persons so charged may be tried together.

(2)   On the trial of two or more persons indicted for jointly handling any stolen goods the jury may find any of the accused guilty if the jury are satisfied that he handled all or any of the stolen goods, whether or not he did so jointly with the other accused or any of them.

(3)   Where a person is being proceeded against for handling stolen goods (but not for any offence other than handling stolen goods), then at any stage of the proceedings, if evidence has been given of his having or arranging to have in his possession the goods the subject of the charge, or of his undertaking or assisting in, or arranging to undertake or assist in, their retention, removal, disposal or realisation, the following evidence shall be admissible for the purpose of proving that he knew or believed the goods to be stolen goods:—

(a)   evidence that he has had in his possession, or has undertaken or assisted in the retention, removal, disposal or realisation of, stolen goods from any theft taking place not earlier than twelve months before the offence charged; and

(b)   (provided that seven days' notice in writing has been given to him of the intention to prove the conviction) evidence that he has within the five years preceding the date of the offence charged been convicted of theft or of handling stolen goods.

(4)   In any proceedings for the theft of anything in the course of transmission (whether by post or otherwise), or for handling stolen goods from such a theft, a statutory declaration made by any person that he despatched or received or failed to receive any goods or postal packet, or that any goods or postal packet when despatched or received by him were in a particular state or condition, shall be admissible as evidence of the facts stated in the declaration, subject to the following conditions:—

(a)   a statutory declaration shall only be admissible where and to the extent to which oral evidence to the like effect would have been admissible in the proceedings; and

(b)   a statutory declaration shall only be admissible if at least seven days before the hearing or trial a copy of it has been given to the person charged, and he has not, at least three days before the hearing or trial or within such further time as the court may in special circumstances allow, given the prosecutor written notice requiring the attendance at the hearing or trial of the person making the declaration.

[(4A)   Where the proceedings mentioned in subsection (4) above are proceedings before a magistrates' court inquiring into an offence as examining justices that subsection shall have effect with the omission of the words from 'subject to the following conditions' to the end of the subsection.]

(5)   This section is to be construed in accordance with section 24 of this Act; and in subsection (3)(b) above the reference to handling stolen goods shall include any corresponding offence committed before the commencement of this Act.

30.   Husband and wife

(1)   This Act shall apply in relation to the parties to a marriage, and to property belonging to the wife or husband whether or not by reason of an interest derived from the marriage, as it would apply if they were not married and any such interest subsisted independently of the marriage.

(2)   Subject to subsection (4) below, a person shall have the same right to bring proceedings against that person's wife or husband for any offence (whether under this Act or otherwise), as if they were not married.

[(3)   *Repealed by the Police and Criminal Evidence Act 1984, s. 18, Sched. 7.*]

(4)   Proceedings shall not be instituted against a person for any offence of stealing or doing unlawful damage to property which at the time of the offence belongs to that person's wife or husband, or for any attempt, incitement or conspiracy to commit such an offence, unless the proceedings are instituted by or with the consent of the Director of Public Prosecutions:

Provided that—

(a)   this subsection shall not apply to proceedings against a person for an offence—

(i)   if that person is charged with committing the offence jointly with the wife or husband; or

(ii)   if by virtue of any judicial decree or order (wherever made) that person and the wife or husband are at the time of the offence under no obligation to cohabit [*and*

(b)   *Repealed by the Criminal Jurisdiction Act 1975, s. 14(5), Sched. 6.*]

(5)   Notwithstanding [section 6 of the Prosecution of Offences Act 1979] subsection (4) of this section shall apply—

(a)   to an arrest (if without warrant) made by the wife or husband, and

(b)   to a warrant of arrest issued on an information laid by the wife or husband.

31.   Effect on civil proceedings and rights

(1)   A person shall not be excused, by reason that to do so may incriminate that person or the wife or husband of that person of an offence under this Act—

(a)   from answering any question put to that person in proceedings for the recovery or administration of any property, for the execution of any trust or for an account of any property or dealings with property; or

(b)   from complying with any order made in any such proceedings;

but no statement or admission made by a person in answering a question put or complying with an order made as aforesaid shall, in proceedings for an offence under this Act, be admissible in evidence against that person or (unless they married after the making of the statement of admission) against the wife or husband of that person.

(2)   Notwithstanding any enactment to the contrary, where property has been stolen or obtained by fraud or other wrongful means, the title to that or any other property shall not be affected by reason only of the conviction of the offender.

CRIMINAL DAMAGE ACT 1971
(1971, c. 48)

9.   Evidence in connection with offences under this Act

A person shall not be excused, by reason that to do so may incriminate that person or the wife or husband of that person of an offence under this Act—

(a) from answering any question put to that person in proceedings for the recovery or administration of any property, for the execution of any trust or for an account of any property or dealings with property; or

(b) from complying with any order made in any such proceedings;

but no statement or admission made by a person in answering a question put or complying with an order made as aforesaid shall, in proceedings for an offence under the Act, be admissible in evidence against that person or (unless they married after the making of the statement or admission) against the wife or husband of that person.

MISUSE OF DRUGS ACT 1971
(1971, c. 38)

5. Restriction of possession of controlled drugs

(1) Subject to any regulations under section 7 of this Act for the time being in force, it shall not be lawful for a person to have a controlled drug in his possession.

(2) Subject to section 28 of this Act and to subsection (4) below, it is an offence for a person to have a controlled drug in his possession in contravention of subsection (1) above.

(3) Subject to section 28 of this Act, it is an offence for a person to have a controlled drug in his possession, whether lawfully or not, with intent to supply it to another in contravention of section 4(1) of this Act.

(4) In any proceedings for an offence under subsection (2) above in which it is proved that the accused had a controlled drug in his possession, it shall be a defence for him to prove—

(a) that, knowing or suspecting it to be a controlled drug, he took possession of it for the purpose of preventing another from committing or continuing to commit an offence in connection with that drug and that as soon as possible after taking possession of it he took all such steps as were reasonably open to him to destroy the drug or to deliver it into the custody of a person lawfully entitled to take custody of it; or

(b) that, knowing or suspecting it to be a controlled drug, he took possession of it for the purpose of delivering it into the custody of a person lawfully entitled to take custody of it and that as soon as possible after taking possession of it he took all such steps as were reasonably open to him to deliver it into the custody of such a person.

(5) ...

(6) Nothing in subsection (4) ... above shall prejudice any defence which it is open to a person charged with an offence under this section to raise apart from that subsection.

REHABILITATION OF OFFENDERS ACT 1974
(1974, c. 53)

4. Effect of rehabilitation

(1) Subject to sections 7 and 8 below, a person who has become a rehabilitated person for the purposes of this Act in respect of a conviction shall be treated for all purposes in law as a person who has not committed or been charged with or prosecuted for or convicted of or sentenced for the offence or offences which were the subject of that conviction; and, notwithstanding the provisions of any other enactment or rule of law to the contrary, but subject as aforesaid—

(a) no evidence shall be admissible in any proceedings before a judicial authority exercising its jurisdiction or functions in Great Britain to prove that any such person has committed or been charged with or prosecuted for or convicted of or sentenced for any offence which was the subject of a spent conviction; and

(b)   a person shall not, in any such proceedings, be asked, and, if asked, shall not be required to answer, any question relating to his past which cannot be answered without acknowledging or referring to a spent conviction or spent convictions or any circumstances ancillary thereto.

(2)   Subject to the provisions of any order made under subsection (4) below, where a question seeking information with respect to a person's previous convictions, offences, conduct or circumstances is put to him or to any other person otherwise than in proceedings before a judicial authority—

(a)   the question shall be treated as not relating to spent convictions or to any circumstances ancillary to spent convictions, and the answer thereto may be framed accordingly; and

(b)   the person questioned shall not be subjected to any liability or otherwise prejudiced in law by reason of any failure to acknowledge or disclose a spent conviction or any circumstances ancillary to a spent conviction in his answer to the question.

(3)   Subject to the provisions of any order made under subsection (4) below,—

(a)   any obligation imposed on any person by any rule of law or by the provisions of any agreement or arrangement to disclose any matters to any other person shall not extend to requiring him to disclose a spent conviction or any circumstances ancillary to a spent conviction (whether the conviction is his own or another's); and

(b)   a conviction which has become spent or any circumstances ancillary thereto, or any failure to disclose a spent conviction or any such circumstances, shall not be a proper ground for dismissing or excluding a person from any office, profession, occupation or employment, or for prejudicing him in any way in any occupation or employment.

(4)   The Secretary of State may by order—

(a)   make such provisions as seems to him appropriate for excluding or modifying the application of either or both of paragraphs (a) and (b) of subsection (2) above in relation to questions put in such circumstances as may be specified in the order;

(b)   provide for such exceptions from the provisions of subsection (3) above as seem to him appropriate, in such cases or classes of case, and in relation to convictions of such a description, as may be specified in the order.

(5)   For the purposes of this section and section 7 below any of the following are circumstances ancillary to a conviction, that is to say—

(a)   the offence or offences which were the subject of that conviction;

(b)   the conduct constituting that offence or those offences; and

(c)   any process or proceedings preliminary to the conviction, any sentence imposed in respect of that conviction, any proceedings (whether by way of appeal or otherwise) for reviewing that conviction or any such sentence, and anything done in pursuance of or undergone in compliance with any such sentence.

(6)   For the purposes of this section and section 7 below 'proceedings before a judicial authority' includes, in addition to proceedings before any of the ordinary courts of law, proceedings before any tribunal, body or person having power—

(a)   by virtue of any enactment, law, custom or practice;

(b)   under the rules governing any association, institution, profession, occupation or employment; or

(c)   under any provision of an agreement providing for arbitration with respect to questions arising thereunder;

to determine any question affecting the rights, privileges, obligations or liabilities of any person, or to receive evidence affecting the determination of any such question.

5.   Rehabilitation periods for particular sentences

(1)   The sentences excluded from rehabilitation under this Act are—

(a)   a sentence of imprisonment for life;

(b) a sentence of imprisonment [youth custody] [detention in a young offender institution] or corrective training for a term exceeding thirty months;

(c) a sentence of preventive detention; . . .

(d) a sentence of detention during Her Majesty's pleasure or for life under section 90 or 91 of the Powers of Criminal Court (Sentencing) Act 2000 [or under section 205(2) or (3) of the Criminal Procedure (Scotland) Act 1975,] or a sentence of detention for a term exceeding thirty months passed under section 91 of the said Act of 2000 [(young offenders convicted of grave crimes) or under section 206 of the said Act of 1975 (detention of children convicted on indictment)] [or a corresponding court-martial punishment]; [and

(e) a sentence of custody for life]

and any other sentence is a sentence subject to rehabilitation under this Act.

[(1A) In subsection (1)(d) above 'corresponding court-martial punishment' means a punishment awarded under section 71A(3) or (4) of the Army Act 1955, section 71A(3) or (4) of the Air Force Act 1955 or section 43A(3) or (4) of the Naval Discipline Act 1957.]

(2) For the purposes of this Act—

(a) the rehabilitation period applicable to a sentence specified in the first column of Table A below is the period specified in the second column of that Table in relation to that sentence, or, where the sentence was imposed on a person who was under seventeen years of age at the date of his conviction, half that period; and

(b) the rehabilitation period applicable to a sentence specified in the first column of Table B below is the period specified in the second column of that Table in relation to that sentence;

reckoned in either case from the date of the conviction in respect of which the sentence was imposed.

Table A
Rehabilitation periods subject to reduction by half for persons under 17

Sentence	Rehabilitation period
A sentence of imprisonment [detention in a young offender institution] [or youth custody] or corrective training for a term exceeding six months but not exceeding thirty months.	Ten years.
A sentence of cashiering, discharge with ignominy or dismissal with disgrace from Her Majesty's service.	Ten years.
A sentence of imprisonment [detention in a young offender institution] [or youth custody] for a term not exceeding six months.	Seven years.
A sentence of dismissal from Her Majesty's service.	Seven years.
Any sentence of detention in respect of a conviction in service disciplinary proceedings.	Five years.
A fine or any other sentence subject to rehabilitation under this Act, not being a sentence to which Table B below or any of subsections (3) or (8) below applies.	Five years.

Table B
Rehabilitation periods for certain sentences confined to young offenders

Sentence	Rehabilitation period
A sentence of Borstal training.	Seven years.
[A custodial order under Schedule 5A to the Army Act 1955 or the Air Force Act 1955, or under Schedule 4A to the Naval Discipline Act 1957, where the maximum period of detention specified in the order is more than six months.	Seven years.]
[A custodial order under section 71AA of the Army Act 1955 or the Air Force Act 1955, or under section 43AA of the Naval Discipline Act 1957, where the maximum period of detention specified in the order is more than six months.	Seven years.]
A sentence of detention for a term exceeding six months but not exceeding thirty months passed under section 91 of the Power of Criminal Courts (Sentencing) Act 2000 or under section [206 of the Criminal Procedure (Scotland) Act 1975].	Five years.
A sentence of detention for a term not exceeding six months passed under either of those provisions.	Three years.
An order for detention in a detention centre made under [section 4 of the Criminal Justice Act 1982,] section 4 of the Criminal Justice Act 1961 ...	Three years.
[A custodial order under any of the Schedules to the said Acts of 1955 and 1957 mentioned above, where the maximum period of detention specified in the order is six months or less.	Three years.]
[A custodial order under section 71AA of the said Acts of 1955, or section 43AA of the said Act of 1957, where the maximum period of detention specified in the order is six months or less.	Three years.]

(3)   The rehabilitation period applicable—
  (a)   to an order discharging a person absolutely for an offence; and
  (b)   to the discharge by a children's hearing under section 43(2) of the Social Work (Scotland) Act 1968 of the referral of a child's case;
shall be six months from the date of conviction.

(4)   Where in respect of a conviction a person was conditionally discharged, bound over to keep the peace or be of good behaviour, the rehabilitation period applicable to the sentence shall be one year from the date of conviction or a period beginning with that date and ending when the order for conditional discharge or (as the case may be) the recognisance or bond of caution to keep the peace or be of good behaviour ceases to have effect, whichever is the longer.

(4A)   Where in respect of a conviction a probation order was made, the rehabilitation period applicable to the sentence shall be—
  (a)   in the case of a person aged eighteen years or over at the date of his conviction, five years from the date of conviction;
  (b)   in the case of a person aged under the age of eighteen years at the date of his conviction, two and a half years from the date of conviction or a period beginning with the date of conviction and ending when the order in question ceases or ceased to have effect, whichever is the longer.

(4B)   Where in respect of a conviction a referral order (within the meaning of the Powers of Criminal Courts (Sentencing) Act 2000) is made in respect of the person convicted, the rehabilitation period applicable to the sentence shall be—
  (a)   if a youth offender contract takes effect under section 23 of that Act between him and a youth offender panel, the period beginning with the date of conviction and ending on the date when (in accordance with section 24 of that Act) the contract ceases to have effect;

(b) if no such contract so takes effect, the period beginning with the date of conviction and having the same length as the period for which such a contract would (ignoring any order under paragraph 11 or 12 of Schedule 1 to that Act) have had effect had one so taken effect.

(4C) Where in respect of a conviction an order is made in respect of the person convicted under paragraph 11 or 12 of Schedule 1 to the Powers of Criminal Courts (Sentencing) Act 2000 (extension of period for which youth offender contract has effect), the rehabilitation period applicable to the sentence shall be—

(a) if a youth offender contract takes effect under section 23 of that Act between the offender and a youth offender panel, the period beginning with the date of conviction and ending on the date when (in accordance with section 24 of that Act) the contract ceases to have effect;

(b) if no such contract so takes effect, the period beginning with the date accordance with the order such a contract would have had effect had one so taken effect.

(5) Where in respect of a conviction any of the following sentences was imposed, that is to say—

(a) an order under section 57 of the Children and Young Persons Act 1933 or section 61 of the Children and Young Persons (Scotland) Act 1937 committing the person convicted to the care of a fit person;

(b) a supervision order under any provision of either of those Acts or of the Children and Young Persons Act 1963;

[(c) an order under section 413 of the Criminal Procedure (Scotland) Act 1975 committing a child for the purpose of his undergoing residential training;]

(d) an approved school order under section 61 of the said Act of 1937;

(e) a care order or a supervision order under section 63(1) of the Powers of Criminal Courts (Sentencing) Act 2000; or

(f) a supervision requirement under any provision of the Social Work (Scotland) Act 1968;

[(g) a community supervision order under Schedule 5A to the Army Act 1955 or the Air Force Act 1955, or under Schedule 4A to the Naval Discipline Act 1957;

(h) a reception order under any of those Schedules;]

the rehabilitation period applicable to the sentence shall be one year from the date of conviction or a period beginning with that date and ending when the order or requirement ceases or ceased to have effect, whichever is the longer.

(6) Where in respect of a conviction any of the following orders was made, that is to say—

(a) an order under section 54 of the said Act of 1933 committing the person convicted to custody in a remand home;

(b) an approved school order under section 57 of the said Act of 1933; or

(c) an attendance centre order under section 60 of the Powers of Criminal Courts (Sentencing) Act 2000;

the rehabilitation period applicable to the sentence shall be a period beginning with the date of conviction and ending one year after the date on which the order ceases or ceased to have effect; or

(d) a secure training order under section 1 of the Criminal Justice and Public Order Act 1994.

(6A) Where in respect of a conviction a detention and training order was made under section 100 of the Powers of Criminal Courts (Sentencing) Act 2000, the rehabilitation period applicable to the sentence shall be—

(a) in the case of a person aged fifteen years or over at the date of his conviction, five years if the order was, and three and a half years if the order was not, for a term exceeding six months;

(b)   in the case of a person aged under fifteen years at the date of his conviction, a period beginning with that date and ending one year after the date on which the order ceases to have effect.

(7)   Where in respect of a conviction a hospital order under [Part III of the Mental Health Act 1983] or under [Part VI of the Mental Health (Scotland) Act 1984] (with or without [a restriction order]) was made, the rehabilitation period applicable to the sentence shall be the period of five years from the date of conviction or a period beginning with that date and ending two years after the date on which the hospital order ceases or ceased to have effect, whichever is the longer.

(8)   Where in respect of a conviction an order was made imposing on the person convicted any disqualification, disability, prohibition or other penalty, the rehabilitation period applicable to the sentence shall be a period beginning with the date of conviction and ending on the date on which the disqualification, disability, prohibition or penalty (as the case may be) ceases or ceased to have effect.

(9)   For the purposes of this section—

(a)   'sentence of imprisonment' includes a sentence of detention [under section 207 or 415 of the Criminal Procedure (Scotland) Act 1975] and a sentence of penal servitude, and 'term of imprisonment' shall be construed accordingly;

(b)   consecutive terms of imprisonment or of detention under section 91 of the Powers of Criminal Courts (Sentencing) Act 2000 or (section 206 of the said Act 1975)], and terms which are wholly or partly concurrent (being terms of imprisonment or detention imposed in respect of offences of which a person was convicted in the same proceedings) shall be treated as a single term;

(c)   no account shall be taken of any subsequent variation, made by a court in dealing with a person in respect of a suspended sentence of imprisonment, or the term originally imposed; and

(d)   a sentence imposed by a court outside Great Britain shall be treated as a sentence of that one of the descriptions mentioned in this section which most nearly corresponds to the sentence imposed.

(10)   References in this section to the period during which a probation order, or a care order or supervision order under the Powers of Criminal Courts (Sentencing) Act 2000, or a supervision requirement under the Social Work (Scotland) Act 1968, is or was in force include references to any period during which any order or requirement to which this subsection applies, being an order or requirement made or imposed directly or indirectly in substitution for the first-mentioned order or requirement, is or was in force.

This subsection applies—

(a)   to any such order or requirement as is mentioned above in this subsection;

(b)   to any order having effect under section 25(2) of the Children and Young Persons Act 1969 as if it were a training school order in Northern Ireland; and

(c)   to any supervision order made under section 72(2) of the said Act of 1968 and having effect as a supervision order under the Children and Young Persons Act (Northern Ireland) 1950.

[(10A)   The reference in subsection (5) above to the period during which a reception order has effect includes a reference to any subsequent period during which by virtue of the order having been made the Social Work (Scotland) Act 1968 or the Children and Young Persons Act (Northern Ireland) 1968 has effect in relation to the person in respect of whom the order was made and subsection (10) above shall accordingly have effect in relation to any such subsequent period.]

(11)   The Secretary of State may by order—

(a)   substitute different periods or terms for any of the periods or terms mentioned in subsections (1) to (8) above; and

(b)   substitute a different age for the age mentioned in subsection (2)(a) above.

7. Limitations on rehabilitation under this Act, etc.

(1)   Nothing in section 4(1) above shall affect—

(a)   any right of Her Majesty, by virtue of Her Royal prerogative or otherwise, to grant a free pardon, to quash any conviction or sentence, or to commute any sentence;

(b)   the enforcement by any process or proceedings of any fine or other sum adjudged to be paid by or imposed on a spent conviction;

(c)   the issue of any process for the purpose of proceedings in respect of any breach of a condition or requirement applicable to a sentence imposed in respect of a spent conviction; or

(d)   the operation of any enactment by virtue of which, in consequence of any conviction, a person is subject, otherwise than by way of sentence, to any disqualification, disability, prohibition or other penalty the period of which extends beyond the rehabilitation period applicable in accordance with section 6 above to the conviction.

(2)   Nothing in section 4(1) above shall affect the determination of any issue, or prevent the admission or requirement of any evidence, relating to a person's previous convictions or to circumstances ancillary thereto—

(a)   in any criminal proceedings before a court in Great Britain (including any appeal or reference in a criminal matter);

(b)   in any service disciplinary proceedings or in any proceedings on appeal from any service disciplinary proceedings;

(bb)   in any proceedings on an application for a sex offence order under section 2 or, as the case may be, 20 of the Crime and Disorder Act 1998 or in any appeal against the making of such an order;

(c)   in any proceedings relating to adoption or to the guardianship, wardship, marriage, custody, care or control of, or access to, any minor, or to the provision by any person of accommodation, care or schooling for minors;

(d)   in any care proceedings under section 1 of the Powers of Criminal Courts (Sentencing) Act 2000 or on appeal from any such proceedings, or in any proceedings relating to the variation or discharge of a care order or supervision order under that Act;

(e)   in any proceedings before a children's hearing under the Social Work (Scotland) Act 1968 or on appeal from any such hearing; or

(f)   in any proceedings in which he is a party or a witness, provided that, on the occasion when the issue or the admission or requirement of the evidence falls to be determined, he consents to the determination of the issue or, as the case may be, the admission or requirement of the evidence notwithstanding the provisons of section 4(1); [or,

(g)   ...]

In the application of this subsection to Scotland, 'minor' means a child under the age of eighteen, including a pupil child.

(3)   If at any stage in any proceedings before a judicial authority in Great Britain (not being proceedings to which, by virtue of any of paragraphs (a) to (e) of subsection (2) above or of any order for the time being in force under subsection (4) below, section 4(1) above has no application, or proceedings to which section 8 below applies) the authority is satisfied, in the light of any considerations which appear to it to be relevant (including any evidence which has been or may thereafter be put before it), that justice cannot be done in the case except by admitting or requiring evidence relating to a person's spent convictions or to circumstances ancillary thereto, that authority may admit or, as the case may be, require the evidence in question notwithstanding the provisions of subsection (1) of section 4 above, and may determine any issue to which the evidence relates in disregard, so far as necessary, of those provisions.

(4)   The Secretary of State may by order exclude the application of section 4(1) above in relation to any proceedings specified in the order (other than proceedings to

which section 8 below applies) to such extent and for such purposes as may be so specified.

(5)   No order made by a court with respect to any person otherwise than on a conviction shall be included in any list or statement of that person's previous convictions given or made to any court which is considering how to deal with him in respect of any offence.

SEXUAL OFFENCES (AMENDMENT) ACT 1976
(1976, c. 82)

1.   Meaning of 'rape' etc.

(2)   It is hereby declared that if at a trial for a rape offence the jury has to consider whether a man believed that a woman or man was consenting to sexual intercourse, the presence or absence of reasonable grounds for such a belief is a matter to which the jury is to have regard, in conjunction with any other relevant matters, in considering whether he so believed.

PROTECTION OF CHILDREN ACT 1978
(1978, c. 37)

1.   Indecent photographs of children

(1)   It is an offence for a person—

(a)   to take, or permit to be taken, or to make any indecent photograph or pseudo-photograph of a child; or

(b)   to distribute or show such indecent photographs or pseudo-photographs; or

(c)   to have in his possession such indecent photographs or pseudo-photographs, with a view to their being distributed or shown by himself or others; or

(d)   to publish or cause to be published any advertisement likely to be understood as conveying that the advertiser distributes or shows such indecent photographs or pseudo-photographs, or intends to do so.

(2)   For purposes of this Act, a person is to be regarded as distributing an indecent photograph or pseudo-photograph if he parts with possession of it to, or exposes or offers it for acquisition by another person.

(3)   Proceedings for an offence under this Act shall not be instituted except by or with the consent of the Director of Public Prosecutions.

(4)   Where a person is charged with an offence under subsection (1)(b) or (c), it shall be a defence for him to prove—

(a)   that he had a legitimate reason for distributing or showing the photographs or pseudo-photographs or (as the case may be) having them in his possession; or

(b)   that he had not himself seen the photographs or pseudo-photographs and did not know, nor had any cause to suspect, them to be indecent.

(5)   References in the Children and Young Persons Act 1933 (except in sections 15 and 99) to the offences mentioned in Schedule 1 to that Act shall include an offence under subsection (1)(a) above.

2.   Evidence

(1), (2)   . . .

(3)   In proceedings under this Act relating to indecent photographs of children a person is to be taken as having been a child at any material time if it appears, from the evidence as a whole, that he was then under the age of 16.

MAGISTRATES' COURTS ACT 1980
(1980, c. 43)

Committal proceedings

4. General nature of committal proceedings

(1)   The functions of examining justices may be discharged by a single justice.

(2)   Examining justices shall sit in open court except where any enactment contains an express provision to the contrary and except where it appears to them as respects the whole or any part of committal proceedings that the ends of justice would not be served by their sitting in open court.

(3)   Subject to subsection (4) below and section 102 below, evidence [tendered] before examining justices shall be [tendered] in the presence of the accused. . . .

(4)   Examining justices may allow evidence to be [tendered] before them in the absence of the accused if—

(a)   they consider that by reason of his disorderly conduct before them it is not practicable for the evidence to be [tendered] in his presence, or

(b)   he cannot be present for reasons of health but is represented by [a legal representative] and has consented to the evidence being [tendered] in his absence.

5. Adjournment of inquiry

(1)   A magistrates' court may, before beginning to inquire into an offence as examining justices, or at any time during the inquiry, adjourn the hearing, and if it does so shall remand the accused.

(2)   The court shall when adjourning fix the time and place at which the hearing is to be resumed; and the time fixed shall be that at which the accused is required to appear or be brought before the court in pursuance of the remand [or would be required to be brought before the court but for section 128(3A) below].

[5A. Evidence which is admissible

(1)   Evidence falling within subsection (2) below, and only that evidence, shall be admissible by a magistrates' court inquiring into an offence as examining justices.

(2)   Evidence falls within this subsection if it—

(a)   is tendered by or on behalf of the prosecutor; and

(b)   falls within subsection (3) below.

(3)   The following evidence falls within this subsection—

(a)   written statements complying with section 5B below;

(b)   the documents or other exhibits (if any) referred to in such statements;

(c)   depositions complying with section 5C below;

(d)   the documents or other exhibits (if any) referred to in such depositions;

(e)   statements complying with section 5D below;

(f)   documents falling within section 5E below.

(4)   In this section 'document' means anything in which information of any description is recorded.

5B. Written statements

(1)   For the purposes of section 5A above a written statement complies with this section if—

(a)   the conditions falling within subsection (2) below are met, and

(b)   such of the conditions falling within subsection (3) below as apply are met.

(2)   The conditions falling within this subsection are that—

(a)   the statement purports to be signed by the person who made it;

(b)   the statement contains a declaration by that person to the effect that it is true to the best of his knowledge and belief and that he made the statement knowing that, if it were tendered in evidence, he would be liable to prosecution if he wilfully stated in it anything which he knew to be false or did not believe to be true;

    (c)   before the statement is tendered in evidence a copy of the statement is given, by or on behalf of the prosecutor, to each of the other parties to the proceedings.

    (3)   The conditions falling within this subsection are that—

    (a)   if the statement is made by a person under 18 years old, it gives his age;

    (b)   if it is made by a person who cannot read it, it is read to him before he signs it and is accompanied by a declaration by the person who so read the statement to the effect that it was so read;

    (c)   if it refers to any other document as an exhibit, the copy given to any other party to the proceedings under subsection (2)(c) above is accompanied by a copy of that document or by such information as may be necessary to enable the party to whom it is given to inspect that document or a copy of it.

    (3A)   In the case of a statement which indicates in pursuance of subsection (3)(a) of this section that the person making it has not attained the age of 14, subsection (2)(b) of this section shall have effect as if for the words from 'made' onwards there were substituted the words 'understands the importance of telling the truth in it' (inserted herein as from a day to be appointed by the Children and Young Persons Act 1969, Schedule 5, paragraph 55 as amended by the Criminal Procedure Investigations Act 1996, Schedule 1, para. 21).

    (4)   So much of any statement as is admitted in evidence by virtue of this section shall, unless the court commits the accused for trial by virtue of section 6(2) below or the court otherwise directs, be read aloud at the hearing; and where the court so directs an account shall be given orally of so much of any statement as is not read aloud.

    (5)   Any document or other object referred to as an exhibit and identified in a statement admitted in evidence by virtue of this section shall be treated as if it had been produced as an exhibit and identified in court by the maker of the statement.

    (6)   In this section 'document' means anything in which information of any description is recorded.

5C.   Depositions

    (1)   For the purposes of section 5A above a deposition complies with this section if—

    (a)   a copy of it is sent to the prosecutor under section 97A(9) below,

    (b)   the condition falling within subsection (2) below is met, and

    (c)   the condition falling within subsection (3) below is met, in a case where it applies.

    (2)   The condition falling within this subsection is that before the magistrates' court begins to inquire into the offence concerned as examining justices a copy of the deposition is given, by or on behalf of the prosecutor, to each of the other parties to the proceedings.

    (3)   The condition falling within this subsection is that, if the deposition refers to any other document as an exhibit, the copy given to any other party to the proceedings under subsection (2) above is accompanied by a copy of that document or by such information as may be necessary to enable the party to whom it is given to inspect that document or a copy of it.

    (4)   So much of any deposition as is admitted in evidence by virtue of this section shall, unless the court commits the accused for trial by virtue of section 6(2) below or the court otherwise directs, be read aloud at the hearing; and where the court so directs an account shall be given orally of so much of any deposition as is not read aloud.

    (5)   Any document or other object referred to as an exhibit and identified in a deposition admitted in evidence by virtue of this section shall be treated as if it had been produced as an exhibit and identified in court by the person whose evidence is taken as the deposition.

(6)   In this section 'document' means anything in which information of any description is recorded.

5D.   Statements

(1)   For the purposes of section 5A above a statement complies with this section if the conditions falling within subsection (2) to (4) below are met.

(2)   The condition falling within this subsection is that, before the committal proceedings begin, the prosecutor notifies the magistrates' court and each of the other parties to the proceedings that he believes—

(a)   that the statement might by virtue of section 23 or 24 of the Criminal Justice Act 1988 (statements in certain documents) be admissible as evidence if the case came to trial, and

(b)   that the statement would not be admissible as evidence otherwise than by virtue of section 23 or 24 of that Act if the case came to trial.

(3)   The condition falling within this subsection is that—

(a)   the prosecutor's belief is based on information available to him at the time he makes the notification,

(b)   he has reasonable grounds for his belief, and

(c)   he gives the reasons for his belief when he makes the notification.

(4)   The condition falling within the subsection is that when the court or a party is notified as mentioned in subsection (2) above a copy of the statement is given, by or on behalf of the prosecutor, to the court or the party concerned.

(5)   So much of any statement as is in writing and is admitted in evidence by virtue of this section shall, unless the court commits the accused for trial by virtue of section 6(2) below or the court otherwise directs, be read aloud at the hearing; and where the court so directs an account shall be given orally of so much of any statement as is not read aloud.

5E.   Other documents

(1)   The following documents fall within this section—

(a)   any document which by virtue of any enactment is evidence in proceedings before a magistrates' court inquiring into an offence as examining justices;

(b)   any document which by virtue of any enactment is admissible, or may be used, or is to be admitted or received, in or as evidence in such proceedings;

(c)   any document which by virtue of any enactment may be considered in such proceedings;

(d)   any document whose production constitutes proof in such proceedings by virtue of any enactment;

(e)   any document by the production of which evidence may be given in such proceedings by virtue of any enactment.

(2)   In subsection (1) above—

(a)   references to evidence include references to prima facie evidence;

(b)   references to any enactment include references to any provision of this Act.

(3)   So much of any document as is admitted in evidence by virtue of this section shall, unless the court commits the accused for trial by virtue of section 6(2) below or the court otherwise directs, be read aloud at the hearing; and where the court so directs an account shall be given orally of so much of any document as is not read aloud.

(4)   In this section 'document' means anything in which information of any description is recorded.

5F.   Proof by production of copy

(1)   Where a statement, deposition or document is admissible in evidence by virtue of section 5B, 5C, 5D or 5E above it may be proved by the production of—

(a)   the statement, deposition or document, or

(b)   a copy of it or the material part of it.

(2)   Subsection (1)(b) above applies whether or not the statement, deposition or document is still in existence.

(3)   It is immaterial for the purposes of this section how many removes there are between a copy and the original.

(4)   In this section 'copy', in relation to a statement, deposition or document, means anything onto which information recorded in the statement, deposition or document has been copied, by whatever means and whether directly or indirectly.]

6.   Application for dismissal

[(1)   A magistrates' court inquiring into an offence as examining justices shall on consideration of the evidence—

(a)   commit the accused for trial if it is of opinion that there is sufficient evidence to put him on trial by jury for any indictable offence;

(b)   discharge him if it is not of that opinion and he is in custody for no other cause than the offence under inquiry;

but the preceding provisions of this subsection have effect subject to the provisions of this and any other Act relating to the summary trial of indictable offences.

(2)   If a magistrates' court inquiring into an offence as examining justices is satisfied that all the evidence tendered by or on behalf of the prosecutor falls within section 5A(3) above, it may commit the accused for trial for the offence without consideration of the contents of any statements, depositions or other documents, and without consideration of any exhibits which are not documents, unless—

(a)   the accused or one of the accused has no legal representative acting for him in the case, or

(b)   a legal representative for the accused or one of the accused, as the case may be, has requested the court to consider a submission that there is insufficient evidence to put that accused on trial by jury for the offence;

and subsection (1) above shall not apply to a committal for trial under this subsection.]

98.   Evidence on oath

Subject to the provisions of any enactment or rule of law authorising the reception of unsworn evidence, evidence given before a magistrates' court shall be given on oath.

101.   Onus of proving exceptions, etc.

Where the defendant to an information or complaint relies for his defence on any exception, exemption, proviso, excuse or qualification, whether or not it accompanies the description of the offence or matter of complaint in the enactment creating the offence or on which the complaint is founded, the burden of proving the exception, exemption, proviso, excuse or qualification shall be on him; and this notwithstanding that the information or complaint contains an allegation negativing the exception, exemption, proviso, excuse or qualification.

[103.   Evidence of persons under 14 in committal proceedings for assault, sexual offences etc.

[(1)   In any proceedings before a magistrates' court inquiring as examining justices into an offence to which this section applies, a statement made in writing by or taken in writing from a child shall be admissible in evidence of any matter.]

(2)   This section applies—

(a)   to an offence which involves an assault, or injury or a threat of injury to, a person;

(b)   to an offence under section 1 of the Children and Young Persons Act 1933 (cruelty to persons under 16);

(c)   to an offence under the Sexual Offences Act 1956, the Indecency with Children Act 1960, the Sexual Offences Act 1967, section 54 of the Criminal Law Act 1977 or the Protection of Children Act 1978; and

(d) to an offence which consists of attempting or conspiring to commit, or of aiding, abetting, counselling, procuring or inciting the commission of, an offence falling within paragraph (a), (b) or (c) above.

(3), (4) ...

[(5) In this section'child' has the same meaning as in section 53 of the Criminal Justice Act 1991.]]

104. Proof of previous convictions

Where a person is convicted of a summary offence by a magistrates' court, other than a juvenile court, and—

(a) it is proved to the satisfaction of the court, on oath or in such other manner as may be prescribed, that not less than 7 days previously a notice was served on the accused in the prescribed form and manner specifying any alleged previous conviction of the accused of a summary offence proposed to be brought to the notice of the court in the event of his conviction of the offence charged; and

(b) the accused is not present in person before the court,

the court may take account of any such previous conviction so specified as if the accused had appeared and admitted it.

107. False statements in declaration proving service, etc.

If, in any solemn declaration, certificate or other writing made or given for the purpose of its being used in pursuance of the rules as evidence of the service of any document or the handwriting or seal of any person, a person makes a statement that he knows to be false in a material particular, or recklessly makes any statement that is false in a material particular, he shall be liable on summary conviction to imprisonment for a term not exceeding 6 months or a fine not exceeding [level 3 on the standard scale] or both.

CRIMINAL ATTEMPTS ACT 1981
(1981, c. 47)

1. Attempting to commit an offence

(1) If, with intent to commit an offence to which this section applies, a person does an act which is more than merely preparatory to the commission of the offence, he is guilty of attempting to commit the offence.

(1A) Subject to section 8 of the Computer Misuse Act 1990 (relevance of external law) if this subsection applies to an act, what the person doing it had in view shall be treated as an offence to which this section applies.

(1B) Subsection (1A) above applies to an act if—

(a) it is done in England and Wales; and

(b) it would fall within subsection (1) above as more than merely preparatory to the commission of an offence under section 3 of the Computer Misuse Act 1990 but for the fact that the offence, if completed, would not be an offence triable in England and Wales.

(2) A person may be guilty of attempting to commit an offence to which this section applies even though the facts are such that the commission of the offence is impossible.

(3) In any case where—

(a) apart from this subsection a person's intention would not be regarded as having amounted to an intent to commit an offence; but

(b) if the facts of the case had been as he believed them to be, his intention would be so regarded,

then, for the purposes of subsection (1) above, he shall be regarded as having had an intent to commit that offence.

(4) This section applies to any offence which, if it were completed, would be triable in England and Wales as an indictable offence, other than—

    (a)   conspiracy (at common law or under section 1 of the Criminal Law Act 1977 or any other enactment);

    (b)   aiding, abetting, counselling, procuring or suborning the commission of an offence;

    (c)   offences under section 4(1) (assisting offenders) or 5(1) (accepting or agreeing to accept consideration for not disclosing information about an arrestable offence) of the Criminal Law Act 1967.

1A   Extended jurisdiction in relation to certain attempts

    (1)   If this section applies to an act, what the person doing the act had in view shall be treated as an offence to which section 1(1) above applies.

    (2)   This section applies to an act if—

    (a)   it is done in England and Wales, and

    (b)   it would fall within section 1(1) above as more than merely preparatory to the commission of a Group A offence but for the fact that that offence, if completed, would not be an offence triable in England and Wales.

    (3)   In this section 'Group A offence' has the same meaning as in Part I of the Criminal Justice Act 1993.

    (4)   Subsection (1) above is subject to the provisions of section 6 of the Act of 1993 (relevance of external law).

    (5)   Where a person does an act to which this section applies, the offence which he commits shall for all purposes be treated as the offence of attempting to commit the relevant Group A offence.

2.   Application of procedural and other provisions to offences under s.1

    (1)   Any provision to which this section applies shall have effect with respect to an offence under section 1 above of attempting to commit an offence as it has effect with respect to the offence attempted.

    (2)   This section applies to provisions of any of the following descriptions made by or under any enactment (whenever passed)—

    (a)   provisions whereby proceedings may not be instituted or carried on otherwise than by, or on behalf or with the consent of, any person (including any provisions which also make other exceptions to the prohibition);

    (b)   provisions conferring power to institute proceedings;

    (c)   provisions as to the venue of proceedings;

    (d)   provisions whereby proceedings may not be instituted after the expiration of a time limit;

    (e)   provisions conferring a power of arrest or search;

    (f)   provisions conferring a power of seizure and detention of property;

    (g)   provisions whereby a person may not be convicted [or committed for trial] on the uncorroborated evidence of one witness (including any provision requiring the evidence of not less than two credible witnesses);

    (h)   provisions conferring a power of forfeiture, including any power to deal with anything liable to be forfeited;

    (i)   provisions whereby, if an offence committed by a body corporate is proved to have been committed with the consent or connivance of another person, that person also is guilty of the offence.

3.   Offences of attempt under other enactments

    (1)   Subsections (2) to (5) below shall have effect, subject to subsection (6) below and to any inconsistent provision in any other enactment, for the purpose of determining whether a person is guilty of an attempt under a special statutory provision.

    (2)   For the purposes of this Act an attempt under a special statutory provision is an offence which—

(a)   is created by an enactment other than section 1 above, including an enactment passed after this Act; and

(b)   is expressed as an offence of attempting to commit another offence (in this section referred to as 'the relevant full offence').

(3)   A person is guilty of an attempt under a special statutory provision if, with intent to commit the relevant full offence, he does an act which is more than merely preparatory to the commission of that offence.

(4)   A person may be guilty of an attempt under a special statutory provision even though the facts are such that the commission of the relevant full offence is impossible.

(5)   In any case where—

(a)   apart from this subsection a person's intention would not be regarded as having amounted to an intent to commit the relevant full offence; but

(b)   if the facts of the case had been as he believed them to be, his intention would be so regarded,

then, for the purposes of subsection (3) above, he shall be regarded as having had an intent to commit that offence.

(6)   Subsections (2) to (5) above shall not have effect in relation to an act done before the commencement of this Act.

4.   Trial and penalties

(1)   A person guilty by virtue of section 1 above of attempting to commit an offence shall—

(a)   if the offence attempted is murder or any other offence the sentence for which is fixed by law, be liable on conviction on indictment to imprisonment for life; and

(b)   if the offence attempted is indictable but does not fall within paragraph (a) above, be liable on conviction on indictment to any penalty to which he would have been liable on conviction on indictment of that offence; and

(c)   if the offence attempted is triable either way, be liable on summary conviction to any penalty to which he would have been liable on summary conviction of that offence.

(2)   In any case in which a court may proceed to summary trial of an information charging a person with an offence and an information charging him with an offence under section 1 above of attempting to commit it or an attempt under a special statutory provision, the court may, without his consent, try the informations together.

(3)   Where, in proceedings against a person for an offence under section 1 above, there is evidence sufficient in law to support a finding that he did an act falling within subsection (1) of that section, the question whether or not his act fell within that subsection is a question of fact.

(4)   Where, in proceedings against a person for an attempt under a special statutory provision, there is evidence sufficient in law to support a finding that he did an act falling within subsection (3) of section 3 above, the question whether or not his act fell within that subsection is a question of fact.

(5)   Subsection (1) above shall have effect—

(a)   subject to section 37 of and Schedule 2 to the Sexual Offences Act 1956 (mode of trial of and penalties for attempts to commit certain offences under that Act); and

(b)   notwithstanding anything—

(i)   in section 32(1) (no limit to fine on conviction on indictment) of the Criminal Law Act 1977; or

(ii)   in section 78(1) and (2) (maximum of six months' imprisonment on summary conviction unless express provision made to the contrary) of the Powers of Criminal Courts (Sentencing) Act 2000.

CONTEMPT OF COURT ACT 1981
(1981, c. 49)

10. Sources of information

No court may require a person to disclose, nor is any person guilty of contempt of court for refusing to disclose, the source of information contained in a publication for which he is responsible, unless it be established to the satisfaction of the court that disclosure is necessary in the interests of justice or national security or for the prevention of disorder or crime.

CRIMINAL JUSTICE ACT 1982
(1982, c. 48)

Unsworn statements

72. Abolition of right of accused to make unsworn statement

(1)   Subject to subsections (2) and (3) below, in any criminal proceedings the accused shall not be entitled to make a statement without being sworn, and accordingly, if he gives evidence, he shall do so (subject to sections 55 and 56 of the Youth Justice and Criminal Evidence Act 1999) on oath and be liable to cross-examination; but this section shall not affect the right of the accused, if not represented by counsel or a solicitor, to address the court or jury otherwise than on oath on any matter on which, if he were so represented, counsel or a solicitor could address the court or jury on his behalf.

(2)   Nothing in subsection (1) above shall prevent the accused making a statement without being sworn—

(a)   if it is one which he is required by law to make personally; or

(b)   if he makes it by way of mitigation before the court passes sentence upon him.

(3)   Nothing in this section applies—

(a)   to a trial; or

(b)   to proceedings before a magistrates' court acting as examining justices,

which began before the commencement of this section.

POLICE AND CRIMINAL EVIDENCE ACT 1984
(1984, c. 60)

PART I
POWERS TO STOP AND SEARCH

1. Power of constable to stop and search persons, vehicles etc.

(1)   A constable may exercise any power conferred by this section—

(a)   in any place to which at the time when he proposes to exercise the power the public or any section of the public has access, on payment or otherwise, as of right or by virtue of express or implied permission; or

(b)   in any other place to which people have ready access at the time when he proposes to exercise the power but which is not a dwelling.

(2)   Subject to subsection (3) to (5) below, a constable—

(a)   may search—

(i)   any person or vehicle;

(ii)   anything which is in or on a vehicle, for stolen or prohibited articles or any article to which subsection (8A) below applies; and

(b)   may detain a person or vehicle for the purpose of such a search.

(3)   This section does not give a constable power to search a person or vehicle or anything in or on a vehicle unless he has reasonable grounds for suspecting that he will find stolen or prohibited articles or any article to which subsection (8A) below applies.

(4)   If a person is in a garden or yard occupied with and used for the purposes of a dwelling or on other land so occupied and used, a constable may not search him in the exercise of the power conferred by this section unless the constable has reasonable grounds for believing—

(a)   that he does not reside in the dwelling; and

(b)   that he is not in the place in question with the express or implied permission of a person who resides in the dwelling.

(5)   If a vehicle is in a garden or yard occupied with and used for the purposes of a dwelling or on other land so occupied and used, a constable may not search the vehicle or anything in or on it in the exercise of the power conferred by this section unless he has reasonable grounds for believing—

(a)   that the person in charge of the vehicle does not reside in the dwelling; and

(b)   that the vehicle is not in the place in question with the express or implied permission of a person who resides in the dwelling.

(6)   If in the course of such a search a constable discovers an article which he has reasonable grounds for suspecting to be a stolen or prohibited article or any article to which subsection (8A) below applies, he may seize it.

(7)   An article is prohibited for the purposes of this Part of this Act if it is—

(a)   an offensive weapon; or

(b)   an article—

(i)   made or adapted for use in the course of or in connection with an offence to which this sub-paragraph applies; or

(ii)   intended by the person having it with him for such use by him or by some other person.

(8)   The offences to which subsection (7)(b)(i) above applies are—

(a)   burglary;

(b)   theft;

(c)   offences under section 12 of the Theft Act 1968 (taking motor vehicle or other conveyance without authority); and

(d)   offences under section 15 of that Act (obtaining property by deception).

(8A)   This subsection applies to any article in relation to which a person has committed, or is committing or is going to commit an offence under section 139 of the Criminal Justice Act 1988.

(9)   In this Part of this Act 'offensive weapon' means any article—

(a)   made or adapted for use for causing injury to persons; or

(b)   intended by the person having it with him for such use by him or by some other person.

2.   Provisions relating to search under section 1 and other powers

(1)   A constable who detains a person or vehicle in the exercise—

(a)   of the power conferred by section 1 above; or

(b)   of any other power—

(i)   to search a person without first arresting him; or

(ii)   to search a vehicle without making an arrest,

need not conduct a search if it appears to him subsequently—

(i)   that no search is required; or

(ii)   that a search is impracticable.

(2)   If a constable contemplates a search, other than a search of an unattended vehicle, in the exercise—

(a)   of the power conferred by section 1 above; or

(b)   of any other power, except the power conferred by section 6 below and the power conferred by section 27(2) of the Aviation Security Act 1982—

(i)   to search a person without first arresting him; or

  (ii)   to search a vehicle without making an arrest,
it shall be his duty, subject to subsection (4) below, to take reasonable steps before he
commences the search to bring to the attention of the appropriate person—
  (i)   if the constable is not in uniform, documentary evidence that he is a
constable; and
  (ii)   whether he is in uniform or not, the matter specified in subsection (3)
below;
and the constable shall not commence the search until he has performed that duty.
  (3)   The matters referred to in subsection (2)(ii) above are—
  (a)   the constable's name and the name of the police station to which he is
attached;
  (b)   the object of the proposed search;
  (c)   the constable's grounds for proposing to make it; and
  (d)   the effect of section 3(7) or (8) below, as may be appropriate.
  (4)   A constable need not bring the effect of section 3(7) or (8) below to the attention
of the appropriate person if it appears to the constable that it will not be practicable to
make the record in section 3(1) below.
  (5)   In this section 'the appropriate person' means—
  (a)   if the constable proposes to search a person, that person; and
  (b)   if he proposes to search a vehicle, or anything in or on a vehicle, the person in
charge of the vehicle.
  (6)   On completing a search of an unattended vehicle or anything in or on such a
vehicle in the exercise of any such power as is mentioned in subsection (2) above a
constable shall leave a notice—
  (a)   stating that he has searched it;
  (b)   giving the name of the police station to which he is attached;
  (c)   stating that an application for compensation for any damage caused by the
search may be made to that police station; and
  (d)   stating the effect of section 3(8) below.
  (7)   The constable shall leave the notice inside the vehicle unless it is not reasonably
practicable to do so without damaging the vehicle.
  (8)   The time for which a person or vehicle may be detained for the purposes of such
a search is such time as is reasonably required to permit a search to be carried out either
at the place where the person or vehicle was first detained or nearby.
  (9)   Neither the power conferred by section 1 above nor any other power to detain
and search a person without first arresting him or to detain and search a vehicle without
making an arrest is to be construed—
  (a)   as authorising a constable to require a person to remove any of his clothing in
public other than an outer coat, jacket or gloves; or
  (b)   as authorising a constable not in uniform to stop a vehicle.
  (10)   This section and section 1 above apply to vessels, aircraft and hovercraft as
they apply to vehicles.

3. Duty to make records concerning searches

  (1)   Where a constable has carried out a search in the exercise of any such power as
is mentioned in section 2(1) above, other than a search—
  (a)   under section 6 below; or
  (b)   under section 27(2) of the Aviation Security Act 1982, he shall make a record
of it in writing unless it is not practicable to do so.
  (2)   If—
  (a)   a constable is required by subsection (1) above to make a record of a search; but
  (b)   it is not practicable to make the record on the spot,
he shall make it as soon as practicable after the completion of the search.

(3)　The record of a search of a person shall include a note of his name, if the constable knows it, but a constable may not detain a person to find out his name.

(4)　If a constable does not know the name of a person whom he has searched, the record of the search shall include a note otherwise describing that person.

(5)　The record of a search of a vehicle shall include a note describing the vehicle.

(6)　The record of a search of a person or a vehicle—

  (a)　shall state—

    (i)　the object of the search;

    (ii)　the grounds for making it;

    (iii)　the date and time when it was made;

    (iv)　the place where it was made;

    (v)　whether anything, and if so what, was found;

    (vi)　whether any, and if so what, injury to a person or damage to property appears to the constable to have resulted from the search; and

  (b)　shall identify the constable making it.

(7)　If a constable who conducted a search of a person made a record of it, the person who was searched shall be entitled to a copy of the record if he asks for one before the end of the period specified in subsection (9) below.

(8)　If—

  (a)　the owner of a vehicle which has been searched or the person who was in charge of the vehicle at the time when it was searched asks for a copy of the record of the search before the end of the period specified in subsection (9) below; and

  (b)　the constable who conducted the search made a record of it,

the person who made the request shall be entitled to a copy.

(9)　The period mentioned in subsections (7) and (8) above is the period of 12 months beginning with the date on which the search was made.

(10)　The requirements imposed by this section with regard to records of searches of vehicles shall apply also to records of searches of vessels, aircraft and hovercraft.

4.　Road checks

(1)　This section shall have effect in relation to the conducting of road checks by police officers for the purpose of ascertaining whether a vehicle is carrying—

  (a)　a person who has committed an offence other than a road traffic offence or a vehicles excise offence;

  (b)　a person who is a witness to such an offence;

  (c)　a person intending to commit such an offence; or

  (d)　a person who is unlawfully at large.

(2)　For the purposes of this section a road check consists of the exercise in a locality of the power conferred by section 163 of the Road Traffic Act 1988 in such a way as to stop during the period for which its exercise in that way in that locality continues all vehicles or vehicles selected by any criterion.

(3)　Subject to subsection (5) below, there may only be such a road check if a police officer of the rank of superintendent or above authorises it in writing.

(4)　An officer may only authorise a road check under subsection (3) above—

  (a)　for the purpose specified in subsection (1)(a) above, if he has reasonable grounds—

    (i)　for believing that the offence is a serious arrestable offence; and

    (ii)　for suspecting that the person is, or is about to be, in the locality in which vehicles would be stopped if the road check were authorised;

  (b)　for the purpose specified in subsection (1)(b) above, if he has reasonable grounds for believing that the offence is a serious arrestable offence;

  (c)　for the purpose specified in subsection (1)(c) above, if he has reasonable grounds—

(i)   for believing that the offence would be a serious arrestable offence; and

(ii)   for suspecting that the person is, or is about to be, in the locality in which vehicles would be stopped if the road check were authorised;

(d)   for the purpose specified in subsection (1)(d) above, if he has reasonable grounds for suspecting that the person is, or is about to be, in that locality.

(5)   An officer below the rank of superintendent may authorise such a road check if it appears to him that it is required as a matter of urgency for one of the purposes specified in subsection (1) above.

(6)   If an authorisation is given under subsection (5) above, it shall be the duty of the officer who gives it—

(a)   to make a written record of the time at which he gives it; and

(b)   to cause an officer of the rank of superintendent or above to be informed that it has been given.

(7)   The duties imposed by subsection (6) above shall be performed as soon as it is practicable to do so.

(8)   An officer to whom a report is made under subsection (6) above may, in writing, authorise the road check to continue.

(9)   If such an officer considers that the road checks should not continue, he shall record in writing—

(a)   the fact that it took place; and

(b)   the purpose for which it took place.

(10)   An officer giving an authorisation under this section shall specify the locality in which vehicles are to be stopped.

(11)   An officer giving an authorisation under this section, other than an authorisation under subsection (5) above—

(a)   shall specify a period, not exceeding seven days, during which the road check may continue; and

(b)   may direct that the road check—

(i)   shall be continuous; or

(ii)   shall be conducted at specified times, during that period.

(12)   If it appears to an officer of the rank of superintendent or above that a road check ought to continue beyond the period for which it has been authorised he may, from time to time, in writing specify a further period, not exceeding seven days, during which it may continue.

(13)   Every written authorisation shall specify—

(a)   the name of the officer giving it;

(b)   the purpose of the road check; and

(c)   the locality in which vehicles are to be stopped.

(14)   The duties to specify the purposes of a road check imposed by subsections (9) and (13) above include duties to specify any relevant serious arrestable offence.

(15)   Where a vehicle is stopped in a road check, the person in charge of the vehicle at the time when it is stopped shall be entitled to obtain a written statement of the purpose of the road check if he applies for such a statement not later than the end of the period of twelve months from the day on which the vehicle was stopped.

(16)   Nothing in this section affects the exercise by police officers of any power to stop vehicles for purposes other than those specified in subsection (1) above.

5.   Reports of recorded searches and of road checks

(1)   Every annual report—

(a)   under [section 22 of the Police Act 1996]; or

(b)   made by the Commissioner of Police of the Metropolis, shall contain information—

(i)   about searches recorded under section 3 above which have been carried out in the area to which the report relates during the period to which it relates; and

(ii)   about road checks authorised in that area during that period under section 4 above.

[(1A)   Every annual report under section 57 of the Police Act 1997 (reports by Director General of the National Crime Squad) shall contain information—

(a)   about searches recorded under section 3 above which have been carried out by members of the National Crime Squad during the period to which the report relates, and

(b)   about road checks authorised by members of the National Crime Squad during that period under section 4 above.]

(2)   The information about searches shall not include information about specific searches but shall include—

(a)   the total number of searches in each month during the period to which the report relates—

(i)   for stolen articles;

(ii)   for offensive weapons or articles to which section 1(8A) above applies; and

(iii)   for other prohibited articles;

(b)   the total number of persons arrested in each such month in consequence of searches of each of the descriptions specified in paragraph (a)(i) to (iii) above.

(3)   The information about road checks shall include information—

(a)   about the reason for authorising each road check; and

(b)   about the result of each of them.

6.   Statutory undertakers etc.

(1)   A constable employed by statutory undertakers may stop, detain and search any vehicle before it leaves a goods area included in the premises of the statutory undertakers.

(1A)   Without prejudice to any powers under subsection (1) above, a constable employed by the British Railways Board may stop, detain and search any vehicle before it leaves a goods area which is included in the premises of any successor of the British Railways Board and is used wholly or mainly for the purpose of a relevant undertaking.

(2)   In this section 'goods area' means any area used wholly or mainly for the storage or handling of goods.

(3)   For the purposes of section 6 of the Public Stores Act 1875, any person appointed under the Special Constables Act 1923 to be a special constable within any premises which are in the possession or under the control of British Nuclear Fuels Limited shall be deemed to be a constable deputed by a public department and any goods and chattels belonging to or in the possession of British Nuclear Fuels Limited shall be deemed to be Her Majesty's Stores.

(4)   In the application of subsection (3) above to Northern Ireland, for the reference to the Special Constables Act 1923 there shall be substituted a reference to paragraph 1(2) of Schedule 2 to the Emergency Laws (Miscellaneous Provisions) Act 1947.

7.   Part I — supplementary

(1)   The following enactments shall cease to have effect—

(a)   section 8 of the Vagrancy Act 1824;

(b)   section 66 of the Metropolitan Police Act 1839;

(c)   section 11 of the Canals (Offences) Act 1840;

(d)   section 19 of the Pedlars Act 1871;

(e)   section 33 of the County of Merseyside Act 1980; and

(f)   section 42 of the West Midlands County Council Act 1980.

(2)   There shall also cease to have effect—

(a)   so much of any enactment contained in an Act passed before 1974, other than—

(i)   an enactment contained in a public general Act; or
(ii)   an enactment relating to statutory undertakers, as confers power on a constable to search for stolen or unlawfully obtained goods; and
(b)   so much of any enactment relating to statutory undertakers as provides that such a power shall not be exercisable after the end of a specified period.
(3)   In this Part of this Act 'statutory undertakers' means persons authorised by any enactment to carry on any railway, light railway, road transport, water transport, canal, inland navigation, dock or harbour undertaking.

PART II
POWERS OF ENTRY, SEARCH AND SEIZURE

Search warrants

8.   Power of justice of the peace to authorise entry and search of premises
(1)   If on an application made by a constable a justice of the peace is satisfied that there are reasonable grounds for believing—
(a)   that a serious arrestable offence has been committed; and
(b)   that there is material on premises specified in the application which is likely to be of substantial value (whether by itself or together with other material) to the investigation of the offence; and
(c)   that the material is likely to be relevant evidence; and
(d)   that it does not consist of or include items subject to legal privilege, excluded material or special procedure material; and
(e)   that any of the conditions specified in subsection (3) below applies,
he may issue a warrant authorising a constable to enter and search the premises.
(2)   A constable may seize and retain anything for which a search has been authorised under subsection (1) above.
(3)   The conditions mentioned in subsection (1)(e) above are—
(a)   that it is not practicable to communicate with any person entitled to grant entry to the premises;
(b)   that it is practicable to communicate with a person entitled to grant entry to the premises but it is not practicable to communicate with any person entitled to grant access to the evidence;
(c)   that entry to the premises will not be granted unless a warrant is produced;
(d)   that the purpose of a search may be frustrated or seriously prejudiced unless a constable arriving at the premises can secure immediate entry to them.
(4)   In this Act 'relevant evidence', in relation to an offence, means anything that would be admissible in evidence at a trial for the offence.
(5)   The power to issue a warrant conferred by this section is in addition to any such power otherwise conferred.
(6)   This section applies in relation to a relevant offence (as defined in section 28D of the Immigration Act 1971) as it applies to a serious arrestable offence.

9.   Special provisions as to access
(1)   A constable may obtain access to excluded material or special procedure material for the purposes of a criminal investigation by making an application under Schedule 1 below and in accordance with that Schedule.
(2)   Any Act (including a local Act) passed before this Act under which a search of premises for the purposes of a criminal investigation could be authorised by the issue of a warrant to a constable shall cease to have effect so far as it relates to the authorisation of searches—
(a)   for items subject to legal privilege; or
(b)   for excluded material; or

(c)   for special procedure material consisting of documents or records other than documents.

(2A)   Section 4 of the Summary Jurisdiction (Process) Act 1881 (c. 24) (which includes provision for the execution of process of English courts in Scotland) and section 29 of the Petty Sessions (Ireland) Act 1851 (c. 93) (which makes equivalent provision for execution in Northern Ireland) shall each apply to any process issued by a circuit judge under Schedule 1 to this Act as it applies to process issued by a magistrates' court under the Magistrates' Courts Act 1980 (c. 43).

10.   Meaning of 'items subject to legal privilege'

(1)   Subject to subsection (2) below, in this Act 'items subject to legal privilege' means—

[(a)   communications between a professional legal adviser and his client or any person representing his client made in connection with the giving of legal advice to the client;]

[(b)]   communications between a professional legal adviser and his client or any person representing his client or between such an adviser or his client or any such representative and any other person made in connection with or in contemplation of legal proceedings and for the purpose of such proceedings; and

(c)   items enclosed with or referred to in such communications and made—

(i)   in connection with the giving of legal advice; or

(ii)   in connection with or in contemplation of legal proceedings and for the purposes of such proceedings,

when they are in the possession of a person who is entitled to possession of them.

(2)   Items held with the intention of furthering a criminal purpose are not items subject to legal privilege.

11.   Meaning of 'excluded material'

(1)   Subject to the following provisions of this section, in this Act 'excluded material' means—

(a)   personal records which a person has acquired or created in the course of any trade, business, profession or other occupation or for the purposes of any paid or unpaid office and which he holds in confidence;

(b)   human tissue or tissue fluid which has been taken for the purposes of diagnosis or medical treatment and which a person holds in confidence;

(c)   journalistic material which a person holds in confidence and which consists—

(i)   of documents; or

(ii)   of records other than documents.

(2)   A person holds material other than journalistic material in confidence for the purposes of this section if he holds it subject—

(a)   to an express or implied undertaking to hold it in confidence; or

(b)   to a restriction on disclosure or an obligation of secrecy contained in any enactment, including an enactment contained in an Act passed after this Act.

(3)   A person holds journalistic material in confidence for the purposes of this section if—

(a)   he holds it subject to such an undertaking, restriction or obligation; and

(b)   it has been continuously held (by one or more persons) subject to such an undertaking, restriction or obligation since it was first acquired or created for the purposes of journalism.

12.   Meaning of 'personal records'

In this Part of this Act 'personal records' means documentary and other records concerning an individual (whether living or dead) who can be identified from them and relating—

(a)   to his physical or mental health;

(b)   to spiritual counselling or assistance given or to be given to him; or

(c)   to counselling or assistance given or to be given to him, for the purposes of his personal welfare, by any voluntary organisation or by any individual who—

(i)   by reason of his office or occupation has responsibilities for his personal welfare; or

(ii)   by reason of an order of a court has responsibilities for his supervision.

13. Meaning of 'journalistic material'

(1)   Subject to subsection (2) below, in this Act 'journalistic material' means material acquired or created for the purposes of journalism.

(2)   Material is only journalistic material for the purposes of this Act if it is in the possession of a person who acquired or created it for the purposes of journalism.

(3)   A person who receives material from someone who intends that the recipient shall use it for the purposes of journalism is to be taken to have acquired it for those purposes.

14. Meaning of 'special procedure material'

(1)   In this Act 'special procedure material' means—

(a)   material to which subsection (2) below applies; and

(b)   journalistic material, other than excluded material.

(2)   Subject to the following provisions of this section, this subsection applies to material, other than items subject to legal privilege and excluded material, in the possession of a person who—

(a)   acquired or created it in the course of any trade, business, profession or other occupation or for the purpose of any paid or unpaid office; and

(b)   holds it subject—

(i)   to an express or implied undertaking to hold it in confidence; or

(ii)   to a restriction or obligation such as is mentioned in section 11(2)(b) above.

(3)   Where material is acquired—

(a)   by an employee from his employer and in the course of his employment; or

(b)   by a company from an associated company,

it is only special procedure material if it was special procedure material immediately before the acquisition.

(4)   Where material is created by an employee in the course of his employment, it is only special procedure material if it would have been special procedure material had his employer created it.

(5)   Where material is created by a company on behalf of an associated company, it is only special procedure material if it would have been special procedure material had the associated company created it.

(6)   A company is to be treated as another's associated company for the purposes of this section if it would be so treated under section 302 of the Income and Corporation Taxes Act 1970.

15. Search warrants — safeguards

(1)   This section and section 16 below have effect in relation to the issue to constables under any enactment, including an enactment contained in an Act passed after this Act, of warrants to enter and search premises; and an entry on or search of premises under a warrant is unlawful unless it complies with this section 16 below.

(2)   Where a constable applies for any such warrant, it shall be his duty—

(a)   to state—

(i)   the ground on which he makes the application; and

(ii)   the enactment under which the warrant would be issued;

(b)   to specify the premises which it is desired to enter and search; and

(c)   to identify, so far as is practicable, the articles or persons to be sought.

(3)   An application for such a warrant shall be made ex parte and supported by an information in writing.

(4)   The constable shall answer on oath any question that the justice of the peace or judge hearing the application asks him.

(5)   A warrant shall authorise an entry on one occasion only.

(6)   A warrant—

   (a)   shall specify—

      (i)   the name of the person who applies for it;

      (ii)   the date on which it is issued;

      (iii)   the enactment under which it is issued; and

      (iv)   the premises to be searched; and

   (b)   shall identify, so far as is practicable, the articles or persons to be sought.

(7)   Two copies shall be made of a warrant.

(8)   The copies shall be clearly certified as copies.

16.   Execution of warrants

(1)   A warrant to enter and search premises may be executed by any constable.

(2)   Such a warrant may authorise persons to accompany any constable who is executing it.

(3)   Entry and search under a warrant must be within one month from the date of its issue.

(4)   Entry and search under a warrant must be at a reasonable hour unless it appears to the constable executing it that the purpose of a search may be frustrated on an entry at a reasonable hour.

(5)   Where the occupier of premises which are to be entered and searched is present at the time when a constable seeks to execute a warrant to enter and search them, the constable—

   (a)   shall identify himself to the occupier and, if not in uniform, shall produce to him documentary evidence that he is a constable;

   (b)   shall produce a warrant to him; and

   (c)   shall supply him with a copy of it.

(6)   Where—

   (a)   the occupier of such premises is not present at the time when a constable seeks to execute such a warrant; but

   (b)   some other person who appears to the constable to be in charge of the premises is present,

subsection (5) above shall have effect as if any reference to the occupier were a reference to that other person.

(7)   If there is no person present who appears to the constable to be in charge of the premises, he shall leave a copy of the warrant in a prominent place on the premises.

(8)   A search under a warrant may only be a search to the extent required for the purpose for which the warrant was issued.

(9)   A constable executing a warrant shall make an endorsement on it stating—

   (a)   whether the articles or persons sought were found; and

   (b)   whether any articles were seized, other than articles which were sought.

(10)   A warrant which—

   (a)   has been executed; or

   (b)   has not been executed within the time authorised for its execution,

shall be returned—

      (i)   if it was issued by a justice of the peace, to the chief executive to the justices for the petty sessions for which he acts; and

(ii)   if it was issued by a judge, to the appropriate officer of the court from which he issued it.

(11)   A warrant which is returned under subsection (10) above shall be retained for 12 months from its return—

(a)   by the chief executive to the justices, if it was returned under paragraph (i) of that subsection; and

(b)   by the appropriate officer, if it was returned under paragraph (ii).

(12)   If during the period for which a warrant is to be retained the occupier of the premises to which it relates asks to inspect it, he shall be allowed to do so.

Entry and search without search warrant

17.   Entry for purpose of arrest etc.

(1)   Subject to the following provisions of this section, and without prejudice to any other enactment, a constable may enter and search any premises for the purpose—

(a)   of executing—

(i)   a warrant of arrest issued in connection with or arising out of criminal proceedings; or

(ii)   a warrant of commitment issued under section 76 of the Magistrates' Courts Act 1980;

(b)   of arresting a person for an arrestable offence;

(c)   of arresting a person for an offence under—

(i)   section 1 (prohibition of uniforms in connection with political objects), of the Public Order Act 1936;

(ii)   any enactment contained in sections 6 to 8 or 10 of the Criminal Law Act 1977 (offences relating to entering and remaining on property);

(iii)   section 4 of the Public Order Act 1986 (fear or provocation of violence);

(iv)   section 76 of the Criminal Justice and Public Order Act 1994 (failure to comply with interim possession order);

(ca)   of arresting, in pursuance of section 32(1A) of the Children and Young Persons Act 1969, any child or young person who has been remanded or committed to local authority accommodation under section 23(1) of that Act;

(cb)   of recapturing any person who is, or is deemed for any purpose to be, unlawfully at large while liable to be detained—

(i)   in a prison, remand centre, young offender institution or secure housing centre, or

(ii)   in pursuance of section 92 of the Powers of Criminal Courts (Sentencing) Act 2000 (dealing with children and young persons guilty of grave crimes), in any other place.

(d)   of recapturing a person who is unlawfully at large and whom he is pursuing; or

(e)   of saving life or limb or preventing serious damage to property.

(2)   Except for the purpose specified in paragraph (e) of subsection (1) above, the powers of entry and search conferred by this section—

(a)   are only exercisable if the constable has reasonable grounds for believing that the person whom he is seeking is on the premises; and

(b)   are limited, in relation to premises consisting of two or more separate dwellings, to powers to enter and search—

(i)   any parts of the premises which the occupiers of any dwelling comprised in the premises use in common with the occupiers of any other such dwelling; and

(ii)   any such dwelling in which the constable has reasonable grounds for believing that the person whom he is seeking may be.

(3)   The powers of entry and search conferred by this section are only exercisable for the purposes specified in subsection (1)(c)(ii) or (iv) above by a constable in uniform.

(4)   The power of search conferred by this section is only a power to search to the extent that is reasonably required for the purpose for which the power of entry is exercised.

(5)   Subject to subsection (6) below, all the rules of common law under which a constable has power to enter premises without a warrant are hereby abolished.

(6)   Nothing in subsection (5) above affects any power of entry to deal with or prevent a breach of the peace.

18.   Entry and search after arrest

(1)   Subject to the following provisions of this section, a constable may enter and search any premises occupied or controlled by a person who is under arrest for an arrestable offence, if he has reasonable grounds for suspecting that there is on the premises evidence, other than items subject to legal privilege, that relates—

(a)   to that offence; or

(b)   to some other arrestable offence which is connected with or similar to that offence.

(2)   A constable may seize and retain anything for which he may search under subsection (1) above.

(3)   The power to search conferred by subsection (1) above is only a power to search to the extent that is reasonably required for the purpose of discovering such evidence.

(4)   Subject to subsection (5) below, the powers conferred by this section may not be exercised unless an officer of the rank of inspector or above has authorised them in writing.

(5)   A constable may conduct a search under subsection (1) above—

(a)   before taking the person to a police station; and

(b)   without obtaining an authorisation under subsection (4) above,

if the presence of that person at a place other than a police station is necessary for the effective investigation of the offence.

(6)   If a constable conducts a search by virtue of subsection (5) above, he shall inform an officer of the rank of inspector or above that he has made the search as soon as practicable after he has made it.

(7)   An officer who—

(a)   authorises a search; or

(b)   is informed of a search under subsection (6) above,

shall make a record in writing—

(i)   of the grounds for the search; and

(ii)   of the nature of the evidence that was sought.

(8)   If the person who was in occupation or control of the premises at the time of the search is in police detention at the time the record is to be made, the officer shall make the record as part of his custody record.

Seizure etc.

19.   General power of seizure etc.

(1)   The powers conferred by subsections (2), (3) and (4) below are exercisable by a constable who is lawfully on any premises.

(2)   The constable may seize anything which is on the premises if he has reasonable grounds for believing—

(a)   that it has been obtained in consequence of the commission of an offence; and

(b)   that it is necessary to seize it in order to prevent it being concealed, lost, damaged, altered or destroyed.

(3) The constable may seize anything which is on the premises if he has reasonable grounds for believing—

(a) that it is evidence in relation to an offence which he is investigating or any other offence; and

(b) that it is necessary to seize it in order to prevent it being concealed, lost, altered or destroyed.

(4) The constable may require any information which is contained in a computer and is accessible from the premises to be produced in a form in which it can be taken away and in which it is visible and legible if he has reasonable grounds for believing—

(a) that—

(i) it is evidence in relation to an offence which he is investigating or any other offence; or

(ii) it has been obtained in consequence of the commission of an offence; and

(b) that it is necessary to do so in order to prevent it being concealed, lost, tampered with or destroyed.

(5) The powers conferred by this section are in addition to any power otherwise conferred.

(6) No power of seizure conferred on a constable under any enactment (including an enactment contained in an Act passed after this Act) is to be taken to authorise the seizure of an item which the constable exercising the power has reasonable grounds for believing to be subject to legal privilege.

20. Extension of powers of seizure to computerised information

(1) Every power of seizure which is conferred by an enactment to which this section applies on a constable who has entered premises in the exercise of a power conferred by an enactment shall be construed as including a power to require any information contained in a computer and accessible from the premises to be produced in a form in which it can be taken away and in which it is visible and legible.

(2) This section applies—

(a) to any enactment contained in an Act passed before this Act;

(b) to sections 8 and 18 above;

(c) to paragraph 13 of Schedule 1 to this Act; and

(d) to any enactment contained in an Act passed after this Act.

21. Access and copying

(1) A constable who seizes anything in the exercise of a power conferred by any enactment, including an enactment contained in an Act passed after this Act, shall, if so requested by a person showing himself—

(a) to be the occupier of premises on which it was seized; or

(b) to have had custody or control of it immediately before the seizure,

provide that person with a record of what he seized.

(2) The officer shall provide the record within a reasonable time from the making of the request for it.

(3) Subject to subsection (8) below, if a request for permission to be granted access to anything which—

(a) has been seized by a constable; and

(b) is retained by the police for the purpose of investigating an offence,

is made to the officer in charge of the investigation by a person who had custody or control of the thing immediately before it was so seized or by someone acting on behalf of such a person, the officer shall allow the person who made the request access to it under the supervision of a constable.

(4) Subject to subsection (8) below, if a request for a photograph or copy of any such thing is made to the officer in charge of the investigation by a person who had

custody or control of the thing immediately before it was so seized, or by someone acting on behalf of such a person, the officer shall—

(a)   allow the person who made the request access to it under the supervision of a constable for the purpose of photographing or copying it; or

(b)   photograph or copy it, or cause it to be photographed or copied.

(5)   A constable may also photograph or copy, or have photographed or copied, anything which he has power to seize, without a request being made under subsection (4) above.

(6)   Where anything is photographed or copied under subsection (4)(b) above, the photograph or copy shall be supplied to the person who made the request.

(7)   The photograph or copy shall be so supplied within a reasonable time from the making of the request.

(8)   There is no duty under this section to grant access to, or to supply a photograph or copy of, anything if the officer in charge of the investigation for the purposes of which it was seized has reasonable grounds for believing that to do so would prejudice—

(a)   that investigation;

(b)   the investigation of an offence other than the offence for the purposes of investigating which the thing was seized; or

(c)   any criminal proceedings which may be brought as a result of—

(i)   the investigation of which he is in charge; or

(ii)   any such investigation as is mentioned in paragraph (b) above.

22. Retention

(1)   Subject to subsection (4) below, anything which has been seized by a constable or taken away by a constable following a requirement made by virtue of section 19 or 20 above may be retained so long as is necessary in all the circumstances.

(2)   Without prejudice to the generality of subsection (1) above—

(a)   anything seized for the purposes of a criminal investigation may be retained, except as provided by subsection (4) below,—

(i)   for use as evidence at a trial for an offence; or

(ii)   for forensic examination or for investigation in connection with an offence; and

(b)   anything may be retained in order to establish its lawful owner, where there are reasonable grounds for believing that it has been obtained in consequence of the commission of an offence.

(3)   Nothing seized on the ground that it may be used—

(a)   to cause physical injury to any person;

(b)   to damage property;

(c)   to interfere with evidence; or

(d)   to assist in escape from police detention or lawful custody,

may be retained when the person from whom it was seized is no longer in police detention or the custody of a court or is in the custody of a court but has been released on bail.

(4)   Nothing may be retained for either of the purposes mentioned in subsection (2)(a) above if a photograph or copy would be sufficient for that purpose.

(5)   Nothing in this section affects any power of a court to make an order under section 1 of the Police (Property) Act 1897.

(6)   This section also applies to anything retained by the police under section 28H(5) of the Immigration Act 1971.

Supplementary

23. Meaning of 'premises' etc.
In this Act—

'premises' includes any place and, in particular, includes—
  (a)   any vehicle, vessel, aircraft or hovercraft;
  (b)   any offshore installation; and
  (c)   any tent or movable structure; and
'offshore installation' has the meaning given to it by section 1 of the Mineral Workings (Offshore Installations) Act 1971.

PART III
ARREST

24.   Arrest without warrant for arrestable offences

  (1)   The powers of summary arrest conferred by the following subsections shall apply—
  (a)   to offences for which the sentence is fixed by law;
  (b)   to offences for which a person of 18 years of age or over (not previously convicted) may be sentenced to imprisonment for a term of five years (or might be so sentenced but for the restrictions imposed by section 33 of the Magistrates' Courts Act 1980); and
  (c)   to the offences to which subsection (2) below applies,
and in this Act 'arrestable offence' means any such offence.
  (2)   The offences to which this subsection applies are—
  (a)   offences for which a person may be arrested under the customs and excise Acts, as defined in section 1(1) of the Customs and Excise Management Act 1979;
  (b)   offences under the Official Secrets Act 1920 that are not arrestable offences by virtue of the term of imprisonment for which a person may be sentenced in respect of them;
  (bb)   offences under any provision of the Official Secrets Act 1989 except section 8(1), (4) or (5);
  (c)   offences under section 22 (causing prostitution of women) or 23 (procuration of girl under 21) of the Sexual Offences Act 1956;
  (d)   offences under section 12(1) (taking motor vehicle or other conveyance without authority etc.) or 25(1) (going equipped for stealing, etc.) of the Theft Act 1968;
  (e)   any offence under the Football (Offences) Act 1991.
  (f)   an offence under section 2 of the Obscene Publications Act 1959 (publication of obscene matter);
  (g)   an offence under section 1 of the Protection of Children Act 1978 (indecent photographs and pseudo-photographs of children);
  (ga)   an offence under section 1 of the Sexual Offences Act 1985 (kerb-crawling);
  (gb)   an offence under subsection (4) of section 170 of the Road Traffic Act 1988 (failure to stop and report an accident) in respect of an accident to which that section applies by virtue of subsection (1)(a) of that section (accidents causing personal injury);
  (h)   an offence under section 166 of the Criminal Justice and Public Order Act 1994 (sale of tickets by unauthorised persons);
  (i)   an offence under section 19 of the Public Order Act 1986 (publishing etc. material intended or likely to stir up racial hatred);
  (j)   an offence under section 167 of the Criminal Justice and Public Order Act 1994 (touting for car hire services);
  [(k)   an offence under section 1(1) of the Prevention of Crime Act 1953 (prohibition of the carrying of offensive weapons without lawful authority or reasonable excuse);
  (l)   an offence under section 139(1) of the Criminal Justice Act 1988 (offence of having article with blade or point in public place);

(m)   an offence under section 139A(1) or (2) of the Criminal Justice Act 1988 (offence of having article with blade or point (or offensive weapon) on school premises).]

(n)   an offence under section 2 of the Protection from Harassment Act (harassment).

(o)   an offence under section 60(8)(b) of the Criminal Justice and Public Order Act 1994 (failing to comply with requirements to remove mask etc.);

(p)   an offence falling within section 32(1)(a) of the Crime and Disorder Act 1998 (racially aggravated harassment);

(q)   an offence under section 14J or 21C of the Football Spectators Act 1989 (failure to comply with requirements imposed by or under a banning order or a notice under section 21B).

(3)   Without prejudice to section 2 of the Criminal Attempts Act 1981, the powers of summary arrest conferred by the following subsections shall also apply to the offences of—

(a)   conspiring to commit any of the offences mentioned in subsection (2) above;

(b)   attempting to commit any such offence [other than an offence under section 12(1) of the Theft Act 1968];

(c)   inciting, aiding, abetting, counselling or procuring any such offence;

and such offences are also arrestable offences for the purposes of this Act.

(4)   Any person may arrest without a warrant—

(a)   anyone who is in the act of committing an arrestable offence;

(b)   anyone whom he has reasonable grounds for suspecting to be committing such an offence.

(5)   Where an arrestable offence has been committed, any person may arrest without a warrant—

(a)   anyone who is guilty of the offence;

(b)   anyone whom he has reasonable grounds for suspecting to be guilty of it.

(6)   Where a constable has reasonable grounds for suspecting that an arrestable offence has been committed, he may arrest without a warrant anyone whom he has reasonable grounds for suspecting to be guilty of the offence.

(7)   A constable may arrest without a warrant—

(a)   anyone who is about to commit an arrestable offence;

(b)   anyone whom he has reasonable grounds for suspecting to be about to commit an arrestable offence.

25.   General arrest conditions

(1)   Where a constable has reasonable grounds for suspecting that any offence which is not an arrestable offence has been committed or attempted, or is being committed or attempted, he may arrest the relevant person if it appears to him that service of a summons is impracticable or inappropriate because any of the general arrest conditions is satisfied.

(2)   In this section 'the relevant person' means any person whom the constable has reasonable grounds to suspect of having committed or having attempted to commit the offence or of being in the course of committing or attempting to commit it.

(3)   The general arrest conditions are—

(a)   that the name of the relevant person is unknown to, and cannot be readily ascertained by, the constable;

(b)   that the constable has reasonable grounds for doubting whether a name furnished by the relevant person as his name is his real name;

(c)   that—

(i)   the relevant person has failed to furnish a satisfactory address for service; or

(ii)   the constable has reasonable grounds for doubting whether an address furnished by the relevant person is a satisfactory address for service;

(d)   that the constable has reasonable grounds for believing that arrest is necessary to prevent the relevant person—
>   (i)   causing physical injury to himself or any other person;
>   (ii)   suffering physical injury;
>   (iii) causing loss of or damage to property;
>   (iv)   committing an offence against public decency; or
>   (v)   causing an unlawful obstruction of the highway;

(e)   that the constable has reasonable grounds for believing that arrest is necessary to protect a child or other vulnerable person from the relevant person.

(4)   For the purposes of subsection (3) above an address is a satisfactory address for service if it appears to the constable—

(a)   that the relevant person will be at it for a sufficiently long period for it to be possible to serve him with a summons; or

(b)   that some other person specified by the relevant person will accept service of a summons for the relevant person at it.

(5)   Nothing in subsection (3)(d) above authorises the arrest of a person under sub-paragraph (iv) of that paragraph except where members of the public going about their normal business cannot reasonably be expected to avoid the person to be arrested.

(6)   This section shall not prejudice any power of arrest conferred apart from this section.

26.   Repeal of statutory powers of arrest without warrant or order

(1)   Subject to subsection (2) below, so much of any Act (including a local Act) passed before this Act as enables a constable—

(a)   to arrest a person for an offence without a warrant; or

(b)   to arrest a person otherwise than for an offence without a warrant or an order of a court,

shall cease to have effect.

(2)   Nothing in subsection (1) above affects the enactments specified in Schedule 2 to this Act.

27.   Fingerprinting of certain offenders

(1)   If a person—

(a)   has been convicted of a recordable offence;

(b)   has not at any time been in police detention for the offence; and

(c)   has not had his fingerprints taken—
>   (i)   in the course of the investigation of the offence by the police; or
>   (ii)   since the conviction,

any constable may at any time not later than one month after the date of the conviction require him to attend a police station in order that his fingerprints may be taken.

(1A)   Where a person convicted of a recordable offence has already had his fingerprints taken as mentioned in paragraph (c) of subsection (1) above, that fact (together with any time when he has been in police detention for the offence) shall be disregarded for the purposes of that subsection if—

(a)   the fingerprints taken on the previous occasion do not constitute a complete set of his fingerprints; or

(b)   some or all of the fingerprints taken on the previous occasion are not of sufficient quality to allow satisfactory analysis, comparison or matching.

(1B)   Subsections (1) and (1A) above apply—

(a)   where a person has been given a caution in respect of a recordable offence which, at the time of the caution, he has admitted, or

(b)   where a person has been warned or reprimanded under section 65 of the Crime and Disorder Act 1998 (c. 37) for a recordable offence, as they apply where a person has been convicted of an offence, and references in this section to a conviction shall be construed accordingly.

(2)   A requirement under subsection (1) above—

(a)   shall give the person a period of at least 7 days within which he must so attend; and

(b)   may direct him to so attend at a specified time of day or between specified times of a day.

(3)   Any constable may arrest without warrant a person who has failed to comply with a requirement under subsection (1) above.

(4)   The Secretary of State may by regulations make provision for recording in national police records convictions for such offences as are specified in the regulations.

(5)   Regulations under this section shall be made by statutory instrument and shall be subject to annulment in pursuance of a resolution of either House of Parliament.

28.   Information to be given on arrest

(1)   Subject to subsection (5) below, where a person is arrested, otherwise than by being informed that he is under arrest, the arrest is not lawful unless the person arrested is informed that he is under arrest as soon as is practicable after his arrest.

(2)   Where a person is arrested by a constable, subsection (1) above applies regardless of whether the fact of the arrest is obvious.

(3)   Subject to subsection (5) below, no arrest is lawful unless the person arrested is informed of the ground for the arrest at the time of, or as soon as is practicable after, the arrest.

(4)   Where a person is arrested by a constable, subsection (3) above applies regardless of whether the ground for the arrest is obvious.

(5)   Nothing in this section is to be taken to require a person to be informed—

(a)   that he is under arrest; or

(b)   of the ground for the arrest,

if it was not reasonably practicable for him to be so informed by reason of his having escaped from arrest before the information could be given.

29.   Voluntary attendance at police station etc.

Where for the purpose of assisting with an investigation a person attends voluntarily at a police station or at any other place where a constable is present or accompanies a constable to a police station or any such other place without having been arrested—

(a)   he shall be entitled to leave at will unless he is placed under arrest;

(b)   he shall be informed at once that he is under arrest if a decision is taken by a constable to prevent him from leaving at will.

30.   Arrest elsewhere than at police station

(1)   Subject to the following provisions of this section, where a person—

(a)   is arrested by a constable for an offence; or

(b)   is taken into custody by a constable after being arrested for an offence by a person other than a constable,

at any place other than a police station, he shall be taken to a police station by a constable as soon as practicable after the arrest.

(2)   Subject to subsections (3) and (5) below, the police station to which an arrested person is taken under subsection (1) above shall be a designated police station.

(3)   A constable to whom this subsection applies may take an arrested person to any police station unless it appears to the constable that it may be necessary to keep the arrested person in police detention for more than six hours.

(4)   Subsection (3) above applies—

(a)   to a constable who is working in a locality covered by a police station which is not a designated police station; and

(b) to a constable belonging to a body of constables maintained by an authority other than a police authority.

(5) Any constable may take an arrested person to any police station if—

(a) either of the following conditions is satisfied—

(i) the constable has arrested him without the assistance of any other constable and no other constable is available to assist him;

(ii) the constable has taken him into custody from a person other than a constable without the assistance of any other constable and no other constable is available to assist him; and

(b) it appears to the constable that he will be unable to take the arrested person to a designated police station without the arrested person injuring himself, the constable or some other person.

(6) If the first police station to which an arrested person is taken after his arrest is not a designated police station, he shall be taken to a designated police station not more than six hours after his arrival at the first police station unless he is released previously.

(7) A person arrested by a constable at a place other than a police station shall be released if a constable is satisfied, before the person arrested reaches a police station, that there are no grounds for keeping him under arrest.

(8) A constable who releases a person under subsection (7) above shall record the fact that he has done so.

(9) The constable shall make the record as soon as is practicable after the release.

(10) Nothing in subsection (1) above shall prevent a constable delaying taking a person who has been arrested to a police station if the presence of that person elsewhere is necessary in order to carry out such investigations as it is reasonable to carry out immediately.

. . .

(11) Where there is delay in taking a person who has been arrested to a police station after his arrest, the reasons for the delay shall be recorded when he first arrives at a police station.

(12) Nothing in subsection (1) above shall be taken to affect—

(a) paragraphs 16(3) or 18(1) of Schedule 2 to the Immigration Act 1971;

(b) section 34(1) of the Criminal Justice Act 1972; or

(c) any provision of the Terrorism Act 2000.

(13) Nothing in subsection (10) above shall be taken to affect paragraph 18(3) of Schedule 2 to the Immigration Act 1971.

31. Arrest for further offence

Where—

(a) a person—

(i) has been arrested for an offence; and

(ii) is at a police station in consequence of that arrest; and

(b) it appears to a constable that, if he were released from that arrest, he would be liable to arrest for some other offence,

he shall be arrested for that other offence.

32. Search upon arrest

(1) A constable may search an arrested person, in any case where the person to be searched has been arrested at a place other than a police station, if the constable has reasonable grounds for believing that the arrested person may present a danger to himself or others.

(2) Subject to subsections (3) to (5) below, a constable shall also have power in any such case—

(a) to search the arrested person for anything—

(i) which he might use to assist him to escape from lawful custody; or

(ii)   which might be evidence relating to an offence; and

(b)   to enter and search any premises in which he was when arrested or immediately before he was arrested for evidence relating to the offence for which he has been arrested.

(3)   The power to search conferred by subsection (2) above is only a power to search to the extent that is reasonably required for the purpose of discovering any such thing or any such evidence.

(4)   The powers conferred by this section to search a person are not to be construed as authorising a constable to require a person to remove any of his clothing in public other than an outer coat, jacket or gloves but they do authorise a search of a person's mouth.

(5)   A constable may not search a person in the exercise of the power conferred by subsection (2)(a) above unless he has reasonable grounds for believing that the person to be searched may have concealed on him anything for which a search is permitted under that paragraph.

(6)   A constable may not search premises in the exercise of the power conferred by subsection (2)(b) above unless he has reasonable grounds for believing that there is evidence for which a search is permitted under that paragraph on the premises.

(7)   In so far as the power of search conferred by subsection (2)(b) above relates to premises consisting of two or more separate dwellings, it is limited to a power to search—

(a)   any dwelling in which the arrest took place or in which the person arrested was immediately before his arrest; and

(b)   any parts of the premises which the occupier of any such dwelling uses in common with the occupiers of any other dwellings comprised in the premises.

(8)   A constable searching a person in the exercise of the power conferred by subsection (1) above may seize and retain anything he finds, if he has reasonable grounds for believing that the person searched might use it to cause physical injury to himself or to any other person.

(9)   A constable searching a person in the exercise of the power conferred by subsection (2)(a) above may seize and retain anything he finds, other than an item subject to legal privilege, if he has reasonable grounds for believing—

(a)   that he might use it to assist him to escape from lawful custody; or

(b)   that it is evidence of an offence or has been obtained in consequence of the commission of an offence.

(10)   Nothing in this section shall be taken to affect the power conferred by section 43 of the Terrorism Act 2000.

. . .

PART IV
DETENTION

Detention — conditions and duration

34.   Limitations on police detention

(1)   A person arrested for an offence shall not be kept in police detention except in accordance with the provisions of this Part of this Act.

(2)   Subject to subsection (3) below, if at any time a custody officer—

(a)   becomes aware, in relation to any person in police detention, that the grounds for the detention of that person have ceased to apply and

(b)   is not aware of any other grounds on which the continued detention of that person could be justified under the provisions of this Part of this Act,

it shall be the duty of the custody officer, subject to subsection (4) below, to order his immediate release from custody.

(3)   No person in police detention shall be released except on the authority of a custody officer at the police station where his detention was authorised, or if it was authorised at more than one station, a custody officer at the station where it was last authorised.

(4)   A person who appears to the custody officer to have been unlawfully at large when he was arrested is not to be released under subsection (2) above.

(5)   A person whose release is ordered under subsection (2) above shall be released without bail unless it appears to the custody officer—

(a)   that there is need for further investigation of any matter in connection with which he was detained at any time during the period of his detention; or

(b)   that proceedings may be taken against him in respect of any such matter, and if it so appears, he shall be released on bail.

(6)   For the purposes of this Part of this Act a person arrested under section 6(5) of the Road Traffic Act 1988 is arrested for an offence.

(7)   For the purposes of this Part of this Act a person who returns to a police station to answer to bail or is arrested under section 46A below shall be treated as arrested for an offence and the offence in connection with which he was granted bail shall be deemed to be that offence.

35.   Designated police stations

(1)   The chief officer of police for each police area shall designate the police stations in his area which, subject to section 30(3) and (5) above, are to be the stations in that area to be used for the purpose of detaining arrested persons.

(2)   A chief officer's duty under subsection (1) above is to designate police stations appearing to him to provide enough accommodation for that purpose.

(3)   Without prejudice to section 12 of the Interpretation Act 1978 (continuity of duties) a chief officer—

(a)   may designate a station which was not previously designated; and

(b)   may direct that a designation of a station previously made shall cease to operate.

(4)   In this Act 'designated police station' means a police station designated under this section.

36.   Custody officers at police stations

(1)   One or more custody officers shall be appointed for each designated police station.

(2)   A custody officer for a designated police station shall be appointed—

(a)   by the chief officer of police for the area in which the designated police station is situated; or

(b)   by such other police officer as the chief officer of police for that area may direct.

(3)   No officer may be appointed a custody officer unless he is of at least the rank of sergeant.

(4)   An officer of any rank may perform the functions of a custody officer at a designated police station if a custody officer is not readily available to perform them.

(5)   Subject to the following provisions of this section and to section 39(2) below, none of the functions of a custody officer in relation to a person shall be performed by an officer who at the time when the function fails to be performed is involved in the investigation of an offence for which that person is in police detention at that time.

(6)   Nothing in subsection (5) above is to be taken to prevent a custody officer—

(a)   performing any function assigned to custody officers—

(i)   by this Act; or

(ii)   by a code of practice issued under this Act;

(b) carrying out the duty imposed on custody officers by section 39 below;

(c) doing anything in connection with the identification of a suspect; or

(d) doing anything under sections 7 and 8 of the Road Traffic Act 1988.

(7) Where an arrested person is taken to a police station which is not a designated police station, the functions in relation to him which at a designated police station would be the functions of a custody officer shall be performed—

(a) by an officer who is not involved in the investigation of an offence for which he is in police detention, if such an officer is readily available; and

(b) if no such officer is readily available, by the officer who took him to the station or any other officer.

(8) References to a custody officer in the following provisions of this Act include references to an officer other than a custody officer who is performing the functions of a custody officer by virtue of subsection (4) or (7) above.

(9) Where by virtue of subsection (7) above an officer of a force maintained by a police authority who took an arrested person to a police station is to perform the functions of a custody officer in relation to him, the officer shall inform an officer who—

(a) is attached to a designated police station; and

(b) is of at least the rank of inspector,

that he is to do so.

(10) The duty imposed by subsection (9) above shall be performed as soon as it is practicable to perform it.

37. Duties of custody officer before charge

(1) Where—

(a) a person is arrested for an offence—

(i) without a warrant; or

(ii) under a warrant not endorsed for bail,

the custody officer at each police station where he is detained after his arrest shall determine whether he has before him sufficient evidence to charge that person with the offence for which he was arrested and may detain him at the police station for such period as is necessary to enable him to do so.

(2) If the custody officer determines that he does not have such evidence before him, the person arrested shall be released either on bail or without bail, unless the custody officer has reasonable grounds for believing that his detention without being charged is necessary to secure or preserve evidence relating to an offence for which he is under arrest or to obtain such evidence by questioning him.

(3) If the custody officer has reasonable grounds for so believing, he may authorise the person arrested to be kept in police detention.

(4) Where a custody officer authorises a person who has not been charged to be kept in police detention, he shall, as soon as is practicable, make a written record of the grounds for the detention.

(5) Subject to subsection (6) below, the written record shall be made in the presence of the person arrested who shall at that time be informed by the custody officer of the grounds for his detention.

(6) Subsection (5) above shall not apply where the person arrested is, at the time when the written record is made—

(a) incapable of understanding what is said to him;

(b) violent or likely to become violent; or

(c) in urgent need of medical attention.

(7) Subject to section 41(7) below, if the custody officer determines that he has before him sufficient evidence to charge the person arrested with the offence for which he was arrested, the person arrested—

(a)   shall be charged; or
(b)   shall be released without charge, either on bail or without bail.
(8)   Where—
(a)   a person is released under subsection (7)(b) above; and
(b)   at the time of his release a decision whether he should be prosecuted for the offence for which he was arrested has not been taken,
it shall be the duty of the custody officer so to inform him.
(9)   If the person arrested is not in a fit state to be dealt with under subsection (7) above, he may be kept in police detention until he is.
(10)   The duty imposed on the custody officer under subsection (1) above shall be carried out by him as soon as practicable after the person arrested arrives at the police station or, in the case of a person arrested at the police station, as soon as practicable after the arrest.
(15)   In this Part of this Act—
'arrested juvenile' means a person arrested with or without a warrant who appears to be under the age of 17;
'endorsed for bail' means endorsed with a direction for bail in accordance with section 117(2) of the Magistrates' Courts Act 1980.

38.   Duties of custody officer after charge
(1)   Where a person arrested for an offence otherwise than under a warrant endorsed for bail is charged with an offence, the custody officer shall, subject to section 25 of the Criminal Justice and Public Order Act 1994, order his release from police detention, either on bail or without bail, unless—
(a)   if the person arrested is not an arrested juvenile—
(i)   his name or address cannot be ascertained or the custody officer has reasonable grounds for doubting whether a name or address furnished by him as his name or address is his real name or address;
(ii)   the custody officer has reasonable grounds for believing that the person arrested will fail to appear in court to answer to bail;
(iii)   in the case of a person arrested for an imprisonable offence, the custody officer has reasonable grounds for believing that the detention of the person arrested is necessary to prevent him from committing an offence;
(iiia)   in the case of a person who has attained the age of 18, the custody officer has reasonable grounds for believing that the detention of the person is necessary to enable a sample to be taken from him under section 63B below;
(iv)   in the case of a person arrested for an offence which is not an imprisonable offence, the custody officer has reasonable grounds for believing that the detention of the person arrested is necessary to prevent him from causing physical injury to any other person or from causing loss of or damage to property;
(v)   the custody officer has reasonable grounds for believing that the detention of the person arrested is necessary to prevent him from interfering with the administration of justice or with the investigation of offences or of a particular offence; or
(vi)   the custody officer has reasonable grounds for believing that the detention of the person arrested is necessary for his own protection;
(b)   if he is an arrested juvenile—
(i)   any of the requirements of paragraph (a) above is satisfied; or
(ii)   the custody officer has reasonable grounds for believing that he ought to be detained in his own interests.
(2)   If the release of a person arrested is not required by subsection (1) above, the custody officer may authorise him to be kept in police detention but may not authorise a person to be kept in police detention by virtue of subsection (1)(a)(iiia) after the end of the period of six hours beginning with when he was charged with the offence.

(2A)   The custody officer, in taking the decisions required by subsection (1)(a) and (b) above (except (a)(i) and (vi) and (b)(ii)), shall have regard to the same considerations as those which a court is required to have regard to in taking the corresponding decisions under paragraph 2 of Part I of Schedule 1 to the Bail Act 1976.

(3)   Where a custody officer authorises a person who has been charged to be kept in police detention, he shall, as soon as practicable, make a written record of the grounds for the detention.

(4)   Subject to subsection (5) below, the written record shall be made in the presence of the person charged who shall at that time be informed by the custody officer of the grounds for his detention.

(5)   Subsection (4) above shall not apply where the person charged is, at the time when the written record is made—

(a)   incapable of understanding what is said to him;

(b)   violent or likely to become violent; or

(c)   in urgent need of medical attention.

(6)   Where a custody officer authorises an arrested juvenile to be kept in police detention under subsection (1) above, the custody officer shall, unless he certifies—

(a)   that, by reason of such circumstances as are specified in the certificate, it is impracticable for him to do so; or

(b)   in the case of an arrested juvenile who has attained the age of 15 years, that no secure accommodation is available and that keeping him in other local authority accommodation would not be adequate to protect the public from serious harm from him,
secure that the arrested juvenile is moved to local authority accommodation.

(6A)   In this section, 'local authority accommodation' means accommodation provided by or on behalf of a local authority (within the meaning of the Children Act 1989);

'secure accommodation' means accommodation provided for the purpose of restricting liberty;

'sexual offence' and 'violent offence' have the same meanings as in the Powers of Criminal Courts (Sentencing) Act 2000.

(6B)   Where an arrested juvenile is moved to local authority accommodation under subsection (6) above, it shall be lawful for any person acting on behalf of the authority to detain him.

(7)   A certificate made under subsection (6) above in respect of an arrested juvenile shall be produced to the court before which he is first brought thereafter.

(7A)   In this section 'imprisonable offence' has the same meaning as in Schedule 1 to the Bail Act 1976.

(8)   In this Part of this Act 'local authority' has the same meaning as in the Children Act 1989.

39.   Responsibilities in relation to persons detained

(1)   Subject to subsections (2) and (4) below, it shall be the duty of the custody officer at a police station to ensure—

(a)   that all persons in police detention at that station are treated in accordance with this Act and any code of practice issued under it and relating to the treatment of persons in police detention; and

(b)   that all matters relating to such persons which are required by this Act or by such codes of practice to be recorded are recorded in the custody records relating to such persons.

(2)   If this custody officer, in accordance with any code of practice issued under this Act, transfers or permits the transfer of a person in police detention—

(a)   to the custody of a police officer investigating an offence for which that person is in police detention; or

(b)   to the custody of an officer who has charge of that person outside the police station,

the custody officer shall cease in relation to that person to be subject to the duty imposed on him by subsection (1)(a) above; and it shall be the duty of the officer to whom the transfer is made to ensure that he is treated in accordance with the provisions of this Act and of any such codes of practice as are mentioned in subsection (1) above.

(3)   If the person detained is subsequently returned to the custody of the custody officer, it shall be the duty of the officer investigating the offence to report to the custody officer as to the manner in which this section and the codes of practice have been complied with while that person was in his custody.

(4)   If an arrested juvenile is moved to local authority accommodation under section 38(6) above, the custody officer shall cease in relation to that person to be subject to the duty imposed on him by subsection (1) above.

(6)   Where—

(a)   an officer of higher rank than the custody officer gives directions relating to a person in police detention; and

(b)   the directions are at variance—

(i)   with any decision made or action taken by the custody officer in the performance of a duty imposed on him under this Part of this Act; or

(ii)   with any decision or action which would but for the directions have been made or taken by him in the performance of such a duty,

the custody officer shall refer the matter at once to an officer of the rank of superintendent or above who is responsible for the police station for which the custody officer is acting as custody officer.

40.   Review of police detention

(1)   Reviews of the detention of each person in police detention in connection with the investigation of an offence shall be carried out periodically in accordance with the following provisions of this section—

(a)   in the case of a person who has been arrested and charged, by the custody officer; and

(b)   in the case of a person who has been arrested but not charged, by an officer of at least the rank of inspector who has not been directly involved in the investigation.

(2)   The officer to whom it falls to carry out a review is referred to in this section as a 'review officer'.

(3)   Subject to subsection (4) below—

(a)   the first review shall be not later than six hours after the detention was first authorised;

(b)   the second review shall be not later than nine hours after the first;

(c)   subsequent reviews shall be at intervals of not more than nine hours.

(4)   A review may be postponed—

(a)   if, having regard to all the circumstances prevailing at the latest time for it specified in subsection (3) above, it is not practicable to carry out the review at that time;

(b)   without prejudice to the generality of paragraph (a) above—

(i)   if at that time the person in detention is being questioned by a police officer and the review officer is satisfied that an interruption of the questioning for the purpose of carrying out the review would prejudice the investigation in connection with which he is being questioned; or

(ii)   if at that time no review officer is readily available.

(5)   If a review is postponed under subsection (4) above it shall be carried out as soon as practicable after the latest time specified for it in subsection (3) above.

(6)   If a review is carried out after postponement under subsection (4) above, the fact that it was so carried out shall not affect any requirement of this section as to the time at which any subsequent review is to be carried out.

(7)   The review officer shall record the reasons for any postponement of a review in the custody record.

(8)   Subject to subsection (9) below, where the person whose detention is under review has not been charged before the time of the review, section 37(1) to (6) above shall have effect in relation to him, but with the substitution—

(a)   of references to the person whose detention is under review for references to the person arrested;

(b)   of references to the review officer for references to the custody officer.

(9)   Where a person has been kept in police detention by virtue of section 37(9) above, section 37(1) to (6) shall not have effect in relation to him but it shall be the duty of the review officer to determine whether he is yet in a fit state.

(10)   Where the person whose detention is under review has been charged before the time of the review, section 38(1) to (6) above shall have effect in relation to him, but with the substitution of references to the person whose detention is under review for references to the person arrested.

(11)   Where—

(a)   an officer of higher rank than the review officer gives directions relating to a person in police detention; and

(b)   the directions are at variance—

(i)   with any decision made or action taken by the review officer in the performance of a duty imposed on him under this Part of this Act; or

(ii)   with any decision or action which would but for the directions have been made or taken by him in the performance of such a duty,

the review officer shall refer the matter at once to an officer of the rank of superintendent or above who is responsible for the police station for which the review officer is acting as review officer in connection with the detention.

(12)   Before determining whether to authorise a person's continued detention the review officer shall give—

(a)   that person (unless he is asleep); or

(b)   any solicitor representing him who is available at the time of the review,

an opportunity to make representations to him about the detention.

(13)   Subject to subsection (14) below, the person whose detention is under review or his solicitor may make representations under subsection (12) above either orally or in writing.

(14)   The review officer may refuse to hear oral representations from the person whose detention is under review if he considers that he is unfit to make such representations by reason of his condition or behaviour.

40A   Use of telephone for review under s. 40

(1)   This section applies, notwithstanding anything in section 40 above, where in the case of a person who has been arrested but not charged—

(a)   it is not reasonably practicable for an officer of at least the rank of inspector to be present in the police station where that person is held to carry out any review of that person's detention that is required by subsection (1)(b) of that section; and

(b)   the review is not one which regulations under section 45A below authorise to be carried out using video-conferencing facilities, or is one which it is not reasonably practicable, in the circumstances, to carry out using any such facilities.

(2)   The review may be carried out by an officer of at least the rank of inspector who has access to a means of communication by telephone to persons in the police station where the arrested person is held.

(3)   Where any review is carried out under this section by an officer who is not present at the station where the arrested person is held—

(a)   any obligation of that officer to make a record in connection with the carrying out of the review shall have effect as an obligation to cause another officer to make the record;

(b)   any requirement for the record to be made in the presence of the arrested person shall apply to the making of that record by that other officer; and

(c)   the requirements under section 40(12) and (13) above for—

(i)   the arrested person, or

(ii)   solicitor representing him,

to be given any opportunity to make representations (whether in writing or orally to that officer shall have effect as a requirement for that person, or such a solicitor, to be given an opportunity to make representations in a manner authorised by subsection (4) below.

(4)   Representations are made in a manner authorised by this subsection—

(a)   in a case where facilities exist for the immediate transmission of written representations to the officer carrying out the review, if they are made either—

(i)   orally by telephone to that officer; or

(ii)   in writing to that officer by means of those facilities;

and

(b)   in any other case, if they are made orally by telephone to that officer.

(5)   In this section 'video-conferencing facilities' has the same meaning as in section 45A below.

41.   Limits on period of detention without charge

(1)   Subject to the following provisions of this section and to sections 42 and 43 below, a person shall not be kept in police detention for more than 24 hours without being charged.

(2)   The time from which the period of detention of a person is to be calculated (in this Act referred to as 'the relevant time')—

(a)   in the case of a person to whom this paragraph applies, shall be—

(i)   the time at which that person arrives at the relevant police station; or

(ii)   the time 24 hours after the time of that person's arrest,

whichever is the earlier;

(b)   in the case of a person arrested outside England and Wales, shall be—

(i)   the time at which that person arrives at the first police station to which he is taken in the police area in England or Wales in which the offence for which he was arrested is being investigated; or

(ii)   the time 24 hours after the time of that person's entry into England and Wales,

whichever is the earlier;

(c)   in the case of a person who—

(i)   attends voluntarily at a police station; or

(ii)   accompanies a constable to a police station without having been arrested, and is arrested at the police station, the time of his arrest;

(d)   in any other case, except where subsection (5) below applies, shall be the time at which the person arrested arrives at the first police station to which he is taken after his arrest.

(3)   Subsection (2)(a) above applies to a person if—

(a)   his arrest is sought in one police area in England and Wales;

(b)   he is arrested in another police area; and

(c)   he is not questioned in the area in which he is arrested in order to obtain evidence in relation to an offence for which he is arrested;
and in sub-paragraph (i) of that paragraph 'the relevant police station' means the first police station to which he is taken in the police area in which his arrest was sought.

(4)   Subsection (2) above shall have effect in relation to a person arrested under section 31 above as if every reference in it to his arrest or his being arrested were a reference to his arrest or his being arrested for the offence for which he was originally arrested.

(5)   If—

(a)   a person is in police detention in a police area in England and Wales ('the first area'); and

(b)   his arrest for an offence is sought in some other police area in England and Wales ('the second area'); and

(c)   he is taken to the second area for the purposes of investigating that offence, without being questioned in the first area in order to obtain evidence in relation to it, the relevant time shall be—

(i)   the time 24 hours after he leaves the place where he is detained in the first area; or

(ii)   the time at which he arrives at the first police station to which he is taken in the second area,
whichever is the earlier.

(6)   When a person who is in police detention at a police station is removed to hospital because he is in need of medical treatment, any time during which he is being questioned in hospital or on the way there or back by a police officer for the purpose of obtaining evidence relating to an offence shall be included in any period which falls to be calculated for the purposes of this Part of this Act, but any other time while he is in hospital or on his way there or back shall not be so included.

(7)   Subject to subsection (8) below, a person who at the expiry of 24 hours after the relevant time is in police detention and has not been charged shall be released at that time either on bail or without bail.

(8)   Subsection (7) above does not apply to a person whose detention for more than 24 hours after the relevant time has been authorised or is otherwise permitted in accordance with section 42 or 43 below.

(9)   A person released under subsection (7) above shall not be re-arrested without a warrant for the offence for which he was previously arrested unless new evidence justifying a further arrest has come to light since his release; but this subsection does not prevent an arrest under section 46A below.

42.   Authorisation of continued detention

(1)   Where a police officer of the rank of superintendent or above who is responsible for the police station at which a person is detained has reasonable grounds for believing that—

(a)   the detention of that person without charge is necessary to secure or preserve evidence relating to an offence for which he is under arrest or to obtain such evidence by questioning him;

(b)   the offence for which he is under arrest is a serious arrestable offence; and

(c)   the investigation is being conducted diligently and expeditiously,
he may authorise the keeping of that person in police detention for a period expiring at or before 36 hours after the relevant time.

(2)   Where an officer such as is mentioned in subsection (1) above has authorised the keeping of a person in police detention for a period expiring less than 36 hours after the relevant time, such an officer may authorise the keeping of that person in police detention for a further period expiring not more than 36 hours after that time if the

conditions specified in subsection (1) above are still satisfied when he gives the authorisation.

(3)   If it is proposed to transfer a person in police detention to another police area, the officer determining whether or not to authorise keeping him in detention under subsection (1) above shall have regard to the distance and the time the journey would take.

(4)   No authorisation under subsection (1) above shall be given in respect of any person—

    (a)   more than 24 hours after the relevant time; or

    (b)   before the second review of his detention under section 40 above has been carried out.

(5)   Where an officer authorises the keeping of a person in police detention under subsection (1) above, it shall be his duty—

    (a)   to inform that person of the grounds for his continued detention; and

    (b)   to record the grounds in that person's custody record.

(6)   Before determining whether to authorise the keeping of a person in detention under subsection (1) or (2) above, an officer shall give—

    (a)   that person; or

    (b)   any solicitor representing him who is available at the time when it falls to the officer to determine whether to give the authorisation,

an opportunity to make representations to him about the detention.

(7)   Subject to subsection (8) below, the person in detention or his solicitor may make representations under subsection (6) above either orally or in writing.

(8)   The officer to whom it falls to determine whether to give the authorisation may refuse to hear oral representations from the person in detention if he considers that he is unfit to make such representations by reason of his condition or behaviour.

(9)   Where—

    (a)   an officer authorises the keeping of a person in detention under subsection (1) above; and

    (b)   at the time of the authorisation he has not yet exercised a right conferred on him by section 56 or 58 below,

the officer—

    (i)   shall inform him of that right;

    (ii)   shall decide whether he should be permitted to exercise it;

    (iii)   shall record the decision in his custody record; and

    (iv)   if the decision is to refuse to permit the exercise of the right, shall also record the grounds for the decision in that record.

(10)   Where an officer has authorised the keeping of a person who has not been charged in detention under subsection (1) or (2) above, he shall be released from detention, either on bail or without bail, not later than 36 hours after the relevant time, unless—

    (a)   he has been charged with an offence; or

    (b)   his continued detention is authorised or otherwise permitted in accordance with section 43 below.

(11)   A person released under subsection (10) above shall not be re-arrested without a warrant for the offence for which he was previously arrested unless new evidence justifying a further arrest has come to light since his release; but this subsection does not prevent an arrest under section 46A below.

43.   Warrants of further detention

(1)   Where, on an application on oath made by a constable and supported by an information, a magistrates' court is satisfied that there are reasonable grounds for

believing that the further detention of the person to whom the application relates is justified, it may issue a warrant of further detention authorising the keeping of that person in police detention.

(2)   A court may not hear an application for a warrant of further detention unless the person to whom the application relates—

(a)   has been furnished with a copy of the information; and

(b)   has been brought before the court for the hearing.

(3)   The person to whom the application relates shall be entitled to be legally represented at the hearing and, if he is not so represented but wishes to be so represented—

(a)   the court shall adjourn the hearing to enable him to obtain representation; and

(b)   he may be kept in police detention during the adjournment.

(4)   A person's further detention is only justified for the purposes of this section or section 44 below if—

(a)   his detention without charge is necessary to secure or preserve evidence relating to an offence for which he is under arrest or to obtain such evidence by questioning him;

(b)   an offence for which he is under arrest is a serious arrestable offence; and

(c)   the investigation is being conducted diligently and expeditiously.

(5)   Subject to subsection (7) below, an application for a warrant of further detention may be made—

(a)   at any time before the expiry of 36 hours after the relevant time; or

(b)   in a case where—

(i)   it is not practicable for the magistrates' court to which the application will be made to sit at the expiry of 36 hours after the relevant time; but

(ii)   the court will sit during the 6 hours following the end of that period, at any time before the expiry of the said 6 hours.

(6)   In a case to which subsection (5)(b) above applies—

(a)   the person to whom the application relates may be kept in police detention until the application is heard; and

(b)   the custody officer shall make a note in that person's custody record—

(i)   of the fact that he was kept in police detention for more than 36 hours after the relevant time; and

(ii)   of the reason why he was so kept.

(7)   If—

(a)   an application for a warrant of further detention is made after the expiry of 36 hours after the relevant time; and

(b)   it appears to the magistrates' court that it would have been reasonable for the police to make it before the expiry of that period, the court shall dismiss the application.

(8)   Where on an application such as is mentioned in subsection (1) above a magistrates' court is not satisfied that there are reasonable grounds for believing that the further detention of the person to whom the application relates is justified, it shall be its duty—

(a)   to refuse the application; or

(b)   to adjourn the hearing of it until a time not later than 36 hours after the relevant time.

(9)   The person to whom the application relates may be kept in police detention during the adjournment.

(10)   A warrant of further detention shall—

(a)   state the time at which it is issued;

(b)   authorise the keeping in police detention of the person to whom it relates for the period stated in it.

(11) Subject to subsection (12) below, the period stated in a warrant of further detention shall be such period as the magistrates' court thinks fit, having regard to the evidence before it.

(12) The period shall not be longer than 36 hours.

(13) If it is proposed to transfer a person in police detention to a police area other than that in which he is detained when the application for a warrant of further detention is made, the court hearing the application shall have regard to the distance and the time the journey would take.

(14) Any information submitted in support of an application under this section shall state—

(a) the nature of the offence for which the person to whom the application relates has been arrested;

(b) the general nature of the evidence on which that person was arrested;

(c) what inquiries relating to the offence have been made by the police and what further inquiries are proposed by them;

(d) the reasons for believing the continued detention of that person to be necessary for the purposes of such further inquiries.

(15) Where an application under this section is refused, the person to whom the application relates shall forthwith be charged or, subject to subsection (16) below, released, either on bail or without bail.

(16) A person need not be released under subsection (15) above—

(a) before the expiry of 24 hours after the relevant time; or

(b) before the expiry of any longer period for which his continued detention is or has been authorised under section 42 above.

(17) Where an application under this section is refused, no further application shall be made under this section in respect of the person to whom the refusal relates, unless supported by evidence which has come to light since the refusal.

(18) Where a warrant of further detention is issued, the person to whom it relates shall be released from police detention, either on bail or without bail, upon or before the expiry of the warrant unless he is charged.

(19) A person released under subsection (18) above shall not be re-arrested without a warrant for the offence for which he was previously arrested unless new evidence justifying a further arrest has come to light since his release; but this subsection does not prevent an arrest under section 46A below.

44. Extension of warrants of further detention

(1) On an application made by a constable and supported by an information a magistrates' court may extend a warrant of further detention issued under section 43 above if it is satisfied that there are reasonable grounds for believing that the further detention of the person to whom the application relates is justified.

(2) Subject to subsection (3) below, the period for which a warrant of further detention may be extended shall be such period as the court thinks fit, having regard to the evidence before it.

(3) The period shall not—

(a) be longer than 36 hours; or

(b) end later than 96 hours after the relevant time.

(4) Where a warrant of further detention has been extended under subsection (1) above, or further extended under this subsection, for a period ending before 96 hours after the relevant time, on an application such as is mentioned in that subsection a magistrates' court may further extend the warrant if it is satisfied as there mentioned; and subsections (2) and (3) above apply to such further extensions as they apply to extensions under subsection (1) above.

(5)   A warrant of further detention shall, if extended under this section, be endorsed with a note of the period of the extension.

(6)   Subsections (2), (3), (14) and (15) of section 43 above shall apply to an application made under this section as they apply to an application made under that section.

(7)   Where an application under this section is refused, the person to whom the application relates shall forthwith be charged or, subject to subsection (8) below, released, either on bail or without bail.

(8)   A person need not be released under subsection (7) above before the expiry of any period for which a warrant of further detention issued in relation to him has been extended or further extended on an earlier application made under this section.

45.   Detention before charge — supplementary

(1)   In sections 43 and 44 of this Act 'magistrates' court' means a court consisting of two or more justices of the peace sitting otherwise than in open court.

(2)   Any reference in this Part of this Act to a period of time or a time of day is to be treated as approximate only.

45A   Use of video-conferencing facilities for decisions about detention

(1)   Subject to the following provisions of this section, the Secretary of State may by regulations provide that, in the case of an arrested person who is held in a police station, some or all of the functions mentioned in subsection (2) may be performed (notwithstanding anything in the preceding provisions of this Part) by an officer who—

(a)   is not present in that police station; but

(b)   has access to the use of video-conferencing facilities that enable him to communicate with persons in that station.

(2)   Those functions are—

(a)   the functions in relation to an arrested person taken to a police station that is not a designated police station which, in the case of an arrested person taken to a station that is a designated police station, are functions of a custody officer under section 37, 38 or 40 above; and

(b)   the function of carrying out a review under section 40(1)(b) above (review, by an officer of at least the rank of inspector, of the detention of person arrested but not charged).

(3)   Regulations under this section shall specify the use to be made in the performance of the functions mentioned in subsection (2) above of the facilities mentioned in subsection (1) above.

(4)   Regulations under this section shall not authorise the performance of any of the functions mentioned in subsection (2)(a) above by such an officer as is mentioned in subsection (1) above unless he is a custody officer for a designated police station.

(5)   Where any functions mentioned in subsection (2) above are performed in a manner authorised by regulations under this section—

(a)   any obligation of the officer performing those functions to make a record in connection with the performance of those functions shall have effect as an obligation to cause another officer to make the record; and

(b)   any requirement for the record to be made in the presence of the arrested person shall apply to the making of that record by that other officer.

(6)   Where the functions mentioned in subsection (2)(b) are performed in a manner authorised by regulations under this section, the requirements under section 40(12) and (13) above for—

(a)   the arrested person, or

(b)   a solicitor representing him,

to be given any opportunity to make representations (whether in writing or orally) to the person performing those functions shall have effect as a requirement for that person, or such a solicitor, to be given an opportunity to make representations in a manner authorised by subsection (7) below.

(7) Representations are made in a manner authorised by this subsection—

(a) in a case where facilities exist for the immediate transmission of written representations to the officer performing the functions, if they are made either—

(i) orally to that officer by means of the video-conferencing facilities used by him for performing those functions; or

(ii) in writing to that officer by means of the facilities available for the immediate transmission of the representations; and

(b) in any other case if they are made orally to that officer by means of the video-conferencing facilities used by him for performing the functions.

(8) Regulations under this section may make different provision for different cases and may be made so as to have effect in relation only to the police stations specified or described in the regulations.

(9) Regulations under this section shall be made by statutory instrument and shall be subject to annulment in pursuance of a resolution of either House of Parliament.

(10) Any reference in this section to video-conferencing facilities, in relation to any functions, is a reference to any facilities (whether a live television link or other facilities) by means of which the functions may be performed with the officer performing them, the person in relation to whom they are performed and any legal representative of that person all able to both see and to hear each other.

Detention — miscellaneous

46. Detention after charge

(1) Where a person—

(a) is charged with an offence; and

(b) after being charged—

(i) is kept in police detention; or

(ii) is detained by a local authority in pursuance of arrangements made under section 38(6) above,

he shall be brought before a magistrates' court in accordance with the provisions of this section.

(2) If he is to be brought before a magistrates' court for the petty sessions area in which the police station at which he was charged is situated, he shall be brought before such a court as soon as is practicable and in any event not later than the first sitting after he is charged with the offence.

(3) If no magistrates' court for that area is due to sit either on the day on which he is charged or on the next day, the custody officer for the police station at which he was charged shall inform the clerk to the justices for the area that there is a person in the area to whom subsection (2) above applies.

(4) If the person charged is to be brought before a magistrates' court for a petty sessions area other than that in which the police station at which he was charged is situated, he shall be removed to that area as soon as is practicable and brought before such a court as soon as is practicable after his arrival in the area and in any event not later than the first sitting of a magistrates' court for that area after his arrival in the area.

(5) If no magistrates' court for that area is due to sit either on the day on which he arrives in the area or on the next day—

(a) he shall be taken to a police station in the area; and

(b) the custody officer at that station shall inform the clerk to the justices for the area that there is a person in the area to whom subsection (4) applies.

(6) Subject to subsection (8) below, where a clerk to the justices for a petty sessions area has been informed—

(a)   under subsection (3) above that there is a person in the area to whom subsection (2) above applies; or

(b)   under subsection (5) above that there is a person in the area to whom subsection (4) above applies,

the clerk shall arrange for a magistrates' court to sit not later than the day next following the relevant day.

(7)   In this section 'the relevant day'—

(a)   in relation to a person who is to be brought before a magistrates' court for the petty sessions area in which the police station at which he was charged is situated, means the day on which he was charged; and

(b)   in relation to a person who is to be brought before a magistrates' court for any other petty sessions area, means the day on which he arrives in the area.

(8)   Where the day next following the relevant day is Christmas Day, Good Friday or a Sunday, the duty of the clerk under subsection (6) above is a duty to arrange for a magistrates' court to sit not later than the first day after the relevant day which is not one of those days.

(9)   Nothing in this section requires a person who is in hospital to be brought before a court if he is not well enough.

46A.   Power of arrest for failure to answer to police bail

(1)   A constable may arrest without a warrant any person who, having been released on bail under this Part of this Act subject to a duty to attend at a police station, fails to attend at that police station at the time appointed for him to do so.

(2)   A person who is arrested under this section shall be taken to the police station appointed as the place at which he is to surrender to custody as soon as practicable after the arrest.

(3)   For the purposes of—

(a)   section 30 above (subject to the obligation in subsection (2) above), and

(b)   section 31 above,

an arrest under this section shall be treated as an arrest for an offence.

47.   Bail after arrest

(1)   Subject to subsection (2) below, a release on bail of a person under this Part of this Act shall be a release on bail granted in accordance with sections 3, 3A, 5 and 5A of the Bail Act 1976 as they apply to bail granted by a constable.

(1A)   The normal powers to impose conditions of bail shall be available to him where a custody officer releases a person on bail under section 38(1) above (including that subsection as applied by section 40(10) above) but not in any other cases.

In this subsection, 'the normal powers to impose conditions of bail' has the meaning given in section 3(b) of the Bail Act 1976.

(2)   Nothing in the Bail Act 1976 shall prevent the re-arrest without warrant of a person released on bail subject to a duty to attend at a police station if new evidence justifying a further arrest has come to light since his release.

(3)   Subject to subsections (3A) and (4) below, in this Part of this Act references to 'bail' are references to bail subject to a duty—

(a)   to appear before a magistrates' court at such time and such place; or

(b)   to attend at such police station at such time,

as the custody officer may appoint.

(3A)   Where a custody officer grants bail to a person subject to a duty to appear before a magistrates' court, he shall appoint for the appearance—

(a)   a date which is not later than the first sitting of the court after the person is charged with the offence; or

(b)   where he is informed by the justices' chief executive for the relevant petty sessions area that the appearance cannot be accommodated until a later date, that later date.

(4)   Where a custody officer has granted bail to a person subject to a duty to appear at a police station, the custody officer may give notice in writing to that person that his attendance at the police station is not required.

(6)   Where a person who has been granted bail and has either attended at the police station in accordance with the grant of bail or has been arrested under section 46A above is detained at a police station, any time during which he was in police detention prior to being granted bail shall be included as part of any period which falls to be calculated under this Part of this Act.

(7)   Where a person who was released on bail subject to a duty to attend at a police station is re-arrested, the provisions of this Part of this Act shall apply to him as they apply to a person arrested for the first time but this subsection does not apply to a person who is arrested under section 46A above or has attended a police station in accordance with the grant of bail (and who accordingly is deemed by section 34(7) above to have been arrested for an offence).

(8)   In the Magistrates' Courts Act 1980—

(a)   the following section shall be substituted for section 43—

'43.   Bail on arrest

(1)   Where a person has been granted bail under the Police and Criminal Evidence Act 1984 subject to a duty to appear before a magistrates' court, the court before which he is to appear may appoint a later time as the time at which he is to appear and may enlarge the recognizances of any sureties for him at that time.

(2)   The recognizance of any surety for any person granted bail subject to a duty to attend at a police station may be enforced as if it were conditioned for his appearance before a magistrates' court for the petty sessions area in which the police station named in the recognizance is situated.'; and

(b)   the following subsection shall be substituted for section 117(3)—

'(3)   Where a warrant has been endorsed for bail under subsection (1) above—

(a)   where the person arrested is to be released on bail on his entering into a recognizance without sureties, it shall not be necessary to take him to a police station, but if he is so taken, he shall be released from custody on his entering into the recognizance; and

(b)   where he is to be released on his entering into a recognizance with sureties, he shall be taken to a police station on his arrest, and the custody officer there shall (subject to his approving any surety tendered in compliance with the endorsement) release him from custody as directed in the endorsement.'.

47A.   Early administrative hearings conducted by justices' clerk

Where a person has been charged with an offence at a police station, any requirement imposed under this Part for the person to appear or be brought before a magistrates' court shall be taken to be satisfied if the person appears or is brought before the clerk to the justices for a petty sessions area in order for the clerk to conduct a hearing under section 50 of the Crime and Disorder Act 1998 (early administrative hearings).

48.   Remands to police detention

In section 128 of the Magistrates' Courts Act 1980—

(a)   in subsection (7) for the words 'the custody of a constable' there shall be substituted the words 'detention at a police station';

(b)   after subsection (7) there shall be inserted the following subsection—

'(8)   Where a person is committed to detention at a police station under subsection (7) above—

(a)   he shall not be kept in such detention unless there is a need for him to be so detained for the purposes of inquiries into other offences;

(b)   if kept in such detention, he shall be brought back from the magistrates' court which committed him as soon as that need ceases;

(c)   he shall be treated as a person in police detention to whom the duties under section 39 of the Police and Criminal Evidence Act 1984 (responsibilities in relation to persons detained) relate;

(d)   his detention shall be subject to periodic review at the times set out in section 40 of that Act (review of police detention).'.

49.   Police detention to count towards custodial sentence

(1)   In subsection (1) of section 67 of the Criminal Justice Act 1967 (computation of custodial sentences) for the words from 'period', in the first place where it occurs, to 'the offender' there shall be substituted the words 'relevant period, but where he'.

(2)   The following subsection shall be inserted after that subsection—

'(1A)   In subsection (1) above "relevant period" means—

(a)   any period during which the offender was in police detention in connection with the offence for which the sentence was passed; or

(b)   any period during which he was in custody—

(i)   by reason only of having been committed to custody by an order of a court made in connection with any proceedings relating to that sentence or the offence for which it was passed or any proceedings from which those proceedings arose; or

(ii)   by reason of his having been so committed and having been concurrently detained otherwise than by order of a court.'.

(3)   The following subsections shall be added after subsection (6) of that section—

'(7)   A person is in police detention for the purposes of this section—

(a)   at any time when he is in police detention for the purposes of the Police and Criminal Evidence Act 1984; and

(b)   at any time when he is detained under section [14] of the Prevention of Terrorism (Temporary Provisions) Act 1984.

(8)   No period of police detention shall be taken into account under this section unless it falls after the coming into force of section 49 of the Police and Criminal Evidence Act 1984.'.

50.   Records of detention

(1)   Each police force shall keep written records showing on an annual basis—

(a)   the number of persons kept in police detention for more than 24 hours and subsequently released without charge;

(b)   the number of applications for warrants of further detention and the results of the applications; and

(c)   in relation to each warrant of further detention—

(i)   the period of further detention authorised by it;

(ii)   the period which the person named in it spent in police detention on its authority; and

(iii)   whether he was charged or released without charge.

(2)   Every annual report—

(a)   under [section 22 of the Police Act 1996]; or

(b)   made by the Commissioner of Police of the Metropolis,

shall contain information about the matters mentioned in subsection (1) above in respect of the period to which the report relates.

51.   Savings

Nothing in this Part of this Act shall affect—

(a)   the powers conferred on immigration officers by section 4 of and Schedule 2 to the Immigration Act 1971 (administrative provisions as to control on entry etc.);

(b)   the powers conferred by or by virtue of section 41 of, or Schedule 7 to, the Terrorism Act 2000 (Powers of Arrest and Detention);

(c)   any duty of a police officer under—

    (i)   section 129, 190 or 202 of the Army Act 1955 (duties of governors of prisons and others to receive prisoners, deserters, absentees and persons under escort);

    (ii)   section 129, 190 or 202 of the Air Force Act 1955 (duties of governors of prisons and others to receive prisoners, deserters, absentees and persons under escort);

    (iii)   section 107 of the Naval Discipline Act 1957 (duties of governors of civil prisons etc.); or

    (iv)   paragraph 5 of Schedule 5 to the Reserve Forces Act 1980 (duties of governors of civil prisons); or

(d)   any right of a person in police detention to apply for a writ of habeas corpus or other prerogative remedy.

PART V
QUESTIONING AND TREATMENT OF PERSONS BY POLICE

53.   Abolition of certain powers of constables to search persons

(1)   Subject to subsection (2) below, there shall cease to have effect any Act (including a local Act) passed before this Act in so far as it authorises—

(a)   any search by a constable of a person in police detention at a police station; or

(b)   an intimate search of a person by a constable;

and any rule of common law which authorises a search such as is mentioned in paragraph (a) or (b) above is abolished.

54.   Searches of detained persons

(1)   The custody officer at a police station shall ascertain and record or cause to be recorded everything which a person has with him when he is—

(a)   brought to the station after being arrested elsewhere or after being committed to custody by an order or sentence of a court; or

(b)   arrested at the station or detained there, as a person falling within section 34(7), under section 37 above.

(2)   In the case of an arrested person the record shall be made as part of his custody record.

(3)   Subject to subsection (4) below, a custody officer may seize and retain any such thing or cause any such thing to be seized and retained.

(4)   Clothes and personal effects may only be seized if the custody officer—

(a)   believes that the person from whom they are seized may use them—

    (i)   to cause physical injury to himself or any other person;

    (ii)   to damage property;

    (iii)   to interfere with evidence; or

    (iv)   to assist him to escape; or

(b)   has reasonable grounds for believing that they may be evidence relating to an offence.

(5)   Where anything is seized, the person from whom it is seized shall be told the reason for the seizure unless he is—

(a)   violent or likely to become violent; or

(b)   incapable of understanding what is said to him.

(6)   Subject to subsection (7) below, a person may be searched if the custody officer considers it necessary to enable him to carry out his duty under subsection (1) above and to the extent that the custody officer considers necessary for that purpose.

(6A)   A person who is in custody at a police station or is in police detention otherwise than at a police station may at any time be searched in order to ascertain whether he has with him anything which he could use for any of the purposes specified in subsection 4(a) above.

(6B)   Subject to subsection (6C) below, a constable may seize and detain, or cause to be seized and detained, anything found in such a search.

(6C)   A constable may only seize clothes and personal effects in the circumstances specified in subsection (4) above.

(7)   An intimate search may not be conducted under this section.

(8)   A search under this section shall be carried out by a constable.

(9)   The constable carrying out a search shall be of the same sex as the person searched.

55.   Intimate searches

(1)   Subject to the following provisions of this section, if an officer of at least the rank of inspector has reasonable grounds for believing—

(a)   that a person who has been arrested and is in police detention may have concealed on him anything which—

(i)   he could use to cause physical injury to himself or others; and

(ii)   he might so use while he is in police detention or in the custody of a court;

or

(b)   that such a person—

(i)   may have a Class A drug concealed on him; and

(ii)   was in possession of it with the appropriate criminal intent before his arrest,

he may authorise an intimate search of that person.

(2)   An officer may not authorise an intimate search of a person for anything unless he has reasonable grounds for believing that it cannot be found without his being intimately searched.

(3)   An officer may give an authorisation under subsection (1) above orally or in writing but, if he gives it orally, he shall confirm it in writing as soon as is practicable.

(4)   An intimate search which is only a drug offence search shall be by way of examination by a suitably qualified person.

(5)   Except as provided by subsection (4) above, an intimate search shall be by way of examination by a suitably qualified person unless an officer of at least the rank of inspector considers that this is not practicable.

(6)   An intimate search which is not carried out as mentioned in subsection (5) above shall be carried out by a constable.

(7)   A constable may not carry out an intimate search of a person of the opposite sex.

(8)   No intimate search may be carried out except—

(a)   at a police station;

(b)   at a hospital;

(c)   at a registered medical practitioner's surgery; or

(d)   at some other place used for medical purposes.

(9)   An intimate search which is only a drug offence search may not be carried out at a police station.

(10)   If an intimate search of a person is carried out, the custody record relating to him shall state—

(a)   which parts of his body were searched; and

(b)   why they were searched.

(11)   The information required to be recorded by subsection (10) above shall be recorded as soon as practicable after the completion of the search.

(12)   The custody officer at a police station may seize and retain anything which is found on an intimate search of a person, or cause any such thing to be seized and retained—

(a)   if he believes that the person from whom it is seized may use it—

(i)   to cause physical injury to himself or any other person;

(ii)   to damage property;

(iii)   to interfere with evidence; or

(iv)   to assist him to escape; or

(b)   if he has reasonable grounds for believing that it may be evidence relating to an offence.

(13)   Where anything is seized under this section, the person from whom it is seized shall be told the reason for the seizure unless he is—

(a)   violent or likely to become violent; or

(b)   incapable of understanding what is said to him.

(14)–(16)   [Information to be contained in annual reports.]

(17)   In this section—

'the appropriate criminal intent' means an intent to commit an offence under—

(a)   section 5(3) of the Misuse of Drugs Act 1971 (possession of controlled drug with intent to supply to another); or

(b)   section 68(2) of the Customs and Excise Management Act 1979 (exportation etc. with intent to evade a prohibition or restriction);

'Class A drug' has the meaning assigned to it by section 2(1)(b) of the Misuse of Drugs Act 1971;

'drug offence search' means an intimate search for a Class A drug which an officer has authorised by virtue of subsection (1)(b) above; and

'suitably qualified person' means—

(a)   a registered medical practitioner; or

(b)   a registered nurse.

56.   Right to have someone informed when arrested

(1)   Where a person has been arrested and is being held in custody in a police station or other premises, he shall be entitled, if he so requests, to have one friend or relative or other person who is known to him or who is likely to take an interest in his welfare told, as soon as is practicable except to the extent that delay is permitted by this section, that he has been arrested and is being detained there.

(2)   Delay is only permitted—

(a)   in the case of a person who is in police detention for a serious arrestable offence; and

(b)   if an officer of at least the rank of inspector authorises it.

(3)   In any case the person in custody must be permitted to exercise the right conferred by subsection (1) above within 36 hours from the relevant time, as defined in section 41(2) above.

(4)   An officer may give an authorisation under subsection (2) above orally or in writing but, if he gives it orally, he shall confirm it in writing as soon as is practicable.

(5)   Subject to subsection (5A) below an officer may only authorise delay where he has reasonable grounds for believing that telling the named person of the arrest—

(a)   will lead to interference with or harm to evidence connected with a serious arrestable offence or interference with or physical injury to other persons; or

(b)   will lead to the alerting of other persons suspected of having committed such an offence but not yet arrested for it; or

(c)   will hinder the recovery of any property obtained as a result of such an offence.

(5A)   An officer may also authorise delay where the serious arrestable offence is a drug trafficking offence or an offence to which Part VI of the Criminal Justice Act 1988 applies (offences in respect of which confiscation orders under that Part may be made) and the officer has reasonable grounds for believing—

(a)   where the offence is a drug trafficking offence, that the detained person has benefited from drug trafficking and that the recovery of the value of that person's proceeds of drug trafficking will be hindered by telling the named person of the arrest; and

(b)   where the offence is one to which Part VI of the Criminal Justice Act 1988 applies, that the detained person has benefited from the offence and that the recovery of the value of the property obtained by that person from or in connection with the offence or of the pecuniary advantage derived by him from or in connection with it will be hindered by telling the named person of the arrest.

(6)   If a delay is authorised—

(a)   the detained person shall be told the reason for it, and

(b)   the reason shall be noted on his custody record.

(7)   The duties imposed by subsection (6) above shall be performed as soon as is practicable.

(8)   The rights conferred by this section on a person detained at a police station or other premises are exercisable whenever he is transferred from one place to another; and this section applies to each subsequent occasion on which they are exercisable as it applies to the first such occasion.

(9)   There may be no further delay in permitting the exercise of the right conferred by subsection (1) above once the reason for authorising delay ceases to subsist.

(10)   Nothing in this section applies to a person arrested or detained under the terrorism provisions.

57.   Additional rights of children and young persons

The following subsections shall be substituted for section 34(2) of the Children and Young Persons Act 1933—

'(2)   Where a child or young person is in police detention, such steps as are practicable shall be taken to ascertain the identity of a person responsible for his welfare.

(3)   If it is practicable to ascertain the identity of a person responsible for the welfare of the child or young person, that person shall be informed, unless it is not practicable to do so—

(a)   that the child or young person has been arrested;

(b)   why he has been arrested; and

(c)   where he is being detained.

(4)   Where information falls to be given under subsection (3) above, it shall be given as soon as it is practicable to do so.

(5)   For the purposes of this section the persons who may be responsible for the welfare of a child or young person are—

(a)   his parent or guardian; or

(b)   any other person who has for the time being assumed responsibility for his welfare.

(6)   If it is practicable to give a person responsible for the welfare of the child or young person the information required by subsection (3) above, that person shall be given it as soon as it is practicable to do so.

(7)   If it appears that at the time of his arrest a supervision order, as defined in section 163 of the Powers of Criminal Courts (Sentencing) Act 2000 or Part IV of the Children Act 1989, is in force in respect of him, the person responsible for his supervision shall also be informed as described in subsection (3) above as soon as it is reasonably practicable to do so.

(8)   The reference to a parent or guardian in subsection (5) above is—

(a)   in the case of a child or young person in the care of a local authority, a reference to that authority; and

(b)   in the case of a child or young person in the care of a voluntary organisation in which parental rights and duties with respect to him are vested by virtue of a resolution under section 64(1) of the Child Care Act 1980, a reference to that organisation.

(9)   The rights conferred on a child or young person by subsections (2) to (8) above are in addition to his rights under section 56 of the Police and Criminal Evidence Act 1984.

(10)   The reference in subsection (2) above to a child or young person who is in police detention includes a reference to a child or young person who has been detained under the terrorism provisions; and in subsection (3) above 'arrest' includes such detention.

(11)   In subsection (10) above 'the terrorism provisions' has the meaning assigned to it by section 65 of the Police and Criminal Evidence Act 1984.'.

58.   Access to legal advice

(1)   A person arrested and held in custody in a police station or other premises shall be entitled, if he so requests, to consult a solicitor privately at any time.

(2)   Subject to subsection (3) below, a request under subsection (1) above and the time at which it was made shall be recorded in the custody record.

(3)   Such a request need not be recorded in the custody record of a person who makes it at a time while he is at a court after being charged with an offence.

(4)   If a person makes such a request, he must be permitted to consult a solicitor as soon as is practicable except to the extent that delay is permitted by this section.

(5)   In any case he must be permitted to consult a solicitor within 36 hours from the relevant time, as defined in section 41(2) above.

(6)   Delay in compliance with a request is only permitted—

(a)   in the case of a person who is in police detention for a serious arrestable offence; and

(b)   if an officer of at least the rank of superintendent authorises it.

(7)   An officer may give an authorisation under subsection (6) above orally or in writing but, if he gives it orally, he shall confirm it in writing as soon as is practicable.

(8)   Subject to subsection (8A) below an officer may only authorise delay where he has reasonable grounds for believing that the exercise of the right conferred by subsection (1) above at the time when the person detained desires to exercise it—

(a)   will lead to interference with or harm to evidence connected with a serious arrestable offence or interference with or physical injury to other persons; or

(b)   will lead to the alerting of other persons suspected of having committed such an offence but not yet arrested for it; or

(c)   will hinder the recovery of any property obtained as a result of such an offence.

(8A)   An officer may also authorise delay where the serious arrestable offence is a drug trafficking offence [or an offence to which Part VI of the Criminal Justice Act 1988 applies] and the officer has reasonable grounds for believing—

[(a)   where the offence is a drug trafficking offence, that the detained person has benefited from drug trafficking and that the recovery of the value of that person's proceeds of drug trafficking will be hindered by the exercise of the right conferred by subsection (1) above; and

(b)   where the offence is one to which Part VI of the Criminal Justice Act 1988 applies, that the detained person has benefited from the offence and that the recovery of the value of the property obtained by that person from or in connection with the offence or of the pecuniary advantage derived by him from or in connection with it will be hindered by the exercise of the right conferred by subsection (1) above.]

(9)   If delay is authorised—

(a)   the detained person shall be told the reason for it; and

(b)   the reason shall be noted on his custody record.

(10)   The duties imposed by subsection (9) above shall be performed as soon as is practicable.

(11)   There may be no further delay in permitting the exercise of the right conferred by subsection (1) above once the reason for authorising delay ceases to subsist.

(12)   Nothing in this section applies to a person arrested or detained under the terrorism provisions.

60.   Tape-recording of interviews

(1)   It shall be the duty of the Secretary of State—

(a)   to issue a code of practice in connection with the tape-recording of interviews of persons suspected of the commission of criminal offences which are held by police officers at police stations; and

(b)   to make an order requiring the tape-recording of interviews of persons suspected of the commission of criminal offences, or of such descriptions of criminal offences as may be specified in the order, which are so held, in accordance with the code as it has effect for the time being.

(2)   An order under subsection (1) above shall be made by statutory instrument and shall be subject to annulment in pursuance of a resolution of either House of Parliament.

60A.   Visual recording of interviews

(1)   The Secretary of State shall have power—

(a)   to issue a code of practice for the visual recording of interviews held by police officers at police stations; and

(b)   to make an order requiring the visual recording of interviews so held, and requiring the visual recording to be in accordance with the code for the time being in force under this section.

(2)   A requirement imposed by an order under this section may be imposed in relation to such cases or police stations in such areas, or both, as may be specified or described in the order.

(3)   An order under subsection (1) above shall be made by statutory instrument and shall be subject to annulment in pursuance of a resolution of either House of Parliament.

(4)   In this section—

(a)   references to any interview are references to an interview of a person suspected of a criminal offence; and

(b)   references to a visual recording include references to a visual recording in which an audio recording is comprised.

61.   Fingerprinting

(1)   Except as provided by this section no person's fingerprints may be taken without the appropriate consent.

(2)   Consent to the taking of a person's fingerprints must be in writing if it is given at a time when he is at a police station.

(3)   The fingerprints of a person detained at a police station may be taken without the appropriate consent—

(a)   if an officer of at least the rank of inspector authorises them to be taken; or

(b)   if—

(i)   he has been charged with a recordable offence or informed that he will be reported for such an offence; and

(ii)   he has not had his fingerprints taken in the course of the investigation of the offence by the police.

(3A)   Where a person charged with a recordable offence or informed that he will be reported for such an offence has already had his fingerprints taken as mentioned in paragraph (b)(ii) of subsection (3) above, that fact shall be disregarded for the purposes of that subsection if—

(a)   the fingerprints taken on the previous occasion do not constitute a complete set of his fingerprints; or

(b)   some or all of the fingerprints taken on the previous occasion are not of sufficient quality to allow satisfactory analysis, comparison or matching (whether in the case in question or generally).

(4)   An officer may only give an authorisation under subsection (3)(a) above if he has reasonable grounds—

(a)   for suspecting the involvement of the person whose fingerprints are to be taken in a criminal offence; and

(b)   for believing that his fingerprints will tend to confirm or disprove his involvement.

(4A)   The fingerprints of a person who has answered to bail at a court or police station may be taken without the appropriate consent at the court or station if—

(a)   the court, or

(b)   an officer of at least the rank of inspector,
authorises them to be taken.

(4B)   A court or officer may only give an authorisation under subsection (4A) if—

(a)   the person who has answered to bail has answered to it for a person whose fingerprints were taken on a previous occasion and there are reasonable grounds for believing that he is not the same person; or

(b)   the person who has answered to bail claims to be a different person from a person whose fingerprints were taken on a previous occasion.

(5)   An officer may give an authorisation under subsection (3)(a) or (4A) above orally or in writing but, if he gives it orally, he shall confirm it in writing as soon as is practicable.

(6)   Any person's fingerprints may be taken without the appropriate consent if—

(a)   he has been convicted of a recordable offence;

(b)   he has been given a caution in respect of a recordable offence which, at the time of the caution, he has admitted; or

(c)   he has been warned or reprimanded under section 65 of the Crime and Disorder Act 1998 (c. 37) for a recordable offence.

(7)   In a case where by virtue of subsection (3) or (6) above a person's fingerprints are taken without the appropriate consent—

(a)   he shall be told the reason before his fingerprints are taken; and

(b)   the reason shall be recorded as soon as is practicable after the fingerprints are taken.

(7A)   If a person's fingerprints are taken at a police station, whether with or without the appropriate consent—

(a)   before the fingerprints are taken, an officer shall inform him that they may be the subject of a speculative search; and

(b)   the fact that the person has been informed of this possibility shall be recorded as soon as is practicable after the fingerprints have been taken; and

(8)   If he is detained at a police station when the fingerprints are taken, the reason for taking them and in the case falling within subsection (7A) above, the fact referred to in paragraph (b) of that subsection shall be recorded on his custody record.

(8A) Where a person's fingerprints are taken electronically, they must be taken only in such manner, and using such devices, as the Secretary of State has approved for the purposes of electronic fingerprinting.

(9) Nothing in this section—

(a) affects any power conferred by paragraph 18(2) of Schedule 2 to the Immigration Act 1971; or

(b) applies to a person arrested or detained under the terrorism provisions.

62. Intimate samples

(1) Subject to section 63B below an intimate sample may be taken from a person in police detention only—

(a) if a police officer of at least the rank of inspector authorises it to be taken; and

(b) if the appropriate consent is given.

(1A) An intimate sample may be taken from a person who is not in police detention but from whom, in the course of the investigation of an offence, two or more non-intimate samples suitable for the same means of analysis have been taken which have proved insufficient—

(a) if a police officer of at least the rank of inspector authorises it to be taken; and

(b) if the appropriate consent is given.

(2) An officer may only give an authorisation under subsection (1) or (1A) above if he has reasonable grounds—

(a) for suspecting the involvement of the person from whom the sample is to be taken in a recordable offence; and

(b) for believing that the sample will tend to confirm or disprove his involvement.

(3) An officer may give an authorisation under subsection (1) or (1A) above orally or in writing but, if he gives it orally, he shall confirm it in writing as soon as is practicable.

(4) The appropriate consent must be given in writing.

(5) Where—

(a) an authorisation has been given; and

(b) it is proposed that an intimate sample shall be taken in pursuance of the authorisation,

an officer shall inform the person from whom the sample is to be taken—

(i) of the giving of the authorisation; and

(ii) of the grounds for giving it.

(6) The duty imposed by subsection (5)(ii) above includes a duty to state the nature of the offence in which it is suspected that the person from whom the sample is taken has been involved.

(7) If an intimate sample is taken from a person—

(a) the authorisation by virtue of which it was taken;

(b) the grounds for giving the authorisation; and

(c) the fact that the appropriate consent was given,

shall be recorded as soon as is practicable after the sample is taken.

(7A) If an intimate sample is taken from a person at a police station—

(a) before the sample is taken, an officer shall inform him that it may be the subject of a speculative search; and

(b) the fact that the person has been informed of this possibility shall be recorded as soon as practicable after the sample has been taken; and

(8) If an intimate sample is taken from a person detained at a police station, the matters required to be recorded by subsection (7) or (7A) above shall be recorded in his custody record.

(9) An intimate sample, other than a sample of urine or dental impression, may only be taken from a person by a registered medical practitioner or a registered nurse and a dental impression may only be taken by a registered dentist.

(10)   Where the appropriate consent to the taking of an intimate sample from a person was refused without good cause, in any proceedings against that person for an offence—
(a)   the court, in determining—
(i)   whether to [commit that person for trial; or]
(ii)   whether there is a case to answer; and
(aa)   a judge, in deciding whether to grant an application made by the accused under—
(i)   section 6 of the Criminal Justice Act 1987 (application for dismissal of charge of serious fraud in respect of which notice of transfer has been given under section 4 of that Act); or
(ii)   paragraph 5 of Schedule 6 to the Criminal Justice Act 1991 (application for dismissal of charge of violent or sexual offence involving child in respect of which notice of transfer has been given under section 53 of that Act); and
(b)   the court or jury, in determining whether that person is guilty of the offence charged,
may draw such inferences from the refusal as appear proper.
(11)   Nothing in this section affects sections 4 to 11 of the Road Traffic Act 1988.
(12)   Nothing in this section applies to a person arrested or detained under the terrorism provisions; and subsection (1A) shall not apply where the non-intimate samples mentioned in that subsection were taken under paragraph 10 of Schedule 8 to the Terrorism Act 2000.

63.   Other samples

(1)   Except as provided by this section, a non-intimate sample may not be taken from a person without the appropriate consent.
(2)   Consent to the taking of a non-intimate sample must be given in writing.
(3)   A non-intimate sample may be taken from a person without the appropriate consent if—
(a)   he is in police detention or is being held in custody by the police on the authority of a court; and
(b)   an officer of at least the rank of inspector authorises it to be taken without the appropriate consent.
(3A)   A non-intimate sample may be taken from a person (whether or not he falls within subsection (3)(a) (above) without the appropriate consent if—
(a)   he has been charged with a recordable offence or informed that he will be reported for such an offence; and
(b)   either he has not had a non-intimate sample taken from him in the course of the investigation of the offence by the police or he has had a non-intimate sample taken from him but either it was not suitable for the same means of analysis or, though so suitable, the sample proved insufficient.
(3B)   A non-intimate sample may be taken from a person without the appropriate consent if he has been convicted of a recordable offence.
(3C)   A non-intimate sample may also be taken from a person without the appropriate consent if he is a person to whom section 2 of the Criminal Evidence (Amendment) Act 1997 applies (persons detained following acquittal on grounds of insanity or finding of unfitness to plead).
(4)   An officer may only give an authorisation under subsection (3) above if he has reasonable grounds—
(a)   for suspecting the involvement of the person from whom the sample is to be taken in a recordable offence; and
(b)   for believing that the sample will tend to confirm or disprove his involvement.
(5)   An officer may give an authorisation under subsection (3) above orally or in writing but, if he gives it orally, he shall confirm it in writing as soon as is practicable.

(5A) An officer shall not give an authorisation under subsection (3) above for the taking from any person of a non-intimate sample consisting of a skin impression if—

(a) a skin impression of the same part of the body has already been taken from that person in the course of the investigation of the offence; and

(b) the impression previously taken is not one that has proved insufficient.

(6) Where—

(a) an authorisation has been given; and

(b) it is proposed that a non-intimate sample shall be taken in pursuance of the authorisation,

an officer shall inform the person from whom the sample is to be taken—

(i) of the giving of the authorisation; and

(ii) of the grounds for giving it.

(7) The duty imposed by subsection (6)(ii) above, includes a duty to state the nature of the offence in which it is suspected that the person from whom the sample is to be taken has been involved.

(8) If a non-intimate sample is taken from a person by virtue of subsection (3) above—

(a) the authorisation by virtue of which it was taken; and

(b) the grounds for giving the authorisation,

shall be recorded as soon as is practicable after the sample is taken.

(8A) In a case whereby by virtue of subsection (3A), (3B) or (3C) above a sample is taken from a person without the appropriate consent—

(a) he shall be told the reason before the sample is taken; and

(b) the reason shall be recorded as soon as practicable after the sample is taken.

(8B) If a non-intimate sample is taken from a person at a police station, whether with or without the appropriate consent—

(a) before the sample is taken, an officer shall inform him that it may be the subject of a speculative search; and

(b) the fact that the person has been informed of this possibility shall be recorded as soon as practicable after the sample has been taken.

(9) If a non-intimate sample is taken from a person detained at a police station, the matters required to be recorded by subsection (8) or (8A) or (8B) above shall be recorded in his custody record.

(9A) Subsection (3B) above shall not apply to any person convicted before 10 April 1995 unless he is a person to whom section 1 of the Criminal Evidence (Amendment) Act 1997 applies (persons imprisoned or detained by virtue of pre-existing conviction for sexual offence etc.).

[(10) Nothing in this section applies to a person arrested or detained under the terrorism provisions.]

63A. Fingerprints and samples: supplementary provisions

(1) Where a person has been arrested on suspicion of being involved in a recordable offence or has been charged with such an offence or has been informed that he will be reported for such an offence, fingerprints or samples or the information derived from samples taken under any power conferred by this Part of this Act from the person may be checked against—

(a) other fingerprints or samples to which the person seeking to check has access and which are held by or on behalf of any one or more relevant law enforcement authorities or which are held in connection with or as a result of an investigation of an offence;

(b) information derived from other samples if the information is contained in records to which the person seeking to check has access and which are held as mentioned in paragraph (a) above.

(1A)   In subsection (1) above 'relevant law-enforcement authority' means—
   (a)   a police force;
   (b)   the National Criminal Intelligence Service;
   (c)   the National Crime Squad;
   (d)   a public authority (not falling within paragraphs (a) to (c)) with functions in any part of the British Islands which consist of or include the investigation of crimes or the charging of offenders;
   (e)   any person with functions in any country or territory outside the United Kingdom which—
      (i)   correspond to those of a police force; or
      (ii)   otherwise consist of or include the investigation of conduct contrary to the law of that country or territory, or the apprehension of persons guilty of such conduct;
   (f)   any person with functions under any international agreement which consist of or include the investigation of conduct which is—
      (i)   unlawful under the law of one or more places,
      (ii)   prohibited by such an agreement, or
      (iii)   contrary to international law,
or the apprehension of persons guilty of such conduct.
   (1B)   The reference in subsection (1A) above to a police force is a reference to any of the following—
   (a)   any police force maintained under section 2 of the Police Act 1996 (c. 16) (police forces in England and Wales outside London);
   (b)   the metropolitan police force;
   (c)   the City of London police force;
   (d)   any police force maintained under or by virtue of section 1 of the Police (Scotland) Act 1967 (c. 77);
   (e)   the Police Service of Northern Ireland;
   (f)   the Police Service of Northern Ireland Reserve;
   (g)   the Ministry of Defence Police;
   (h)   the Royal Navy Regulating Branch;
   (i)   the Royal Military Police;
   (j)   the Royal Air Force Police;
   (k)   the Royal Marines Police;
   (l)   the British Transport Police;
   (m)   the States of Jersey Police Force;
   (n)   the salaried police force of the Island of Guernsey;
   (o)   the Isle of Man Constabulary.
   (1C)   Where—
   (a)   fingerprints or samples have been taken from any person in connection with the investigation of an offence but otherwise than in circumstances to which subsection (1) above applies, and
   (b)   that person has given his consent in writing to the use in a speculative search of the fingerprints or of the samples and of information derived from them,
the fingerprints or, as the,case may be, those samples and that information may be checked against any of the fingerprints, samples or information mentioned in paragraph (a) or (b) of that subsection.
   (1D)   A consent given for the purposes of subsection (1C) above shall not be capable of being withdrawn.
   (2)   Where a sample of hair other than pubic hair is to be taken the sample may be taken either by cutting hairs or by plucking hairs with their roots so long as no more are plucked than the person taking the sample reasonably considers to be necessary for a sufficient sample.

(3) Where any power to take a sample is exercisable in relation to a person the sample may be taken in a prison or other institution to which the Prison Act 1952 applies.

(3A) Where—

(a) the power to take a non-intimate sample under section 63(3B) above is exercisable in relation to any person who is detained under Part III of the Mental Health Act 1983 in pursuance of—

(i) a hospital order or interim hospital order made following his conviction for the recordable offence in question, or

(ii) a transfer direction given at a time when he was detained in pursuance of any sentence or order imposed following that conviction, or

(b) the power to take a non-intimate sample under section 63(3C) above is exercisable in relation to any person,

the sample may be taken in the hospital in which he is detained under that Part of that Act. Expressions used in this subsection and in the Mental Health Act 1983 have the same meaning as in that Act.

(3B) Where the power to take a non-intimate sample under section 63(3B) above is exercisable in relation to a person detained in pursuance of directions of the Secretary of State under section 92 of the Powers of Criminal Courts (Sentencing) Act 2000 the sample may be taken at the place where he is so detained.

(4) Any constable may, within the allowed period, require a person who is neither in police detention nor held in custody by the police on the authority of a court to attend a police station in order to have a sample taken where—

(a) the person has been charged with a recordable offence or informed that he will be reported for such an offence and either he has not had a sample taken from him in the course of the investigation of the offence by the police or he has had a sample so taken from him but either it was not suitable for the same means of analysis or, though so suitable, the sample proved insufficient; or

(b) the person has been convicted of a recordable offence and either he has not had a sample taken from him since the conviction or he has had a sample taken from him (before or after his conviction) but either it was not suitable for the same means of analysis or, though so suitable, the sample proved insufficient.

(5) The period allowed for requiring a person to attend a police station for the purpose specified in subsection (4) above is—

(a) in the case of a person falling within paragraph (a), one month beginning with the date of the charge or of his being informed as mentioned in that paragraph or one month beginning with the date on which the appropriate officer is informed of the fact that the sample is not suitable for the same means of analysis or has proved insufficient, as the case may be;

(b) in the case of a person falling within paragraph (b), one month beginning with the date of the conviction or one month beginning with the date on which the appropriate officer is informed of the fact that the sample is not suitable for the same means of analysis or has proved insufficient, as the case may be.

(6) A requirement under subsection (4) above—

(a) shall give the person at least 7 days within which he must so attend; and

(b) may direct him to attend at a specified time of day or between specified times of day.

(7) Any constable may arrest without a warrant a person who has failed to comply with a requirement under subsection (4) above.

(8) In this section 'the appropriate officer' is—

(a) in the case of a person falling within subsection (4)(a), the officer investigating the offence with which that person has been charged or as to which he was informed that he would be reported;

(b)   in the case of a person falling within subsection (4)(b), the officer in charge of the police station from which the investigation of the offence of which he was convicted was conducted.

63B.   Testing for presence of Class A drugs

(1)   A sample of urine or a non-intimate sample may be taken from a person in police detention for the purpose of ascertaining whether he has any specified Class A drug in his body if the following conditions are met.

(2)   The first condition is—

(a)   that the person concerned has been charged with a trigger offence; or

(b)   that the person concerned has been charged with an offence and a police officer of at least the rank of inspector, who has reasonable grounds for suspecting that the misuse by that person of any specified Class A drug caused or contributed to the offence, has authorised the sample to be taken.

(3)   The second condition is that the person concerned has attained the age of 18.

(4)   The third condition is that a police officer has requested the person concerned to give the sample.

(5)   Before requesting the person concerned to give a sample, an officer must—

(a)   warn him that if, when so requested, he fails without good cause to do so he may be liable to prosecution, and

(b)   in a case within subsection (2)(b) above, inform him of the giving of the authorisation and of the grounds in question.

(6)   A sample may be taken under this section only by a person prescribed by regulations made by the Secretary of State by statutory instrument. No regulations shall be made under this subsection unless a draft has been laid before, and approved by resolution of, each House of Parliament.

(7)   Information obtained from a sample taken under this section may be disclosed—

(a)   for the purpose of informing any decision about granting bail in criminal proceedings (within the meaning of the Bail Act 1976) to the person concerned;

(b)   where the person concerned is in police detention or is remanded in or committed to custody by an order of a court or has been granted such bail, for the purpose of informing any decision about his supervision;

(c)   where the person concerned is convicted of an offence, for the purpose of informing any decision about the appropriate sentence to be passed by a court and any decision about his supervision or release;

(d)   for the purpose of ensuring that appropriate advice and treatment is made available to the person concerned.

(8)   A person who fails without good cause to give any sample which may be taken from him under this section shall be guilty of an offence.

63C.   Testing for presence of Class A drugs: supplementary

(1)   A person guilty of an offence under section 63B above shall be liable on summary conviction to imprisonment for a term not exceeding three months, or to a fine not exceeding level 4 on the standard scale, or to both.

(2)   A police officer may give an authorisation under section 63B above orally or in writing but, if he gives it orally, he shall confirm it in writing as soon as is practicable.

(3)   If a sample is taken under section 63B above by virtue of an authorisation, the authorisation and the grounds for the suspicion shall be recorded as soon as is practicable after the sample is taken.

(4)   If the sample is taken from a person detained at a police station, the matters required to be recorded by subsection (3) above shall be recorded in his custody record.

(5)   Subsections (11) and (12) of section 62 above apply for the purposes of section 63B above as they do for the purposes of that section; and section 63B above does not prejudice the generality of sections 62 and 63 above.

(6)   In section 63B above—

'Class A drug' and 'misuse' have the same meanings as in the Misuse of Drugs Act 1971;

'specified' (in relation to a Class A drug) and 'trigger offence' have the same meanings as in Part III of the Criminal Justice and Court Services Act 2000.

As to the definitions in subsection (6), see section 70 of, and Schedule 6 to, the 2000 Act, post, Appendix J–78, J–133 in this supplement.

64.   Destruction of fingerprints and samples

(1A)   Where—

(a)   fingerprints or samples are taken from a person in connection with the investigation of an offence, and

(b)   subsection (3) below does not require them to be destroyed,

the fingerprints or samples may be retained after they have fulfilled the purposes for which they were taken but shall not be used by any person except for purposes related to the prevention or detection of crime, the investigation of an offence or the conduct of a prosecution.

(1B)   In subsection (1A) above—

(a)   the reference to using a fingerprint includes a reference to allowing any check to be made against it under section 63A(1) or (1C) above and to disclosing it to any person;

(b)   the reference to using a sample includes a reference to allowing any check to be made under section 63A(1) or (1C) above against it or against information derived from it and to disclosing it or any such information to any person;

(c)   the reference to crime includes a reference to any conduct which—

(i)   constitutes one or more criminal offences (whether under the law of a part of the United Kingdom or of a country or territory outside the United Kingdom); or

(ii)   is, or corresponds to, any conduct which, if it all took place in any one part of the United Kingdom, would constitute one or more criminal offences; and

(d)   the references to an investigation and to a prosecution include references, respectively, to any investigation outside the United Kingdom of any crime or suspected crime and to a prosecution brought in respect of any crime in a country or territory outside the United Kingdom.

(3)   If—

(a)   fingerprints or samples are taken from a person in connection with the investigation of an offence; and

(b)   that person is not suspected of having committed the offence,

they must, except as provided by the following provisions of this section, be destroyed as soon as they have fulfilled the purpose for which they were taken.

(3AA)   Samples and fingerprints are not required to be destroyed under subsection (3) above if—

(a)   they were taken for the purposes of the investigation of an offence of which a person has been convicted; and

(b)   a sample or, as the case may be, fingerprint was also taken from the convicted person for the purposes of that investigation.

(3AB)   Subject to subsection (3AC) below, where a person is entitled under subsection (3) above to the destruction of any fingerprint or sample taken from him (or would be but for subsection (3AA) above), neither the fingerprint nor the sample, nor any information derived from the sample, shall be used—

(a)   in evidence against the person who is or would be entitled to the destruction of that fingerprint or sample; or

(b)   for the purposes of the investigation of any offence;

and subsection (1B) above applies for the purposes of this subsection as it applies for the purposes of subsection (1A) above.

(3AC)   Where a person from whom a fingerprint or sample has been taken consents in writing to its retention—

(a)   that sample need not be destroyed under subsection (3) above;

(b)   subsection (3AB) above shall not restrict the use that may be made of the fingerprint or sample or, in the case of a sample, of any information derived from it; and

(c)   that consent shall be treated as comprising a consent for the purposes of section 63A(1C) above;

and a consent given for the purpose of this subsection shall not be capable of being withdrawn.

(3AD)   For the purposes of subsection (3AC) above it shall be immaterial whether the consent is given at, before or after the time when the entitlement to the destruction of the fingerprint or sample arises.

(4)   Proceedings which are discontinued are to be treated as concluded for the purposes of this section.

(5)   If fingerprints are destroyed—

(a)   any copies of the fingerprints shall also be destroyed; and

(b)   any chief officer of police controlling access to computer data relating to the fingerprints shall make access to the data impossible, as soon as it is practicable to do so.

(6)   A person who asks to be allowed to witness the destruction of his fingerprints or copies of them shall have a right to witness it.

(6A)   If—

(a)   subsection (5)(b) above falls to be complied with; and

(b)   the person to whose fingerprints the data relate asks for a certificate that it has been complied with,

such a certificate shall be issued to him, not later than the end of the period of three months beginning with the day on which he asks for it, by the responsible chief officer of police or a person authorised by him or on his behalf for the purposes of this section.

(6B)   In this section—

'the responsible chief officer of police' means the chief officer of police in whose police area the computer data were put on to the computer.

(7)   Nothing in this section—

(a)   affects any power conferred by paragraph 18(2) of Schedule 2 to the Immigration Act 1971 or section 20 of the Immigration and Asylum Act 1999 (disclosure of police information to the Secretary of State for use for immigration purposes); or

(b)   applies to a person arrested or detained under the terrorism provisions.

65.   Part V — supplementary

(1)   In this Part of this Act—

'analysis', in relation to a skin impression, includes comparison and matching;

'appropriate consent' means—

(a)   in relation to a person who has attained the age of 17 years, the consent of that person;

(b)   in relation to a person who has not attained that age but has attained the age of 14 years, the consent of that person and his parent or guardian; and

(c)   in relation to a person who has not attained the age of 14 years, the consent of his parent or guardian;

['drug trafficking' and 'drug trafficking offence' have the same meaning as in the Drug Trafficking Offences Act 1994;]

'fingerprints', in relation to any person, means a record (in any form and produced by any method) of the skin pattern and other physical characteristics or features of—

    (a)   any of that person's fingers; or

    (b)   either of his palms;

'intimate sample' means

    (a)   a sample of blood, semen or any other tissue fluid, urine or pubic hair;

    (b)   a dental impression;

    (c)   a swab taken from a person's body orifice other than the mouth.

'intimate search' means a search which consists of the physical examination of a person's body orifices other than the mouth;

'non-intimate sample' means—

    (a)   a sample of hair other than pubic hair;

    (b)   a sample taken from a nail or from under a nail;

    (c)   a swab taken from any part of a person's body including the mouth but not any other body orifice;

    (d)   saliva;

    (e)   a skin impression;

'registered dentist' has the same meaning as in the Dentists Act 1984;

'skin impression', in relation to any person, means any record (other than a fingerprint) which is a record (in any form and produced by any method) of the skin pattern and other physical characteristics or features of the whole or any part of his foot or of any other part of his body;

'speculative search', in relation to a person's fingerprints or samples, means such a check against other fingerprints or samples or against information derived from other samples as is referred to in section 63A(1) above;

'sufficient' and 'insufficient', in relation to a sample, (subject to subsection (2) below) means sufficient or insufficient (in point of quantity or quality) for the purpose of enabling information to be produced by the means of analysis used or to be used in relation to the sample.

['the terrorism provisions' means —

    (a)   section 41 of the Terrorism Act 2000 and any provision of Schedule 7 to that Act conferring a power of arrest or detention]; and

'terrorism' has the meaning given in section 1 of that Act;

[— references in this Part to any person's proceeds of drug trafficking are to be construed in accordance with the Drug Trafficking Offences Act 1994.]

(2)   References in this Part of this Act to a sample's proving insufficient include references to where, as a consequence of—

    (a)   the loss, destruction or contamination of the whole or any part of the sample,

    (b)   any damage to the whole or a part of the sample, or

    (c)   the use of the whole or a part of the sample for an analysis which produced no results or which produced results some or all of which must be regarded, in the circumstances, as unreliable,

the sample has become unavailable or insufficient for the purpose of enabling information, or information of a particular description, to be obtained by means of analysis of the sample.

PART VI
CODES OF PRACTICE—GENERAL

66. Codes of practice

The Secretary of State shall issue codes of practice in connection with—

    (a)   the exercise by police officers of statutory powers—

    (i)   to search a person without first arresting him; or

    (ii)   to search a vehicle without making an arrest;

  (b)   the detention, treatment, questioning and identification of persons by police officers;

  (c)   searches of premises by police officers; and

  (d)   the seizure of property found by police officers on persons or premises.

(2)   Codes shall (in particular) include provision in connection with the exercise by police officers of powers under section 63B above.

67. Codes of practice—supplementary

(1)   When the Secretary of State proposes to issue a code of practice to which this section applies, he shall prepare and publish a draft of the code, shall consider any representations made to him about the draft and may modify the draft accordingly.

(2)   This section applies to a code of practice under section 60, 60A or 66 above.

(3)   The Secretary of State shall lay before both Houses of Parliament a draft of any code of practice prepared by him under this section.

(4)   When the Secretary of State has laid the draft of a code before Parliament, he may bring the code into operation by order made by statutory instrument.

(5)   No order under subsection (4) above shall have effect until approved by a resolution of each House of Parliament.

(6)   An order bringing a code of practice into operation may contain such transitional provisions or savings as appear to the Secretary of State to be necessary or expedient in connection with the code of practice thereby brought into operation.

(7)   The Secretary of State may from time to time revise the whole or any part of a code of practice to which this section applies and issue that revised code; and the foregoing provisions of this section shall apply (with appropriate modifications) to such a revised code as they apply to the first issue of a code.

(7A)   Subject to subsection (7B) below, the Secretary of State may by order provide that a code of practice for the time being in force is to be treated as having effect with such modifications as may be set out in the order.

(7B)   The effect of the modifications made by an order under subsection (7A) above must be confined to one or more of the following—

  (a)   the effect of the code in relation to such area of England and Wales as may be specified in the order;

  (b)   the effect of the code during such period, not exceeding two years, as may be so specified;

  (c)   the effect of the order in relation to such offences or descriptions of offender as may be so specified.

(7C)   An order under subsection (7A) above shall be made by statutory instrument and shall be subject to annulment in pursuance of a resolution of either House of Parliament.

(9)   Persons other than police officers who are charged with the duty of investigating offences or charging offenders shall in the discharge of that duty have regard to any relevant provision of such a code.

(10)   A failure on the part—

  (a)   of a police officer to comply with any provision of such a code; or

  (b)   of any person other than a police officer who is charged with the duty of investigating offences or charging offenders to have regard to any relevant provision of such a code in the discharge of that duty,

shall not of itself render him liable to any criminal or civil proceedings.

(11)   In all criminal and civil proceedings any such code shall be admissible in evidence; and if any provision of such a code appears to the court or tribunal conducting the proceedings to be relevant to any question arising in the proceedings it shall be taken into account in determining that question.

(12)   In this section 'criminal proceedings' includes—

(a)   proceedings in the United Kingdom or elsewhere before a court-martial constituted under the Army Act 1955, the Air Force Act 1955 or the Naval Discipline Act 1957 or a disciplinary court constituted under section [52G] of the said Act of 1957;

(b)   proceedings before the Courts-Martial Appeal Court; and

(c)   proceedings before a Standing Civilian Court.

PART VII
DOCUMENTARY EVIDENCE IN CRIMINAL PROCEEDINGS

71.   Microfilm copies
In any proceedings the contents of a document may (whether or not the document is still in existence) be proved by the production of an enlargement of a microfilm copy of that document or of the material part of it, authenticated in such manner as the court may approve.

Where the proceedings concerned are proceedings before a magistrates' court inquiring into an offence as examining justices this section shall have effect with the omission of the words 'authenticated in such manner as the court may approve'.

72.   Part VII—supplementary
(1)   In this Part of this Act—

'copy' in relation to a document means anything onto which information recorded in the document has been copied, by whatever means and whether directly or indirectly, and 'statement' means any representation of fact however made; and 'proceedings' means criminal proceedings, including—

(a)   proceedings in the United Kingdom or elsewhere before a court-martial constituted under the Army Act 1955 or the Air Force Act 1955 or the Naval Discipline Act 1957;

(b)   proceedings in the United Kingdom or elsewhere before the Courts-Martial Appeal Court—

(i)   on an appeal from a court-martial so constituted; or

(ii)   on a reference under section 34 of the Courts-Martial (Appeals) Act 1968; and

(c)   proceedings before a Standing Civilian Court.

(2)   Nothing in this Part of this Act shall prejudice any power of a court to exclude evidence (whether by preventing questions from being put or otherwise) at its discretion.

PART VIII
EVIDENCE IN CRIMINAL PROCEEDINGS—GENERAL

Convictions and acquittals

73.   Proof of convictions and acquittals
(1)   Where in any proceedings the fact that a person has in the United Kingdom been convicted or acquitted of an offence otherwise than by a Service court is admissible in evidence, it may be proved by producing a certificate of conviction or, as the case may be, of acquittal relating to that offence, and proving that the person named in the certificate as having been convicted or acquitted of the offence is the person whose conviction or acquittal of the offence is to be proved.

(2)   For the purposes of this section a certificate of conviction or of acquittal—

(a)   shall, as regards a conviction or acquittal on indictment, consist of a certificate, signed by the clerk of the court where the conviction or acquittal took place, giving the substance and effect (omitting the formal parts) of the indictment and of the conviction or acquittal; and

(b)   shall, as regards a conviction or acquittal on a summary trial, consist of a copy of the conviction or of the dismissal of the information, signed by the clerk of the court where the conviction or acquittal took place or by the clerk of the court, if any, to which a memorandum of the conviction or acquittal was sent;
and a document purporting to be a duly signed certificate of conviction or acquittal under this section shall be taken to be such a certificate unless the contrary is proved.

(3)   In subsection (2) above 'proper officer' means:

(a)   in relation to a magistrates' court in England and Wales, the justices' chief executive for the court; and

(b)   in relation to any other court, the clerk of a court, his deputy and to any other person having the custody of the court record.

(4)   The method of proving a conviction or acquittal authorised by this section shall be in addition to and not to the exclusion of any other authorised manner of proving a conviction or acquittal.

74.   Conviction as evidence of commission of offence

(1)   In any proceedings the fact that a person other than the accused has been convicted of an offence by or before any court in the United Kingdom or by a Service court outside the United Kingdom shall be admissible in evidence for the purpose of proving, where to do so is relevant to any issue in those proceedings, that that person committed that offence, whether or not any other evidence of his having committed that offence is given.

(2)   In any proceedings in which by virtue of this section a person other than the accused is proved to have been convicted of an offence by or before any court in the United Kingdom or by a Service court outside the United Kingdom, he shall be taken to have committed that offence unless the contrary is proved.

(3)   In any proceedings where evidence is admissible of that fact that the accused has committed an offence, in so far as that evidence is relevant to any matter in issue in the proceedings for a reason other than a tendency to show in the accused a disposition to commit the kind of offence with which he is charged, if the accused is proved to have been convicted of the offence—

(a)   by or before any court in the United Kingdom; or

(b)   by a Service court outside the United Kingdom,
he shall be taken to have committed that offence unless the contrary is proved.

(4)   Nothing in this section shall prejudice—

(a)   the admissibility in evidence of any conviction which would be admissible apart from this section; or

(b)   the operation of any enactment whereby a conviction or a finding of fact in any proceedings is for the purposes of any other proceedings made conclusive evidence of any fact.

75.   Provisions supplementary to section 74

(1)   Where evidence that a person has been convicted of an offence is admissible by virtue of section 74 above, then without prejudice to the reception of any other admissible evidence for the purpose of identifying the facts on which the conviction was based—

(a)   the contents of any document which is admissible as evidence of the conviction; and

(b)   the contents of the information, complaint, indictment or charge-sheet on which the person in question was convicted,
shall be admissible in evidence for that purpose.

(2)   Where in any proceedings the contents of any document are admissible in evidence by virtue of subsection (1) above, a copy of that document, or of the material part of it, purporting to be certified or otherwise authenticated by or on behalf of the

court or authority having custody of that document shall be admissible in evidence and shall be taken to be a true copy of that document or part unless the contrary is shown.

(3)   Nothing in any of the following—

(a)   section 14 of the Powers of Criminal Courts (Sentencing) Act 2000 (under which a conviction leading to probation or discharge is to be disregarded except as mentioned in that section);

(b)   section 392 of the Criminal Procedure (Scotland) Act 1975 (which makes similar provision in respect of convictions on indictment in Scotland); and

(c)   section 8 of the Probation Act (Northern Ireland) 1950 (which corresponds to section 13 of the Powers of Criminal Courts Act 1973) or any legislation which is in force in Northern Ireland for the time being and corresponds to that section,

shall affect the operation of section 74 above; and for the purposes of that section any order made by a court of summary jurisdiction in Scotland under section 182 or section 183 of the said Act of 1975 shall be treated as a conviction.

(4)   Nothing in section 74 above shall be construed as rendering admissible in any proceedings evidence of any conviction other than a subsisting one.

Confessions

76.   Confessions

(1)   In any proceedings a confession made by an accused person may be given in evidence against him in so far as it is relevant to any matter in issue in the proceedings and is not excluded by the court in pursuance of this section.

(2)   If, in any proceedings where the prosecution proposes to give in evidence a confession made by an accused person, it is represented to the court that the confession was or may have been obtained—

(a)   by oppression of the person who made it; or

(b)   in consequence of anything said or done which was likely, in the circumstances existing at the time, to render unreliable any confession which might be made by him in consequence thereof,

the court shall not allow the confession to be given in evidence against him except in so far as the prosecution proves to the court beyond reasonable doubt that the confession (notwithstanding that it may be true) was not obtained as aforesaid.

(3)   In any proceedings where the prosecution proposes to give in evidence a confession made by an accused person, the court may of its own motion require the prosecution, as a condition of allowing it to do so, to prove that the confession was not obtained as mentioned in subsection (2) above.

(4)   The fact that a confession is wholly or partly excluded in pursuance of this section shall not affect the admissibility in evidence—

(a)   of any facts discovered as a result of the confession; or

(b)   where the confession is relevant as showing that the accused speaks, writes or expresses himself in a particular way, of so much of the confession as is necessary to show that he does so.

(5)   Evidence that a fact to which this subsection applies was discovered as a result of a statement made by an accused person shall not be admissible unless evidence of how it was discovered is given by him or on his behalf.

(6)   Subsection (5) above applies—

(a)   to any fact discovered as a result of a confession which is wholly excluded in pursuance of this section; and

(b)   to any fact discovered as a result of a confession which is partly so excluded, if the fact is discovered as a result of the excluded part of the confession.

(7)   Nothing in Part VII of this Act shall prejudice the admissibility of a confession made by an accused person.

(8)   In this section 'oppression' includes torture, inhuman or degrading treatment, and the use or threat of violence (whether or not amounting to torture).

(9)   Where the proceedings mentioned in subsection (1) above are proceedings before a magistrates' court inquiring into an offence as examining justices this section shall have effect with the omission of

(a)   in subsection (1) the words 'and is not excluded by the court in pursuance of this section', and

(b)   subsection (2) to (6) and (8).

77. Confessions by mentally handicapped persons

(1)   Without prejudice to the general duty of the court at a trial on indictment to direct the jury on any matter on which it appears to the court appropriate to do so, where at such a trial—

(a)   the case against the accused depends wholly or substantially on a confession by him; and

(b)   the court is satisfied—

(i)   that he is mentally handicapped; and

(ii)   that the confession was not made in the presence of an independent person,

the court shall warn the jury that there is special need for caution before convicting the accused in reliance on the confession, and shall explain that the need arises because of the circumstances mentioned in paragraphs (a) and (b) above.

(2)   In any case where at the summary trial of a person for an offence it appears to the court that a warning under subsection (1) above would be required if the trial were on indictment, the court shall treat the case as one in which there is a special need for caution before convicting the accused on his confession.

(3)   In this section—

'independent person' does not include a police officer or a person employed for, or engaged on, police purposes;

'mentally handicapped', in relation to a person, means that he is in a state of arrested or incomplete development of mind which includes significant impairment of intelligence and social functioning; and

'police purposes' has the meaning assigned to it by section 101(2) of the Police Act 1996.

78. Exclusion of unfair evidence

(1)   In any proceedings the court may refuse to allow evidence on which the prosecution proposes to rely to be given if it appears to the court that, having regard to all the circumstances, including the circumstances in which the evidence was obtained, the admission of the evidence would have such an adverse effect on the fairness of the proceedings that the court ought not to admit it.

(2)   Nothing in this section shall prejudice any rule of law requiring a court to exclude evidence.

(3)   This section shall not apply in the case of proceedings before a magistrates' court inquiring into an offence as examining justices.

79. Time for taking accused's evidence

If at the trial of any person for an offence—

(a)   the defence intends to call two or more witnesses to the facts of the case; and

(b)   those witnesses include the accused,

the accused shall be called before the other witness or witnesses unless the court in its discretion otherwise directs.

80. Competence and compellability of accused's spouse

(2)   In any proceedings the wife or husband of a person charged in the proceedings shall, subject to subsection (4) below, be compellable to give evidence on behalf of that person.

(2A)   In any proceedings the wife or husband of a person charged in the proceedings shall, subject to subsection (4) below, be compellable—

(a)   to give evidence on behalf of any other person charged in the proceedings but only in respect of any specified offence with which that other person is charged; or

(b)   to give evidence for the prosecution but only in respect of any specified offence with which any person is charged in the proceedings.

(3)   In relation to the wife or husband of a person charged in any proceedings, an offence is a specified offence for the purposes of subsection (2A) above if—

(a)   it involves an assault on, or injury or a threat of injury to, the wife or husband or a person who was at the material time under the age of 16;

(b)   it is a sexual offence alleged to have been committed in respect of a person who was at the material time under that age; or

(c)   it consists of attempting or conspiring to commit, or of aiding, abetting, counselling, procuring or inciting the commission of, an offence falling within paragraph (a) or (b) above.

(4)   No person who is charged in any proceedings shall be compellable by virtue of subsection (2) or (2A) above to give evidence in the proceedings.

(4A)   References in this section to a person charged in any proceedings do not include a person who is not, or is no longer, liable to be convicted of any offence in the proceedings (whether as a result of pleading guilty or for any other reason).

(5)   In any proceedings a person who has been but is no longer married to the accused shall be compellable to give evidence as if that person and the accused had never been married.

(6)   Where in any proceedings the age of any person at any time is material for the purposes of subsection (3) above, his age at the material time shall for the purposes of that provision be deemed to be or to have been that which appears to the court to be or to have been his age at that time.

(7)   In subsection (3)(b) above 'sexual offence' means an offence under the Sexual Offences Act 1956, the Indecency with Children Act 1960, the Sexual Offences Act 1967, section 54 of the Criminal Law Act 1977 or the Protection of Children Act 1978.

(9)   Section 1(d) of the Criminal Evidence Act 1898 (communications between husband and wife) and section 43(1) of the Matrimonial Causes Act 1965 (evidence as to marital intercourse) shall cease to have effect.

80A.   The failure of the wife or husband of a person charged in any proceedings to give evidence shall not be made the subject of any comment by the prosecution.

81.   Advance notice of expert evidence in Crown Court

(1)   Crown Court Rules may make provision for—

(a)   requiring any party to proceedings before the Court to disclose to the other party or parties any expert evidence which he proposes to adduce in the proceedings; and

(b)   prohibiting a party who fails to comply in respect of any evidence with any requirement imposed by virtue of paragraph (a) above from adducing that evidence without the leave of the court.

(2)   Crown Court Rules made by virtue of this section may specify the kinds of expert evidence to which they apply and may exempt facts or matters of any description specified in the rules.

PART VIII
SUPPLEMENTARY

82.   Part VIII — interpretation

(1)   In this Part of this Act—

'confession' includes any statement wholly or partly adverse to the person who made it, whether made to a person in authority or not and whether made in words or otherwise;

'court-martial' means a court-martial constituted under the Army Act 1955, the Air Force Act 1955 or the Naval Discipline Act 1957 or a disciplinary court constituted under section 52G of the said Act of 1957;

'proceedings' means criminal proceedings, including—

(a)   proceedings in the United Kingdom or elsewhere before a court-martial; and

(b)   proceedings in the United Kingdom or elsewhere before the Courts-Martial Appeal Court—

(i)   on an appeal from a court-martial; or

(ii)   on a reference under section 34 of the Courts-Martial (Appeals) Act 1968; and

(c)   proceedings before a Standing Civilian Court; and

'Service court' means a court-martial or a Standing Civilian Court.

(2)   In this Part of this Act references to conviction before a Service court are references—

(a)   as regards a court-martial constituted under the Army Act 1955 or the Air Force Act 1955, to a finding of guilty which is, or falls to be treated as, a finding of the court duly confirmed;

(b)   as regards—

(i)   a court-martial; or

(ii)   a disciplinary court;

constituted under the Naval Discipline Act 1957, to a finding of guilty which is, or falls to be treated as, the finding of the court;

and 'convicted' shall be construed accordingly.

(3)   Nothing in this Part of this Act shall prejudice any power of a court to exclude evidence (whether by preventing questions from being put or otherwise) at its discretion.

PART X
POLICE — GENERAL

107.   Police officers performing duties of higher rank

(1)   For the purpose of any provision of this Act or any other Act under which a power in respect of the investigation of offences or the treatment of persons in police custody is exercisable only by or with the authority of a police officer of at least the rank of superintendent, an officer of the rank of chief inspector shall be treated as holding the rank of superintendent if—

(a)   he has been authorised by an officer holding a rank above the rank of superintendent to exercise the power or, as the case may be, to give his authority for its exercise, or

(b)   he is acting during the absence of an officer holding the rank of superintendent who has authorised him, for the duration of that absence, to exercise the power, or as the case may be, to give his authority for its exercise.

(2)   For the purpose of any provision of this Act or any other Act under which such a power is exercisable only by or with the authority of an officer of at least the rank of inspector, an officer of the rank of sergeant shall be treated as holding the rank of inspector if he has been authorised by an officer of at least the rank of superintendent to exercise the power or, as the case may be, to give this authority for its exercise.

108.   Deputy chief constables

(1)   The office of deputy chief constable is hereby abolished.

(6)   In section 23(2) of the Police (Scotland) Act 1967 (under which a chief constable affected by an amalgamation holds the rank of assistant chief constable) for the word 'assistant' there shall be substituted the word 'deputy'.

110.   Functions of special constables in Scotland
Subsection (6) of section 17 of the Police (Scotland) Act 1967 (restriction on functions of special constables) is hereby repealed.

111.   Regulations for Police Forces and Police Cadets — Scotland
(1)   In section 26 to the Police (Scotland) Act 1967 (regulations as to government and administration of police forces)—
    (a)   after subsection (1) there shall be inserted the following subsection—
      '(1A)   Regulations under this section may authorise the Secretary of State, the police authority or the chief constable to make provision for any purpose specified in the regulations.'; and
    (b)   at the end there shall be inserted the following subsection—
      '(10)   Any statutory instrument made under this section shall be subject to annulment in pursuance of a resolution of either House of Parliament.'.
(2)   In section 27 of the said Act of 1967 (regulations for police cadets) in subsection (3) for the word '(9)' there shall be substituted the words '(1A), (9) and (10)'.

PART XI

MISCELLANEOUS AND SUPPLEMENTARY

113.   Application of Act to Armed Forces
(1)   The Secretary of State may by order direct that any provision of this Act which relates to investigations of offences conducted by police officers or to persons detained by the police shall apply, subject to such modifications as he may specify, to investigations of offences conducted under the Army Act 1955, the Air Force Act 1955 or the Naval Discipline Act 1957 or to persons under arrest under any of those Acts.
(2)   Section 67(9) above shall not have effect in relation to investigations of offences conducted under the Army Act 1955, the Air Force Act 1955 or the Naval Discipline Act 1957.
(3)   The Secretary of State shall issue a code of practice, or a number of such codes, for persons other than police officers who are concerned with enquiries into offences under the Army Act 1955, the Air Force Act 1955 or the Naval Discipline Act 1957.
(4)   Without prejudice to the generality of subsection (3) above, a code issued under that subsection may contain provisions, in connection with enquiries into such offences, as to the following matters—
    (a)   the tape-recording of interviews;
    (b)   searches of persons and premises; and
    (c)   the seizure of things found on searches.
(5)   If the Secretary of State lays before both Houses of Parliament a draft of a code of practice under this section, he may by order bring the code into operation.
(6)   An order bringing a code of practice into operation may contain such transitional provisions or savings as appear to the Secretary of State to be necessary or expedient in connection with the code of practice thereby brought into operation.
(7)   The Secretary of State may from time to time revise the whole or any part of a code of practice issued under this section and issue that revised code, and the foregoing provisions of this section shall apply (with appropriate modifications) to such a revised code as they apply to the first issue of a code.
(8)   A failure on the part of any person to comply with any provision of a code of practice issued under this section shall not of itself render him liable to any criminal or civil proceedings except those to which this subsection applies.
(9)   Subsection (8) above applies—

(a)   to proceedings under any provision of the Army Act 1955 or the Air Force Act 1955 other than section 70; and

(b)   to proceedings under any provision of the Naval Discipline Act 1957 other than section 42.

(10)   In all criminal and civil proceedings any such code shall be admissible in evidence and if any provision of such a code appears to the court or tribunal conducting the proceedings to be relevant to any question arising in the proceedings it shall be taken into account in determining that question.

(11)   In subsection (10) above 'criminal proceedings' includes—

(a)   proceedings in the United Kingdom or elsewhere before a court-martial constituted under the Army Act 1955, the Air Force Act 1955 or the Naval Discipline Act 1957 or a disciplinary court constituted under section 52G of the said Act of 1957;

(b)   proceedings before the Courts-Martial Appeal Court; and

(c)   proceedings before a Standing Civilian Court.

(12)   Parts VII and VIII of this Act have effect for the purposes of proceedings—

(a)   before a court-martial constituted under the Army Act 1955 or the Air Force Act 1955;

(b)   before a Courts-Martial Appeal Court; and

(c)   before a Standing Civilian Court,

subject to any modifications which the Secretary of State may by order specify.

(13)   An order under this section shall be made by statutory instrument and shall be subject to annulment in pursuance of a resolution of either House of Parliament.

114.   Application of Act to Customs and Excise

(1)   'Arrested', 'arresting', 'arrest' and 'to arrest' shall respectively be substituted for 'detained', 'detaining', 'detention' and 'to detain' wherever in the customs and excise Acts, as defined in section 1(1) of the Customs and Excise Management Act 1979, those words are used in relation to persons.

(2)   The Treasury may by order direct—

(a)   that any provision of this Act which relates to investigations of offences conducted by police officers or to persons detained by the police shall apply, subject to such modifications as the order may specify, to investigations conducted by officers of Customs and Excise of offences which relate to assigned matters, as defined in section 1 of the Customs and Excise Management Act 1979, or to persons detained by officers of Customs and Excise; and

(b)   that, in relation to investigations of offences conducted by officers of Customs and Excise—

(i)   this Act shall have effect as if the following section were inserted after section 14—

'14A.   Exception for Customs and Excise

Material in the possession of a person who acquired or created it in the course of any trade, business, profession or other occupation or for the purpose of any paid or unpaid office and which relates to an assigned matter, as defined in section 1 of the Customs and Excise Management Act 1979, is neither excluded material nor special procedure material for the purposes of any enactment such as is mentioned in section 9(2) above.'; and

(ii)   section 55 above shall have effect as if it related only to things such as are mentioned in subsection (1)(a) of that section; and

(c)   that in relation to customs detention (as defined in any order made under this subsection) the Bail Act 1976 shall have effect as if references in it to a constable were references to an officer of Customs and Excise of such grade as may be specified in the order.

(3)   Nothing in any order under subsection (2) above shall be taken to limit any powers exercisable under section 164 of the Customs and Excise Management Act 1979.

(4)   In this section 'officers of Customs and Excise' means officers commissioned by the Commissioners of Customs and Excise under section 6(3) of the Customs and Excise Management Act 1979.

(5)   An order under this section shall be made by statutory instrument and shall be subject to annulment in pursuance of a resolution of either House of Parliament.

114A   Power to apply Act to officers of the Secretary of State etc.

(1)   The Secretary of State may by order direct that—
(a)   the provisions of Schedule 1 to this Act so far as they relate to special procedure material, and
(b)   the other provisions of this Act so far as they relate to the provisions falling within paragraph (a) above,
shall apply, with such modifications as may be specified in the order, for the purposes of investigations falling within subsection (2) as they apply for the purposes of investigations of offences conducted by police officers.

(2)   An investigation falls within this subsection if—
(a)   it is conducted by an officer of the department of the Secretary of State for Trade and Industry or by another person acting on that Secretary of State's behalf;
(b)   it is conducted by that officer or other person in the discharge of a duty to investigate offences; and
(c)   the investigation relates to a serious arrestable offence or to anything which there are reasonable grounds for suspecting has involved the commission of a serious arrestable offence.

(3)   The investigations for the purposes of which provisions of this Act may be applied with modifications by an order under this section include investigations of offences committed, or suspected of having been committed, before the coming into force of the order or of this section.

(4)   An order under this section shall be made by statutory instrument and shall be subject to annulment in pursuance of a resolution of either House of Parliament.

115.   Expenses

Any expenses of a Minister of the Crown incurred in consequence of the provisions of this Act, including any increase attributable to those provisions in sums payable under any other Act, shall be defrayed out of money provided by Parliament.

116.   Meaning of 'serious arrestable offence'

(1)   This section has effect for determining whether an offence is a serious arrestable offence for the purposes of this Act.

(2)   The following arrestable offences are always serious—
(a)   an offence (whether at common law or under any enactment) specified in Part I of Schedule 5 to this Act; and
(b)   an offence under an enactment specified in Part II of that Schedule; and
(c)   any of the offences mentioned in paragraphs (a) to (f) of section 1(3) of the Drug Trafficking Act 1994.

(3)   Subject to subsection (4) below, any other arrestable offence is serious only if its commission—
(a)   has led to any of the consequences specified in subsection (6) below; or
(b)   is intended or is likely to lead to any of those consequences.

(4)   An arrestable offence which consists of making a threat is serious if carrying out the threat would be likely to lead to any of the consequences specified in subsection (6) below.

(6)   The consequences mentioned in subsections (3) and (4) above are

(a)   serious harm to the security of the State or to public order;

(b)   serious interference with the administration of justice or with the investigation of offences or of a particular offence;

(c)   the death of any person;

(d)   serious injury to any person;

(e)   substantial financial gain to any person; and

(f)   serious financial loss to any person.

(7)   Loss is serious for the purposes of this section, if having regard to all the circumstances, it is serious for the person who suffers it.

(8)   In this section 'injury' includes any disease and any impairment of a person's physical or mental condition.

117.   Power of constable to use reasonable force

Where any provision of this Act—

(a)   confers a power on a constable; and

(b)   does not provide that the power may only be exercised with the consent of some person, other than a police officer,

the officer may use reasonable force, if necessary, in the exercise of the power.

118.   General interpretation

(1)   In this Act—

'arrestable offence' has the meaning assigned to it by section 24 above;

'designated police station' has the meaning assigned to it by section 35 above;

'document' means anything in which information of any description is recorded;

'item subject to legal privilege' has the meaning assigned to it by section 10 above;

'parent or guardian' means—

(a)   in the case of a child or young person in the care of a local authority, that authority;

(b)   in the case of a child or young person in the care of a voluntary organisation in which parental rights and duties with respect to him are vested by virtue of a resolution under section 64(1) of the Child Care Act 1980, that organisation;

'premises' has the meaning assigned to it by section 23 above;

'record offence' means any offence to which regulations under section 27 above apply;

'vessel' includes any ship, boat, raft or other apparatus constructed or adapted for floating on water.

(2)   A person is in police detention for the purposes of this Act if—

(a)   he has been taken to a police station after being arrested for an offence or after being arrested under section 41 of the Terrorism Act 2000;

(b)   he is arrested at a police station after attending voluntarily at the station or accompanying a constable to it,

and is detained there or is detained elsewhere in the charge of a constable, except that a person who is at a court after being charged is not in police detention for those purposes.

119.   Amendments and repeals

(1)   The enactments mentioned in Schedule 6 to this Act shall have effect with the amendments there specified.

(2)   The enactments mentioned in Schedule 7 to this Act (which include enactments already obsolete or unnecessary) are repealed to the extent specified in the third column of that Schedule.

(3)   The repeals in Parts II and IV of Schedule 7 to this Act have effect only in relation to criminal proceedings.

120.   Extent
(1)   Subject to the following provisions of this section, this Act extends to England and Wales only.

(2)   The following extend to Scotland only—

section 108(4) and (5);

section 110;

section 111;

section 112(1); and

section 119(2), so far as it relates to the provisions of the Pedlars Act 1871 repealed by Part VI of Schedule 7.

(3)   The following extend to Northern Ireland only—

section 6(4), and

section 112(2).

(4)   The following extend to England and Wales and Scotland—

section 6(1) and (2);

section 7;

section 83(2), so far as it relates to paragraph 8 of Schedule 4;

section 108(1) and (6);

section 109; and

section 119(2), so far as it relates to section 19 of the Pedlars Act 1871.

(5)   The following extend to England and Wales, Scotland and Northern Ireland—

section 6(3);

section 9(2A);

section 83(2), so far as it relates to paragraph 7(1) of Schedule 4; and

section 114(1).

(6)   So far as they relate to proceedings before courts-martial and Standing Civilian Courts, the relevant provisions extend to any place at which such proceedings may be held.

(7)   So far as they relate to proceedings before the Courts-Martial Appeal Court, the relevant provisions extend to any place at which such proceedings may be held.

(8)   In this section 'the relevant provisions' means—

   (a)   subsection (11) of section 67 above;

   (b)   subsection (12) of that section as far as it relates to subsection (11);

   (c)   Parts VII and VIII of this Act, except paragraph 10 of Schedule 3;

   (d)   subsections (2) and (8) to (12) of section 113 above; and

   (e)   subsection (13) of that section, so far as it relates to an order under subsection (12).

(9)   Except as provided by the foregoing provisions of this section, section 113 above extends to any place to which the Army Act 1955, the Air Force Act 1955 or the Naval Discipline Act 1957 extends.

(9A)   Section 119(1), so far as it relates to any provision amended by Part II of Schedule 6, extends to any place to which that provision extends.

(11)   Section 119(2), so far as it relates—

   (a)   to any provision contained in—

the Army Act 1955;

the Air Force Act 1955;

the Armed Forces Act 1981; or

the Value Added Tax Act 1983;

   (b)   to any provision mentioned in Part VI of Schedule 7, other than section 18 of the Pedlars Act 1871, extends to any place to which that provision extends.

(12)   So far as any of the following—
section 115;
in section 118, the definition of 'document';
this section;
section 121; and
section 122,
has effect in relation to any other provision of this Act, it extends to any place to which
that provision extends.

121.   Commencement

(1)   This Act, except section 120 above, this section and section 122 below, shall
come into operation on such day as the Secretary of State may by order made by
statutory instrument appoint, and different days may be so appointed for different
provisions and for different purposes.

(2)   Different days may be appointed under this section for the coming force of
section 60 above in different areas.

(3)   When an order under this section provides by virtue of subsection (2) above that
section 60 above shall come into force in an area specified in the order, the duty imposed
on the Secretary of State by that section shall be construed as a duty to make an order
under it in relation to interviews in that area.

(4)   An order under this section may make such transitional provision as appears to
the Secretary of State to be necessary or expedient in connection with the provisions
thereby brought into operation.

122.   Short title

This Act may be cited as the Police and Criminal Evidence Act 1984.

SCHEDULES

(Section 9)   SCHEDULE 1
                                    SPECIAL PROCEDURE

Making of orders by circuit judge

1.   If on an application made by a constable a circuit judge is satisfied that one or
other of the sets of access conditions is fulfilled, he may make an order under paragraph
4 below.

2.   The first set of access conditions is fulfilled if—
 (a)   there are reasonable grounds for believing—
  (i)   that a serious arrestable offence has been committed;
  (ii)   that there is material which consists of special procedure material or
includes special procedure material and does not also include excluded material on
premises specified in the application;
  (iii)   that the material is likely to be of substantial value (whether by itself or
together with other material) to the investigation in connection with which the
application is made; and
  (iv)   that the material is likely to be relevant evidence;
 (b)   other methods of obtaining the material—
  (i)   have been tried without success; or
  (ii)   have not been tried because it appeared that they were bound to fail; and
 (c)   it is in the public interest, having regard—
  (i)   to the benefit likely to accrue to the investigation if the material is obtained;
and
  (ii)   to the circumstances under which the person in possession of the material
holds it,

that the material should be produced or that access to it should be given.

3.   The second set of access conditions is fulfilled if—

(a)   there are reasonable grounds for believing that there is material which consists of or includes excluded material or special procedure material on premises specified in the application;

(b)   but for section 9(2) above a search of the premises for that material could have been authorised by the issue of a warrant to a constable under an enactment other than this Schedule; and

(c)   the issue of such a warrant would have been appropriate.

4.   An order under this paragraph is an order that the person who appears to the circuit judge to be in possession of the material to which the application relates shall—

(a)   produce it to a constable for him to take away; or

(b)   give a constable access to it,

not later than the end of the period of seven days from the date of the order or the end of such longer period as the order may specify.

5.   Where the material consists of information contained in a computer—

(a)   an order under paragraph 4(a) above shall have effect as an order to produce the material in a form in which it can be taken away and in which it is visible and legible; and

(b)   an order under paragraph 4(b) above shall have effect as an order to give a constable access to the material in a form in which it is visible and legible.

6.   For the purposes of sections 21 and 22 above material produced in pursuance of an order under paragraph 4(a) above shall be treated as if it were material seized by a constable.

Notices of applications for orders

7.   An application for an order under paragraph 4 above shall be made inter partes.

8.   Notice of an application for such an order may be served on a person either by delivering it to him or by leaving it at his proper address or by sending it by post to him in a registered letter or by the recorded delivery service.

9.   Such a notice may be served—

(a)   on a body corporate, by serving it on the body's secretary or clerk or other similar officer; and

(b)   on a partnership, by serving it on one of the partners.

10.   For the purposes of this Schedule, and of section 7 of the Interpretation Act 1978 in its application to this Schedule, the proper address of a person, in the case of secretary or clerk or other similar officer of a body corporate, shall be that of the registered or principal office of that body, in the case of a partner of a firm shall be that of the principal office of the firm, and in any other case shall be the last known address of the person to be served.

11.   Where notice of an application for an order under paragraph 4 above has been served on a person, he shall not conceal, destroy, alter or dispose of the material to which the application relates except—

(a)   with the leave of a judge; or

(b)   with the written permission of a constable,

until—

(i)   the application is dismissed or abandoned; or

(ii)   he has complied with an order under paragraph 4 above made on the application.

Issue of warrants by circuit judge

12.   If on an application made by a constable a circuit judge—

(a)   is satisfied—

(i)   that either set of access conditions is fulfilled; and
(ii)   that any of the further conditions set out in paragraph 14 below is also
fulfilled; or
(b)   is satisfied—
(i)   that the second set of access conditions is fulfilled; and
(ii)   that an order under paragraph 4 above relating to the material has not been
complied with,
he may issue a warrant authorising a constable to enter and search the premises.

13.   A constable may seize and retain anything for which a search has been
authorised under paragraph 12 above.

14.   The further conditions mentioned in paragraph 12(a)(ii) above are—
(a)   that it is not practicable to communicate with any person entitled to grant
entry to the premises to which the application relates;
(b)   that it is practicable to communicate with a person entitled to grant entry to
the premises but it is not practicable to communicate with any person entitled to grant
access to the material;
(c)   that the material contains information which—
(i)   is subject to a restriction or obligation such as is mentioned in section
11(2)(b) above; and
(ii)   is likely to be disclosed in breach of it if a warrant is not issued;
(d)   that service of notice of an application for an order under paragraph 4 above
may seriously prejudice the investigation.

15.—(1)   If a person fails to comply with an order under paragraph 4 above, a circuit
judge may deal with him as if he had committed a contempt of the Crown Court.

(2)   Any enactment relating to contempt of the Crown Court shall have effect in
relation to such a failure as if it were such a contempt.

Costs

16.   The costs of any application under this Schedule and of anything done or to be
done in pursuance of an order made under it shall be in the discretion of the judge.

(Section 26)

SCHEDULE 2
PRESERVED POWERS OF ARREST

1892 c.43.   Section 17(2) of the Military Lands Act 1892.
1911 c.27.   Section 12(1) of the Protection of Animals Act 1911.
1920 c.55.   Section 2 of the Emergency Powers Act 1920.
1936 c.6.   Section 7(3) of the Public Order Act 1936.
1952 c.52.   Section 49 of the Prison Act 1952.
1952 c.67.   Section 13 of the Visiting Forces Act 1952.
1955 c.18.   Sections 186 and 190B of the Army Act 1955.
1955 c.19.   Sections 186 and 190B of the Air Force Act 1955.
1957 c.53.   Sections 104 and 105 of the Naval Discipline Act 1957.
1959 c.37.   Section 1(3) of the Street Offences Act 1959.
1969 c.54.   Section 32 of the Children and Young Persons Act 1969.
1971 c.77.   Section 24(2) of the Immigration Act 1971 and paragraphs 17, 24 and 33
             of Schedule 2 and paragraph 7 of Schedule 3 of that Act.
1976 c.63.   Section 7 of the Bail Act 1976.
1977 c.45.   Sections 6(6), 7(11), 8(4), 9(7) and 10(5) of the Criminal Law
             Act 1977.

1980 c.9.   Schedule 5 to the Reserve Forces Act 1980.
1981 c.22.   Sections 60(5) and 61(1) of the Animal Health Act 1981.
1983 c.2.   Rule 36 in Schedule 1 to the Representation of the People Act 1983.
1983 c.20.   Sections 18, 35(10), 36(8), 38(7), 136(1) and 138 of the Mental Health
             Act 1983.
1984 c.47.   Section 5(5) of the Repatriation of Prisoners Act 1984.

(Section 70)   PART II
                 PROVISIONS SUPPLEMENTARY TO SECTION 69

8.   In any proceedings where it is desired to give a statement in evidence in
accordance with section 69 above, a certificate—
    (a)   identifying the document containing the statement and describing the manner
in which it was produced;
    (b)   giving such particulars of any device involved in the production of that
document as may be appropriate for the purpose of showing that the document was
produced by a computer;
    (c)   dealing with any of the matters mentioned in subsection (1) of section 69
above; and
    (d)   purporting to be signed by a person occupying a responsible position in
relation to the operation of the computer,
shall be evidence of anything stated in it; and for the purposes of this paragraph it shall
be sufficient for a matter to be stated to the best of the knowledge and belief of the
person stating it.
    9.   Notwithstanding paragraph 8 above, a court may require oral evidence to be
given of anything of which evidence could be given by a certificate under that paragraph,
but the preceding provisions of this paragraph shall not apply where the court is a
magistrates' court inquiring into an offence as examining justices.
    10.   Any person who in a certificate tendered under paragraph 8 above in a
magistrates' court, the Crown Court or the Court of Appeal makes a statement which
he knows to be false or does not believe to be true shall be guilty of an offence and
liable—
    (a)   on conviction on indictment to imprisonment for a term not exceeding two
years or to a fine or to both;
    (b)   on summary conviction to imprisonment for a term not exceeding six months
or to a fine not exceeding the statutory maximum (as defined in section 74 of the
Criminal Justice Act 1982) or to both.
    11.   In estimating the weight, if any, to be attached to a statement regard shall be had
to all the circumstances from which any inference can reasonably be drawn as to the
accuracy or otherwise of the statement and, in particular—
    (a)   to the question whether or not the information which the information
contained in the statement reproduces or is derived from was supplied to the relevant
computer, or recorded for the purpose of being supplied to it, contemporaneously with
the occurrence or existence of the facts dealt with in that information; and
    (b)   to the question whether or not any person concerned with the supply of
information to that computer, or with the operation of that computer or any equipment
by means of which the document containing the statement was produced by it, had any
incentive to conceal or misrepresent the facts.
    12.   For the purposes of paragraph 11 above information shall be taken to be
supplied to a computer whether it is supplied directly or (with or without human
intervention) by means of any appropriate equipment.

(Section 116)   SCHEDULE 5

SERIOUS ARRESTABLE OFFENCES

PART I

OFFENCES MENTIONED IN SECTION 116(2)(a)

1. Treason.
2. Murder.
3. Manslaughter.
4. Rape.
5. Kidnapping.
6. Incest with a girl under the age of 13.
7. Buggery with a person under the age of 16.
8. Indecent assault which constitutes an act of gross indecency.
9. An offence under section 170 of the Customs and Excise Management Act 1979 of being knowingly concerned, in relation to any goods, in the fraudulent evasion or attempt at evasion of a prohibition in force with respect to the goods under section 42 of the Customer Consolidation Act 1876 (prohibition on importing indecent or obscene articles).

PART II

OFFENCES MENTIONED IN SECTION 116(2)(b)

Explosive Substances Act 1883 (c. 3)
1. Section 2 (causing explosion likely to endanger life or property).

Sexual Offences Act 1956 (c. 69)
2. Section 5 (intercourse with a girl under the age of 13).

Firearms Act 1968 (c. 27)
3. Section 16 (possession of firearms with intent to injure).
4. Section 17(1) (use of firearms and imitation firearms to resist arrest).
5. Section 18 (carrying firearms with criminal intent).

Taking of Hostages Act 1982 (c. 28)
7. Section 1 (hostage-taking).

Aviation Security Act 1982 (c. 36)
8. Section 1 (hi-jacking).

[Criminal Justice Act 1988 (c. 33)
9. Section 134 (torture).]

[Road Traffic Act 1988 (c. 52)
[10.] Section 1 (causing death by [dangerous] driving).
      Section 3A (causing death by careless driving when under the influence of drink or drugs).]

[Aviation and Maritime Security Act 1990 (c. 31)
11. Section 1 (endangering safety at aerodromes).
12. Section 9 (hi-jacking of ships).
13. Section 10 (seizing or exercising control of fixed platforms).]

Protection of Children Act 1978 (c.37)
14. Section 1 (indecent photographs and pseudo-photographs of children).

Obscene Publications Act 1959 (c. 66)
15. Section 2 (publication of obscene matter).

(Section 119)   SCHEDULE 6

MINOR AND CONSEQUENTIAL AMENDMENTS

PART I

ENGLAND AND WALES

Game Act 1831 (c. 32)

1.   The following section shall be inserted after section 31 of the Game Act 1831—

'**31A   Powers of constables in relation to trespassers**

The powers conferred by section 31 above to require a person found on land as mentioned in that section to quit the land and to tell his christian name, surname, and place of abode shall also be exercisable by a police constable.'.

Metropolitan Police Act 1839 (c. 47)

2.   In section 39 of the Metropolitan Police Act 1839 (fairs within the metropolitan police district) after the word 'amusement' there shall be inserted the words 'shall be guilty of an offence'.

Railway Regulation Act 1840 (c. 97)

3.   In section 16 of the Railway Regulation Act 1840 (persons obstructing officers of railway company or trespassing upon railway) for the words from 'and' in the third place where it occurs to 'justice,' in the third place where it occurs there shall be substituted the words ', upon conviction by a magistrates' court, at the discretion of the court,'.

London Hackney Carriages Act 1843 (c. 86)

4.   In section 27 of the London Hackney Carriages Act 1843 (no person to act as driver of carriage without consent of proprietor) for the words after 'constable' there shall be substituted the words 'if necessary, to take charge of the carriage and every horse in charge of any person unlawfully acting as a driver or as a conductor and to deposit the same in some place of safe custody until the same can be applied for by the proprietor.'.

Town Gardens Protection Act 1863 (c. 13)

5.   In section 5 of the Town Gardens Protection Act 1863 (penalty for injuring garden) for the words from the beginning to 'district' there shall be substituted the words 'Any person who throws any rubbish into any such garden, or trespasses therein, or gets over the railings or fence, or steals or damages the flowers or plants, or commits any nuisance therein, shall be guilty of an offence and'.

Parks Regulation Act 1872 (c. 15)

6.   The following section shall be substituted for section 5 of the Parks Regulation Act 1872 (apprehension of offender whose name or residence is not known)—

'5.   Any person who—

   (a)   within the view of a park constable acts in contravention of any of the said regulations in the park where the park constable has jurisdiction; and

   (b)   when required by any park constable or by any police constable to give his name and address gives a false name or false address.

shall be liable on summary conviction to a penalty of an amount not exceeding level 1 on the standard scale, as defined in section 75 of the Criminal Justice Act 1982.'.

Dogs (Protection of Livestock) Act 1953 (c. 28)

7.   In the Dogs (Protection of Livestock) Act 1953 the following section shall be inserted after section 2—

'**2A.   Power of justice of the peace to authorise entry and search**

If on an application made by a constable a justice of the peace is satisfied that there are reasonable grounds for believing—

   (a)   that an offence under this Act has been committed; and

(b)   that the dog in respect of which the offence has been committed is on premises specified in the application.
he may issue a warrant authorising a constable to enter and search the premises in order to identify the dog.

Army Act 1955 (c. 18)
Air Force Act 1955 (c. 19)
8.   The following subsection shall be substituted for section 195(3) of the Army Act 1955 and section 195(3) of the Air Force Act 1955—
'(3)   A constable may seize any property which he has reasonable grounds for suspecting of having been the subject of an offence against this section.'.

Sexual Offences Act 1956 (c. 69)
9.   At the end of section 41 of the Sexual Offences Act 1956 (power to arrest in case of soliciting by men) there shall be added the words 'but a constable may only do so in accordance with section 25 of the Police and Criminal Evidence Act 1984.'.

Game Laws (Amendment) Act 1960 (c. 36)
10.   In subsection (1) of section 2 of the Game Laws (Amendment) Act 1960 (power of police to enter on land) for the words 'purpose of exercising any power conferred on him by the foregoing section' there shall be substituted the words
'purpose—
(a)   of exercising in relation to him the powers under section 31 of the Game Act 1831 which section 31A of the Act confers on police constables; or
(b)   of arresting him in accordance with section 25 of the Police and Criminal Evidence Act 1984.'.
11.   In subsection (1) of section 4 of that Act (enforcement powers) for the words from 'under', in the first place where it occurs, to 'thirty-one' there shall be substituted the words ', in accordance with section 25 of the Police and Criminal Evidence Act 1984, for an offence under section one or section nine of the Night Poaching Act 1828, or under section thirty'.

Betting, Gaming and Lotteries Act 1963 (c.2)
12.   The following subsection shall be substituted for subsection (2) of section 8 of the Betting, Gaming and Lotteries Act 1963 (prohibition of betting in streets and public places)—
'(2) Where a person is found committing an offence under this section, any constable may seize and detain any article liable to be forfeited under this section.'.

Police Act 1964 (c. 48)
14.   In section 7(1) of the Police Act 1964 (other members of police forces) after the words 'chief constable' there shall be inserted the words ', deputy chief constable'.
15.   In section 29(2) of that Act (removal of chief constables) for the words 'the deputy or an assistant chief constable' there shall be substituted the words 'a deputy or assistant chief constable'.

Criminal Law Act 1967 (c. 58)
17.   The following subsection shall be inserted after section 4(1) of the Criminal Law Act 1967—
'(1A)   In this section and section 5 below "arrestable offence" has the meaning assigned to it by section 24 of the Police and Criminal Evidence Act 1984.'.

Theatres Act 1968 (c. 54)
18.   In section 15(1) of the Theatres Act 1968 (powers of entry and inspection); for the words 'fourteen days' there shall be substituted the words 'one month'.

Children and Young Persons Act 1969 (c. 54)
    19. In the Children and Young Persons Act 1969—
      (b) the following section shall be substituted for section 29—
    '29. Recognisance on release of arrested child or young person
A child or young person arrested in pursuance of a warrant shall not be released unless he or his parent or guardian (with or without sureties) enters into a recognisance for such amount as the custody officer at the police station where he is detained considers will secure his attendance at the hearing of the charge; and the recognisance entered into in pursuance of this section may, if the custody officer thinks fit, be conditioned for the attendance of the parent or guardian at the hearing in addition to the child or young person.'.

Immigration Act 1971 (c. 77)
    20. In section 25(3) of the Immigration Act 1971 for the words 'A constable or' there shall be substituted the word 'An'.

Criminal Justice Act 1972 (c. 71)
    21. In subsection (1) of section 34 of the Criminal Justice Act 1972 (powers of constable to take drunken offender to treatment centre) for the words from the beginning to 'section the' there shall be substituted the words 'On arresting an offender for an offence under—
      (a) section 12 of the Licensing Act 1872; or
      (b) section 91(1) of the Criminal Justice Act 1967, a'.

Animal Health Act 1981 (c. 22)
    24. In subsection (5) of section 60 of the Animal Health Act 1981 (enforcement powers) for the words 'a constable or other officer' there shall be substituted the words 'an officer other than a constable'.

Wildlife and Countryside Act 1981 (c. 69)
    25. In subsection (2) of section 19 of the Wildlife and Countryside Act 1981 (enforcement powers) after the words 'subsection (1)' there shall be inserted the words 'or arresting a person, in accordance with section 25 of the Police and Criminal Evidence Act 1984, for such an offence'.

Mental Health Act 1983 (c. 20)
    26. In section 135(4) of the Mental Health Act 1983 for the words 'the constable to whom it is addressed', in both places where they occur, there shall be substituted the words 'a constable'.

PART II
OTHER AMENDMENTS

Army Act 1955 (c. 18)
    28.—(1) The Army Act 1955 shall be amended as follows.
    (2) In section 99—
      (a) in subsection (1), after the word 'below' there shall be inserted the words 'and to service modifications'; and
      (b) the following subsections shall be inserted after that subsection—
        '(1A) In this section 'service modifications' means such modifications as the Secretary of State may by regulations made by statutory instrument prescribe, being modifications which appear to him to be necessary or proper for the purposes of proceedings before a court-martial; and it is hereby declared that in this section—
          'rules' includes rules contained in or made by virtue of an enactment; and
          'enactment' includes an enactment contained in an Act passed after this Act.

(1B)   Regulations under subsection (1A) above may not modify section 99A below.

(1C)   Regulations under subsection (1A) above shall be subject to annulment in pursuance of a resolution of either House of Parliament.'.

(3)   In section 99A(1) for the word 'Section' there shall be substituted the words 'Without prejudice to section 99 above, section'.

(4)   The following section shall be inserted after section 200—

'**200A.   False statements in computer record certificates**

(1)   Any person who in a certificate tendered under paragraph 8 of Schedule 3 to the Police and Criminal Evidence Act 1984 (computer records) in evidence before a court-martial makes a statement which he knows to be false or does not believe to be true shall be guilty of an offence and liable—

(a)   on conviction on indictment to imprisonment for a term not exceeding two years or to a fine or to both;

(b)   on summary conviction to imprisonment for a term not exceeding six months or to a fine not exceeding the statutory maximum or to both.

(2)   In this section 'statutory maximum' has the meaning given by section 74 of the Criminal Justice Act 1982.'.

Air Force Act 1955 (c. 19)

29.—(1)   The Air Force Act 1955 shall be amended as follows.

(2)   In section 99—

(a)   in subsection (1), after the word 'below' there shall be inserted the words 'and to service modifications'; and

(b)   the following subsections shall be inserted after that subsection—

'(1A)   In this section 'service modifications' means such modifications as the Secretary of State may by regulations made by statutory instrument prescribe, being modifications which appear to him to be necessary or proper for the purpose of proceedings before a court-martial; and it is hereby declared that in this section—

'rules' include rules contained in or made by virtue of an enactment; and

'enactment' includes an enactment contained in an Act passed after this Act.

(1B)   Regulations under subsection (1A) above may not modify section 99A below.

(1C)   Regulations under subsection (1A) above shall be subject to annulment in pursuance of a resolution of either House of Parliament.'.

(3)   In section 99A(1) for the word 'Section' there shall be substituted the words 'Without prejudice to section 99 above, section'.

(4)   The following section shall be inserted after section 200—

'**200A.   False statements in computer record certificates**

(1)   Any person who in a certificate tendered under paragraph 8 of Schedule 3 to the Police and Criminal Evidence Act 1984 (computer records) in evidence before a court-martial makes a statement which he knows to be false or does not believe to be true shall be guilty of an offence and liable—

(a)   on conviction on indictment to imprisonment for a term not exceeding two years or to a fine or to both;

(b)   on summary conviction to imprisonment for a term not exceeding six months or to a fine not exceeding the statutory maximum or to both.

(2)   In this section 'statutory maximum' has the meaning given by section 74 of the Criminal Justice Act 1982.'.

Police (Scotland) Act 1967 (c. 77)

30.   In section 6(2) of the Police (Scotland) Act 1967 (constables below rank of assistant chief constable) for the words 'an assistant chief constable or a constable

holding the office of deputy chief constable' there shall be substituted the words 'a deputy chief constable or an assistant chief constable'.

31.   In section 7(1) of that Act (ranks) after the words 'chief constable,' there shall be inserted the words 'deputy chief constable,'.

32.   In section 26(7) of that Act (disciplinary authority) immediately before the words 'deputy chief constable' there shall be inserted the word 'any'.

33.   In section 31(2) of that Act (compulsory retirement of chief constable etc.) for the words 'the deputy or an assistant chief constable' there shall be substituted the words 'a deputy or assistant chief constable'.

Courts-Martial (Appeals) Act 1968 (c. 20)

34.—(1)   The following section shall be inserted after section 37 of the Courts-Martial (Appeals) Act 1968—

'**37A.   False statements in computer record certificates**

(1)   Any person who in a certificate tendered under paragraph 8 of Schedule 3 to the Police and Criminal Evidence Act 1984 (computer records) in evidence before the Appeal Court makes a statement which he knows to be false and does not believe to be true shall be guilty of an offence and liable—

(a)   on conviction on indictment to imprisonment for a term not exceeding two years or to a fine or to both;

(b)   on summary conviction to imprisonment for a term not exceeding six months or to a fine not exceeding the statutory maximum or to both.

(2)   Proceedings for an offence under this section committed outside the United Kingdom may be taken, and the offence may for all incidental purposes be treated as having been committed, in any place in the United Kingdom.

(3)   In this section 'statutory maximum' has the meaning given by section 74 of the Criminal Justice Act 1982.'

House of Commons Disqualification Act 1975 (c. 24)
Northern Ireland Assembly Disqualification Act 1975 (c. 25)

35.   In Part II of Schedule 1 to the House of Commons Disqualification Act 1975 and Part II of Schedule 1 to the Northern Ireland Assembly Disqualification Act 1975 (bodies of which all members are disqualified under those Acts) there shall be inserted at the appropriate place in alphabetical order—

'The Police Complaints Authority'.

Armed Forces Act 1976 (c. 52)

36.   The following paragraph shall be inserted after paragraph 17 of Schedule 3 to the Armed Forces Act 1976 (Standing Civilian Courts)—

'17A.   Section 20A of that Act (false statements in computer record certificates) shall have effect as if the reference to a court-martial in subsection (1) included a reference to a Standing Civilian Court.'.

Customs and Excise Management Act 1979 (c. 2)

37.   The following subsection shall be substituted for section 138(4) of the Customs and Excise Management Act 1979—

'(4)   Where any person has been arrested by a person who is not an officer—

(a)   by virtue of this section; or

(b)   by virtue of section 24 of the Police and Criminal Evidence Act 1984 in its application to offences under the customs and excise Acts,

the person arresting him shall give notice of the arrest to an officer at the nearest convenient office of customs and excise.'.

38.   In section 161 of that Act—

(a)   in subsection (3), for the words from 'that officer' to the end of the subsection there shall be substituted the words 'any officer and any person accompanying an officer

to enter and search the building or place named in the warrant within one month from
that day'; and

(b)   in subsection (4), for the words 'person named in a warrant under subsection
(3) above' there shall be substituted the words 'other person so authorised'.

Betting and Gaming Duties Act 1981 (c. 63)

39.   In the following provisions of the Betting and Gaming Duties Act 1981, namely—

(a)   section 15(2);
(b)   paragraph 16(1) of Schedule 1;
(c)   paragraph 17(1) of Schedule 3; and
(d)   paragraph 17(1) of Schedule 4,

for the words 'fourteen days' there shall be substituted the words 'one month'.

Car Tax Act 1983 (c. 53)

40.   In paragraph 7(3) of Schedule 1 to the Car Tax Act 1983 for the words 'fourteen
days' there shall be substituted the words 'one month'.

Value Added Tax Act 1983 (c. 55)

41.   In Schedule 7 to the Value-Added Tax Act 1983—

(a)   the following sub-paragraph shall be substituted for paragraph 7(5)—

'(5)   A statement contained in a document produced by a computer shall not
by virtue of sub-paragraph (3) of this paragraph be admissible in evidence—

(b)   in criminal proceedings in England and Wales except in accordance
with sections 68 to 70 of the Police and Criminal Evidence Act 1984;

(c)   in civil proceedings in Scotland, except in accordance with sections
13 and 14 of the Law Reform (Miscellaneous Provisions) (Scotland) Act
1968;

(d)   in criminal proceedings in Scotland, except in accordance with the said
sections 13 and 14, which shall, for the purposes of this paragraph, apply with the
necessary modifications to such proceedings;

(e)   in civil proceedings in Northern Ireland, except in accordance with
sections 2 and 3 of the Civil Evidence Act (Northern Ireland) 1971; and

(f)   in criminal proceedings in Northern Ireland, except in accordance with
the said sections 2 and 3, which shall, for the purposes of this paragraph, apply
with the necessary modifications to such proceedings.';

(b)   in paragraph 7(6), for the words from 'under the corresponding' to the end of
the sub-paragraph there shall be substituted the words 'section 13(4) of the Law Reform
(Miscellaneous Provisions) (Scotland) Act 1968 or section 2(4) of the Civil Evidence
Act (Northern Ireland) 1971'; and

(c)   in paragraph 10(3), for the words '14 days' there shall be substituted the
words 'one month'.

POLICE AND CRIMINAL EVIDENCE ACT 1984
REVISED CODES OF PRACTICE A-D

EFFECTIVE 10 APRIL 1995

[AS AMENDED 1 MARCH 1999]

PACE CODE OF PRACTICE FOR THE EXERCISE BY POLICE OFFICERS
OF STATUTORY POWERS OF STOP AND SEARCH (CODE A)

1.   General
1.1   This code of practice must be readily available at all police stations for
consultation by police officers, detained persons and members of the public.

1.2   The notes for guidance included are not provisions of this code, but are guidance to police officers and others about its application and interpretation. Provisions in the annexes to the code are provisions of this code.

1.3   This code governs the exercise by police officers of statutory powers to search a person without first arresting him or to search a vehicle without making an arrest. The main stop and search powers to which this code applies at the time the code was prepared are set out in Annex A, but that list should not be regarded as definitive.

1.4   This code does not apply to the following powers of stop and search:
    (i)   Aviation Security Act 1982, s. 27(2);
    (ii)   Police and Criminal Evidence Act 1984, s. 6(1) (which relates specifically to powers of constables employed by statutory undertakers on the premises of the statutory undertakers).

1.5   This code applies to stops and searches under powers:
    (a)   requiring reasonable grounds for suspicion that articles unlawfully obtained or possessed are being carried;
    (b)   authorised under section 60 of the Criminal Justice and Public Order Act 1994, (as amended by section 8 of the Knives Act 1997), based upon a reasonable belief that incidents involving serious violence may take place or that people are carrying dangerous instruments or offensive weapons within any locality in the police area [See Note 1A];
    (c)   authorised under section 13A of the Prevention of Terrorism (Temporary Provisions) Act 1989, (as amended by section 81 of the Criminal Justice and Public Order Act 1994 and section 1 of the Prevention of Terrorism (Additional Powers) Act 1996);
    (d)   authorised under section 13B of the Prevention of Terrorism (Temporary Provisions) Act 1989, (as inserted by section 1 of the Prevention of Terrorism (Additional Powers) Act 1996);
    (e)   exercised under paragraph 4(2) of Schedule 5 to the Prevention of Terrorism (Temporary Provisions) Act 1989.
[See Note 1AA]

(a)   Powers requiring reasonable suspicion

1.6   Whether a reasonable ground for suspicion exists will depend on the circumstances in each case, but there must be some objective basis for it. An officer will need to consider the nature of the article suspected of being carried in the context of other factors such as the time and the place, and the behaviour of the person concerned or those with him. Reasonable suspicion may exist, for example, where information has been received such as a description of an article being carried or of a suspected offender; a person is seen acting covertly or warily or attempting to hide something; or a person is carrying a certain type of article at an unusual time or in a place where a number of burglaries or thefts are known to have taken place recently. But the decision to stop and search must be based on all the facts which bear on the likelihood that an article of a certain kind will be found.

1.6A   For example, reasonable suspicion may be based upon reliable information or intelligence which indicates that members of a particular group or gang, or their associates, habitually carry knives unlawfully or weapons or controlled drugs.

1.7   Subject to the provision in paragraph 1.7AA below, reasonable suspicion can never be supported on the basis of personal factors alone without supporting intelligence or information. For example, a person's colour, age, hairstyle or manner of dress, or the fact that he is known to have a previous conviction for possession of an unlawful article, cannot be used alone or in combination with each other as the sole basis on which to search that person. Nor may it be founded on the basis of stereotyped images of certain persons or groups as more likely to be committing offences.

1.7AA   However, where there is reliable information or intelligence that members of a group or gang who habitually carry knives unlawfully or weapons or controlled drugs, and wear a distinctive item of clothing or other means of identification to indicate membership of it, the members may be identified by means of that distinctive item of clothing or other means of identification. [See Note 1H]

1.7A   Where a police officer has reasonable grounds to suspect that a person is in innocent possession of a stolen or prohibited article or other item for which he is empowered to search, the power of stop and search exists notwithstanding that there would be no power of arrest. However every effort should be made to secure the person's co-operation in the production of the article before resorting to the use of force.

(b)   Authorisation under section 60 of the Criminal Justice and Public Order Act 1994, as amended by section 8 of the Knives Act 1997

1.8   Authority to exercise the powers of stop and search under section 60 of the Criminal Justice and Public Order Act 1994, as amended by section 8 of the Knives Act 1997, may be given where it is reasonably believed that incidents involving serious violence may take place in any locality in the police area, and it is expedient to use these powers to prevent their occurrence, or that persons are carrying dangerous instruments or offensive weapons without good reason in any locality in any police area. Authorisation may only be given by an officer of the rank of inspector or above, in writing, specifying the grounds on which it was given, the locality in which the powers may be exercised and the period of time for which they are in force. The period authorised shall be no longer than appears reasonably necessary to prevent, or try to prevent incidents of serious violence, or to deal with the problem of carrying dangerous instruments or offensive weapons and it may not exceed 24 hours. If an inspector gives an authorisation, he must, as soon as practicable, inform an officer of or above the rank of superintendent. An officer of or above the rank of superintendent may direct that the period shall be extended for a further 24 hours if violence or the carrying of dangerous instruments or offensive weapons has occurred or is suspected to have occurred and the continued use of the powers is considered necessary to prevent or deal with further such activity. That direction must also be given in writing at the time or as soon as practicable afterwards. [See Notes 1A, 1F and 1G]

(c)   Authorisation under section 13A of the Prevention of Terrorism (Temporary Provisions) Act 1989, as inserted by section 81 of the Criminal Justice and Public Order Act 1994 and amended by the Prevention of Terrorism (Additional Powers) Act 1996

1.8A   (Removed)

1.9   An authorisation given under section 13A of the Prevention of Terrorism (Temporary Provisions) Act 1989 gives a constable in uniform the power to stop and search any vehicle, its driver and any passengers for articles which could be used for terrorist purposes. A constable may exercise the power whether or not he has any grounds for suspecting the presence of such articles.

1.10   Authority for the use of the power may be given where it appears expedient to do so to prevent acts of terrorism. The authorisation must:
      (i)   be given by an officer of the rank of assistant chief constable (or equivalent or above);
      (ii)   be in writing (it may be given orally at first but should be confirmed in writing by the officer who gave it as soon as reasonably practicable);

(iii)   be signed, dated and timed by the officer giving the authorisation;

(iv)   state the geographical area in which the power may be used (i.e. whether it applies to the whole or only a specific part of his force area); and

(v)   specify the time and date that the authorisation starts and ends (up to a maximum of 28 days from the time the authorisation was given).

1.11   Further use of the power requires a new authorisation.

[See Notes 1F, 1G and 1I]

(d)   Authorisation under section 13B of the Prevention of Terrorism (Temporary Provisions) Act 1989, as inserted by section 1 of the Prevention of Terrorism (Additional Powers) Act 1996

1.12   An authorisation given under section 13B of the Prevention of Terrorism (Temporary Provisions) Act 1989 gives a constable in uniform the power to stop a pedestrian and search him, or anything carried by him, for articles which could be used for terrorist purposes. A constable may exercise the power whether or not he has any grounds for suspecting the presence of such articles.

1.13   Authority for the use of the power may be given where it appears expedient to do so to prevent acts of terrorism. The authorisation must be given in exactly the same way as explained in paragraph 1.10 (and may in fact be combined with a section 13A authorisation). However, the officer giving an authorisation under section 13B must cause the Secretary of State to be informed, as soon as reasonably practicable, that such an authorisation has been given. The authorisation may take effect before the Secretary of State has decided whether to confirm it. But it ceases to have effect if it is not confirmed by the Secretary of State within 48 hours of its having been given.

1.14   Following notification of the authorisation, the Secretary of State may:

(i)   cancel the authorisation with immediate effect or with effect from such other time as he may direct;

(ii)   confirm it but for a shorter period than that specified in the authorisation (which may not be more than 28 days); or

(iii)   confirm the authorisation as given.

1.15   Further use of the power requires a new authorisation.

1.16   The selection of persons stopped under sections 13A and 13B of the Prevention of Terrorism (Temporary Provision) Act 1989 should reflect an objective assessment of the threat posed by the various terrorist groups active in Great Britain. The powers should not be used to stop and search for reasons unconnected with terrorism. Officers should take particular care not to discriminate against members of ethnic minorities in the exercise of these powers. There may be circumstances, however, where it is appropriate for officers to take account of a person's ethnic origin in selecting persons to be stopped in response to a specific terrorist threat (for example, some international terrorist groups are associated with particular ethnic identities).

[See Notes 1F, 1G and 1I]

Notes for Guidance

1A   Section 60 is amended by section 25 of the Crime and Disorder Act 1998 to provide a power to demand the removal of face coverings where an authority referred to in paragraph 1.8 above is given. The officer exercising the power must reasonably believe that someone is wearing the face covering wholly or mainly for the purpose of concealing identity. There is also a power to seize face coverings where the officer believes that a person intends to wear them for this purpose. **There is not a power to**

stop and search for face coverings. An officer may seize any face covering which he comes across when exercising a power of search for something else, or which he sees being carried, and which he reasonably believes is intended to be used for concealing anyone's identity.

1AA   It is important to ensure that powers of stop and search are used responsibly by those who exercise them and those who authorise their use. An officer should bear in mind that he may be required to justify the authorisation or use of the powers to a senior officer and in court, and that misuse of the powers is likely to be harmful to the police effort in the long term and can lead to mistrust of the police by the community. Regardless of the power exercised, all police officers should be careful to ensure that the selection and treatment of those questioned or searched is based upon objective factors and not upon personal prejudice. It is also particularly important to ensure that any person searched is treated courteously and considerately. Where there may be religious sensitivities about asking someone to remove a face covering using the powers in section 25 of the Crime and Disorder Act 1998, for example in the case of a Muslim woman wearing a face covering for religious purposes, the officer should permit the item to be removed out of public view. Where practicable, the item should be removed in the presence of an officer of the same sex as the person and out of sight of anyone of the opposite sex. In all cases, the officer must reasonably believe that the person is wearing the item in question *wholly or mainly* to conceal his or her identity.

1B   This code does not affect the ability of an officer to speak to or question a person in the ordinary course of his duties (and in the absence of reasonable suspicion) without detaining him or exercising any element of compulsion. It is not the purpose of the code to prohibit such encounters between the police and the community with the co-operation of the person concerned and neither does it affect the principle that all citizens have a duty to help police officers to prevent crime and discover offenders.

1C   (Not Used)

1D   Nothing in this code affects

(a)   the routine searching of persons entering sports grounds or other premises with their consent, or as a condition of entry; or

(b)   the ability of an officer to search a person in the street with his consent where no search power exists. In these circumstances, an officer should always make it clear that he is seeking the consent of the person concerned to the search being carried out by telling the person that he need not consent and that without his consent he will not be searched.

1E   If an officer acts in an improper manner this will invalidate a voluntary search. Juveniles, people suffering from a mental handicap or mental disorder and others who appear not to be capable of giving an informed consent should not be subject to a voluntary search.

1F   It is for the authorising officer to determine the period of time during which the powers mentioned in paragraph 1.5(b), (c) and (d) may be exercised. The officer should set the minimum period he considers necessary to deal with the risk of violence, the carrying of knives or offensive weapons, or terrorism. A direction to extend the period authorised under the powers mentioned in paragraph 1.5(b) may be given only once. Thereafter further use of the powers requires a new authorisation. There is no provision to extend an authorisation of the powers mentioned in paragraph 1.5(c) and (d); further use of the powers requires a new authorisation.

1G   It is for the authorising officer to determine the geographical area in which the use of the powers are to be authorised. In doing so he may wish to take into account factors such as the nature and venue of the anticipated incident, the numbers of people who may be in the immediate area of any possible incident, their access to surrounding areas and the anticipated level of violence. The officer should not set a geographical area which is wider than that he believes necessary for the purpose of preventing anticipated violence, the carrying of knives or offensive weapons, or terrorism. It is particularly important to ensure that constables exercising such powers are fully aware of where they may be used. If the area specified is smaller than the whole force area, the officer giving the authorisation should specify either the streets which form the boundary of the area or a divisional boundary within the force area. If the power is to be used in response to a threat or incident that straddles police force areas, an officer from each of the forces concerned will need to give an authorisation.

1H   Other means of identification might include jewellery, insignias, tattoos or other features which are known to identify members of the particular gang or group.

1I   An officer who has authorised the use of powers under section 13B of the Prevention of Terrorism (Temporary Provisions) Act 1989 must take immediate steps to send a copy of the authorisation to the National Joint Unit, Metropolitan Police Special Branch, who will forward it to the Secretary of State. The Secretary of State should be informed of the reasons for the authorisation. The National Joint Unit will inform the force concerned, within 48 hours of the authorisation being made, whether the Secretary of State has confirmed or cancelled or altered the authorisation. The National Joint Unit should also be sent a copy of all section 13A authorisations for national monitoring purposes.

2.   Action before a search is carried out

(a)   Searches requiring reasonable suspicion

2.1   Where an officer has the reasonable grounds for suspicion necessary to exercise a power of stop and search, he may detain the person concerned for the purposes of and with a view to searching him. There is no power to stop or detain a person against his will in order to find grounds for a search.

2.2   Before carrying out a search the officer may question the person about his behaviour or his presence in circumstances which gave rise to the suspicion, since he may have a satisfactory explanation which will make a search unnecessary. If, as a result of any questioning preparatory to a search, or other circumstances which come to the attention of the officer, there cease to be reasonable grounds for suspecting that an article is being carried of a kind for which there is a power of stop and search, no search may take place. [See Note 2A]

2.3   The reasonable grounds for suspicion which are necessary for the exercise of the initial power to detain may be confirmed or eliminated as a result of the questioning of a person detained for the purposes of a search (or such questioning may reveal reasonable grounds to suspect the possession of a different kind of unlawful article from that originally suspected); but the reasonable grounds for suspicion without which any search or detention for the purposes of a search is unlawful cannot be retrospectively provided by such questioning during his detention or by his refusal to answer any question put to him.

(b)   All searches

2.4   Before any search of a detained person or attended vehicle takes place the officer must take reasonable steps to give the person to be searched or in charge of the vehicle the following information:
        (i)   his name (except in the case of enquiries linked to the investigation of terrorism, in which case he shall give his warrant or other identification number) and the name of the police station to which he is attached;

(ii)   the object of the search; and

(iii)   his grounds or authorisation for undertaking it.

2.5   If the officer is not in uniform he must show his warrant card. In doing so in the case of enquiries linked to the investigation of terrorism, the officer need not reveal his name. Stops and searches under the powers mentioned in paragraphs 1.5 (b) and (c) may be undertaken only by a constable in uniform.

2.6   Unless it appears to the officer that it will not be practicable to make a record of the search, he must also inform the person to be searched (or the owner or person in charge of a vehicle that is to be searched, as the case may be) that he is entitled to a copy of the record of the search if he asks for it within a year. If the person wishes to have a copy and is not given one on the spot, he shall be advised to which police station he should apply.

2.7   If the person to be searched, or in charge of a vehicle to be searched, does not appear to understand what is being said, or there is any doubt about his ability to understand English, the officer must take reasonable steps to bring the information in paragraphs 2.4 and 2.6 to his attention. If the person is deaf or cannot understand English and has someone with him then the officer must try to establish whether the person can interpret or otherwise help him to give the required information.

Note for Guidance

2A   In some circumstances preparatory questioning may be unnecessary, but in general a brief conversation or exchange will be desirable, not only as a means of avoiding unsuccessful searches but to explain the grounds for the stop/search, to gain co-operation and reduce any tension there might be surrounding the stop/search. Where a person is lawfully detained for the purpose of a search, but no search in the event takes place, the detention will not thereby have been rendered unlawful.

3.   Conduct of the search

3.1   Every reasonable effort must be made to reduce to the minimum the embarrassment that a person being searched may experience.

3.2   The co-operation of the person to be searched shall be sought in every case, even if he initially objects to the search. A forcible search may be made only if it has been established that the person is unwilling to co-operate (e.g. by opening a bag) or resists. Although force may only be used as a last resort, reasonable force may be used if necessary to conduct a search or to detain a person or vehicle for the purposes of a search.

3.3   The length of time for which a person or vehicle may be detained will depend on the circumstances, but must in all circumstances, be reasonable and not extend beyond the time taken for the search. Where the exercise of the power requires reasonable suspicion, the thoroughness and extent of a search must depend on what is suspected of being carried, and by whom. If the suspicion relates to a particular article which is seen to be slipped into a person's pocket, then, in the absence of other grounds for suspicion or an opportunity for the article to be moved elsewhere, the search must be confined to that pocket. In the case of a small article which can readily be concealed, such as a drug, and which might be concealed anywhere on the person, a more extensive search may be necessary. In the case of searches mentioned in paragraph 1.5(b), (c), (d) and (e), which do not require reasonable grounds for suspicion, the officer may make any reasonable search to find what he is empowered to search for. [See Note 3B]

3.4   The search must be conducted at or nearby the place where the person or vehicle was first detained.

3.5   Searches in public must be restricted to superficial examination of outer clothing. There is no power to require a person to remove any clothing in public other than an outer coat, jacket or gloves (other than under sections 13A and 13B of the Prevention of Terrorism (Temporary Provisions) Act 1989, which grant a constable in addition the power to require a person to remove in public any headgear and footwear, or under section 60 of the Criminal Justice and Public Order Act 1994 as amended by the Crime and Disorder Act 1998, which grants a constable power to require the removal of any item worn to conceal identity). Where on reasonable grounds it is considered necessary to conduct a more thorough search (e.g. by requiring a person to take off a T-shirt), this shall be done out of public view for example, in a police van or police station if there is one nearby. Any search involving the removal of more than an outer coat, jacket, gloves, headgear or footwear, or any other item concealing identity, may only be made by an officer of the same sex as the person searched and may not be made in the presence of anyone of the opposite sex unless the person being searched specifically requests it. [See Note 3A and 3C]. No search involving exposure of intimate parts of the body may take place in a police van. All searches involving exposure of intimate parts of the body shall be conducted in accordance with paragraph 11 of Annex A to Code C. The other provisions of Code C do not apply to persons at police stations for the purposes of searches under stop and search powers.

3.5A   The powers under sections 13A and 13B of the Prevention of Terrorism (Temporary Provisions) Act 1989 allow a constable to search only for articles which could be used for terrorist purposes. The powers must not be used for any other purpose (for example to search for drugs in the absence of reasonable grounds for suspicion). However, this would not prevent a search being carried out under other powers if, in course of exercising powers under sections 13A or 13B, the police officer formed reasonable grounds for suspicion.

Notes for Guidance

3A   A search in the street itself should be regarded as being in public for the purposes of paragraph 3.5 above, even though it may be empty at the time a search begins. Although there is no power to require a person to do so, there is nothing to prevent an officer from asking a person to voluntarily remove more than an outer coat, jacket or gloves (and headgear or footwear under section 13A and 13B of the Prevention of Terrorism (Temporary Provisions) Act 1989) in public.

3B   As a search of a person in public should be superficial examination of outer clothing, such searches should be completed as soon as possible.

3C   Where there may be religious sensitivities about asking someone to remove headgear using a power under section 13A or 13B of the Prevention of Terrorism (Temporary Provisions) Act 1989, the police officer should offer to carry out the search out of public view (for example, in a police van or police station if there is one nearby).

4.   Action after a search is carried out

(a)   General

4.1   An officer who has carried out a search must make a written record unless it is not practicable to do so, on account of the numbers to be searched or for some other operational reason, e.g. in situations involving public disorder.

4.2   The records must be completed as soon as practicable – on the spot unless circumstances (e.g. other immediate duties or very bad weather) make this impracticable.

4.3   The record must be made on the form provided for this purpose (the national search record).

4.4   In order to complete the search record the officer shall normally seek the name, address and date of birth of the person searched, but under the search procedures there is no obligation on a person to provide these details and no power to detain him if he is unwilling to do so.

4.5   The following information must always be included in the record of a search even if the person does not wish to identify himself or give his date of birth:
      (i)   the name of the person searched, or (if he withholds it) a description of him;
      (ii)   a note of the person's ethnic origin; [See Note 4DA]
      (iii)   when a vehicle is searched, a description of it, including its registration number; [See Note 4B]
      (iv)   the object of the search;
      (v)   the grounds for making it;
      (vi)   the date and time it was made;
      (vii)   the place where it was made;
      (viii)   its results;
      (ix)   a note of any injury or damage to property resulting from it;
      (x)   the identity of the officer making it (except in the case of enquiries linked to the investigation of terrorism, in which case the record shall state the officer's warrant or other identification number and duty station). [See Note 4A]

4.6   A record is required for each person and each vehicle searched. However, if a person is in a vehicle and both are searched, and the object and grounds of the search are the same, only one record need be completed.

4.7   The record of the grounds for making a search must, briefly but informatively, explain the reason for suspecting the person concerned, whether by reference to his behaviour or other circumstances; or in the case of those searches mentioned in paragraph 1.5 (b), (c), (d) and (e) by stating the authority provided to carry out such a search. [See Note 4D]

4.7A   The driver of a vehicle which is stopped in accordance with the powers mentioned in paragraphs 1.5 (b) and (c) may obtain a written statement to that effect within twelve months from the day the vehicle was stopped. A written statement may be similarly obtained by any person if he is searched in accordance with the powers mentioned in paragraph 1.5 (b) and (d) (see paragraph 2.6). The statement may form part of the national search record or be supplied on a separate document. [See Note 4C]

(b)   Unattended vehicles

4.8   After searching an unattended vehicle, or anything in or on it, an officer must leave a notice in it (or on it, if things in or on it have been searched without opening it) recording the fact that it has been searched.

4.9   The notice should include the name of the police station to which the officer concerned is attached and state where a copy of the record of the search may be obtained and where any application for compensation should be directed.

4.10   The vehicle must if practicable be left secure.

Notes for Guidance

4A   Where a search is conducted by more than one officer the identity of all the officers engaged in the search must be recorded on the search record.

4B   Where a vehicle has not been allocated a registration number (e.g. a rally car or a trials motorbike) that part of the requirements under 4.5 (iii) does not apply.

4C   In paragraph 4.7A, a written statement means a record that a person or vehicle was stopped under the powers contained in paragraph 1.5 (b), (c) or (d) of this code.

4D   It is important for national monitoring purposes to specify in the record whether a stop and search under the Prevention of Terrorism (Temporary Provisions) Act 1989 were made under section 13A or section 13B powers.

4DA   Supervising officers, in monitoring the exercise of officers' stop and search powers, should consider in particular whether there is any evidence that officers are exercising their discretion on the basis of stereotyped images of certain persons or groups contrary to the provisions of this code. It is important that any such evidence should be addressed. Supervising officers should take account of the information about the ethnic origin of those stopped and searched which is collected and published under section 95 of the Criminal Justice Act 1991.

ANNEX A
SUMMARY OF MAIN STOP AND SEARCH POWERS (See paragraph 1.3)

POWER	OBJECT OF SEARCH	EXTENT OF SEARCH	WHERE EXERCISABLE
Unlawful articles general			
1. Public Stores Act 1875, s. 6	HM Stores stolen or unlawfully obtained	Persons, vehicles and vessels	Anywhere where the constabulary powers are exercisable
2. Firearms Act 1968, s. 47	Firearms	Persons and Vehicles	A public place, or anywhere in the case of reasonable suspicion of offences of carrying firearms with criminal intent or trespassing with firearms
3. Misuse of Drugs Act 1971, s. 23	Controlled drugs	Persons and vehicles	Anywhere
4. Customs and Excise Management Act 1979, s. 163	Goods: (a) on which duty has not been paid; (b) being unlawfully removed, imported or exported; (c) otherwise liable to forfeiture to HM Customs and Excise	Vehicles and vessels only	Anywhere
5. Aviation Security Act 1982, s. 27(1)	Stolen or unlawfully obtained goods	Airport employees and vehicles carrying airport employees, or aircraft or any vehicle in a cargo area whether or not carrying an employee.	Any designated airport

6. Police and Criminal Evidence Act 1984, s. 1	Stolen goods; articles for use in certain Theft Act offences; offensive weapons, including bladed or sharply-pointed articles (except folding pocket-knives with a bladed cutting edge not exceeding 3 inches).	Persons and vehicles	Where there is public access
Police and Criminal Evidence Act 1984, s. 6(3) (by a constable of the United Kingdom Atomic Energy Authority Constabulary in respect of property owned or controlled by British Nuclear Fuels plc)	HM Stores (in the form of goods and chattels belonging to British Nuclear Fuels plc)	Persons, vehicles and vessels	Anywhere where the constabulary powers are exercisable
7. Sporting Events (Control of Alcohol etc.) Act 1985, s. 7	Intoxicating liquor	Persons, coaches and trains	Designated sports grounds or coaches and trains travelling to or from a designated sporting event
8. Crossbows Act 1987, s. 4 (except crossbows with a draw weight of less than 1.4 kilograms)	Crossbows or parts of crossbows	Persons and vehicles	Anywhere except dwellings
Evidence of game and wild-life offences			
9. Poaching Prevention Act 1862, s. 2	Game or poaching equipment	Persons and vehicles	A public place
10. Deer Act 1991, s. 12	Evidence of offences under the Act	Persons and vehicles	Anywhere except dwellings
11. Conservation of Seals Act 1970, s. 4	Seals or hunting equipment	Vehicles only	Anywhere
12. Badgers Act 1992, s. 11	Evidence of offences under the Act	Persons and vehicles	Anywhere
13. Wildlife and Countryside Act 1981, s. 19	Evidence of wildlife offences	Persons and vehicles	Anywhere except dwellings

Other

14. Prevention of Terrorism (Temporary Provisions) Act 1989, s. 15(3)	Evidence of liability to arrest under section 14 of the Act	Persons and vehicles	Anywhere
15. Prevention of Terrorism (Temporary Provisions) Act 1989, s. 13A as inserted by section 81 of the Criminal Justice and Public Order Act 1994	Articles which could be used for a purpose connected with the commission, preparation or instigation of acts of terrorism	Persons and vehicles	Anywhere within the area or locality authorised under subsection (1)
16. Prevention of Terrorism (Temporary Provisions) Act 1989, paragraph 4(2) of Schedule 5	Anything relevant to determining if a person being examined falls within paragraph 2(a) to (c) of Schedule 5	Persons, vehicles, vessels etc.	At designated ports and airports
17. Section 60 Criminal Justice and Public Order Act 1994	Offensive weapons or dangerous instruments to prevent incidents of serious violence	Persons and vehicles	Anywhere within a locality authorised under subsection (1)

CODE OF PRACTICE FOR THE SEARCHING OF PREMISES BY POLICE OFFICERS AND THE SEIZURE OF PROPERTY FOUND BY POLICE OFFICERS ON PERSONS OR PREMISES (CODE B)

1. General

1.1   This code of practice must be readily available at all police stations for consultation by police officers, detained persons and members of the public.

1.2   The notes for guidance included are not provisions of this code, but are guidance to police officers and others about its application and interpretation.

1.3   This code applies to the following searches of premises:

(a)   undertaken for the purposes of an investigation into an alleged offence, with the occupier's consent, other than searches made in the following circumstances:

— routine scenes of crime searches

— calls to a fire or a burglary made by or on behalf of an occupier or searches following the activation of fire or burglar alarms

— searches to which paragraph 4.4 applies

— bomb threat calls;

(b)   under powers conferred by sections 17, 18 and 32 of the Police and Criminal Evidence Act 1984;

(c)   undertaken in pursuance of a search warrant issued in accordance with section 15 of, or Schedule 1 to the Police and Criminal Evidence Act 1984, or section 15 of, or Schedule 7 to the Prevention of Terrorism (Temporary Provisions) Act 1989.

'Premises' for the purpose of this code is defined in section 23 of the Police and Criminal Evidence Act 1984. It includes any place and, in particular, any vehicle, vessel, aircraft, hovercraft, tent or movable structure. It also includes any offshore installation as defined in section 1 of the Mineral Workings (Offshore Installations) Act 1971.

1.3A   Any search of a person who has not been arrested which is carried out during a search of premises shall be carried out in accordance with Code A.

1.3B   This code does not apply to the exercise of a statutory power to enter premises or to inspect goods, equipment or procedures if the exercise of that power is not dependent on the existence of grounds for suspecting that an offence may have been committed and the person exercising the power has no reasonable grounds for such suspicion.

2.   Search warrants and production orders

(a)   Action to be taken before an application is made

2.1   Where information is received which appears to justify an application, the officer concerned must take reasonable steps to check that the information is accurate, recent and has not been provided maliciously or irresponsibly. An application may not be made on the basis of information from an anonymous source where corroboration has not been sought.

2.2   The officer shall ascertain as specifically as is possible in the circumstances the nature of the articles concerned and their location.

2.3   The officer shall also make reasonable enquiries to establish what, if anything, is known about the likely occupier of the premises and the nature of the premises themselves; and whether they have been previously searched and if so how recently; and to obtain any other information relevant to the application.

2.4   No application for a search warrant may be made without the authority of an officer of at least the rank of inspector (or, in a case of urgency where no officer of this rank is readily available, the senior officer on duty). No application for a production order or warrant under Schedule 1 to the Police and Criminal Evidence Act 1984, or under Schedule 7 to the Prevention of Terrorism (Temporary Provisions) Act 1989, may be made without the authority of an officer of at least the rank of superintendent.

2.5   Except in a case of urgency, if there is reason to believe that a search might have an adverse effect on relations between the police and the community then the local police community liaison officer shall be consulted before it takes place. In urgent cases, the local police community liaison officer should be informed of the search as soon as practicable after it has been made. [See Note 2B]

(b)   Making an application

2.6   An application for a search warrant must be supported by an information in writing, specifying:
      (i)   the enactment under which the application is made;
      (ii)   as specifically as is reasonably practicable the premises to be searched and the object of the search; and
      (iii)   the grounds on which the application is made (including, where the purpose of the proposed search is to find evidence of an alleged offence, an indication of how the evidence relates to the investigation).

2.7   An application for a search warrant under paragraph 12(a) of Schedule 1 to the Police and Criminal Evidence Act 1984, or under Schedule 7 to the Prevention of Terrorism (Temporary Provisions) Act 1989, shall also, where appropriate, indicate why it is believed that service of notice of an application for a production order may seriously prejudice the investigation.

2.8   If an application is refused, no further application may be made for a warrant to search those premises unless supported by additional grounds.

Notes for Guidance

2A   The identity of an informant need not be disclosed when making an application, but the officer concerned should be prepared to deal with any questions the magistrate or judge may have about the accuracy of previous information provided by that source or other related matters.

2B   The local police/community consultative group, where it exists, or its equivalent, should be informed as soon as practicable after a search has taken place where there is reason to believe that it might have had an adverse effect on relations between the police and the community.

3.   Entry without warrant

(a)   Making an arrest etc.

3.1   The conditions under which an officer may enter and search premises without a warrant are set out in section 17 of the Police and Criminal Evidence Act 1984.

(b)   Search after arrest of premises in which arrest takes place or in which the arrested person was present immediately prior to arrest

3.2   The powers of an officer to search premises in which he has arrested a person or where the person was immediately before he was arrested are as set out in section 32 of the Police and Criminal Evidence Act 1984.

(c) Search after arrest of premises other than those in which arrest takes place

3.3   The specific powers of an officer to search premises occupied or controlled by a person who has been arrested for an arrestable offence are as set out in section 18 of the Police and Criminal Evidence Act 1984. They may not (unless subsection 5 of section 18 applies) be exercised unless an officer of the rank of inspector or above has given authority in writing. That authority should (unless wholly impracticable) be given on the Notice of Powers and Rights (see paragraph 5.7(i)). The record of the search required by section 18(7) of the Act shall be made in the custody record, where there is one. In the case of enquiries linked to the investigation of terrorism, the authorising officer shall use his warrant or other identification number.

4.   Search with consent

4.1   Subject to paragraph 4.4 below, if it is proposed to search premises with the consent of a person entitled to grant entry to the premises the consent must, if practicable, be given in writing on the notice of Powers and Rights before the search takes place. The officer must make enquiries to satisfy himself that the person is in a position to give such consent. [See Note 4B and paragraph 5.7(i)]

4.2   Before seeking consent the officer in charge of the search shall state the purpose of the proposed search and inform the person concerned that he is not obliged to consent and that anything seized may be produced in evidence. If at the time the person is not suspected of an offence, the officer shall tell him so when stating the purpose of the search.

4.3   An officer cannot enter and search premises or continue to search premises under 4.1 above if the consent has been given under duress or is withdrawn before the search is completed.

4.4   It is unnecessary to seek consent under paragraphs 4.1 and 4.2 above where in the circumstances this would cause disproportionate inconvenience to the person concerned. [Note 4C]

Notes for Guidance

4A   In the case of a lodging house or similar accommodation a search should not be made on the basis solely of the landlord's consent unless the tenant or occupier is unavailable and the matter is urgent.

4B   Where it is intended to search premises under the authority of a warrant or a power of entry and search without warrant, and the co-operation of the occupier of the premises is obtained in accordance with paragraph 5.4 below, there is no additional requirement to obtain written consent as at paragraph 4.1 above.

4C   Paragraph 4.4 is intended in particular to apply to circumstances where it is reasonable to assume that innocent occupiers would agree to, and expect that, police should take the proposed action. Examples are where a suspect has fled from the scene of a crime or to evade arrest and it is necessary quickly to check surrounding gardens and readily accessible places to see whether he is hiding; or where police have arrested someone in the night after a pursuit and it is necessary to make a brief check of gardens along the route of the pursuit to see whether stolen or incriminating articles have been discarded.

5.   Searching of premises: general considerations

(a)   Time of searches

5.1   Searches made under warrant must be made within one calendar month from the date of issue of the warrant.

5.2   Searches must be made at a reasonable hour unless this might frustrate the purpose of the search. [See Note 5A]

5.3   A warrant authorises an entry on one occasion only.

(b)   Entry other than with consent

5.4   The officer in charge shall first attempt to communicate with the occupier or any other person entitled to grant access to the premises by explaining the authority under which he seeks entry to the premises and ask the occupier to allow him to do so, unless:

      (i)   the premises to be searched are known to be unoccupied;

      (ii)   the occupier and any other person entitled to grant access are known to be absent; or

      (iii)   there are reasonable grounds for believing that to alert the occupier or any other person entitled to grant access by attempting to communicate with him would frustrate the object of the search or endanger the officers concerned or other persons.

5.5   Where the premises are occupied the officer shall identify himself (by warrant or other identification number in the case of inquiries linked to the investigation of terrorism) and, if not in uniform, show his warrant cards (but in so doing in the case of enquiries linked to the investigation of terrorism, the officer need not reveal his name); and state the purpose of the search and the grounds for undertaking it, before a search begins, unless sub-paragraph 5.4 (iii) applies.

5.6   Reasonable force may be used if necessary to enter premises if the officer in charge is satisfied that the premises are those specified in any warrant, or in exercise of the powers described in 3.1 to 3.3 above, and where:

      (i)   the occupier or any other person entitled to grant access has refused a request to allow entry to his premises;

      (ii)   it is impossible to communicate with the occupier or any other person entitled to grant access; or

      (iii)   any of the provisions of 5.4(i) to (iii) apply.

(c)   Notice of powers and rights

5.7   If an officer conducts a search to which this code applies he shall, unless it is impracticable to do so, provide the occupier with a copy of a notice in a standard format:

      (i)   specifying whether the search is made under warrant, or with consent, or in the exercise of the powers described in 3.1 to 3.3 above (the format of the notice shall provide for authority or consent to be indicated where appropriate — see 3.3 and 4.1 above);

      (ii)   summarising the extent of the powers of search and seizure conferred in the Act;

      (iii)   explaining the rights of the occupier, and of the owner of property seized in accordance with the provisions of 6.1 to 6.5 and 6.8 below, set out in the Act and in this code;

      (iv)   explaining that compensation may be payable in appropriate cases for damage caused in entering and searching premises, and giving the address to which an application for compensation should be directed; and

      (v)   stating that a copy of this code is available to be consulted at any police station.

5.8   If the occupier is present, copies of the notice mentioned above, and of the warrant (if the search is made under warrant) should if practicable be given to the occupier before the search begins, unless the officer in charge of the search reasonably believes that to do so would frustrate the object of the search or endanger the officers concerned or other persons. If the occupier is not present, copies of the notice, and of the warrant where appropriate, should be left in a prominent place on the premises or appropriate part of the premises and endorsed with the name of the officer in charge of the search (except in the case of inquiries linked to the investigation of terrorism, in which case the officer's warrant or other identification number should be given), the name of the police station to which he is attached and the date and time of the search. The warrant itself should be endorsed to show that this has been done.

(d)   Conduct of searches

5.9   Premises may be searched only to the extent necessary to achieve the object of the search, having regard to the size and nature of whatever is sought. A search under warrant may not continue under the authority of that warrant once all the things specified in it have been found, or the officer in charge of the search is satisfied that they are not on the premises.

5.10   Searches must be conducted with due consideration for the property and privacy of the occupier of the premises searched, and with no more disturbance than necessary. Reasonable force may be used only where this is necessary because the co-operation of the occupier cannot be obtained or is insufficient for the purpose.

5.11   If the occupier wishes to ask a friend, neighbour or other person to witness the search then he must be allowed to do so, unless the officer in charge has reasonable grounds for believing that this would seriously hinder the investigation or endanger the officers concerned or other people. A search need not be unreasonably delayed for this purpose.

(e)   Leaving premises

5.12   If premises have been entered by force the officer in charge shall, before leaving them, satisfy himself that they are secure either by arranging for the occupier or his agent to be present or by any other appropriate means.

(f)   Search under Schedule 1 to the Police and Criminal Evidence Act 1984

5.13   An officer of the rank of inspector or above shall take charge of and be present at any search made under a warrant issued under Schedule 1 to the Police and Criminal Evidence Act 1984 or under Schedule 7 to the Prevention of Terrorism (Temporary Provisions) Act 1989. He is responsible for ensuring that the search is conducted with discretion and in such a manner as to cause the least possible disruption to any business or other activities carried on in the premises.

5.14   After satisfying himself that material may not be taken from the premises without his knowledge, the officer in charge of the search shall ask for the documents or other records concerned to be produced. He may also, if he considers it to be necessary, ask to see the index to files held on the premises, if there is one; and the officers conducting the search may inspect any files which, according to the index, appear to contain any of the material sought. A more extensive search of the premises may be made only if the person responsible for them refuses to produce the material sought, or to allow access to the index; if it appears that the index is inaccurate or incomplete; or if for any other reason the officer in charge has reasonable grounds for believing that such a search is necessary in order to find the material sought. [See Note 5B]

Notes for Guidance

5A   In determining at what time to make a search, the officer in charge should have regard, among other considerations, to the times of day at which the occupier of the premises is likely to be present, and should not search at a time when he, or any other person on the premises, is likely to be asleep unless not doing so is likely to frustrate the purpose of the search.

5B   In asking for documents to be produced in accordance with paragraph 5.14 above, officers should direct the request to a person in authority and with responsibility for the documents.

5C   If the wrong premises are searched by mistake, everything possible should be done at the earliest opportunity to allay any sense of grievance. In appropriate cases assistance should be given to obtain compensation.

6.   Seizure and retention of property

(a)   Seizure

6.1   Subject to paragraph 6.2 below, an officer who is searching any premises under any statutory power or with the consent of the occupier may seize:
  (a)   anything covered by a warrant; and
  (b)   anything which he has reasonable grounds for believing is evidence of an offence or has been obtained in consequence of the commission of an offence.
Items under (b) may only be seized where this is necessary to prevent their concealment, alteration, loss, damage or destruction.

6.2   No item may be seized which is subject to legal privilege (as defined in section 10 of the Police and Criminal Evidence Act 1984).

6.3   An officer who decides that it is not appropriate to seize property because of an explanation given by the person holding it, but who has reasonable grounds for believing that it has been obtained in consequence of the commission of an offence by some person, shall inform the holder of his suspicions and shall explain that, if he disposes of the property, he may be liable to civil or criminal proceedings.

6.4   An officer may photograph or copy, or have photographed or copied, any document or other article which he has power to seize in accordance with paragraph 6.1 above.

6.5   Where an officer considers that a computer may contain information that could be used in evidence, he may require the information to be produced in a form that can be taken away and in which it is visible and legible.

(b)   Retention

6.6   Subject to paragraph 6.7 below, anything which has been seized in accordance with the above provisions may be retained only for as long as is necessary in the circumstances. It may be retained, among other purposes:
  (i)   for use as evidence at a trial for an offence;
  (ii)   for forensic examination or for other investigation in connection with an offence; or
  (iii) where there are reasonable grounds for believing that it has been stolen or obtained by the commission of an offence, in order to establish its lawful owner.

6.7   Property shall not be retained in accordance with 6.6 (i) and (ii) (i.e., for use as evidence or for the purposes of investigation) if a photograph or copy would suffice for those purposes.

(c)   Rights of owners etc.

6.8   If property is retained the person who had custody or control of it immediately prior to its seizure must on request be provided with a list or description of the property within a reasonable time.

6.9   He or his representative must be allowed supervised access to the property to examine it or have it photographed or copied, or must be provided with a photograph or copy, in either case within a reasonable time of any request and at his own expense, unless the officer in charge of an investigation has reasonable grounds for believing that this would prejudice the investigation of an offence or any criminal proceedings. In this case a record of the grounds must be made.

Note for Guidance

6A   Any person claiming property seized by the police may apply to a magistrate's court under the Police (Property) Act 1897 for its possession, and should, where appropriate, be advised of this procedure.

7.   Action to be taken after searches

7.1   Where premises have been searched in circumstances to which this code applies, other than in the circumstances covered by paragraph 1.3(a), the officer in charge of the search shall, on arrival at a police station, make or have made a record of the search. The record shall include:

(i)   the address of the premises searched;
(ii)   the date, time and duration of the search;
(iii)   the authority under which the search was made. Where the search was made in the exercise of a statutory power to search premises without warrant, the record shall include the power under which the search was made; and where the search was made under warrant, or with written consent, a copy of the warrant or consent shall be appended to the record or kept in a place identified in the record;
(iv)   the names of all the officers who conducted the search (except in the case of enquiries linked to the investigation of terrorism, in which case the record shall state the warrant or other identification number and duty station of each officer concerned);
(v)   the names of any persons on the premises if they are known;
(vi)   either a list of any articles seized or a note of where such a list is kept and, if not covered by a warrant, the reason for their seizure;
(vii)   whether force was used, and, if so, the reason why it was used;
(viii)   details of any damage caused during the search, and the circumstances in which it was caused.

7.2   Where premises have been searched under warrant, the warrant shall be endorsed to show:

(i)   whether any articles specified in the warrant were found;
(ii)   whether any other articles were seized;
(iii)   the date and time at which it was executed;
(iv)   the names of the officers who executed it (except in the case of enquiries linked to the investigation of terrorism, in which case the warrant or other identification number and duty station of each officer concerned shall be shown);
(v)   whether a copy, together with a copy of the notice of powers and rights was handed to the occupier; or whether it was endorsed as requested by paragraph 5.8, and left on the premises together with the copy notice and, if so, where.

7.3   Any warrant which has been executed or which has not been executed within one calendar month of its issue shall be returned, if it was issued by a justice of the peace, to the clerk to the justices for the petty sessions area concerned or, if issued by a judge, to the appropriate officer of the court from which he issued it.

8.   Search registers

8.1 A search register shall be maintained at each sub-divisional police station. All records which are required to be made by this code shall be made, copied, or referred to in the register.

CODE OF PRACTICE FOR THE DETENTION, TREATMENT AND QUESTIONING OF PERSONS BY POLICE OFFICERS (CODE C)

1. General

1.1   All persons in custody must be dealt with expeditiously, and released as soon as the need for detention has ceased to apply.

1.1A   A custody officer is required to perform the functions specified in this code as soon as is practicable. A custody officer shall not be in breach of this code in the event of delay provided that the delay is justifiable and that every reasonable step is taken to prevent unnecessary delay. The custody record shall indicate where a delay has occurred and the reason why. [See Note 1H]

1.2   This code of practice must be readily available at all police stations for consultation by police officers, detained persons and members of the public.

1.3   The notes for guidance included are not provisions of this code, but are guidance to police officers and others about its application and interpretation. Provisions in the annexes to this code are provisions of this code.

1.4   If an officer has any suspicion, or is told in good faith, that a person of any age may be mentally disordered or mentally handicapped, or mentally incapable of understanding the significance of questions put to him or his replies, then that person shall be treated as a mentally disordered or mentally handicapped person for the purposes of this code. [See Note 1G]

1.5   If anyone appears to be under the age of 17 then he shall be treated as a juvenile for the purposes of this code in the absence of clear evidence to show that he is older.

1.6   If a person appears to be blind or seriously visually handicapped, deaf, unable to read, unable to speak or has difficulty orally because of a speech impediment, he should be treated as such for the purposes of this code in the absence of clear evidence to the contrary.

1.7   In this code 'the appropriate adult' means:
    (a)   in the case of a juvenile:
        (i)   his parent or guardian (or, if he is in care, the care authority or voluntary organisation. The term 'in care' is used in this code to cover all cases in which a juvenile is 'looked after' by a local authority under the terms of the Children Act 1989);
        (ii)   a social worker; or
        (iii)   failing either of the above, another responsible adult aged 18 or over who is not a police officer or employed by the police.
    (b)   in the case of a person who is mentally disordered or mentally handicapped:
        (i)   a relative, guardian or other person responsible for his care or custody;
        (ii)   someone who has experience of dealing with mentally disordered or mentally handicapped persons but is not a police officer or employed by the police (such as an approved social worker as defined by the Mental Health Act 1983 or a specialist social worker); or
        (iii)   failing either of the above, some other responsible adult aged 18 or over who is not a police officer or employed by the police.
[See Note 1E]

1.8   Whenever this code requires a person to be given certain information he does not have to be given it if he is incapable at the time of understanding what is said to him or is violent or likely to become violent or is in urgent need of medical attention, but he must be given it as soon as practicable.

1.9   Any reference to a custody officer in this code includes an officer who is performing the functions of a custody officer.

1.10   Subject to paragraph 1.12, this code applies to people who are in custody at police stations in England and Wales whether or not they have been arrested for an offence and to those who have been removed to a police station as a place of safety under section 135 and 136 of the Mental Health Act 1983. Section 15 (reviews and extensions of detention) however applies solely to people in police detention, for example those who have been brought to a police station under arrest for an offence or have been arrested at a police station for an offence after attending there voluntarily.

1.11   Persons in police detention include persons taken to a police station after being arrested under section 14 of the Prevention of Terrorism (Temporary Provisions) Act 1989 or under paragraph 6 of schedule 5 to that Act by an examining officer who is a constable.

1.12   This code does not apply to the following groups of people in custody:
   (i)   people who have been arrested by officers from a police force in Scotland exercising their powers of detention under section 137(2) of the Criminal Justice and Public Order Act 1994 (Cross Border powers of arrest etc.);
   (ii)   people arrested under section 3(5) of the Asylum and Immigration Appeals Act 1993 for the purpose of having their fingerprints taken;
   (iii)   people who have been served a notice advising them of their detention under powers contained in the Immigration Act 1971;
   (iv)   convicted or remanded prisoners held in police cells on behalf of the prison service under the Imprisonment (Temporary Provisions) Act 1980;
but the provisions on conditions of detention and treatment in sections 8 and 9 of this code must be considered as the minimum standards of treatment for such detainees.

Notes for Guidance

1A   Although certain sections of this code (e.g., section 9 — treatment of detained persons) apply specifically to persons in custody at police stations, those there voluntarily to assist with an investigation should be treated with no less consideration (e.g., offered refreshments at appropriate times) and enjoy an absolute right to obtain legal advice or communicate with anyone outside the police station.

1B   This code does not affect the principle that all citizens have a duty to help police officers to prevent crime and discover offenders. This is a civic rather than a legal duty; but when a police officer is trying to discover whether, or by whom, an offence has been committed he is entitled to question any person from whom he thinks useful information can be obtained, subject to the restrictions imposed by this code. A person's declaration that he is unwilling to reply does not alter this entitlement.

1C   A person, including a parent or guardian, should not be an appropriate adult if he is suspected of involvement in the offence in question, is the victim, is a witness, is involved in the investigation or has received admissions prior to attending to act as the appropriate adult. If the parent of a juvenile is estranged from the juvenile, he should not be asked to act as the appropriate adult if the juvenile expressly and specifically objects to his presence.

1D   If a juvenile admits an offence to or in the presence of a social worker other than during the time that the social worker is acting as the appropriate adult for that juvenile, another social worker should be the appropriate adult in the interest of fairness.

1E   In the case of people who are mentally disordered or mentally handicapped, it may in certain circumstances be more satisfactory for all concerned if the appropriate adult is someone who has experience or training in their care rather than a relative lacking such qualifications. But if the person himself prefers a relative to a better qualified stranger or objects to a particular person as the appropriate adult, his wishes should if practicable be respected.

1EE   A person should always be given an opportunity, when an appropriate adult is called to the police station, to consult privately with a solicitor in the absence of the appropriate adult if they wish to do so.

1F   A solicitor or lay visitor who is present at the police station in that capacity may not act as the appropriate adult.

1G   The generic term 'mental disorder' is used throughout this code. 'Mental disorder' is defined in section 1(2) of the Mental Health Act 1983 as 'mental illness, arrested or incomplete development of mind, psychopathic disorder and any other disorder or disability of mind'. It should be noted that 'mental disorder' is different from 'mental handicap' although the two are dealt with similarly throughout this code. Where the custody officer has any doubt as to the mental state or capacity of a person detained an appropriate adult should be called.

1H   Paragraph 1.1A is intended to cover the kinds of delays which may occur in the processing of detained persons because, for example, a large number of suspects are brought into the police station simultaneously to be placed in custody, or interview rooms are all being used, or where there are difficulties in contacting an appropriate adult, solicitor or interpreter.

1I   It is important that the custody officer reminds the appropriate adult and the detained person of the right to legal advice and records any reasons for waiving it in accordance with section 6 of this code.

2.   Custody records

2.1   A separate custody record must be opened as soon as practicable for each person who is brought to a police station under arrest or is arrested at the police station having attended there voluntarily. All information which has to be recorded under this code must be recorded as soon as practicable in the custody record unless otherwise specified. Any audio or video recording made in the custody area is not part of the custody record.

2.2   In the case of any action requiring the authority of an officer of a specified rank, his name and rank must be noted in the custody record. The recording of names does not apply to officers dealing with persons detained under the Prevention of Terrorism (Temporary Provisions) Act 1989. Instead the record shall state the warrant or other identification number and duty station of such officers.

2.3   The custody officer is responsible for the accuracy and completeness of the custody record and for ensuring that the record or a copy of the record accompanies a detained person if he is transferred to another police station. The record shall show the time of and reason for transfer and the time a person is released from detention.

2.4   A solicitor or appropriate adult must be permitted to consult the custody record of a person detained as soon as practicable after their arrival at the police station. When a person leaves police detention or is taken before a court, he or his legal representative or his appropriate adult shall be supplied on request with a copy of the custody record as soon as practicable. This entitlement lasts for 12 months after his release.

2.5   The person who has been detained, the appropriate adult, or the legal representative shall be permitted to inspect the original custody record after the person has left police detention provided they give reasonable notice of their request. A note of any such inspection shall be made in the custody record.

2.6   All entries in custody records must be timed and signed by the maker. In the case of a record entered on a computer this shall be timed and contain the operator's identification. Warrant or other identification numbers shall be used rather than names in the case of detention under the Prevention of Terrorism (Temporary Provisions) Act 1989.

2.7   The fact and time of any refusal by a person to sign a custody record when asked to do so in accordance with the provisions of this code must itself be recorded.

3.   Initial action

(a)   Detained persons: normal procedure

3.1   When a person is brought to a police station under arrest or is arrested at the police station having attended there voluntarily the custody officer must tell him clearly of the following rights and of the fact that they are continuing rights which may be exercised at any stage during the period in custody.
    (i)   the right to have someone informed of his arrest in accordance with section 5 below;
    (ii)   the right to consult privately with a solicitor in accordance with section 6 below, and the fact that independent legal advice is available free of charge; and
    (iii)   the right to consult this and the other codes of practice.
[See Note 3E]

3.2   In addition the custody officer must give the person a written notice setting out the above three rights, the right to a copy of the custody record in accordance with paragraph 2.4 above and the caution in the terms prescribed in section 10 below. The notice must also explain the arrangements for obtaining legal advice. The custody officer must also give the person an additional written notice briefly setting out his entitlements while in custody. [See Notes 3A and 3B] The custody officer shall ask the person to sign the custody record to acknowledge receipt of these notices and any refusal to sign must be recorded on the custody record.

3.3   A citizen of an independent Commonwealth country or a national of a foreign country (including the Republic of Ireland) must be informed as soon as practicable of his rights of communication with his High Commission, Embassy or Consulate (see Section 7).

3.4   The custody officer shall note on the custody record any comment the person may make in relation to the arresting officer's account but shall not invite comment. If the custody officer authorises a person's detention he must inform him of the grounds as soon as practicable and in any case before that person is then questioned about any offence. The custody officer shall note any comment the person may make in respect of the decision to detain him but, again, shall not invite comment. The custody officer shall not put specific questions to the person regarding his involvement in any offence, nor in respect of any comments he may make in response to the arresting officer's account or the decision to place him in detention. Such an exchange is likely to constitute an interview as defined by paragraph 11.1A and would require the associated safeguards included in section 11. [See also paragraph 11.13 in respect of unsolicited comments]

3.5   The custody officer shall ask the detained person whether at this time he would like legal advice (see paragraph 6.5). The person shall be asked to sign the custody record to confirm his decision. The custody officer is responsible for ensuring that in confirming any decision the person signs in the correct place.

3.5A   If video cameras are installed in the custody area, notices which indicate that cameras are in use shall be prominently displayed. Any request by a detained person or other person to have video cameras switched off shall be refused.

(b)   Detained persons: special groups

3.6   If the person appears to be deaf or there is doubt about his hearing or speaking ability or ability to understand English, and the custody officer cannot establish effective communication, the custody officer must as soon as practicable call an interpreter, and ask him to provide the information required above. [See Section 13]

3.7   If the person is a juvenile, the custody officer must, if it is practicable, ascertain the identity of a person responsible for his welfare. That person may be his parent or guardian (or, if he is in care, the care authority or voluntary organisation) or any other person who has, for the time being, assumed responsibility for his welfare. That person must be informed as soon as practicable that the juvenile has been arrested, why he has been arrested and where he is detained. This right is in addition to the juvenile's right in section 5 of the code not to be held incommunicado. [See Note 3C]

3.8   In the case of a juvenile who is known to be subject to a supervision order, reasonable steps must also be taken to notify the person supervising him.

3.9   If the person is a juvenile, is mentally handicapped or appears to be suffering from a mental disorder, then the custody officer must, as soon as practicable, inform the appropriate adult (who in the case of a juvenile may or may not be a person responsible for his welfare, in accordance with paragraph 3.7 above) of the grounds for his detention and his whereabouts, and ask the adult to come to the police station to see the person.

3.10   It is imperative that a mentally disordered or mentally handicapped person who has been detained under section 136 of the Mental Health Act 1983 should be assessed as soon as possible. If that assessment is to take place at the police station, an approved social worker and a registered medical practitioner should be called to the police station as soon as possible in order to interview and examine the person. Once the person has been interviewed and examined and suitable arrangements have been made for his treatment or care, he can no longer be detained under section 136. The person should not be released until he has been seen by both the approved social worker and the registered medical practitioner.

3.11   If the appropriate adult is already at the police station, then the provisions of paragraphs 3.1 to 3.5 above must be complied with in his presence. If the appropriate adult is not at the police station when the provisions of paragraphs 3.1 to 3.5 above are complied with, then these provisions must be complied with again in the presence of the appropriate adult once that person arrives.

3.12   The person should be advised by the custody officer that the appropriate adult (where applicable) is there to assist and advise him and that he can consult privately with the appropriate adult at any time.

3.13   If, having been informed of the right to legal advice under paragraph 3.11 above, either the appropriate adult or the person detained wishes legal advice to be taken, then the provisions of section 6 of this code apply. [See Note 3G]

3.14   If the person is blind or seriously visually handicapped or is unable to read, the custody officer should ensure that his solicitor, relative, the appropriate adult or some other person likely to take an interest in him (and not involved in the investigation) is available to help in checking any documentation. Where this code requires written consent or signification, then the person who is assisting may be asked to sign instead if the detained person so wishes. [See Note 3F]

(c)   Persons attending a police station voluntarily

3.15   Any person attending a police station voluntarily for the purpose of assisting with an investigation may leave at will unless placed under arrest. If it is decided that he should not be allowed to do so then he must be informed at once that he is under arrest and brought before the custody officer, who is responsible for ensuring that he is notified of his rights in the same way as other detained persons. If he is not placed under arrest but is cautioned in accordance with section 10 below, the officer who gives the caution must at the same time inform him that he is not under arrest, that he is not obliged to remain at the police station but that if he remains at the police station he may obtain free legal advice if he wishes. The officer shall point out that the right to legal advice includes the right to speak with a solicitor on the telephone and ask him if he wishes to do so.

3.16   If a person who is attending the police station voluntarily (in accordance with paragraph 3.15) asks about his entitlement to legal advice, he should be given a copy of the notice explaining the arrangements for obtaining legal advice. (See paragraph 3.2.)

(d)   Documentation

3.17   The grounds for a person's detention shall be recorded, in his presence if practicable.

3.18   Action taken under paragraphs 3.6 to 3.14 shall be recorded.

Notes for Guidance

3A   The notice of entitlements is intended to provide detained persons with brief details of their entitlements over and above the statutory rights which are set out in the notice of rights. The notice of entitlements should list the entitlements contained in this code, including visits and contact with outside parties (including special provisions for Commonwealth citizens and foreign nationals), reasonable standards of physical comfort, adequate food and drink, access to toilets and washing facilities, clothing, medical attention, and exercise where practicable. It should also mention the provisions relating to the conduct of interviews, the circumstances in which an appropriate adult should be available to assist the detained person and his statutory rights to make representation whenever the period of his detention is reviewed.

3B   In addition to the notices in English, translations should be available in Welsh, the main ethnic minority languages and the principal European languages whenever they are likely to be helpful.

3C   If the juvenile is in the care of a local authority or voluntary organisation but is living with his parents or other adults responsible for his welfare then, although there is no legal obligation on the police to inform them, they as well as the authority or organisation should normally be contacted unless suspected of involvement in the offence concerned. Even if a juvenile in care is not living with his parents, consideration should be given to informing them as well.

3D   Most local authority Social Services Departments can supply a list of interpreters who have the necessary skills and experience to interpret for the deaf at police interviews. The local Community Relations Council may be able to provide similar information in cases where the person concerned does not understand English. [See Section 13]

3E   The right to consult the codes of practice under paragraph 3.1 above does not entitle the person concerned to delay unreasonably any necessary investigative or administrative action while he does so. Procedures requiring the provision of breath, blood or urine specimens under the terms of the Road Traffic Act 1988 need not be delayed.

3F   Blind or seriously visually handicapped persons may be unwilling to sign police documents. The alternative of their representative signing on their behalf seeks to protect the interests of both police and suspects.

3G   The purpose of paragraph 3.13 is to protect the rights of a juvenile, mentally disordered or mentally handicapped person who may not understand the significance of what is being said to him. If such a person wishes to exercise the right to legal advice the appropriate action should be taken straightaway and not delayed until the appropriate adult arrives.

4. Detained persons' property

(a)   Action

4.1   The custody officer is responsible for:
    (a)   ascertaining:
        (i)   what property a detained person has with him when he comes to the police station (whether on arrest, re-detention on answering to bail, commitment to prison custody on the order or sentence of a court, on lodgement at the police station with a view to his production in court from such custody, on arrival at a police station on transfer from detention at another station or from hospital or on detention under section 135 or 136 of the Mental Health Act 1983);
        (ii)   what property he might have acquired for an unlawful or harmful purpose while in custody.
    (b)   the safekeeping of any property which is taken from him and which remains at the police station.
To these ends the custody officer may search him or authorise his being searched to the extent that he considers necessary (provided that a search of intimate parts of the body or involving the removal of more than outer clothing may only be made in accordance with Annex A to this code). A search may only be carried out by an officer of the same sex as the person searched. [See Note 4A]

4.2   A detained person may retain clothing and personal effects at his own risk unless the custody officer considers that he may use them to cause harm to himself or others, interfere with evidence, damage property or effect an escape or they are needed as evidence. In this event the custody officer may withhold such articles as he considers necessary. If he does so he must tell the person why.

4.3   Personal effects are those items which a person may lawfully need or use or refer to while in detention but do not include cash and other items of value.

(b)   Documentation

4.4   The custody officer is responsible for recording all property brought to the police station that a detained person had with him, or had taken from him on arrest. The detained person shall be allowed to check and sign the record of property as correct. Any refusal to sign should be recorded.

4.5   If a detained person is not allowed to keep any article of clothing or personal effects the reason must be recorded.

Notes for Guidance

4A   Section 54(1) of PACE and paragraph 4.1 require a detained person to be searched where it is clear that the custody officer will have continuing duties in relation to that person or where that person's behaviour or offence makes an inventory appropriate. They do not require every detained person to be searched. Where, for example, it is clear that a person will only be detained for a short period and is not to be placed in a cell, the custody officer may decide not to search him. In such a case the custody record will be endorsed 'not searched', paragraph 4.4 will not apply, and the person will be invited to sign the entry. Where the person detained refuses to sign, the custody officer will be obliged to ascertain what property he has on him in accordance with paragraph 4.1.

4B   Paragraph 4.4 does not require the custody officer to record on the custody record property in the possession of the person on arrest, if by virtue of its nature, quantity or size, it is not practicable to remove it to the police station.

4C   Paragraph 4.4 above is not to be taken as requiring that items of clothing worn by the person be recorded unless withheld by the custody officer in accordance with paragraph 4.2.

5.   Right not to be held incommunicado

(a)   Action

5.1   Any person arrested and held in custody at a police station or other premises may on request have one person known to him or who is likely to take an interest in his welfare informed at public expense as soon as practicable of his whereabouts. If the person cannot be contacted the person who has made the request may choose up to two alternatives. If they too cannot be contacted the person in charge of detention or of the investigation has discretion to allow further attempts until the information has been conveyed. [See Notes 5C and 5D]

5.2   The exercise of the above right in respect of each of the persons nominated may be delayed only in accordance with Annex B to this code.

5.3   The above right may be exercised on each occasion that a person is taken to another police station.

5.4   The person may receive visits at the custody officer's discretion. [See Note 5B]

5.5   Where an enquiry as to the whereabouts of the person is made by a friend, relative or person with an interest in his welfare, this information shall be given, if he agrees and if Annex B does not apply. [See Note 5D]

5.6   Subject to the following condition, the person should be supplied with writing materials on request and allowed to speak on the telephone for a reasonable time to one person. [See Notes 5A and 5E] Where an officer of the rank of Inspector or above considers that the sending of a letter or the making of a telephone call may result in:
    (a)   any of the consequences set out in the first and second paragraph of Annex B and the person is detained in connection with an arrestable or a serious arrestable offence, for which purpose, any reference to a serious arrestable offence in Annex B includes an arrestable offence; or
    (b)   either of the consequences set out in paragraph 8 of Annex B and the person is detained under the Prevention of Terrorism (Temporary Provisions) Act 1989, that officer can deny or delay the exercise of either or both these privileges. However, nothing in this section permits the restriction or denial of the rights set out in sections 5.1 and 6.1.

5.7   Before any letter or message is sent, or telephone call made, the person shall be informed that what he says in any letter, call or message (other than in the case of a communication to a solicitor) may be read or listened to as appropriate and may be given in evidence. A telephone call may be terminated if it is being abused. The costs can be at public expense at the discretion of the custody officer.

(b)   Documentation

5.8   A record must be kept of:
    (a)   any request made under this section and the action taken on it;
    (b)   any letters, messages or telephone calls made or received or visits received;
and
    (c)   any refusal on the part of the person to have information about himself or his whereabouts given to an outside enquirer. The person must be asked to countersign the record accordingly and any refusal to sign should be recorded.

Notes for Guidance

5A   An interpreter may make a telephone call or write a letter on a person's behalf.

5B   In the exercise of his discretion the custody officer should allow visits where possible in the light of the availability of sufficient manpower to supervise a visit and any possible hindrance to the investigation.

5C   If the person does not know of anyone to contact for advice or support or cannot contact a friend or relative, the custody officer should bear in mind any local voluntary bodies or other organisations who might be able to offer help in such cases. But if it is specifically legal advice that is wanted, then paragraph 6.1 below will apply.

5D   In some circumstances it may not be appropriate to use the telephone to disclose information under paragraphs 5.1 and 5.5 above.

5E   The telephone call at paragraph 5.6 is in addition to any communication under paragraphs 5.1 and 6.1.

6.   Right to legal advice

(a)   Action

6.1   Subject to the provisos in Annex B all people in police detention must be informed that they may at any time consult and communicate privately, whether in person, in writing or by telephone with a solicitor, and that independent legal advice is available free of charge from the duty solicitor. [See paragraph 3.1 and Note 6B and Note 6J]

6.2   [Not Used]

6.3   A poster advertising the right to have legal advice must be prominently displayed in the charging area of every police station. [See Note 6H]

6.4   No police officer shall at any time do or say anything with the intention of dissuading a person in detention from obtaining legal advice.

6.5   The exercise of the right of access to legal advice may be delayed only in accordance with Annex B to this code. Whenever legal advice is requested (and unless Annex B applies) the custody officer must act without delay to secure the provision of such advice to the person concerned. If, on being informed or reminded of the right to legal advice, the person declines to speak to a solicitor in person, the officer shall point out that the right to legal advice includes the right to speak with a solicitor on the telephone and ask him if he wishes to do so. If the person continues to waive his right to legal advice the officer shall ask him the reasons for doing so, and any reasons shall be recorded on the custody record or the interview record as appropriate. Reminders of the right to legal advice must be given in accordance with paragraphs 3.5, 11.2, 15.3, 16.4 and 16.5 of this code and paragraphs 2.15(ii) and 5.2 of Code D. Once it is clear that a person neither wishes to speak to a solicitor in person nor by telephone he should cease to be asked his reasons. [See Note 6K]

6.6   A person who wants legal advice may not be interviewed or continue to be interviewed until he has received it unless:

(a)   Annex B applies; or

(b)   an officer of the rank of superintendent or above has reasonable grounds for believing that:

(i)   delay will involve an immediate risk of harm to persons or serious loss of, or damage to, property; or

(ii)   where a solicitor, including a duty solicitor, has been contacted and has agreed to attend, awaiting his arrival would cause unreasonable delay to the process of investigation; or

(c)   The solicitor nominated by the person, or selected by him from a list:

(i)   cannot be contacted; or

(ii)   has previously indicated that he does not wish to be contacted; or

(iii)   having been contacted, has declined to attend;

and the person has been advised of the Duty Solicitor Scheme (where one is in operation) but has declined to ask for the duty solicitor, or the duty solicitor is unavailable. (In these circumstances the interview may be started or continued without further delay provided that an officer of the rank of Inspector or above has given agreement for the interview to proceed in those circumstances — See Note 6B).

(d)   the person who wanted legal advice changes his mind.

In these circumstances the interview may be started or continued without further delay provided that the person has given his agreement in writing or on tape to being interviewed without receiving legal advice and that an officer of the rank of Inspector or above, having inquired into the person's reasons for his change of mind, has given authority for the interview to proceed. Confirmation of the person's agreement, his change of mind, his reasons where given and the name of the authorising officer shall be recorded in the taped or written interview record at the beginning or recommencement of interview. [See Note 6I]

6.7   Where 6.6(b)(i) applies, once sufficient information to avert the risk has been obtained, questioning must cease until the person has received legal advice or 6.6(a), (b)(ii), (c) or (d) apply.

6.8   Where a person has been permitted to consult a solicitor and the solicitor is available (i.e., present at the station or on his way to the station or easily contactable by telephone) at the time the interview begins or is in progress, he must be allowed to have his solicitor present while he is interviewed.

6.9   The solicitor may only be required to leave the interview if his conduct is such that the investigating officer is unable properly to put questions to the suspect. [See Notes 6D and 6E]

6.10   If the investigating officer considers that a solicitor is acting in such a way, he will stop the interview and consult an officer not below the rank of superintendent, if one is readily available, and otherwise an officer not below the rank of inspector who is not connected with the investigation. After speaking to the solicitor, the officer who has been consulted will decide whether or not the interview should continue in the presence of that solicitor. If he decides that it should not, the suspect will be given the opportunity to consult another solicitor before the interview continues and that solicitor will be given an opportunity to be present at the interview.

6.11   The removal of a solicitor from an interview is a serious step and, if it occurs, the officer of superintendent rank or above who took the decision will consider whether the incident should be reported to the Law Society. If the decision to remove the solicitor has been taken by an officer below the rank of superintendent, the facts must be reported to an officer of superintendent rank or above who will similarly consider whether a report to the Law Society would be appropriate. Where the solicitor concerned is a duty solicitor, the report should be both to the Law Society and to the Legal Aid Board.

6.12   In Codes of Practice issued under the Police and Criminal Evidence Act 1984, 'solicitor' means a solicitor who holds a current practising certificate, a trainee solicitor, a duty solicitor representative or an accredited representative included on the register of representatives maintained by the Legal Aid Board. If a solicitor wishes to send a non-accredited or probationary representative to provide advice on his behalf, then that person shall be admitted to the police station for this purpose unless an officer of the rank of inspector or above considers that such a visit will hinder the investigation of crime and directs otherwise. (Hindering the investigation of a crime does not include giving proper legal advice to a detained person in accordance with Note 6D.) Once admitted to the police station, the provisions of paragraphs 6.6 to 6.10 apply.

6.13   In exercising his discretion under pargraph 6.12, the officer should take into account in particular whether the identity and status of the non-accredited or probationary representative have been [satisfactorily] established; whether he is of suitable character to provide legal advice (a person with a criminal record is unlikely to be suitable unless the conviction was for a minor offence and is not of recent date); and any other matters in any written letter of authorisation provided by the solicitor on whose behalf the clerk or legal executive is attending the police station. [See Note 6F]

6.14   If the inspector refuses access to a non-accredited or probationary representative or a decision is taken that such a person should not be permitted to remain at an interview, he must forthwith notify a solicitor on whose behalf the non-accredited or probationary representative was to have acted or was acting, and give him an opportunity to make alternative arrangements. The detained person must also be informed and the custody record noted.

6.15   If a solicitor arrives at the station to see a particular person, that person must (unless Annex B applies) be informed of the solicitor's arrival whether or not he is being interviewed and asked whether he would like to see him. This applies even if the person concerned has already declined legal advice or having requested it, subsequently agreed to be interviewed without having received advice. The solicitor's attendance and the detained person's decision must be noted in the custody record.

(b)   Documentation

6.16   Any request for legal advice and the action taken on it shall be recorded.

6.17   If a person has asked for legal advice and an interview is begun in the absence of a solicitor or his representative (or the solicitor or his representative has been required to leave an interview), a record shall be made in the interview record.

Notes for Guidance

6A   In considering whether paragraph 6.6(b) applies, the officer should where practicable ask the solicitor for an estimate of the time that he is likely to take in coming to the station, and relate this information to the time for which detention is permitted, the time of day (i.e., whether the period of rest required by paragraph 12.2 is imminent) and the requirements of other investigations in progress. If the solicitor says that he is on his way to the station or that he will set off immediately, it will not normally be appropriate to begin an interview before he arrives. If it appears that it will be necessary to begin an interview before the solicitor's arrival he should be given an indication of how long police would be able to wait before paragraph 6.6(b) applies so that he has an opportunity to make arrangements for legal advice to be provided by someone else.

6B   A person who asks for legal advice should be given an opportunity to consult a specific solicitor or another solicitor from that solicitor's firm or the duty solicitor. If advice is not available by these means, or he does not wish to consult the duty solicitor, the person should be given an opportunity to choose a solicitor from a list of those willing to provide legal advice. If this solicitor is unavailable, he may choose up two alternatives. If these attempts to secure legal advice are unsuccessful, the custody officer has discretion to allow further attempts until a solicitor has been contacted and agrees to provide legal advice. Apart from carrying out his duties under Note 6B, a police officer must not advise the suspect about any particular firm of solicitors.

6C   [Not Used]

6D   A detained person has a right to free legal advice and to be represented by a solicitor. The solicitor's only role in the police station is to protect and advance the legal rights of his client. On occasions this may require the solicitor to give advice which has the effect of his client avoiding giving evidence which strengthens a prosecution case. The solicitor may intervene in order to seek clarification or to challenge an improper question to his client or the manner in which it is put, or to advise his client not to reply to particular questions, or if he wishes to give his client further legal advice. Paragraph 6.9 will only apply if the solicitor's approach or conduct prevents or unreasonably obstructs proper questions being put to the suspect or his response being recorded. Examples of unacceptable conduct include answering questions on a suspect's behalf or providing written replies for him to quote.

6E   In a case where an officer takes the decision to exclude a solicitor, he must be in a position to satisfy the court that the decision was properly made. In order to do this he may need to witness what is happening himself.

6F   If an officer of at least the rank of inspector considers that a particular solicitor or firm of solicitors is persistently sending non-accredited or probationary representatives who are unsuited to provide legal advice, he should inform an officer of at least the rank of superintendent, who may wish to take the matter up with the Law Society.

6G   Subject to the constraints of Annex B, a solicitor may advise more than one client in an investigation if he wishes. Any question of a conflict of interest is for the solicitor under his professional code of conduct. If, however, waiting for a solicitor to give advice to one client may lead to unreasonable delay to the interview with another, the provisions of paragraph 6.6(b) may apply.

6H   In addition to the poster in English advertising the right to legal advice, a poster or posters containing translations into Welsh, the main ethnic minority languages and the principal European languages should be displayed wherever they are likely to be helpful and it is practicable to do so.

6I   Paragraph 6.6(d) requires the authorisation of an officer of the rank of Inspector or above, to the continuation of an interview, where a person who wanted legal advice changes his mind. It is permissible for such authorisation to be given over the telephone, if the authorising officer is able to satisfy himself as to the reason for the person's change of mind and is satisfied that it is proper to continue the interview in those circumstances.

6J   Where a person chooses to speak to a solicitor on the telephone, he should be allowed to do so in private unless this is impractical because of the design and layout of the custody area or the location of telephones.

6K   A person is not obliged to give reasons for declining legal advice and should not be pressed if he does not wish to do so.

7. Citizens of Independent Commonwealth countries or foreign nationals

(a) Action

7.1   Any citizen of an independent Commonwealth country or a national of a foreign country (including the Republic of Ireland) may communicate at any time with his High Commission, Embassy or Consulate. He must be informed of this right as soon as practicable. He must also be informed as soon as practicable of his right, upon request to have his High Commission, Embassy or Consulate told of his whereabouts and the grounds for his detention. Such a request should be acted upon as soon as practicable.

7.2   If a person is detained who is a citizen of an independent Commonwealth or foreign country with which a bilateral consular convention or agreement is in force requiring notification of arrest, the appropriate High Commission, Embassy or Consulate shall be informed as soon as practicable, subject to paragraph 7.4 below. The countries to which this applies as an 1 January 1995 are listed in Annex F.

7.3   Consular officers may visit one of their nationals who is in police detention to talk to him and, if required, to arrange for legal advice. Such visits shall take place out of the hearing of a police officer.

7.4   Notwithstanding the provisions of consular conventions, where the person is a political refugee (whether for reasons of race, nationality, political opinion or religion) or is seeking political asylum, a consular officer shall not be informed of the arrest of one of his nationals or given access to or information about him except at the person's express request.

(b) Documentation

7.5   A record shall be made when a person is informed of his rights under this section and of any communications with a High Commission, Embassy or Consulate.

Note for Guidance

7A   The exercise of the rights in this section may not be interfered with even though Annex B applies.

8. Conditions of Detention

(a) Action

8.1   So far as is practicable, not more than one person shall be detained in each cell.

8.2   Cells in use must be adequately heated, cleaned and ventilated. They must be adequately lit, subject to such dimming as is compatible with safety and security to allow people detained overnight to sleep. No additional restraints shall be used within a locked cell unless absolutely necessary, and then only suitable handcuffs. In the case of a mentally handicapped or mentally disordered person, particular care must be taken when deciding whether to use handcuffs. [See Annex E paragraph 13]

8.3   Blankets, mattresses, pillows and other bedding supplied should be of a reasonable standard and in a clean and sanitary condition. [See Note 8B]

8.4   Access to toilet and washing facilities must be provided.

8.5   If it is necessary to remove a person's clothes for the purposes of investigation, for hygiene or health reasons or for cleaning, replacement clothing of a reasonable standard of comfort and cleanliness shall be provided. A person may not be interviewed unless adequate clothing has been offered to him.

8.6   At least two light meals and one main meal shall be offered in any period of 24 hours. [See Note 8C] Drinks should be provided at mealtimes and upon reasonable request between mealtimes. Whenever necessary, advice shall be sought from the police surgeon on medical or dietary matters. As far as practicable, meals provided shall offer a varied diet and meet any special dietary needs or religious beliefs that the person may have; he may also have meals supplied by his family or friends at his or their own expense. [See Note 8B]

8.7   Brief outdoor exercise shall be offered daily if practicable.

8.8   A juvenile shall not be placed in a police cell unless no other secure accommodation is available and the custody officer considers that it is not practicable to supervise him if he is not placed in a cell or the custody officer considers that a cell provides more comfortable accommodation than other secure accommodation in the police station. He may not be placed in a cell with a detained adult.

8.9   Reasonable force may be used if necessary for the following purposes:
       (i)   to secure compliance with reasonable instructions, including instructions given in pursuance of the provisions of a code of practice; or
       (ii)   to prevent escape, injury, damage to property or the destruction of evidence.

8.10   People detained shall be visited every hour, and those who are drunk, at least every half hour. A person who is drunk shall be roused and spoken to on each visit. (See Note 8A] Should the custody officer feel in any way concerned about the person's condition, for example because he fails to respond adequately when roused, then the officer shall arrange for medical treatment in accordance with paragraph 9.2 of this code.

(b)   Documentation

8.11   A record must be kept of replacement clothing and meals offered.

8.12   If a juvenile is placed in a cell, the reason must be recorded.

Notes for Guidance

8A   Whenever possible juveniles and other persons at risk should be visited more frequently.

8B   The provisions in paragraphs 8.3 and 8.6 respectively regarding bedding and a varied diet are of particular importance in the case of a person detained under the Prevention of Terrorism (Temporary Provisions) Act 1989, immigration detainees and others who are likely to be detained for an extended period.

8C   Meals should so far as practicable be offered at recognised meal times.

9.   Treatment of Detained Persons

(a)   General

9.1   If a complaint is made by or on behalf of a detained person about his treatment since his arrest, or it comes to the notice of any officer that he may have been treated improperly, a report must be made as soon as practicable to an officer of the rank of inspector or above who is not connected with the investigation. If the matter concerns a possible assault or the possibility of the unnecessary or unreasonable use of force then the police surgeon must also be called as soon as practicable.

(b) Medical treatment

9.2   The custody officer must immediately call the police surgeon (or, in urgent cases,
— for example, where a person does not show signs of sensibility or awareness, — must
send the person to hospital or call the nearest available medical practitioner) if a person
brought to a police station or already detained there:

(a)   appears to be suffering from physical illness or a mental disorder; or

(b)   is injured; or

(c)   [Not Used]

(d)   fails to respond normally to questions or conversation (other than through
drunkenness alone); or

(e)   otherwise appears to need medical attention.

This applies even if the person makes no request for medical attention and whether or
not he has recently had medical treatment elsewhere (unless brought to the police
station direct from hospital). It is not intended that the contents of this paragraph
should delay the transfer of a person to a place of safety under section 136 of the Mental
Health Act 1983 where that is applicable. Where an assessment under that Act is to take
place at the police station, the custody officer has discretion not to call the police
surgeon so long as he believes that the assessment by a registered medical practitioner
can be undertaken without undue delay. [See Note 9A]

9.3   If it appears to the custody officer, or he is told, that a person brought to the police
station under arrest may be suffering from an infectious disease of any significance he
must take steps to isolate the person and his property until he has obtained medical
directions as to where the person should be taken, whether fumigation should take place
and what precautions should be taken by officers who have been or will be in contact
with him.

9.4   If a detained person requests a medical examination the police surgeon must be
called as soon as practicable. He may in addition be examined by a medical practitioner
of his own choice at his own expense.

9.5   If a person is required to take or apply any medication in compliance with medical
directions, but prescribed before the person's detention, the custody officer should
consult the police surgeon prior to the use of the medication. The custody officer is
responsible for the safekeeping of any medication and for ensuring that the person is
given the opportunity to take or apply medication which the police surgeon has
approved. However no police officer may administer medicines which are also
controlled drugs subject to the Misuse of Drugs Act 1971 for this purpose. A person
may administer a controlled drug to himself only under the personal supervision of the
police surgeon. The requirement for personal supervision will have been satisfied if the
custody officer consults the police surgeon (this may be done by telephone) and both the
police surgeon and the custody officer are satisfied that, in all the circumstances, self
administration of the controlled drug will not expose the detained person, police officers
or anyone to the risk of harm or injury. If so satisfied, the police surgeon may authorise
the custody officer to permit the detained person to administer the controlled drug. If
the custody officer is in any doubt, the police surgeon should be asked to attend. Such
consultation should be noted in the custody record.

9.6   If a detained person has in his possession or claims to need medication relating to
a heart condition, diabetes, epilepsy or a condition of comparable potential seriousness
then, even though paragraph 9.2 may not apply, the advice of the police surgeon must
be obtained.

(c) Documentation

9.7   A record must be made of any arrangements made for an examination by a police surgeon under paragraph 9.1 above and of any complaint reported under that paragraph together with any relevant remarks by the custody officer.

9.8   A record must be kept of any request for a medical examination under paragraph 9.4, of the arrangements for any examination made, and of any medical directions to the police.

9.9   Subject to the requirements of section 4 above the custody record shall include not only a record of all medication that a detained person has in his possession on arrival at the police station but also a note of any such medication he claims he needs but does not have with him.

Notes for Guidance

9A   The need to call a police surgeon need not apply to minor ailments or injuries which do not need attention. However, all such ailments or injuries must be recorded in the custody record and any doubt must be resolved in favour of calling the police surgeon.

9B   It is important to remember that a person who appears to be drunk or behaving abnormally may be suffering from illness or the effects of drugs or may have sustained injury (particularly head injury) which is not apparent, and that someone needing or addicted to certain drugs may experience harmful effects within a short time of being deprived of their supply. Police should therefore always call the police surgeon when in any doubt, and act with all due speed.

9C   If a medical practitioner does not record his clinical findings in the custody record, the record must show where they are recorded.

10.   Cautions

(a) When a caution must be given

10.1   A person whom there are grounds to suspect of an offence must be cautioned before any questions about it (or further questions if it is his answers to previous questions which provide the grounds for suspicion) are put to him regarding his involvement or suspected involvement in that offence if his answers or his silence (i.e., failure or refusal to answer a question or to answer satisfactorily) may be given in evidence to a court in a prosecution. He therefore need not be cautioned if questions are put for other purposes, for example, solely to establish his identity or his ownership of any vehicle or to obtain information in accordance with any relevant statutory requirement (see paragraph 10.5C) or in furtherance of the proper and effective conduct of a search (for example to determine the need to search in the exercise of powers of stop and search or to seek co-operation while carrying out a search), or to seek verification of a written record in accordance with paragraph 11.13.

10.2   Whenever a person who is not under arrest is initially cautioned or is reminded that he is under caution (see paragraph 10.5) he must at the same time be told that he is not under arrest and is not obliged to remain with the officer (see paragraph 3.15).

10.3   A person must be cautioned upon arrest for an offence unless:
   (a)   it is impracticable to do so by reason of his condition or behaviour at the time;
or
   (b)   he has already been cautioned immediately prior to arrest in accordance with paragraph 10.1 above.

(b)   Action: general

10.4   The caution shall be in the following terms:

> You do not have to say anything. But it may harm your defence if you do not mention when questioned something which you later rely on in court. Anything you do say may be given in evidence.

10.5   When there is a break in questioning under caution the interviewing officer must ensure that the person being questioned is aware that he remains under caution. If there is any doubt the caution should be given again in full when the interview resumes. [See Note 10A]

Special warnings under sections 36 and 37 of the Criminal Justice and Public Order Act 1994

10.5A   When a suspect who is interviewed after arrest fails or refuses to answer certain questions, or to answer them satisfactorily, after due warning, a court or jury may draw such inferences as appear proper under sections 36 and 37 of the Criminal Justice and Public Order Act 1994. This applies when:

    (a)   a suspect is arrested by a constable and there is found on his person, or in or on his clothing or footwear, or otherwise in his possession, or in the place where he was arrested, any objects, marks or substances, or marks on such objects, and the person fails or refuses to account for the objects, marks or substances found; or

    (b)   an arrested person was found by a constable at a place at or about the time the offence for which he was arrested, is alleged to have been committed, and the person fails or refuses to account for his presence at that place.

10.5B   For an inference to be drawn from a suspect's failure or refusal to answer a question about one of these matters or to answer it satisfactorily, the interviewing officer must first tell him in ordinary language:

    (a)   what offence he is investigating;

    (b)   what fact he is asking the suspect to account for;

    (c)   that he believes this fact may be due to the suspect's taking part in the commission of the offence in question;

    (d)   that a court may draw a proper inference if he fails or refuses to account for the fact about which he is being questioned;

    (e)   that a record is being made of the interview and that it may be given in evidence if he is brought to trial.

10.5C   Where, despite the fact that a person has been cautioned, failure to co-operate may have an effect on his immediate treatment, he should be informed of any relevant consequences and that they are not affected by the caution. Examples are when his refusal to provide his name and address when charged may render him liable to detention, or when his refusal to provide particulars and information in accordance with a statutory requirement, for example, under the Road Traffic Act 1988, may amount to an offence or may make him liable to arrest.

(c)   Juveniles, the mentally disordered and the mentally handicapped

10.6   If a juvenile or a person who is mentally disordered or mentally handicapped is cautioned in the absence of the appropriate adult, the caution must be repeated in the adult's presence.

(d)   Documentation

10.7   A record shall be made when a caution is given under this section, either in the officer's pocket book or in the inteview record as appropriate.

Notes for Guidance

10A   In considering whether or not to caution again after a break, the officer should bear in mind that he may have to satisfy a court that the person understood that he was still under caution when the interview resumed.

10B   [Not Used]

10C   If it appears that a person does not understand what the caution means, the officer who has given it should go on to explain it in his own words.

10D   [Not Used]

11. Interviews: general

(a)   Action

11.1A   An interview is the questioning of a person regarding his involvement or suspected involvement in a criminal offence or offences which, by virtue of paragraph 10.1 of Code C, is required to be carried out under caution. Procedures undertaken under section 7 of the Road Traffic Act 1988 do not constitute interviewing for the purpose of this code.

11.1   Following a decision to arrest a suspect he must not be interviewed about the relevant offence except at a police station (or other authorised place of detention) unless the consequent delay would be likely:

    (a)   to lead to interference with or harm to evidence connected with an offence or interference with or physical harm to other persons; or

    (b)   to lead to the alerting of other persons suspected of having committed an offence but not yet arrested for it; or

    (c)   to hinder the recovery of property obtained in consequence of the commission of an offence.

Interviewing in any of these circumstances should cease once the relevant risk has been averted or the necessary questions have been put in order to attempt to avert that risk.

11.2   Immediately prior to the commencement or re-commencement of any interview at a police station or other authorised place of detention, the interviewing officer shall remind the suspect of his entitlement to free legal advice and the interview can be delayed for him to obtain legal advice (unless the exceptions in paragraph 6.6 or Annex C apply). It is the responsibility of the interviewing officer to ensure that all such reminders are noted in the record of interview.

11.2A   At the beginning of an interview carried out in a police station, the interviewing officer, after cautioning the suspect, shall put to him any significant statement or silence which occurred before his arrival at the police station, and shall ask him whether he confirms or denies that earlier statement or silence and whether he wishes to add anything. A 'significant' statement or silence is one which appears capable of being used in evidence against the suspect, in particular a direct admission of guilt, or failure or refusal to answer a question or to answer it satisfactorily, which might give rise to an inference under Part III of the Criminal Justice and Public Order Act 1994.

11.3   No police officer may try to obtain answers to questions or to elicit a statement by the use of oppression. Except as provided for in paragraph 10.5C, no police officer shall indicate, except in answer to a direct question, what action will be taken on the part of the police if the person being interviewed answers questions, makes a statement or refuses to do either. If the person asks the officer directly what action will be taken in the event of his answering questions, making a statement or refusing to do either, then the officer may inform the person what action the police propose to take in that event provided that action is itself proper and warranted.

11.4   As soon as a police officer who is making enquiries of any person about an offence believes that a prosecution should be brought against him and that there is sufficient evidence for it to succeed, he should ask the person if he has anything further to say. If the person indicates that he has nothing more to say the officer shall without delay cease to question him about that offence. This should not, however, be taken to prevent officers in revenue cases or acting under the confiscation provisions of the Criminal Justice Act 1988 or the Drug Trafficking Offences Act 1986 from inviting suspects to complete a formal question and answer record after the interview is concluded.

(b)   Interview records

11.5   (a)   An accurate record must be made of each interview with a person suspected of an offence, whether or not the interview takes place at a police station.

(b)   The record must state the place of the interview, the time it begins and ends, the time the record is made (if different), any breaks in the interview and the names of all those present; and must be made on the forms provided for this purpose or in the officer's pocket-book or in accordance with the code of practice for the tape-recording of police interviews with suspects.

(c)   The record must be made during the course of the interview, unless in the investigating officer's view this would not be practicable or would interfere with the conduct of the interview, and must constitute either a verbatim record of what has been said or, failing this, an account of the interview which adequately and accurately summarises it.

11.6   The requirement to record the names of all those present at an interview does not apply to police officers interviewing persons detained under the Prevention of Terrorism (Temporary Provisions) Act 1989. Instead the record shall state the warrant or other identification number and duty station of such officers.

11.7   If an interview record is not made during the course of the interview it must be made as soon as practicable after its completion.

11.8   Written interview records must be timed and signed by the maker.

11.9   If an interview record is not completed in the course of the interview the reason must be recorded in the officer's pocket book.

11.10   Unless it is impracticable the person interviewed shall be given the opportunity to read the interview record and to sign it as correct or to indicate the respects in which he considers it inaccurate. If the interview is tape-recorded the arrangements set out in the relevant code of practice apply. If the person concerned cannot read or refuses to read the record or to sign it, the senior police officer present shall read it over to him and ask him whether he would like to sign it as correct (or make his mark) or to indicate the respects in which he considers it inaccurate. The police officer shall then certify on the interview record itself what has occurred. [See Note 11D]

11.11   If the appropriate adult or the person's solicitor is present during the interview, he should also be given an opportunity to read and sign the interview record (or any written statement taken down by a police officer).

11.12   Any refusal by a person to sign an interview record when asked to do so in accordance with the provisions of this code must itself be recorded.

11.13   A written record should also be made of any comments made by a suspected person, including unsolicited comments, which are outside the context of an interview but which might be relevant to the offence. Any such record must be timed and signed by the maker. Where practicable the person shall be given the opportunity to read that record and to sign it as correct or to indicate the respects in which he considers it inaccurate. Any refusal to sign should be recorded. [See Note 11D]

(c) Juveniles, the mentally disordered and the mentally handicapped

11.14 A juvenile or a person who is mentally disordered or mentally handicapped, whether suspected or not, must not be interviewed or asked to provide or sign a written statement in the absence of the appropriate adult unless paragraph 11.1 or Annex C applies.

11.15 Juveniles may only be interviewed at their places of education in exceptional circumstances and then only where the principal or his nominee agrees. Every effort should be made to notify both the parent(s) or other person responsible for the juvenile's welfare and the appropriate adult (if this is a different person) that the police want to interview the juvenile and reasonable time should be allowed to enable the appropriate adult to be present at the interview. Where awaiting the appropriate adult would cause unreasonable delay and unless the interviewee is suspected of an offence against the educational establishment, the principal or his nominee can act as the appropriate adult for the purposes of the interview.

11.16 Where the appropriate adult is present at an interview, he should be informed that he is not expected to act simply as an observer; and also that the purposes of his presence are, first, to advise the person being questioned and to observe whether or not the interview is being conducted properly and fairly, and, secondly, to facilitate communication with the person being interviewed.

Notes for Guidance

11A [Not Used]

11B It is important to bear in mind that, although juveniles or persons who are mentally disordered or mentally handicapped are often capable of providing reliable evidence, they may, without knowing or wishing to do so, be particularly prone in certain circumstances to provide information which is unreliable, misleading or self-incriminating. Special care should therefore always be exercised in questioning such a person, and the appropriate adult should be involved, if there is any doubt about a person's age, mental state or capacity. Because of the risk of unreliable evidence it is also important to obtain corroboration of any facts admitted whenever possible.

11C It is preferable that a juvenile is not arrested at his place of education unless this is unavoidable. Where a juvenile is arrested at his place of education, the principal or his nominee must be informed.

11D When a suspect agrees to read records of interviews and of other comments and to sign them as correct, he should be asked to endorse the record with words such as 'I agree that this is a correct record of what was said' and add his signature. Where the suspect does not agree with the record, the officer should record the details of any disagreement and then ask the suspect to read these details and then sign them to the effect that they accurately reflect his disagreement. Any refusal to sign when asked to do so shall be recorded.

12. Interviews in police stations

(a) Action

12.1 If a police officer wishes to interview, or conduct enquiries which require the presence of a detained person the custody officer is responsible for deciding whether to deliver him into his custody.

12.2   In any period of 24 hours a detained person must be allowed a continuous period of at least 8 hours for rest, free from questioning, travel or any interruption by police officers in connection with the investigation concerned. This period should normally be at night. The period of rest may not be interrupted or delayed, except at the request of the person, his appropriate adult or his legal representative, unless there are reasonable grounds for believing that it would:

(i)   involve a risk of harm to persons or serious loss of, or damage to, property;

(ii)   delay unnecessarily the person's release from custody; or

(iii)   otherwise prejudice the outcome of the investigation.

If a person is arrested at a police station after going there voluntarily, the period of 24 hours runs from the time of his arrest and not the time of arrival at the police station. Any action which is required to be taken in accordance with section 8 of this code, or in accordance with medical advice or at the request of the detained person, his appropriate adult or his legal representative, does not constitute an interruption to the rest period such that a fresh period must be allowed.

12.3   A detained person may not be supplied with intoxicating liquor except on medical directions. No person who is unfit through drink or drugs to the extent that he is unable to appreciate the significance of questions put to him and his answers may be questioned about an alleged offence in that condition except in accordance with Annex C. [See Note 12B]

12.4   As far as practicable interviews shall take place in interview rooms which must be adequately heated, lit and ventilated.

12.5   Persons being questioned or making statements shall not be required to stand.

12.6   Before the commencement of an interview each interviewing officer shall identify himself and any other officers present by name and rank to the person being interviewed, except in the case of persons detained under the Prevention of Terrorism (Temporary Provisions) Act 1989 when each officer shall identify himself by his warrant or other identification number and rank rather than his name.

12.7   Breaks from interviewing shall be made at recognised meal times. Short breaks for refreshment shall also be provided at intervals of approximately two hours, subject to the interviewing officer's discretion to delay a break if there are reasonable grounds for believing that it would:

(i)   involve a risk of harm to persons or serious loss of, or damage to, property;

(ii)   delay unnecessarily the person's release from custody; or

(iii)   otherwise prejudice the outcome of the investigation.

[See Note 12C]

12.8   If in the course of the interview a complaint is made by the person being questioned or on his behalf concerning the provisions of this code then the interviewing officer shall:

(i)   record it in the interview record; and

(ii)   inform the custody officer, who is then responsible for dealing with it in accordance with section 9 of this code.

(b)   Documentation

12.9   A record must be made of the times at which a detained person is not in the custody of the custody officer, and why; and of the reason for any refusal to deliver him out of that custody.

12.10   A record must be made of any intoxicating liquor supplied to a detained person, in accordance with paragraph 12.3 above.

12.11 Any decision to delay a break in an interview must be recorded, with grounds, in the interview record.

12.12 All written statements made at police stations under caution shall be written on the forms provided for the purpose.

12.13 All written statements made under caution shall be taken in accordance with Annex D to this code.

Notes for Guidance

12A If the interview has been contemporaneously recorded and the record signed by the person interviewed in accordance with paragraph 11.10 above, or has been tape recorded, it is normally unnecessary to ask for a written statement. Statements under caution should normally be taken in these circumstances only at the person's express wish. An officer may, however, ask him whether or not he wants to make such a statement.

12B The police surgeon can give advice about whether or not a person is fit to be interviewed in accordance with paragraph 12.3 above.

12C Meal breaks should normally last at least 45 minutes and shorter breaks after two hours should last at least 15 minutes. If the interviewing officer delays a break in accordance with paragraph 12.7 of this code and prolongs the interview, a longer break should then be provided. If there is a short interview, and a subsequent short interview is contemplated, the length of the break may be reduced if there are reasonable grounds to believe that this is necessary to avoid any of the consequences in paragraph 12.7 (i) to (iii).

13. Interpreters

(a) General

13.1 Information on obtaining the services of a suitably qualified interpreter for the deaf or for persons who do not understand English is given in Note for Guidance 3D.

(b) Foreign languages

13.2 Except in accordance with paragraph 11.1 or unless Annex C applies, a person must not be interviewed in the absence of a person capable of acting as interpreter if:
    (a) he has difficulty in understanding English;
    (b) the interviewing officer cannot himself speak the person's own language; and
    (c) the person wishes an interpreter to be present.

13.3 The interviewing officer shall ensure that the interpreter makes a note of the interview at the time in the language of the person being interviewed for use in the event of his being called to give evidence, and certifies its accuracy. He shall allow sufficient time for the interpreter to make a note of each question and answer after each has been put or given and interpreted. The person shall be given an opportunity to read it or have it read to him and sign it as correct or to indicate the respects in which he considers it inaccurate. If the interview is tape-recorded the arrangements set out in the relevant code of practice apply.

13.4 In the case of a person making a statement in a language other than English:
    (a) the interpreter shall take down the statement in the language in which it is made;
    (b) the person making the statement shall be invited to sign it; and
    (c) an official English translation shall be made in due course.

(c) Deaf people and people with a speech handicap

13.5   If a person appears to be deaf or there is doubt about his hearing or speaking ability, he must not be interviewed in the absence of an interpreter unless he agrees in writing to be interviewed without one or paragraph 11.1 or Annex C applies.

13.6   An interpreter should also be called if a juvenile is interviewed and the parent or guardian present as the appropriate adult appears to be deaf or there is doubt about his hearing or speaking ability, unless he agrees in writing that the interview should proceed without one or paragraph 11.1 or Annex C applies.

13.7   The interviewing officer shall ensure that the interpreter is given an opportunity to read the record of the interview and to certify its accuracy in the event of his being called to give evidence.

(d) Additional rules for detained persons

13.8   All reasonable attempts should be made to make clear to the detained person that interpreters will be provided at public expense.

13.9   Where paragraph 6.1 applies and the person concerned cannot communicate with the solicitor, whether because of language, hearing or speech difficulties, an interpreter must be called. The interpreter may not be a police officer when interpretation is needed for the purposes of obtaining legal advice. In all other cases a police officer may only interpret if he first obtains the detained person's (or the appropriate adult's) agreement in writing or if the interview is tape-recorded in accordance with Code E.

13.10   When a person is charged with an offence who appears to be deaf or there is doubt about his hearing or speaking ability or ability to understand English, and the custody officer cannot establish effective communication, arrangements must be made for an interpreter to explain as soon as practicable the offence concerned and any other information given by the custody officer.

(e) Documentation

13.11   Action taken to call an interpreter under this section and any agreement to be interviewed in the absence of an interpreter must be recorded.

Note for Guidance

13A   If the interpreter is needed as a prosecution witness at the person's trial, a second interpreter must act as the court interpreter.

14.   Questioning: special restrictions

14.1   If a person has been arrested by one police force on behalf of another and the lawful period of detention in respect of that offence has not yet commenced in accordance with section 41 of the Police and Criminal Evidence Act 1984 no questions may be put to him about the offence while he is in transit between the forces except in order to clarify any voluntary statement made by him.

14.2   If a person is in police detention at a hospital he may not be questioned without the agreement of a responsible doctor. [See Note 14A]

Note for Guidance

14A   If questioning takes place at a hospital under paragraph 14.2 (or on the way to or from a hospital) the period concerned counts towards the total period of detention permitted.

15. Reviews and extensions of detention

(a) Action

15.1   The review officer is responsible under section 40 of the Police and Criminal Evidence Act 1984 (or, in terrorist cases, under Schedule 3 to the Prevention of Terrorism (Temporary Provisions) Act 1989) for determining whether or not a person's detention continues to be necessary. In reaching a decision he shall provide an opportunity to the detained person himself to make representations (unless he is unfit to do so because of his condition or behaviour) or to his solicitor or the appropriate adult if available at the time. Other persons having an interest in the person's welfare may make representations at the review officer's discretion.

15.2   The same persons may make representations to the officer determining whether further detention should be authorised under section 42 of the Act or under Schedule 3 to the 1989 Act. [See Note 15A]

15.2A   After hearing any representations, the review officer or officer determining whether further detention should be authorised shall note any comment the person may make if the decision is to keep him in detention. The officer shall not put specific questions to the suspect regarding his involvement in any offence, nor in respect of any comments he may make in response to the decision to keep him in detention. Such an exchange is likely to constitute an interview as defined by paragraph 11.1A and would require the associated safeguards included in section 11. [See also paragraph 11.13]

(b) Documentation

15.3   Before conducting a review the review officer must ensure that the detained person is reminded of his entitlement to free legal advice (see paragraph 6.5). It is the responsibility of the review officer to ensure that all such reminders are noted in the custody record.

15.4   The grounds for and extent of any delay in conducting a review shall be recorded.

15.5   Any written representations shall be retained.

15.6   A record shall be made as soon as practicable of the outcome of each review and application for a warrant of further detention or its extension.

Notes for Guidance

15A   If the detained person is likely to be asleep at the latest time when a review of detention or an authorisation of continued detention may take place, the appropriate officer should bring it forward so that the detained person may make representations without being woken up.

15B   An application for a warrant of further detention or its extension should be made between 10am and 9pm, and if possible during normal court hours. It will not be practicable to arrange for a court to sit specially outside the hours of 10am to 9pm. If it appears possible that a special sitting may be needed (either at a weekend, Bank/Public Holiday or on a weekday outside normal court hours but between 10am and 9pm) then the clerk to the justices should be given notice and informed of this possibility, while the court is sitting if possible.

15C   If in the circumstances the only practicable way of conducting a review is over the telephone then this is permissible, provided that the requirements of section 40 of the Police and Criminal Evidence Act 1984 or of Schedule 3 to the Prevention of Terrorism (Temporary Provisions) Act 1989 are observed. However, a review to decide whether to authorise a person's continued detention under section 42 of the 1984 Act must be done in person rather than over the telephone.

16.   Charging of detained persons

(a)   Action

16.1   When an officer considers that there is sufficient evidence to prosecute a detained person, and that there is sufficient evidence for a prosecution to succeed, and that the person has said all that he wishes to say about the offence, he should without delay (and subject to the following qualification) bring him before the custody officer who shall then be responsible for considering whether or not he should be charged. When a person is detained in respect of more than one offence it is permissible to delay bringing him before the custody officer until the above conditions are satisfied in respect of all the offences (but see paragraph 11.4). Any resulting action should be taken in the presence of the appropriate adult if the person is a juvenile or mentally disordered or mentally handicapped.

16.2   When a detained person is charged with or informed that he may be prosecuted for an offence he shall be cautioned in the terms:

> You do not have to say anything. But it may harm your defence if you do not mention now something which you later rely on in court. Anything you do say may be given in evidence.

16.3   At the time a person is charged he shall be given a written notice showing particulars of the offence with which he is charged and including the name of the officer in the case (in terrorist cases, the officer's warrant or other identification number instead), his police station and the reference number for the case. So far as possible the particulars of the charge shall be stated in simple terms, but they shall also show the precise offence in law with which he is charged. The notice shall begin with the following words:

> You are charged with the offence(s) shown below. You do not have to say anything. But it may harm your defence if you do not mention now something which you later rely on in court. Anything you do say may be given in evidence.

If the person is a juvenile or is mentally disordered or mentally handicapped the notice shall be given to the appropriate adult.

16.4   If at any time after a person has been charged with or informed he may be prosecuted for an offence, a police officer wishes to bring to the notice of the person any written statement made by another person or the content of an interview with another person, he shall hand to that person a true copy of any such written statement or bring to his attention the content of the interview record, but shall say or do nothing to invite any reply or comment save to warn him that he does not have to say anything but that anything he does say may be given in evidence and to remind him of his right to legal advice in accordance with paragraph 6.5 above. If the person cannot read then the officer may read it to him. If the person is a juvenile or mentally disordered or mentally handicapped the copy shall also be given to, or the interview record brought to the attention of, the appropriate adult.

16.5   Questions relating to an offence may not be put to a person after he has been charged with that offence, or informed that he may be prosecuted for it, unless they are necessary for the purpose of preventing or minimising harm or loss to some other person or to the public or for clearing up an ambiguity in a previous answer or statement, or where it is in the interests of justice that the person should have put to him and have an opportunity to comment on information concerning the offence which has come to light since he was charged or informed that he might be prosecuted. Before any such questions are put to him, he shall be warned that he does not have to say anything but that anything he does say may be given in evidence and reminded of his right to legal advice in accordance with paragraph 6.5 above. [See Note 16A]

16.6   Where a juvenile is charged with an offence and the custody officer authorises his continued detention he must try to make arrangements for the juvenile to be taken into the care of a local authority to be detained pending appearance in court unless he certifies that it is impracticable to do so, or, in the case of a juvenile of at least 12 years of age, no secure accommodation is available and there is a risk to the public of serious harm from that juvenile, in accordance with section 38(6) of the Police and Criminal Evidence Act 1984, as amended by Section 59 of the Criminal Justice Act 1991 and section 24 of the Criminal Justice and Public Order Act 1994. [See Note 16B]

(b)   Documentation

16.7   A record shall be made of anything a detained person says when charged.

16.8   Any questions put after charge and answers given relating to the offence shall be contemporaneously recorded in full on the forms provided and the record signed by that person or, if he refuses, by the interviewing officer and any third parties present. If the questions are tape-recorded the arrangements set out in Code E apply.

16.9   If it is not practicable to make arrangements for the transfer of a juvenile into local authority care in accordance with paragraph 16.6 above the custody officer must record the reasons and make out a certificate to be produced before the court together with the juvenile.

Notes for Guidance

16A   The service of the Notice of Intended Prosecution under sections 1 and 2 of the Road Traffic Offenders Act 1988 does not amount to informing a person that he may be prosecuted for an offence and so does not preclude further questioning in relation to that offence.

16B   Except as provided for in 16.6 above, neither a juvenile's behviour nor the nature of the offence with which he is charged provides grounds for the custody officer to decide that it is impracticable to seek to arrange for his transfer to the care of the local authority. Similarly, the lack of secure local authority accommodation shall not make it impracticable for the custody officer to transfer him. The availability of secure accommodation is only a factor in relation to a juvenile aged 12 or over when the local authority accommodation would not be adequate to protect the public from serious harm from the juvenile. The obligation to transfer a juvenile to local authority accommodation applies as much to a juvenile charged during the daytime as it does to a juvenile to be held overnight, subject to a requirement to bring the juvenile before a court under section 46 of the Police and Criminal Evidence Act 1984.

ANNEX A
INTIMATE AND STRIP SEARCHES (see paragraph 4.1)

A.   Intimate search

1.   An 'intimate search' is a search which consists of the physical examination of a person's body orifices other than the mouth.

(a)   Action

2.   Body orifices may be searched only if an officer of the rank of superintendent or above has reasonable grounds for believing:
        (a)   that an article which could cause physical injury to a detained person or others at the police station has been concealed; or

(b)   that the person has concealed a Class A drug which he intended to supply to another or to export; and

(c)   that in either case an intimate search is the only practicable means of removing it.

The reasons why an intimate search is considered necessary shall be explained to the person before the search takes place.

3.   An intimate search may only be carried out by a registered medical practitioner or registered nurse, unless an officer of at least the rank of superintendent considers that this is not practicable and the search is to take place under sub-paragraph 1(a) above.

4.   An intimate search under sub-paragraph 1(a) above may take place only at a hospital, surgery, other medical premises or police station. A search under sub-paragraph 1(b) may take place only at a hospital, surgery or other medical premises.

5.   An intimate search at a police station of a juvenile or a mentally disordered or mentally handicapped person may take place only in the presence of the appropriate adult of the same sex (unless the person specifically requests the presence of a particular adult of the opposite sex who is readily available). In the case of a juvenile the search may take place in the absence of the appropriate adult only if the juvenile signifies in the presence of the appropriate adult that he prefers the search to be done in his absence and the appropriate adult agrees. A record should be made of the juvenile's decision and signed by the appropriate adult.

6.   Where an intimate search under sub-paragraph 2(a) above is carried out by a police officer, the officer must be of the same sex as the person searched. Subject to paragraph 5 above, no person of the opposite sex who is not a medical practitioner or nurse shall be present, nor shall anyone whose presence is unnecessary but a minimum of two people, other than the person searched, must be present during the search. The search shall be conducted with proper regard to the sensitivity and vulnerability of the person in these circumstances.

(b)   Documentation

7.   In the case of an intimate search the custody officer shall as soon as practicable record which parts of the person's body were searched, who carried out the search, who was present, the reasons for the search and its result.

8.   If an intimate search is carried out by a police officer, the reason why it is impracticable for a suitably qualified person to conduct it must be recorded.

B.   Strip search

9.   A strip search is a search involving the removal of more than outer clothing.

(a)   Action

10.   A strip search may take place only if it is considered necessary to remove an article which a person would not be allowed to keep, and the officer reasonably considers that the person might have concealed such an article. Strip searches shall not be routinely carried out where there is no reason to consider that articles have been concealed.

The conduct of strip searches

11.   The following procedures shall be observed when strip searches are conducted:

(a)   a police officer carrying out a strip search must be of the same sex as the person searched;

(b)   the search shall take place in an area where the person being searched cannot be seen by anyone who does not need to be present, nor by a member of the opposite sex (except an appropriate adult who has been specifically requested by the person being searched);

(c)   except in cases of urgency, where there is a risk of serious harm to the person detained or to others, whenever a strip search involves exposure of intimate parts of the body, there must be at least two people present other than the person searched, and if the search is of a juvenile or a mentally disordered or mentally handicapped person, one of the people must be the appropriate adult. Except in urgent cases as above, a search of a juvenile may take place in the absence of the appropriate adult only if the juvenile signifies in the presence of the appropriate adult that he prefers the search to be done in his absence and the appropriate adult agrees. A record shall be made of the juvenile's decision and signed by the appropriate adult. The presence of more than two people, other than an appropriate adult, shall be permitted only in the most exceptional circumstances

(d)   the search shall be conducted with proper regard to the sensitivity and vulnerability of the person in these circumstances and every reasonable effort shall be made to secure the person's co-operation and minimise embarrassment. People who are searched should not normally be required to have all their clothes removed at the same time, for example, a man shall be allowed to put on his shirt before removing his trousers, and a woman shall be allowed to put on her blouse and upper garments before further clothing is removed;

(e)   where necessary to assist the search, the person may be required to hold his or her arms in the air or to stand with his or her legs apart and to bend forward so that a visual examination may be made of the genital and anal areas provided that no physical contact is made with any body orifice;

(f)   if, during a search, articles are found, the person shall be asked to hand them over. If articles are found within any body orifice other than the mouth, and the person refuses to hand them over, their removal would constitute an intimate search, which must be carried out in accordance with the provisions of Part A of this Annex;

(g)   a strip search shall be conducted as quickly as possible, and the person searched allowed to dress as soon as the procedure is complete.

(b)   Documentation

12.   A record shall be made on the custody record of a strip search including the reason it was considered necessary to undertake it, those present and any result.

ANNEX B
DELAY IN NOTIFYING ARREST OR ALLOWING ACCESS TO LEGAL ADVICE

A.   Persons detained under the Police and Criminal Evidence Act 1984

(a)   Action

1.   The rights set out in sections 5 or 6 of the code or both may be delayed if the person is in police detention in connection with a serious arrestable offence, has not yet been charged with an offence and an officer of the rank of superintendent or above has reasonable grounds for believing that the exercise of either right:

(i)   will lead to interference with or harm to evidence connected with a serious arrestable offence or interference with or physical injury to other persons; or

(ii)   will lead to the alerting of other persons suspected of having committed such an offence but not yet arrested for it; or

(iii)   will hinder the recovery of property obtained as a result of such an offence.
[See Note B3]

2. These rights may also be delayed where the serious arrestable offence is either:

(i)   a drug trafficking offence and the officer has reasonable grounds for believing that the detained person has benefited from drug trafficking, and that the recovery of the value of that person's proceeds of drug trafficking will be hindered by the exercise of either right or;

(ii)   an offence to which Part VI of the Criminal Justice Act 1988 (covering confiscation orders) applies and the officer has reasonable grounds for believing that the detained person has benefited from the offence, and that the recovery of the value of the property obtained by that person from or in connection with the offence or if the pecuniary advantage derived by him from or in connection with it will be hindered by the exercise of either right.

3. Access to a solicitor may not be delayed on the grounds that he might advise the person not to answer any questions or that the solicitor was initially asked to attend the police station by someone else, provided that the person himself then wishes to see the solicitor. In the latter case the detained person must be told that the solicitor has come to the police station at another person's request, and must be asked to sign the custody record to signify whether or not he wishes to see the solicitor.

4. These rights may be delayed only for as long as is necessary and, subject to paragraph 9 below, in no case beyond 36 hours after the relevant time as defined in section 41 of the Police and Criminal Evidence Act 1984. If the above grounds cease to apply within this time, the person must as soon as practicable be asked if he wishes to exercise either right, the custody record must be noted accordingly, and action must be taken in accordance with the relevant section of the code.

5. A detained person must be permitted to consult a solicitor for a reasonable time before any court hearing.

(b)   Documentation

6. The grounds for action under this Annex shall be recorded and the person informed of them as soon as practicable.

7. Any reply given by a person under paragraphs 4 or 9 must be recorded and the person asked to endorse the record in relation to whether he wishes to receive legal advice at this point.

B. Persons detained under the Prevention of Terrorism (Temporary Provisions) Act 1989

(a)   Action

8. The rights set out in sections 5 or 6 of this code or both may be delayed if paragraph 1 above applies or if an officer of the rank of superintendent or above has reasonable grounds for believing that the exercise of either right:

(a)   will lead to interference with the gathering of information about the commission, preparation or instigation of acts of terrorism; or

(b)   by alerting any person, will make it more difficult to prevent an act of terrorism or to secure the apprehension, prosecution or conviction of any person in connection with the commission, preparation or instigation of an act of terrorism.

9. These rights may be delayed only for as long as is necessary and in no case beyond 48 hours from the time of arrest. If the above grounds cease to apply within this time, the person must as soon as practicable be asked if he wishes to exercise either right, the custody record must be noted accordingly, and action must be taken in accordance with the relevant section of this code.

10. Paragraphs 3 and 5 above apply.

(b)   Documentation

11.   Paragraphs 6 and 7 above apply.

Notes for Guidance

B1   Even if Annex B applies in the case of a juvenile, or a person who is mentally disordered or mentally handicapped, action to inform the appropriate adult (and the person responsible for a juvenile's welfare, if that is a different person) must nevertheless be taken in accordance with paragraph 3.7 and 3.9 of this code.

B2   In the case of Commonwealth citizens and foreign nationals see Note 7A.

B3   Police detention is defined in section 118(2) of the Police and Criminal Evidence Act 1984.

B4   The effect of paragraph 1 above is that the officer may authorise delaying access to a specific solicitor only if he has reasonable grounds to believe that that specific solicitor will, inadvertently or otherwise, pass on a message from the detained person or act in some other way which will lead to any of the three results in paragraph 1 coming about. In these circumstances the officer should offer the detained person access to a solicitor (who is not the specific solicitor referred to above) on the Duty Solicitor Scheme.

B5   The fact that the grounds for delaying notification of arrest under paragraph 1 above may be satisfied does not automatically mean that the grounds for delaying access to legal advice will also be satisfied.

ANNEX C
VULNERABLE SUSPECTS: URGENT INTERVIEWS AT POLICE STATIONS

1.   When an interview is to take place in a police station or other authorised place of detention if, and only if, an officer of the rank of superintendent or above considers that delay will lead to the consequences set out in paragraph 11.1 (a) to (c) of this Code:

(a)   a person heavily under the influence of drink or drugs may be interviewed in that state; or

(b)   a juvenile or a person who is mentally disordered or mentally handicapped may be interviewed in the absence of the appropriate adult; or

(c)   a person who has difficulty in understanding English or who has a hearing disability may be interviewed in the absence of an interpreter.

2.   Questioning in these circumstances may not continue once sufficient information to avert the immediate risk has been obtained.

3.   A record shall be made of the grounds for any decision to interview a person under paragraph 1 above.

Note for Guidance

C1   The special groups referred to in this Annex are all particularly vulnerable. The provisions of the annex, which override safeguards designed to protect them and to minimise the risk of interviews producing unreliable evidence, should be applied only in exceptional cases of need.

ANNEX D
WRITTEN STATEMENTS UNDER CAUTION (see paragraph 12.13)

(a)   Written by a person under caution

1.   A person shall always be invited to write down himself what he wants to say.

2.   Where the person wishes to write it himself, he shall be asked to write out and sign before writing what he wants to say, the following:

> I make this statement of my own free will. I understand that I do not have to say anything but that it may harm my defence if I do not mention when questioned something which I later rely on in court. This statement may be given in evidence.

3.   Any person writing his own statement shall be allowed to do so without any prompting except that a police officer may indicate to him which matters are material or question any ambiguity in the statement.

(b)   Written by a police officer

4.   If a person says that he would like someone to write it for him, a police officer shall write the statement, but, before starting, he must ask him to sign, or make his mark, to the following:

> I, ..., wish to make a statement. I want someone to write down what I say. I understand that I need not say anything but that it may harm my defence if I do not mention when questioned something which I later rely on in court. This statement may be given in evidence.

5.   Where a police officer writes the statement, he must take down the exact words spoken by the person making it and he must not edit or paraphrase it. Any questions that are necessary (e.g., to make it more intelligible) and the answers given must be recorded contemporaneously on the statement form.

6.   When the writing of a statement by a police officer is finished the person making it shall be asked to read it and to make any corrections, alterations or additions he wishes. When he has finished reading it he shall be asked to write and sign or make his mark on the following certificate at the end of the statement:

> I have read the above statement, and I have been able to correct, alter or add anything I wish. This statement is true. I have made it of my own free will.

7.   If the person making the statement cannot read, or refuses to read it, or to write the above mentioned certificate at the end of it or to sign it, the senior police officer present shall read it over to him whether he would like to correct, alter or add anything and to put his signature or make his mark at the end. The police officer shall then certify on the statement itself what has occurred.

ANNEX E
SUMMARY OF PROVISIONS RELATING TO MENTALLY DISORDERED AND MENTALLY HANDICAPPED PEOPLE

1.   If an officer has any suspicion or is told in good faith that a person of any age, may be mentally disordered or mentally handicapped, or mentally incapable of understanding the significance of questions put to him or his replies, then that person shall be treated as a mentally disordered or mentally handicapped for the purposes of this code. (See paragraph 1.4.)

2.   In the case of a person who is mentally disordered or mentally handicapped, 'the appropriate adult' means:
    (a)   a relative, guardian or some other person responsible for his care or custody;
    (b)   someone who has experience of dealing with mentally disordered or mentally handicapped people but is not a police officer or employed by the police; or
    (c)   failing either of the above, some other responsible adult aged 18 or over who is not a police officer or employed by the police.

(See paragraph 1.7(b).)

3.   If the custody officer authorises the detention of a person who is mentally handicapped or appears to be suffering from a mental disorder he must as soon as practicable inform the appropriate adult of the grounds for the person's detention and his whereabouts, and ask the adult to come to the police station to see the person. If the appropriate adult is already at the police station when information is given as required in paragraphs 3.1 to 3.5 the information must be given to the detained person in the appropriate adult's presence. If the appropriate adult is not at the police station when the provisions of 3.1 to 3.5 are complied with then these provisions must be complied with again in the presence of the appropriate adult once that person arrives. [See paragraphs 3.9 and 3.11]

4.   If the appropriate adult, having been informed of the right to legal advice, considers that legal advice should be taken, the provisions of section 6 of the code apply as if the mentally disordered or mentally handicapped person has requested access to legal advice. (See paragraph 3.13. And Note E2.)

5.   If a person brought to a police station appears to be suffering from mental disorder or is incoherent other than through drunkenness alone, or if a detained person subsequently appears to be mentally disordered, the custody officer must immediately call the police surgeon or, in urgent cases, send the person to hospital or call the nearest available medical practitioner. It is not intended that these provisions should delay the transfer of a person to a place of safety under section 136 of the Mental Health Act 1983 where that is applicable. Where an assessment under that Act is to take place at the police station, the custody officer has discretion not to call the police surgeon so long as he believes that the assessment by a registered medical practitioner can be undertaken without undue delay. (See paragraph 9.2.)

6.   It is imperative that a mentally disordered or mentally handicapped person who has been detained under section 136 of the Mental Health Act 1983 should be assessed as soon as possible. If that assessment is to take place at the police station, an approved social worker and a registered medical practitioner should be called to the police station as soon as possible in order to interview and examine the person. Once the person has been interviewed and examined and suitable arrangements have been made for his treatment or care, he can no longer be detained under section 136.   The person should not be released until he has been seen by both the approved social worker and the registered medical practitioner. (See paragraph 3.10.)

7.   If a mentally disordered or mentally handicapped person is cautioned in the absence of the appropriate adult, the caution must be repeated in the adult's presence. (See paragraph 10.6.)

8.   A mentally disordered or mentally handicapped person must not be interviewed or asked to provide or sign a written statement in the absence of the appropriate adult unless the provisions of paragraph 11.1 or Annex C of this code apply. Questioning in these circumstances may not continue in the absence of the appropriate adult once sufficient information to avert the risk has been obtained. A record shall be made of the grounds for any decision to begin an interview in these circumstances. [See paragraphs 11.1 and 11.14 and Annex C]

9.   Where the appropriate adult is present at an interview, he should be informed that he is not expected to act simply as an observer; and also that the purposes of his presence are, first, to advise the person being interviewed and to observe whether or not the interview is being conducted properly and fairly, and, secondly to facilitate communication with the person being interviewed. (See paragraph 11.16.)

10. If the detention of a mentally disordered or mentally handicapped person is reviewed by a review officer or a superintendent, the appropriate adult must, if available at the time, be given opportunity to make representations to the officer about the need for continuing detention. (See paragraph 15.1 and 15.2.)

11. If the custody officer charges a mentally disordered or mentally handicapped person with an offence or takes such other action as is appropriate when there is sufficient evidence for a prosecution this must be done in the presence of the appropriate adult. The written notice embodying any charge must be given to the appropriate adult. (See paragraphs 16.1 to 16.3.)

12. An intimate or strip search of a mentally disordered or mentally handicapped person may take place only in the presence of the appropriate adult of the same sex, unless the person specifically requests the presence of a particular adult of the opposite sex. A strip search may take place in the absence of an appropriate adult only in cases of urgency where there is a risk of serious harm to the person detained or to others. [See Annex A, paragraphs 5 and 11(c)]

13. Particular care must be taken when deciding whether to use handcuffs to restrain a mentally disordered or mentally handicapped person in a locked cell. [See paragraph 8.2]

Notes for Guidance

E1 In the case of mentally disordered or mentally handicapped people, it may in certain circumstances be more satisfactory for all concerned if the appropriate adult is someone who has experience or training in their care rather than a relative lacking such qualifications. But if the person himself prefers a relative to a better qualified stranger or objects to a particular person as the appropriate adult, his wishes should if practicable be respected. [See Note 1E]

E2 The purpose of the provision at paragraph 3.13 is to protect the rights of a mentally disordered or mentally handicapped person who does not understand the significance of what is being said to him. If the person wishes to exercise the right to legal advice, the appropriate action should be taken and not delayed until the appropriate adult arrives. [See Note 3G] A mentally disordered or mentally handicapped person should always be given an opportunity, when an appropriate adult is called to the police station, to consult privately with a solicitor in the absence of the appropriate adult if he wishes to do so. [See Note 1EE].

E3 It is important to bear in mind that although persons who are mentally disordered or mentally handicapped are often capable of providing reliable evidence, they may, without knowing or wishing to do so, be particularly prone in certain circumstances to provide information which is unreliable, misleading or self-incriminating. Special care should therefore always be exercised in questioning such a person, and the appropriate adult involved, if there is any doubt about a person's mental state or capacity. Because of the risk of unreliable evidence, it is important to obtain corroboration of any facts admitted whenever possible. [See Note 11B]

E4 Because of the risks referred to in Note E3, which the presence of the appropriate adult is intended to minimise, officers of superintendent rank or above should exercise their discretion to authorise the commencement of an interview in the adult's absence only in exceptional cases, where it is necessary to avert an immediate risk of serious harm. [See Annex C, sub-paragraph 1(1) and Note C1]

ANNEX F
COUNTRIES WITH WHICH BILATERAL CONSULAR CONVENTIONS OR AGREEMENTS REQUIRING NOTIFICATION OF THE ARREST AND DETENTION OF THEIR NATIONALS ARE IN FORCE AS AT 1 JANUARY 1995

Armenia
Austria
Azerbaijan
Belarus
Belgium
Bosnia-Hercegovina
Bulgaria
China*
Croatia
Cuba
Czech Republic
Denmark
Egypt
France
Georgia
German Federal Republic
Greece
Hungary

Kazakhstan
Kyrgyzstan
Macedonia
Mexico
Moldova
Mongolia
Norway
Poland
Romania
Russia
Slovak Republic
Slovenia
Spain
Sweden
Tajikistan
Turkmenistan
Ukraine
USA
Uzbekistan
Yugoslavia

*Police are required to inform Chinese officials of arrest/detention in the Manchester consular district only. This comprises Derbyshire, Durham, Greater Manchester, Lancashire, Merseyside, North, South and West Yorkshire, and Tyne and Wear.

THE POLICE AND CRIMINAL EVIDENCE ACT 1984 (CODES OF PRACTICE) (MODIFICATION) ORDER 2001
(2001 No. 2254)

Whereas, in pursuance of sections 60(1)(a) and 66 of the Police and Criminal Evidence Act 1984, the Secretary of State issued codes of practice in connection with, amongst other matters:

(a)   the detention, treatment and questioning of persons by police officers; and
(b)   the identification of persons by police officers;

And whereas section 66(2) of that Act requires codes to include provision in connection with the exercise by police officers of powers under section 63B of that Act:

Now, therefore, the Secretary of State, in exercise of the powers conferred on him by section 67(7A) of that Act, hereby orders as follows:

1.   This Order may be cited as the Police and Criminal Evidence Act 1984 (Codes of Practice) (Modification) Order 2001 and shall come into force on 16 July 2001.

2.   Subject to article 3 below, the codes of practice in force shall have effect with the modifications set out in the Schedule to this Order.

3.   The modifications to the codes of practice made by article 2 shall have effect for a period of two years from the date on which this Order comes into force, and shall have effect only in the following police areas:

(a) Staffordshire;
(b) Nottinghamshire;
(c) the metropolitan police district.

Article 2   SCHEDULE

MODIFICATIONS TO CODES OF PRACTICE

1. In code C,
(1) after paragraph 1.5 insert the following:
1.5A If anyone appears to be under the age of 18 then he shall be exempt from drug testing under section 17 of this code in the absence of clear evidence to show that he is older; and
(2) after section 16, insert the following:

17 Testing persons for the presence of specified Class A drugs

(a) Action

17.1 A sample of urine or a non-intimate sample may be taken from a person in police detention for the purpose of ascertaining whether he has any specified Class A drugs in his body if:
(a) that person has been charged with a trigger offence, or
(b) he has been charged with any offence and a police officer of inspector rank or above, who has reasonable grounds for suspecting that the misuse by that person of any specified Class A drug caused or contributed to the offence has authorised the sample to be taken.

17.2 The person from whom the sample is taken must have attained the age of 18.

17.3 A police officer must have requested the person concerned to give the sample.

17.4 Before requesting a sample from the person concerned, an officer must:
(a) inform him that the purpose of taking the sample is for drug testing under the Police and Criminal Evidence Act 1984. This is to ascertain whether he has a specified Class A drug present in his body;
(b) warn him that if, when requested, he fails without good cause to provide a sample he may be liable to prosecution;
(c) where the taking of the sample has been authorised by an inspector or above under paragraph 17.1(b) of this code, inform him that the authorisation has been given and the grounds for giving it;
(d) remind him of the following rights, which may be exercised at any stage during the period in custody:
(i) the right to have someone informed of his arrest [see section 5];
(ii) the right to consult privately with a solicitor and the fact that independent legal advice is available free of charge [see section 6]; and
(iii) the right to consult these codes of practice [see note 3E].

17.5 Authorisation by an officer of the rank of inspector or above may be given orally or in writing, but if it is given orally it must be confirmed in writing as soon as practicable.

17.6 Custody officers may authorise continued detention for up to six hours from the time of charge to enable a sample to be taken.

(b) Documentation

17.7 If a sample is taken following authorisation by an officer of the rank of inspector or above, the authorisation and the grounds for suspicion must be recorded in the custody record.

17.8   The giving of a warning on the consequences of failure to provide a specimen must be recorded in the custody record.

17.9   The time of charge and the time at which the sample was given must be recorded in the custody record.

(c)   General

17.10   A sample may only be taken by a prescribed person.

17.11   Force may not be used to take any sample for the purpose of drug testing.

17.12   The terms 'Class A drug' and 'misuse' have the same meaning as in the Misuse of Drugs 1971. 'Specified' (in relation to a Class A drug) and 'trigger offence' have the same meanings as in Part III of the Criminal Justice and Court Services Act 2000.

17.13   Any sample taken:
(a)   may not be used for any purpose other than to ascertain whether the person concerned has a specified Class A drug present in his body; and
(b)   must be retained until court proceedings have been concluded.

Notes for Guidance

17A   When warning a person who is asked to provide a urine or non-intimate sample in accordance with paragraph 17.1, the following form of words may be used:
You do not have to provide a sample, but I must warn you that if you fail or refuse without good cause to do so, you will commit an offence for which you may be imprisoned, or fined, or both.

17B   A sample has to be sufficient and suitable. A sufficient sample is sufficient in quantity and quality to enable drug testing analysis to take place. A suitable sample is one, which by its nature, is suitable for a particular form of drug analysis.

17C   A prescribed person in paragraph 17.10 is one who is prescribed in regulations made by the Secretary of State under section 63B(6) of the Police and Criminal Evidence Act 1984.

17D   The retention of the sample in paragraph 17.13 allows for the sample to be sent to the Forensic Science Service laboratory for confirmatory testing and analysis if the detainee disputes the test. But such samples, and the information derived from them, may not be subsequently used in the investigation of any offence or in evidence against the persons from whom they were taken.

17E   The trigger offences are: from the Theft Act 1968 — theft, robbery, burglary, aggravated burglary, taking a motor vehicle (or other conveyance) without authority, aggravated vehicle-taking, obtaining property by deception, going equipped for stealing etc.; and from the Misuse of Drugs Act 1971 (but only if committed in respect of a specified Class A drug) — producing and supplying a controlled drug, possessing a controlled drug, possessing a controlled drug with intent to supply.

2.   In Code D, after paragraph 5H, insert the following:
5G   Samples of urine and non-intimate samples taken in accordance with sections 63B and 63C of the Police and Criminal Evidence Act 1984 may not be used for identification purposes in accordance with this code.

EXPLANATORY NOTE
(This note is not part of the Order)

Section 63B of the Police and Criminal Evidence Act 1984 gives police officers a new power to undertake tests for the presence of specified Class A drugs in relation to certain persons in police detention. Section 66(2) of the 1984 Act provides that codes in connection with these powers must be in place before the powers are exercised. This Order puts in place modifications to the Police and Criminal Evidence Act 1984 codes of practice to provide for drug testing within police detention. The modifications are only to have effect for 2 years and extend only to named police areas where the drug testing provisions are to be piloted.

CODE OF PRACTICE FOR THE IDENTIFICATION OF PERSONS BY POLICE OFFICERS (CODE D)

1. General

1.1   This code of practice must be readily available at all police stations for consultation by police officers, detained persons and members of the public.

1.2   The notes for guidance included are not provisions of this code, but are guidance to police officers and others about its application and interpretation. Provisions in the Annexes to the code are provisions of this code.

1.3   If an officer has any suspicion, or is told in good faith, that a person of any age may be suffering from mental disorder or mentally handicapped, or mentally incapable of understanding the significance of questions put to him or his replies, then that person shall be treated as a mentally disordered or mentally handicapped person for the purposes of this code.

1.4   If anyone appears to be under the age of 17 then he shall be treated as a juvenile for the purposes of this code in the absence of clear evidence to show that he is older.

1.5   If a person appears to be blind or seriously visually handicapped, deaf, unable to read, unable to speak or has difficulty orally because of a speech impediment, he should be treated as such for the purposes of this code in the absence of clear evidence to the contrary.

1.6   In this code the term 'appropriate adult' has the same meaning as in paragraph 1.7 of Code C, and the term 'solicitor' has the same meaning as in paragraph 6.12 of Code C.

1.7   Any reference to a custody officer in this code includes an officer who is performing the functions of a custody officer.

1.8   Where a record is made under this code of any action requiring the authority of an officer of a specified rank, his name (except in the case of enquiries linked to the investigation of terrorism, in which case the officer's warrant or other identification number shall be given) and rank must be included in the record.

1.9   All records must be timed and signed by the maker. Warrant or other identification numbers should be used rather than names in the case of detention under the Prevention of Terrorism (Temporary Provision) Act 1989.

1.10   In the case of a detained person records are to be made in his custody record unless otherwise specified.

1.11   In the case of any procedure requiring a person's consent, the consent of a person who is mentally disordered or mentally handicapped is only valid if given in the presence of the appropriate adult; and in the case of a juvenile the consent of his parent or guardian is required as well as his own (unless he is under 14, in which case the consent of his parent or guardian is sufficient in its own right). [See Note 1E]

1.12   In the case of a person who is blind or seriously visually handicapped or unable to read, the custody officer should ensure that his solicitor, relative, the appropriate adult or some other person likely to take an interest in him (and not involved in the investigation) is available to help in checking any documentation. Where this code requires written consent or signification, then the person who is assisting may be asked to sign instead if the detained person so wishes. [See Note 1F]

1.13   In the case of any procedure requiring information to be given to or sought from a suspect, it must be given or sought in the presence of the appropriate adult if the suspect is mentally disordered, mentally handicapped or a juvenile. If the appropriate adult is not present when the information is first given or sought, the procedure must be repeated in his presence when he arrives. If the suspect appears to be deaf or there is doubt about his hearing or speaking ability or ability to understand English, and the officer cannot establish effective communication, the information must be given or sought through an interpreter.

1.14   Any procedure in this code involving the participation of a person (whether as a suspect or a witness) who is mentally disordered, mentally handicapped or a juvenile must take place in the presence of the appropriate adult; but the adult must not be allowed to prompt any identification of a suspect by a witness.

1.15   Subject to paragraph 1.16 below, nothing in this code affects any procedure under:
    (i)   Sections 4 to 11 of the Road Traffic Act 1988 or sections 15 and 16 of the Road Traffic Offenders Act 1988; or
    (ii)   paragraph 18 of Schedule 2 to the Immigration Act 1971; or
    (iii)   the Prevention of Terrorism (Temporary Provisions) Act 1989; section 15(9), paragraph 8(5) of Schedule 2, and paragraph 7(5) of Schedule 5.

1.16   Notwithstanding paragraph 1.15, the provisions of section 3 below on the taking of fingerprints, and of section 5 below on the taking of body samples, do apply to people detained under section 14 of, or paragraph 6 of Schedule 5 to, the Prevention of Terrorism (Temporary Provisions) Act 1989. (In the case of fingerprints, section 61 of PACE is modified by section 15(10) of, and paragraph 7(6) of Schedule 5 to, the 1989 Act.) In the case of samples, sections 62 and 63 of PACE are modified by section 15(11) of and paragraph 7(6A) of Schedule 5 to the 1989 Act. The effect of both of these modifications is to allow fingerprints and samples to be taken in terrorist cases to help determine whether a person is or has been involved in terrorism, as well as where there are reasonable grounds for suspecting that person's involvement in a particular offence. There is, however, no statutory requirement (and, therefore, no requirement under paragraph 3.4 below) to destroy fingerprints or body samples taken in terrorist cases, no requirement to tell the people from whom these were taken that they will be destroyed, and no statutory requirement to offer such people an opportunity to witness the destruction of their fingerprints.

1.17   In this code, references to photographs, negatives and copies include reference to images stored or reproduced through any medium.

1.18   This code does not apply to those groups of people listed in paragraph 1.12 of Code C.

Notes for Guidance

1A   A person, including a parent or guardian, should not be the appropriate adult if he is suspected of involvement in the offence, is the victim, is a witness, is involved in the investigation or has received admissions prior to attending to act as the appropriate adult. If the parent of a juvenile is estranged from the juvenile, he should not be asked to act as the appropriate adult if the juvenile expressly and specifically objects to his presence.

1B   If a juvenile admits an offence to or in the presence of a social worker other than during the time that the social worker is acting as the appropriate adult for that juvenile, another social worker should be the appropriate adult in the interest of fairness.

1C   In the case of people who are mentally disordered or mentally handicapped, it may in certain circumstances be more satisfactory for all concerned if the appropriate adult is someone who has experience or training in their care rather than a relative lacking such qualifications. But if the person himself prefers a relative to a better-qualified stranger, or objects to a particular person as the appropriate adult, his wishes should if practicable be respected.

1D   A solicitor or lay visitor who is present at the station in that capacity may not act as the appropriate adult.

1E   For the purposes of paragraph 1.11 above, the consent required to be given by a parent or guardian may be given, in the case of a juvenile in the care of a local authority or voluntary organisation, by that authority or organisation.

1F   Persons who are blind, seriously visually handicapped or unable to read may be unwilling to sign police documents. The alternative of their representative signing on their behalf seeks to protect the interests of both police and suspects.

1G   Further guidance about fingerprints and body samples is given in Home Office circulars.

1H   The generic term 'mental disorder' is used throughout this code. 'Mental disorder' is defined in section 1(2) of the Mental Health Act 1983 as 'mental illness, arrested or incomplete development of mind, psychopathic disorder and any other disorder or disability of mind'. It should be noted that 'mental disorder' is different from 'mental handicap' although the two are dealt with similarly throughout this code. Where the custody officer has any doubt as to the mental state or capacity of a person detained an appropriate adult should be called.

2.   Identification by witnesses

2.0   A record shall be made of the description of the suspect as first given by a potential witness. This must be done before the witness takes part in the forms of identification listed in paragraph 2.1 or Annex D of this code. The record may be made or kept in any form provided that details of the description as first given by the witness can accurately be produced from it in a written form which can be provided to the suspect or his solicitor in accordance with this code. A copy shall be provided to the suspect or his solicitor before any procedures under paragraph 2.1 of this code are carried out. [See Note 2D]

(a) Cases where the suspect is known

2.1   In a case which involves disputed identification evidence, and where the identity of the suspect is known to the police and he is available (See Note 2E), the methods of identification by witnesses which may be used are:

(i)   a parade;
(ii)   a group identification;
(iii)   a video film;
(iv)   a confrontation.

2.2   The arrangements for, and conduct of, these types of identification shall be the responsibility of an officer in uniform not below the rank of inspector who is not involved with the investigation ('the identification officer'). No officer involved with the investigation of the case against the suspect may take any part in these procedures.

Identification parade

2.3   Whenever a suspect disputes an identification, an identification parade shall be held if the suspect consents unless paragraphs 2.4 or 2.7 or 2.10 apply. A parade may also be held if the officer in charge of the investigation considers that it would be useful, and the suspect consents.

2.4   A parade need not be held if the identification officer considers that, whether by reason of the unusual appearance of the suspect or for some other reason, it would not be practicable to assemble sufficient people who resembled him to make a parade fair.

2.5   Any parade must be carried out in accordance with Annex A. A video recording or colour photograph shall be taken of the parade.

2.6   If a suspect refuses or, having agreed, fails to attend an identification parade or the holding of a parade is impracticable, arrangements must if practicable be made to allow the witnesses an opportunity of seeing him in a group identification, a video identification, or a confrontation (see below).

Group identification

2.7   A group identification takes place where the suspect is viewed by a witness amongst an informal group of people. The procedure may take place with the consent and co-operation of a suspect or covertly where a suspect has refused to co-operate with an identification parade or a group identification or has failed to attend. A group identification may also be arranged if the officer in charge of the investigation considers, whether because of fear on the part of the witness or for some other reason, that it is, in the circumstances, more satisfactory than a parade.

2.8   The suspect should be asked for his consent to a group identification and advised in accordance with paragraphs 2.15 and 2.16 of this code. However, where consent is refused the identification officer has the discretion to proceed with a group identification if it is practicable to do so.

2.9   A group identification shall be carried out in accordance with Annex E. A video recording or colour photograph shall be taken of the group identification in accordance with Annex E.

Video film identification

2.10   The identification officer may show a witness a video film of a suspect if the investigating officer considers, whether because of the refusal of the suspect to take part in an identification parade or group identification or other reasons, that this would in the circumstances be the most satisfactory course of action.

2.11   The suspect should be asked for his consent to a video identification and advised in accordance with paragraphs 2.15 and 2.16. However, where such consent is refused the identification officer has the discretion to proceed with a video identification if it is practicable to do so.

2.12   A video identification must be carried out in accordance with Annex B.

Confrontation

2.13   If neither a parade, a group identification nor a video identification procedure is arranged, the suspect may be confronted by the witness. Such a confrontation does not require the suspect's consent, but may not take place unless none of the other procedures are practicable.

2.14   A confrontation must be carried out in accordance with Annex C.

Notice to suspect

2.15   Before a parade takes place or a group identification or video identification is arranged, the identification officer shall explain to the suspect:

(i)   the purposes of the parade or group identification or video identification;

(ii)   the fact that he is entitled to free legal advice;

(iii)   the procedures for holding it (including his right to have a solicitor or friend present);

(iv)   where appropriate the special arrangements for juveniles;

(v)   where appropriate the special arrangements for mentally disordered and mentally handicapped persons;

(vi)   that he does not have to take part in a parade, or co-operate in a group identification, or with the making of a video film and, if it is proposed to hold a group identification or video identification, his entitlement to a parade if this can practicably be arranged;

(vii)   if he does not consent to take part in a parade or co-operate in a group identification or with the making of a video film, his refusal may be given in evidence in any subsequent trial and police may proceed covertly without his consent or make other arrangements to test whether a witness identifies him;

(vii)a   that if he should significantly alter his appearance between the taking of any photograph at the time of his arrest or after charge and any attempt to hold an identification procedure, this may be given in evidence if the case comes to trial; and the officer may then consider other forms of identification;

(vii)b   that a video or photograph may be taken of him when he attends for any identification procedure;

(viii)   whether the witness had been shown photographs, photofit, identikit or similar pictures by the police during the investigation before the identity of the suspect became known; [See Note 2B]

(ix)   that if he changes his appearance before a parade it may not be practicable to arrange one on the day in question or subsequently and, because of his change of appearance, the identification officer may then consider alternative methods of identification;

(x)   that he or his solicitor will be provided with details of the description of the suspect as first given by any witnesses who are to attend the parade, group identification, video identification or confrontation.

2.16   This information must also be contained in a written notice which must be handed to the suspect. The identification officer shall give the suspect a reasonable opportunity to read the notice, after which he shall be asked to sign a second copy of the notice to indicate whether or not he is willing to take part in the parade or group identification or co-operate with the making of a video film. The signed copy shall be retained by the identification officer.

(b) Cases where the identity of the suspect is not known

2.17   A police officer may take a witness to a particular neighbourhood or place to see whether he can identify the person whom he said he saw on the relevant occasion. Before doing so, where practicable a record shall be made of any description given by the witness of the suspect. Care should be taken however not to direct the witness's attention to any individual.

2.18   A witness must not be shown photographs or photofit, identikit or similar pictures if the identity of the suspect is known to the police and he is available to stand on an identification parade. If the identity of the suspect is not known, the showing of such pictures to a witness must be done in accordance with Annex D. (See paragraph 2.15(viii) and Note 2E.)

(c)   Documentation

2.19   The identification officer shall make a record of the parade, group identification or video identification on the forms provided.

2.20   If the identification officer considers that it is not practicable to hold a parade, he shall tell the suspect why and record the reason.

2.21   A record shall be made of a person's refusal to co-operate in a parade, group identification or video identification.

(d)   Showing films and photographs of incidents

2.21A   Nothing in this code inhibits an investigating officer from showing a video film or photographs of an incident to the public at large through the national, or local media, or to police officers, for the purposes of recognition and tracing suspects. However when such material is shown to potential witnesses (including police officers [see Note 2A] for the purpose of obtaining identification evidence, it shall be shown on an individual basis so as to avoid any possibility of collusion, and the showing shall, as far as possible, follow the principles for Video Film Identification (see paragraph 2.10) or Identification by Photographs (see paragraph 2.18) as appropriate).

2.21B   Where such a broadcast or publication is made a copy of the material released by the police to the media for the purposes of recognising or tracing the suspect shall be kept and the suspect or his solicitor should be allowed to view such material before any procedures under paragraph 2.1 of this Code are carried out [see Notes 2D and 2E] provided it is practicable to do so and would not unreasonably delay the investigation. Each witness who is involved in the procedure shall be asked by the investigating officer after they have taken part whether they have seen any broadcast or published films or photographs relating to the offence and their replies shall be recorded.

Notes for Guidance

2A   Except for the provision of Annex D paragraph 1, a police officer who is a witness for the purposes of this part of the code is subject to the same principles and procedures as a civilian witness.

2B   Where a witness attending an identification parade has previously been shown photographs or photofit, identikit or similar pictures, it is the responsibility of the officer in charge of the investigation to make the identification officer aware that this is the case.

2C   [Not Used]

2D   Where it is proposed to show photographs to a witness in accordance with Annex D, it is the responsibility of the officer in charge of the investigation to confirm to the officer responsible for supervising and directing the showing that the first description of the suspect given by that witness has been recorded. If this description has not been recorded, the procedure under Annex D must be postponed. (See Annex D paragraph 1A)

2E   References in this section to a suspect being 'known' means there is sufficient information known to the police to justify the arrest of a particular person for suspected involvement in the offence. A suspect being 'available' means that he is immediately available to take part in the procedure or he will become available within a reasonably short time.

3.   Identification by fingerprints

(a)   Action

3.1   A person's fingerprints may be taken only with his consent or if paragraph 3.2 applies. If he is at a police station consent must be in writing. In either case the person must be informed of the reason before they are taken and that they will be destroyed as soon as practicable if paragraph 3.4 applies. He must be told that he may witness their destruction if he asks to do so within five days of being cleared or informed that he will not be prosecuted.

3.2   Powers to take fingerprints without consent from any person over the age of ten years are provided by sections 27 and 61 of the Police and Criminal Evidence Act 1984. These provide that fingerprints may be taken without consent:
    (a)   from a person detained at a police station if an officer of at least the rank of superintendent has reasonable grounds for suspecting that the fingerprints will tend to confirm or disprove his involvment in a criminal offence and the officer authorises the fingerprints to be taken;
    (b)   from a person detained at a police station who has been charged with a recordable offence or informed that he will be reported for such an offence and he has not previously had his fingerprints taken in relation to that offence;
    (c)   from a person convicted of a recordable offence. Section 27 of the Police and Criminal Evidence Act 1984 provides power to require such a person to attend a police station for the purposes of having his fingerprints taken if he has not been in police detention for the offence nor had his fingerprints taken in the course of the investigation of the offence or since conviction.
Reasonable force may be used if necessary to take a person's fingerprints without his consent.

3.2A   A person whose fingerprints are to be taken with or without consent shall be informed beforehand that his prints may be subject of a speculative search against other fingerprints. [See Note 3B]

3.3   [Not Used]

3.4   The fingerprints of a person and all copies of them taken in that case must be destroyed as soon as practicable if:
    (a)   he is prosecuted for the offence concerned and cleared; or
    (b)   he is not prosecuted (unless he admits the offence and is cautioned for it).
An opportunity of witnessing the destruction must be given to him if he wishes and if, in accordance with paragraph 3.1, he applies within five days of being cleared or informed that he will not be prosecuted.

3.5   When fingerprints are destroyed, access to relevant computer data shall be made impossible as soon as it is practicable to do so.

3.6   References to fingerprints include palm prints.

(b)   Documentation

3.7   A record must be made as soon as possible of the reason for taking a person's fingerprints without consent and of their destruction. If force is used a record shall be made of the circumstances and those present.

3.8   A record shall be made when a person has been informed under the terms of paragraph 3.2A that his fingerprints may be subject of a speculative search.

Notes for Guidance

3A   References to recordable offences in this code relate to those offences for which convictions may be recorded in national police records. (See section 27(4) of the Police and Criminal Evidence Act 1984.) The recordable offences to which this code applies at the time when the code was prepared, are any offences which carry a sentence of imprisonment on conviction (irrespective of the period, or the age of the offender or actual sentence passed) and non-imprisonable offences under section 1 of the Street Offences Act 1959 (loitering or soliciting for purposes of prostitution), section 43 of the Telecommunications Act 1984 (improper use of public telecommunications system), section 25 of the Road Traffic Act 1988 (tampering with motor vehicles), section 1 of the Malicious Communications Act 1988 (sending letters etc. with intent to cause distress or anxiety) and section 139(1) of the Criminal Justice Act 1988 (having article with a blade or point in a public place).

3B   A speculative search means that a check may be made against other fingerprints contained in records held by or on behalf of the police or held in connection with or as a result of an investigation of an offence.

4.   Photographs

(a)   Action

4.1   The photograph of a person who has been arrested may be taken at a police station only with his written consent or if paragraph 4.2 applies. In either case he must be informed of the reason for taking it and that the photograph will be destroyed if paragraph 4.4 applies. He must be told that if he should significantly alter his appearance between the taking of the photograph and any attempt to hold an identification procedure this may be given in evidence if the case comes to trial. He must be told that he may witness the destruction of the photograph or be provided with a certificate confirming its destruction if he applies within five days of being cleared or informed that he will not be prosecuted.

4.2   The photograph of a person who has been arrested may be taken without consent if:

(i)   he is arrested at the same time as other persons, or at a time when it is likely that other persons will be arrested, and a photograph is necessary to establish who was arrested, at what time and at what place;

(ii)   he has been charged with, or reported for a recordable offence and has not yet been released or brought before a court [see Note 3A]; or

(iii)   he is convicted of such an offence and his photograph is not already on record as a result of (i) or (ii). There is no power of arrest to take a photograph in pursuance of this provision which applies only where the person is in custody as a result of the exercise of another power (e.g., arrest for fingerprinting under section 27 of the Police and Criminal Evidence Act 1984);

(iv)   an officer of at least the rank of superintendent authorises it, having reasonable grounds for suspecting the involvement of the person in a criminal offence and where there is identification evidence in relation to that offence.

4.3   Force may not be used to take a photograph.

4.4   Where a person's photograph has been taken in accordance with this section, the photograph, negatives and all copies taken in that particular case must be destroyed if:

(a)   he is prosecuted for the offence and cleared unless he has a previous conviction for a recordable offence; or

(b)   he has been charged but not prosecuted (unless he admits the offence and is cautioned for it or he has a previous conviction for a recordable offence).

An opportunity of witnessing the destruction or a certificate confirming the destruction must be given to him if he so requests, provided that, in accordance with paragraph 4.1, he applies within five days of being cleared or informed that he will not be prosecuted. [See Note 4B]

(b)   Documentation

4.5   A record must be made as soon as possible of the reason for taking a person's photograph under this section without consent and of the destruction of any photographs.

Notes for Guidance

4A   The admissibility and value of identification evidence may be compromised if a potential witness in an identification procedure views any photographs of the suspect otherwise than in accordance with the provisions of this code.

4B   This paragraph is not intended to require the destruction of copies of a police gazette in cases where, for example, a remand prisoner has escaped from custody, or a person in custody is suspected of having committed offences in other force areas, and a photograph of the person concerned is circulated in a police gazette for information.

5.   Identification by body samples and impressions

(a)   Action

Intimate samples

5.1   Intimate samples may be taken from a person in police detention only:

(i)   if an officer of the rank of superintendent or above has reasonable grounds to believe that such an impression or sample will tend to confirm or disprove the suspect's involvement in a recordable offence and gives authorisation for a sample to be taken; and

(ii)   with the suspect's written consent.

5.1A   Where two or more non-intimate samples have been taken from a person in the course of an investigation of an offence and the samples have proved unsuitable or insufficient for a particular form of analysis and that person is not in police detention, an intimate sample may be taken from him if a police officer of at least the rank of superintendent authorises it to be taken, and the person concerned gives his written consent. [See Note 5B and Note 5E]

5.2   Before a person is asked to provide an intimate sample he must be warned that if he refuses without good cause, his refusal may harm his case if it comes to trial. [See Note 5A] If he is in police detention and not legally represented, he must also be reminded of his entitlement to have free legal advice (see paragraph 6.5 of Code C) and the reminder must be noted in the custody record. If paragraph 5.1A above applies and the person is attending a police station voluntarily, the officer shall explain the entitlement to free legal advice as provided for in accordance with paragraph 3.15 of Code C.

5.3   Except for samples of urine or saliva, intimate samples may be taken only by a registered medical or dental practitioner as appropriate.

Non-intimate samples

5.4   A non-intimate sample may be taken from a detained person only with his written consent or if paragraph 5.5 applies.

5.5   A non-intimate sample may be taken from a person without consent in accordance with the provisions of section 63 of the Police and Criminal Evidence Act 1984, as amended by section 55 of the Criminal Justice and Public Order Act 1994. The principal circumstances provided for are as follows:

    (i)   if an officer of the rank of superintendent or above has reasonable grounds to believe that the sample will tend to confirm or disprove the person's involvement in a recordable offence and gives authorisation for a sample to be taken; or

    (ii)   where the person has been charged with a recordable offence or informed that he will be reported for such an offence; and he has not had a non-intimate sample taken from him in the course of the investigation or if he has had a sample taken from him, it has proved unsuitable or insufficient for the same form of analysis [See Note 5B]; or

    (iii)   if the person has been convicted of a recordable offence after the date on which this code comes into effect. Section 63A of the Police and Criminal Evidence Act 1984, as amended by section 56 of the Criminal Justice and Public Order Act 1994, describes the circumstances in which a constable may require a person convicted of a recordable offence to attend a police station in order that a non-intimate sample may be taken.

5.6   Where paragraph 5.5 applies, reasonable force may be used if necessary to take non-intimate samples.

(b)   Destruction

5.7   [Not Used]

5.8   Except in accordance with paragraph 5.8A below, where a sample or impression has been taken in accordance with this section it must be destroyed as soon as practicable if:

    (a)   the suspect is prosecuted for the offence concerned and cleared; or

    (b)   he is not prosecuted (unless he admits the offence and is cautioned for it).

5.8A   In accordance with section 64 of the Police and Criminal Evidence Act 1984 as amended by section 57 of the Criminal Justice and Public Order Act 1994 samples need not be destroyed if they were taken for the purpose of an investigation of an offence for which someone has been convicted, and from whom a sample was also taken. [See Note 5F]

(c)   Documentation

5.9   A record must be made as soon as practicable of the reasons for taking a sample or impression and of its destruction. If force is used a record shall be made of the circumstances and those present. If written consent is given to the taking of a sample or impression, the fact must be recorded in writing.

5.10   A record must be made of the giving of a warning required by paragraph 5.2 above. A record shall be made of the fact that a person has been informed under the terms of paragraph 5.11A below that samples may be subject of a speculative search.

(d)   General

5.11   The terms intimate and non-intimate samples are defined in section 65 of the Police and Criminal Evidence Act 1984, as amended by section 58 of the Criminal Justice and Public Order Act 1994, as follows:

    (a)   'intimate sample' means a dental impression or a sample of blood, semen or any other tissue fluid, urine, or pubic hair, or a swab taken from a person's body orifice other than the mouth;

    (b)   'non-intimate sample' means:

     (i)   a sample of hair (other than pubic hair) which includes hair plucked with the root [See Note 5C];

     (ii)   a sample taken from a nail or from under a nail;

     (iii) a swab taken from any part of a person's body including the mouth but not any other body orifice;

     (iv) saliva;

     (v)   a footprint or similar impression of any part of a person's body other than a part of his hand.

5.11A   A person from whom an intimate or non-intimate sample is to be taken shall be informed beforehand that any sample taken may be the subject of a speculative search. [See Note 5D]

5.11B   The suspect must be informed, before an intimate or non-intimate sample is taken, of the grounds on which the relevant authority has been given, including where appropriate the nature of the suspected offence.

5.12   Where clothing needs to be removed in circumstances likely to cause embarrassment to the person, no person of the opposite sex who is not a medical practitioner or nurse shall be present, (unless in the case of a juvenile, that juvenile specifically requests the presence of a particular adult of the opposite sex who is readily available) nor shall anyone whose presence is unnecessary. However, in the case of a juvenile this is subject to the overriding proviso that such a removal of clothing may take place in the absence of the appropriate adult only if the juvenile signifies in the presence of the appropriate adult that he prefers the search to be done in his absence and the appropriate adult agrees.

Notes for Guidance

5A   In warning a person who is asked to provide an intimate sample in accordance with paragraph 5.2, the following form of words may be used:

> You do not have to [provide this sample] [allow this swab or impression to be taken], but I must warn you that if you refuse without good cause, your refusal may harm your case if it comes to trial.

5B   An insufficient sample is one which is not sufficient either in quantity or quality for the purpose of enabling information to be provided for the purpose of a particular form of analysis such as DNA analysis. An unsuitable sample is one which, by its nature, is not suitable for a particular form of analysis.

5C   Where hair samples are taken for the purpose of DNA analysis (rather than for other purposes such as making a visual match) the suspect should be permitted a reasonable choice as to what part of the body he wishes the hairs to be taken from. When hairs are plucked they should be plucked individually unless the suspect prefers otherwise and no more should be plucked than the person taking them reasonably considers necessary for a sufficient sample.

5D   A speculative search means that a check may be made against other samples and information derived from other samples contained in records or held by or on behalf of the police or held in connection with or as a result of an investigation of an offence.

5E   Nothing in paragraph 5.1A prevents intimate samples being taken for elimination purposes with the consent of the person concerned but the provisions of paragraph 1.11, relating to the role of the appropriate adult, should be applied.

5F   The provisions for the retention of samples in 5.8A allow for all samples in a case to be available for any subsequent miscarriage of justice investigation. But such samples

— and the information derived from them — may not be used in the investigation of any offence or in evidence against the person who would otherwise be entitled to their destruction.

ANNEX A
IDENTIFICATION PARADES

(a) General

1. A suspect must be given a reasonable opportunity to have a solicitor or friend present, and the identification officer shall ask him to indicate on a second copy of the notice whether or not he so wishes.

2. A parade may take place either in a normal room or in one equipped with a screen permitting witnesses to see members of the parade without being seen. The procedures for the composition and conduct of the parade are the same in both cases, subject to paragraph 7 below (except that a parade involving a screen may take place only when the suspect's solicitor, friend or appropriate adult is present or the parade is recorded on video).

2A Before the parade takes place the suspect or his solicitor shall be provided with details of the first description of the suspect by any witnesses who are to attend the parade. The suspect or his solicitor should also be allowed to view any material released to the media by the police for the purpose of recognising or tracing the suspect, provided it is practicable to do so and would not unreasonably delay the investigation.

(b) Parades involving prison inmates

3. If an inmate is required for identification, and there are no security problems about his leaving the establishment, he may be asked to participate in a parade or video identification. (A group identification, however, may not be arranged other than in the establishment or inside a police station.)

4. A parade may be held in a Prison Department establishment, but shall be conducted as far as practicable under normal parade rules. Members of the public shall make up the parade unless there are serious security or control objections to their admission to the establishment. In such cases, or if a video or group identification is arranged within the establishment, other inmates may participate. If an inmate is the suspect, he should not be required to wear prison uniform for the parade unless the other persons taking part are other inmates in uniform or are members of the public who are prepared to wear prison uniform for the occasion.

(c) Conduct of the parade

5. Immediately before the parade, the identification officer must remind the suspect of the procedures governing its conduct and caution him in the terms of paragraph 10.4 of Code C.

6. All unauthorised persons must be excluded from the place where the parade is held.

7. Once the parade has been formed, everything afterwards in respect of it shall take place in the presence and hearing of the suspect and of any interpreter, solicitor, friend or appropriate adult who is present (unless the parade involves a screen, in which case everything said to or by any witness at the place where the parade is held must be said in the hearing and presence of the suspect's solicitor, friend or appropriate adult or be recorded on video).

8. The parade shall consist of at least eight persons (in addition to the suspect) who so far as possible resemble the suspect in age, height, general appearance and position in

life. One suspect only shall be included in a parade unless there are two suspects of roughly similar appearance in which case they may be paraded together with at least twelve other persons. In no circumstances shall more than two suspects be included in one parade and where there are separate parades they shall be made up of different persons.

9.   Where all members of a similar group are possible suspects, separate parades shall be held for each member of the group unless there are two suspects of similar appearance when they may appear on the same parade with at least twelve other members of the group who are not suspects. Where police officers in uniform form an identification parade, any numerals or other identifying badge shall be concealed.

10.   When the suspect is brought to the place where the parade is to be held, he shall be asked by the identification officer whether he has any objection to the arrangements for the parade or to any of the other participants in it. The suspect may obtain advice from his solicitor or friend, if present, before the parade proceeds. Where practicable, steps shall be taken to remove the grounds for objection. Where it is not practicable to do so, the officer shall explain to the suspect why his objections cannot be met.

11.   The suspect may select his own position in the line. Where there is more than one witness, the identification officer must tell the suspect, after each witness has left the room, that he can if he wishes change position in the line. Each position in the line must be clearly numbered, whether by means of a numeral laid on the floor in front of each parade member or by other means.

12.   The identification officer is responsible for ensuring that, before they attend the parade, witnesses are not able to:

(i)   communicate with each other about the case or overhear a witness who has already seen the parade;
(ii)   see any member of the parade;
(iii)   on that occasion see or be reminded of any photograph or description of the suspect or be given any other indication of his identity; or
(iv)   on that occasion, see the suspect either before or after the parade.

13.   The officer conducting a witness to a parade must not discuss with him the composition of the parade, and in particular he must not disclose whether a previous witness has made any identification.

14.   Witnesses shall be brought in one at a time. Immediately before the witness inspects the parade, the identification officer shall tell him that the person he saw may or may not be on the parade and if he cannot make a positive identification he should say so but that he should not make a decision before looking at each member of the parade at least twice. The officer shall then ask him to look at each member of the parade at least twice, taking as much care and time as he wishes. When the officer is satisfied that the witness has properly looked at each member of the parade, he shall ask him whether the person he himself saw on an earlier relevant occasion is on the parade.

15.   The witness should make an identification by indicating the number of the person concerned.

16.   If the witness makes an identification after the parade has ended the suspect and, if present, his solicitor, interpreter or friend shall be informed. Where this occurs, consideration should be given to allowing the witness a second opportunity to identify the suspect.

17.   If a witness wishes to hear any parade member speak, adopt any specified posture or see him move, the identification officer shall first ask whether he can identify any

persons on the parade on the basis of appearance only. When the request is to hear members of the parade speak, the witness shall be reminded that the participants in the parade have been chosen on the basis of physical appearance only. Members of the parade may then be asked to comply with the witness's request to hear them speak, to see them move or to adopt any specified posture.

17A.   Where video films or photographs have been released to the media by the police for the purpose of recognising or tracing the suspect, the investigating officer shall ask each witness after the parade whether he has seen any broadcast or published films or photographs relating to the offence and shall record his reply.

18.   When the last witness has left, the identification officer shall ask the suspect whether he wishes to make any comments on the conduct of the parade.

(d)   Documentation

19.   A colour photograph or a video film of the parade shall be taken. A copy of the photograph or video film shall be supplied on request to the suspect or his solicitor within a reasonable time.

20.   The photograph or video film taken in accordance with paragraph 19 and held by the police shall be destroyed or wiped clean at the conclusion of the proceedings unless the person concerned is convicted or admits the offence and is cautioned for it.

21.   If the identification officer asks any person to leave a parade because he is interfering with its conduct the circumstances shall be recorded.

22.   A record must be made of all those present at a parade or group identification whose names are known to the police.

23.   If prison inmates make up a parade the circumstances must be recorded.

24.   A record of the conduct of any parade must be made on the forms provided.

ANNEX B
VIDEO IDENTIFICATION

(a)   General

1.   Where a video parade is to be arranged the following procedures must be followed.

2.   Arranging, supervising and directing the making and showing of a video film to be used in a video identification must be the responsibility of an identification officer or identification officers who have no direct involvement with the relevant case.

3.   The film must include the suspect and at least eight other people who so far as possible resemble the suspect in age, height, general appearance and position in life. Only one suspect shall appear on any film unless there are two suspects of roughly similar appearance in which case they may be shown together with at least twelve other persons.

4.   The suspect and other persons shall as far as possible be filmed in the same positions or carrying out the same activity and under identical conditions.

5.   Provision must be made for each person filmed to be identified by number.

6.   If police officers are filmed, any numerals or other identifying badges must be concealed. If a prison inmate is filmed either as a suspect or not, then either all or none of the persons filmed should be in prison uniform.

7.   The suspect and his solicitor, friend, or appropriate adult must be given a reasonable opportunity to see the complete film before it is shown to witnesses. If he has

a reasonable objection to the video film or any of its participants, steps should, if practicable be taken to remove the grounds for objection. If this is not practicable the identification officer shall explain to the suspect and/or his representative why his objections cannot be met and record both the objection and the reason on the forms provided.

8. The suspect's solicitor, or where one is not instructed the suspect himself, where practicable should be given reasonable notification of the time and place that it is intended to conduct the video identification in order that a representative may attend on the behalf of the suspect. The suspect himself may not be present when the film is shown to the witness(es). In the absence of a person representing the suspect the viewing itself shall be recorded on video. No unauthorised persons may be present.

8A. Before the video identification takes place the suspect or his solicitor shall be provided with details of the first description of the suspect by any witnesses who are to attend the parade. The suspect or his solicitor should also be allowed to view any material released to the media by the police for the purpose of recognising or tracing the suspect, provided it is practicable to do so and would not unreasonably delay the investigation.

(b) Conducting the video identification

9. The identification officer is responsible for ensuring that, before they see the film, witnesses are not able to communicate with each other about the case or overhear a witness who has seen the film. He must not discuss with the witness the composition of the film and must not disclose whether a previous witness has made any identification.

10. Only one witness may see the film at a time. Immediately before the video identification takes place the identification officer shall tell the witness that the person he saw may or may not be on the video film. The witness should be advised that at any point he may ask to see a particular part of the tape again or to have a particular picture frozen for him to study. Furthermore, it should be pointed out that there is no limit on how many times he can view the whole tape or any part of it. However, he should be asked to refrain from making a positive identification or saying that he cannot make a positive identification until he has seen the entire film at least twice.

11. Once the witness has seen the whole film at least twice and has indicated that he does not want to view it or any part of it again, the identification officer shall ask the witness to say whether the individual he saw in person on an earlier occasion has been shown on the film and, if so, to identify him by number. The identification officer will then show the film of the person identified again to confirm the identification with the witness.

12. The identification officer must take care not to direct the witness's attention to any one individual on the video film, or give any other indication of the suspect's identity. Where a witness has previously made an identification by photographs, or a photofit, identikit or similar picture has been made, the witness must not be reminded of such a photograph or picture once a suspect is available for identification by other means in accordance with this code. Neither must he be reminded of any description of the suspect.

12A Where video films or photographs have been released to the media by the police for the purpose of recognising or tracing the suspect, the investigating officer shall ask each witness after the parade whether he has seen any broadcast or published films or photographs relating to the offence and shall record his reply.

(c) Tape security and destruction

13.   It shall be the responsibility of the identification officer to ensure that all relevant tapes are kept securely and their movements accounted for. In particular, no officer involved in the investigation against the suspect shall be permitted to view the video film prior to it being shown to any witness.

14.   Where a video film has been made in accordance with this section all copies of it held by the police must be destroyed if:
 (a)   he is prosecuted for the offence and cleared; or
 (b)   he is not prosecuted (unless he admits the offence and is cautioned for it).
An opportunity of witnessing the destruction must be given to him if he so requests within five days of being cleared or informed that he will not be prosecuted.

(d)   Documentation

15.   A record must be made of all those participating in or seeing the video whose names are known to the police.

16.   A record of the conduct of the video identification must be made on the forms provided.

ANNEX C
CONFRONTATION BY A WITNESS

1.   The identification officer is responsible for the conduct of any confrontation of a suspect by a witness.

2.   Before the confrontation takes place, the identification officer must tell the witness that the person he saw may or may not be the person he is to confront and that if he cannot make a positive identification he should say so.

2A   Before the confrontation takes place, the suspect or his solicitor shall be provided with details of the first description of the suspect given by any witness who is to attend the confrontation. The suspect or his solicitor should also be allowed to view any material released by the police to the media for the purposes of recognising or tracing the suspect provided that it is practicable to do so and would not unreasonably delay the investigation.

3.   The suspect shall be confronted independently by each witness, who shall be asked 'Is this the person?' Confrontation must take place in the presence of the suspect's solicitor, interpreter or friend, unless this would cause unreasonable delay.

4.   The confrontation should normally take place in the police station, either in a normal room or in one equipped with a screen permitting a witness to see the suspect without being seen. In both cases the procedures are the same except that a room equipped with a screen may be used only when the suspect's solicitor, friend or appropriate adult is present or the confrontation is recorded on video.

5.   Where video films or photographs have been released to the media by the police for the purposes of recognising or tracing the suspect, the investigating officer shall ask each witness after the procedure whether he has seen any broadcast or published films or photographs relating to the offence and shall record his reply.

ANNEX D
SHOWING OF PHOTOGRAPHS

(a)   Action

1.   An officer of the rank of sergeant or above shall be responsible for supervising and directing the showing of photographs. The actual showing may be done by a constable or a civilian police employee.

1A   The officer must confirm that the first description of the suspect given by the witness has been recorded before the witness is shown the photographs. If he is unable to confirm that the description has been recorded, he shall postpone the showing.

2.   Only one witness shall be shown photographs at any one time. He shall be given as much privacy as practicable and shall not be allowed to communicate with any other witness in the case.

3.   The witness shall be shown not less than twelve photographs at a time which shall, as far as possible, all be of a similar type.

4.   When the witness is shown the photographs, he shall be told that the photograph of the person he saw may or may not be amongst them. He shall not be prompted or guided in any way but shall be left to make any selection without help.

5.   If a witness makes a positive identification from photographs, then, unless the person identified is otherwise eliminated from enquiries, other witnesses shall not be shown photographs. But both they and the witness who has made the identification shall be asked to attend an identification parade or group or video identification if practicable unless there is no dispute about the identification of the suspect.

6.   Where the use of a photofit, identikit or similar picture has led to there being a suspect available who can be asked to appear on a parade, or participate in a video or group identification, the picture shall not be shown to other potential witnesses.

7.   Where a witness attending an identification parade has previously been shown photographs or photofit, identikit or similar pictures (and it is the responsibility of the officer in charge of the investigation to make the identification officer aware that this is the case) then the suspect and his solicitor must be informed of this fact before the identity parade takes place.

8.   None of the photographs used shall be destroyed, whether or not an identification is made, since they may be required for production in court. The photographs should be numbered and a separate photograph taken of the frame or part of the album from which the witness made an identification as an aid to reconstituting it.

(b)   Documentation

9.   Whether or not an identification is made, a record shall be kept of the showing of photographs and of any comment made by the witness.

ANNEX E
GROUP IDENTIFICATION

(a)   General

1.   The purpose of the provisions of this Annex is to ensure that as far as possible, group identifications follow the principles and procedures for identification parades so that the conditions are fair to the suspect in the way they test the witness's ability to make an identification.

2. Group identifications may take place either with the suspect's consent and co-operation or covertly without his consent.

3. The location of the group identification is a matter for the identification officer, although he may take into account any representations made by the suspect, appropriate adult, his solicitor or friend. The place where the group identification is held should be one where other people are either passing by, or waiting around informally, in groups such that the suspect is able to join them and be capable of being seen by the witness at the same time as others in the group. Examples include people leaving an escalator, pedestrians walking through a shopping centre, passengers on railway and bus stations waiting in queues or groups or where people are standing or sitting in groups in other public places.

4. If the group identification is to be held covertly, the choice of locations will be limited by the places where the suspect can be found and the number of other people present at that time. In these cases, suitable locations might be along regular routes travelled by the suspect, including buses or trains, or public places he frequents.

5. Although the number, age, sex, race and general description and style of clothing of other people present at the location cannot be controlled by the identification officer, in selecting the location he must consider the general appearance and number of people likely to be present. In particular, he must reasonably expect that over the period the witness observes the group, he will be able to see, from time to time, a number of others (in addition to the suspect) whose appearance is broadly similar to that of the suspect.

6. A group identification need not be held if the identification officer believes that because of the unusual appearance of the suspect, none of the locations which it would be practicable to use satisfy the requirements of paragraph 5 necessary to make the identification fair.

7. Immediately after a group identification procedure has taken place (with or without the suspect's consent), a colour photograph or a video should be taken of the general scene, where this is practicable, so as to give a general impression of the scene and the number of people present, Alternatively, if it is practicable, the group identification may be video recorded.

8. If it is not practicable to take the photograph or video film in accordance with paragraph 7, a photograph or film of the scene should be taken later at a time determined by the identification officer, if he considers that it is practicable to do so.

9. An identification carried out in accordance with this code remains a group identification notwithstanding that at the time of being seen by the witness the suspect was on his own rather than in a group.

10. The identification officer need not be in uniform when conducting a group identification.

11. Before the group identification takes place the suspect or his solicitor should be provided with details of the first description of the suspect by any witnesses who are to attend the identification. The suspect or his solicitor should also be allowed to view any material released by the police to the media for the purposes of recognising or tracing the suspect provided that it is practicable to do so and would not unreasonably delay the investigation.

12. Where video films or photographs have been released to the media by the police for the purposes of recognising or tracing the suspects, the investigating officer shall ask each witness after the procedure whether he has seen any broadcast or published films or photographs relating to the offence and shall record his reply.

(b)   Identification with the consent of the suspect

13.   A suspect must be given a reasonable opportunity to have a solicitor or friend present. The identification officer shall ask him to indicate on a second copy of the notice whether or not he so wishes.

14.   The witness, identification officer and suspect's solicitor, appropriate adult, friend or any interpreter for the witness, if present may be concealed from the sight of the persons in the group which they are observing if the identification officer considers that this facilitates the conduct of the identification.

15.   The officer conducting a witness to a group identification must not discuss with the witness the forthcoming group identification and in particular he must not disclose whether a previous witness has made any identification.

16.   Anything said to or by the witness during the procedure regarding the identification should be said in the presence and hearing of the identification officer and, if present, the suspect's solicitor, appropriate adult, friend or any interpreter for the witness.

17.   The identification officer is responsible for ensuring that before they attend the group identification witnesses are not able to:
  (i)   communicate with each other about the case or overhear a witness who has already been given an opportunity to see the suspect in the group;
  (ii)   on that occasion see the suspect; or
  (iii)   on that occasion see or be reminded of any photographs or description of the suspect or be given any other indication of his identity.

18.   Witnesses shall be brought to the place where they are to observe the group one at a time. Immediately before the witness is asked to look at the group, the identification officer shall tell him that the person he saw may or may not be in the group and if he cannot make a positive identification he should say so. The witness shall then be asked to observe the group in which the suspect is to appear. The way in which the witness should do this will depend on whether the group is moving or stationary.

Moving group

19.   When the group in which the suspect is to appear is moving, for example, leaving an escalator, the provisions of paragraphs 20 to 23 below should be followed.

20.   If two or more suspects consent to a group identification, each should be the subject of separate identification procedures. These may however be conducted consecutively on the same occasion.

21.   The identification officer shall tell the witness to observe the group and ask him to point out any person he thinks he saw on the earlier relevant occasion. When the witness makes such an indication the officer shall, if it is practicable, arrange for the witness to take a closer look at the person he has indicated and ask him whether he can make a positive identification. If this is not practicable, the officer shall ask the witness how sure he is that the person he has indicated is the relevant person.

22.   The witness should continue to observe the group for the period which the identification officer reasonably believes is necessary in the circumstances for the witness to be able to make comparisons between the suspect and other persons of broadly similar appearance to the suspect in accordance with paragraph 5.

23.   Once the identification officer has informed the witness in accordance with paragraph 21, the suspect should be allowed to take any position in the group he wishes.

Stationary groups

24.   When the group in which the suspect is to appear is stationary, for example, people waiting in a queue, the provisions of paragraphs 25 to 28 below should be followed.

25.   If two or more suspects consent to a group identification, each should be the subject of separate identification procedures unless they are of broadly similar appearance when they may appear in the same group. Where separate group identifications are held, the groups must be made up of different persons.

26.   The suspect may take any position in the group he wishes. Where there is more than one witness, the identification officer must tell the suspect, out of the sight and hearing of any witness, that he can if he wishes change his position in the group.

27.   The identification officer shall ask the witness to pass along or amongst the group and to look at each person in the group at least twice, taking as much care and time as is possible according to the circumstances, before making an identification. When he has done this, the officer shall ask him whether the person he saw on an earlier relevant occasion is in the group and to indicate any such person by whatever means the identificaton officer considers appropriate in the circumstances. If this is not practicable, the officer shall ask the witness to point out any person he thinks he saw on the earlier relevant occasion.

28.   When the witness makes an indication in accordance with paragraph 27, the officer shall, if it is practicable, arrange for the witness to take a closer look at the person he has indicated and ask him whether he can make a positive identification. If this is not practicable, the officer shall ask the witness how sure he is that the person he has indicated is the relevant person.

All cases

29.   If the suspect unreasonably delays joining the group, or having joined the group, deliberately conceals himself from the sight of the witness, the identification officer may treat this as a refusal to co-operate in a group identification.

30.   If the witness identifies a person other than the suspect, an officer should inform that person what has happened and ask if they are prepared to give their name and address. There is no obligation upon any member of the public to give these details. There shall be no duty to record any details of any other member of the public present in the group or at the place where the procedure is conducted.

31.   When the group identification has been completed, the identification officer shall ask the suspect whether he wishes to make any comments on the conduct of the procedure.

32.   If he has not been previously informed the identification officer shall tell the suspect of any identifications made by the witnesses.

(c)   Identification without suspect's consent

33.   Group identifications held covertly without the suspect's consent should so far as is practicable follow the rules for conduct of group identification by consent.

34.   A suspect has no right to have a solicitor, appropriate adult or friend present as the identification will, of necessity, take place without the knowledge of the suspect.

35.   Any number of suspects may be identified at the same time.

(d) Identifications in police stations

36.   Group identifications should only take place in police stations for reasons of safety, security, or because it is impracticable to hold them elsewhere.

37.   The group identification may take place either in a room equipped with a screen permitting witnesses to see members of the group without being seen, or anywhere else in the police station that the identification officer considers appropriate.

38.   Any of the additional safeguards applicable to identification parades should be followed if the identification officer consider it is practicable to do so in the circumstances.

(e) Identifications involving prison inmates

39.   A group identification involving a prison inmate may only be arranged in the prison or at a police station.

40.   Where a group identification takes place involving a prison inmate, whether in a prison or in a police station, the arrangements should follow those in paragraphs 36 to 38 of this Annex. If a group identification takes place within a prison other inmates may participate. If an inmate is the suspect he should not be required to wear prison uniform for the group identification unless the other persons taking part are wearing the same uniform.

(f) Documentation

41.   Where a photograph or video film is taken in accordance with paragraph 7 or 8, a copy of the photograph or video film shall be supplied on request to the suspect or his solicitor within a reasonable time.

42.   If the photograph or film includes the suspect, it and all copies held by the police shall be destroyed or wiped clean at the conclusion of the proceedings unless the person is convicted or admits the offence and is cautioned for it.

43.   A record of the conduct of any group identification must be made on the forms provided. This shall include anything said by the witness or the suspect about any identifications or the conduct of the procedure and any reasons why it was not practicable to comply with any of the provisions of this code governing the conduct of group identifications.

CODE OF PRACTICE ON TAPE RECORDING OF INTERVIEWS WITH SUSPECTS (CODE E)

1. General

1.1   This code of practice must be readily available for consultation by police officers, detained persons and members of the public at every police station to which an order made under section 60(1)(b) of the Police and Criminal Evidence Act 1984 applies.

1.2   The notes for guidance included are not provisions of this code. They form guidance to police officers and others about its application and interpretation.

1.3   Nothing in this code shall be taken as detracting in any way from the requirements of the Code of Practice for the Detention, Treatment and Questioning of Persons by Police Officers (Code C). [See Note 1A]

1.4   This code does not apply to those groups of people listed in paragraph 1.12 of Code C.

1.5   In this code the term 'appropriate adult' has the same meaning as in paragraph 1.7 of Code C; and the term 'solicitor' has the same meaning as in paragraph 6.12 of Code C.

Notes for Guidance

1A   As in Code C, references to custody officers include those carrying out the functions of a custody officer.

2.   Recording and the sealing of master tapes

2.1   Tape recording of interviews shall be carried out openly to instil confidence in its reliability as an impartial and accurate record of the interview. [See Note 2A]

2.2   One tape, referred to in this code as the master tape, will be sealed before it leaves the presence of the suspect. A second tape will be used as a working copy. The master tape is either one of the two tapes used in a twin deck machine or the only tape used in a single deck machine. The working copy is either the second tape used in a twin deck machine or a copy of the master tape made by a single deck machine. [See Notes 2B and 2C]

Notes for Guidance

2A   Police Officers will wish to arrange that, as far as possible, tape recording arrangements are unobtrusive. It must be clear to the suspect, however, that there is no opportunity to interfere with the tape recording equipment or the tapes.

2B   The purpose of sealing the master tape before it leaves the presence of the suspect is to establish his confidence that the integrity of the tape is preserved. Where a single deck machine is used the working copy of the master tape must be made in the presence of the suspect and without the master tape having left his sight. The working copy shall be used for making further copies where the need arises. The recorder will normally be capable of recording voices and have a time coding or other security device.

2C   Throughout this code any reference to 'tapes' shall be construed as 'tape', as appropriate, where a single deck machine is used.

3.   Interviews to be tape recorded

3.1   Subject to paragraph 3.2 below, tape recording shall be used at police stations for any interview:
       (a)   with a person who has been cautioned in accordance with section 10 of Code C in respect of an indictable offence (including an offence triable either way) [see Notes 3A and 3B];
       (b)   which takes place as a result of a police officer exceptionally putting further questions to a suspect about an offence described in sub-paragraph (a) above after he has been charged with, or informed he may be prosecuted for, that offence [see Note 3C]; or
       (c)   in which a police officer wishes to bring to the notice of a person, after he has been charged with, or informed he may be prosecuted for an offence described in sub-paragraph (a) above, any written statement made by another person, or the content of an interview with another person [see Note 3D].

3.2   Tape recording is not required in respect of the following:
       (a)   an interview with a person arrested under section 14(1)(a) or Schedule 5, para 6 of the Prevention of Terrorism (Temporary Provisions) Act 1989 or an interview with a person being questioned in respect of an offence where there are reasonable grounds for suspecting that it is connected to terrorism or was committed in furtherance of the objectives of an organisation engaged in terrorism. This sub-paragraph applies only

where the terrorism is connected with the affairs of Northern Ireland or is terrorism of any other description except terrorism connected solely with the affairs of the United Kingdom or any part of the United Kingdom other than Northern Ireland. 'Terrorism' has the meaning given by section 20(1) of the Prevention of Terrorism (Temporary Provisions) Act 1989 [see Notes 3E, 3F, 3G and 3H];

3.3   The custody officer may authorise the interviewing officer not to tape record the interview:

  (a)   where it is not reasonably practicable to do so because of failure of the equipment or the non-availability of a suitable interview room or recorder and the authorising officer considers on reasonable grounds that the interview should not be delayed until the failure has been rectified or a suitable room or recorder becomes available [see Note 3J]; or

  (b)   where it is clear from the outset that no prosecution will ensue.

In such cases the interview shall be recorded in writing and in accordance with section 11 of Code C. In all cases the custody officer shall make a note in specified terms of the reasons for not tape recording. [See Note 3K]

3.4   Where an interview takes place with a person voluntarily attending the police station and the police officer has grounds to believe that person has become a suspect (i.e., the point at which he should be cautioned in accordance with paragraph 10.1 of Code C) the continuation of the interview shall be tape recorded, unless the custody officer gives authority in accordance with the provisions of paragraph 3.3 above for the continuation of the interview not to be recorded.

3.5   The whole of each interview shall be tape recorded, including the taking and reading back of any statement.

Notes for Guidance

3A   Nothing in this code is intended to preclude tape recording at police discretion of interviews at police stations with persons cautioned in respect of offences not covered by paragraph 3.1, or responses made by interviewees after they have been charged with, or informed they may be prosecuted for, an offence, provided that this code is complied with.

3B   Attention is drawn to the restrictions in paragraph 12.3 of Code C on the questioning of persons unfit through drink or drugs to the extent that they are unable to appreciate the significance of questions put to them or of their answers.

3C   Circumstances in which a suspect may be questioned about an offence after being charged with it are set out in paragraph 17.5 of Code C.

3D   Procedures to be followed when a person's attention is drawn after charge to a statement made by another person are set out in paragraph 17.4 of Code C. One method of bringing the content of an interview with another person to the notice of a suspect may be to play him a tape recording of that interview.

3E   Section 14(1)(a) of the Prevention of Terrorism (Temporary Provisions) Act 1989, permits the arrest without warrant of a person reasonably suspected to be guilty of an offence under sections 2, 8, 9, 10 or 11 of the Act.

3F   Section 14(1) of the Prevention of Terrorism (Temporary Provisions) Act 1989 says 'terrorism means the use of violence for political ends and includes any use of violence for the purpose of putting the public or any section of the public in fear'.

3G   It should be noted that the provisions of paragraph 3.2 apply only to those suspected of offences connected with terrorism connected with Northern Ireland, or with terrorism of any other description other than terrorism connected solely with the affairs of the United Kingdom or any part of the United Kingdom other than Northern Ireland, or offences committed in furtherance of such terrorism. Any interviews with those suspected of offences connected with terrorism of any other description or in furtherance of the objectives of an organisation engaged in such terrorism should be carried out in compliance with the rest of this code.

3H   When it only becomes clear during the course of an interview which is being tape recorded that the interviewee may have committed an offence to which paragraph 3.2 applies the interviewing officer should turn off the tape recorder.

3J   Where practicable, priority should be given to tape recording interviews with persons who are suspected of more serious offences.

3K   A decision not to tape record an interview for any reason may be the subject of comment in court. The authorising officer should therefore be prepared to justify his decision in each case.

4.   The interview

(a)   Commencement of interviews

4.1   When the suspect is brought into the interview room the police officer shall without delay, but in the sight of the suspect, load the tape recorder with clean tapes and set it to record. The tapes must be unwrapped or otherwise opened in the presence of the suspect. [See Note 4A]

4.2   The police officer shall then tell the suspect formally about the tape recording. He shall say:
  (a)   that the interview is being tape recorded;
  (b)   his name and rank and the name and rank of any other police officer present except in the case of enquiries linked to the investigation of terrorism where warrant or other identification numbers shall be stated rather than names;
  (c)   the name of the suspect and any other party present (e.g., a solicitor);
  (d)   the date, time of commencement and place of the interview; and
  (e)   that the suspect will be given a notice about what will happen to the tapes.
[See Note 4B]

4.3   The police officer shall then caution the suspect in the following terms:

You do not have to say anything. But it may harm your defence if you do not mention when questioned something which you later rely on in court. Anything you do say may be given in evidence.

Minor deviations do not constitute a breach of this requirement provided that the sense of the caution is preserved. [See Note 4C]

4.3A   The police officer shall remind the suspect of his right to free and independent legal advice and that he can speak to a solicitor on the telephone in accordance with paragraph 6.5 of Code C.

4.3B   The police officer shall then put to the suspect any significant statement or silence (i.e., failure or refusal to answer a question or to answer it satisfactorily) which occurred before the start of the tape-recorded interview, and shall ask him whether he confirms or denies that earlier statement or silence or whether he wishes to add anything. A 'significant' statement or silence means one which appears capable of being used in evidence against the suspect, in particular a direct admission of guilt, or failure or refusal to answer a question or to answer it satisfactorily, which might give rise to an inference under Part III of the Criminal Justice and Public Order Act 1994.

Special warnings under Sections 36 and 37 of the Criminal Justice and Public Order Act 1994

4.3C   When a suspect who is interviewed after arrest fails or refuses to answer certain questions, or to answer them satisfactorily, after due warning, a court or jury may draw a proper inference from this silence under sections 36 and 37 of the Criminal Justice and Public Order Act 1994. This applies when:

(a)   a suspect is arrested by a constable and there is found on his person, or in or on his clothing or footwear, or otherwise in his possession, or in the place where he was arrested, any objects, marks or substances, or marks on such objects, and the person fails or refuses to account for the objects, marks or substances found; or

(b)   an arrested person was found by a constable at a place at or about the time the offence for which he was arrested, is alleged to have been committed, and the person fails or refuses to account for his presence at that place.

4.3D   For an inference to be drawn from a suspect's failure or refusal to answer a question about one of these matters or to answer it satisfactorily, the interviewing officer must first tell him in ordinary language:

(a)   what offence he is investigating;

(b)   what fact he is asking the suspect to account for;

(c)   that he believes this fact may be due to the suspect's taking part in the commission of the offence in question;

(d)   that a court may draw a proper inference from his silence if he fails or refuses to account for the fact about which he is being questioned;

(e)   that a record is being made of the interview and may be given in evidence if he is brought to trial.

4.3E   Where, despite the fact that a person has been cautioned, failure to co-operate may have an effect on his immediate treatment, he should be informed of any relevant consequences and that they are not affected by the caution. Examples are when his refusal to provide his name and address when charged may render him liable to detention, or when his refusal to provide particulars and information in accordance with a statutory requirement, for example, under the Road Traffic Act 1988, may amount to an offence or may make him liable to arrest.

(b)   Interviews with the deaf

4.4   If the suspect is deaf or there is doubt about his hearing ability, the police officer shall take a contemporaneous note of the interview in accordance with the requirements of Code C, as well as tape record it in accordance with the provisions of this code. [See Notes 4E and 4F]

(c)   Objections and complaints by the suspect

4.5   If the suspect raises objections to the interview being tape recorded either at the outset or during the interview or during a break in the interview, the police officer shall explain the fact that the interview is being tape recorded and that the provisions of this code require that the suspect's objections should be recorded on tape. When any objections have been recorded on tape or the suspect has refused to have his objections recorded, the police officer may turn off the recorder. In this eventuality he shall say that he is turning off the recorder and give his reasons for doing so and then turn it off. The police officer shall then make a written record of the interview in accordance with section 11 of Code C. If, however, the police officer reasonably considers that he may proceed to put questions to the suspect with the tape recorder still on, he may do so. [See Note 4G]

4.6   If in the course of an interview a complaint is made by the person being questioned, or on his behalf, concerning the provisions of this code or of Code C, then the officer shall act in accordance with paragraph 12.8 of Code C. [See Notes 4H and 4J]

4.7   If the suspect indicates that he wishes to tell the police officer about matters not directly connected with the offence of which he is suspected and that he is unwilling for these matters to be recorded on tape, he shall be given the opportunity to tell the police officer about these matters after the conclusion of the formal interview.

(d)   Changing tapes

4.8   When the recorder indicates that the tapes have only a short time left to run, the police officer shall tell the suspect that the tapes are coming to an end and round off that part of the interview. If the police officer wishes to continue the interview but does not already have a second set of tapes, he shall obtain a set. The suspect shall not be left unattended in the interview room. The police officer will remove the tapes from the tape recorder and insert the new tapes which shall be unwrapped or otherwise opened in the suspect's presence. The tape recorder shall then be set to record on the new tapes. Care must be taken, particularly when a number of sets of tapes have been used, to ensure that there is no confusion between the tapes. This may be done by marking the tapes with an identification number immediately they are removed from the tape recorder.

(e)   Taking a break during interview

4.9   When a break is to be taken during the course of an interview and the interview room is to be vacated by the suspect, the fact that a break is to be taken, the reason for it and the time shall be recorded on tape. The tapes shall then be removed from the tape recorder and the procedures for the conclusion of an interview set out in paragraph 4.14 below followed.

4.10   When a break is to be a short one and both the suspect and a police officer are to remain in the interview room the fact that a break is to be taken, the reasons for it and the time shall be recorded on tape. The tape recorder may be turned off; there is, however, no need to remove the tapes and when the interview is recommenced the tape recording shall be continued on the same tapes. The time at which the interview recommences shall be recorded on tape.

4.11   When there is a break in questioning under caution the interviewing officer must ensure that the person being questioned is aware that he remains under caution. If there is any doubt the caution must be given again in full when the interview resumes. [See Notes 4K and 4L]

(f)   Failure of recording equipment

4.12   If there is a failure of equipment which can be rectified quickly, for example by inserting new tapes, the appropriate procedures set out in paragraph 4.8 shall be followed, and when the recording is resumed the officer shall explain what has happened and record the time the interview recommences. If, however, it will not be possible to continue recording on that particular tape recorder and no replacement recorder or recorder in another interview room is readily available, the interview may continue without being tape recorded. In such circumstances the procedures in paragraphs 3.3 above for seeking the authority of the custody officer will be followed. [See Note 4M]

(g)   Removing tapes from the recorder

4.13   Where tapes are removed from the recorder in the course of an interview, they shall be retained and the procedures set out in paragraph 4.15 below followed.

(h)   Conclusion of interview

4.14   At the conclusion of the interview, the suspect shall be offered the opportunity to clarify anything he has said and to add anything he may wish.

4.15   At the conclusion of the interview, including the taking and reading back of any written statement, the time shall be recorded and the tape recorder switched off. The master tape shall be sealed with a master tape label and treated as an exhibit in accordance with the force standing orders. The police officer shall sign the label and ask the suspect and any third party present to sign it also. If the suspect or third party refuses to sign the label, an officer of at least the rank of inspector, or if one is not available the custody officer, shall be called into the interview room and asked to sign it. In the case of enquiries linked to the investigation of terrorism, an officer who signs the label shall use his warrant or other identification number.

4.16   The suspect shall be handed a notice which explains the use which will be made of the tape recording and the arrangements for access to it and that a copy of the tape shall be supplied as soon as practicable if the person is charged or informed that he will be prosecuted.

Notes for Guidance

4A   The police officer should attempt to estimate the likely length of the interview and ensure that the appropriate number of clean tapes and labels with which to seal the master copies are available in the interview room.

4B   It will be helpful for the purpose of voice identification if the officer asks the suspect and any other persons present to identify themselves.

4C   If it appears that a person does not understand what the caution means, the officer who has given it should go on to explain it in his own words.

4D   [Not Used]

4E   This provision is intended to give the deaf equivalent rights of first hand access to the full interview record as other suspects.

4F   The provisions of paragraphs 13.2, 13.5 and 13.9 of Code C on interpreters for the deaf or for interviews with suspects who have difficulty in understanding English continue to apply. In a tape recorded interview there is no requirement on the interviewing officer to ensure that the interpreter makes a separate note of interview as prescribed in section 13 of Code C.

4G   The officer should bear in mind that a decision to continue recording against the wishes of the suspect may be the subject of comment in court.

4H   Where the custody officer is called immediately to deal with the complaint, wherever possible the tape recorder should be left to run until the custody officer has entered the interview room and spoken to the person being interviewed. Continuation or termination of the interview should be at the discretion of the interviewing officer pending action by an inspector under paragraph 9.1 of Code C.

4H   [Not Used]

4J   Where the complaint is about a matter not connected with this code of practice or Code C, the decision to continue with the interview is at the discretion of the interviewing officer. Where the interviewing officer decides to continue with the interview the person being interviewed shall be told that the complaint will be brought to the attention of the custody officer at the conclusion of the interview. When the interview is concluded the interviewing officer must, as soon as practicable, inform the custody officer of the existence and nature of the complaint made.

4K In considering whether to caution again after a break, the officer should bear in mind that he may have to satisfy a court that the person understood that he was still under caution when the interview resumed.

4L The officer should bear in mind that it may be necessary to show to the court that nothing occurred during a break in an interview or between interviews which influenced the suspect's recorded evidence. The officer should consider, therefore, after a break in an interview or at the beginning of a subsequent interview summarising on tape the reason for the break and confirming this with the suspect.

4M If one of the tapes breaks during the interview it should be sealed as a master tape in the presence of the suspect and the interview resumed where it left off. The unbroken tape should be copied and the original sealed as a master tape in the suspect's presence, if necessary after the interview. If equipment for copying the unbroken tape is not readily available, both tapes should be sealed in the suspect's presence and the interview begun again. If the tape breaks when a single deck machine is being used and the machine is one where a broken tape cannot be copied on available equipment, the tape should be sealed as a master tape in the suspect's presence and the interview begun again.

5. After the interview

5.1 The police officer shall make a note in his notebook of the fact that the interview has taken place and has been recorded on tape, its time, duration and date and the identification number of the master tape.

5.2 Where no proceedings follow in respect of the person whose interview was recorded the tapes must nevertheless be kept securely in accordance with paragraph 6.1 and Note 6A.

Notes for Guidance

5A Any written record of a tape recorded interview shall be made in accordance with national guidelines approved by the Secretary of State.

6. Tape security

6.1 The officer in charge of each police station at which interviews with suspects are recorded shall make arrangements for master tapes to be kept securely and their movements accounted for on the same basis as other material which may be used for evidential purposes, in accordance with force standing orders. [See Note 6A]

6.2 A police officer has no authority to break the seal on a master tape which is required for criminal proceedings. If it is necessary to gain access to the master tape, the police officer shall arrange for its seal to be broken in the presence of a representative of the Crown Prosecution Service. The defendant or his legal adviser shall be informed and given a reasonable opportunity to be present. If the defendant or his legal representative is present he shall be invited to reseal and sign the master tape. If either refuses or neither is present this shall be done by the representative of the Crown Prosecution Service. [See Notes 6B and 6C]

6.3 Where no criminal proceedings result it is the responsibility of the chief officer of police to establish arrangements for the breaking of the seal on the master tape, where this becomes necessary.

Notes for Guidance

6A   This section is concerned with the security of the master tape which will have been sealed at the conclusion of the interview. Care should, however, be taken of working copies of tapes since their loss or destruction may lead unnecessarily to the need to have access to master tapes.

6B   If the tape has been delivered to the Crown Court for their keeping after committal for trial the crown prosecutor will apply to the chief clerk of the Crown Court centre for the release of the tape for unsealing by the crown prosecutor.

6C   Reference to the Crown Prosecution Service or to the crown prosecutor in this part of the code shall be taken to mean any other body or person with a statutory responsibility for prosecution for whom the police conduct any tape recorded interviews.

ROAD TRAFFIC REGULATION ACT 1984
(1984, c. 27)

89.   Speeding offences generally

(1)   A person who drives a motor vehicle on a road at a speed exceeding a limit imposed by or under any enactment to which this section applies shall be guilty of an offence.

(2)   A person prosecuted for such an offence shall not be liable to be convicted solely on the evidence of one witness to the effect that, in the opinion of the witness, the person prosecuted was driving the vehicle at a speed exceeding a specified limit.

(3)   The enactments to which this section applies are—

(a)   any enactment contained in this Act except section 17(2);

(b)   section 2 of the Parks Regulation (Amendment) Act 1926; and

(c)   any enactment not contained in this Act, but passed after 1st September 1960, whether before or after the passing of this Act.

If a person who employs other persons to drive motor vehicles on roads publishes or issues any time-table or schedule, or gives any directions, under which any journey, or any stage or part of any journey, is to be completed within some specified time, and it is not practicable in the circumstances of the case of that journey (or that stage or part of it) to be completed in the specified time without the commission of such an offence as is mentioned in subsection (1) above, the publication or issue of the time-table or schedule, or the giving of the directions may be produced as prima facie evidence that the employer procured or (as the case may be) incited the persons employed by him to drive the vehicles to commit such an offence.

PROSECUTION OF OFFENCES ACT 1985
(1985, c. 23)

25.   Consents to prosecutions etc.

(1)   This section applies to any enactment which prohibits the institution or carrying on of proceedings for any offence except—

(a)   with the consent (however expressed) of a Law Officer of the Crown or the Director; or

(b)   where the proceedings are instituted or carried on by or on behalf of a Law Officer of the Crown or the Director;

and so applies whether or not there are other exceptions to the prohibition (and in particular whether or not the consent is an alternative to the consent of any other authority or person).

(2)   An enactment to which this section applies—

(a) shall not prevent the arrest without warrant, or the issue or execution of a warrant for the arrest, of a person for any offence, or the remand in custody or on bail of a person charged with any offence; and

(b) shall be subject to any enactment concerning the apprehension or detention of children or young persons.

(3) In this section 'enactment' includes any provision having effect under or by virtue of any Act; and this section applies to enactments whenever passed or made.

26. Consents to be admissible in evidence

Any document purporting to be the consent of a Law Officer of the Crown, the Director or a Crown Prosecutor for, or to—

(a) the institution of any criminal proceedings; or

(b) the institution of criminal proceedings in any particular form;

and to be signed by a Law Officer of the Crown, the Director or, as the case may be, a Crown Prosecutor shall be admissible as prima facie evidence without further proof.

PUBLIC ORDER ACT 1986
(1986, c. 64)

5. Harassment, alarm or distress

(1) A person is guilty of an offence if he—

(a) uses threatening, abusive or insulting words or behaviour, or disorderly behaviour, or

(b) displays any writing, sign or other visible representation which is threatening, abusive or insulting,

within the hearing or sight of a person likely to be caused harassment, alarm or distress thereby.

(2) An offence under this section may be committed in a public or a private place, except that no offence is committed where the words or behaviour are used, or the writing, sign or other visible representation is displayed, by a person inside a dwelling and the other person is also inside that or another dwelling.

(3) It is a defence for the accused to prove—

(a) that he had no reason to believe that there was any person within hearing or sight who was likely to be caused harassment, alarm or distress, or

(b) that he was inside a dwelling and had no reason to believe that the words or behaviour used, or the writing, sign or other visible representation displayed, would be heard or seen by a person outside that or any other dwelling, or

(c) that his conduct was reasonable.

(4) A constable may arrest a person without warrant if—

(a) he engages in offensive conduct which a constable warns him to stop, and

(b) he engages in further offensive conduct immediately or shortly after the warning.

(5) In subsection (4) 'offensive conduct' means conduct the constable reasonably suspects to constitute an offence under this section, and the conduct mentioned in paragraph (a) and the further conduct need not be of the same nature.

(6) A person guilty of an offence under this section is liable on summary conviction to a fine not exceeding level 3 on the standard scale.

CRIMINAL JUSTICE ACT 1987
(1987, c. 38)

1. The Serious Fraud Office

(1) A Serious Fraud Office shall be constituted for England and Wales and Northern Ireland.

(2)   The Attorney General shall appoint a person to be the Director of the Serious Fraud Office (referred to in this Part of this Act as 'the Director'), and he shall discharge his functions under the superintendence of the Attorney General.

(3)   The Director may investigate any suspected offence which appears to him on reasonable grounds to involve serious or complex fraud.

(4)   The Director may, if he thinks fit, conduct any such investigation in conjunction either with the police or with any other person who is, in the opinion of the Director, a proper person to be concerned in it.

(5)   The Director may—

(a)   institute and have the conduct of any criminal proceedings which appear to him to relate to such fraud; and

(b)   take over the conduct of any such proceedings at any stage.

(6)   The Director shall discharge such other functions in relation to fraud as may from time to time be assigned to him by the Attorney General.

(7)   The Director may designate for the purposes of subsection (5) above any member of the Serious Fraud Office who is—

(a)   a barrister in England and Wales or Northern Ireland;

(b)   a solicitor of the Supreme Court; or

(c)   a solicitor of the Supreme Court of Judicature of Northern Ireland.

(8)   Any member so designated shall, without prejudice to any functions which may have been assigned to him in his capacity as a member of that Office, have all the powers of the Director as to the institution and conduct of proceedings but shall exercise those powers under the direction of the Director.

(12)   Any member so designated who is a barrister in Northern Ireland or a solicitor of the Supreme Court of Judicature of Northern Ireland shall have—

(a)   in any court the rights of audience enjoyed by solicitors of the Supreme Court of Judicature of Northern Ireland and, in the Crown Court in Northern Ireland, such additional rights of audience as may be given by virtue of subsection (14) below; and

(b)   in the Crown Court in Northern Ireland, the rights of audience enjoyed by barristers employed by the Director of Public Prosecutions for Northern Ireland.

(13)   Subject to subsection (14) below, the reference in subsection (12)(a) above to rights of audience enjoyed by solicitors of the Supreme Court of Judicature of Northern Ireland is a reference to such rights enjoyed in the Crown Court in Northern Ireland as restricted by any direction given by the Lord Chief Justice of Northern Ireland under section 50 of the Judicature (Northern Ireland) Act 1978.

(14)   For the purpose of giving any member so designated who is a barrister in Northern Ireland or a solicitor of the Supreme Court of Judicature of Northern Ireland additional rights of audience in the Crown Court in Northern Ireland, the Lord Chief Justice of Northern Ireland may direct that any direction given by him under the said section 50 shall not apply to such members.

(15)   Schedule 1 to this Act shall have effect.

(16)   For the purposes of this section (including that Schedule) references to the conduct of any proceedings include references to the proceedings being discontinued and to the taking of any steps (including the bringing of appeal and making of representations in respect of applications for bail) which may be taken in relation to them.

(17)   In the application of this section (including that Schedule) to Northern Ireland references to the Attorney General are to be construed as references to him in his capacity as Attorney General for Northern Ireland.

2.   Director's investigation powers

(1)   The powers of the Director under this section shall be exercisable, but only for the purposes of an investigation under section 1 above, [or, on a request made by the

authority entitled to make such a request,] in any case in which it appears to him that there is good reason to do so for the purpose of investigating the affairs, or any aspect of the affairs, of any person.

(1A) The authorities entitled to request the Director to exercise his powers under this section are—

(a) the Attorney-General of the Isle of Man, Jersey or Guernsey, acting under legislation corresponding to section 1 of this Act and having effect in the Island whose Attorney-General makes the request; and

(b) the Secretary of State acting under section 4(2A) of the Criminal Justice (International Co-operation) Act 1990, in response to a request received by him from an overseas court, tribunal or authority (an 'overseas authority').

(1B) The Director shall not exercise his powers on a request from the Secretary of State acting in reponse to a request received from an overseas authority within subsection (1A)(b) above unless it appears to the Director on reasonable grounds that the offence in respect of which he has been requested to obtain evidence involves serious or complex fraud.

(2) The Director may by notice in writing require the person whose affairs are to be investigated ('the person under the investigation') or any other person whom he has reason to believe has relevant information to [answer questions or otherwise furnish information with respect to any matter relevant to the investigation at a specified place and either at a specified time or forthwith].

(3) The Director may by notice in writing require the person under investigation or any other person to produce at [such place as may be specified in the notice and either forthwith or at such time as may be so specified] any specified documents which appear to the Director to relate to any matter relevant to the investigation or any documents of a specified [description] which appear to him so to relate; and—

(a) if any such documents are produced, the Director may—

(i) take copies or extracts from them;

(ii) require the person producing them to provide an explanation of any of them;

(b) if any such documents are not produced, the Director may require the person who was required to produce them to state, to the best of his knowledge and belief, where they are.

(4) Where, on information on oath laid by a member of the Serious Fraud Office, a justice of the peace if satisfied, in relation to any documents, that there are reasonable grounds for believing—

(a) that—

(i) a person has failed to comply with an obligation under this section to produce them;

(ii) it is not practicable to serve a notice under subsection (3) above in relation to them; or

(iii) the service of such a notice in relation to them might seriously prejudice the investigation; and

(b) that they are on premises specified in the information,
he may issue such a warrant as is mentioned in subsection (5) below.

(5) the warrant referred to above is a warrant authorising any constable—

(a) to enter (using such force as is reasonably necessary for the purpose) and search the premises, and

(b) to take possession of any documents appearing to be documents of the description specified in the information or to take in relation to any documents so appearing any other steps which may appear to be necessary for preserving them and preventing interference with them.

(6) Unless it is not practicable in the circumstances, a constable executing a warrant issued under subsection (4) above shall be accompanied by an appropriate person.

(7)   In subsection (6) above 'appropriate person' means—
    (a)   a member of the Serious Fraud Office; or
    (b)   some person who is not a member of that Office but whom the Director has authorised to accompany the constable.

(8)   A statement by a person in response to a requirement imposed by virtue of this section may only be used in evidence against him—
    (a)   on a prosecution for an offence under subsection (14) below; or
    (b)   on a prosecution for some other offence where in giving evidence he makes a statement inconsistent with it.

(8A)   Any evidence obtained by the Director for use by an overseas authority shall be furnished by him to the Secretary of State for transmission to the overseas authority which requested it.

(8B)   If in order to comply with the request of the overseas authority it is necessary for any evidence obtained by the Director to be accompanied by any certificate, affidavit or other verifying document, the Director shall also furnish for transmission such document of that nature as may be specified by the Secretary of State when asking the Director to obtain the evidence.

(8C)   Where any evidence obtained by the Director for use by an overseas authority consists of a document the original or a copy shall be transmitted, and where it consists of any other article the article itself or a description, photograph or other representation of it shall be transmitted, as may be necessary in order to comply with the request of the overseas authority; and

(8D)   However, the statement may not be used against that person by virtue of paragraph (b) of subsection (8) unless evidence relating to it is adduced, or a question relating to it is asked, by or on behalf of that person in the proceedings arising out of the prosecution.

(9)   A person shall not under this section be required to disclose any information or produce any document which he would be entitled to refuse to disclose or produce on grounds of legal professional privilege in proceedings in the High Court, except that a lawyer may be required to furnish the name and address of his client.

(10)   A person shall not under this section be required to disclose information or produce a document in respect of which he owes an obligation of confidence by virtue of carrying on any banking business unless—
    (a)   the person to whom the obligation of confidence is owed consents to the disclosure or production; or
    (b)   the Director has authorised the making of the requirement or, if it is impracticable for him to act personally, a member of the Serious Fraud Office designated by him for the purposes of this subsection has done so.

(11)   Without prejudice to the power of the Director to assign functions to members of the Serious Fraud Office, the Director may authorise any competent investigator (other than a constable) who is not a member of that Office to exercise on his behalf all or any of the powers conferred by this section, but no such authority shall be granted except for the purpose of investigating the affairs, or any aspect of the affairs, of a person specified in the authority.

(12)   No person shall be bound to comply with any requirement imposed by a person exercising powers by virtue of any authority granted under subsection (11) above unless he has, if required to do so, produced evidence of his authority.

(13)   Any person who without reasonable excuse fails to comply with a requirement imposed on him under this section shall be guilty of an offence and liable on summary conviction to imprisonment for a term not exceeding six months or to a fine not exceeding level 5 on the standard scale or to both.

(14)   A person who, in purported compliance with a requirement under this section—

(a)   makes a statement which he knows to be false or misleading in a material particular; or

(b)   recklessly makes a statement which is false or misleading in a material particular,

shall be guilty of an offence.

(15)   A person guilty of an offence under subsection (14) above shall—

(a)   on conviction on indictment, be liable to imprisonment for a term, not exceeding two years or to a fine or to both; and

(b)   on summary conviction, be liable to imprisonment for a term not exceeding six months or to a fine not exceeding the statutory maximum, or to both.

(16)   Where any person—

(a)   knows or suspects that an investigation by the police or the Serious Fraud Office into serious or complex fraud is being or is likely to be carried out; and

(b)   falsifies, conceals, destroys or otherwise disposes of, or causes or permits the falsification, concealment, destruction or disposal of documents which he knows or suspects are or would be relevant to such an investigation,

he shall be guilty of an offence unless he proves that he had no intention of concealing the facts disclosed by the documents from persons carrying out such an investigation.

(17)   A person guilty of an offence under subsection (16) above shall—

(a)   on conviction on indictment, be liable to impriment for a term not exceeding 7 years or to a fine or to both; and

(b)   on summary conviction, be liable to imprisonment for a term not exceeding 6 months or to a fine not exceeding the statutory maximum or to both.

(18)   In this section, 'documents' includes information recorded in any form and, in relation to information recorded otherwise than in legible form, references to its production include references to producing a copy of the information in legible form [; and 'evidence' (in relation to subsection (1A)(b), (8A), (8B) and (8C) above) includes documents and other articles.]

(19)   . . .; and in the application of this section to Northern Ireland, subsection (4) above shall have effect as if for the references to information there were substituted references to a complaint.

CRIMINAL JUSTICE ACT 1988
(1988, c. 33)

23.   First-hand hearsay

(1)   Subject—

(a)   to subsection (4) below; and

(b)   to paragraph 1A of Schedule 2 to the Criminal Appeal Act 1968 (evidence given orally at original trial to be given orally at retrial),

a statement made by a person in a document shall be admissible in criminal proceedings as evidence of any fact of which direct oral evidence by him would be admissible if—

(i)   the requirements of one of the paragraphs of subsection (2) below are satisfied; or

(ii)   the requirements of subsection (3) below are satisfied.

(2)   The requirements mentioned in subsection (1)(i) above are—

(a)   that the person who made the statement is dead or by reason of his bodily or mental condition unfit to attend as a witness;

(b)   that—

(i)   the person who made the statement is outside the United Kingdom; and

(ii)   it is not reasonably practicable to secure his attendance; or

(c)   that all reasonable steps have been taken to find the person who made the statement, but that he cannot be found.

(3)   The requirements mentioned in subsection (1)(ii) above are—

(a)   that the statement was made to a police officer or some other person charged with the duty of investigating offences or charging offenders; and

(b)   that the person who made it does not give oral evidence through fear or because he is kept out of the way.

(4)   Subsection (1) above does not render admissible a confession made by an accused person that would not be admissible under section 76 of the Police and Criminal Evidence Act 1984.

(5)   This section shall not apply to proceedings before a magistrates' court inquiring into an offence as examining justices.

24.   Business etc. documents

(1)   Subject—

(a)   to subsections (3) and (4) below; and

(b)   to paragraph 1A of Schedule 2 to the Criminal Appeal Act 1968,

a statement in a document shall be admissible in criminal proceedings as evidence of any fact of which direct oral evidence would be admissible, if the following conditions are satisfied—

(i)   the document was created or received by a person in the course of a trade, business, profession or other occupation, or as the holder of a paid or unpaid office; and

(ii)   the information contained in the document was supplied by a person (whether or not the maker of the statement) who had, or may reasonably be supposed to have had, personal knowledge of the matters dealt with.

(2)   Subsection (1) above applies whether the information contained in the document was supplied directly or indirectly but if it was supplied indirectly, only if each person through whom it was supplied received it—

(a)   in the course of a trade, business, profession or other occupation; or

(b)   as the holder of a paid or unpaid office.

(3)   Subsection (1) above does not render admissible a confession made by an accused person that would not be admissible under section 76 of the Police and Criminal Evidence Act 1984.

(4)   A statement prepared otherwise than in accordance with section 3 of the Criminal Justice (International Co-operation) Act 1990 below or an order under paragraph 6 of Schedule 13 to this Act or under section 30 or 31 below for the purposes—

(a)   of pending or contemplated criminal proceedings; or

(b)   of a criminal investigation,

shall not be admissible by virtue of subsection (1) above unless—

(i)   the requirements of one of the paragraphs of subsection (2) of section 23 above are satisfied; or

(ii)   the requirements of subsection (3) of that section are satisfied; or

(iii)   the person who made the statement cannot reasonably be expected (having regard to the time which has elapsed since he made the statement and to all the circumstances) to have any recollection of the matters dealt with in the statement.

(5)   This section shall not apply before a magistrates' court inquiring into an offence as examining justices.

25.   Principles to be followed by court

(1)   If, having regard to all the circumstances—

(a)   the Crown Court—

(i)   on a trial on indictment;

(ii)   on an appeal from a magistrates' court;

(iii)   on the hearing of an application under section 6 of the Criminal Justice Act 1987 (applications for dismissal or charges of fraud transferred from magistrates' court or Crown Court);

(iv)   on the hearing of an application under paragraph 5 of Schedule 6 to the Criminal Justice Act 1991 (applications for dismissal of charges in certain cases involving children transferred from magistrates' courts to Crown Court); or

(b)   the criminal division of the Court of Appeal; or

(c)   a magistrates' court on a trial of an information,

is of the opinion that in the interests of justice a statement which is admissible by virtue of section 23 or 24 above nevertheless ought not to be admitted, it may direct that the statement shall not be admitted.

(2)   Without prejudice to the generality of subsection (1) above, it shall be the duty of the court to have regard—

(a)   to the nature and source of the document containing the statement and to whether or not, having regard to its nature and source and to any other circumstances that appear to the court to be relevant, it is likely that the document is authentic;

(b)   to the extent to which the statement appears to supply evidence which would otherwise not be readily available;

(c)   to the relevance of the evidence that it appears to supply to any issue which is likely to have to be determined in the proceedings; and

(d)   to any risk, having regard in particular to whether it is likely to be possible to controvert the statement if the person making it does not attend to give oral evidence in the proceedings, that its admission or exclusion will result in unfairness to the accused or, if there is more than one, to any of them.

26.   Statements in documents that appear to have been prepared for purposes of criminal proceedings or investigations

Where a statement which is admissible in criminal proceedings by virtue of section 23 or 24 above appears to the court to have been prepared, otherwise than in accordance with section 3 of the Criminal Justice (International Co-operation) Act 1990 below or an order under paragraph 6 of Schedule 13 to this Act or under section 30 or 31 below, for the purposes—

(a)   of pending or contemplated criminal proceedings; or

(b)   of a criminal investigation,

the statement shall not be given in evidence in any criminal proceedings without the leave of the court, and the court shall not give leave unless it is of the opinion that the statement ought to be admitted in the interests of justice; and in considering whether its admission would be in the interests of justice, it shall be the duty of the court to have regard—

(i)   to the contents of the statement;

(ii)   to any risk, having regard in particular to whether it is likely to be possible to controvert the statement if the person making it does not attend to give oral evidence in the proceedings, that its admission or exclusion will result in unfairness to the accused or, if there is more than one, to any of them; and

(iii)   to any other circumstances that appear to the court to be relevant.

This section shall not apply to proceedings before a magistrates' court inquiring into an offence as examining justices.

27.   Proof of statements contained in documents

Where a statement contained in a document is admissible as evidence in criminal proceedings, it may be proved—

(a)   by the production of that document; or

(b)   (whether or not that document is still in existence) by the production of a copy of that document, or of the material part of it,

authenticated in such manner as the court may approve; and it is immaterial for the purposes of this subsection how many removes there are between a copy and the original.

This section shall not apply to proceedings before a magistrates' court inquiring into an offence as examining justices.

28. Documentary evidence—supplementary

(1) Nothing in this Part of this Act shall prejudice—

(a) the admissibility of a statement not made by a person while giving oral evidence in court which is admissible otherwise than by virtue of this Part of this Act; or

(b) any power of a court to exclude at its discretion a statement admissible by virtue of this Part of this Act.

(2) Schedule 2 to this Act shall have effect for the purpose of supplementing this Part of this Act.

PART III
OTHER PROVISIONS ABOUT EVIDENCE IN CRIMINAL PROCEEDINGS

30. Expert reports

(1) An expert report shall be admissible as evidence in criminal proceedings, whether or not the person making it attends to give oral evidence in those proceedings.

(2) If it is proposed that the person making the report shall not give oral evidence, the report shall only be admissible with the leave of the court.

(3) For the purpose of determining whether to give leave the court shall have regard—

(a) to the contents of the report;

(b) to the reasons why it is proposed that the person making the report shall not give oral evidence;

(c) to any risk, having regard in particular to whether it is likely to be possible to controvert statements in the report if the person making it does not attend to give oral evidence in the proceedings, that its admission or exclusion will result in unfairness to the accused or, if there is more than one, to any of them; and

(d) to any other circumstances that appear to the court to be relevant.

(4) An expert report, when admitted, shall be evidence of any fact or opinion of which the person making it could have given oral evidence.

(4A) Where the proceedings mentioned in subsection (1) above are proceedings before a magistrates' court inquiring into an offence as examining justices this section shall have effect with the omission of—

(a) in subsection (1) the words 'whether or not the person making it attends to give oral evidence in those proceedings', and

(b) subsections (2) to (4).

(5) In this section 'expert report' means a written report by a person dealing wholly or mainly with matters on which he is (or would if living be) qualified to give expert evidence.

31. Form of evidence and glossaries

For the purpose of helping members of juries to understand complicated issues of fact or technical terms Crown Court Rules may make provision:

(a) as to the furnishing of evidence in any form, notwithstanding the existence of admissible material from which the evidence to be given in that form would be derived; and

(b) as to the furnishing of glossaries for such purposes as may be specified;

in any case where the court gives leave for, or requires, evidence or a glossary to be so furnished.

This section shall not apply to proceedings before a magistrates' court inquiring into an offence as examining justices.

32. Evidence through television links

(1)   A person other than the accused may give evidence through a live television link in proceedings to which subsection (1A) below applies if:

(a)   the witness is outside the United Kingdom.

but evidence may not be so given without the leave of the court.

(1A)   This subsection applies:

(a)   to trials on indictment, appeals to the criminal division of the Court of Appeal and hearings of references under section 9 of the Criminal Appeal Act 1995; and

(b)   to proceedings in youth courts, appeals to the Crown Court arising out of such proceedings and hearings of references under section 11 of the Criminal Appeal Act 1995 so arising.

(3)   A statement made on oath by a witness outside the United Kingdom and given in evidence through a link by virtue of this section shall be treated for the purposes of section 1 of the Perjury Act 1911 as having been made in the proceedings in which it is given in evidence.

(3B)   A place appointed under subsection (3A) above may be outside the petty sessions area for which it is appointed; but it shall be deemed to be in that area for the purpose of the jurisdiction of the justices acting for that area

(3C)   Where—

(a)   the court gives leave for a person to give evidence through a live television link, and

(b)   the leave is given by virtue of subsection (1)(b) above,

then, subject to subsection (3D) below, the person concerned may not give evidence otherwise than through a live television link.

(3D)   In a case falling within subsection (3C) above the court may give permission for the person to give evidence otherwise than through a live television link if it appears to the court to be in the interests of justice to give such permission.

(4)   Without prejudice to the generality of any enactment conferring power to make rules to which this subsection applies, such rules may make such provision as appears to the authority making them to be necessary or expedient for the purposes of this section.

(5)   The rules to which subsection (4) above applies are:

Magistrates' Courts Rules;

Crown Court Rules;

and

Criminal Appeal Rules.

34. Abolition of requirement of corroboration for unsworn evidence of children

(2)   Any requirement whereby at a trial on indictment it is obligatory for the court to give the jury a warning about convicting the accused on the uncorroborated evidence of a child is abrogated.

(3)   Unsworn evidence admitted by virtue of section 56 of the Youth Justice and Criminal Evidence Act 1999 may corroborate evidence (sworn or unsworn) given by any other person.

SCHEDULE 2
DOCUMENTARY EVIDENCE—SUPPLEMENTARY

1.   Where a statement is admitted as evidence in criminal proceedings by virtue of Part II of this Act—

(a)   any evidence which, if the person making the statement had been called as a witness, would have been admissible as relevant to his credibility as a witness shall be admissible for that purpose in those proceedings;

(b)   evidence may, with the leave of the court, be given of any matter which, if that person had been called as a witness, could have been put to him in cross-examination as relevant to his credibility as a witness but of which evidence could not have been adduced by the cross-examining party; and

(c)   evidence tending to prove that that person, whether before or after making the statement, made (whether orally or not) some other statement which is inconsistent with it shall be admissible for the purpose of showing that he has contradicted himself.

2.   A statement which is given in evidence by virtue of Part II of this Act shall not be capable of corroborating evidence given by the person making it.

3.   In estimating the weight, if any, to be attached to such a statement regard shall be had to all the circumstances from which any inference can reasonably be drawn as to its accuracy or otherwise.

4.   Without prejudice to the generality of any enactment conferring power to make them—

(a)   Crown Court Rules;

(b)   Criminal Appeal Rules; and

(c)   rules under section 144 of the Magistrates' Courts Act 1980,

may make such provision as appears to the authority making any of them to be necessary or expedient for the purposes of Part II of this Act.

5.—(1)   In Part II of this Act—

'document' means anything in which information of any description is recorded;

'copy', in relation to a document, means anything onto which information recorded in the document has been copied, by whatever means and whether directly or indirectly; and

'statement' means any representation of fact, however made.

(2)   For the purposes of Part II of this Act evidence which, by reason of a defect of speech or hearing, a person called as a witness gives in writing or by signs shall be treated as given orally.

6.   In Part II of this Act 'confession' has the meaning assigned to it by section 82 of the Police and Criminal Evidence Act 1984.

SCHEDULE 13

1.   In this Schedule—

'procedural instruments' means—

(a)   rules under section 103 of the Army Act 1955 or section 103 of the Air Force Act 1955;

(b)   rules under section 58 of the Naval Discipline Act 1957;

(c)   rules under section 49 of the Courts-Martial (Appeals) Act 1968; and

(d)   orders under paragraph 12 of Schedule 3 to the Armed Forces Act 1976; and

'Service courts' means—

(a)   courts-martial constituted under the Army Act 1955 or the Air Force Act 1955;

(b)   courts-martial constituted under the Naval Discipline Act 1957 and disciplinary courts constituted under section 52G of that Act;

(c)   the Courts-Martial Appeal Court; and

(d)   Standing Civilian Courts.

First-hand hearsay

2.   Sections 23 and 24 above shall have effect in relation to proceedings in the United Kingdom or elsewhere before Service courts with the substitution of the following sub-paragraph for section 23(2)(b)(i)—

'(i)   the person who made the statement is not in the country where the court is sitting; and'.

Documentary evidence

3.   Section 25 above shall have effect in relation to proceedings in the United Kingdom or elsewhere before Service courts as if such proceedings were mentioned in subsection (1) of that section.

4.   In section 26 above—

(a)   the reference to criminal proceedings in paragraph (a) includes summary proceedings under section 76B of the Army Act 1955, section 76B of the Air Force Act 1955 or section 52D of the Naval Discipline Act 1957; and

(b)   in paragraph (b) 'criminal investigation' includes any investigation which may lead—

(i)   to proceedings before a court-martial or Standing Civilian Court; or

(ii)   to summary proceedings such as are mentioned in sub-paragraph (a) above.

5.   Without prejudice to the generality of any enactment conferring power to make them, procedural instruments may make such provision as appears to the authority making any of them to be necessary or expedient for the purposes of Part II of this Act.

Letters of request etc.

6.—(1)   In section 29 above 'criminal proceedings' does not include proceedings before a Service court, but the Secretary of State may by order make provision as to letters of request or corresponding documents for such proceedings.

(2)   An order under this paragraph may make different provision for different classes of case.

(3)   The power to make an order under this paragraph shall be exercisable by statutory instrument and a statutory instrument containing any such order shall be subject to annulment in pursuance of a resolution of either House of Parliament.

(4)   Without prejudice to the generality of any enactment conferring power to make procedural instruments, procedural instruments may make such provision as appears to the authority making them to be necessary or expedient in relation to letters of request or corresponding documents for proceedings before a Service court.

Form of evidence and glossaries

7.   For the purpose of helping members—

(a)   of courts-martial constituted under the Army Act 1955 or the Air Force Act 1955; or

(b)   of courts-martial constituted under the Naval Discipline Act 1957 or disciplinary courts constituted under section 52G of that Act,

to understand complicated issues of fact or technical terms rules under section 103 of either of the first two of those Acts and rules under section 58 of the Naval Discipline Act 1957 may make provision—

(i)   as to the furnishing of evidence in any form, notwithstanding the existence of admissible material from which the evidence to be given in that form would be derived; and

(ii)   as to the furnishing of glossaries for such purposes as may be specified;

in any case where the court gives leave for, or requires, evidence or a glossary to be so furnished.

Use of television links

8.—(1)   The Secretary of State may by order direct that section 32(1) to (3) above shall have effect in relation—

(a)   to proceedings before Service courts; or

(b)   to proceedings or proceedings of specified descriptions before Service courts in specified places.

(2)   If an order is made under this paragraph—

(a)   subsection (1) of section 32 above shall have effect in relation to any court to which the order applies with the substitution of the following paragraph for paragraph (a)—

'(a)   the witness is not in the country where the court is sitting; or';

(3)   An order under this paragraph may provide that section 32(1) or (3) above shall have effect in relation to any court to which the order applies subject to such modifications as may be specified in the order, in addition to the modifications for which sub-paragraph (2) above provides.

(4)   The power to make an order conferred by this paragraph shall be exercisable by statutory instrument and a statutory instrument containing any such order shall be subject to annulment in pursuance of a resolution of either House of Parliament.

(5)   Without prejudice to the generality of any enactment conferring power to make procedural instruments, procedural instruments may make such provision as appears to the authority making them to be necessary or expedient for the purposes of section 32(1) to (3) above in their application to proceedings such as are mentioned in sub-paragraph (1) above by virtue of an order under that sub-paragraph.

(6)   In this paragraph 'modifications' includes additions, omissions and amendments.

ROAD TRAFFIC OFFENDERS ACT 1988
(1988, c. 53)

11.   Evidence by certificate as to driver, user or owner

(1)   In any proceedings in England and Wales for an offence to which this section applies, a certificate in the prescribed form, purporting to be signed by a constable and certifying that a person specified in the certificate stated to the constable—

(a)   that a particular mechanically propelled vehicle was being driven or used by, or belonged to, that person on a particular occasion, or

(b)   that a particular mechanically propelled vehicle on a particular occasion was used by, or belonged to, a firm and that he was, at the time of the statement, a partner in that firm, or

(c)   that a particular mechanically propelled vehicle on a particular occasion was used by, or belonged to, a corporation and that he was, at the time of the statement, a director, officer or employee of that corporation,

shall be admissible as evidence for the purpose of determining by whom the vehicle was being driven or used, or to whom it belonged, as the case may be, on that occasion.

(2)   Nothing in subsection (1) above makes a certificate admissible as evidence in proceedings for an offence except in a case where and to the like extent to which oral evidence to the like effect would have been admissible in those proceedings.

(3)   Nothing in subsection (1) above makes a certificate admissible as evidence in proceedings for an offence—

(a)   unless a copy of it has, not less than seven days before the hearing or trial, been served in the prescribed manner on the person charged with the offence, or

(b)   if that person, not later than three days before the hearing or trial or within such further time as the court in special circumstances allow, serves a notice in the prescribed form and manner on the prosecutor requiring the attendance at the trial of the person who signed the certificate.

(3A)   Where the proceedings mentioned in subsection (1) above are proceedings before a magistrates' court inquiring into an offence as examining justices this section shall have effect with the omission of—

(a)   subsection (2), and

(b)   in subsection (3), paragraph (b) and the word 'or' immediately preceding it.

12.   Proof, in summary proceedings, of identity of driver of vehicle

(1)   Where on the summary trial in England and Wales of an information for an offence to which this subsection applies—

(a)   it is proved to the satisfaction of the court, on oath or in manner prescribed by rules made under section 144 of the Magistrates' Courts Act 1980, that a requirement under section 172(2) of the Road Traffic Act 1988 to give information as to the identity of the driver of a particular vehicle on the particular occasion to which the information relates has been served on the accused by post, and

(b)   a statement in writing is produced to the court purporting to be signed by the accused that the accused was the driver of that vehicle on that occasion,

the court may accept that statement as evidence that the accused was the driver of that vehicle on that occasion.

(2)   Schedule 1 to this Act shows the offences to which subsection (1) above applies.

(3)   Where on the summary trial in England and Wales of an information for an offence to which section 112 of the Road Traffic Regulation Act 1984 applies—

(a)   it is proved to the satisfaction of the court, on oath or in manner prescribed by rules made under section 144 of the Magistrates' Courts Act 1980, that a requirement under section 112(2) of the Road Traffic Regulation Act 1984 to give information as to the identity of the driver of a particular vehicle on the particular occasion to which the information relates has been served on the accused by post, and

(b)   a statement in writing is produced to the court purporting to be signed by the accused that the accused was the driver of that vehicle on that occasion,

the court may accept that statement as evidence that the accused was the driver of that vehicle on that occasion.

(4)   In summary proceedings in Scotland . . .

13.   Admissibility of records as evidence

(1)   This section applies to a statement contained in a document purporting to be—

(a)   a part of the records maintained by the Secretary of State in connection with any functions exercisable by him by virtue of Part III of the Road Traffic Act 1988 or a part of any other records maintained by the Secretary of State with respect to vehicles, or

(b)   a copy of a document forming part of those records, or

(c)   a note of any information contained in those records,

and to be authenticated by a person authorised in that behalf by the Secretary of State.

(2)   A statement to which this section applies shall be admissible in any proceedings as evidence (in Scotland, sufficient evidence) of any fact stated in it to the same extent as oral evidence of that fact is admissible in those proceedings.

(3)   In the preceding subsections, except in Scotland—

'copy', in relation to a document, means anything onto which information recorded in the document has been copied, by whatever means and whether directly or indirectly;

'document' means anything in which information of any description is recorded; and

'statement' means any representation of fact, however made.

[(3A)   In any case where—

(a)   a person is convicted by a magistrates' court of a summary offence under the Traffic Acts or the Road Traffic (Driver Licensing and Information Systems) Act 1989,

(b)   a statement to which this section applies is produced to the court in the proceedings,

(c)   the statement specifies an alleged previous conviction of the accused of an offence involving obligatory endorsment or an order made on the conviction, and

(d)   the accused is not present in the person before the court when the statement is produced,

the court may take account of the previous conviction or order as if the accused had appeared and admitted it.

(3B)   Section 104 of the Magistrates' Courts Act 1980 (under which the previous convictions may be adduced in the absence of the accused after giving him seven days' notice of them) does not limit the effect of subsection (3A) above.]

(4)   In any case where—

(a)   a statement to which this section applies is produced to a magistrates' court in any proceedings for an offence involving obligatory or discretionary disqualification [other than a summary offence under any of the enactments mentioned in subsection (3A) above],

(b)   the statement specifies an alleged previous conviction of an accused person of any such offence or any order made on the conviction,

(c)   it is proved to the satisfaction of the court, on oath or in such manner as may be prescribed by rules under section 144 of the Magistrates' Courts Act 1980, that not less than seven days before the statement is so produced a notice was served on the accused, in such form and manner as may be so prescribed, specifying the previous conviction or order and stating that it is proposed to bring it to the notice of the court in the event of or, as the case may be, in view of his conviction, and

(d)   the accused is not present in person before the court when the statement is so produced,

the court may take account of the previous conviction or order as if the accused had appeared and admitted it.

(5)   Nothing in the preceding provisions of this section enables evidence to be given in respect of any matter other than a matter of a description prescribed by regulations made by the Secretary of State.

(6)   The power to make regulations under this section shall be exercisable by statutory instrument, which shall be subject to annulment in pursuance of a resolution of either House of Parliament.

(7)   Where the proceedings mentioned in subsection (2) above are proceedings before a magistrates' court inquiring into an offence as examining justices this section shall have effect as if—

(a)   in subsection (2) the words 'to the same extent as oral evidence of that fact is admissible in those proceedings' were omitted;

(b)   in subsection (4) the word 'and' were inserted at the end of paragraph (a);

(c)   in subsection (4), paragraphs (c) and (d) and the words 'as if the accused had appeared and admitted it' were omitted.

16.   Documentary evidence as to specimens in such proceedings

(1)   Evidence of the proportion of alcohol or a drug in a specimen of breath, blood or urine may, subject to subsections (3) and (4) below and to section 15(5) of this Act, be given by the production of a document or documents purporting to be whichever of the following is appropriate, that is to say—

(a)   a statement automatically produced by the device by which the proportion of alcohol in a specimen of breath was measured and a certificate signed by a constable (which may but need not be contained in the same document as the statement) that the statement relates to a specimen provided by the accused at the date and time shown in the statement, and

(b)   a certificate signed by an authorised analyst as to the proportion of alcohol or any drug found in a specimen of blood or urine identified in the certificate.

(2)   Subject to subsections (3) and (4) below, evidence that a specimen of blood was taken from the accused with his consent by a medical practitioner may be given by the

production of a document purporting to certify that fact and to be signed by a medical practitioner.

(3) Subject to subsection (4) below—

(a) a document purporting to be such a statement or such a certificate (or both such a statement and such a certificate) as is mentioned in subsection (1)(a) above is admissible in evidence on behalf of the prosecution in pursuance of this section only if a copy of it either has been handed to the accused when the document was produced or has been served on him not later than seven days before the hearing, and

(b) any other document is so admissible only if a copy of it has been served on the accused not later than seven days before the hearing.

(4) A document purporting to be a certificate (or so much of a document as purports to be a certificate) is not so admissible if the accused, not later than three days before the hearing or within such further time as the court may in special circumstances allow, has served notice on the prosecutor requiring the attendance at the hearing of the person by whom the document purports to be signed.

(5) (Applies to Scotland only.)

(6) A copy of a certificate required by this section to be served on the accused or a notice required by this section to be served on the prosecutor may be served personally or sent by registered post or recorded delivery service.

(6A) Where the proceedings mentioned in section 15(1) of this Act are proceedings before a magistrates' court inquiring into an offence as examining justices this section shall have effect with the omission of subsection (4).

(7) In this section 'authorised analyst' means—

(a) any person possessing the qualifications prescribed by regulations made under section 27 of the Food Safety Act 1990 as qualifying persons for appointment as public analysts under those Acts, and

(b) any other person authorised by the Secretary of State to make analyses for the purposes of this section.

18. Evidence by certificate as to registration of driving instructors and licences to give instruction

(1) A certificate signed by the Registrar and stating that, on any date—

(a) a person's name was, or was not, in the register,

(b) the entry of a person's name was made in the register or a person's name was removed from it,

(c) a person was, or was not, the holder of a current licence under section 129 of the Road Traffic Act 1988, or

(d) a licence under that section granted to a person came into force or ceased to be in force,

shall be evidence, and in Scotland sufficient evidence, of the facts stated in the certificate in pursuance of this section.

(2) A certificate so stating and purporting to be signed by the Registrar shall be deemed to be so signed unless the contrary is proved.

(3) In this section 'current licence', 'Registrar' and 'register' have the same meanings as in Part V of the Road Traffic Act 1988.

CHILDREN ACT 1989
(1989, c. 41)

96. Evidence given by, or with respect to, children

(1) Subsection (2) applies where a child who is called as a witness in any civil proceedings does not, in the opinion of the court, understand the nature of an oath.

(2)   The child's evidence may be heard by the court if, in its opinion—

(a)   he understands that it is his duty to speak the truth; and

(b)   he has sufficient understanding to justify his evidence being heard.

(3)   The Lord Chancellor may by order make provision for the admissibility of evidence which would otherwise be inadmissible under any rule of law relating to hearsay.

(4)   An order under subsection (3) may only be made with respect to—

(a)   civil proceedings in general or such civil proceedings, or class of civil proceedings, as may be prescribed; and

(b)   evidence in connection with the upbringing, maintenance or welfare of a child.

(5)   An order under subsection (3)—

(a)   may, in particular, provide for the admissibility of statements which are made orally or in a prescribed form or which are recorded by any prescribed method of recording;

(b)   may make different provision for different purposes and in relation to different descriptions of court; and

(c)   may make such amendments and repeals in any enactment relating to evidence (other than in this Act) as the Lord Chancellor considers necessary or expedient in consequence of the provision made by the order.

(6)   Subsection (5)(b) is without prejudice to section 104(4).

(7)   In this section—

'civil proceedings' means civil proceedings, before any tribunal, in relation to which the strict rules of evidence apply, whether as a matter of law or agreement between the parties, and reference to 'the court' shall be construed accordingly; and

'prescribed' means prescribed by an order under subsection (3).

98.   Self-incrimination

(1)   In any proceedings in which a court is hearing an application for an order under Part IV or V, no person shall be excused from—

(a)   giving evidence on any matter; or

(b)   answering any question put to him in the course of his giving evidence,

on the ground that doing so might incriminate him or his spouse of an offence.

(2)   A statement or admission made in such proceedings shall not be admissible in evidence against the person making it or his spouse in proceedings for an offence other than perjury.

PREVENTION OF TERRORISM (TEMPORARY PROVISIONS) ACT 1989
(1989, c. 4)

PART I
PROSCRIBED ORGANISATIONS

1.   Proscribed organisations

(1)   Any organisation for the time being specified in Schedule 1 to this Act is a proscribed organisation for the purposes of this Act; and any organisation which passes under a name mentioned in that Schedule shall be treated as proscribed whatever relationship (if any) it has to any other organisation of the same name.

(2)   The Secretary of State may by order made by statutory instrument—

(a)   add to Schedule 1 to this Act any organisation that appears to him to be concerned in, or in promoting or encouraging, terrorism occurring in the United Kingdom and connected with the affairs of Northern Ireland;

(b)   remove an organisation from that Schedule.

(3)   No order shall be made under this section unless—

(a)   a draft of the order has been laid before and approved by a resolution of each House of Parliament; or

(b)   it is declared in the order that it appears to the Secretary of State that by reason of urgency it is necessary to make the order without a draft having been so approved.

(4)   An order under this section of which a draft has not been approved under subsection (3) above—

(a)   shall be laid before Parliament; and

(b)   shall cease to have effect at the end of the period of forty days beginning with the day on which it was made unless, before the end of that period, the order has been approved by a resolution of each House of Parliament, but without prejudice to anything previously done or to the making of a new order.

(5)   In reckoning for the purposes of subsection (4) above any period of forty days, no account shall be taken of any period during which Parliament is dissolved or prorogued or during which both Houses are adjourned for more than four days.

(6)   In this section 'organisation' includes any association or combination of persons.

2.   Membership, support and meetings

(1)   Subject to subsection (3) below, a person is guilty of an offence if he—

(a)   belongs or professes to belong to a proscribed organisation;

(b)   solicits or invites support for a proscribed organisation other than support with money or other property; or

(c)   arranges or assists in the arrangement or management of, or addresses, any meeting of three or more persons (whether or not it is a meeting to which the public are admitted) knowing that the meeting is—

(i)   to support a proscribed organisation;

(ii)   to further the activities of such an organisation; or

(iii)   to be addressed by a person belonging or professing to belong to such an organisation.

(2)   A person guilty of an offence under subsection (1) above is liable—

(a)   on conviction on indictment, to imprisonment for a term not exceeding ten years or a fine or both;

(b)   on summary conviction, to imprisonment for a term not exceeding six months or a fine not exceeding the statutory maximum or both.

(3)   A person belonging to a proscribed organisation is not guilty of an offence under this section by reason of belonging to the organisation if he shows—

(a)   that he became a member when it was not a proscribed organisation under the current legislation; and

(b)   that he has not since he became a member taken part in any of its activities at any time while it was a proscribed organisation under that legislation.

(4)   In subsection (3) above 'the current legislation', in relation to any time, means whichever of the following was in force at that time—

(a)   the Prevention of Terrorism (Temporary Provisions) Act 1974;

(b)   the Prevention of Terrorism (Temporary Provisions) Act 1976;

(c)   the Prevention of Terrorism (Temporary Provisions) Act 1984; or

(d)   this Act.

(5)   The reference in subsection (3) above to a person becoming a member of an organisation is a reference to the only or last occasion on which he became a member.

2A.   Evidence and inferences

(1)   This section applies where a person is charged with an offence under section 2(1)(a) above; and references here to a specified organisation must be construed in accordance with section 2B below.

(2)   Subsection (3) below applies if a police officer of or above the rank of superintendent states in oral evidence that in his opinion the accused—

    (a)   belongs to an organisation which is specified, or

    (b)   belonged at a particular time to an organisation which was then specified.

(3)   If this subsection applies—

    (a)   the statement shall be admissible as evidence of the matter stated, but

    (b)   the accused shall not be committed for trial in England and Wales, or be found to have a case to answer or be convicted, solely on the basis of the statement.

(4)   Subsection (6) below applies if evidence is given that—

    (a)   at any time before being charged with the offence the accused, on being questioned under caution by a constable, failed to mention a fact which is material to the offence and which he could reasonably be expected to mention, and

    (b)   before being questioned he was permitted to consult a solicitor.

(5)   Subsection (6) below also applies if evidence is given that—

    (a)   on being charged with the offence or informed by a constable that he might be prosecuted for it the accused failed to mention a fact which is material to the offence and which he could reasonably be expected to mention, and

    (b)   before being charged or informed he was permitted to consult a solicitor.

(6)   If this subsection applies—

    (a)   the court or jury, in considering any question whether the accused belongs or belonged at a particular time to a specified organisation, may draw from the failure inferences relating to that question, but

    (b)   the accused shall not be committed for trial in England and Wales, or be found to have a case to answer or be convicted, solely on the basis of the inferences.

(7)   Subject to any directions by the court, evidence tending to establish the failure may be given before or after evidence tending to establish the fact which the accused is alleged to have failed to mention.

(8)   This section does not—

    (a)   prejudice the admissibility of evidence admissible apart from this section;

    (b)   preclude the drawing of inferences which could be drawn apart from this section;

    (c)   prejudice an enactment providing (in whatever words) that an answer or evidence given by a person in specified circumstances is not admissible in evidence against him or some other person in any proceedings or class of proceedings (however described, and whether civil or criminal).

(9)   In subsection (8)(c) above the reference to giving evidence is a reference to giving it in any manner (whether by giving information, making discovery or disclosure, producing documents or otherwise).

(10)   In any proceedings in Scotland for an offence under section 2(1)(a) above in which the accused is charged with belonging to a specified organisation, where the court or jury draws an inference as mentioned in subsection (6) above any evidence that he belongs or, as the case may be, belonged to the organisation shall be sufficient evidence of that matter.

(11)   In this section 'police officer' means a member of—

    (a)   a police force within the meaning of the Police Act 1996 or the Police (Scotland) Act 1967, or

    (b)   the Royal Ulster Constabulary.

(12)   This section does not apply to a statement made or failure occurring before the day on which the Criminal Justice (Terrorism and Conspiracy) Act 1998 was passed.

2B.   Specified organisations

(1)   For the purposes of section 2A above an organisation is specified at a particular time if at that time—

(a)   it is specified under section 3(8) of the Northern Ireland (Sentences) Act 1998 or under subsection (2) below, and

(b)   it is, or forms part of, an organisation which is proscribed for the purposes of this Act.

(2)   If the condition in subsection (3) below is satisfied the Secretary of State may by order specify an organisation which is not specified under section 3(8) of the Northern Ireland (Sentences) Act 1998.

(3)   The condition is that the Secretary of State believes that the organisation—

(a)   is concerned in terrorism connected with the affairs of Northern Ireland, or in promoting or encouraging it, and

(b)   has not established or is not maintaining a complete and unequivocal ceasefire.

(4)   An order under this section shall be made by statutory instrument; and no order shall be made unless a draft has been laid before, and approved by resolution of, each House of Parliament.

(2)   For the purposes of section 27 of the Prevention of Terrorism (Temporary Provisions) Act 1989 (duration etc.) sections 2A and 2B of that Act shall be treated as having been continued in force by the order under subsection (6) of section 27 which has effect when this Act is passed.

3.   Display of support in public

(1)   Any person who in a public place—

(a)   wears any item of dress; or

(b)   wears, carries or displays any article,

in such a way or in such circumstances as to arouse reasonable apprehension that he is a member or supporter of a proscribed organisation, is guilty of an offence and liable on summary conviction to imprisonment for a term not exceeding six months or a fine not exceeding level 5 on the standard scale or both.

(2)   (*Applies to Scotland only.*)

(3)   In this section 'public place' includes any highway or, in Scotland, any road within the meaning of the Roads (Scotland) Act 1984 and any premises to which at the material time the public have, or are permitted to have, access, whether on payment or otherwise.

PART II
EXCLUSION ORDERS

4.   Exclusion orders: general

(1)   The Secretary of State may exercise the powers conferred on him by this Part of this Act in such a way as appears to him expedient to prevent acts of terrorism to which this Part of this Act applies.

(2)   The acts of terrorism to which this Part of this Act applies are acts of terrorism connected with the affairs of Northern Ireland.

(3)   An order under section 5, 6 or 7 below is referred to in this Act as an 'exclusion order'.

(4)   Schedule 2 to this Act shall have effect with respect to the duration of exclusion orders, the giving of notices, the right to make representations, powers of removal and detention and other supplementary matters for this Part of this Act.

(5)   The exercise of the detention powers conferred by that Schedule shall be subject to supervision in accordance with Schedule 3 to this Act.

5.   Orders excluding persons from Great Britain

(1)   If the Secretary of State is satisfied that any person—

(a)   is or has been concerned in the commission, preparation or instigation of acts of terrorism to which this Part of this Act applies; or

(b) is attempting or may attempt to enter Great Britain with a view to being concerned in the commission, preparation or instigation of such acts of terrorism,
the Secretary of State may make an exclusion order against him.

(2)   An exclusion order under this section is an order prohibiting a person from being in, or entering, Great Britain.

(3)   In deciding whether to make an exclusion order under this section against a person who is ordinarily resident in Great Britain, the Secretary of State shall have regard to the question whether that person's connection with any country or territory outside Great Britain is such as to make it appropriate that such an order should be made.

(4)   An exclusion order shall not be made under this section against a person who is a British citizen and who—

(a) is at the time ordinarily resident in Great Britain and has then been ordinarily resident in Great Britain throughout the last three years; or

(b) is at the time subject to an order under section 6 below.

6.   Orders excluding persons from Northern Ireland

(1)   If the Secretary of State is satisfied that any person—

(a) is or has been concerned in the commission, preparation or instigation of acts of terrorism to which this Part of this Act applies; or

(b) is attempting or may attempt to enter Northern Ireland with a view to being concerned in the commission, preparation or instigation of such acts of terrorism,
the Secretary of State may make an exclusion order against him.

(2)   An exclusion order under this section is an order prohibiting a person from being in, or entering, Northern Ireland.

(3)   In deciding whether to make an exclusion order under this section against a person who is ordinarily resident in Northern Ireland, the Secretary of State shall have regard to the question whether that person's connection with any country or territory outside Northern Ireland is such as to make it appropriate that such an order should be made.

(4)   An exclusion order shall not be made under this section against a person who is a British citizen and who—

(a) is at the time ordinarily resident in Northern Ireland and has then been ordinarily resident in Northern Ireland throughout the last three years; or

(b) is at the time subject to an order under section 5 above.

7.   Orders excluding persons from the United Kingdom

(1)   If the Secretary of State is satisfied that any person—

(a) is or has been concerned in the commission, preparation or instigation of acts of terrorism to which this Part of this Act applies; or

(b) is attempting or may attempt to enter Great Britain or Northern Ireland with a view to being concerned in the commission, preparation or instigation of such acts of terrorism,
the Secretary of State may make an exclusion order against him.

(2)   An exclusion order under this section is an order prohibiting a person from being in, or entering, the United Kingdom.

(3)   In deciding whether to make an exclusion order under this section against a person who is ordinarily resident in the United Kingdom, the Secretary of State shall have regard to the question whether that person's connection with any country or territory outside the United Kingdom is such as to make it appropriate that such an order should be made.

(4)   An exclusion order shall not be made under this section against a person who is a British citizen.

8. Offences in respect of exclusion orders

(1)   A person who is subject to an exclusion order is guilty of an offence if he fails to comply with the order at a time after he has been, or has become liable to be, removed under Schedule 2 to this Act.

(2)   A person is guilty of an offence—

(a)   if he is knowingly concerned in arrangements for securing or facilitating the entry into Great Britain, Northern Ireland or the United Kingdom of a person whom he knows, or has reasonable grounds for believing, to be an excluded person; or

(b)   if he knowingly harbours such a person in Great Britain, Northern Ireland or the United Kingdom.

(3)   In subsection (2) above 'excluded person' means—

(a)   in relation to Great Britain, a person subject to an exclusion order made under section 5 above who has been, or has become liable to be, removed from Great Britain under Schedule 2 to this Act;

(b)   in relation to Northern Ireland, a person subject to an exclusion order made under section 6 above who has been, or has become liable to be, removed from Northern Ireland under that Schedule; and

(c)   in relation to the United Kingdom, a person subject to an exclusion order made under section 7 above who has been, or has become liable to be, removed from the United Kingdom under that Schedule.

(4)   A person guilty of an offence under this section is liable—

(a)   on conviction on indictment, to imprisonment for a term not exceeding five years or a fine or both;

(b)   on summary conviction, to imprisonment for a term not exceeding six months or a fine not exceeding the statutory maximum or both.

PART III
FINANCIAL ASSISTANCE FOR TERRORISM

9. Contributions towards acts of terrorism

(1)   A person is guilty of an offence if he—

(a)   solicits or invites any other person to give, lend or otherwise make available, whether for consideration or not, any money or other property; . . .

(b)   receives or accepts from any other person, whether for consideration or not, any money or other property; [or

(c)   uses or has possession of, whether for consideration or not, any money or other property,]

intending that it shall be applied or used for the commission of, or in furtherance of or in connection with, acts of terrorism to which this section applies or having reasonable cause to suspect that it may be so used or applied.

(2)   A person is guilty of an offence if he—

(a)   gives, lends or otherwise makes available to any other person, whether for consideration or not, any money or other property; or

(b)   enters into or is otherwise concerned in an arrangement whereby money or other property is or is to be made available to another person,

knowing or having reasonable cause to suspect that it will or may be applied or used as mentioned in subsection (1) above.

(3)   The acts of terrorism to which this section applies are—

(a)   acts or terrorism connected with the affairs of Northern Ireland; and

(b)   subject to subsection (4) below, acts of terrorism of any other description except acts connected solely with the affairs of the United Kingdom or any part of the United Kingdom other than Northern Ireland.

(4)   Subsection (3)(b) above does not apply to an act done or to be done outside the United Kingdom unless it constitutes or would constitute an offence triable in the United Kingdom.

(5)   In proceedings against a person for an offence under this section in relation to an act within subsection (3)(b) above done or to be done outside the United Kingdom—

(a)   the prosecution need not prove that that person knew or had reasonable cause to suspect that the act constituted or would constitute such an offence as is mentioned in subsection (4) above; but

(b)   it shall be a defence to prove that he did not know and had no reasonable cause to suspect that the facts were such that the act constituted or would constitute such an offence.

10.   Contributions to resources of proscribed organisations

(1)   A person is guilty of an offence if he—

(a)   solicits or invites any other person to give, lend or otherwise make available, whether for consideration or not, any money or other property for the benefit of a proscribed organisation;

(b)   gives, lends or otherwise makes available or receives or accepts [or uses or has possession of], whether for consideration or not, any money or other property for the benefit of such an organisation; or

(c)   enters into or is otherwise concerned in an arrangement whereby money or other property is or is to be made available for the benefit of such an organisation.

(2)   In proceedings against a person for an offence under subsection (1)(b) above it is a defence to prove that he did not know and had no reasonable cause to suspect that the money or property was for the benefit of a proscribed organisation; and in proceedings against a person for an offence under subsection (1)(c) above it is a defence to prove that he did not know and had no reasonable cause to suspect that the arrangement related to a proscribed organisation.

(3)   In this section and sections 11 and 13 below 'proscribed organisation' includes a proscribed organisation for the purposes of [section 30 of the Northern Ireland (Emergency Provisions) Act 1996].

11.   Assisting in retention or control of terrorist funds

(1)   A person is guilty of an offence if he enters into or is otherwise concerned in an arrangement whereby the retention or control by or on behalf of another person of terrorist funds is facilitated, whether by concealment, removal from the jurisdiction, transfer to nominees or otherwise.

(2)   In proceedings against a person for an offence under this section it is a defence to prove that he did not know and had no reasonable cause to suspect that the arrangement related to terrorist funds.

(3)   In this section and section 12 below 'terrorist funds' means—

(a)   funds which may be applied or used for the commission of, or in furtherance of or in connection with, acts of terrorism to which section 9 above applies;

(b)   the proceeds of the commission of such acts of terrorism or of activities engaged in furtherance of or in connection with such acts; and

(c)   the resources of a proscribed organisation.

(4)   Paragraph (b) of subsection (3) includes any property which in whole or in part directly or indirectly represents such proceeds as are mentioned in that paragraph; and paragraph (c) of that subsection includes any money or other property which is or is to be applied or made available for the benefit of a proscribed organisation.

12.   Disclosure of information about terrorist funds

(1)   A person may notwithstanding any restriction on the disclosure of information imposed by [statute or otherwise] disclose to a constable a suspicion or belief that any

money or other property is or is derived from terrorist funds or any matter on which such a suspicion or belief is based.

(2)   A person who enters into or is otherwise concerned in any such transaction or arrangement as is mentioned in section 9, 10 or 11 above does not commit an offence under that section if he is acting with the express consent of a constable or if—

(a)   he discloses to a constable his suspicion or belief that the money or other property concerned is or is derived from terrorist funds or any matter on which such a suspicion or belief is based; and

(b)   the disclosure is made after he enters into or otherwise becomes concerned in the transaction or arrangement in question but is made on his own initiative and as soon as it is reasonable for him to make it,

but paragraphs (a) and (b) above do not apply in a case where, having disclosed any such suspicion, belief or matter to a constable and having been forbidden by a constable to enter into or otherwise be concerned in the transaction or arrangement in question, he nevertheless does so.

[(2A)   For the purposes of subsection (2) above a person who uses or has possession of money or other property shall be taken to be concerned in a transaction or arrangement.]

(3)   In proceedings against a person for an offence under section 9(1)(b) [or (c)] or (2), 10(1)(b) or (c) or 11 above it is a defence to prove—

(a)   that he intended to disclose to a constable such a suspicion, belief or matter as is mentioned in paragraph (a) of subsection (2) above; and

(b)   that there is a reasonable excuse for his failure to make the disclosure as mentioned in paragraph (b) of that subsection.

[(4)   In the case of a person who was in employment at the relevant time, subsections (1) to (3) above shall have effect in relation to disclosures, and intended disclosures, to the appropriate person in accordance with the procedure established by his employer for the making of such disclosures as they have effect in relation to disclosures, and intended disclosures, to a constable.

(5)   No constable or other person shall be guilty of an offence under section 9(1)(b) or (c) or (2) or 10(1)(b) or (c) above in respect of anything done by him in the course of acting in connection with the enforcement, or intended enforcement, of any provision of this Act or of any other enactment relating to terrorism or the proceeds or resources of terrorism.

(6)   For the purposes of subsection (5) above, having possession of any property shall be taken to be doing an act in relation to it.]

13. Penalties and forfeiture

(1)   A person guilty of an offence under section 9, 10 or 11 above is liable—

(a)   on conviction on indictment, to imprisonment for a term not exceeding fourteen years or a fine or both;

(b)   on summary conviction, to imprisonment for a term not exceeding six months or a fine not exceeding the statutory maximum or both.

(2)   Subject to the provisions of this section, the court by or before which a person is convicted of an offence under section 9(1) or (2)(a) above may order the forfeiture of any money or other property—

(a)   which, at the time of the offence, he had in his possession or under his control; and

(b)   which, at that time—

(i)   in the case of an offence under subsection (1) of section 9, he intended should be applied or used, or had reasonable cause to suspect might be applied or used as mentioned in that subsection;

(ii)   in the case of an offence under subsection (2)(a) of that section, he knew or had reasonable cause to suspect would or might be applied or used as mentioned in subsection (1) of that section.

(3)   Subject to the provisions of this section, the court by or before which a person is convicted of an offence under section 9(2)(b), 10(1)(c) or 11 above may order the forfeiture of the money or other property to which the arrangement in question related and which, in the case of an offence under section 9(2)(b), he knew or had reasonable cause to suspect would or might be applied or used as mentioned in section 9(1) above.

(4)   Subject to the provisions of this section, the court by or before which a person is convicted of an offence under section 10(1)(a) or (b) above may order the forfeiture of any money or other property which, at the time of the offence, he had in his possession or under his control for the use or benefit of a proscribed organisation.

(5)   The court shall not under this section make an order forfeiting any money or other property unless the court considers that the money or property may, unless forfeited, be applied or used as mentioned in section 9(1) above but the court may, in the absence of evidence to the contrary, assume that any money or property may be applied or used as there mentioned.

(6)   Where a person other than the convicted person claims to be the owner of or otherwise interested in anything which can be forfeited by an order under this section, the court shall, before making such an order in respect of it, give him an opportunity to be heard.

(7)   (*Applies to Scotland only.*)

(8)   Schedule 4 to this Act shall have effect in relation to orders under this section.

[13A.   Powers to stop and search vehicles etc. and persons

(1)   Where it appears to—

(a)   any officer of police of or above the rank or commander of the metropolitan police, as respects the metropolitan police [district];

(b)   any officer of police of or above the rank of commander of the City of London police, as respects the City of London; or

(c)   any officer of police of or above the rank of assistant chief constable for any other police area,

that it is expedient to do so in order to prevent acts of terrorism to which this section applies he may give an authorisation that the powers to stop and search vehicles and persons conferred by this section shall be exercisable at any place within his area or a specified locality in his area for a specified period not exceeding twenty eight days.

(2)   the acts of terrorism to which this section applies are—

(a)   acts of terrorism connected with the affairs of Northern Ireland; and

(b)   acts of terrorism of any other description except acts connected solely with the affairs of the United Kingdom or any part of the United Kingdom other than Northern Ireland.

(3)   This section confers on any constable in uniform power—

(a)   to stop any vehicle;

(b)   to search any vehicle, its driver or any passenger for articles of a kind which could be used for a purpose connected with the commission, preparation or instigation of acts of terrorism to which this section applies;

(c)   . . .

[(4)   A constable may exercise his powers under this section whether or not he has any grounds for suspecting the presence of articles of that kind.

(4A)   Nothing in this section authorises a constable to require a person to remove any of his clothing in public other than any headgear, footwear, outer coat, jacket or gloves.]

(5)   This section applies (with the necessary modifications) to ships and aircraft as it applies to vehicles.

(6)   A person is guilty of an offence if he—

(a)   fails to stop ... the vehicle when required to do so by a constable in the exercise of his powers under this section; or

(b)   wilfully obstructs a constable in the exercise of those powers.

(7)   A person guilty of an offence under subsection (6) above shall be liable on summary conviction to imprisonment for a term not exceeding six months or a fine not exceeding level 5 on the standard scale or both.

(8)   If it appears to a police officer of the rank [mentioned] in subsection (1)(a), (b) or (c) (as the case may be) that the exercise of the powers conferred by this section ought to continue beyond the period for which their exercise has been authorised under this section he may, from time to time, authorise the exercise of those powers for a further period, not exceeding twenty eight days.

(9)   Where a vehicle is stopped by a constable under this section, the driver shall be entitled to obtain a written statement that the vehicle was stopped under the powers conferred by this section if he applies for a statement not later than the end of the period of twelve months from the day on which the vehicle was stopped; ...

[(10)   An authorisation under this section may be given in writing or orally but if given orally must be confirmed in writing by the person giving it as soon as is reasonably practicable.

(10A)   In this section 'specified' means specified in an authorisation under this section.]

(11)   Nothing in this section affects the exercise by constables of any power to stop vehicles for purposes other than those specified in subsection (1) above.]

[13B.   Power to stop and search pedestrians

(1)   Where it appears to a police officer of the rank mentioned in subsection (1)(a), (b) or (as the case may be) (c) of section 13A above that it is expedient to do so in order to prevent acts of terrorism to which that section applies, he may give an authorisation that the powers to stop and search persons conferred by this section shall be exercisable at any place within his area or a locality in his area which is specified in the authorisation.

(2)   This section confers on any constable in uniform power to stop any pedestrian and search him, or anything carried by him, for articles of a kind which could be used for a purpose connected with the commission, preparation or instigation of such acts of terrorism.

(3)   A constable may exercise his powers under this section whether or not he has any grounds for suspecting the presence of articles of that kind.

(4)   Nothing in this section authorises a constable to require a person to remove any of his clothing in public other than any headgear, footwear, outer coat, jacket or gloves.

(5)   A person is guilty of an offence if he—

(a)   fails to stop when required to do so by a constable in the exercise of his powers under this section; or

(b)   wilfully obstructs a constable in the exercise of those powers.

(6)   A person guilty of an offence under subsection (5) above shall be liable on summary conviction to imprisonment for a term not exceeding six months or a fine not exceeding level 5 on the standard scale or both.

(7)   An authorisation under this section may be given in writing or orally but if given orally must be confirmed in writing by the person giving it as soon as is reasonably practicable.

(8)   A person giving an authorisation under this section must cause the Secretary of State to be informed, as soon as is reasonably practicable, that it was given.

(9)   An authorisation under this section—

(a)   may be cancelled by the Secretary of State with effect from such time as he may direct;

(b) ceases to have effect if it is not confirmed by the Secretary of State before the end of the period of 48 hours beginning with the time when it was given; but

(c) if confirmed, continues in force—

(i) for such period, not exceeding 28 days beginning with the day on which it was given, as may be specified in the authorisation; or

(ii) for such shorter period as the Secretary of State may direct.

(10) If a person is stopped by a constable under this section, he shall be entitled to obtain a written statement that he was stopped under the powers conferred by this section if he applies for such a statement not later than the end of the period of twelve months from the day on which he was stopped.]

14. Arrest and detention of suspected persons

(1) Subject to subsection (2) below, a constable may arrest without warrant a person whom he has reasonable grounds for suspecting to be—

(a) a person guilty of an offence under section 2, 8, 9, 10 or 11 above or under section 30 of the Northern Ireland (Emergency Provisions) Act 1996;

(b) a person who is or has been concerned in the commission, preparation or instigation of acts of terrorism to which this section applies; or

(c) a person subject to an exclusion order.

(2) The acts of terrorism to which this section applies are—

(a) acts of terrorism connected with the affairs of Northern Ireland; and

(b) acts of terrorism of any other description except acts connected solely with the affairs of the United Kingdom or any part of the United Kingdom other than Northern Ireland.

(3) The power of arrest conferred by subsection (1)(c) above is exercisable only—

(a) in Great Britain if the exclusion order was made under section 5 above; and

(b) in Northern Ireland if it was made under section 6 above.

(4) Subject to subsection (5) below, a person arrested under this section shall not be detained in right of the arrest for more than forty-eight hours after his arrest.

(5) The Secretary of State may, in any particular case, extend the period of forty-eight hours mentioned in subsection (4) above by a period or periods specified by him, but any such further period or periods shall not exceed five days in all and if an application for such an extension is made the person detained shall as soon as practicable be given written notice of that fact and of the time when the application was made.

(6) The exercise of the detention powers conferred by this section shall be subject to supervision in accordance with Schedule 3 to this Act.

(7) The provisions of this section are without prejudice to any power of arrest exercisable apart from this section.

15. Provisions supplementary to s. 14

(1) If a justice of the peace is satisfied that there are reasonable grounds for suspecting that a person whom a constable believes to be liable to arrest under section 14(1)(b) above is to be found on any premises he may grant a search warrant authorising any constable to enter those premises for the purpose of searching for and arresting that person.

(2) (*Applies to Scotland only.*)

(3) In any circumstances in which a constable has power under section 14 above to arrest a person, he may also, for the purpose of ascertaining whether he has in his possession any document or other article which may constitute evidence that he is a person liable to arrest, stop that person and search him.

(4) Where a constable has arrested a person under that section for any reason other than the commission of a criminal offence, he, or any other constable, may search him

for the purpose of ascertaining whether he has in his possession any document or other article which may constitute evidence that he is a person liable to arrest.

(5)   A search of a person under subsection (3) or (4) above may only be carried out by a person of the same sex.

(6)   A person detained under section 14 above shall be deemed to be in legal custody at any time when he is so detained and may be detained in such a place as the Secretary of State may from time to time direct.

(7)   The following provisions (requirement to bring accused person before the court after his arrest) shall not apply to a person detained in right of an arrest under section 14 above—

(a)   (*applies to Scotland only*);

[(b)   Article 47 of the Police and Criminal Evidence (Northern Ireland) Order 1989;]

(c)   section 50(3) of the Children and Young Persons Act (Northern Ireland) 1968.

(8)   (*Applies to Scotland only.*)

(9)   Where a person is detained under section 14 above, any constable or prison officer, or any other person authorised by the Secretary of State, may take all such steps as may be reasonably necessary for photographing, measuring or otherwise identifying him.

(10)   Section 61(1) to (8) of the Police and Criminal Evidence Act 1984 (fingerprinting) shall apply to the taking of a person's fingerprints by a constable under subsection (9) above as if for subsection (4) there were substituted—

'(4)   An officer may only give an authorisation under subsection (3)(a) above for the taking of a person's fingerprints if he is satisfied that it is necessary to do so in order to assist in determining—

(a)   whether that person is or has been concerned in the commission, preparation or instigation of acts of terrorism to which section 14 of the Prevention of Terrorism (Temporary Provisions) Act 1989 applies; or

(b)   whether he is subject to an exclusion order under that Act;

or if the officer has reasonable grounds for suspecting that person's involvement in an offence under any of the provisions mentioned in subsection (1)(a) of that section and for believing that his fingerprints will tend to confirm or disprove his involvement.'

[(11) Section 62(1) to (11) of the Police and Criminal Evidence Act 1984 (regulation of taking of intimate samples) shall apply to the taking of an intimate sample from a person under subsection (9) above as if—

(a)   for subsection (2) there were substituted—

'(2)   An officer may only give an authorisation under subsection (1) or (1A) above for the taking of an intimate sample if he is satisfied that it is necessary to do so in order to assist in determining—

(a)   whether that person is or has been concerned in the commission, preparation or instigation of acts of terrorism to which section 14 of the Prevention of Terrorism (Temporary Provisions) Act 1989 applies; or

(b)   whether he is subject to an exclusion order under that Act;

or if the officer has reasonable grounds for suspecting that person's involvement in an offence under any of the provisions mentioned in subsection (1)(a) of that section and for believing that an intimate sample will tend to confirm or disprove his involvement'; and

(b)   in subsection (6), after the word 'includes', there were inserted the words 'where relevant'.

(12)   In this section, 'intimate sample' has the same meaning as in section 65 of the Police and Criminal Evidence Act 1984.

(13)   Section 63(1) to (9) of the Police and Criminal Evidence Act 1984 (regulation of taking of non-intimate samples) shall apply to the taking of a non-intimate sample from a person by a constable under subsection (9) above as if—

(a)   for subsection (4) there were substituted—

'(4)   An officer may only give an authorisation under subsection (3) above for the taking of a non-intimate sample if he is satisfied that it is necessary to do so in order to assist in determining—

(a)   whether that person is or has been concerned in the commission, preparation or instigation of acts of terrorism to which section 14 of the Prevention of Terrorism (Temporary Provisions) Act 1989 applies; or

(b)   whether he is subject to an exclusion order under that Act;

or if the officer has reasonable grounds for suspecting that person's involvement in an offence under any of the provisions mentioned in subsection (1)(a) of that section and for believing that a non-intimate sample will tend to confirm or disprove his involvement'; and

(b)   in subsection (7), after the word 'includes' there were inserted the words 'where relevant'.

(14)   In this section, 'non-intimate sample' has the same meaning as in section 65 of the Police and Criminal Evidence Act 1984.]

16.   Port and border controls

(1)   Schedule 5 to this Act shall have effect for conferring powers to examine persons [or goods] arriving in or leaving Great Britain or Northern Ireland and for connected purposes.

(2)   The exercise of the examination and detention powers conferred by paragraphs 2 and 6 of that Schedule shall be subject to supervision in accordance with Schedule 3 to this Act.

(3)   The designated ports for the purposes of paragraph 8 of Schedule 5 to this Act shall be those specified in Schedule 6 to this Act but the Secretary of State may by order add any port to, or remove any port from, that Schedule.

(4)   Without prejudice to the provisions of Schedule 5 to this Act with respect to persons who enter or leave Northern Ireland by land or who seek to do so, the Secretary of State may by order make such further provisions with respect to those persons as appears to him to be expedient.

(5)   The power to make orders under this section shall be exercisable by statutory instrument.

(6)   An order under subsection (4) above may contain transitional provisions and savings and shall be subject to annulment in pursuance of a resolution of either House of Parliament.

[PART IVA

OFFENCES AGAINST PUBLIC SECURITY

16A.   Possession of articles for suspected terrorist purposes

(1)   A person is guilty of an offence if he has any article in his possession in circumstances giving rise to a reasonable suspicion that the article is in his possession for a purpose connected with the commission, preparation or instigation of acts of terrorism to which this section applies.

(2)   The acts of terrorism to which this section applies are—

(a)   acts of terrorism connected with the affairs of Northern Ireland; and

(b)   acts of terrorism of any other description except acts connected solely with the affairs of the United Kingdom or any part of the United Kingdom other than Northern Ireland.

(3)   It is a defence for a person charged with an offence under this section to prove that at the time of the alleged offence the article in question was not in his possession for such a purpose as is mentioned in subsection (1) above.

(4)   Where a person is charged with an offence under this section and it is proved that at the time of the alleged offence—

(a)   he and that article were both present in any premises; or

(b)   the article was in premises of which he was the occupier or which he habitually used otherwise than as a member of the public,

the court may accept the fact proved as sufficient evidence of his possessing that article at that time unless it is further proved that he did not at that time know of its presence in the premises in question, or, if he did know, that he had no control over it.

(5)   A person gulity of an offence under this section is liable—

(a)   on conviction on indictment, to imprisonment for a term not exceeding ten years or a fine or both;

(b)   on summary conviction, to imprisonment for a term not exceeding six months or a fine not exceeding the statutory maximum or both.

(6)   This section applies to vessels, aircraft and vehicles as it applies to premises.]

[16B.   Unlawful collection, etc. of information

(1)   No person shall, without lawful authority or reasonable excuse (the proof of which lies on him)—

(a)   collect or record any information which is of such a nature as is likely to be useful to terrorists in planning or carrying out any act of terrorism to which this section applies; or

(b)   have in his possession any record or document containing any such information as is mentioned in paragraph (a) above.

(2)   The acts of terrorism to which this section applies are—

(a)   acts of terrorism connected with the affairs of Northern Ireland; and

(b)   acts of terrorism of any other description except acts connected solely with the affairs of the United Kingdom or any part of the United Kingdom other than Northern Ireland.

(3)   In subsection (1) above the reference to recording information includes a reference to recording it by means of photography or by any other means.

(4)   Any person who contravenes this section is guilty of an offence and liable—

(a)   on conviction on indictment, to imprisonment for a term not exceeding ten years or a fine or both;

(b)   on summary conviction, to imprisonment for a term not exceeding six months or a fine not exceeding the statutory maximum or both.

(5)   The court by or before which a person is convicted of an offence under this section may order the forfeiture of any record or document mentioned in subsection (1) above which is found in his possession.]

[PART IVB
CORDONS AND PROTECTIVE POWERS

16C.   Power to impose a police cordon

(1)   If it appears to a police officer of at least the rank of superintendent that it is expedient to do so in connection with an investigation into the commission, preparation or instigation of an act of terrorism to which this section applies, he may authorise a cordon to be imposed on an area specified by him in the authorisation.

(2)   If it appears to a constable below the rank of superintendent that it is necessary for him to do so as a matter of great urgency, he may exercise the power given to a superintendent by subsection (1) above.

(3)   The acts of terrorism to which this section applies are—

(a)   acts or terrorism connected with the affairs of Northern Ireland; and
(b)   acts of terrorism of any other description except acts connected solely with the affairs of the United Kingdom or any part of the United Kingdom other than Northern Ireland.

(4)   The powers that may be exercised within an area on which a cordon has been imposed under this section are set out in Schedule 6A to this Act.

(5)   Schedule 6A also makes further provision with respect to cordoned areas.]

[16D   Parking prohibitions and restrictions and the removal of vehicles

(1)   If it appears to an appropriate officer that it is expedient to do so in order to prevent acts of terrorism to which section 16C above applies he may give an authorisation for the purposes of this section.

(2)   An authorisation—
(a)   may be given in writing or orally but if given orally must be confirmed in writing by the person giving it as soon as is reasonably practicable; and
(b)   has effect—
(i)   in relation to such roads, or parts of roads, as may be specified; and
(ii)   for such period, not exceeding 28 days, as may be specified.

(3)   Only roads, or parts of roads, which are within the police area of the officer giving the authorisation may be specified.

(4)   An authorisation gives any constable power to prohibit or restrict the leaving of vehicles, or their remaining at rest, on any specified road, or part of a road.

(5)   The power conferred by subsection (4) above is to be exercised by placing the appropriate traffic sign on, or on any structure which is on, the road or part of the road concerned.

(6)   If the driver or other person in charge of a vehicle which has been permitted to remain at rest in contravention of any prohibition or restriction imposed under subsection (4) above fails to move the vehicle when ordered to do so by a constable in uniform, he is guilty of an offence.

(7)   A person is guilty of an offence if he leaves a vehicle, or permits a vehicle to remain at rest, on a road in contravention of a prohibition or restriction imposed under this section.

(8)   It is a defence for any person charged with an offence under this section to prove that he had lawful authority or some other reasonable excuse for the act or omission in question.

(9)   A person guilty of an offence under subsection (6) above is liable on summary conviction to imprisonment for a term not exceeding three months or a fine not exceeding level 4 on the standard scale or both.

(10)   A person guilty of an offence under subsection (7) above is liable on summary conviction to a fine not exceeding level 4 on the standard scale.

(11)   If it appears to an appropriate officer that the exercise of the powers conferred by this section ought to continue beyond the period for which their exercise has been authorised under this section he may, from time to time, authorise the exercise of those powers for a further period, not exceeding 28 days.

(12)   The fact that a person has a current disabled person's badge does not—
(a)   exempt him from any prohibition or restriction imposed under this section; or
(b)   constitute lawful authority, or a reasonable excuse, for failing to comply with any order given under this section.

(13)   In this section—
'appropriate officer' means—
(a)   any police officer of or above the rank of commander of the Metropolitan police, as respects the Metropolitan police district;
(b)   any police officer of or above the rank of commander of the City of London police, as respects the City of London; or

(c)   any police officer of or above the rank of assistant chief constable of a force maintained for any other police area;
'authorisation' means an authorisation given under this section;
'disabled person's badge' has the same meaning as in section 142 of the Road Traffic Regulation Act 1984;
'driver' means, in relation to a vehicle which has been left on any road, the person who was driving it when it was left there;
'road' has the same meaning as in the Road Traffic Act 1988;
'specified' means specified in an authorisation;
'traffic sign' has the meaning given in section 142(1) of the Road Traffic Regulation Act 1984; and
'vehicle' has the same meaning as in section 99(5) of the Act of 1984.
    (14)   A constable exercising powers under this section may suspend a parking place; and any such suspension is to be treated for the purposes of section 99 of the Act of 1984 (removal of vehicles illegally parked etc.), and any regulations in force under that section, as a restriction imposed under this section.
    (15)   The powers conferred by this section are additional to any other powers which a constable has either at common law or under or by virtue of any other enactment and are not to be taken to affect any of those other powers.]

PART V
INFORMATION, PROCEEDINGS AND INTERPRETATION

17.   Investigation of terrorist activities
    (1)   Schedule 7 to this Act shall have effect for conferring powers to obtain information for the purposes of terrorist investigations, that is to say—
        (a)   investigations into—
            (i)   the commission, preparation or instigation of acts of terrorism to which section 14 above applies; or
            (ii)   any other act which appears to have been done in furtherance of or in connection with such acts or terrorism, including any act which appears to constitute an offence under section 2, 9, 10 [11, 18 or 18A of this Act] or [section 29 or 30 of the Northern Ireland (Emergency Provisions) Act 1996]; or
            (iii)   without prejudice to sub-paragraph (ii) above, the resources of a pro- scribed organisation within the meaning of this Act or a proscribed organisation for the purposes of [section 30 of the said Act of 1996] and
        (b)   investigations into whether there are grounds justifying the making of an order under section 1(2)(a) above or [section 30(3) of the Act of 1996].
    [(2)   A person is guilty of an offence if, knowing or having reasonable cause to suspect that a constable is acting, or is proposing to act, in connection with a terrorist investigation which is being, or is about to be, conducted, he—
        (a)   discloses to any other person information or any other matter which is likely to prejudice the investigation or proposed investigation, or
        (b)   falsifies, conceals or destroys or otherwise disposes of, or causes or permits the falsification, concealment, destruction or disposal of, material which is or is likely to be relevant to the investigation, or proposed investigation.
    (2A)   A person is guilty of an offence if, knowing or having reasonable cause to suspect that a disclosure ('the disclosure') has been made to a constable under section 12, 18 or 18A of this Act or . . ., he—
        (a)   discloses to any other person information or any other matter which is likely to prejudice any investigation which might be conducted following the disclosure; or
        (b)   falsifies, conceals or destroys or otherwise disposes of, or causes or permits the falsification, concealment, destruction or disposal of, material which is or is likely to be relevant to any such investigation.

(2B)   A person is guilty of an offence if, knowing or having reasonable cause to suspect that a disclosure ('the disclosure') of a kind mentioned in section 12(4) or 18A(5) of this Act ... has been made, he—

(a)   discloses to any person information or any other matter which is likely to prejudice any investigation which might be conducted following the disclosure; or

(b)   falsifies, conceals or destroys or otherwise disposes of, or causes or permits the falsification, concealment, destruction or disposal of, material which is or is likely to be relevant to any such investigation.

(2C)   Nothing in subsections (2) to (2B) above makes it an offence for a professional legal adviser to disclose any information or other matter—

(a)   to, or to a representative of, a client of his in connection with the giving by the adviser of legal advice to the client; or

(b)   to any person—

(i)   in contemplation of, or in connection with, legal proceedings; and

(ii)   for the purpose of those proceedings.

(2D)   Subsection (2C) above does not apply in relation to any information or other matter which is disclosed with a view to furthering any criminal purpose.

(2E)   No constable or other person shall be guilty of an offence under this section in respect of anything done by him in the course of acting in connection with the enforcement, or intended enforcement, of any provision of this Act or of any other enactment relating to terrorism or the proceeds or resources of terrorism.]

(3)   In proceedings against a person for an offence under subsection (2)(a) above it is a defence to prove—

(a)   that he did not know and had no reasonable cause to suspect that the disclosure was likely to prejudice the investigation [or proposed investigation]; or

(b)   that he had lawful authority or reasonable excuse for making the disclosure.

[(3A)   In proceedings against a person for an offence under subsection (2A)(a) or (2B)(a) above it is a defence to prove—

(a)   that he did not know and had no reasonable cause to suspect that his disclosure was likely to prejudice the investigation in question; or

(b)   that he had lawful authority or reasonable excuse for making his disclosure.]

(4)   In proceedings against a person for an offence under subsection (2)(b) above it is a defence to prove that he had no intention of concealing any information contained in the material in question from [any person conducting, or likely to be conducting, the investigation or proposed investigation].

[(4A)   In proceedings against a person for an offence under subsection (2A)(b) or (2B)(b) above, it is a defence to prove that he had no intention of concealing any information contained in the material in question from any person who might carry out the investigation in question.]

(5)   A person guilty of an offence under subsection (2) [(2A) or (2B)] above is liable—

(a)   on conviction on indictment, to imprisonment for a term not exceeding five years or a fine or both;

(b)   on summary conviction, to imprisonment for a term not exceeding six months or a fine not exceeding the statutory maximum or both.

[(6)   For the purposes of subsection (1) above, as it applies in relation to any offence under section 18 or 18A below ... 'act' includes omission.]

18.   Information about acts of terrorism

(1)   A person is guilty of an offence if he has information which he knows or believes might be of material assistance—

(a)   in preventing the commission by any other person of an act of terrorism connected with the affairs of Northern Ireland; or

(b)   in securing the apprehension, prosecution or conviction of any other person for an offence involving the commission, preparation or instigation of such an act, and fails without reasonable excuse to disclose that information as soon as reasonably practicable—

    (i)   in England and Wales, to a constable;

    (ii)   (*applies to Scotland only*); or

    (iii)   in Northern Ireland, to a constable or a member of Her Majesty's Forces.

(2)   A person guilty of an offence under this section is liable—

    (a)   on conviction on indictment, to imprisonment for a term not exceeding five years or a fine or both;

    (b)   on summary conviction, to imprisonment for a term not exceeding six months or a fine not exceeding the statutory maximum or both.

(3)   Proceedings for an offence under this section may be taken, and the offence may for the purposes of those proceedings be treated as having been committed, in any place where the person to be charged is or has at any time been since he first knew or believed that the information might be of material assistance as mentioned in subsection (1) above.

[18A.   Failure to disclose knowledge or suspicion of offences under sections 9 to 11

(1)   A person is guilty of an offence if—

    (a)   he knows, or suspects, that another person is providing financial assistance for terrorism;

    (b)   the information, or other matter, on which that knowledge or suspicion is based came to his attention in the course of his trade, profession, business or employment; and

    (c)   he does not disclose the information or other matter to a constable as soon as is reasonably practicable after it comes to his attention.

(2)   Subsection (1) above does not make it an offence for a professional legal adviser to fail to disclose any information or other matter which has come to him in privileged circumstances.

(3)   It is a defence to a charge of committing an offence under this section that the person charged had a reasonable excuse for not disclosing the information or other matter in question.

(4)   Where a person discloses to a constable—

    (a)   his suspicion or belief that another person is providing financial assistance for terrorism; or

    (b)   any information or other matter on which that suspicion or belief is based;

the disclosure shall not be treated as a breach of any restriction imposed by statute or otherwise.

(5)   Without prejudice to subsection (3) or (4) above, in the case of a person who was in employment at the relevant time, it is a defence to a charge of committing an offence under this section that he disclosed the information or other matter in question to the appropriate person in accordance with the procedure established by his employer for the making of such disclosures.

(6)   A disclosure to which subsection (5) above applies shall not be treated as a breach of any restriction imposed by statute or otherwise.

(7)   In this section 'providing financial assistance for terrorism' means doing any act which constitutes an offence under section 9, 10 or 11 above or, in the case of an act done otherwise than in the United Kingdom, which would constitute such an offence if done in the United Kingdom.

(8)   For the purposes of subsection (7) above, having possession of any property shall be taken to be doing an act in relation to it.

(9)   For the purposes of this section, any information or other matter comes to a professional legal adviser in privileged circumstances if it is communicated, or given, to him—
  (a)   by, or by a representative of, a client of his in connection with the giving by the adviser of legal advice to the client;
  (b)   by, or by a representative of, a person seeking legal advice from the adviser; or
  (c)   by any person—
    (i)   in contemplation of, or in connection with, legal proceedings; and
    (ii)   for the purpose of those proceedings.
(10)   No information or other matter shall be treated as coming to a professional legal adviser in privileged circumstances if it is communicated or given with a view to furthering any criminal purpose.
(11)   A person guilty of an offence under this section shall be liable—
  (a)   on summary conviction, to imprisonment for a term not exceeding six months or a fine not exceeding the statutory maximum or to both; or
  (b)   on conviction on indictment, to imprisonment for a term not exceeding five years or a fine or to both.]

19.   Prosecutions and evidence
(1)   Proceedings shall not be instituted—
  (a)   in England and Wales for an offence under section 2, 3, 8, 9, 10, 11, 17[, 18 or 18A] above or Schedule 7 to this Act except by or with the consent of the Attorney General;
  [(aa)   In England and Wales for an offence under section 13A [13B], 16A [16B or 16D or under Schedule 6A] except by or with the consent of the Director of Public Prosecutions;]
  (b)   in Northern Ireland for an offence under section 8, 9, 10, 11, 17[, 18 or 18A] above or Schedule 7 to this Act except by or with the consent of the Attorney General for Northern Ireland.
(2)   Any document purporting to be an order, notice or direction made or given by the Secretary of State for the purposes of any provision of this Act and to be signed by him or on his behalf shall be received in evidence, and shall, until the contrary is proved, be deemed to be made or given by him.
(3)   A document bearing a certificate purporting to be signed by or on behalf of the Secretary of State and stating that the document is a true copy of such an order, notice or direction shall, in any legal proceedings, be evidence, and in Scotland sufficient evidence, of the order, notice or direction.

[19A.   Extension of certain offences to Crown servants and exemptions for regulators etc.
(1)   The Secretary of State may by regulations provide that, in such circumstances as may be prescribed, sections 9 to 11, 17 and 18A above, shall apply to such persons in the public service of the Crown, or such categories of person in that service, as may be prescribed.
(2)   Section 18A of this Act shall not apply to—
  (a)   any person designated by regulations made by the Secretary of State for the purpose of this paragraph; or
  (b)   in such circumstances as may be prescribed, any person who falls within such category of person as may be prescribed for the purpose of this paragraph.
(3)   The Secretary of State may designate, for the purpose of paragraph (a) of subsection (2) above, any person appearing to him to be performing regulatory, supervisory, investigative or registration functions.
(4)   The categories of person prescribed by the Secretary of State, for the purpose of paragraph (b) of subsection (2) above, shall be such categories of person connected with

the performance by any designated person of regulatory, supervisory, investigative or registration functions as he considers it appropriate to prescribe.

(5) In this section—

'the Crown' includes the Crown in right of Her Majesty's Government in Northern Ireland; and

'prescribed' means prescribed by regulations made by the Secretary of State.

(6) The power to make regulations under this section shall be exercisable by statutory instrument.

(7) Any such instrument shall be subject to annulment in pursuance of a resolution of either House of Parliament.]

20. Interpretation

(1) In this Act—

'aircraft' includes hovercraft;

'captain' means master of a ship or commander of an aircraft;

[. . .]

'examining officer' has the meaning given in paragraph 1 of Schedule 5 to this Act;

'exclusion order' has the meaning given by section 4(3) above but subject to section 25(3) below;

'the Islands' means the Channel Islands or the Isle of Man;

'port' includes airport and hoverport;

'premises' includes any place and in particular includes—

    (a) any vehicle, vessel or aircraft;

    (b) any offshore installation as defined in section 1 of the Mineral Workings (Offshore Installations) Act 1971; and

    (c) any tent or moveable structure;

'property' includes property wherever situated and whether real or personal, heritable or moveable and things in action and other intangible or incorporeal property;

'ship' includes every description of vessel used in navigation;

'terrorism' means the use of violence for political ends, and includes any use of violence for the purpose of putting the public or any section of the public in fear;

[. . .]

'vehicle' includes a train and carriages forming part of a train.

(2) A constable or examining officer may, if necessary, use reasonable force for the purpose of exercising any powers conferred on him under or by virtue of any provision of this act other than paragraph 2 of Schedule 5; but this subsection is without prejudice to any provision of this Act, or of any instrument made under it, which implies that a person may use reasonable force in connection with that provision.

(3) The powers conferred by Part II and section 16 of, and Schedules 2 and 5 to, this Act shall be exercisable notwithstanding the rights conferred by section 1 of the Immigration Act 1971 (general principles regulating entry into and staying in the Untied Kingdom).

(4) Any reference in a provision of this act to a person having been concerned in the commission, preparation or instigation of acts of terrorism shall be taken to be a reference to his having been so concerned at any time, whether before or after the passing of this Act.

PART VII
SUPPLEMENTARY

25. Consequential amendments, repeals and transitional provisions

(1) The enactments mentioned in Schedule 8 to this Act shall have effect with the amendments there specified, being amendments consequential on the provisions of this Act.

(2)   The enactments mentioned in Part I of Schedule 9 to this Act are hereby repealed to the extent specified in the third column of that Schedule; and the Orders mentioned in Part II of that Schedule are hereby revoked.

(3)   Any exclusion order in force under any provision of Part II of the Prevention of Terrorism (Temporary Provisions) Act 1984 ('the former Act') shall have effect as if made under the corresponding provision of Part II of this Act and references in this Act to an exclusion order shall be construed accordingly.

(4)   Any person who immediately before 22 March 1989 is being detained under any provision of the former Act or of an order made under section 13 of that Act shall be treated as lawfully detained under the corresponding provision of this act.

(5)   Paragraph 2 of Schedule 5 to this Act shall not apply in relation to a person whose examination under any corresponding provision of an order made under section 13 of the former Act has begun but has not been concluded before the coming into force of that paragraph, and that provision shall continue to apply to him but any reference in this Act to examination under that paragraph shall include a reference to examination under that corresponding provision.

(6)   The expiry of the former Act and its repeal by this Act shall not affect the operation of any Order in Council extending it to any of the Channel Islands or the Isle of Man; but any such Order may be revoked as if made under section 28(3) below and, notwithstanding anything contained in any such Order, shall continue in operation until revoked.

27. Commencement and duration

(1)   Subject to subsections (2), (3) and (4) below, this Act shall come into force on 22 March 1989.

(2)   ...

(3)   Schedule 3 and paragraphs 8 to 10, 18 to 20, 28 to 30 and 34 of Schedule 4 shall come into force on such day as the Secretary of State may appoint by an order made by statutory instrument; and different days may be appointed for different provisions and for England and Wales, for Scotland and for Northern Ireland.

(4)   The repeal by Schedule 9 of paragraph 9 of Schedule 7 shall come into force on the coming into force of the Land Registration Act 1988.

(5)   The provisions of Parts I to V of this Act and of subsection (6)(c) below shall remain in force until 22 March 1990 and shall then expire unless continued in force by an order under subsection (6) below.

(6)   The Secretary of State may by order made by statutory instrument provide—

(a)   that all or any of those provisions which are for the time being in force (including any in force by virtue of an order under this paragraph or paragraph (c) below) shall continue in force for a period not exceeding twelve months from the coming into operation of the order;

(b)   that all or any of those provisions which are for the time being in force shall cease to be in force; or

(c)   that all or any of those provisions which are not for the time being in force shall come into force again and remain in force for a period not exceeding twelve months from the coming into operation of the order.

(7)   No order shall be made under subsection (6) above unless—

(a)   a draft of the order has been laid before and approved by a resolution of each House of Parliament; or

(b)   it is declared in the order that it appears to the Secretary of State that by reason of urgency it is necessary to make the order without a draft having been so approved.

(8)   An order under that subsection of which a draft has not been approved under section (7) above—

(a)   shall be laid before Parliament; and

(b)   shall cease to have effect at the end of the period of forty days beginning with the day on which it was made unless, before the end of that period, the order has been approved by a resolution of each House of Parliament, but without prejudice to anything previously done or to the making of a new order.

(9)   In reckoning for the purposes of subsection (8) above the period of forty days no account shall be taken of any period during which Parliament is dissolved or prorogued or during which both Houses are adjourned for more than four days.

(10)   In subsection (5) above the reference to Parts I to V of this Act does not include a reference to the provisions of Parts III and V so far as they have effect in Northern Ireland and relate to proscribed organisations for the purposes of [section 30 of the Northern Ireland (Emergency Provisions) Act 1996] or offences or orders under that section.

[(11)   The provisions excluded by subsection (10) above from subsection (5) shall remain in force until 15 June 1997 and then expire but shall be—

(a)   included in the provisions to which subsection (3) of section 62 of the said Act of 1996 applies (provisions that can be continued in force, repealed or revived by order); and

(b)   treated as part of that Act for the purposes of subsection (10) of that section (repeal at end of two years).]

(12)   . . .

28.   Short title and extent

(1)   This Act may be cited as the Prevention of Terrorism (Temporary Provisions) Act 1989.

(2)   This Act extends to the whole of the United Kingdom except that—

(a)   Part I[, sections 13A [13B] and 15(1) and [Parts IVA and IVB]] do not extend to Northern Ireland and . . . Part III of Schedule 4 and the repeal in Schedule 9 relating to the Explosives Act 1875 extend only to Northern Ireland;

(b)   section 15(10) [to (14)], Part I of Schedule 4 . . . paragraph 7(6) [to (6D)] of Schedule 5[, paragraph 7 of Schedule 6A and paragraph 2A of Schedule 7] extend only to England and Wales;

(c)   (applies to Scotland only);

(d)   Part I of Schedule 7 [except paragraph 2A] extends only to England, Wales and Northern Ireland; and

(e)   subject to paragraph (a) above, the amendments and repeals in Schedules 8 and 9 have the same extent as the enactments to which they refer.

(3)   Her Majesty may by Order in Council direct that any of the provisions of this Act shall extend, with such exceptions, adaptations and modifications, if any, as may be specified in the Order, to any of the Channel Islands and the Isle of Man.

CRIMINAL JUSTICE (INTERNATIONAL CO-OPERATION) ACT 1990
(1990, c. 5)

PART I
CRIMINAL PROCEEDINGS AND INVESTIGATIONS

Mutual service of process

1.   Service of overseas process in United Kingdom

(1)   This section has effect where the Secretary of State receives from the government of, or other authority in, a country or territory outside the United Kingdom—

(a)   a summons or other process requiring a person to appear as defendant or attend as a witness is criminal proceedings in that country or territory; or

(b)   a document issued by a court exercising criminal jurisdiction in that country or territory and recording a decision of the court made in the exercise of that jurisdiction,
together with a request for it to be served on a person in the United Kingdom.

(2)   The Secretary of State or, where the person to be served is in Scotland, the Lord Advocate may cause the process or document to be served by post or, if the request is for personal service, direct the chief officer of police for the area in which that person appears to be to cause it to be personally served on him.

(3)   Service by virtue of this section of any such process as is mentioned in subsection (1)(a) above shall not impose any obligation under the law of any part of the United Kingdom to comply with it.

(4)   Any such process served by virtue of this section shall be accompanied by a notice—

(a)   stating the effect of subsection (3) above;

(b)   indicating that the person on whom it is served may wish to seek advice as to the possible consequences of his failing to comply with the process under the law of the country or territory where it was issued; and

(c)   indicating that under that law he may not, as a witness, be accorded the same rights and privileges as would be accorded to him in criminal proceedings in the United Kingdom.

(5)   Where a chief officer of police is directed under this section to cause any process or document to be served he shall after it has been served forthwith inform the Secretary of State or, as the case may be, the Lord Advocate when and how it was served and (if possible) furnish him with a receipt signed by the person on whom it was served; and if the chief officer has been unable to cause the process or document to be served he shall forthwith inform the Secretary of State or, as the case may be, the Lord Advocate of that fact and of the reason.

(6)   In the application of this section to Northern Ireland for references to a chief officer of police there shall be substituted references to the Chief Constable of the Royal Ulster Constabulary.

2.   Service of United Kingdom process overseas

(1)   Process of the following descriptions, that is to say—

(a)   a summons requiring a person charged with an offence to appear before a court in the United Kingdom; and

(b)   a summons or order requiring a person to attend before a court in the United Kingdom for the purpose of giving evidence in criminal proceedings,
may be issued or made notwithstanding that the person in question is outside the United Kingdom and may be served outside the United Kingdom in accordance with arrangements made by the Secretary of State.

(2)   In relation to Scotland subsection (1) above applies to any document which may competently be served on any accused person or on any person who may give evidence in criminal proceedings.

(3)   Service of any process outside the United Kingdom by virtue of this section shall not impose any obligation under the law of any part of the United Kingdom to comply with it and accordingly failure to do so shall not constitute contempt of any court or be a ground for issuing a warrant to secure the attendance of the person in question or, in Scotland, for imposing any penalty.

(4)   Subsection (3) above is without prejudice to the service of any process (with the usual consequences for non-compliance) on the person in question if subsequently effected in the United Kingdom.

Mutual provision of evidence

3. Overseas evidence for use in United Kingdom

(1) Where on an application made in accordance with subsection (2) below it appears to a justice of the peace or a judge or, in Scotland, to a sheriff or a judge—

(a) that an offence has been committed or that there are reasonable grounds for suspecting that an offence has been committed; and

(b) that proceedings in respect of the offence have been instituted or that the offence is being investigated,

he may issue a letter ('a letter of request') requesting assistance in obtaining outside the United Kingdom such evidence as is specified in the letter for use in the proceedings or investigation.

(2) An application under subsection (1) above may be made by a prosecuting authority or, if proceedings have been instituted, by the person charged in those proceedings.

(3) A prosecuting authority which is for the time being designated for the purposes of this section by an order made by the Secretary of State by statutory instrument may itself issue a letter of request if—

(a) it is satisfied as to the matters mentioned in subsection (1)(a) above; and

(b) the offence in question is being investigated or the authority has instituted proceedings in respect of it.

(4) Subject to subsection (5) below, a letter of request shall be sent to the Secretary of State for transmission either—

(a) to a court or tribunal specified in the letter and exercising jurisdiction in the place where the evidence is to be obtained; or

(b) to any authority recognised by the government of the country or territory in question as the appropriate authority for receiving requests for assistance of the kind to which this section applies.

(5) In cases of urgency a letter of request may be sent direct to such a court or tribunal as is mentioned in subsection (4)(a) above.

(6) In this section 'evidence' includes documents and other articles.

(7) Evidence obtained by virtue of a letter of request shall not without the consent of such an authority as is mentioned in subsection (4)(b) above be used for any purpose other than that specified in the letter; and when any document or other article obtained pursuant to a letter of request is no longer required for that purpose (or for any other purpose for which such consent has been obtained), it shall be returned to such an authority unless that authority indicates that the document or article need not be returned.

(8) In exercising the discretion conferred by section 25 of the Criminal Justice Act 1988 (exclusion of evidence otherwise admissible in relation to a statement contained in evidence taken pursuant to a letter of request the court shall have regard—

(a) to whether it was possible to challenge the statement by questioning the person who made it; and

(b) if proceedings have been instituted, to whether the local law allowed the parties to the proceedings to be legally represented when the evidence was being taken.

(9) In Scotland evidence obtained by virtue of a letter of request shall, without being sworn to by witnesses, be received in evidence in so far as that can be done without unfairness to either party.

(10) In the application of this section to Northern Ireland for the reference in subsection (1) to a justice of the peace there shall be substituted a reference to a resident magistrate and for the reference in subsection (8) to section 25 of the Criminal Justice Act 1988 there shall be substituted a reference to Article 5 of the Criminal Justice (Evidence, Etc.) (Northern Ireland) Order 1988.

4.   United Kingdom evidence for use overseas
(1)   This section has effect where the Secretary of State receives—
(a)   from a court or tribunal exercising criminal jurisdiction in a country or territory outside the United Kingdom or a prosecuting authority in such a country or territory; or
(b)   from any other authority in such a country or territory which appears to him to have the function of making requests of the kind to which this section applies,
a request for assistance in obtaining evidence in the United Kingdom in connection with criminal proceedings that have been instituted, or a criminal investigation that is being carried on, in that country or territory.
(2)   If the Secretary of State or, if the evidence is to be obtained in Scotland, the Lord Advocate is satisfied—
(a)   that an offence under the law of the country or territory in question has been committed or that there are reasonable grounds for suspecting that such an offence has been committed; and
(b)   that proceedings in respect of that offence have been instituted in that country or territory or that an investigation into the offence is being carried on there,
he may, if he thinks fit, by a notice in writing nominate a court in England, Wales or Northern Ireland or, as the case may be, Scotland to receive such of the evidence to which the request relates as may appear to the court to be appropriate for the purpose of giving effect to the request.
(2A)   Except where the evidence is to be obtained as is mentioned in subsection (2B) below, if the Secretary of State is satisfied—
(a)   that an offence under the law of the country or territory in question has been committed or that there are reasonable grounds for suspecting that such an offence has been committed; and
(b)   that proceedings in respect of that offence have been instituted in that country or territory or that an investigation into that offence is being carried on there,
and it appears to him that the request relates to an offence involving serious or complex fraud, he may, if he thinks fit, refer the request or any part of the request to the Director of the Serious Fraud Office for him to obtain such of the evidence to which the request or part referred relates as may appear to the Director to be appropriate for giving effect to the request or part referred.
(2B)   Where the evidence is to be obtained in Scotland, if the Lord Advocate is satisfied as to the matters mentioned in paragraphs (a) and (b) of subsection (2A) above and it appears to him that the request relates to an offence involving serious or complex fraud, he may, if he thinks fit, give a direction under section 51 of the Criminal Justice (Scotland) Act 1987.
(3)   Where it appears to the Secretary of State or, as the case may be, the Lord Advocate that the request relates to a fiscal offence in respect of which proceedings have not yet been instituted he shall not exercise his powers under subsection (2), (2A) or (2B) above unless—
(a)   the request is from a country or territory which is a member of the Commonwealth or is made pursuant to a treaty to which the United Kingdom is a party; or
(b)   he is satisfied that the conduct constituting the offence would constitute an offence of the same or a similar nature if it had occurred in the United Kingdom.
(4)   For the purpose of satisfying himself as to the matters mentioned in subsection (2)(a) and (b) or (2A)(a) and (b) above the Secretary of State or, as the case may be, the Lord Advocate shall regard as conclusive a certificate issued by such authority in the country or territory in question as appears to him to be appropriate.
(5)   In this section 'evidence' includes documents and other articles.
(6)   Schedule 1 to this Act shall have effect with respect to the proceedings before a nominated court in pursuance of a notice under subsection (2) above.

5. Transfer of United Kingdom prisoner to give evidence or assist investigation overseas

(1) The Secretary of State may, if he thinks fit, issue a warrant providing for any person ('a prisoner') serving a sentence in a prison or other institution to which the Prison Act 1952 or the Prisons (Scotland) Act 1989 applies to be transferred to a country or territory outside the United Kingdom for the purpose—

(a) of giving evidence in criminal proceedings there; or

(b) of being identified in, or otherwise by his presence assisting, such proceedings or the investigation of an offence.

(2) No warrant shall be issued under this section in respect of any prisoner unless he has consented to being transferred as mentioned in subsection (1) above and that consent may be given either—

(a) by the prisoner himself; or

(b) in circumstances in which it appears to the Secretary of State inappropriate, by reason of the prisoner's physical or mental condition or his youth, for him to act for himself, by a person appearing to the Secretary of State to be an appropriate person to act on his behalf;

but a consent once given shall not be capable of being withdrawn after the issue of the warrant.

(3) The effect of a warrant under this section shall be to authorise—

(a) the taking of the prisoner to a place in the United Kingdom and his delivery at a place of departure from the United Kingdom into the custody of a person representing the appropriate authority of the country or territory to which the prisoner is to be transferred; and

(b) the bringing of the prisoner back to the United Kingdom and his transfer in custody to the place where he is liable to be detained under the sentence to which he is subject.

(4) Where a warrant has been issued in respect of a prisoner under this section he shall be deemed to be in legal custody at any time when, being in the United Kingdom or on board a British ship, British aircraft or British hovercraft, he is being taken under the warrant to or from any place or being kept in custody under the warrant.

(5) A person authorised by or for the purposes of the warrant to take the prisoner to or from any place or to keep him in custody shall have all the powers, authority, protection and privileges—

(a) of a constable in the part of the United Kingdom in which that person is for the time being; or

(b) if he is outside the United Kingdom, of a constable in the part of the United Kingdom to or from which the prisoner is to be taken under the warrant.

(6) If the prisoner escapes or is unlawfully at large, he may be arrested without warrant by a constable and taken to any place to which he may be taken under the warrant issued under this section.

(7) In subsection (4) above—

'British aircraft' means a British-controlled aircraft within the meaning of section 92 of the Civil Aviation Act 1982 (application of criminal law to aircraft) or one of Her Majesty's aircraft;

'British hovercraft' means a British-controlled hovercraft within the meaning of that section as applied in relation to hovercraft by virtue of provisions made under the Hovercraft Act 1968 or one of Her Majesty's hovercraft;

'British ship' means a British ship for the purposes of the Merchant Shipping Acts 1894 to 1988 or one of Her Majesty's ships;

and in this subsection references to Her Majesty's aircraft, hovercraft or ships are references to aircraft, hovercraft or, as the case may be, ships belonging to or exclusively employed in the service of Her Majesty in right of the Government of the United Kingdom.

(8)   In subsection (6) above 'constable', in relation to any part of the United Kingdom, means any person who is a constable in that or any other part of the United Kingdom or any person who, at the place in question has, under any enactment including subsection (5) above, the powers of a constable in that or any other part of the United Kingdom.

(9)   The section applies to a person in custody awaiting trial or sentence and a person committed to prison for default in paying a fine as it applies to a prisoner and the reference in subsection (3)(b) above to a sentence shall be construed accordingly.

(10)   In the application of this section to Northern Ireland for the reference in subsection (1) to the Prison Act 1952 there shall be substituted a reference to the Prison Act (Northern Ireland) 1953.

6.   Transfer of overseas prisoner to give evidence or assist investigation in the United Kingdom
(1)   This section has effect where—
(a)   a witness order has been made or a witness summons or citation issued in criminal proceedings in the United Kingdom in respect of a person ('a prisoner') who is detained in custody in a country or territory outside the United Kingdom by virtue of a sentence or order of a court or tribunal exercising criminal jurisdiction in that country or territory; or
(b)   it appears to the Secretary of State that it is desirable for a prisoner to be identified in, or otherwise by his presence to assist, such proceedings or the investigation in the United Kingdom of an offence.

(2)   If the Secretary of State is satisfied that the appropriate authority in the country or territory where the prisoner is detained will make arrangements for him to come to the United Kingdom to give evidence pursuant to the witness order, witness summons or citation or, as the case may be, for the purpose mentioned in subsection (1)(b) above, he may issue a warrant under this section.

(3)   No warrant shall be issued under this section in respect of any prisoner unless he has consented to being brought to the United Kingdom to give evidence as aforesaid or, as the case may be, for the purpose mentioned in subsection (1)(b) above but a consent once given shall not be capable of being withdrawn after the issue of the warrant.

(4)   The effect of the warrant shall be to authorise—
(a)   the bringing of the prisoner to the United Kingdom;
(b)   the taking of the prisoner to, and his detention in custody at, such place or places in the United Kingdom as are specified in the warrant; and
(c)   the returning of the prisoner to the country or territory from which he has come.

(5)   Subsections (4) to (8) of section 5 above shall have effect in relation to a warrant issued under this section as they have effect in relation to a warrant issued under that section.

(6)   A person shall not be subject to the Immigration Act 1971 in respect of his entry into or presence in the United Kingdom in pursuance of a warrant under this section but if the warrant ceases to have effect while he is still in the United Kingdom—
(a)   he shall be treated for the purposes of that Act as if he has then illegally entered the United Kingdom; and
(b)   the provisions of Schedule 2 to that Act shall have effect accordingly except that paragraph 20(1) (liability of carrier for expenses of custody etc. of illegal entrant) shall not have effect in relation to directions for his removal given by virtue of this subsection.

(7)   This section applies to a person detained in custody in a country or territory outside the United Kingdom in consequence of having been transferred there—

(a)   from the United Kingdom under the Repatriation of Prisoners Act 1984; or

(b)   under any similar provision or arrangement from any other country or territory,

as it applies to a person detained as mentioned in subsection (1) above.

Additional co-operation powers

7.   Search etc. for material relevant to overseas investigation

(1)   Part II of the Police and Criminal Evidence Act 1984 (powers of entry, search and seizure) shall have effect as if references to serious arrestable offences in section 8 of and Schedule 1 to that Act included any conduct which is an offence under the law of a country or territory outside the United Kingdom and would constitute a serious arrestable offence if it had occurred in any part of the United Kingdom.

(2)   If, on an application made by a constable, a justice of the peace is satisfied—

(a)   that criminal proceedings have been instituted against a person in a country or territory outside the United Kingdom or that a person has been arrested in the course of a criminal investigation carried on there;

(b)   that the conduct constituting the offence which is the subject of the proceedings or investigation would constitute an arrestable offence within the meaning of the said Act of 1984 if it had occurred in any part of the United Kingdom; and

(c)   that there are reasonable grounds for suspecting that there is on premises in the United Kingdom occupied or controlled by that person evidence relating to the offence other than items subject to legal privilege within the meaning of that Act,

he may issue a warrant authorising a constable to enter and search those premises and to seize any such evidence found there.

(3)   The power to search conferred by subsection (2) above is only a power to search to the extent that is reasonably required for the purpose of discovering such evidence as is there mentioned.

(4)   No application for a warrant or order shall be made by virtue of subsection (1) or (2) above except in pursuance of a direction given by the Secretary of State in response to a request received—

(a)   from a court or tribunal exercising criminal jurisdiction in the overseas country or territory in question or a prosecuting authority in that country or territory; or

(b)   from any other authority in that country or territory which appears to him to have the function of making requests for the purposes of this section;

and any evidence seized by a constable by virtue of this section shall be furnished by him to the Secretary of State for transmission to that court, tribunal or authority.

(5)   If in order to comply with the request it is necessary for any such evidence to be accompanied by any certificate, affidavit or other verifying document the constable shall also furnish for transmission such document of that nature as may be specified in the direction given by the Secretary of State.

(6)   Where the evidence consists of a document the original or a copy shall be transmitted, and where it consists of any other article the article itself or a description, photograph or other representation of it shall be transmitted, as may be necessary in order to comply with the request.

(7)   The Treasury may by order direct that any powers which by virtue of this section are exercisable by a constable shall also be exercisable by, or by any person acting under the direction of, an officer commissioned by the Commissioners of Customs and Excise under section 6(3) of the Customs and Excise Management Act 1979; and the Secretary of State may by order direct that any of those powers shall also be exercisable by a person or any other description specified in the order.

(8)   An order under subsection (7) above shall be made by statutory instrument subject to annulment in pursuance of a resolution of either House of Parliament.

(9)   In the application of this section to Northern Ireland for references to the Police and Criminal Evidence Act 1984, to Part II and section 8 of and to Schedule 1

to that Act there shall be substituted references to the Police and Criminal Evidence (Northern Ireland) Order 1989, to Part III and Article 10 of and to Schedule 1 to that Order.

9. Enforcement of overseas forfeiture orders

(1)   Her Majesty may by Order in Council provide for the enforcement in the United Kingdom of any order which—

(a)   is made by a court in a country or territory outside the United Kingdom designated for the purposes of this section by the Order in Council; and

(b)   is for the forfeiture and destruction, or the forfeiture and other disposal, of anything in respect of which an offence to which this section applies has been committed or which was used in connection with the commission of such an offence.

(2)   Without prejudice to the generality of subsection (1) above an Order in Council under this section may provide for the registration by a court in the United Kingdom of any order as a condition of its enforcement and prescribe requirements to be satisfied before an order can be registered.

(3)   An Order in Council under this section may include such supplementary and incidental provisions as appear to Her Majesty to be necessary or expedient and may apply for the purposes of the Order (with such modifications as appear to Her Majesty to be appropriate) any provisions relating to confiscation or forfeiture orders under any other enactment.

(4)   An Order in Council under this section may make different provision for different cases.

(5)   No Order in Council shall be made under this section unless a draft of it has been laid before and approved by a resolution of each House of Parliament.

(6)   This section applies to any offence which corresponds to or is similar to an offence under the Misuse of Drugs Act 1971, a drug trafficking offence as defined in section 1(3) of the Drug Trafficking Act 1994, an offence to which section 1 of the Criminal Justice (Scotland) Act 1987 relates or an offence to which Part VI of the Criminal Justice Act 1988 applies.

Supplementary

10. Rules of court

(1)   Provision may be made by rules of court for any purpose for which it appears to the authority having power to make the rules that it is necessary or expedient that provision should be made in connection with any of the provisions of this Part of this Act.

(2)   Rules made for the purposes of Schedule 1 to this Act may, in particular, make provision with respect to the persons entitled to appear or take part in the proceedings to which that Schedule applies and for excluding the public from any such proceedings.

(3)   An Order in Council under section 9 above may authorise the making of rules of court for any purpose specified in the Order.

(4)   Rules of court made under this section by the High Court in Scotland shall be made by Act of Adjournal.

(5)   This section is without prejudice to the generality of any existing power to make rules.

11. Application to courts-martial etc.

(1)   Section 2 above applies also to a summons requiring a person charged with a civil offence to appear before a service court (whether or not in the United Kingdom) or to attend before such a court for the purpose of giving evidence in proceedings for such an offence; and a warrant may be issued under section 6 above where—

(a)   such a summons has been issued in respect of a prisoner within the meaning of that section; or

(b)   it appears to the Secretary of State that it is desirable for such a prisoner to be identified in, or otherwise by his presence to assist, such proceedings or the investigation or such an offence.

(2)   Section 5 above applies also to a person serving a sentence of detention imposed by a service court or detained in custody awaiting trial by such a court.

(3)   In this section 'a civil offence' has the same meaning as in the Army Act 1955, the Air Force Act 1955 and the Naval Discipline Act 1957 and 'service court' means a court-martial constituted under any of those Acts or a Standing Civilian Court.

PART IV
GENERAL

30.   Expenses and receipts

(1)   Any expenses incurred by the Secretary of State under this Act shall be defrayed out of money provided by Parliament.

(2)   Any money representing cash forfeited under Part III of this Act or accrued interest thereon shall be paid into the Consolidated Fund.

31.   Consequential and other amendments, repeals and revocation

(1)   The enactments and instruments mentioned in Schedule 4 to this Act shall have effect with the amendments there specified, being amendments consequential on or otherwise relating to the provisions of this Act.

(2)   For the avoidance of doubt it is hereby declared that the amendment by that Schedule of the definition of 'drug trafficking offence' in section 38(1) of the Drug Trafficking Offences Act 1986 applies to that definition as applied by any other enactment, including this Act.

(3)   The enactments mentioned in Schedule 5 to this Act are hereby repealed to the extent specified in the third column of that Schedule.

(4)   Article 9 of the Criminal Justice (Evidence, Etc.) (Northern Ireland) Order 1988 is hereby revoked.

32.   Short title, commencement and extent

(1)   This Act may be cited as the Criminal Justice (International Co-operation) Act 1990.

(2)   This Act shall come into force on such day as may be appointed by the Secretary of State by an order made by statutory instrument and different days may be appointed for different provisions and different purposes and for different parts of the United Kingdom.

(3)   This Act extends to Northern Ireland.

(4)   Her Majesty may by Order in Council direct that the provisions of this Act and those provisions of the Drug Trafficking Act 1994 which re-enact provisions of this Act shall extend, with such exceptions and modifications as appear to Her Majesty to be appropriate, to any of the Channel Islands, the Isle of Man or any colony.

SCHEDULES

Section 4(6)   SCHEDULE 1

UNITED KINGDOM EVIDENCE FOR USE OVERSEAS: PROCEEDINGS OF
NOMINATED COURT

Securing attendance of witnesses

1.   The court shall have the like powers for securing the attendance of a witness for the purpose of the proceedings as it has for the purpose of other proceedings before the court.

2.   In Scotland the court shall have power to issue a warrant to officers of law to cite witnesses for the purpose of the proceedings and section 320 of the Criminal Procedure (Scotland) Act 1975 shall apply in relation to such a witness.

Power to administer oaths

3.   The court may in the proceedings take evidence on oath.

Privilege of witnesses

4.—(1)   A person shall not be compelled to give in the proceedings any evidence which he could not be compelled to give—

    (a)   in criminal proceedings in the part of the United Kingdom in which the nominated court exercises jurisdiction; or

    (b)   subject to sub-paragraph (2) below, in criminal proceedings in the country or territory from which the request for the evidence has come.

(2)   Sub-paragraph (1)(b) above shall not apply unless the claim of the person questioned to be exempt from giving the evidence is conceded by the court, tribunal or authority which made the request.

(3)   Where such a claim made by any person is not conceded as aforesaid he may (subject to the other provisions of this paragraph) be required to give the evidence to which the claim relates but the evidence shall not be transmitted to the court, tribunal or authority which requested it if a court in the country or territory in question, on the matter being referred to it, upholds the claim.

(4)   Without prejudice to sub-paragraph (1) above a person shall not be compelled under this Schedule to give any evidence if his doing so would be prejudicial to the security of the United Kingdom; and a certificate signed by or on behalf of the Secretary of State or, where the court is in Scotland, by or on behalf of the Lord Advocate to the effect that it would be so prejudicial for that person to do so shall be conclusive evidence of that fact.

(5)   Without prejudice to sub-paragraph (1) above a person shall not be compelled under this Schedule to give any evidence in his capacity as an officer or servant of the Crown.

(6)   In this paragraph references to giving evidence include references to answering any question and to producing any document or other article and the reference in sub-paragraph (3) above to the transmission of evidence given by a person shall be construed accordingly.

Transmission of evidence

5.—(1)   The evidence received by the court shall be furnished to the Secretary of State or, in Scotland, the Lord Advocate for transmission to the court, tribunal or authority that made the request.

(2)   If in order to comply with the request it is necessary for the evidence to be accompanied by any certificate, affidavit or other verifying document, the court shall also furnish for transmission such document of that nature as may be specified in the notice nominating the court.

(3)   Where the evidence consists of a document the original or a copy shall be transmitted, and where it consists of any other article the article itself or a description, photograph or other representation of it shall be transmitted, as may be necessary in order to comply with the request.

Supplementary

6.   For the avoidance of doubt it is hereby declared that the Bankers Books' Evidence Act 1879 applies to the proceedings as it applies to other proceedings before the court.

7.   No order for costs shall be made in the proceedings.

Section 31(1)   SCHEDULE 4

CONSEQUENTIAL AND OTHER AMENDMENTS

The Misuse of Drugs Act 1971

1.   In section 27(1) of the Misuse of Drugs Act 1971 after '1986' there shall be inserted the words 'or an offence to which section 1 of the Criminal Justice (Scotland) Act 1987 relates'.

The Magistrates' Courts Act 1980

2.   After section 97(2) of the Magistrates' Courts Act 1980 there shall be inserted—
    '(2A)   A summons may also be issued under subsection (1) above if the justice is satisfied that the person in question is outside the British Islands but no warrant shall be issued under subsection (2) above unless the justice is satisfied by evidence on oath that the person in question is in England or Wales.'

The Criminal Justice Act 1982

3.   At the end of Part II of Schedule 1 to the Criminal Justice Act 1982 there shall be inserted—
    'Criminal Justice (International Co-operation) Act 1990 (c. 5)
    Section 14 (concealing or transferring proceeds of drug trafficking).'

The Drug Trafficking Offences Act 1986

4.—(1)   The Drug Trafficking Offences Act 1986 shall be amended as follows.
    (2)   In section 2(4) after the words 'section 24 of this Act' there shall be inserted the words 'or section 14 of the Criminal Justice (International Co-operation) Act 1990'.
    (3)   In the definition of 'drug trafficking' in section 38(1) after paragraph (c) there shall be inserted—
        '(d)   manufacturing or supplying a scheduled substance within the meaning of section 12 of the Criminal Justice (International Co-operation) Act 1990 where the manufacture or supply is an offence under that section;'.
    (4)   In the definition of 'drug trafficking offence' in section 38(1) after paragraph (d) there shall be inserted—
        '(dd)   an offence under sections 12, 14 or 19 of the Criminal Justice (International Co-operation) Act 1990;',
and in paragraph (e) for '(d)' there shall be substituted '(dd)'.

The Criminal Justice (Scotland) Act 1987

5.—(1)   The Criminal Justice (Scotland) Act 1987 shall be amended as follows.
    (2)   In section 1—
        (a)   in subsection (2) after paragraph (c) there shall be inserted—
        '(cc)   an offence under sections 12, 14 or 19 of the Criminal Justice (International Co-operation) Act 1990;',
and in paragraph (d) for 'or (c)' there shall be substituted ', (c) or (cc)';
        (b)   in subsection (6) after paragraph (d) there shall be inserted—
        '(e)   manufacturing or supplying a scheduled substance within the meaning of section 12 of the Criminal Justice (International Co-operation) Act 1990 where the manufacture or supply is an offence under that section;'.
    (3)   In section 3(3) after the words 'section 43 of this Act' there shall be inserted the words 'or section 14 of the Criminal Justice (International Co-operation) Act 1990'.
    (4)   In section 5(2) the words from 'at the date' to 'first occurs)', the words 'on that date' and the words 'as at that date' shall cease to have effect.

The Criminal Justice Act 1988

6.—(1) The Criminal Justice Act 1988 shall be amended as follows.

(2) In sections 24(4) and 26 for the words 'section 29 below' there shall be substituted the words 'section 3 of the Criminal Justice (International Co-operation) Act 1990'.

(3) In paragraph 6(1) of Schedule 13 for the words 'In section 29 above "criminal proceedings" does not include proceedings before a Service court' there shall be substituted the words 'No application shall be made under section 3 of the Criminal Justice (International Co-operation) Act 1990 in relation to any offence which is or is to be the subject to proceedings before a Service court'.

The Magistrates' Courts (Northern Ireland) Order 1981

7. In Article 118(2) of the Magistrates' Courts (Northern Ireland) Order 1981 after the words 'a person' there shall be inserted the words 'in Northern Ireland'.

The Criminal Justice (Evidence, Etc.) (Northern Ireland) Order 1988

8. In Articles 4(4) and 6 of the Criminal Justice (Evidence, etc.) (Northern Ireland) Order 1988 for the words 'Article 9' there shall be substituted the words 'section 3 of the Criminal Justice (International Co-operation) Act 1990'.

CRIMINAL PROCEDURE (INSANITY AND UNFITNESS TO PLEAD) ACT 1991
(1991, c. 25)

1. Acquittals on grounds of insanity

(1) A jury shall not return a special verdict under section 2 of the Trial of Lunatics Act 1883 (acquittal on ground of insanity) except on the written or oral evidence of two or more registered medical practitioners at least one of whom is duly approved.

(2) Subsections (2) and (3) of section 54 of the Mental Health Act 1983 ('the 1983 Act') shall have effect with respect to proof of the accused's mental condition for the purposes of the said section 2 as they have effect with respect to proof of an offender's mental condition for the purpose of section 37(2)(a) of that Act.

2. Findings of unfitness to plead etc.

For section 4 of the Criminal Procedure (Insanity) Act 1964 ('the 1964 Act') there shall be substituted the following sections—

'**4. Finding of unfitness to plead**

(1) This section applies where on the trial of a person the question arises (at the instance of the defence or otherwise) whether the accused is under a disability, that is to say, under any disability such that apart from this Act it would constitute a bar to his being tried.

(2) If, having regard to the nature of the supposed disability, the court are of opinion that it is expedient to do so and in the interests of the accused, they may postpone consideration of the question of fitness to be tried until any time up to the opening of the case for the defence.

(3) If, before the question of fitness to be tried falls to be determined, the jury return a verdict of acquittal on the count or each of the counts on which the accused is being tried, that question shall not be determined.

(4) Subject to subsections (2) and (3) above, the question of fitness to be tried shall be determined as soon as it arises.

(5) The question of fitness to be tried shall be determined by a jury and—

(a) where it falls to be determined on the arraignment of the accused and the trial proceeds, the accused shall be tried by a jury other than that which determined that question;

(b)   where it falls to be determined at any later time, it shall be determined by a separate jury or by the jury by whom the accused is being tried, as the court may direct.

(6)   A jury shall not make a determination under subsection (5) above except on the written or oral evidence of two or more registered medical practitioners at least one of whom is duly approved.

4A.   Finding that the accused did the act or made the omission charged against him

(1)   This section applies where in accordance with section 4(5) above it is determined by a jury that the accused is under a disability.

(2)   The trial shall not proceed or further proceed but it shall be determined by a jury—

(a)   on the evidence (if any) already given in the trial; and

(b)   on such evidence as may be adduced or further adduced by the prosecution, or adduced by a person appointed by the court under this section to put the case for the defence,

whether they are satisfied, as respects the count or each of the counts on which the accused was to be or was being tried, that he did the act or made the omission charged against him as the offence.

(3)   If as respects that count or any of those counts the jury are satisfied as mentioned in subsection (2) above, they shall make a finding that the accused did the act or made the omission charged against him.

(4)   If as respects that count or any of those counts the jury are not so satisfied, they shall return a verdict of acquittal as if on the count in question the trial had proceeded to a conclusion.

(5)   A determination under subsection (2) above shall be made—

(a)   where the question of disability was determined on the arraignment of the accused, by a jury other than that which determined that question; and

(b)   where that question was determined at any later time, by the jury by whom the accused was being tried.'

3.   Powers to deal with persons not guilty by reason of insanity or unfit to plead etc.

For section 5 of the 1964 Act there shall be substituted the following section—

'5.   Powers to deal with persons not guilty by reason of insanity or unfit to plead etc.

(1)   This section applies where—

(a)   a special verdict is returned that the accused is not guilty by reason of insanity; or

(b)   findings are recorded that the accused is under a disability and that he did the act or made the omission charged against him.

(2)   Subject to subsection (3) below, the court shall either—

(a)   make an order that the accused be admitted, in accordance with the provisions of Schedule 1 to the Criminal Procedure (Insanity and Unfitness to Plead) Act 1991, to such hospital as may be specified by the Secretary of State; or

(b)   where they have the power to do so by virtue of section 5 of that Act, make in respect of the accused such one of the following orders as they think most suitable in all the circumstances of the case, namely—

(i)   a guardianship order within the meaning of the Mental Health Act 1983;

(ii)   a supervision and treatment order within the meaning of Schedule 2 to the said Act of 1991; and

(iii)   an order for his absolute discharge.

(3)   Paragraph (b) of subsection (2) above shall not apply where the offence to which the special verdict or findings relate is an offence the sentence for which is fixed by law.'

4.   Corresponding provisions with respect to appeals

(1)   For section 6 of the Criminal Appeal Act 1968 ('the 1968 Act') there shall be substituted the following section—

'**6.   Substitution of finding of insanity or findings of unfitness to plead etc.**

(1)   This section applies where, on an appeal against conviction, the Court of Appeal, on the written or oral evidence of two or more registered medical practitioners at least one of whom is duly approved, are of opinion—

(a)   that the proper verdict would have been one of not guilty by reason of insanity; or

(b)   that the case is not one where there should have been a verdict of acquittal, but there should have been findings that the accused was under a disability and that he did the act or made the omission charged against him.

(2)   Subject to subsection (3) below, the Court of Appeal shall either—

(a)   make an order that the appellant be admitted, in accordance with the provisions of Schedule 1 to the Criminal Procedure (Insanity and Unfitness to Plead) Act 1991, to such hospital as may be specified by the Secretary of State; or

(b)   where they have the power to do so by virtue of section 5 of that Act, make in respect of the appellant such one of the following orders as they think most suitable in all the circumstances of the case, namely—

(i)   a guardianship order within the meaning of the Mental Health Act 1983;

(ii)   a supervision and treatment order within the meaning of Schedule 2 to the said Act of 1991; and

(iii)   an order for his absolute discharge.

(3)   Paragraph (b) of subsection (2) above shall not apply where the offence to which the appeal relates is an offence the sentence for which is fixed by law.'

(2)   For section 14 of the 1968 Act there shall be substituted the following sections—

'**14.   Substitution of findings of unfitness to plead etc.**

(1)   This section applies where, on an appeal under section 12 of this Act, the Court of Appeal, on the written or oral evidence of two or more registered medical practitioners at least one of whom is duly approved, are of opinion that—

(a)   the case is not one where there should have been a verdict of acquittal; but

(b)   there should have been findings that the accused was under a disability and that he did the act or made the omission charged against him.

(2)   Subject to subsection (3) below, the Court of Appeal shall either—

(a)   make an order that the appellant be admitted, in accordance with the provisions of Schedule 1 to the Criminal Procedure (Insanity and Unfitness to Plead) Act 1991, to such hospital as may be specified by the Secretary of State; or

(b)   where they have the power to do so by virtue of section 5 of that Act, make in respect of the appellant such one of the following orders as they think most suitable in all the circumstances of the case, namely—

(i)   a guardianship order within the meaning of the Mental Health Act 1983;

(ii)   a supervision and treatment order within the meaning of Schedule 2 to the said Act of 1991; and

(iii)   an order for his absolute discharge.

(3)   Paragraph (b) of subsection (2) above shall not apply where the offence to which the appeal relates is an offence the sentence for which is fixed by law.

14A.   Substitution of verdict of acquittal
(1)   This section applies where, in accordance with section 13(4)(b) of this Act, the Court of Appeal substitute a verdict of acquittal and the Court, on the written or oral evidence of two or more registered medical practitioners at least one of whom is duly approved, are of opinion—
(a)   that the appellant is suffering from mental disorder of a nature or degree which warrants his detention in a hospital for assessment (or for assessment followed by medical treatment) for at least a limited period; and
(b)   that he ought to be so detained in the interests of his own health or safety or with a view to the protection of other persons.
(2)   The Court of Appeal shall make an order that the appellant be admitted for assessment, in accordance with the provisions of Schedule 1 to the Criminal Procedure (Insanity and Unfitness to Plead) Act 1991, to such hospital as may be specified by the Secretary of State.'

5.   Orders under 1964 and 1968 Acts
(1)   The provisions of Schedule 1 to this Act shall apply in relation to the following orders, namely—
(a)   any order made by the Crown Court under section 5 of the 1964 Act that the accused be admitted to hospital; and
(b)   any order made by the Court of Appeal under section 6, 14 or 14A of the 1968 Act that the appellant be so admitted.
(2)   The 1983 Act shall have effect, in its application to guardianship orders within the meaning of that Act, as if the reference in section 37(1) to a person being convicted before the Crown Court of such an offence as is there mentioned included references—
(a)   to a special verdict being returned that the accused is not guilty by reason of insanity, or to findings being recorded that the accused is under a disability and that he did the act or made the omission charged against him; and
(b)   to the Court of Appeal being, on an appeal against conviction or under section 12 of the 1968 Act, of such opinion as is mentioned in section 6(1) or 14(1) of that Act; and in relation to guardianship orders made by virtue of this subsection, references in the 1983 Act to the offender shall be construed accordingly.
(3)   The power to make a supervision and treatment order within the meaning given by Part I of Schedule 2 to this Act shall be exercisable, subject to and in accordance with Part II of that Schedule—
(a)   by the Crown Court in cases to which section 5 of the 1964 Act applies; and
(b)   by the Court of Appeal in cases to which section 6 to 14 of the 1968 Act applies:
and Part III of that Schedule shall have effect with respect to the revocation and amendment of such orders.
(4)   Section 12(1) of the Powers of Criminal Courts (Sentencing) Act 2000 shall have effect, in its application to orders for absolute discharge, as if—
(a)   the reference to a person being convicted by or before a court of such an offence as is there mentioned included such references as are mentioned in subsection (2)(a) and (b) above; and
(b)   the reference to the court being of opinion that it is inexpedient to inflict punishment included a reference to it thinking that an order for absolute discharge would be most suitable in all the circumstances of the case.

6.   Interpretation etc.
(1)   In this Act—

'the 1964 Act' means the Criminal Procedure (Insanity) Act 1964;

'the 1968 Act' means the Criminal Appeal Act 1968;

'the 1983 Act' means the Mental Health Act 1983;

'duly approved', in relation to a registered medical practitioner, means approved for the purposes of section 12 of the 1983 Act by the Secretary of State as having special experience in the diagnosis or treatment of mental disorder; local probation board means a local probation board established under section 4 of the Criminal Justice and Court Services Act 2000.

(2)   Other expressions used in this Act which are also used in the 1983 Act have the same meanings as in Part III of that Act; and references to that Act in sections 137 to 139 of that Act shall include references to Schedule 1 to this Act.

7.   Minor and consequential amendments

The enactments mentioned in Schedule 3 to this Act shall have effect subject to the amendments there specified, being minor amendments or amendments consequential on the preceding provisions of this Act.

8.   Transitional provisions, savings and repeals

(1)   The following provisions, namely—

     (a)   sections 1 to 3 above;

     (b)   so far as relating to the making of orders or orders made under the 1964 Act, section 5 above and Schedules 1 and 2 to this Act; and

     (c)   so far as relating to the repeals in the 1964 Act, the repeal in Schedule 5 to the 1968 Act and the repeal of paragraph 18(b) of Schedule 4 to the 1983 Act, subsection (3) below and Schedule 4 to this Act,

shall not apply where the accused was arraigned before the commencement of this Act.

(2)   The following provisions, namely—

     (a)   section 4 above;

     (b)   so far as relating to the making of orders or orders made under the 1968 Act, section 5 above and Schedules 1 and 2 to this Act;

     (c)   paragraphs 2 to 4 of Schedule 3 to this Act and, so far as relating to those paragraphs, section 7 above; and

     (d)   so far as relating to repeals not mentioned in subsection (1)(c) above, subsection (3) below and Schedule 4 to this Act,

shall not apply where the hearing of the appeal began before that commencement.

(3)   The enactments mentioned in Schedule 4 to this Act are hereby repealed to the extent specified in the third column of that Schedule.

9.   Short title, commencement and extent

(1)   This Act may be cited as the Criminal Procedure (Insanity and Unfitness to Plead) Act 1991.

(2)   This Act shall come into force on such day as the Secretary of State may by order made by statutory instrument appoint.

(3)   This Act extends to England and Wales only.

SCHEDULES

Section 5(1)   SCHEDULE 1

ORDERS FOR ADMISSION TO HOSPITAL

1.—(1)   An admission order, that is to say, an order for admission to hospital made—

     (a)   by the Crown Court under section 5 of the 1964 Act; or

     (b)   by the Court of Appeal under section 6, 14 or 14A of the 1968 Act, shall be sufficient authority for any person acting under the authority of the Secretary of State to take the person to whom the order relates and convey him at any time within the relevant period to the hospital specified by the Secretary of State.

(2)   The court by which any such order is made may give such directions as it thinks fit for the conveyance of a person to whom the order relates to a place of safety and his detention there pending his admission to the hospital within the relevant period.

(3)   Where a person is admitted within the relevant period to the hospital specified by the Secretary of State, the admission order shall be sufficient authority for the managers to detain him in accordance with the provisions of the 1983 Act referred to in paragraphs 2 and 3 below, as those provisions apply by virtue of those paragraphs.

(4)   The relevant period for the purposes of this paragraph is—

(a)   in relation to an admission order made otherwise than under section 14A of the 1968 Act, the period of two months;

(b)   in relation to an admission order excepted by paragraph (a) above, the period of seven days,

beginning (in either case) with the date on which the order in question was made.

2.—(1)   A person who is admitted to a hospital in pursuance of an admission order made otherwise than under section 14A of the 1968 Act shall be treated for the purposes of the 1983 Act—

(a)   as if he had been so admitted in pursuance of a hospital order within the meaning of that Act made on the date of the admission order; and

(b)   if the court so directs, as if an order restricting his discharge had been made under section 41 of that Act, either without limitation of time or during such period as may be specified in the direction.

(2)   Where the offence to which the special verdict, findings or appeal relates is an offence the sentence for which is fixed by law, the court shall give a direction under subparagraph (1)(b) above without specifying any period.

(3)   In the application of subsection (5) of section 40 of the 1983 Act to admission orders made under section 5 of the 1964 Act, that subsection shall have effect as if the reference to a conviction included a reference to a special verdict and to findings that the accused was under a disability and that he did the act or made the omission charged against him.

(4)   In section 47 of the 1983 Act (which relates to the removal to hospital of persons serving sentences of imprisonment and is applied by subsection (5) of that section to persons in other forms of detention), references to a person serving a sentence of imprisonment shall be construed as not including references to a person subject to an admission order made under section 6 or 14 of the 1968 Act.

3.   A person who is admitted to a hospital in pursuance of an admission order made under section 14A of the 1968 Act shall be treated for the purposes of Part II of the 1983 Act as if he had been admitted (on the date of the admission order) in pursuance of an application for admission for assessment duly made under the said Part II.

4.—(1)   If, while a person is detained in pursuance of an admission order made by virtue of section 5(1)(b) of the 1964 Act (findings of unfitness to plead etc.), the Secretary of State, after consultation with the responsible medical officer, is satisfied that that person can properly be tried, the Secretary of State may remit that person for trial either—

(a)   to the court of trial; or

(b)   to a prison;

and on his arrival at the court or prison, the order shall cease to have effect.

(2)   For the purpose of sub-paragraph (1) above, a person shall not be treated as detained in pursuance of such an order as is there mentioned if—

(a)   no direction has been given in his case under paragraph 2(1)(b) above; or

(b)   the Secretary of State has directed under section 42(1) of the 1983 Act that he shall cease to be subject to the special restrictions set out in section 41(3) of that Act.

(3)   In relation to persons ordered under section 2 of the Criminal Lunatics Act 1800 to be kept in custody, sub-paragraphs (1) and (2) above shall apply as if the order were such an order as is mentioned in sub-paragraph (1) above.

Section 5(3)   SCHEDULE 2
                   SUPERVISION AND TREATMENT ORDERS
                              PART I
                            PRELIMINARY

1.—(1)   In this Schedule 'supervision and treatment order' means an order requiring the person in respect of whom it is made ('the supervised person')—
      (a)   to be under the supervision of a social worker or an officer of the local probation board ('the supervising officer') for a period specified in the order of not more than two years; and
      (b)   to submit, during the whole of that period or such part of it as may be specified in the order, to treatment by or under the direction of a registered medical practitioner with a view to the improvement of his mental condition.
(2)   The Secretary of State may by order direct that sub-paragraph (1) above shall be amended by substituting, for the period specified in that sub-paragraph as originally enacted or as previously amended under this sub-paragraph, such period as may be specified in the order.
(3)   An order under sub-paragraph (2) above may make in paragraph 8(2) below any amendment which the Secretary of State thinks necessary in consequence of any substitution made by the order.
(4)   The power of the Secretary of State to make orders under sub-paragraph (2) above shall be exercisable by statutory instrument which shall be subject to annulment in pursuance of a resolution of either House of Parliament.

                              PART II
                   MAKING AND EFFECT OF ORDERS

                Circumstances in which orders may be made

2.—(1)   The court shall not make a supervision and treatment order unless it is satisfied—
      (a)   that, having regard to all the circumstances of the case, the making of such an order is the most suitable means of dealing with the accused or appellant; and
      (b)   on the written or oral evidence of two or more registered medical practitioners, at least one of whom is duly approved, that the mental condition of the accused or appellant—
            (i)   is such as requires and may be susceptible to treatment; but
            (ii)   is not such as to warrant the making of an admission order within the meaning of Schedule 1 to this Act, or the making of a guardianship order within the meaning of the 1983 Act.
(2)   The court shall not make a supervision and treatment order unless it is also satisfied—
      (a)   that the supervising officer intended to be specified in the order is willing to undertake the supervision; and
      (b)   that arrangements have been made for the treatment intended to be specified in the order (including arrangements for the reception of the accused or appellant where he is to be required to submit to treatment as a resident patient).
(3)   Subsections (2) and (3) of section 54 of the 1983 Act shall have effect with respect to proof of a person's mental condition for the purposes of sub-paragraph (1) above as they have effect with respect to proof of an offender's mental condition for the purposes of section 37(2)(a) of that Act.

Making of orders and general requirements

3.—(1) A supervision and treatment order shall either—

(a) specify the local social services authority area in which the supervised person resides or will reside, and require him to be under the supervision of a social worker of the local social services authority for that area; or

(b) specify the petty sessions area in which that person resides or will reside, and require him to be under the supervision of a probation officer appointed for or assigned to that area.

(2) Before making such an order, the court shall explain to the supervised person in ordinary language—

(a) the effect of the order (including any requirements proposed to be included in the order in accordance with paragraph 5 below); and

(b) that a magistrates' court has power under paragraphs 6 to 8 below to review the order on the application either of the supervised person or of the supervising officer.

(3) After making such an order, the court shall forthwith give copies of the order to a probation officer assigned to the court, and he shall give a copy—

(a) to the supervised person;

(b) to the supervising officer; and

(c) to the person in charge of any institution in which the supervised person is required by the order to reside.

(4) After making such an order, the court shall also send to the justices' chief executive for the petty sessions area in which the supervised person resides or will reside ('the petty sessions area concerned')—

(a) a copy of the order; and

(b) such documents and information relating to the case as it considers likely to be of assistance to a court acting for that area in the exercise of its functions in relation to the order.

(5) Where such an order is made, the supervised person shall keep in touch with the supervising officer in accordance with such instructions as he may from time to time be given by the officer and shall notify him of any change of address.

Obligatory requirements as to medical treatment

4.—(1) A supervision and treatment order shall include a requirement that the supervised person shall submit, during the whole of the period specified in the order or during such part of that period as may be so specified, to treatment by or under the direction of a registered medical practitioner with a view to the improvement of his mental condition.

(2) The treatment required by any such order shall be such one of the following kinds of treatment as may be specified in the order, that is to say—

(a) treatment as a resident patient in an independent hospital or care home within the meaning of the Care Standards Act 2000 or in a hospital, not being a special hospital within the meaning of the National Health Service Act 1977;

(b) treatment as a non-resident patient at such institution or place as may be specified in the order; and

(c) treatment by or under the direction of such registered medical practitioner as may be so specified;

but the nature of the treatment shall not be specified in the order except as mentioned in paragraph (a), (b) or (c) above.

(3) While the supervised person is under treatment as a resident patient in pursuance of a requirement of a supervision and treatment order, the supervising officer shall carry out the supervision to such extent only as may be necessary for the purpose of the revocation or amendment of the order.

(4)   Where the medical practitioner by whom or under whose direction the supervised person is being treated for his mental condition in pursuance of a supervision and treatment order is of the opinion that part of the treatment can be better or more conveniently given in or at an institution or place which—

(a)   is not specified in the order; and

(b)   is one in or at which the treatment of the supervised person will be given by or under the direction of a registered medical practitioner,

he may, with the consent of the supervised person, make arrangements for him to be treated accordingly.

(5)   Such arrangements as are mentioned in sub-paragraph (4) above may provide for the supervised person to receive part of his treatment as a resident patient in an institution or place notwithstanding that the institution or place is not one which could have been specified for that purpose in the supervision and treatment order.

(6)   Where any such arrangements as are mentioned in sub-paragraph (4) above are made for the treatment of a supervised person—

(a)   the medical practitioner by whom the arrangements are made shall give notice in writing to the supervising officer, specifying the institution or place in or at which the treatment is to be carried out; and

(b)   the treatment provided for by the arrangements shall be deemed to be treatment to which he is required to submit in pursuance of the supervision and treatment order.

Optional requirements as to residence

5.—(1)   Subject to sub-paragraphs (2) and (3) below, a supervision and treatment order may include requirements as to the residence of the supervised person.

(2)   Before making such an order containing any such requirement, the court shall consider the home surroundings of the supervised person.

(3)   Where such an order requires the supervised person to reside in an approved hostel or any other institution, the period for which he is so required to reside shall be specified in the order.

PART III
REVOCATION AND AMENDMENT OF ORDERS

Revocation of order in interests of health or welfare

6.   Where a supervision and treatment order is in force in respect of any person and, on the application of the supervised person or the supervising officer, it appears to a magistrates' court acting for the petty sessions area concerned that, having regard to circumstances which have arisen since the order was made, it would be in the interests of the health or welfare of the supervised person that the order should be revoked, the court may revoke the order.

Amendment of order by reason of change of residence

7.—(1)   This paragraph applies where, at any time while a supervision and treatment order is in force in respect of any person, a magistrates' court acting for the petty sessions area concerned is satisfied that the supervised person proposes to change, or has changed, his residence from the area specified in the order to another local social services authority area or petty sessions area.

(2)   Subject to sub-paragraph (3) below, the court may, and on the application of the supervising officer shall, amend the supervision and treatment order by substituting the other area for the area specified in the order.

(3)   The court shall not amend under this paragraph a supervision and treatment order which contains requirements which in the opinion of the court, cannot be

complied with unless the supervised person continues to reside in the area specified in the order unless, in accordance with paragraph 8 below, it either—

(a)   cancels those requirements; or

(b)   substitutes for those requirements other requirements which can be complied with if the supervised person ceases to reside in that area.

Amendment of requirements of order

8.—(1)   Without prejudice to the provisions of paragraph 7 above, but subject to sub-paragraph (2) below, a magistrates' court for the petty sessions area concerned may, on the application of the supervised person or the supervising officer, by order amend a supervision and treatment order—

(a)   by cancelling any of the requirements of the order; or

(b)   by inserting in the order (either in addition to or in substitution for any such requirement) any requirement which the court could include if it were the court by which the order was made and were then making it.

(2)   The power of a magistrates' court under sub-paragraph (1) above shall not include power to amend an order by extending the period specified in it beyond the end of two years from the day of the original order.

Amendment of requirements in pursuance of medical report

9.—(1)   Where the medical practitioner by whom or under whose direction the supervised person is being treated for his mental condition in pursuance of any requirement of a supervision and treatment order—

(a)   is of the opinion mentioned in sub-paragraph (2) below; or

(b)   is for any reason unwilling to continue to treat or direct the treatment of the supervised person,

he shall make a report in writing to that effect to the supervising officer and that officer shall apply under paragraph 8 above to a magistrates' court for the petty sessions area concerned for the variation or cancellation of the requirement.

(2)   The opinion referred to in sub-paragraph (1) above is—

(a)   that the treatment of the supervised person should be continued beyond the period specified in the supervision and treatment order;

(b)   that the supervised person needs different treatment, being treatment of a kind to which he could be required to submit in pursuance of such an order;

(c)   that the supervised person is not susceptible to treatment; or

(d)   that the supervised person does not require further treatment.

Supplemental

10.—(1)   On the making under paragraph 6 above of an order revoking a supervision and treatment order, the clerk to the court shall forthwith give copies of the revoking order to the supervising officer.

(2)   A supervising officer to whom in accordance with the sub-paragraph (1) above copies of a revoking order are given shall give a copy to the supervised person and to the person in charge of any institution in which the supervised person was required by the order to reside.

11.—(1)   On the making under paragraph 7 or 8 above of any order amending a supervision and treatment order, the clerk to the court shall forthwith—

(a)   if the order amends the supervision and treatment order otherwise than by substituting a new area or a new place for the one specified in the supervision and treatment order, give copies of the amending order to the supervising officer;

(b)   if the order amends the supervision and treatment order in the manner excepted by paragraph (a) above, send to the clerk to the justices for the new petty sessions area concerned—

(i)   copies of the amending order; and

(ii)   such documents and information relating to the case as he considers likely to be of assistance to a court acting for that area in exercising its functions in relation to the order;

and in a case falling within paragraph (b) above, the clerk to the justices for that area shall give copies of the amending order to the supervising officer.

(2)   Where in accordance with sub-paragraph (1) above copies of an order are given to the supervising officer, he shall give a copy to the supervised person and to the person in charge of any institution in which the supervised person is or was required by the order to reside.

Section 7   SCHEDULE 3

MINOR AND CONSEQUENTIAL AMENDMENTS

1.—(1)   In subsection (2) of section 8 of the 1964 Act (short title, interpretation etc.), immediately before the definition of 'special verdict' there shall be inserted the following definitions—

"duly approved' in relation to a registered medical practitioner, means approved for the purposes of section 12 of the Mental Health Act 1983 by the Secretary of State as having special experience in the diagnosis or treatment of mental disorder;

'registered medical practitioner' means a fully registered person within the meaning of the Medical Act 1983;'.

(2)   After that subsection there shall be inserted the following subsection—

'(2A)   Subsections (2) and (3) of section 54 of the Mental Health Act 1983 shall have effect with respect to proof of the accused's mental condition for the purposes of section 4 of this Act as they have effect with respect to proof of an offender's mental condition for the purposes of section 37(2)(a) of that Act.'

2.   In section 15(1) of the 1968 Act (right of appeal against finding of disability), for the words from 'a finding' to the end there shall be substituted the words 'findings that he is under a disability and that he did the act or made the omission charged against him, the person may appeal to the Court of Appeal against either or both of those findings'.

3.—(2)   Subsection (2) of that section shall cease to have effect.

(3)   For subsection (3) of that section there shall be substituted the following subsections—

'(3)   Where the Court of Appeal allow an appeal under section 15 of this Act against a finding that the appellant is under a disability—

(a)   the appellant may be tried accordingly for the offence with which he was charged; and

(b)   the Court may make such orders as appear to them necessary or expedient pending any such trial for his custody, release on bail or continued detention under the Mental Health Act 1983;

and Schedule 3 to this Act has effect for applying provisions in Part III of that Act to persons in whose case an order is made by the Court under this subsection.

(4)   Where, otherwise than in a case falling within subsection (3) above, the Court of Appeal allow an appeal under section 15 of this Act against a finding that the appellant did the act or made the omission charged against him, the Court shall, in addition to quashing the finding, direct a verdict of acquittal to be recorded (but not a verdict of not guilty by reason of insanity).'

5.—(1)   In subsection (1) of section 51 of the 1968 Act (interpretation)—

(a)   after the definition of 'the defendant' there shall be inserted the following definition—

"'duly approved", in relation to a registered medical practitioner, means approved for the purposes of section 12 of the Mental Health Act 1983 by the Secretary of State as having special experience in the diagnosis or treatment of mental disorder;'; and

(b) after the definition of 'the judge of the court of trial' there shall be inserted the following definition—

"'registered medical practitioner" means a fully registered person within the meaning of the Medical Act 1983;'.

(2) After subsection (2) of that section there shall be inserted the following subsection—

'(2A) Subsections (2) and (3) of section 54 of the Mental Health Act 1983 shall have effect with respect to proof of the appellant's mental condition for the purposes of section 6, 14 or 14A of this Act as they have effect with respect to proof of an offender's mental condition for the purposes of section 37(2)(a) of that Act.'

6. In section 81(1A) of the Supreme Court Act 1981 (bail), for the words 'finding of disability' there shall be substituted the words 'findings that the accused is under a disability and that he did the act or made the omission charged against him'.

7. In section 16(4)(a) of the Prosecution of Offences Act 1985 (defence costs), for sub-paragraph (iii) there shall be substituted the following sub-paragraph—

'(iii) a finding under the Criminal Procedure (Insanity) Act 1964 that the appellant is under a disability, or that he did the act or made the omission charged against him;'.

8. In section 19(3) of the Prosecution of Offences Act 1985 (provision for orders as to costs in other circumstances), after paragraph (c) there shall be inserted the following paragraph—

'(d) to cover the proper fee or costs of a person appointed by the Crown Court under section 4A of the Criminal Procedure (Insanity) Act 1964 to put the case for the defence.'

ROAD TRAFFIC ACT 1991
(1991, c. 40)

Information

21. Information as to identity of driver etc.

For section 172 of the Road Traffic Act 1988 there shall be substituted—

'172. Duty to give information as to identity of driver etc. in certain circumstances

(1) This section applies—

(a) to any offence under the preceding provisions of this Act except—

(i) an offence under Part V, or

(ii) an offence under section 13, 16, 51(2), 61(4), 67(9), 68(4), 96 or 120, and to an offence under section 178 of this Act,

(b) to any offence under sections 25, 26 or 27 of the Road Traffic Offenders Act 1988,

(c) to any offence against any other enactment relating to the use of vehicles on roads, except an offence under paragraph 8 of Schedule 1 to the Road Traffic (Driver Licensing and Information Systems) Act 1989, and

(d) to manslaughter, or in Scotland culpable homicide, by the driver of a motor vehicle.

(2) Where the driver of a vehicle is alleged to be guilty of an offence to which this section applies—

(a)   the person keeping the vehicle shall give such information as to the identity of the driver as he may be required to give by or on behalf of a chief officer of police, and

(b)   any other person shall if required as stated above give any information which it is in his power to give and may lead to identification of the driver.

(3)   Subject to the following provisions, a person who fails to comply with a requirement under subsection (2) above shall be guilty of an offence.

(4)   A person shall not be guilty of an offence by virtue of paragraph (a) of subsection (2) above if he shows that he did not know and could not with reasonable diligence have ascertained who the driver of the vehicle was.

(5)   Where a body corporate is guilty of an offence under this section and the offence is proved to have been committed with the consent or connivance of, or to be attributable to neglect on the part of, a director, manager, secretary or other similar officer of the body corporate, or a person who was purporting to act in any such capacity, he, as well as the body corporate, is guilty of that offence and liable to be proceeded against and punished accordingly.

(6)   Where the alleged offender is a body corporate, or in Scotland a partnership or an unincorporated association, or the proceedings are brought against him by virtue of subsection (5) above or subsection (11) below, subsection (4) above shall not apply unless, in addition to the matters there mentioned, the alleged offender shows that no record was kept of the persons who drove the vehicle and that the failure to keep a record was reasonable.

(7)   A requirement under subsection (2) may be made by written notice served by post; and where it is so made—

(a)   it shall have effect as a requirement to give the information within the period of 28 days beginning with the day on which the notice is served, and

(b)   the person on whom the notice is served shall not be guilty of an offence under this section if he shows either that he gave the information as soon as reasonably practicable after the end of that period or that it has not been reasonably practicable for him to give it.

(8)   Where the person on whom a notice under subsection (7) above is to be served is a body corporate, the notice is duly served if it is served on the secretary or clerk of that body.

(9)   For the purposes of section 7 of the Interpretation Act 1978 as it applies for the purposes of this section the proper address of any person in relation to the service on him of a notice under subsection (7) above is—

(a)   in the case of the secretary or clerk of a body corporate, that of the registered or principal office of that body or (if the body corporate is the registered keeper of the vehicle concerned) the registered address, and

(b)   in any other case, his last known address at the time of service.

(10)   in this section—

'registered address', in relation to the registered keeper of a vehicle, means the address recorded in the record kept under the Vehicles (Excise) Act 1971 with respect to that vehicle as being that person's address, and

'registered keeper', in relation to a vehicle, means the person in whose name the vehicle is registered under that Act;

and references to the driver of a vehicle include references to the rider of a cycle.

(11)   *(Applies to Scotland only.)*'

Trial

22.   Amendment of Schedule 1 to the Road Traffic Offenders Act 1988

Schedule 1 to this Act, which amends Schedule 1 to the Road Traffic Offenders Act 1988 (procedural requirements applicable in relation to certain offences), shall have effect.

23. Speeding offences etc.: admissibility of certain evidence

For section 20 of the Road Traffic Offenders Act 1988 (admissibility of measurement of speed by radar) there shall be substituted—

'20. Speeding offences etc.: admissibility of certain evidence

(1)   Evidence (which in Scotland shall be sufficient evidence) of a fact relevant to proceedings for an offence to which this section applies may be given by the production of—

(a)   a record produced by a prescribed device, and

(b)   (in the same or another document) a certificate as to the circumstances in which the record was produced signed by a constable or by a person authorised by or on behalf of the chief officer of police for the police area in which the offence is alleged to have been committed;

but subject to the following provisions of this section.

(2)   This section applies to—

(a)   an offence under section 16 of the Road Traffic Regulation Act 1984 consisting in the contravention of a restriction on the speed of vehicles imposed under section 14 of that Act;

(b)   an offence under subsection (4) of section 17 of that Act consisting in the contravention of a restriction on the speed of vehicles imposed under that section;

(c)   an offence under section 88(7) of that Act (temporary minimum speed limits);

(d)   an offence under section 89(1) of that Act (speeding offences generally);

(e)   an offence under section 36(1) of the Road Traffic Act 1988 consisting in the failure to comply with an indication given by a light signal that vehicular traffic is not to proceed.

(3)   The Secretary of State may by order amend subsection (2) above by making additions to or deletions from the list of offences for the time being set out there; and an order under this subsection may make such transitional provision as appears to him to be necessary or expedient.

(4)   A record produced or measurement made by a prescribed device shall not be admissible as evidence of a fact relevant to proceedings for an offence to which this section applies unless—

(a)   the device is of a type approved by the Secretary of State, and

(b)   any conditions subject to which the approval was given are satisfied.

(5)   Any approval given by the Secretary of State for the purposes of this section may be given subject to conditions as to the purposes for which, and the manner and other circumstances in which, any device of the type concerned is to be used.

(6)   In proceedings for an offence to which this section applies, evidence (which in Scotland shall be sufficient evidence)—

(a)   of a measurement made by a device, or of the circumstances in which it was made, or

(b)   that a device was of a type approved for the purposes of this section, or that any conditions subject to which an approval was given were satisfied,

may be given by the production of a document which is signed as mentioned in subsection (1) above and which, as the case may be, gives particulars of the measurement or of the circumstances in which it was made, or states that the device was of such a type or that, to the best of the knowledge and belief of the person making the statement, all such conditions were satisfied.

(7)   For the purposes of this section a document purporting to be a record of the kind mentioned in subsection (1) above, or to be a certificate or other document signed as mentioned in that subsection or in subsection (6) above, shall be deemed to be such a record, or to be so signed, unless the contrary is proved.

(8)   Nothing in subsection (1) or (6) above makes a document admissible as evidence in proceedings for an offence unless a copy of it has, not less than seven days before the hearing or trial, been served on the person charged with the offence; and nothing in those subsections makes a document admissible as evidence of anything other than the matters shown on a record produced by a prescribed device if that person, not less than three days before the hearing or trial or within such further time as the court may in special circumstances allow, serves a notice on the prosecutor requiring attendance at the hearing or trial of the person who signed the document.

(9)   In this section "prescribed device" means device of a description specified in an order made by the Secretary of State.

(10)   The powers to make orders under subsections (3) and (9) above shall be exercisable by statutory instrument, which shall be subject to annulment in pursuance of a resolution of either House of Parliament.'

CRIMINAL JUSTICE ACT 1991
(1991, c. 53)

53.   Notices of transfer in certain cases involving children

(1)   If a person has been charged with an offence to which section 32(2) of the 1988 Act applies (sexual offences and offences involving violence or cruelty) and the Director of Public Prosecutions is of the opinion—

(a)   that the evidence of the offence would be sufficient for the proceedings against the person charged to be transferred to trial;

(b)   that a child who is alleged—

(i)   to be a person against whom the offence was committed; or

(ii)   to have witnessed the commission of the offence,

will be called as a witness at the trial; and

(c)   that, for the purpose of avoiding any prejudice to the welfare of the child, the case should be taken over and proceeded with without delay by the Crown Court,

a notice ('notice of transfer') certifying that opinion may be given by or on behalf of the Director on the magistrates' court in whose jurisdiction the offence has been charged.

(2)   A notice of transfer shall be given not later than the time at which the Director would be required to serve a notice of the prosecution case under section 5 of the Magistrates' Courts Act 1980.

(3)   On the giving of a notice of transfer the functions of the magistrates' court shall cease in relation to the case except as provided by paragraphs 2 and 3 of Schedule 6 to this Act or by pargraph 2 of Schedule 3 to the Access to Justice Act 1999.

(4)   The decision to give a notice of transfer shall not be subject to appeal or liable to be questioned in any court.

(5)   Schedule 6 to this Act (which makes further provision in relation to notices of transfer) shall have effect.

(6)   In this section 'child' means a person who—

(a)   in the case of an offence falling within section 32(2)(a) or (b) of the 1988 Act, is under fourteen years of age or, if he was under that age when any such video recording as is mentioned in section 32A(2) of that Act was made in respect of him, is under fifteen years of age; or

(b)   in the case of an offence falling within section 32(2)(c) of that Act, is under seventeen years of age or, if he was under that age when any such video recording was made in respect of him, is under eighteen years of age.

(7)   Any reference in subsection (6) above to an offence falling within paragraph (a), (b) or (c) of section 32(2) of that Act includes a reference to an offence which consists

of attempting or conspiring to commit, or of aiding, abetting, counselling, procuring or inciting the commission of, an offence falling within that paragraph.

SEXUAL OFFENCES (AMENDMENT) ACT 1992
(1992, c. 34)

1. Anonymity of victims of certain offences

(1)   Where an allegation has been made that an offence to which this Act applies has been committed against a person, no matter relating to that person shall during that person's lifetime be included in any publication.

(2)   Where a person is accused of an offence to which this Act applies, no matter likely to lead members of the public to identify a person as the person against whom the offence is alleged to have been committed ('the complainant') shall during the complainant's lifetime be included in any publication.

(3)   This section—

(a)   does not apply in relation to a person by virtue of subsection (1) at any time after a person has been accused of the offence, and

(b)   in its application in relation to a person by virtue of subsection (2), has effect subject to any direction given under section 3.

(3A)   The matters relating to a person in relation to which the restrictions imposed by subsection (1) or (2) apply (if their inclusion in any publication is likely to have the result mentioned in that subsection) include in particular—

(a)   the person's name,

(b)   the person's address,

(c)   the identity of any school or other educational establishment attended by the person,

(d)   the identity of any place of work, and

(e)   any still or moving picture of the person.

(4)   Nothing in this section prohibits the inclusion in a publication of matter consisting only of a report of criminal proceedings other than proceedings at, or intended to lead to, or on an appeal arising out of, a trial at which the accused is charged with the offence.

2. Offences to which this Act applies

(1)   This Act applies to the following offences against the law of England and Wales—

(a)   any offence under any of the provisions of the Sexual Offences Act 1956 mentioned in subsection (2);

(aa)   rape;

(ab)   burglary with intent to rape;

(b)   any offence under section 128 of the Mental Health Act 1959 (intercourse with mentally handicapped person by hospital staff etc.);

(c)   any offence under section 1 of the Indecency with Children Act 1960 (indecent conduct towards young child);

(d)   any offence under section 54 of the Criminal Law Act 1977 (incitement by man of his grand-daughter, daughter or sister under the age of 16 to commit incest with him);

(e)   any attempt to commit any of the offences mentioned in paragraphs (aa) to (d);

(f)   any conspiracy to commit any of those offences;

(g)   any incitement of another to commit any of those offences;

(h)   aiding, abetting, counselling or procuring the commission of any of the offences mentioned in pargraphs (aa) to (e) and (g).

(2)   The provisions of the Act of 1956 are—
  (a)   section 2 (procurement of a woman by threats);
  (b)   section 3 (procurement of a woman by false pretences);
  (c)   section 4 (administering drugs to obtain intercourse with a woman);
  (d)   section 5 (intercourse with a girl under the age of 13);
  (e)   section 6 (intercourse with a girl between the ages of 13 and 16);
  (f)   section 7 (intercourse with a mentally handicapped person);
  (g)   section 9 (procurement of a mentally handicapped person);
  (h)   section 10 (incest by a man);
  (i)   section 11 (incest by a woman);
  (j)   section 12 (buggery);
  (k)   section 14 (indecent assault on a woman);
  (l)   section 15 (indecent assault on a man);
  (m) section 16 (assault with intent to commit buggery);
  (n)   section 17 (abduction of women by force).
(3)   This Act applies to the following offences against the law of Northern Ireland—
  (a)   rape;
  (b)   burglary with intent to rape;
  (c)   any offence under any of the following provisions of the Offences against the
Person Act 1861—
      (i)   section 52 (indecent assault on a female);
      (ii)   section 53 so far as it relates to abduction of a woman against her will;
      (iii) section 61 (buggery);
      (iv)   section 62 (attempt to commit buggery, assault with intent to commit
buggery or indecent assault on a male);
  (d)   any offence under any of the following provisions of the Criminal Law
Amendment Act 1885—
      (i)   section 3 (procuring unlawful carnal knowledge of woman by threats, false
pretences or administering drugs);
      (ii)   section 4 (unlawful carnal knowledge, or attempted unlawful carnal
knowledge, of a girl under 14);
      (iii) section 5 (unlawful carnal knowledge of a girl under 17);
  (e)   any offence under any of the following provisions of the Punishment of Incest
Act 1908—
      (i)   section 1 (incest, attempted incest by males);
      (ii)   section 2 (incest by females over 16);
  (f)   any offence under section 22 of the Children and Young Persons Act
(Northern Ireland) 1968 (indecent conduct towards child);
  (g)   any offence under Article 9 of the Criminal Justice (Northern Ireland) Order
1980 (inciting girl under 16 to have incestuous sexual intercourse);
  (h)   any offence under any of the following provisions of the Mental Health
(Northern Ireland) Order 1986—
      (i)   Article 122(1)(a) (unalwful sexual intercourse with a woman suffering
from severe mental handicap);
      (ii)   Article 122(1)(b) (procuring a woman suffering from severe mental
handicap to have unlawful sexual intercourse);
      (iii) Article 123 (unlawful sexual intercourse by hospital staff, etc. with a person
receiving treatment for mental disorder);
  (i)   any attempt to commit any of the offences mentioned in paragraphs (a) to (h);
  (j)   any conspiracy to commit any of those offences;
  (k)   any incitement of another to commit any of those offences;
  (l)   aiding, abetting, counselling or procuring the commission of any of the
offences mentioned in paragraphs (a) to (i) and (k).

3.   Power to displace section 1

(1)   If, before the commencement of a trial at which a person is charged with an offence to which this Act applies, he or another person against whom the complainant may be expected to give evidence at the trial, applies to the judge for a direction under this subsection and satisfies the judge—

(a)   that the direction is required for the purpose of inducing persons who are likely to be needed as witnesses at the trial to come forward; and

(b)   that the conduct of the applicant's defence at the trial is likely to be substantially prejudiced if the direction is not given,

the judge shall direct that section 1 shall not, by virtue of the accusation alleging the offence in question, apply in relation to the complainant.

(2)   If at a trial the judge is satisfied—

(a)   that the effect of section 1 is to impose a substantial and unreasonable restriction upon the reporting of proceedings at the trial, and

(b)   that it is in the public interest to remove or relax the restriction,

he shall direct that that section shall not apply to such matter as is specified in the direction.

(3)   A direction shall not be given under subsection (2) by reason only of the outcome of the trial.

(4)   If a person who has been convicted of an offence and has given notice of appeal against the conviction, or notice of an application for leave so to appeal, applies to the appellate court for a direction under this subsection and satisfies the court—

(a)   that the direction is required for the purpose of obtaining evidence in support of the appeal; and

(b)   that the applicant is likely to suffer substantial injustice if the direction is not given,

the court shall direct that section 1 shall not, by virtue of an accusation which alleges an offence to which this Act applies and is specified in the direction, apply in relation to a complainant so specified.

(5)   A direction given under any provision of this section does not affect the operation of section 1 at any time before the direction is given.

(6)   In subsections (1) and (2), 'judge' means—

(a)   in the case of an offence which is to be tried summarily or for which the mode of trial has not been determined, any justice of the peace acting for the petty sessions area concerned; and

(b)   in any other case, any judge of the Crown Court in Englnd and Wales.

(6A)   In its application to Northern Ireland, this section has effect as if—

(a)   in subsection (1) and (2) for any reference to the judge there were substituted a reference to the court; and

(b)   subsection (b) were omitted.

(7)   If, after the commencement of a trial at which a person is charged with an offence to which this Act applies, a new trial of the person for that offence is ordered, the commencement of any previous trial shall be disregarded for the purposes of subsection (1).

4.   Special rules for cases of incest or buggery

(1)   In this section—

'section 10 offence' means an offence under section 10 of the Sexual Offences Act 1956 (incest by a man) or an attempt to commit that offence;

'section 11 offence' means an offence under section 11 of that Act (incest by a woman) or an attempt to commit that offence;

'section 12 offence' means an offence under section 12 of that Act (buggery) or an attempt to commit that offence.

(2)   Section 1 does not apply to a woman against whom a section 10 offence is alleged to have been committed if she is accused of having committed a section 11 offence against the man who is alleged to have committed the section 10 offence against her.

(3)   Section 1 does not apply to a man against whom a section 11 offence is alleged to have been committed if he is accused of having committed a section 10 offence against the woman who is alleged to have committed the section 11 offence against him.

(4)   Section 1 does not apply to a person against whom a section 12 offence is alleged to have been committed if that person is accused of having committed a section 12 offence against the person who is alleged to have committed the section 12 offence against him.

(5)   Subsection (2) does not affect the operation of this Act in relation to anything done at any time before the woman is accused.

(6)   Subsection (3) does not affect the operation of this Act in relation to anything done at any time before the man is accused.

(7)   Subsection (4) does not affect the operation of this Act in relation to anything done at any time before the person mentioned first in that subsection is accused.

(8)   In its application to Northern Ireland, this section has effect as if—

(a)   subsection (1) were omitted;

(b)   for references to a section 10 offence there were substituted references to an offence under section 1 of the Punishment of Incest Act 1908 (incest by a man) or an attempt to commit that offence;

(c)   for references to a section 11 offence there were substituted references to an offence under section 2 of that Act (incest by a woman) or an attempt to commit that offence; and

(d)   for references to a section 12 offence there were substituted references to an offence under section 61 of the Offences against the Person Act 1861 (buggery) or an attempt to commit that offence.

5.   Offences

(1)   If any matter is included in a publication in contravention of section 1, the following persons shall be guilty of an offence and liable on summary conviction to a fine not exceeding level 5 on the standard scale—

(a)   where the publication is a newspaper or periodical, any proprietor, any editor and any publisher of the newspaper or periodical;

(b)   where the publication is a relevnt programme—

(i)   any body corporate or Scottish partnership engaged in providing the progrmme service in which the programme is included; and

(ii)   any person having functions in relation to the programme corresponding to those of an editor of a newspaper;

(c)   in the case of any other publication, any person publishing it.

(2)   Where a person is charged with an offence under this section in respect of the inclusion of any matter in a publication, it shall be a defence, subject to subsection (3), to prove that the publication in which the matter appeared was one in respect of which the person against whom the offence mentioned in section 1 is alleged to have been committed had given written consent to the appearance of matter of that description.

(3)   Written consent is not a defence if it is proved that any person interfered unreasonably with the peace or comfort of the person giving the consent, with intent to obtain it, or that person was under the age of 16 at the time when it was given.

(4)   Proceedings for an offence under this section shall not be instituted except by or with the consent of the Attorney General, if the offence is alleged to have been committed in England and Wales or of the Attorney General for Northern Ireland if the offence is alleged to have been committed in Northern Ireland.

(5)   Where a person is charged with an offence under this section it shall be a defence to prove that at the time of the alleged offence he was not aware, and neither suspected nor had reason to suspect, that the publication included the matter in question.

(5A)   Where—

(a)   a person is charged with an offence under this section, and

(b)   the offence relates to the inclusion of any matter in a publication in contravention of section 1(1),

it shall be a defence to prove that at the time of the alleged offence he was not aware, and neither suspected nor had reason to suspect, that the allegation in question had been made.

(6)   Where an offence under this section committed by a body corporate is proved to have been committed with the consent or connivance of, or to be attributable to any neglect on the part of—

(a)   a director, manager, secretary or other similar officer of the body corporate, or

(b)   a person purporting to act in any such capacity,

he as well as the body corporate shall be guilty of the offence and liable to be proceeded against and punished accordingly.

(7)   In relation to a body corporate whose affairs are managed by its members 'director', in subsection (6), means a member of the body corporate.

(8)   Where an offence under this section is committed by a Scottish partnership and is proved to have been committed with the consent or connivance of a partner, he as well as the partnership shall be guilty of the offence and shall be liable to be proceeded against and punished accordingly.

6.   Interpretation etc.

(1)   In this Act—

'complainant' has the meaning given in section 1(2);

'picture' includes a likeness however produced;

'publication' includes any speech, writing, relevant programme or other communication on whatever form, which is addressed to the public at large or any section of the public (and for this purpose every relevant programme shall be taken to be so addressed), but does not include an indictment or other document prepared for use in particular legal proceedings;

'relevant programme' means a programme included in a programme service, within the meaning of the Broadcasting Act 1990.

(2)   For the purposes of this Act—

(a)   where it is alleged that an offence to which this Act applies has been committed, the fact that any person has consented to an act which, on any prosecution for that offence, would fall to be proved by the prosecution, does not prevent that person from being regarded as a person against whom the alleged offence was committed; and

(b)   where a person is accused of an offence of incest or buggery, the other party to the act in question shall be taken to be a person against whom the offence was committed even though he consented to that act.

(2A)   For the purposes of this Act, where it is alleged or there is an accusation—

(a)   that an offence of conspiracy or incitement of another to commit an offence mentioned in section 2(1)(aa) to (d) or (3)(a) to (h) has been committed, or

(b)   that an offence of aiding, abetting, counselling or procuring the commission of an offence of incitement of another to commit an offence mentioned in section 2(1)(aa) to (d) or (3)(a) to (h) has been committed, the person against whom the substantive offence is alleged to have been intended to be committed shall be regarded as the person against whom the conspiracy or incitement is alleged to have been committed.

In this subsection, 'the substantive offence' means the offence to which the alleged conspiracy or incitement related; and

(b) in subsection (3), after the words 'references in' there shall be inserted the words 'subsection (2A) and in'.

(3) For the purposes of this Act, a person is accused of an offence if—

(a) an information is laid, or (in Northern Ireland) a complaint is made, alleging that he has committed the offence,

(b) he appears before a court charged with the offence,

(c) a court before which he is appearing transfers proceedings against him for trial on a new charge alleging the offence, or

(d) a bill of indictment charging him with the offence is preferred before a court in which he may lawfully be indicted for the offence,

and references in section 3 to an accusation alleging an offence shall be construed accordingly.

(4) Nothing in this Act affects any prohibition or restriction imposed by virtue of any other enactment upon a publication or upon matter included in a relevant programme.

7. Courts-martial

(1) This Act shall have effect with the modifications set out in subsection (2) in any case where, in pursuance of any provision of the Army Act 1955, the Air Force Act 1955 or the Naval Discipline Act 1957, a person is charged with an offence to which this Act applies by virtue of section 2(1).

(2) The modifications are—

(a) any reference to a trial shall be read as a reference to a trial by court-martial;

(c) in section 3(1) any reference to a judge, in relation to the person charged with the offence, shall be read as a reference to the judge advocate appointed to conduct proceedings under section 3(1) relating to the offence (whether or not also appointed to conduct other preliminary proceedings relating to the offence);

(d) in section 3(2), any reference to a judge shall be read as a reference to the judge advocate appointed to be a member of the court-martial; and

(f) for section 6(3)(a) to (d) there shall be substituted 'he is charged, in pursuance of any provision of the Army Act 1955, the Air Force Act 1955 or the Naval Discipline Act 1957, with an offence to which this Act applies'.

(4) In section 36(1) of the Courts-Martial (Appeals) Act 1968 (which provides that certain powers of the Courts-Martial Appeal Court may be exercised by a single judge) after the words 'section 5(1)(d) of that Act' there shall be inserted 'or section 3(4) of the Sexual Offences (Amendment) Act 1992'.

8. Short title, commencement and extent, etc.

(1) This Act may be cited as the Sexual Offences (Amendment) Act 1992.

(2) This Act and the Sexual Offences Acts 1956 to 1976 may be cited together as the Sexual Offences Acts 1956 to 1992.

(3) This section comes into force on the passing of this Act but otherwise this act comes into force on such date as may be appointed by order made by the Secretary of State.

(4) The power to make an order under subsection (3) shall be exercisable by statutory instrument.

(5) Different dates may be appointed for different provisions of this Act and for different purposes.

(6) This Act extends to England nd Wales, Scotland and Northern Ireland.

(7) This Act, so far as it relates to proceedings before a court-martial or the Courts-Martial Appeal Court, applies to such proceedings wherever they may take place (whether in the United Kingdom or elsewhere).

VEHICLE EXCISE AND REGISTRATION ACT 1994
(1994, c. 22)

Evidence

51. Admissions

(1)   This section applies where in any proceedings in England and Wales or Northern Ireland for an offence under section 29, 34 or 43A—

(a)   it is appropriately proved that there has been served on the accused by post a requirement under section 46(1) or (2) to give information as to the identity of—

(i)   the driver of, or a person who used, a particular vehicle, or

(ii)   the person who kept a particular vehicle on a road,

on the particular occasion on which the offence is alleged to have been committed, and

(b)   a statement in writing is produced to the court purporting to be signed by the accused that he was—

(i)   the driver of, or a person who used, that vehicle, or

(ii)   the person who kept that vehicle on a road,

on that occasion.

(2)   Where this section applies, the court may accept the statement as evidence that the accused was—

(a)   the driver of, or a person who used, that vehicle, or

(b)   the person who kept that vehicle on a road,

on that occasion.

(3)   In subsection (1) 'appropriately proved' means proved to the satisfaction of the court—

(a)   on oath, or

(b)   in the manner prescribed—

(i)   in England and Wales, by rules under section 144 of the Magistrates' Courts Act 1980, or

(ii)   in Northern Ireland, by magistrates' courts rules, as defined by Article 2(3) of the Magistrates' Courts (Northern Ireland) Order 1981.

[51A.   Admissions: offences under regulations

(1)   Subsection (2) applies in relation to any proceedings in England, Wales or Northern Ireland against a person for an offence on the grounds that—

(a)   a vehicle has been sold or disposed of by, through or to him and he has failed to furnish particulars prescribed by regulations made by virtue of section 22(1)(d);

(b)   a vehicle has been sold or disposed of by or through him and he has failed to furnish a document prescribed by regulations made by virtue of section 22(1)(dd); or

(c)   he has surrendered, or not renewed, a vehicle licence or is keeping an unlicensed vehicle and has failed to furnish any particulars or make a declaration prescribed by regulations made by virtue of section 22(1D).

(2)   If—

(a)   it is appropriately proved that there has been served on the accused by post a requirement under section 46A to give information as to the identity of the person keeping the vehicle at a particular time, and

(b)   a statement in writing is produced to the court purporting to be signed by the accused that he was keeping the vehicle at that time,

the court may accept the statement as evidence that the accused was keeping the vehicle at that time.

(3)   In subsection (2) 'appropriately proved' has the same meaning as in section 51.]

52.   Records

(1)   A statement to which this section applies is admissible in any proceedings as evidence (or, in Scotland, sufficient evidence) of any fact stated in it with respect to

matters prescribed by regulations made by the Secretary of State to the same extent as oral evidence of that fact is admissible in the proceedings.

(2)   This section applies to a statement contained in a document purporting to be—

(a)   a part of the records maintained by the Secretary of State in connection with any functions exercisable by him under or by virtue of this Act,

(b)   a copy of a document forming part of those records, or

(c)   a note of any information contained in those records,

and to be authenticated by a person authorised to do so by the Secretary of State.

'(3)   In this section as it has effect in England and Wales—

'document' means anything in which information of any description is recorded;

'copy', in relation to a document, means anything onto which information recorded in the document has been copied, by whatever means and whether directly or indirectly; and

'statement' means any representation of fact, however made'.

(6)   Nothing in subsection (4) or (5) limits to civil proceedings the references to proceedings in subsection (1).'.

53.   Burden of proof

Where in any proceedings for an offence under section 29, 34, 37 or 45 any question arises as to—

(a)   the number of vehicles used,

(b)   the character, weight or cylinder capacity of a vehicle,

(c)   the seating capacity of a vehicle, or

(d)   the purpose for which a vehicle has been used,

the burden of proof in respect of the matter lies on the accused.

. . .

55.   Guilty plea by absent accused

(1)   This section applies where, under section 12(2) of the Magistrates' Courts Act 1980 or Article 24(2) of the Magistrates' Courts (Northern Ireland) Order 1981, a person is convicted in his absence of [an offence under section 29 or 35A] and it is appropriately proved that a relevant notice was served on the accused with the summons.

(2)   In subsection (1) 'appropriately proved' means—

(a)   in England and Wales, proved to the satisfaction of the court—

(i)   on oath, or

(ii)   in the manner prescribed by rules under section 144 of the Magistrates' Courts Act 1980, and

(b)   in Northern Ireland, proved to the satisfaction of the court—

(i)   on oath,

(ii)   by affidavit, or

(iii)   in the manner prescribed by magistrates' courts rules, as defined by Article 2(3) of the Magistrates' Courts (Northern Ireland) Order 1981.

(3)   In this section 'relevant notice', in relation to an accused, means a notice stating that, in the event of his being convicted of the offence, it will be alleged that an order requiring him to pay an amount specified in the notice falls to be made by the court—

(a)   in a case within subsection (1)(a), under section 30, or

(b)   in a case within subsection (1)(b), under section 36.

(4)   Where this section applies, the court shall proceed under section 30, or section 36, as if the amount specified in the relevant notice were the amount calculated in accordance with that section.

(5)   The court shall not so proceed if it is stated in the notification purporting to be given by or on behalf of the accused under—

(a)   section 12(2) of the Magistrates' Courts Act 1980, or

(b)   Article 24(2) of the Magistrates' Courts (Northern Ireland) Order 1981,

that the amount specified in the relevant notice is inappropriate.

CRIMINAL JUSTICE AND PUBLIC ORDER ACT 1994
(1994, c. 33)

Corroboration

32.   Abolition of corroboration rules

(1)   Any requirement whereby at a trial on indictment it is obligatory for the court to give the jury a warning about convicting the accused on the uncorroborated evidence of a person merely because that person is—

(a)   an alleged accomplice of the accused, or

(b)   where the offence charged is a sexual offence, the person in respect of whom it is alleged to have been committed,

is hereby abrogated.

(2)   In section 34(2) of the Criminal Justice Act 1988 (abolition of requirement of corroboration warning in respect of evidence of a child) the words from 'in relation to' to the end shall be omitted.

(3)   Any requirement that—

(a)   is applicable at the summary trial of a person for an offence, and

(b)   corresponds to the requirement mentioned in subsection (1) above or that mentioned in section 34(2) of the Criminal Justice Act 1988,

is hereby abrogated.

(4)   Nothing in this section applies in relation to—

(a)   any trial, or

(b)   any proceedings before a magistrates' court as examining justices,

which began before the commencement of this section.

33.   Abolition of corroboration requirements under Sexual Offences Act 1956

(1)   The following provisions of the Sexual Offences Act 1956 (which provide that a person shall not be convicted of the offence concerned on the evidence of one witness only unless the witness is corroborated) are hereby repealed—

(a)   section 2(2) (procurement of woman by threats),

(b)   section 3(2) (procurement of woman by false pretences),

(c)   section 4(2) (administering drugs to obtain or facilitate intercourse),

(d)   section 22(2) (causing prostitution of women), and

(e)   section 23(2) (procuration of girl under twenty-one).

(2)   Nothing in this section applies in relation to—

(a)   any trial, or

(b)   any proceedings before a magistrates' court as examining justices,

which began before the commencement of this section.

Inferences from accused's silence

34.   Effect of accused's failure to mention facts when questioned or charged

(1)   Where, in any proceedings against a person for an offence, evidence is given that the accused—

(a)   at any time before he was charged with the offence, on being questioned under caution by a constable trying to discover whether or by whom the offence had been committed, failed to mention any fact relied on in his defence in those proceedings; or

(b)   on being charged with the offence or officially informed that he might be prosecuted for it, failed to mention any such fact, being a fact which in the circumstances existing at the time the accused could reasonably have been expected to mention when so questioned, charged or informed, as the case may be, subsection (2) below applies.

(2)   Where this subsection applies—

(a)   a magistrates' court inquiring into the offence as examining justices;

(b)   a judge, in deciding whether to grant an application made by the accused under—

(i)   section 6 of the Criminal Justice Act 1987 (application for dismissal of charge of serious fraud in respect of which notice of transfer has been given under section 4 of the act); or

(ii)   paragraph 5 of Schedule 6 to the Criminal Justice Act 1991 (application for dismissal of charge of violent or sexual offence involving child in respect of which notice of transfer has been given under section 53 of that Act);

(c)   the court, in determining whether there is a case to answer; and

(d)   the court or jury, in determining whether the accused is guilty of the offence charged,

may draw such inferences from the failure as appear proper.

(2A)   Where the accused was at an authorised place of detention at the time of failure, subsections (1) and (2) above do not apply if he had not been allowed an opportunity to consult a solicitor prior to being questioned, charged or informed as mentioned in subsection (1) above.

(3)   Subject to any directions by the court, evidence tending to establish the failure may be given before or after evidence tending to establish the fact which the accused is alleged to have failed to mention.

(4)   This section applies in relation to questioning by persons (other than constables) charged with the duty of investigating offences or charging offenders as it applies in relation to questioning by constables; and in subsection (1) above 'officially informed' means informed by a constable or any such person.

(5)   This section does not—

(a)   prejudice the admissibility in evidence of the silence or other reaction of the accused in the face of anything said in his presence relating to the conduct in respect of which he is charged, in so far as evidence thereof would be admissible apart from this section; or

(b)   preclude the drawing of any inference from any such silence or other reaction of the accused which could properly be drawn apart from this section.

(6)   This section does not apply in relation to a failure to mention a fact if the failure occurred before the commencement of this section.

35.   Effect of accused's silence at trial

(1)   At the trial of any person for an offence, subsections (2) and (3) below apply unless—

(a)   the accused's guilt is not in issue; or

(b)   it appears to the court that the physical or mental condition of the accused makes it undesirable for him to give evidence;

but subsection (2) below does not apply if, at the conclusion of the evidence for the prosecution, his legal representative informs the court that the accused will give evidence or, where he is unrepresented, the court ascertains from him that he will give evidence.

(2)   Where this subsection applies, the court shall, at the conclusion of the evidence for the prosecution, satisfy itself (in the case of proceedings on indictment, in the presence of the jury) that the accused is aware that the stage has been reached at which evidence can be given for the defence and that he can, if he wishes, give evidence and that, if he chooses not to give evidence, or having been sworn, without good cause

refuses to answer any question, it will be permissible for the court or jury to draw such inferences as appear proper from his failure to give evidence or his refusal, without good cause, to answer any question.

(3)   Where this subsection applies, the court or jury, in determining whether the accused is guilty of the offence charged, may draw such inferences as appear proper from the failure of the accused to give evidence or his refusal, without good cause, to answer any question.

(4)   This section does not render the accused compellable to give evidence on his own behalf, and he shall accordingly not be guilty of contempt of court by reason of a failure to do so.

(5)   For the purposes of this section a person who, having been sworn, refuses to answer any question shall be taken to do so without good cause unless—

(a)   he is entitled to refuse to answer the question by virtue of any enactment, whenever passed or made, or on the ground of privilege; or

(b)   the court in the exercise of its general discretion excuses him from answering it.

(7)   This section applies—

(a)   in relation to proceedings on indictment for an offence, only if the person charged with the offence is arraigned on or after the commencement of this section;

(b)   in relation to proceedings in a magistrates' court, only if the time when the court begins to receive evidence in the proceedings falls after the commencement of this section.

36.   Effect of accused's failure or refusal to account for objects, substances or marks

(1)   Where—

(a)   a person is arrested by a constable, and there is—

(i)   on his person; or

(ii)   in or on his clothing or footwear; or

(iii)   otherwise in his possession; or

(iv)   in any place in which he is at the time of his arrest,

any object, substance or mark, or there is any mark on any such object; and

(b)   that or another constable investigating the case reasonably believes that the presence of the object, substance or mark may be attributable to the participation of the person arrested in the commission of an offence specified by the constable; and

(c)   the constable informs the person arrested that he so believes, and requests him to account for the presence of the object, substance or mark; and

(d)   the person fails or refuses to do so,

then if, in any proceedings against the person for the offence so specified, evidence of those matters is given, subsection (2) below applies.

(2)   Where this subsection applies—

(a)   a magistrates' court inquiring into the offence as examining justices;

(b)   a judge, in deciding whether to grant an application made by the accused under—

(i)   section 6 of the Criminal Justice Act 1987 (application for dismissal of charge of serious fraud in respect of which notice of transfer has been given under section 4 of that Act); or

(ii)   paragraph 5 of Schedule 6 to the Criminal Justice Act 1991 (application for dismissal of charge of violent or sexual offence involving child in respect of which notice of transfer has been given under section 53 of that Act);

(c)   the court, in determining whether there is a case to answer; and

(d)   the court or jury, in determining whether the accused is guilty of the offence charged, may draw such inferences from the failure or refusal as appear proper.

(3)   Subsections (1) and (2) above apply to the condition of clothing or footwear as they apply to a substance or mark thereon.

(4)   Subsections 1 and 2 above do not apply unless the accused was told in ordinary language by the constable when making the request mentioned in subsection (1)(c) above what the effect of this section would be if he failed or refused to comply with the request.

(4A)   Where the accused was at an authorised place of detention at the time of the failure or refusal, subsections (1) and (2) above do not apply if he had not been allowed an opportunity to consult a solicitor prior to the request being made.

(5)   This section applies in relation to officers of customs and excise as it applies in relation to constables.

(6)   This section does not preclude the drawing of any inference from a failure or refusal of the accused to account for the presence of an object, substance or mark or from the condition of clothing or footwear which could properly be drawn apart from this section.

(7)   This section does not apply in relation to a failure or refusal which occurred before the commencement of this section.

37.   Effect of accused's failure or refusal to account for presence at a particular place

(1)   Where—

(a)   a person arrested by a constable was found by him at a place at or about the time the offence for which he was arrested is alleged to have been committed; and

(b)   that or another constable investigating the offence reasonably believes that the presence of the person at that place and at that time may be attributable to his participation in the commission of the offence; and

(c)   the constable informs the person that he so believes, and requests him to account for that presence; and

(d)   the person fails or refuses to do so,

then if, in any proceedings against the person for the offence, evidence of those matters is given, subsection (2) below applies.

(2)   Where this subsection applies—

(a)   a magistrates' court inquiring into the offence as examining justices;

(b)   a judge, in deciding whether to grant an application made by the accused under—

(i)   section 6 of the Criminal Justice Act 1987 (application for dismissal of charge of serious fraud in respect of which notice of transfer has been given under section 4 of that Act); or

(ii)   paragraph 5 of Schedule 6 to the Criminal Justice Act 1991 (application for dismissal of charge of violent or sexual offence involving child in respect of which notice of transfer has been given under section 53 of that Act);

(c)   the court, in determining whether there is a case to answer; and

(d)   the court or jury, in determining whether the accused is guilty of the offence charged,

may draw such inferences from the failure or refusal as appear proper.

(3)   Subsections (1) and (2) do not apply unless the accused was told in ordinary language by the constable when making the request mentioned in subsection (1)(c) above what the effect of this section would be if he failed or refused to comply with the request.

(3A)   Where the accused was at an authorised place of detention at the time of the failure or refusal, subsections (1) and (2) do not apply if he had not been allowed an opportunity to consult a solicitor prior to the request being made.

(4)   This section applies in relation to officers of customs and excise as it applies in relation to constables.

(5)   This section does not preclude the drawing of any inference from a failure or refusal of the accused to account for his presence at a place which could properly be drawn apart from this section.

(6)   This section does not apply in relation to a failure or refusal which occurred before the commencement of this section.

38.   Interpretation and savings for sections 34, 35, 36 and 37

(1)   In sections 34, 35, 36 and 37 of this Act—
'legal representative' means an authorised advocate or authorised litigator, as defined by section 119(1) of the Courts and Legal Services Act 1990; and
'place' includes any building or part of a building, any vehicle, vessel, aircraft or hovercraft and any other place whatsoever.

(2)   In sections 34(2), 35(3), 36(2) and 37(2), references to an offence charged include references to any other offence of which the accused could lawfully be convicted on that charge.

(2A)   In each of sections 34(2A), 36(4A) and 37(3A) 'authorised place of detention' means—
(a)   a police station; or
(b)   any other place prescribed for the purpose of that provision by the Secretary of State;
and the power to make an order under this subsection shall be exercisable by statutory instrument which shall be subject to annulment on pursuance of a resolution of either House of Parliament.

(3)   A person shall not have the proceedings against him transferred to the Crown Court for trial, have a case to answer or be convicted of an offence solely on an inference drawn from such a failure or refusal as is mentioned in section 34(2), 35(3), 36(2) or 37(2).

(4)   A judge shall not refuse to grant such an application as is mentioned in section 34(2)(b), 36(2)(b) and 37(2)(b) solely on an inference drawn from such a failure as is mentioned in section 34(2), 36(2) or 37(2).

(5)   Nothing in sections 34, 35, 36 or 37 prejudices the operation of a provision of an enactment which provides (in whatever words) that any answer or evidence given by a person in specified circumstances shall not be admissible in evidence against him or some other person in any proceedings or class of proceedings (however described, and whether civil or criminal).

In this subsection, the reference to giving evidence is a reference to giving evidence in any manner, whether by furnishing information, making discovery, producing documents or otherwise.

(6)   Nothing in sections 34, 35, 36 or 37 prejudices any power of a court, in any proceedings, to exclude evidence (whether by preventing questions being put or otherwise) at its discretion.

39.   Power to apply sections 34 to 38 to armed forces

(1)   The Secretary of State may by order direct that any provision of sections 34 to 38 of this Act shall apply, subject to such modifications as he may specify, to any proceedings to which this section applies.

(2)   This section applies—
(a)   to proceedings whereby a charge is dealt with summarily under Part II of the Army Act 1955;
(b)   to proceedings whereby a charge is dealt with summarily under Part II of the Air Force Act 1955;

(c) to proceedings whereby a charge is summarily tried under Part II of the Naval Discipline Act 1957;

(d) to proceedings before a court martial constituted under the Army Act 1955;

(e) to proceedings before a court martial constituted under the Air Force Act 1955;

(f) to proceedings before a court martial constituted under the Naval Discipline Act 1957;

(g) to proceedings before a disciplinary court constituted under section 52G of the Naval Discipline Act 1957;

(h) to proceedings before the Courts-Martial Appeal Court;

(i) to proceedings before a Standing Civilian Court;

and it applies wherever the proceedings take place.

(3) An order under this section shall be made by statutory instrument and shall be subject to annulment in pursuance of a resolution of either House of Parliament.

142. Rape of women and men

For section 1 of the Sexual Offences Act 1956 (rape of a woman) there shall be substituted the following section—

'Rape of woman or man

(1) It is an offence for a man to rape a woman or another man.

(2) A man commits rape if—

(a) he has sexual intercourse with a person (whether vaginal or anal) who at the time of the intercourse does not consent to it; and

(b) at the time he knows that the person does not consent to the intercourse or is reckless as to whether that person consents to it.

(3) A man also commits rape if he induces a married woman to have sexual intercourse with him by impersonating her husband.

(4) Subsection (2) applies for the purpose of any enactment.'.

CRIMINAL APPEAL ACT 1995
(1995, c. 35)

8. The Commission

(1) There shall be a body corporate to be known as the Criminal Cases Review Commission.

(2) The Commission shall not be regarded as the servant or agent of the Crown or as enjoying any status, immunity or privilege of the Crown; and the Commission's property shall not be regarded as property of, or held on behalf of, the Crown.

(3) The Commission shall consist of not fewer than eleven members.

(4) The members of the Commission shall be appointed by Her Majesty on the recommendation of the Prime Minister.

(5) At least one third of the members of the Commission shall be persons who are legally qualified; and for this purpose a person is legally qualified if—

(a) he has a ten year general qualification, within the meaning of section 71 of the Courts and Legal Services Act 1990, or

(b) he is a member of the Bar of Northern Ireland, or solicitor of the Supreme Court of Northern Ireland, of at least ten years' standing.

(6) At least two thirds of the members of the Commission shall be persons who appear to the Prime Minister to have knowledge or experience of any aspect of the criminal justice system and of them at least one shall be a person who appears to him to have knowledge or experience of any aspect of the criminal justice system in Northern Ireland; and for the purposes of this subsection the criminal justice system includes, in particular, the investigation of offences and the treatment of offenders.

(7)   Schedule 1 (further provisions with respect to the Commission) shall have effect.

References to court

9.   Cases dealt with on indictment in England and Wales

(1)   Where a person has been convicted of an offence on indictment in England and Wales, the Commission—

(a)   may at any time refer the conviction to the Court of Appeal, and

(b)   (whether or not they refer the conviction) may at any time refer to the Court of Appeal any sentence (not being a sentence fixed by law) imposed on, or in subsequent proceedings relating to, the conviction.

(2)   A reference under subsection (1) of a person's conviction shall be treated for all purposes as an appeal by the person under section 1 of the 1968 Act against the conviction.

(3)   A reference under subsection (1) of a sentence imposed on, or in subsequent proceedings relating to, a person's conviction on an indictment shall be treated for all purposes as an appeal by the person under section 9 of the 1968 Act against—

(a)   the sentence, and

(b)   any other sentence (not being a sentence fixed by law) imposed on, or in subsequent proceedings relating to, the conviction or any other conviction on the indictment.

(4)   On a reference under subsection (1) of a person's conviction on an indictment the Commission may give notice to the Court of Appeal that any other conviction on the indictment which is specified in the notice is to be treated as referred to the Court of Appeal under subsection (1).

(5)   Where a verdict of not guilty by reason of insanity has been returned in England and Wales in the case of a person, the Commission may at any time refer the verdict to the Court of Appeal; and a reference under this subsection shall be treated for all purposes as an appeal by the person under section 12 of the 1968 Act against the verdict.

(6)   Where a jury in England and Wales has returned findings that a person is under a disability and that he did the act or made the omission charged against him, the Commission may at any time refer either or both of those findings to the Court of Appeal; and a reference under this subsection shall be treated for all purposes as an appeal by the person under section 15 of the 1968 Act against the finding or findings referred.

10.   Cases dealt with on indictment in Northern Ireland

(1)   Where a person has been convicted of an offence on indictment in Northern Ireland, the Commission—

(a)   may at any time refer the conviction to the Court of Appeal, and

(b)   (whether or not they refer the conviction) may at any time refer to the Court of Appeal any sentence (not being a sentence fixed by law) imposed on, or in subsequent proceedings relating to, the conviction.

(2)   A reference under subsection (1) of a person's conviction shall be treated for all purposes as an appeal by the person under section 1 of the 1980 Act against the conviction.

(3)   A reference under subsection (1) of a sentence imposed on, or in subsequent proceedings relating to, a person's conviction on an indictment shall be treated for all purposes as an appeal by the person under section 8 or 9 (as the case may be) of the 1980 Act against—

(a)   the sentence, and

(b)   any other sentence (not being a sentence fixed by law) imposed on, or in subsequent proceedings relating to, the conviction or any other conviction on the indictment.

(4)   On a reference under subsection (1) of a person's conviction on an indictment the Commission may give notice to the Court of Appeal that any other conviction on the indictment which is specified in the notice is to be treated as referred to the Court of Appeal under subsection (1).

(5)   On a reference under subsection (1) the Court of Appeal may not pass any sentence more severe than that passed by the Crown Court.

(6)   Where a finding of not guilty on the ground of insanity has been recorded in Northern Ireland in the case of a person, the Commission may at any time refer the finding to the Court of Appeal; and a reference under this subsection shall be treated for all purposes as an appeal by the person under section 12 of the 1980 Act against the finding.

(7)   Where a jury in Northern Ireland has returned a finding that a person is unfit to be tried, the Commission may at any time refer the finding to the Court of Appeal; and a reference under this subsection shall be treated for all purposes as an appeal by the person under section 13A of the 1980 Act against the finding.

11.   Cases dealt with summarily in England and Wales

(1)   Where a person has been convicted of an offence by a magistrates' court in England and Wales, the Commission—

(a)   may at any time refer the conviction to the Crown Court, and

(b)   (whether or not they refer the conviction) may at any time refer to the Crown Court any sentence imposed on, or in subsequent proceedings relating to, the conviction.

(2)   A reference under subsection (1) of a person's conviction shall be treated for all purposes as an appeal by the person under section 108(1) of the Magistrates' Courts Act 1980 against the conviction (whether or not he pleaded guilty).

(3)   A reference under subsection (1) of a sentence imposed on, or in subsequent proceedings relating to, a person's conviction shall be treated for all purposes as an appeal by the person under section 108(1) of the Magistrates' Courts Act 1980 against—

(a)   the sentence, and

(b)   any other sentence imposed on, or in subsequent proceedings relating to, the conviction or any related conviction.

(4)   On a reference under subsection (1) of a person's conviction the Commission may give notice to the Crown Court that any related conviction which is specified in the notice is to be treated as referred to the Crown Court under subsection (1).

(5)   For the purposes of this section convictions are related if they are convictions of the same person by the same court on the same day.

(6)   On a reference under this section the Crown Court may not award any punishment more severe than that awarded by the court whose decision is referred.

(7)   The Crown Court may grant bail to a person whose conviction or sentence has been referred under this section; and any time during which he is released on bail shall not count as part of any term of imprisonment or detention under his sentence.

12.   Cases dealt with summarily in Northern Ireland

(1)   Where a person has been convicted of an offence by a magistrates' court in Northern Ireland, the Commission—

(a)   may at any time refer the conviction to a county court, and

(b)   (whether or not they refer the conviction) may at any time refer to a county court any sentence imposed on, or in subsequent proceedings relating to, the conviction.

(2)   A reference under subsection (1) of a person's conviction shall be treated for all purposes as an appeal by the person under Article 140(1) of the Magistrates' Courts (Northern Ireland) Order 1981 against the conviction (whether or not he pleaded guilty).

(3)   A reference under subsection (1) of a sentence imposed on, or in subsequent proceedings relating to, a person's conviction shall be treated for all purposes as an appeal by the person under Article 140(1) of the Magistrates' Courts (Northern Ireland) Order 1981 against—
  (a)   the sentence, and
  (b)   any other sentence imposed on, or in subsequent proceedings relating to, the conviction or any related conviction.
(4)   On a reference under subsection (1) of a person's conviction the Commission may give notice to the county court that any related conviction which is specified in the notice is to be treated as referred to the county court under subsection (1).
(5)   For the purposes of this section convictions are related if they are convictions of the same person by the same court on the same day.
(6)   On a reference under this section a county court may not award any punishment more severe than that awarded by the court whose decision is referred.
(7)   The High Court may grant bail to a person whose conviction or sentence has been referred to a county court under this section; and any time during which he is released on bail shall not count as part of any term of imprisonment or detention under his sentence.

13.   Conditions for making of references
(1)   A reference of a conviction, verdict, finding or sentence shall not be made under any of sections 9 to 12 unless—
  (a)   the Commission consider that there is a real possibility that the conviction, verdict, finding or sentence would not be upheld were the reference to be made,
  (b)   the Commission so consider—
    (i)   in the case of a conviction, verdict or finding, because of an argument, or evidence, not raised in the proceedings which led to it or on any appeal or application for leave to appeal against it, or
    (ii)   in the case of a sentence, because of an argument on a point of law, or information, not so raised, and
  (c)   an appeal against the conviction, verdict, finding or sentence has been determined or leave to appeal against it has been refused.
(2)   Nothing in subsection (1)(b)(i) or (c) shall prevent the making of a reference if it appears to the Commission that there are exceptional circumstances which justify making it.

14.   Further provisions about references
(1)   A reference of a conviction, verdict, finding or sentence may be made under any of sections 9 to 12 either after an application has been made by or on behalf of the person to whom it relates or without an application having been so made.
(2)   In considering whether to make a reference of a conviction, verdict, finding or sentence under any of sections 9 to 12 the Commission shall have regard to—
  (a)   any application or representations made to the Commission by or on behalf of the person to whom it relates,
  (b)   any other representations made to the Commission in relation to it, and
  (c)   any other matters which appear to the Commission to be relevant.
(3)   In considering whether to make a reference under section 9 or 10 the Commission may at any time refer any point on which they desire the assistance of the Court of Appeal to that Court for the Court's opinion on it; and on a reference under this subsection the Court of Appeal shall consider the point referred and furnish the Commission with the Court's opinion on the point.
(4)   Where the Commission make a reference under any of sections 9 to 12 the Commission shall—
  (a)   give the court to which the reference is made a statement of the Commission's reasons for making the reference, and

(b)   send a copy of the statement to every person who appears to the Commission to be likely to be a party to any proceedings on the appeal arising from the reference.

(5)   Where a reference under any of sections 9 to 12 is treated as an appeal against any conviction, verdict, finding or sentence, the appeal may be on any ground relating to the conviction, verdict, finding or sentence (whether or not the ground is related to any reason given by the Commission for making the reference).

(6)   In every case in which—

(a)   an application has been made to the Commission by or on behalf of any person for the reference under any of sections 9 to 12 of any conviction, verdict, finding or sentence, but

(b)   the Commission decide not to make a reference of the conviction, verdict, finding or sentence,

the Commission shall give a statement of the reasons for their decision to the person who made the application.

Investigations and assistance

15.   Investigations for Court of Appeal

(1)   Where a direction is given by the Court of Appeal under section 23A(1) of the 1968 Act or section 25A(1) of the 1980 Act the Commission shall investigate the matter specified in the direction in such manner as the Commission think fit.

(2)   Where, in investigating a matter specified in such a direction, it appears to the Commission that—

(a)   another matter (a 'related matter') which is relevant to the determination of the case by the Court of Appeal ought, if possible, to be resolved before the case is determined by that Court, and

(b)   an investigation of the related matter is likely to result in the Court's being able to resolve it,

the Commission may also investigate the related matter.

(3)   The Commission shall—

(a)   keep the Court of Appeal informed as to the progress of the investigation of any matter specified in a direction under section 23A(1) of the 1968 Act or section 25A(1) of the 1980 Act, and

(b)   if they decide to investigate any related matter, notify the Court of Appeal of their decision and keep the Court informed as to the progress of the investigation.

(4)   The Commission shall report to the Court of Appeal on the investigation of any matter specified in direction under section 23A(1) of the 1968 Act or section 25A(1) of the 1980 Act when—

(a)   they complete the investigation of that matter and of any related matter investigated by them, or

(b)   they are directed to do so by the Court of Appeal,

whichever happens first.

(5)   A report under subsection (4) shall include details of any inquiries made by or for the Commission in the investigation of the matter specified in the direction or any related matter investigated by them.

(6)   Such a report shall be accompanied—

(a)   by any statements and opinions received by the Commission in the investigation of the matter specified in the direction or any related matter investigated by them, and

(b)   subject to subsection (7), by any reports so received.

(7)   Such a report need not be accompanied by any reports submitted to the Commission under section 20(6) by an investigating officer.

16. Assistance in connection with prerogative of mercy

(1)   Where the Secretary of State refers to the Commission any matter which arises in the consideration of whether to recommend the exercise of Her Majesty's prerogative of mercy in relation to a conviction and on which he desires their assistance, the Commission shall—

(a)   consider the matter referred, and

(b)   give to the Secretary of State a statement of their conclusions on it;

and the Secretary of State shall, in considering whether so to recommend, treat the Commission's statement as conclusive of the matter referred.

(2)   Where in any case the Commission are of the opinion that the Secretary of State should consider whether to recommend the exercise of Her Majesty's prerogative of mercy in relation to the case they shall give him the reasons for their opinion.

Supplementary powers

17. Power to obtain documents etc.

(1)   This section applies where the Commission believe that a person serving in a public body has possession or control of a document or other material which may assist the Commission in the exercise of any of their functions.

(2)   Where it is reasonable to do so, the Commission may require the person who is the appropriate person in relation to the public body—

(a)   to produce the document or other material to the Commission or to give the Commission access to it, and

(b)   to allow the Commission to take away the document or other material or to make and take away a copy of it in such form as they think appropriate,

and may direct that person that the document or other material must not be destroyed, damaged or altered before the direction is withdrawn by the Commission.

(3)   The documents and other material covered by this section include, in particular, any document or other material obtained or created during any investigation or proceedings relating to—

(a)   the case in relation to which the Commission's function is being or may be exercised, or

(b)   any other case which may be in any way connected with that case (whether or not any function of the Commission could be exercised in relation to that other case).

(4)   The duty to comply with a requirement under this section is not affected by any obligation of secrecy or other limitation on disclosure (including any such obligation or limitation imposed by or by virtue of any enactment) which would otherwise prevent the production of the document or other material to the Commission or the giving of access to it to the Commission.

18. Government documents etc. relating to current or old cases

(1)   Section 17 does not apply to any document or other material in the possession or control of a person serving in a government department if the document or other material—

(a)   is relevant to a case to which this subsection applies, and

(b)   is in the possession or control of the person in consequence of the Secretary of State's consideration of the case.

(2)   Subsection (1) applies to a case if the Secretary of State—

(a)   is, immediately before the day on which the repeal by this Act of section 17 of the 1968 Act or of section 14 of the 1980 Act comes into force, considering the case with a view to deciding whether to make a reference under that section or whether to recommend the exercise of Her Majesty's prerogative of mercy in relation to a conviction by a magistrates' court, or

(b)   has at any earlier time considered the case with a view to deciding whether to make such a reference or whether so to recommend.

(3)   The Secretary of State shall give to the Commission any document or other material which—

(a)   contains representations made to him in relation to any case to which this subsection applies, or

(b)   was received by him in connection with any such case otherwise than from a person serving in a government department,

and may give to the Commission any document or other material which is relevant to any such case but does not fall within paragraph (a) or (b).

(4)   Subsection (3) applies to a case if—

(a)   the Secretary of State is, immediately before the day on which the repeal by this Act of section 17 of the 1968 Act or of section 14 of the 1980 Act comes into force, considering the case with a view to deciding whether to make a reference under that section or whether to recommend the exercise of Her Majesty's prerogative of mercy in relation to a conviction by a magistrates' court, or

(b)   the Secretary of State has at any earlier time considered the case with a view to deciding whether to make such a reference, or whether so to recommend, and the Commission at any time notify him that they wish subsection (3) to apply to the case.

19.   Power to require appointment of investigating officers

(1)   Where the Commission believe that inquiries should be made for assisting them in the exercise of any of their functions in relation to any case they may require the appointment of an investigating officer to carry out the inquiries.

(2)   Where any offence to which the case relates was investigated by persons serving in a public body, a requirement under this section may be imposed—

(a)   on the person who is the appropriate person in relation to the public body, or

(b)   where the public body has ceased to exist, on any chief officer of police or on the person who is the appropriate person in relation to any public body which appears to the Commission to have functions which consist of or include functions similar to any of those of the public body which has ceased to exist.

(3)   Where no offence to which the case relates was investigated by persons serving in a public body, a requirement under this section may be imposed on any chief officer of police.

(4)   A requirement under this section imposed on a chief officer of police may be—

(a)   a requirement to appoint a person serving in the police force in relation to which he is the chief officer of police, or

(b)   a requirement to appoint a person serving in another police force selected by the chief officer.

(5)   A requirement under this section imposed on a person who is the appropriate person in relation to a public body other than a police force may be—

(a)   a requirement to appoint a person serving in the public body, or

(b)   a requirement to appoint a person serving in a police force, or in a public body (other than a police force) having functions which consist of or include the investigation of offences, selected by the appropriate person.

(6)   The Commission may direct—

(a)   that a person shall not be appointed, or

(b)   that a police force or other public body shall not be selected,

under subsection (4) or (5) without the approval of the Commission.

(7)   Where an appointment is made under this section by the person who is the appropriate person in relation to any public body, that person shall inform the Commission of the appointment; and if the Commission are not satisfied with the person appointed they may direct that—

(a) the person who is the appropriate person in relation to the public body shall, as soon as is reasonably practicable, select another person in his place and notify the Commission of the proposal to appoint the other person, and

(b) the other person shall not be appointed without the approval of the Commission.

20. Inquiries by investigating officers

(1) A person appointed as the investigating officer in relation to a case shall undertake such inquiries as the Commission may from time to time reasonably direct him to undertake in relation to the case.

(2) A person appointed as an investigating officer shall be permitted to act as such by the person who is the appropriate person in relation to the public body in which he is serving.

(3) Where the chief officer of an England and Wales police force appoints a member of the Royal Ulster Constabulary as an investigating officer, the member appointed shall have in England and Wales the same powers and privileges as a member of the police force has there as a constable; and where the Chief Constable of the Royal Ulster Constabulary appoints a member of an England and Wales police force as an investigating officer, the member appointed shall have in Northern Ireland the same powers and privileges as a member of the Royal Ulster Constabulary has there as a constable.

(4) The Commission may take any steps which they consider appropriate for supervising the undertaking of inquiries by an investigating officer.

(5) The Commission may at any time direct that a person appointed as the investigating officer in relation to a case shall cease to act as such; but the making of such a direction shall not prevent the Commission from imposing a requirement under section 19 to appoint another investigating officer in relation to the case.

(6) When a person appointed as the investigating officer in relation to a case has completed the inquiries which he has been directed by the Commission to undertake in relation to the case, he shall—

(a) prepare a report of his findings,

(b) submit it to the Commission, and

(c) send a copy of it to the person by whom he was appointed.

(7) When a person appointed as the investigating officer in relation to a case submits to the Commission a report of his findings he shall also submit to them any statements, opinions and reports received by him in connection with the inquiries which he was directed to undertake in relation to the case.

21. Other powers

(1) Sections 17 to 20 are without prejudice to the taking by the Commission of any steps which they consider appropriate for assisting them in the exercise of any of their functions including, in particular—

(a) undertaking, or arranging for others to undertake, inquiries, and

(b) obtaining, or arranging for others to obtain, statements, opinions and reports.

22. Meaning of 'public body' etc.

(1) In sections 17, 19 and 20 and this section 'public body' means—

(a) any police force,

(b) any government department, local authority or other body constituted for purposes of the public service, local government or the administration of justice, or

(c) any other body whose members are appointed by Her Majesty, any Minister or any government department or whose revenues consist wholly or mainly of money provided by Parliament or appropriated by Measure of the Northern Ireland Assembly.

(2) In sections 19 and 20 and this section—

(a) 'police force' includes the Royal Ulster Constabulary and the Royal Ulster Constabulary Reserve, the National Crime Squad and any body of constables maintained otherwise than by a police authority,

(b) references to the chief officer of police—

(i) in relation to the Royal Ulster Constabulary and the Royal Ulster Constabulary Reserve, are to the Chief Constable of the Constabulary,

(ii) in relation to the National Crime Squad, are to the Director General of the Squad, and

(iii) in relation to any other police force maintained otherwise than by a police authority, are to the chief constable.

(c) references to an England and Wales police force are to a police force maintained under section 2 of the Police Act 1996, the metropolitan police force or the City of London police force, or the National Crime Squad,

(d) 'police authority' includes the Service Authority for the National Crime Squad, and

(e) references to a person serving in a police force or to a member of a police force, in relation to the National Crime Squad, mean a police member of that Squad appointed under section 55(1)(b) of the Police Act 1997.

(3) In section 18 and this section—

(a) references to a government department include a Northern Ireland department and the Office of the Director of Public Prosecutions for Northern Ireland, and

(b) 'Minister' means a Minister of the Crown as defined by section 8 of the Ministers of the Crown Act 1975 but also includes the head of a Northern Ireland department.

(4) In sections 17, 19 and 20 'the appropriate person' means—

(a) in relation to a police force, the chief officer of police,

(aa) in relation to the National Crime Intelligence Service, the Director General of that service,

(b) in relation to the Crown Prosecution Service, the Director of Public Prosecutions,

(c) in relation to the Office of the Director of Public Prosecutions for Northern Ireland, that Director,

(d) in relation to the Serious Fraud Office, the Director of the Serious Fraud Office,

(e) in relation to the Inland Revenue, the Commissioners of Inland Revenue,

(f) in relation to the Customs and Excise, the Commissioners of Customs and Excise,

(g) in relation to any government department not within any of the preceding paragraphs, the Minister in charge of the department, and

(h) in relation to any public body not within any of the preceding paragraphs, the public body itself (if it is a body corporate) or the person in charge of the public body (if it is not).

(5) For the purposes of sections 17, 19 and 20—

(a) a justices' chief executive or justices' clerk appointed by, or a member of the staff of, a magistrates' courts committee shall be treated as serving in the committee, and

(b) a person authorised under section 57 of the Northern Ireland (Emergency Provisions) Act 1991 to exercise the powers conferred by Schedule 5 to that Act shall be treated as if he were serving in a public body and he were the appropriate person in relation to the body.

Disclosure of information

23. Offence of disclosure

(1) A person who is or has been a member or employee of the Commission shall not disclose any information obtained by the Commission in the exercise of any of their

functions unless the disclosure of the information is excepted from this section by section 24.

(2) A person who is or has been an investigating officer shall not disclose any information obtained by him in his inquiries unless the disclosure of the information is excepted from this section by section 24.

(3) A member of the Commission shall not authorise—

(a) the disclosure by an employee of the Commission of any information obtained by the Commission in the exercise of any of their functions, or

(b) the disclosure by an investigating officer of any information obtained by him in his inquiries,

unless the authorisation of the disclosure of the information is excepted from this section by section 24.

(4) A person who contravenes this section is guilty of an offence and liable on summary conviction to a fine of an amount not exceeding level 5 on the standard scale.

24. Exceptions from obligations of non-disclosure

(1) The disclosure of information, or the authorisation of the disclosure of information, is expected from section 23 by this section if the information is disclosed, or is authorised to be disclosed—

(a) for the purposes of any criminal, disciplinary or civil proceedings,

(b) in order to assist in dealing with an application made to the Secretary of State for compensation for a miscarriage of justice,

(c) by a person who is a member or an employee of the Commission either to another person who is a member or an employee of the Commission or to an investigating officer,

(d) by an investigating officer to a member or an employee of the Commission,

(e) in any statement or report required by this Act,

(f) in or in connection with the exercise of any function under this Act, or

(g) in any circumstances in which the disclosure of information is permitted by an order made by the Secretary of State.

(2) The disclosure of information is also excepted from section 23 by this section if the information is disclosed by an employee of the Commission, or an investigating officer, who is authorised to disclose the information by a member of the Commission.

(3) The disclosure of information, or the authorisation of the disclosure of information, is also excepted from section 23 by this section if the information is disclosed, or is authorised to be disclosed, for the purposes of—

(a) the investigation of an offence, or

(b) deciding whether to prosecute a person for an offence,

unless the disclosure is or would be prevented by an obligation of secrecy or other limitation on disclosure (including any such obligation or limitation imposed by or by virtue of an enactment) arising otherwise than under that section.

(4) Where the disclosure of information is excepted from section 23 by subsection (1) or (2), the disclosure of the information is not prevented by any obligation of secrecy or other limitation on disclosure (including any such obligation or limitation imposed by or by virtue of an enactment) arising otherwise than under that section.

(5) The power to make an order under subsection (1)(g) is excercisable by statutory instrument which shall be subject to annulment in pursuance of a resolution of either House of Parliament.

25. Consent to disclosure

(1) Where a person on whom a requirement is imposed under section 17 notifies the Commission that any information contained in any document or other material to

which the requirement relates is not to be disclosed by the Commission without his prior consent, the Commission shall not disclose the information without such consent.

(2) Such consent may not be withheld unless—

(a) (apart from section 17) the person would have been prevented by any obligation of secrecy or other limitation on disclosure from disclosing the information to the Commission, and

(b) it is reasonable for the person to withhold his consent to disclosure of the information by the Commission.

(3) An obligation of secrecy or other limitation on disclosure which applies to a person only where disclosure is not authorised by another person shall not be taken for the purposes of subsection (2)(a) to prevent the disclosure by the person of information to the Commission unless—

(a) reasonable steps have been taken to obtain the authorisation of the other person, or

(b) such authorisation could not reasonably be expected to be obtained.

PART IV

SUPPLEMENTARY

30. Interpretation

(1) In this Act—

'the 1968 Act' means the Criminal Appeal Act 1968,

'the 1980 Act' means the Criminal Appeal (Northern Ireland) Act 1980,

'the Commission' means the Criminal Cases Review Commission,

'enactment' includes an enactment comprised in Northern Ireland legislation, and

'investigating officer' means a person appointed under section 19 to carry out inquiries.

(2) In this Act 'sentence'—

(a) in section 9 has the same meaning as in the 1968 Act,

(b) in section 10 has the same meaning as in Part I of the 1980 Act,

(c) in section 11 has the same meaning as in section 108 of the Magistrates' Courts Act 1980, and

(d) in section 12 has the same meaning as in Article 140(1) of the Magistrates' Courts (Northern Ireland) Order 1981.

33. Extent

(1) The provisions of Part I and III and of Schedules 2 and 3 have the same extent as the enactments which they amend or repeal.

(2) Section 8 and Schedule 1 and sections 13 to 25 extend only to England and Wales and Northern Ireland.

(3) Sections 9 and 11 extend only to England and Wales.

(4) Sections 10 and 12 extend only to Northern Ireland.

Section 8   SCHEDULE 1

Evidence

7. A document purporting to be—

(a) duly executed under the seal of the Commission, or

(b) signed on behalf of the Commission,

shall be received in evidence and, unless the contrary is proved, taken to be so executed or signed.

CRIMINAL PROCEDURE AND INVESTIGATIONS ACT 1996
(1996, c. 25)

Other miscellaneous provisions

68.   Use of written statements and depositions at trial
Schedule 2 to this Act (which relates to the use at the trial of written statements and depositions admitted in evidence in committal proceedings) shall have effect.

Section 68   SCHEDULE 2
                              STATEMENTS AND DEPOSITIONS

Statements

1.—(1)   Sub-paragraph (2) applies if—
  (a)   a written statement has been admitted in evidence in proceedings before a magistrates' court inquiring into an offence at examining justices,
  (b)   in those proceedings a person has been committed for trial,
  (c)   for the purposes of section 5A of the Magistrates' Courts Act 1980 the statement complied with section 5B of that Act prior to the committal for trial,
  (d)   the statement purports to be signed by a justice of the peace, and
  (e)   sub-paragraph (3) does not prevent sub-paragraph (2) applying.
  (2)   Where this sub-paragraph applies the statement may without further proof be read as evidence of the trial of the accused, whether for the offence for which he was committed for trial or for any other offence arising out of the same transaction or set of circumstances.
  (3)   Sub-paragraph (2) does not apply if—
  (a)   it is proved that the statement was not signed by the justice by whom it purports to have been signed,
  (b)   the court of trial at its discretion orders that sub-paragraph (2) shall not apply, or
  (c)   a party to the proceedings objects to sub-paragraph (2) applying.
  (4)   If a party to the proceedings objects to sub-paragraph (2) applying the court of trial may order that the objection shall have no effect if the court considers it to be in the interests of justice so to order.

Depositions

2.—(1)   Sub-paragraph (2) applies if—
  (a)   in pursuance of section 97A of the Magistrates' Courts Act 1980 (summons or warrant to have evidence taken as a deposition etc.) a person has had his evidence taken as a deposition for the purposes of proceedings before a magistrates' court inquiring into an offence as examining justices,
  (b)   the deposition has been admitted in evidence in those proceedings,
  (c)   in those proceedings a person has been committed for trial,
  (d)   for the purposes of section 5A of the Magistrates' Courts Act 1980 the deposition complied with section 5C of that Act prior to the committal for trial,
  (e)   the deposition purports to be signed by the justice before whom it purports to have been taken, and
  (f)   sub-paragraph (3) does not prevent sub-paragraph (2) applying.
  (2)   Where this sub-paragraph applies the deposition may without further proof be read as evidence on the trial of the accused, whether for the offence for which he was committed for trial or for any other offence arising out of the same transaction or set of circumstances.
  (3)   Sub-paragraph (2) does not apply if—

(a)   it is proved that the deposition was not signed by the justice by whom it purports to have been signed,

(b)   the court of trial at its discretion orders that sub-paragraph (2) shall not apply, or

(c)   a party to the proceedings objects to sub-paragraph (2) applying.

(4)   If a party to the proceedings objects to sub-paragraph (2) applying the court of trial may order that the objection shall have no effect if the court considers it to be in the interests of justice so to order.

Signatures

3.—(1)   A justice who signs a certificate authenticating one or more relevant statements or depositions shall be treated for the purposes of paragraphs 1 and 2 as signing the statement or deposition or (as the case may be) each of them.

(2)   For this purpose—

(a)   a relevant statement is a written statement made by a person for the purposes of proceedings before a magistrates' court inquiring into an offence as examining justices;

(b)   a relevant deposition is a deposition made in pursuance of section 97A of the Magistrates' Courts Act 1980 for the purposes of such proceedings.

Time limit for objection

4.   Without prejudice to section 84 of the Supreme Court Act 1981 (rules of court) the power to make rules under that section includes power to make provision—

(a)   requiring an objection under paragraph 1(3)(c) or 2(3)(c) to be made within a period prescribed in the rules;

(b)   allowing the court of trial at its discretion to permit such an objection to be made outside any such period.

CRIMINAL EVIDENCE (AMENDMENT) ACT 1997
(1997, c. 17)

Extension of power to take non-intimate body samples without consent

1.   Persons imprisoned or detained by virtue of pre-existing conviction for sexual offence etc.

(1)   This section has effect for removing, in relation to persons to whom this section applies, the restriction on the operation of section 63(3B) of the Police and Criminal Evidence Act 1984 (power to take non-intimate samples without the appropriate consent from persons convicted of recordable offences)—

(a)   which is imposed by the subsection (10) inserted in section 63 by section 55(6) of the Criminal Justice and Public Order Act 1994, and

(b)   by virtue of which section 63(3B) does not apply to persons convicted before 10 April 1995.

(3)   This section applies to a person who was convicted of a recordable offence before 10 April 1995 if—

(a)   that offence was one of the offences listed in Schedule 1 to this Act (which lists certain sexual, violent and other offences), and

(b)   at the relevant time he is serving a sentence of imprisonment in respect of that offence.

(4)   This section also applies to a person who was convicted of a recordable offence before 10 April 1995 if—

(a)   that offence was one of the offences listed in Schedule 1 to this Act, and

(b)   at the relevant time he is detained under Part III of the Mental Health Act 1983 in pursuance of—
    (i)   a hospital order or interim hospital order made following that conviction, or
    (ii)   a transfer direction given at a time when he was serving a sentence of imprisonment in respect of that offence.
Expressions used in this subsection and in the Mental Health Act 1983 have the same meaning as in that Act.

(5)   Where a person convicted of a recordable offence before 10 April 1995 was, following his conviction for that and any other offence or offences, sentenced to two or more terms of imprisonment (whether taking effect consecutively or concurrently), he shall be treated for the purposes of this section as serving a sentence of imprisonment in respect of that offence at any time when serving any of those terms.

(6)   For the purposes of this section, references to a person serving a sentence of imprisonment include references—
    (a)   to his being detained in any institution to which the Prison Act 1952 applies in pursuance of any other sentence or order for detention imposed by a court in criminal proceedings, or
    (b)   to his being detained (otherwise than in any such institution) in pursuance of directions of the Secretary of State under section 53 of the Children and Young Persons Act 1933;
and any reference to a term of imprisonment shall be construed accordingly.

2.   Persons detained following acquittal on grounds of insanity or finding of unfitness to plead

(1)   This section has effect for enabling non-intimate samples to be taken from persons under section 63 of the 1984 Act without the appropriate consent where they are persons to whom this section applies.

(3)   This section applies to a person if—
    (a)   at the relevant time he is detained under Part III of the Mental Health Act 1983 in pursuance of an order made under—
        (i)   section 5(2)(a) of the Criminal Procedure (Insanity) Act 1964 or section 6 or 14 of the Criminal Appeal Act 1968 (finding of insanity or unfitness to plead), or
        (ii)   section 37(3) of the Mental Health Act 1983 (power of magistrates' court to make hospital order without convicting accused); and
    (b)   that order was made on or after the date of the passing of this Act in respect of a recordable offence.

(4)   This section also applies to a person if—
    (a)   at the relevant time he is detained under Part III of the Mental Health Act 1983 in pursuance of an order made under—
        (i)   any of the provisions mentioned in subsection (3)(a), or
        (ii)   section 5(1) of the Criminal Procedure (Insanity) Act 1964 as originally enacted; and
    (b)   that order was made before the date of the passing of this Act in respect of any offence listed in Schedule 1 to this Act.

(5)   Subsection (4)(a)(i) does not apply to any order made under section 14(2) of the Criminal Appeal Act 1968 as originally enacted.

(6)   For the purposes of this section an order falling within subsection (3) or (4) shall be treated as having been made in respect of an offence of a particular description—
    (a)   if, where the order was made following—
        (i)   a finding of not guilty by reason of insanity, or
        (ii)   a finding that the person in question was under a disability and did the act or made the omission charged against him, or

(iii)   a finding for the purposes of section 37(3) of the Mental Health Act 1983 that the person in question did the act or made the omission charged against him, or

(iv)   (in the case of an order made under section 5(1) of the Criminal Procedure (Insanity) Act 1964 as originally enacted) a finding that he was under a disability,

that finding was recorded in respect of an offence of that description; or

(b)   if, where the order was made following the Court of Appeal forming such opinion as is mentioned in section 6(1) or 14(1) of the Criminal Appeal Act 1968, that opinion was formed on an appeal brought in respect of an offence of that description.

(7)   In this section any reference to an Act 'as originally enacted' is a reference to that Act as it had effect without any of the amendments made by the Criminal Procedure (Insanity and Unfitness to Plead) Act 1991.

Supplementary

5. Interpretation
In this Act—

'the 1984 Act' means the Police and Criminal Evidence Act 1984;

'appropriate consent' has the meaning given by section 65 of the 1984 Act;

'non-intimate sample' has the meaning given by section 65 of the 1984 Act;

'recordable offence' means any offence to which regulations under section 27 of the 1984 Act (fingerprinting) apply;

'the relevant time' means, in relation to the exercise of any power to take a non-intimate sample from a person, the time when it is sought to take the sample.

6. Short title, repeal and extent
(1)   This Act may be cited as the Criminal Evidence (Amendment) Act 1997.

(2)   ...

(3)   Section 55(6) of the Criminal Justice and Public Order Act 1994 is repealed.

(4)   This Act extends to England and Wales only.

SCHEDULE 1

LIST OF OFFENCES

Sexual offences and offences of indecency

1. Any offence under the Sexual Offences Act 1956, other than an offence under section 30, 31 or 33 to 36 of that Act.

2. Any offence under section 128 of the Mental Health Act 1959 (intercourse with mentally handicapped person by hospital staff etc.).

3. Any offence under section 1 of the Indecency with Children Act 1960 (indecent conduct towards young child).

4. Any offence under section 54 of the Criminal Law Act 1977 (incitement by man of his grand-daughter, daughter or sister under the age of 16 to commit incest with him).

5. Any offence under section 1 of the Protection of Children Act 1978.

Violent and other offences

6. Any of the following offences—

(a)   murder;

(b)   manslaughter;

(c)   false imprisonment; and

(d)   kidnapping.

7. Any offence under any of the following provisions of the Offences Against the Person Act 1861—

(a)   section 4 (conspiring or soliciting to commit murder);
(b)   section 16 (threats to kill);
(c)   section 18 (wounding with intent to cause grievous bodily harm);
(d)   section 20 (causing grievous bodily harm);
(e)   section 21 (attempting to choke etc. in order to commit or assist in the committing of any indictable offence);
(f)   section 22 (using chloroform etc. to commit or assist in the committing of any indictable offence);
(g)   section 23 (maliciously administering poison etc. so as to endanger life or inflict grievous bodily harm);
(h)   section 24 (maliciously administering poison etc. with intent to injure etc.); and
(i)   section 47 (assault occasioning actual bodily harm).
   8.   Any offence under either of the following provisions of the Explosive Substances Act 1883—
(a)   section 2 (causing explosion likely to endanger life or property); and
(b)   section 3 (attempt to cause explosion, or making or keeping explosive with intent to endanger life or property).
   9.   Any offence under section 1 of the Children and Young Persons Act 1933 (cruelty to person under 16).
   10.   Any offence under section 4(1) of the Criminal Law Act 1967 (assisting offender) committed in relation to the offence of murder.
   11.   Any offence under any of the following provisions of the Firearms Act 1968—
(a)   section 16 (possession of firearm with intent to injure);
(b)   section 17 (use of firearm to resist arrest); and
(c)   section 18 (carrying firearm with criminal intent).
   12.   Any offence under either of the following provisions of the Theft Act 1968—
(a)   section 9 (burglary); and
(b)   section 10 (aggravated burglary);
and any offence under section 12A of that Act (aggravated vehicle-taking) involving an accident which caused the death of any person.
   13.   Any offence under section 1 of the Criminal Damage Act 1971 (destroying or damaging property) required to be charged as arson.
   14.   Any offence under section 2 of the Child Abduction Act 1984 (abduction of child by person other than parent).

Conspiracy, incitement and attempts

   15.   Any offence under section 1 of the Criminal Law Act 1977 of conspiracy to commit any of the offences mentioned in paragraphs 1 to 14.
   16.   Any offence under section 1 of the Criminal Attempts Act 1981 of attempting to commit any of those offences.
   17.   Any offence of inciting another to commit any of those offences.

HUMAN RIGHTS ACT 1998
(1998, c. 42)

Introduction

1.   The Convention Rights
   (1)   In this Act 'the Convention rights' means the rights and fundamental freedoms set out in—
(a)   Articles 2 to 12 and 14 of the Convention,
(b)   Articles 1 to 3 of the First Protocol, and

(c)   Articles 1 and 2 of the Sixth Protocol,
as read with Articles 16 to 18 of the Convention.

(2)   Those Articles are to have effect for the purposes of this Act subject to any designated derogation or reservation (as to which see sections 14 and 15).

(3)   The Articles are set out in Schedule 1.

(4)   The Secretary of State may by order make such amendments to this Act as he considers appropriate to reflect the effect, in relation to the United Kingdom, of a protocol.

(5)   In subsection (4) 'protocol' means a protocol to the Convention—
  (a)   which the United Kingdom has ratified; or
  (b)   which the United Kingdom has signed with a view to ratification.

(6)   No amendment may be made by an order under subsection (4) so as to come into force before the protocol concerned is in force in relation to the United Kingdom.

2.   Interpretation of Convention rights

(1)   A court or tribunal determining a question which has arisen in connection with a Convention right must take into account any—
  (a)   judgment, decision, declaration or advisory opinion of the European Court of Human Rights,
  (b)   opinion of the Commission given in a report adopted under Article 31 of the Convention,
  (c)   decision of the Commission in connection with Article 26 or 27(2) of the Convention, or
  (d)   decision of the Committee of Ministers taken under Article 46 of the Convention,
whenever made or given, so far as, in the opinion of the court or tribunal, it is relevant to the proceedings in which that question has arisen.

(2)   Evidence of any judgment, decision, declaration or opinion of which account may have to be taken under this section is to be given in proceedings before any court or tribunal in such manner as may be provided by rules.

(3)   In this section 'rules' means rules of court or, in the case of proceedings before a tribunal, rules made for the purposes of this section—
  (a)   by the Lord Chancellor or the Secretary of State, in relation to any proceedings outside Scotland;
  (b)   by the Secretary of State, in relation to proceedings in Scotland; or
  (c)   by a Northern Ireland department, in relation to proceedings before a tribunal in Northern Ireland—
    (i)   which deals with transferred matters; and
    (ii)   for which no rules made under paragraph (a) are in force.

Legislation

3.   Interpretation of legislation

(1)   So far as it is possible to do so, primary legislation and subordinate legislation must be read and given effect in a way which is compatible with the Convention rights.

(2)   This section—
  (a)   applies to primary legislation and subordinate legislation whenever enacted;
  (b)   does not affect the validity, continuing operation or enforcement of any incompatible primary legislation; and
  (c)   does not affect the validity, continuing operation or enforcement of any incompatible subordinate legislation if (disregarding any possibility of revocation) primary legislation prevents removal of the incompatibility.

4.   Declaration of incompatibility

(1)   Subsection (2) applies in any proceedings in which a court determines whether a provision of primary legislation is compatible with a Convention right.

(2)   If the court is satisfied that the provision is incompatible with a Convention right, it may make a declaration of that incompatibility.

(3)   Subsection (4) applies in any proceedings in which a court determines whether a provision of subordinate legislation, made in the exercise of a power conferred by primary legislation, is compatible with a Convention right.

(4)   If the court is satisfied—

(a)   that the provision is incompatible with a Convention right, and

(b)   that (disregarding any possibility of revocation) the primary legislation concerned prevents removal of the incompatibility,

it may make a declaration of that incompatibility.

(5)   In this section 'court' means—

(a)   the House of Lords;

(b)   the Judicial Committee of the Privy Council;

(c)   the Courts-Martial Appeal Court;

(d)   in Scotland, the High Court of Justiciary sitting otherwise than as a trial court or the Court of Session;

(e)   in England and Wales or Northern Ireland, the High Court or the Court of Appeal.

(6)   A declaration under this section ('a declaration of incompatibility')—

(a)   does not affect the validity, continuing operation or enforcement of the provision in respect of which it is given; and

(b)   is not binding on the parties to the proceedings in which it is made.

5.   Right of Crown to intervene

(1)   Where a court is considering whether to make a declaration of incompatibility, the Crown is entitled to notice in accordance with rules of court.

(2)   In any case to which subsection (1) applies—

(a)   a Minister of the Crown (or a person nominated by him),

(b)   a member of the Scottish Executive,

(c)   a Northern Ireland Minister,

(d)   a Northern Ireland department,

is entitled, on giving notice in accordance with rules of court, to be joined as a party to the proceedings.

(3)   Notice under subsection (2) may be given at any time during the proceedings.

(4)   A person who has been made a party to criminal proceedings (other than in Scotland) as the result of a notice under subsection (2) may, with leave, appeal to the House of Lords against any declaration of incompatibility made in the proceedings.

(5)   In subsection (4)—

'criminal proceedings' includes all proceedings before the Courts-Martial Appeal Court; and

'leave' means leave granted by the court making the declaration of incompatibility or by the House of Lords.

Public authorities

6.   Acts of public authorities

(1)   It is unlawful for a public authority to act in a way which is incompatible with a Convention right.

(2)   Subsection (1) does not apply to an act if—

(a)   as the result of one or more provisions of primary legislation, the authority could not have acted differently; or

(b)   in the case of one or more provisions of, or made under, primary legislation which cannot be read or given effect in a way which is compatible with the Convention rights, the authority was acting so as to give effect to or enforce those provisions.

(3)   In this section 'public authority' includes—

    (a)   a court or tribunal, and

    (b)   any person certain of whose functions are functions of a public nature,

but does not include either House of Parliament or a person exercising functions in connection with proceedings in Parliament.

(4)   In subsection (3) 'Parliament' does not include the House of Lords in its judicial capacity.

(5)   In relation to a particular act, a person is not a public authority by virtue only of subsection (3)(b) if the nature of the act is private.

(6)   'An act' includes a failure to act but does not include a failure to—

    (a)   introduce in, or lay before, Parliament a proposal for legislation; or

    (b)   make any primary legislation or remedial order.

7. Proceedings

(1)   A person who claims that a public authority has acted (or proposes to act) in a way which is made unlawful by section 6(1) may—

    (a)   bring proceedings against the authority under this Act in the appropriate court or tribunal, or

    (b)   rely on the Convention right or rights concerned in any legal proceedings,

but only if he is (or would be) a victim of the unlawful act.

(2)   In subsection (1)(a) 'appropriate court or tribunal' means such court or tribunal as may be determined in accordance with rules; and proceedings against an authority include a counterclaim or similar proceeding.

(3)   If the proceedings are brought on an application for judicial review, the applicant is to be taken to have a sufficient interest in relation to the unlawful act only if he is, or would be, a victim of that act.

(4)   If the proceedings are made by way of a petition for judicial review in Scotland, the applicant shall be taken to have title and interest to sue in relation to the unlawful act only if he is, or would be, a victim of that act.

(5)   Proceedings under subsection (1)(a) must be brought before the end of—

    (a)   the period of one year beginning with the date on which the act complained of took place; or

    (b)   such longer period as the court or tribunal considers equitable having regard to all the circumstances,

but that is subject to any rule imposing a stricter time limit in relation to the procedure in question.

(6)   In subsection (1)(b) 'legal proceedings' includes—

    (a)   proceedings brought by or at the instigation of a public authority; and

    (b)   an appeal against the decision of a court or tribunal.

(7)   For the purposes of this section, a person is a victim of an unlawful act only if he would be a victim for the purposes of Article 34 of the Convention if proceedings were brought in the European Court of Human Rights in respect of that act.

(8)   Nothing in this Act creates a criminal offence.

(9)   In this section 'rules' means—

    (a)   in relation to proceedings before a court or tribunal outside Scotland, rules made by the Lord Chancellor or the Secretary of State for the purposes of this section or rules of court,

    (b)   in relation to proceedings before a court or tribunal in Scotland, rules made by the Secretary of State for those purposes,

    (c)   in relation to proceedings before a tribunal in Northern Ireland—

        (i)   which deals with transferred matters; and

        (ii)   for which no rules made under paragraph (a) are in force,

rules made by a Northern Ireland department for those purposes, and includes provision made by order under section 1 of the Courts and Legal Services Act 1990.

(10)   In making rules, regard must be had to section 9.

(11)   The Minister who has power to make rules in relation to a particular tribunal may, to the extent he considers it necessary to ensure that the tribunal can provide an appropriate remedy in relation to an act (or proposed act) of a public authority which is (or would be) unlawful as a result of section 6(1), by order add to—

(a)   the relief or remedies which the tribunal may grant; or

(b)   the grounds on which it may grant any of them.

(12)   An order made under subsection (11) may contain such incidental, supplemental, consequential or transitional provision as the Minister making it considers appropriate.

(13)   'The Minister' includes the Northern Ireland department concerned.

8. Judicial remedies

(1)   In relation to any act (or proposed act) of a public authority which the court finds is (or would be) unlawful, it may grant such relief or remedy, or make such order, within its powers as it considers just and appropriate.

(2)   But damages may be awarded only by a court which has power to award damages, or to order the payment of compensation, in civil proceedings.

(3)   No award of damages is to be made unless, taking account of all the circumstances of the case, including—

(a)   any other relief or remedy granted, or order made, in relation to the act in question (by that or any other court), and

(b)   the consequences of any decision (of that or any other court) in respect of that act,

the court is satisfied that the award is necessary to afford just satisfaction to the person in whose favour it is made.

(4)   In determining—

(a)   whether to award damages, or

(b)   the amount of an award,

the court must take into account the principles applied by the European Court of Human Rights in relation to the award of compensation under Article 41 of the Convention.

(5)   A public authority against which damages are awarded is to be treated—

(a)   in Scotland, for the purposes of section 3 of the Law Reform (Miscellaneous Provisions) (Scotland) Act 1940 as if the award were made in an action of damages in which the authority has been found liable in respect of loss or damage to the person to whom the award is made;

(b)   for the purposes of the Civil Liability (Contribution) Act 1978 as liable in respect of damage suffered by the person to whom the award is made.

(6)   In this section—

'court' includes a tribunal;

'damages' means damages for an unlawful act of a public authority; and

'unlawful' means unlawful under section 6(1).

9. Judicial acts

(1)   Proceedings under section 7(1)(a) in respect of a judicial act may be brought only—

(a)   by exercising a right of appeal;

(b)   on an application (in Scotland a petition) for judicial review; or

(c)   in such other forum as may be prescribed by rules.

(2)   That does not affect any rule of law which prevents a court from being the subject of judicial review.

(3)   In proceedings under this Act in respect of a judicial act done in good faith, damages may not be awarded otherwise than to compensate a person to the extent required by Article 5(5) of the Convention.

(4)   An award of damages permitted by subsection (3) is to be made against the Crown; but no award may be made unless the appropriate person, if not a party to the proceedings, is joined.

(5)   In this section—

'appropriate person' means the Minister responsible for the court concerned, or a person or government department nominated by him;

'court' includes a tribunal;

'judge' includes a member of a tribunal, a justice of the peace and a clerk or other officer entitled to exercise the jurisdiction of a court;

'judicial act' means a judicial act of a court and includes an act done on the instructions, or on behalf, of a judge; and

'rules' has the same meaning as in section 7(9).

Remedial action

10.   Power to take remedial action

(1)   This section applies if—

　(a)   a provision of legislation has been declared under section 4 to be incompatible with a Convention right and, if an appeal lies—

　　(i)   all persons who may appeal have stated in writing that they do not intend to do so;

　　(ii)   the time for bringing an appeal has expired and no appeal has been brought within that time; or

　　(iii)   an appeal brought within that time has been determined or abandoned; or

　(b)   it appears to a Minister of the Crown or Her Majesty in Council that, having regard to a finding of the European Court of Human Rights made after the coming into force of this section in proceedings against the United Kingdom, a provision of legislation is incompatible with an obligation of the United Kingdom arising from the Convention.

(2)   If a Minister of the Crown considers that there are compelling reasons for proceeding under this section, he may by order make such amendments to the legislation as he considers necessary to remove the incompatibility.

(3)   If, in the case of subordinate legislation, a Minister of the Crown considers—

　(a)   that it is necessary to amend the primary legislation under which the subordinate legislation in question was made, in order to enable the incompatibility to be removed, and

　(b)   that there are compelling reasons for proceeding under this section,

he may by order make such amendments to the primary legislation as he considers necessary.

(4)   This section also applies where the provision in question is in subordinate legislation and has been quashed, or declared invalid, by reason of incompatibility with a Convention right and the Minister proposes to proceed under paragraph 2(b) of Schedule 2.

(5)   If the legislation is an Order in Council, the power conferred by subsection (2) or (3) is exercisable by Her Majesty in Council.

(6)   In this section 'legislation' does not include a Measure of the Church Assembly or of the General Synod of the Church of England.

(7)   Schedule 2 makes further provision about remedial orders.

21.   Interpretation etc.

(1)   In this Act—

'amend' includes repeal and apply (with or without modifications);
'the appropriate Minister' means the Minister of the Crown having charge of the appropriate authorised government department (within the meaning of the Crown Proceedings Act 1947);
'the Commission' means the European Commission of Human Rights;
'the Convention' means the Convention for the Protection of Human Rights and Fundamental Freedoms, agreed by the Council of Europe at Rome on 4th November 1950 as it has effect for the time being in relation to the United Kingdom;
'declaration of incompatibility' means a declaration under section 4;
'Minister of the Crown' has the same meaning as in the Ministers of the Crown Act 1975;
'Northern Ireland Minister' includes the First Minister and the deputy First Minister in Northern Ireland;
'primary legislation' means any—
    (a)   public general Act;
    (b)   local and personal Act;
    (c)   private Act;
    (d)   Measure of the Church Assembly;
    (e)   Measure of the General Synod of the Church of England;
    (f)   Order in Council—
        (i)   made in exercise of Her Majesty's Royal Prerogative;
        (ii)   made under section 38(1)(a) of the Northern Ireland Constitution Act 1973 or the corresponding provision of the Northern Ireland Act 1998; or
        (iii) amending an Act of a kind mentioned in paragraph (a), (b) or (c);
and includes an order or other instrument made under primary legislation (otherwise than by the National Assembly for Wales, a member of the Scottish Executive, a Northern Ireland Minister or a Northern Ireland department) to the extent to which it operates to bring one or more provisions of that legislation into force or amends any primary legislation;
'the First Protocol' means the protocol to the Convention agreed at Paris on 20th March 1952;
'the Sixth Protocol' means the protocol to the Convention agreed at Strasbourg on 28th April 1983;
'the Eleventh Protocol' means the protocol to the Convention (restructuring the control machinery established by the Convention) agreed at Strasbourg on 11th May 1994;
'remedial order' means an order under section 10;
'subordinate legislation' means any—
    (a)   Order in Council other than one—
        (i)   made in exercise of Her Majesty's Royal Prerogative;
        (ii)   made under section 38(1)(a) of the Northern Ireland Constitution Act 1973 or the corresponding provision of the Northern Ireland Act 1998; or
        (iii) amending an Act of a kind mentioned in the definition of primary legislation;
    (b)   Act of the Scottish Parliament;
    (c)   Act of the Parliament of Northern Ireland;
    (d)   Measure of the Assembly established under section 1 of the Northern Ireland Assembly Act 1973;
    (e)   Act of the Northern Ireland Assembly;
    (f)   order, rules, regulations, scheme, warrant, byelaw or other instrument made under primary legislation (except to the extent to which it operates to bring one or more provisions of that legislation into force or amends any primary legislation);

(g) order, rules, regulations, scheme, warrant, byelaw or other instrument made under legislation mentioned in paragraph (b), (c), (d) or (e) or made under an Order in Council applying only to Northern Ireland;

(h) order, rules, regulations, scheme, warrant, byelaw or other instrument made by a member of the Scottish Executive, a Northern Ireland Minister or a Northern Ireland department in exercise of prerogative or other executive functions of Her Majesty which are exercisable by such a person on behalf of Her Majesty; 'transferred matters' has the same meaning as in the Northern Ireland Act 1998; and 'tribunal' means any tribunal in which legal proceedings may be brought.

(2) The references in paragraphs (b) and (c) of section 2(1) to Articles are to Articles of the Convention as they had effect immediately before the coming into force of the Eleventh Protocol.

(3) The reference in paragraph (d) of section 2(1) to Article 46 includes a reference to Articles 32 and 54 of the Convention as they had effect immediately before the coming into force of the Eleventh Protocol.

(4) The references in section 2(1) to a report or decision of the Commission or a decision of the Committee of Ministers include references to a report or decision made as provided by paragraphs 3, 4 and 6 of Article 5 of the Eleventh Protocol (transitional provisions).

(5) Any liability under the Army Act 1955, the Air Force Act 1955 or the Naval Discipline Act 1957 to suffer death for an offence is replaced by a liability to imprisonment for life or any less punishment authorised by those Acts; and those Acts shall accordingly have effect with the necessary modifications.

22. Short title, commencement, application and extent

(1) This Act may be cited as the Human Rights Act 1998.

(2) Sections 18, 20 and 21(5) and this section come into force on the passing of this Act.

(3) The other provisions of this Act come into force on such day as the Secretary of State may by order appoint; and different days may be appointed for different purposes.

(4) Paragraph (b) of subsection (1) of section 7 applies to proceedings brought by or at the instigation of a public authority whenever the act in question took place; but otherwise that subsection does not apply to an act taking place before the coming into force of that section.

(5) This Act binds the Crown.

(6) This Act extends to Northern Ireland.

(7) Section 21(5), so far as it relates to any provision contained in the Army Act 1955, the Air Force Act 1955 or the Naval Discipline Act 1957, extends to any place to which that provision extends.

YOUTH JUSTICE AND CRIMINAL EVIDENCE ACT 1999
(1999, c. 23)

PART II
GIVING OF EVIDENCE OR INFORMATION FOR PURPOSES OF CRIMINAL PROCEEDINGS
CHAPTER I
SPECIAL MEASURES DIRECTIONS IN CASE OF VULNERABLE AND INTIMIDATED WITNESSES

Preliminary

16. Witnesses eligible for assistance on grounds of age or incapacity

(1) For the purposes of this Chapter a witness in criminal proceedings (other than the accused) is eligible for assistance by virtue of this section—

(a) if under the age of 17 at the time of the hearing; or

(b) if the court considers that the quality of evidence given by the witness is likely to be diminished by reason of any circumstances falling within subsection (2).

(2) The circumstances falling within this subsection are—

(a) that the witness—

(i) suffers from mental disorder within the meaning of the Mental Health Act 1983, or

(ii) otherwise has a significant impairment of intelligence and social functioning;

(b) that the witness has a physical disability or is suffering from a physical disorder.

(3) In subsection (1)(a) 'the time of the hearing', in relation to a witness, means the time when it falls to the court to make a determination for the purposes of section 19(2) in relation to the witness.

(4) In determining whether a witness falls within subsection (1)(b) the court must consider any views expressed by the witness.

(5) In this Chapter references to the quality of a witness's evidence are to its quality in terms of completeness, coherence and accuracy; and for this purpose 'coherence' refers to a witness's ability in giving evidence to give answers which address the questions put to the witness and can be understood both individually and collectively.

17. Witnesses eligible for assistance on grounds of fear or distress about testifying

(1) For the purposes of this Chapter a witness in criminal proceedings (other than the accused) is eligible for assistance by virtue of this subsection if the court is satisfied that the quality of evidence given by the witness is likely to be diminished by reason of fear or distress on the part of the witness in connection with testifying in the proceedings.

(2) In determining whether a witness falls within subsection (1) the court must take into account, in particular—

(a) the nature and alleged circumstances of the offence to which the proceedings relate;

(b) the age of the witness;

(c) such of the following matters as appear to the court to be relevant, namely—

(i) the social and cultural background and ethnic origins of the witness,

(ii) the domestic and employment circumstances of the witness, and

(iii) any religious beliefs or political opinions of the witness;

(d) any behaviour towards the witness on the part of—

(i) the accused,

(ii) members of the family or associates of the accused, or

(iii) any other person who is likely to be an accused or a witness in the proceedings.

(3) In determining that question the court must in addition consider any views expressed by the witness.

(4) Where the complainant in respect of a sexual offence is a witness in proceedings relating to that offence (or to that offence and any other offences), the witness is eligible for assistance in relation to those proceedings by virtue of this subsection unless the witness has informed the court of the witness's wish not to be so eligible by virtue of this subsection.

18. Special measures available to eligible witnesses

(1) For the purposes of this Chapter—

(a) the provision which may be made by a special measures direction by virtue of each of sections 23 to 30 is a special measure available in relation to a witness eligible for assistance by virtue of section 16; and

(b)   the provision which may be made by such a direction by virtue of each of sections 23 to 28 is a special measure available in relation to a witness eligible for assistance by virtue of section 17;
but this subsection has effect subject to subsection (2).

(2)   Where (apart from this subsection) a special measure would, in accordance with subsection (1)(a) or (b), be available in relation to a witness in any proceedings, it shall not be taken by a court to be available in relation to the witness unless—

(a)   the court has been notified by the Secretary of State that relevant arrangements may be made available in the area in which it appears to the court that the proceedings will take place, and

(b)   the notice has not been withdrawn.

(3)   In subsection (2) 'relevant arrangements' means arrangements for implementing the measure in question which cover the witness and the proceedings in question.

(4)   The withdrawal of a notice under that subsection relating to a special measure shall not affect the availability of that measure in relation to a witness if a special measures direction providing for that measure to apply to the witness's evidence has been made by the court before the notice is withdrawn.

(5)   The Secretary of State may by order make such amendments of this Chapter as he considers appropriate for altering the special measures which, in accordance with subsection (1)(a) or (b), are available in relation to a witness eligible for assistance by virtue of section 16 or (as the case may be) section 17, whether—

(a)   by modifying the provisions relating to any measure for the time being available in relation to such a witness,

(b)   by the addition—

(i)   (with or without modifications) of any measure which is for the time being available in relation to a witness eligible for assistance virtue of the other of those sections, or

(ii)   of any new measure, or

(c)   by the removal of any measure.

Special measures directions

19.   Special measures direction relating to eligible witness

(1)   This section applies where in any criminal proceedings—

(a)   a party to the proceedings makes an application for the court to give a direction under this section in relation to a witness in the proceedings other than the accused, or

(b)   the court of its own motion raises the issue whether such a direction should be given.

(2)   Where the court determines that the witness is eligible for assistance by virtue of section 16 or 17, the court must then—

(a)   determine whether any of the special measures available in relation to the witness (or any combination of them) would, in its opinion, be likely to improve the quality of evidence given by the witness; and

(b)   if so—

(i)   determine which of those measures (or combination of them) would, in its opinion, be likely to maximise so far as practicable the quality of such evidence; and

(ii)   give a direction under this section providing for the measure or measures so determined to apply to evidence given by the witness.

(3)   In determining for the purposes of this Chapter whether any special measure or measures would or would not be likely to improve, or to maximise so far as practicable, the quality of evidence given by the witness, the court must consider all the circumstances of the case, including in particular—

(a)   any views expressed by the witness; and

(b)   whether the measure or measures might tend to inhibit such evidence being effectively tested by a party to the proceedings.

(4)   A special measures direction must specify particulars of the provision made by the direction in respect of each special measure which is to apply to the witness's evidence.

(5)   In this Chapter 'special measures direction' means a direction under this section.

(6)   Nothing in this Chapter is to be regarded as affecting any power of a court to make an order or give leave of any description (in the exercise of its inherent jurisdiction or otherwise)—

(a)   in relation to a witness who is not an eligible witness, or

(b)   in relation to an eligible witness where (as, for example, in a case where a foreign language interpreter is to be provided) the order is made or the leave is given otherwise than by reason of the fact that the witness is an eligible witness.

20.   Further provisions about directions: general

(1)   Subject to subsection (2) and section 21(8), a special measures direction has binding effect from the time it is made until the proceedings for the purposes of which it is made are either—

(a)   determined (by acquittal, conviction or otherwise), or

(b)   abandoned,

in relation to the accused or (if there is more than one) in relation to each of the accused.

(2)   The court may discharge or vary (or further vary) a special measures direction if it appears to the court to be in the interests of justice to do so, and may do so either—

(a)   on an application made by a party to the proceedings, if there has been a material change of circumstances since the relevant time, or

(b)   of its own motion.

(3)   In subsection (2) 'the relevant time' means—

(a)   the time when the direction was given, or

(b)   if a previous application has been made under that subsection, the time when the application (or last application) was made.

(4)   Nothing in section 24(2) and (3), 27(4) to (7) or 28(4) to (6) is to be regarded as affecting the power of the court to vary or discharge a special measures direction under subsection (2).

(5)   The court must state in open court its reasons for—

(a)   giving or varying,

(b)   refusing an application for, or for the variation or discharge of, or

(c)   discharging,

a special measures direction and, if it is a magistrates' court, must cause them to be entered in the register of its proceedings.

(6)   Rules of court may make provision—

(a)   for uncontested applications to be determined by the court without a hearing;

(b)   for preventing the renewal of an unsuccessful application for a special measures direction except where there has been a material change of circumstances;

(c)   for expert evidence to be given in connection with an application for, or for varying or discharging, such a direction;

(d)   for the manner in which confidential or sensitive information is to be treated in connection with such an application and in particular as to its being disclosed to, or withheld from, a party to the proceedings.

21.   Special provisions relating to child witnesses

(1)   For the purposes of this section—

(a)   a witness in criminal proceedings is a 'child witness' if he is an eligible witness by reason of section 16(1)(a) (whether or not he is an eligible witness by reason of any other provision of section 16 or 17);

(b)   a child witness is 'in need of special protection' if the offence (or any of the offences) to which the proceedings relate is—

    (i)   an offence falling within section 35(3)(a) (sexual offences etc.), or

    (ii)   an offence falling within section 35(3)(b), (c) or (d) (kidnapping, assaults etc.); and

(c)   a 'relevant recording', in relation to a child witness, is a video recording of an interview of the witness made with a view to its admission as evidence in chief of the witness.

(2)   Where the court, in making a determination for the purposes of section 19(2), determines that a witness in criminal proceedings is a child witness, the court must—

    (a)   first have regard to subsections (3) to (7) below; and

    (b)   then have regard to section 19(2);

and for the purposes of section 19(2), as it then applies to the witness, any special measures required to be applied in relation to him by virtue of this section shall be treated as if they were measures determined by the court, pursuant to section 19(2)(a) and (b)(i), to be ones that (whether on their own or with any other special measures) would be likely to maximise, so far as practicable, the quality of his evidence.

(3)   The primary rule in the case of a child witness is that the court must give a special measures direction in relation to the witness which complies with the following requirements—

    (a)   it must provide for any relevant recording to be admitted under section 27 (video recorded evidence in chief); and

    (b)   it must provide for any evidence given by the witness in the proceedings which is not given by means of a video recording (whether in chief or otherwise) to be given by means of a live link in accordance with section 24.

(4)   The primary rule is subject to the following limitations—

    (a)   the requirement contained in subsection (3)(a) or (b) has effect subject to the availability (within the meaning of section 18(2)) of the special measure in question in relation to the witness;

    (b)   the requirement contained in subsection (2)(a) also has effect subject to section 27(2); and

    (c)   the rule does not apply to the extent that the court is satisfied that compliance with it would not be likely to maximise the quality of the witness's evidence so far as practicable (whether because the application to that evidence of one or more other special measures available in relation to the witness would have that result or for any other reason).

(5)   However, subsection (4)(c) does not apply in relation to a child witness in need of special protection.

(6)   Where a child witness is in need of special protection by virtue of subsection (1)(b)(i), any special measures direction given by the court which complies with the requirement contained in subsection (3)(a) must in addition provide for the special measure available under section 28 (video recorded cross-examination or re-examination) to apply in relation to—

    (a)   any cross-examination of the witness otherwise than by the accused in person, and

    (b)   any subsequent re-examination.

(7)   The requirement contained in subsection (6) has effect subject to the following limitations—

    (a)   it has effect subject to the availability (within the meaning of section 18(2)) of that special measure in relation to the witness; and

    (b)   it does not apply if the witness has informed the court that he does not want that special measure to apply in relation to him.

(8)   Where a special measures direction is given in relation to a child witness who is an eligible witness by reason only of section 16(1)(a), then—

(a)   subject to subsection (9) below, and
(b)   except where the witness has already begun to give evidence in the proceedings,
the direction shall cease to have effect at the time when the witness attains the age of 17.
(9)   Where a special measures direction is given in relation to a child witness who is an eligible witness by reason only of section 16(1)(a) and—
(a)   the direction provides—
(i)   for any relevant recording to be admitted under section 27 as evidence in chief of the witness, or
(ii)   for the special measure available under section 28 to apply in relation to the witness, and
(b)   if it provides for that special measure to so apply, the witness is still under the age of 17 when the video recording is made for the purposes of section 28,
then, so far as it provides as mentioned in paragraph (a)(i) or (ii) above, the direction shall continue to have effect in accordance with section 20(1) even though the witness subsequently attains that age.

22.   Extension of provisions of section 21 to certain witnesses over 17
(1)   For the purposes of this section—
(a)   a witness in criminal proceedings (other than the accused) is a 'qualifying witness' if he—
(i)   is not an eligible witness at the time of the hearing (as defined by section 16(3)), but
(ii)   was under the age of 17 when a relevant recording was made;
(b)   a qualifying witness is 'in need of special protection' if the offence (or any of the offences) to which the proceedings relate is—
(i)   an offence falling within section 35(3)(a) (sexual offences etc.), or
(ii)   an offence falling within section 35(3)(b), (c) or (d) (kidnapping, assaults etc.); and
(c)   a 'relevant recording', in relation to a witness, is a video recording of an interview of the witness made with a view to its admission as evidence in chief of the witness.
(2)   Subsections (2) to (7) of section 21 shall apply as follows in relation to a qualifying witness—
(a)   subsections (2) to (4), so far as relating to the giving of a direction complying with the requirement contained in subsection (3)(a), shall apply to a qualifying witness in respect of the relevant recording as they apply to a child witness (within the meaning of that section);
(b)   subsection (5), so far as relating to the giving of such a direction, shall apply to a qualifying witness in need of special protection as it applies to a child witness in need of special protection (within the meaning of that section); and
(c)   subsection (6) and (7) shall apply to a qualifying witness in need of special protection by virtue of subsection (1)(b)(i) above as they apply to such a child witness as is mentioned in subsection (6).

Special measures

23.   Screening witness from accused
(1)   A special measures direction may provide for the witness, while giving testimony or being sworn in court, to be prevented by means of a screen or other arrangement from seeing the accused.
(2)   But the screen or other arrangement must not prevent the witness from being able to see, and to be seen by—
(a)   the judge or justices (or both) and the jury (if there is one);

(b)   legal representatives acting in the proceedings; and
(c)   any interpreter or other person appointed (in pursuance of the direction or otherwise) to assist the witness.

(3)   Where two or more legal representatives are acting for a party to the proceedings, subsection (2)(b) is to be regarded as satisfied in relation to those representatives if the witness is able to all material times to see and be seen by at least one of them.

24.   Evidence by live link

(1)   A special measures direction may provide for the witness to give evidence by means of a live link.

(2)   Where a direction provides for the witness to give evidence by means of a live link, the witness may not give evidence in any other way without the permission of the court.

(3)   The court may give permission for the purposes of subsection (2) if it appears to the court to be in the interests of justice to do so, and may do so either—
(a)   on an application by a party to the proceedings, if there has been a material change of circumstances since the relevant time, or
(b)   of its own motion.

(4)   In subsection (3) 'the relevant time' means—
(a)   the time when the direction was given, or
(b)   if a previous application has been made under that subsection, the time when the application (or last application) was made.

(5)   Where in proceedings before a magistrates' court—
(a)   evidence is to be given by means of a live link in accordance with a special measures direction, but
(b)   suitable facilities for receiving such evidence are not available at any petty-sessional court-house in which that court can (apart from this subsection) lawfully sit,
the court may sit for the purposes of the whole or any part of those proceedings at a place where such facilities are available and which has been appointed for the purposes of this subsection by the justices acting for the petty sessions area for which the court acts.

(6)   A place appointed under subsection (5) may be outside the petty sessions area for which it is appointed; but (if so) it is to be regarded as being in that area for the purpose of the jurisdiction of the justices acting for that area.

(7)   In this section 'petty-sessional court-house' has the same meaning as in the Magistrates' Courts Act 1980 and 'petty sessions area' has the same meaning as in the Justices of the Peace Act 1997.

(8)   In this Chapter 'live link' means a live television link or other arrangement whereby a witness, while absent from the courtroom or other place where the proceedings are being held, if able to see and hear a person there and to be such and heard by the persons specified in section 23(2)(a) to (c).

25.   Evidence given in private

(1)   A special measures direction may provide for the exclusion from the court, during the giving of the witness's evidence, of persons of any description specified in the direction.

(2)   The persons who may be so excluded do not include—
(a)   the accused,
(b)   legal representatives acting in the proceedings, or
(c)   any interpreter or other person appointed (in pursuance of the direction or otherwise) to assist the witness.

(3)   A special measures direction providing for representatives of news gathering or reporting organisations to be so excluded shall be expressed not to apply to one named person who—

(a)   is a representative of such an organisation, and

(b)   has been nominated for the purpose by one or more such organisations,

unless it appears to the court that no such nomination has been made.

(4)   A special measures direction may only provide for the exclusion of persons under this section where—

(a)   the proceedings relate to a sexual offence; or

(b)   it appears to the court that there are reasonable grounds for believing that any person other than the accused has sought, or will seek, to intimidate the witness in connection with testifying in the proceedings.

(5)   Any proceedings from which persons are excluded under this section (whether or not those persons include representatives of news gathering or reporting organisations) shall nevertheless be taken to be held in public for the purposes of any privilege or exemption from liability available in respect of fair, accurate and contemporaneous reports of legal proceedings held in public.

26.   Removal of wigs and gowns

A special measures direction may provide for the wearing of wigs or gowns to be dispensed with during the giving of the witness's evidence.

27.   Video recorded evidence in chief

(1)   A special measures direction may provide for a video recording of an interview of the witness to be admitted as evidence in chief of the witness.

(2)   A special measures direction may, however, not provide for a video recording, or a part of such a recording, to be admitted under this section if the court is of the opinion, having regard to all the circumstances of the case, that in the interests of justice the recording, or that part of it, should not be so admitted.

(3)   In considering for the purposes of subsection (2) whether any part of a recording should not be admitted under this section, the court must consider whether any prejudice to the accused which might result from that part being so admitted is outweighed by the desirability of showing the whole, or substantially the whole, of the recorded interview.

(4)   Where a special measures direction provides for a recording to be admitted under this section, the court may nevertheless subsequently direct that it is not to be so admitted if—

(a)   it appears to the court that—

(i)   the witness will not be available for cross-examination (whether conducted in the ordinary way or in accordance with any such direction), and

(ii)   the parties to the proceedings have not agreed that there is no need for the witness to be so available; or

(b)   any rules of court requiring disclosure of the circumstances in which the recording was made have not been complied with to the satisfaction of the court.

(5)   Where a recording is admitted under this section—

(a)   the witness must be called by the party tendering it in evidence, unless—

(i)   a special measures direction provides for the witness's evidence on cross-examination to be given otherwise than by testimony in court, or

(ii)   the parties to the proceedings have agreed as mentioned in subsection (4)(a)(ii); and

(b)   the witness may not give evidence in chief otherwise than by means of the recording—

(i)   as to any matter which, in the opinion of the court, has been dealt with adequately in the witness's recorded testimony, or

(ii)   without the permission of the court, as to any other matter which, in the opinion of the court, is dealt with in that testimony.

(6)   Where in accordance with subsection (2) a special measures direction provides for part only of a recording to be admitted under this section, references in subsection

(4) and (5) to the recording or to the witness's recorded testimony are references to the part of the recording or testimony which is to be so admitted.

(7)   The court may give permission for the purposes of subsection (5)(b)(ii) if it appears to the court to be in the interests of justice to do so, and may do so either—

(a)   on an application by a party to the proceedings, if there has been a material change of circumstances since the relevant time, or

(b)   of its own motion.

(8)   In subsection (7) 'the relevant time' means—

(a)   the time when the direction was given, or

(b)   if a previous application has been made under that subsection, the time when the application (or last application) was made.

(9)   The court may, in giving permission for the purposes of subsection (5)(b)(ii), direct that the evidence in question is to be given by the witness by means of a live link; and, if the court so directs, subsections (5) to (7) of section 24 shall apply in relation to that evidence as they apply in relation to evidence which is to be given in accordance with a special measures direction.

(10)   A magistrates' court inquiring into an offence as examining justices under section 6 of the magistrates' Courts Act 1980 may consider any video recording in relation to which it is proposed to apply for a special measures direction providing for it to be admitted at the trial in accordance with this section.

(11)   Nothing in this section affects the admissibility of any video recording which would be admissible apart from this section.

28.   Video recorded cross-examination or re-examination

(1)   Where a special measures direction provides for a video recording to be admitted under section 27 as evidence in chief of the witness, the direction may also provide—

(a)   for any cross-examination of the witness, and any re-examination, to be recorded by means of a video recording; and

(b)   for such a recording to be admitted, so far as it relates to any such cross-examination or re-examination, as evidence of the witness under cross-examination or on re-examination, as the case may be.

(2)   Such a recording must be made in the presence of such persons as rules of court or the direction may provide and in the absence of the accused, but in circumstances in which—

(a)   the judge or justices (or both) and legal representatives acting in the proceedings are able to see and hear the examination of the witness and to communicate with the persons in whose presence the recording is being made, and

(b)   the accused is able to see and hear any such examination and to communicate with any legal representative acting for him.

(3)   Where two or more legal representatives are acting for a party to the proceedings, subsection (2)(a) and (b) are to be regarded as satisfied in relation to those representatives if at all material times they are satisfied in relation to at least one of them.

(4)   Where a special measures direction provides for a recording to be admitted under this section, the court may nevertheless subsequently direct that it is not to be so admitted if any requirement of subsection (2) or rules of court or the direction has not been complied with to the satisfaction of the court.

(5)   Where in pursuance of subsection (1) a recording has been made of any examination of the witness, the witness may not be subsequently cross-examined or re-examined in respect of any evidence given by the witness in the proceedings (whether in any recording admissible under section 27 or this section or otherwise than in such a recording) unless the court gives a further special measures direction making such

provision as is mentioned in subsection (1)(a) and (b) in relation to any subsequent cross-examination, and re-examination, of the witness.

(6) The court may only give such a further direction if it appears to the court—

(a) that the proposed cross-examination is sought by a party to the proceedings as a result of that party having become aware, since the time when the original recording was made in pursuance of subsection (1), of a matter which that party could not with reasonable diligence have ascertained by then, or

(b) that for any other reason it is in the interests of justice to give the further direction.

(7) Nothing in this section shall be read as applying in relation to any cross-examination of the witness by the accused in person (in a case where the accused is to be able to conduct any such cross-examination).

29. Examination of witness through intermediary

(1) A special measures direction may provide for any examination of the witness (however and wherever conducted) to be conducted through an interpreter or other person approved by the court for the purposes of this section ('an intermediary').

(2) The function of an intermediary is to communicate—

(a) to the witness, questions put to the witness, and

(b) to any person asking such questions, the answers given by the witness in reply to them,

and to explain such questions or answers so far as necessary to enable them to be understood by the witness or person in question.

(3) Any examination of the witness in pursuance of subsection (1) must take place in the presence of such persons as rules of court or the direction may provide, but in circumstances in which—

(a) the judge or justices (or both) and legal representatives acting in the proceedings are able to see and hear the examination of the witness and to communicate with the intermediary, and

(b) (except in the case of a video recorded examination) the jury (if there is one) are able to see and hear the examination of the witness.

(4) Where two or more legal representatives are acting for a party to the proceedings, subsection (3)(a) is to be regarded as satisfied in relation to those representatives if at all material times it is satisfied in relation to at least one of them.

(5) A person may not act as an intermediary in a particular case except after making a declaration, in such form as may be prescribed by rules of court, that he will faithfully perform his function as intermediary.

(6) Subsection (1) does not apply to an interview of the witness which is recorded by means of a video recording with a view to its admission as evidence in chief of the witness; but a special measures direction may provide for such a recording to be admitted under section 27 if the interview was conducted through an intermediary and—

(a) that person complied with subsection (5) before the interview began, and

(b) the court's approval for the purposes of this action is given before the direction is given.

(7) Section 1 of the Perjury Act 1911 (perjury) shall apply in relation to a person acting as an intermediary as it applies in relation to a person lawfully sworn as an interpreter in a judicial proceeding; and for this purpose, where a person acts as an intermediary in any proceeding which is not a judicial proceeding for the purposes of that section, that proceeding shall be taken to be part of the judicial proceeding in which the witness's evidence is given.

30. Aids to communication

A special measures direction may provide for the witness, while giving evidence (whether by testimony in court or otherwise), to be provided with such device as the court considers appropriate with a view to enabling questions or answers to be communicated to or by the witness despite any disability or disorder or other impairment which the witness has or suffers form.

Supplementary

31. Status of evidence given under Chapter 1.

(1) Subsections (2) to (4) apply to a statement made by a witness in criminal proceedings which, in accordance with a special measures direction, is not made by the witness in direct oral testimony in court but forms part of the witness's evidence in those proceedings.

(2) The statement shall be treated as if made by the witness in direct oral testimony in court; and accordingly—

(a) it is admissible evidence of any fact of which such testimony from the witness would be admissible;

(b) it is not capable of corroborating any other evidence given by the witness.

(3) Subsection (2) applies to a statement admitted under section 27 or 28 which is not made by the witness on oath even though it would have been required to be made on oath if made by the witness in direct oral testimony in court.

(4) In estimating the weight (if any) to be attached to the statement, the court must have regard to all the circumstances from which an inference can reasonably be drawn (as to the accuracy of the statement or otherwise).

(5) Nothing in this Chapter (apart from subsection (3)) affects the operation of any rule of law relating to evidence in criminal proceedings.

(6) Where any statement made by a person on oath in any proceeding which is not a judicial proceeding for the purposes of section 1 of the Perjury Act 1911 (perjury) is received in evidence in pursuance of a special measures direction, that proceeding shall be taken for the purposes of that section to be part of the judicial proceeding in which the statement is so received in evidence.

(7) Where in any proceeding which is not a judicial proceeding for the purposes of that Act—

(a) a person wilfully makes a false statement otherwise than on oath which is subsequently received in evidence in pursuance of a special measures direction, and

(b) the statement is made in such circumstances that had it been given on oath in any such judicial proceeding that person would have been guilty of perjury,

he shall be guilty of an offence and liable to any punishment which might be imposed on conviction of an offence under section 57(2) (giving of false unsworn evidence in criminal proceedings).

(8) In this section 'statement' includes any representation of fact, whether made in words or otherwise.

32. Warning to jury

Where on a trial on indictment evidence has been given in accordance with a special measures direction, the judge must give the jury such warning (if any) as the judge considers necessary to ensure that the fact that the direction was given in relation to the witness does not prejudice the accused.

33. Interpretation etc. of Chapter 1

(1) In this Chapter—

'eligible witness' means a witness eligible for assistance by virtue of section 16 or 17;

'livelink' has the meaning given by section 24(8);

'quality', in relation to the evidence of a witness, shall be construed in accordance with section 16(5);

'special measures direction' means (in accordance with section 19(5)) a direction under section 19.

(2)   In this Chapter references to the special measures available in relation to a witness shall be construed in accordance with section 18.

(3)   In this Chapter references to a person being able to see or hear, or be seen or heard by, another person are to be read as not applying to the extent that either of them is unable to see or hear by reason of any impairment of eyesight or hearing.

(4)   In the case of any proceedings in which there is more than one accused—

(a)   any reference to the accused in sections 23 to 28 may be taken by a court, in connection with the giving of a special measures direction, as a reference to all or any of the accused, as the court may determine, and

(b)   any such direction may be given on the basis of any such determination.

CHAPTER II
PROTECTION OF WITNESSES FROM CROSS-EXAMINATION BY ACCUSED IN PERSON

General prohibitions

34.   Complainants in proceedings for sexual offences

No person charged with a sexual offence may in any criminal proceedings cross-examine in person a witness who is the complainant, either—

(a)   in connection with that offence, or

(b)   in connection with any other offence (or whatever nature) with which that person is charged in the proceedings.

35.   Child complainants and other child witnesses

(1)   No person charged with an offence to which this section applies may in any criminal proceedings cross-examine in person a protected witness, either—

(a)   in connection with that offence, or

(b)   in connection with any other offence (of whatever nature) with which that person is charged in the proceedings.

(2)   For the purposes of subsection (1) a 'protected witness' is a witness who—

(a)   either is the complainant or is alleged to have been a witness to the commission of the offence to which this section applies, and

(b)   either is a child or falls to be cross-examined after giving evidence in chief (whether wholly or in part)—

(i)   by means of a video recording made (for the purposes of section 27) at a time when the witness was a child, or

(ii)   in any other way at any such time.

(3)   the offences to which this section applies are—

(a)   any offence under—

(i)   the Sexual Offences Act 1956,

(ii)   the Indecency with Children Act 1960,

(iii)   the Sexual Offences Act 1967,

(iv)   section 54 of the Criminal Law Act 1977, or

(v)   the Protection of Children Act 1978;

(b)   kidnapping, false imprisonment or an offence under section 1 or 2 of the Child Abduction Act 1984;

(c)   any offence under section 1 of the Children and Young Persons Act 1933;

(d)   any offence (not within any of the preceding paragraphs) which involves an assault on, or injury or a threat of injury to, any person.

(4)   In this section 'child' means—

(a)   where the offence falls within subsection (3)(a), a person under the age of 17; or

(b)   where the offence of this subsection (3)(b), (c) or (d), a person under the age of 14.

(5)   For the purposes of this section 'witness' includes a witness who is charged with an offence in the proceedings.

Prohibition imposed by court

36.   Direction prohibiting accused from cross-examining particular witness

(1)   This section applies where, in a case where neither of sections 34 and 35 operates to prevent an accused in any criminal proceedings from cross-examining a witness in person—

(a)   the prosecutor makes an application for the court to give a direction under this section in relation to the witness, or

(b)   the court of its own motion raises the issue whether such a direction should be given.

(2)   If it appears to the court—

(a)   that the quality of evidence given by the witness on cross-examination—

(i)   is likely to be diminished if the cross-examination (or further cross-examination) is conducted by the accused in person, and

(ii)   would be likely to be improved if a direction were given under this section, and

(b)   that it would not be contrary to the interests of justice to give such a direction, the court may give a direction prohibiting the accused from cross-examining (or further cross-examining) the witness in person.

(3)   In determining whether subsection (2)(a) applies in the case of a witness the court must have regard, in particular, to—

(a)   any views expressed by the witness as to whether or not the witness is content to be cross-examined by the accused in person;

(b)   the nature of the questions likely to be asked, having regard to the issues in the proceedings and the defence case advanced so far (if any);

(c)   any behaviour on the part of the accused at any stage of the proceedings, both generally and in relation to the witness;

(d)   any relationship (of whatever nature) between the witness and the accused;

(e)   whether any person (other than the accused) is or has at any time been charged in the proceedings with a sexual offence or an offence to which section 35 applies, and (if so) whether section 34 or 35 operates or would have operated to prevent that person from cross-examining the witness in person;

(f)   any direction under section 19 which the court has given, or proposes to give, in relation to the witness.

(4)   For the purposes of this section—

(a)   'witness', in relation to an accused, does not include any other person who is charged with an offence in the proceedings; and

(b)   any reference to the quality of a witness's evidence shall be construed in accordance with section 16(5).

37.   Further provisions about directions under section 36

(1)   Subject to subsection (2), a direction has binding effect from the time it is made until the witness to whom it applies is discharged.

In this section 'direction' means a direction under section 36.

(2)   The court may discharge a direction if it appears to the court to be in the interests of justice to do so, and may do so either—

(a)   on an application made by a party to the proceedings, if there has been a material change of circumstances since the relevant time, or

(b)   of its own motion.

(3)   In subsection (2) 'the relevant time' means—

(a)   the time when the direction was given, or

(b)   if a previous application has been made under that subsection, the time when the application (or last application) was made.

(4)   The court must state in open court its reasons for—

(a)   giving, or

(b)   refusing an application for, or for the discharge of, or

(c)   discharging,

a direction and, if it is a magistrates' court, must cause them to be entered in the register of its proceedings.

(5)   Rules of court may make provision—

(a)   for uncontested applications to be determined by the court without a hearing;

(b)   for preventing the renewal of an unsuccessful application for a direction except where there has been a material change of circumstances;

(c)   for expert evidence to be given in connection with an application for, or for discharging, a direction;

(d)   for the manner in which confidential or sensitive information is to be treated in connection with such an application and in particular as to its being disclosed to, or withheld from, a party to the proceedings.

Cross-examined on behalf of accused

38.   Defence representation for purposes of cross-examination

(1)   This section applies where an accused is prevented from cross-examining a witness in person by virtue of section 34, 35 or 36.

(2)   Where it appears to the court that this section applies, it must—

(a)   invite the accused to arrange for a legal representative to act for him for the purpose of cross-examining the witness; and

(b)   require the accused to notify the court, by the end of such period as it may specify, whether a legal representative is to act for him for that purpose.

(3)   If by the end of the period mentioned in subsection (2)(b) either—

(a)   the accused has notified the court that no legal representative is to act for him for the purpose of cross-examining the witness, or

(b)   no notification has been received by the court and it appears to the court that no legal representative is to so act,

the court must consider whether it is necessary in the interests of justice for the witness to be cross-examined by a legal representative appointed to represent the interests of the accused.

(4)   If the court decides that it is necessary in the interests of justice for the witness to be so cross-examined, the court must appoint a qualified legal representative (chosen by the court) to cross-examine the witness in the interests of the accused.

(5)   A person so appointed shall not be responsible to the accused.

(6)   Rules of court may make provision—

(a)   as to the time when, and the manner in which, subsection (2) is to be complied with;

(b)   in connection with the appointment of a legal representative under subsection (4), and in particular for securing that a person so appointed is provided with evidence or other material relating to the proceedings.

(7)   Rules of court made in pursuance of subsection (6)(b) may make provision for the application, with such modifications as are specified in the rules, of any of the provisions of—

(a)   Part I of the Criminal Procedure and Investigations Act 1996 (disclosure of material in connection with criminal proceedings), or

(b)   the Sexual Offences (Protected Material) Act 1997.

(8)   For the purposes of this section—

(a)   any reference to cross-examination includes (in a case where a direction is given under section 36 after the accused has begun cross-examining the witness) a reference to further cross-examination; and

(b)   'qualified legal representative' means a legal representative who has a right of audience (within the meaning of the Courts and Legal Services Act 1990) in relation to the proceedings before the court.

39.   Warning to jury

(1)   Where on a trial on indictment an accused is prevented from cross-examining a witness in person by virtue of section 34, 35 or 36, the judge must give the jury such warning (if any) as the judge considers necessary to ensure that the accused is not prejudiced—

(a)   by any inferences that might be drawn from the fact that the accused has been prevented from cross-examining the witness in person;

(b)   where the witness has been cross-examined by a legal representative appointed under section 38(4), by the fact that the cross-examination was carried out by such a legal representative and not by a person acting as the accused's own legal representative.

(2)   Subsection (8)(a) of section 38 applies for the purposes of this section as it applies for the purposes of section 38.

CHAPTER III
PROTECTION OF COMPLAINANTS IN PROCEEDINGS FOR SEXUAL
OFFENCES

41.   Restriction on evidence or questions about complainant's sexual history

(1)   If at a trial a person is charged with a sexual offence, then, except with the leave of the court—

(a)   no evidence may be adduced, and

(b)   no question may be asked in cross-examination,

by or on behalf of any accused at the trial, about any sexual behaviour of the complainant.

(2)   The court may give leave in relation to any evidence or question only on an application made by or on behalf of an accused, and may not give such leave unless it is satisfied—

(a)   that subsection (3) or (5) applies, and

(b)   that a refusal of leave might have the result of rendering unsafe a conclusion of the jury or (as the case may be) the court on any relevant issue in the case.

(3)   This subsection applies if the evidence or question relates to a relevant issue in the case and either—

(a)   that issue is not an issue of consent; or

(b)   it is an issue of consent and the sexual behaviour of the complainant to which the evidence or question relates is alleged to have taken place at or about the same time as the event which is the subject matter of the charge against the accused; or

(c)   it is an issue of consent and the sexual behaviour of the complainant to which the evidence or question relates is alleged to have been, in any respect, so similar—

(i)   to any sexual behaviour of the complainant which (according to evidence adduced or to be adduced by or on behalf of the accused) took place as part of the event which is the subject matter of the charge against the accused, or

(ii)   to any other sexual behaviour of the complainant which (according to such evidence) took place at or about the same time as the event,

that the similarity cannot reasonably be explained as a coincidence.

(4)   For the purposes of subsection (3) no evidence or question shall be regarded as relating to a relevant issue in the case if it appears to the court to be reasonable to assume

that the purpose (or main purpose) for which it would be adduced or asked is to establish or elicit material for impugning the credibility of the complainant as a witness.

(5)   This subsection applies if the evidence or question—

(a)   relates to any evidence adduced by the prosecution about any sexual behaviour of the complainant; and

(b)   in the opinion of the court, would go no further than is necessary to enable the evidence adduced by the prosecution to be rebutted or explained by or on behalf of the accused.

(6)   For the purposes of subsections (3) and (5) the evidence or question must relate to a specific instance (or specific instances) of alleged sexual behaviour on the part of the complainant (and accordingly nothing in those subsections is capable of applying in relation to the evidence or question to the extent that it does not so relate).

(7)   Where this section applies in relation to a trial by virtue of the fact that one or more of a number of persons charged in the proceedings is or are charged with a sexual offence—

(a)   it shall cease to apply in relation to the trial if the prosecutor decides not to proceed with the case against that person or those persons in respect of that charge; but

(b)   it shall not cease to do so in the event of that person or those persons pleading guilty to, or being convicted of, that charge.

(8)   Nothing in this section authorises any evidence to be adduced or any question to be asked which cannot be adduced or asked apart from this section.

42.   Interpretation and application of section 41

(1)   In section 41—

(a)   'relevant issue in the case' means any issue falling to be proved by the prosecution or defence in the trial of the accused;

(b)   'issue of consent' means any issue whether the complainant in fact consented to the conduct constituting the offence with which the accused is charged (and accordingly does not include any issue as to the belief of the accused that the complainant so consented);

(c)   'sexual behaviour' means any sexual behaviour or other sexual experience, whether or not involving any accused or other person, but excluding (except in section 41(3)(c)(i) and (5)(a)) anything alleged to have taken place as part of the event which is the subject matter of the charge against the accused; and

(d)   subject to any other made under subsection (2), 'sexual offence' shall be construed in accordance with section 62.

(2)   The Secretary of State may by order make such provision as he considers appropriate for adding or removing, for the purposes of section 41, any offence to or from the offences which are sexual offences for the purposes of this act by virtue of section 62.

(3)   Section 41 applies in relation to the following proceedings as it applies to a trial, namely—

(a)   proceedings before a magistrates' court inquiring into an offence as examining justices,

(b)   the hearing of an application under paragraph 5(1) of Schedule 6 to the Criminal Justice Act 1991 (application to dismiss charge following notice of transfer of case to Crown Court),

(c)   the hearing of an application under paragraph 2(1) of Schedule 3 to the Crime and Disorder Act 1998 (application to dismiss charge by person sent for trial under section 51 of that Act),

(d)   any hearing held, between conviction and sentencing, for the purpose of determining matters relevant to the court's decision as to how the accused is to be dealt with, and

(e)   the hearing of an appeal,
and references (in section 41 or this section) to a person charged with an offence
accordingly include a person convicted of an offence.

43.   Procedure on applications under section 41

(1)   An application for leave shall be heard in private and in the absence of the
complainant.

In this section 'leave' means leave under section 41.

(2)   Where such an application has been determined, the court must state in open
court (but in the absence of the jury, if there is one)—

(a)   its reasons for giving, or refusing, leave, and

(b)   if it gives leave, the extent to which evidence may be adduced or questions
asked in pursuance of the leave,
and, if it is a magistrates' court, must cause those matters to be entered in the register of
its proceedings.

(3)   Rules of court may make provision—

(a)   requiring applications for leave to specify, in relation to each item of evidence
or question to which they relate, particulars of the grounds on which it is asserted that
leave should be given by virtue of subsection (3) or (5) or section 41;

(b)   enabling the court to request a party to the proceedings to provide the court
with information which it considers would assist it in determining an application for
leave;

(c)   for the manner in which confidential or sensitive information is to be treated
in connection with such an application, and in particular as to its being disclosed to, or
withheld from, parties to the proceedings.

CHAPTER IV
REPORTING RESTRICTIONS

Reports relating to persons under 18

44.   Restrictions on reporting alleged offences involving persons under 18

(1)   This section applies (subject to subsection (3)) where a criminal investigation
has begun in respect of—

(a)   an alleged offence against the law of—

(i)   England and Wales, or

(i)   Northern Ireland; or

(b)   an alleged civil offence (other than an offence falling within paragraph (a))
committed (whether or not in the United Kingdom) by a person subject to service law.

(2)   No matter relating to any person involved in the offence shall while he is under
the age of 18 be included in any publication if it is likely to lead members of the public
to identify him as a person involved in the offence.

(3)   The restrictions imposed by subsection (2) cease to apply once there are
proceedings in a court (whether a court in England and Wales, a service court or a court
in Northern Ireland) in respect of the offence.

(4)   For the purposes of subsection (2) any reference to a person involved in the
offence is to—

(a)   a person by whom the offence is alleged to have been committed; or

(b)   if this paragraph applies to the publication in question by virtue of subsection
(5)—

(i)   a person against or in respect of whom the offence is alleged to have been
committed, or

(ii)   a person who is alleged to have been a witness to the commission of the
offence;

except that paragraph (b)(i) does not include a person in relation to whom section 1 of the Sexual Offences (Amendment) Act 1992 (anonymity of victims of certain sexual offences) applies in connection with the offence.

(5) Subsection (4)(b) applies to a publication if—
   (a) where it is a relevant programme, it is transmitted, or
   (b) in the case of any other publication, it is published,
on or after such date as may be specified in an order made by the Secretary of State.

(6) The matters relating to a person in relation to which the restrictions imposed by subsection (2) apply (if their inclusion in any publication is likely to have the result mentioned in that subsection) include in particular—
   (a) his name,
   (b) his address,
   (c) the identity of an school or other educational establishment attended by him,
   (d) the identity of any place of work, and
   (e) any still or moving picture of him.

(7) Any appropriate criminal court may by order dispense, to any extent specified in the order, with the restrictions imposed by subsection (2) in relation to a person if it is satisfied that it is necessary in the interests of justice to do so.

(8) However, when deciding whether to make such an order dispensing (to any extent) with the restrictions imposed by subsection (2) in relation to a person, the court shall have regard to the welfare of that person.

(9) In subsection (7) 'appropriate criminal court' means—
   (a) in a case where this section applies by virtue of subsection (1)(a)(i) or (ii), any court in England and Wales or (as the case may be) in Northern Ireland which has any jurisdiction in, or in relation to, any criminal proceedings (but not a service court unless the offence is alleged to have been committed by a person subject to service law);
   (b) in a case where this section applies by virtue of subsection (1)(b), any court falling within paragraph (a) or a service court.

(10) The power under subsection (7) of a magistrates' court in England and Wales may be exercised by a single justice.

(11) In the case of a decision of a magistrates' court in England and Wales, or a court of summary jurisdiction in Northern Ireland, to make or refuse to make an order under subsection (7), the following persons, namely—
   (a) any person who was a party to the proceedings on the application for the order, and
   (b) with the leave of the Crown Court, any other person,
may, in accordance with rules of court, appeal to the Crown Court against that decision or appear or be represented at the hearing of such an appeal.

(12) On such an appeal the Crown Court—
   (a) may make such order as is necessary to give effect to its determination of the appeal; and
   (b) may also make such incidental or consequential orders as appear to it to be just.

(13) In this section—
   (a) 'civil offence' means an act or omission which, if committed in England and Wales, would be an offence against the law of England and Wales;
   (b) any reference to a criminal investigation, in relation to an alleged offence, is to an investigation conducted by police officers, or other persons charged with the duty of investigation offences, with a view to it being ascertained whether a person should be charged with the offence;
   (c) any reference to a person subject to service law is to—
      (i) a person subject to military law, air-force law or the Naval Discipline Act 1957, or

(ii)   any other person to whom provisions of Part II of the Army Act 1955, Part II of the Air Force Act 1955 or Parts I and II of the Naval Discipline Act 1957 apply (whether with or without any modifications).

45. Power to restrict reporting of criminal proceedings involving persons under 18

(1)   This section applies (subject to subsection (2)) in relation to—

(a)   any criminal proceedings in any court (other than a service court) in England and Wales or Northern Ireland; and

(b)   any proceedings (whether in the United Kingdom or elsewhere) in any service court.

(2)   This section does not apply in relation to any proceedings to which section 49 of the Children and Young Persons Act 1933 applies.

(3)   The court may direct that no matter relating to any person concerned in the proceedings shall while he is under the age of 18 be included in any publication if it is likely to lead members of the public to identify him as a person concerned in the proceedings.

(4)   The court or an appellate court may by direction ('an excepting direction') dispense, to any extent specified in the excepting direction, with the restrictions imposed by a direction under subsection (3) if it is satisfied that it is necessary in the interests of justice to do so.

(5)   The court or an appellate court may also by direction ('an excepting direction') dispense, to any extent specified in the excepting direction, with the restrictions imposed by a direction under subsection (3) if it is satisfied—

(a)   that their effect is to impose a substantial and unreasonable restriction on the reporting of the proceedings, and

(b)   that it is in the public interest to remove or relax that restriction;

but no excepting direction shall be given under this subsection by reason only of the fact that the proceedings have been determined in any way or have been abandoned.

(6)   When deciding whether to make—

(a)   a direction under subsection (3) in relation to a person, or

(b)   an expecting direction under subsection (4) or (5) by virtue of which the restrictions imposed by a direction under subsection (3) would be dispensed with (to any extent) in relation to a person,

the court or (as the case may be) the appellate court shall have regard to the welfare of that person.

(7)   For the purposes of subsection (3) any reference to a person concerned in the proceedings is to a person—

(a)   against or in respect of whom the proceedings are taken, or

(b)   who is a witness in the proceedings.

(8)   the matters relating to a person in relation to which the restrictions imposed by a direction under subsection (3) apply (if their inclusion in any publication is likely to have the result mentioned in that subsection) include in particular—

(a)   his name,

(b)   his address,

(c)   the identity of any school or other educational establishment attended by him,

(d)   the identity of any place of work, and

(e)   any still or moving picture of him.

(9)   A direction under subsection (3) may be revoked by the court or an appellate court.

(10)   An excepting direction—

(a)   may be given at the time the direction under subsection (3) is given or subsequently; and

(b)   may be varied or revoked by the court or an appellate court.

(11)   In this section 'appellate court', in relation to any proceedings in a court, means a court dealing with an appeal (including an appeal by way of case stated) arising out of the proceedings or with any further appeal.

Reports relating to adult witnesses

46.   Power to restrict reports about certain adult witnesses in criminal proceedings

(1)   This section applies where—

(a)   in any criminal proceedings in any court (other than a service court) in England and Wales or Northern Ireland, or

(b)   in any proceedings (whether in the United Kingdom or elsewhere) in any service court,

a party to the proceedings makes an application for the court to give a reporting direction in relation to a witness in the proceedings (other than the accused) who has attained the age of 18.

In this section 'reporting direction' has the meaning given by subsection (6).

(2)   If the court determines—

(a)   that the witness is eligible for protection, and

(b)   that giving a reporting direction in relation to the witness is likely to improve—

(i)   the quality of evidence given by the witness, or

(ii)   the level of co-operation given by the witness to any party to the proceedings in connection with that party's preparation of its case,

the court may give a reporting direction in relation to the witness.

(3)   For the purposes of this section a witness is eligible for protection if the court is satisfied—

(a)   that the quality of evidence given by the witness, or

(b)   the level of co-operation given by the witness to any party to the proceedings in connection with that party's preparation of its case,

is likely to be diminished by reason of fear or distress on the part of the witness in connection with being identified by members of the public as a witness in the proceedings.

(4)   In determining whether a witness is eligible for protection the court must take into account, in particular—

(a)   the nature and alleged circumstances of the offence to which the proceedings relate;

(b)   the age of the witness;

(c)   such of the following matters as appear to the court to be relevant, namely—

(i)   the social and cultural background and ethnic origins of the witness,

(ii)   the domestic and employment circumstances of the witness, and

(iii)   any religious beliefs or political opinions of the witness;

(d)   any behaviour towards the witness on the part of—

(i)   the accused,

(ii)   members of the family or associates of the accused, or

(iii)   any other person who is likely to be an accused or a witness in the proceedings.

(5)   In determining that question the court must in addition consider any views expressed by the witness.

(6)   For the purposes of this section a reporting direction in relation to a witness is a direction that no matter relating to the witness shall during the witness's lifetime be included in any publication if it is likely to lead members of the public to identify him as being a witness in the proceedings.

(7)   The matters relating to a witness in relation to which the restrictions imposed by a reporting direction apply (if their inclusion in any publication is likely to have the result mentioned in subsection (6)) include in particular—

(a)   the witness's name,

(b)   the witness's address,

(c)   the identity of any educational establishment attended by the witness,

(d)   the identity of any place of work, and

(e)   any still or moving picture of the witness.

(8)   In determining whether to give a reporting direction the court shall consider—

(a)   whether it would be in the interests of justice to do so, and

(b)   the public interest in avoiding the imposition of a substantial and unreasonable restriction on the reporting of the proceedings.

(9)   The court or an appellate court may by direction ('an excepting direction') dispense, to any extent specified in the excepting direction, with the restrictions imposed by a reporting direction if—

(a)   it is satisfied that it is necessary in the interests of justice to do so, or

(b)   it is satisfied—

(i)   that the effect of those restrictions is to impose a substantial and unreasonable restriction on the reporting of the proceedings, and

(ii)   that it is in the public interest to remove or relax that restriction;

but no excepting direction shall be given under paragraph (b) by reason only of the fact that the proceedings have been determined in any way or have been abandoned.

(10)   A reporting direction may be revoked by the court or an appellate court.

(11)   An expecting direction—

(a)   may be given at the time the reporting direction is given or subsequently; and

(b)   may be varied or revoked by the court or an appellate court.

(12)   In this section—

(a)   'appellate court', in relation to any proceedings in a court, means a court dealing with an appeal (including an appeal by way of case stated) arising out of the proceedings or with any further appeal;

(b)   references to the quality of a witness's evidence are to its quality in terms of completeness, coherence and accuracy (and for this purpose 'coherence' refers to a witness's ability in giving evidence to give answers which address the questions put to the witness and can be understood both individually and collectively);

(c)   references to the preparation of the case of a party to any proceedings include, where the party is the prosecution, the carrying out of investigations into any offence at any time charged in the proceedings.

Reports relating to directions under Chapter I or II

47.   Restrictions on reporting directions under Chapter I or II

(1)   Except as provided by this section, no publication shall include a report of a matter falling within subsection (2).

(2)   The matters falling within this subsection are—

(a)   a direction under section 19 or 36 or an order discharging, or (in the case of a direction under section 19) varying, such a direction;

(b)   proceedings—

(i)   on an application for such a direction or order, or

(ii)   where the court acts of its own motion to determine whether to give or make any such direction or order.

(3)   The court dealing with a matter falling within subsection (2) may order that subsection (1) is not to apply, or is not to apply to a specified extent, to a report of that matter.

(4)   Where—

    (a)   there is only one accused in the relevant proceedings, and

    (b)   he objects to the making of an order under subsection (3),

the court shall make the order if (and only if) satisfied after hearing the representations of the accused that it is in the interests of justice to do so; and if the order is made it shall not apply to the extent that a report deals with any such objections or representations.

    (5)   Where—

    (a)   there are two or more accused in the relevant proceedings, and

    (b)   one or more of them object to the making of an order under subsection (3),

the court shall make the order if (and only if) satisfied after hearing the representations of each of the accused that it is in the interests of justice to do so; and if the order is made it shall not apply to the extent that a report deals with any such objections or representations.

    (6)   Subsection (1) does not apply to the inclusion in a publication of a report of matters after the relevant proceedings are either—

    (a)   determined (by acquittal, conviction or otherwise), or

    (b)   abandoned,

in relation to the accused or (if there is more than one) in relation to each of the accused.

    (7)   In this section 'the relevant proceedings' means the proceedings to which any such direction as is mentioned in subsection (2) relates or would relate.

    (8)   Nothing in this section affects an prohibition or restriction by virtue of any other enactment on the inclusion of matter in a publication.

Other restrictions

48.   Amendments relating to other reporting restrictions

Schedule 2, which contains amendments relating to reporting restrictions under—

    (a)   the Children and Young Persons Act 1933,

    (b)   the Sexual Offences (Amendment) Act 1976,

    (c)   the Sexual Offences (Northern Ireland) Order 1978,

    (d)   the Sexual Offences (Amendment) Act 1992, and

    (e)   the Criminal Justice (Northern Ireland) Order 1994,

shall have effect.

Offences

49.   Offences under chapter IV

    (1)   This section applies if a publication—

    (a)   includes any matter in contravention of section 44(2) or of a direction under section 45(3) or 46(2); or

    (b)   includes a report in contravention of section 47.

    (2)   Where the publication is a newspaper or periodical, any proprietor, any editor and any publisher of the newspaper or periodical is guilty of an offence.

    (3)   Where the publication is a relevant programme—

    (a)   any body corporate or Scottish partnership engaged in providing the programme service in which the programme is included, and

    (b)   any person having functions in relation to the programme corresponding to those of an editor of a newspaper,

is guilty of an offence.

    (4)   In the case of any other publication, any person publishing it is guilty of an offence.

    (5)   A person guilty of an offence under this section is liable on summary conviction to a fine not exceeding level 5 on the standard scale.

    (6)   Proceedings for an offence under this section in respect of a publication falling within subsection (1)(b) may not be instituted—

(a)   in England and Wales otherwise than by or with the consent of the Attorney General, or

(b)   in Northern Ireland otherwise than by or with the consent of the Attorney General of Northern Ireland.

50. Defences

(1)   Where a person is charged with an offence under section 49 it shall be a defence to prove that at the time of the alleged offence he was not aware, and neither suspected nor had reason to suspect, that the publication included in the matter or report in question.

(2)   Where—

(a)   a person is charged with an offence under section 49, and

(b)   the offence relates to the inclusion of any matter in a publication in contravention of section 44(2),

it shall be a defence to prove that at the time of the alleged offence he was not aware, and neither suspected nor had reason to suspect, that the criminal investigation in question had begun.

(3)   Where—

(a)   paragraphs (a) and (b) or subsection (2) apply, and

(b)   the contravention of section 44(2) does not relate to either—

(i)   the person by whom the offence mentioned in that provision is alleged to have been committed, or

(ii)   (where that offence is one in relation to which section 1 of the Sexual Offences (Amendment) Act 1992 applies) a person who is alleged to be a witness to the commission of the offence,

it shall be a defence to show to the satisfaction of the court that the inclusion in the publication of the matter in question was in the public interest on the ground that, to the extent that they operated to prevent that matter from being so included, the effect of the restrictions imposed by section 44(2) was to impose a substantial and unreasonable restriction on the reporting of matters connected with that offence.

(4)   Subsection (5) applies where—

(a)   paragraphs (a) and (b) of subsection (2) apply, and

(b)   the contravention of section 44(2) relates to a person ('the protected person') who is neither—

(i)   the person mentioned in subsection (3)(b)(i), nor

(ii)   a person within subsection (3)(b)(ii) who is under the age of 16.

(5)   In such a case it shall be a defence, subject to subsection (6), to prove that written consent to the inclusion of the matter in question in the publication had been given—

(a)   by an appropriate person, if at the time when the consent was given the protected person was under the age of 16, or

(b)   by the protected person, if that person was aged 16 or 17 at that time,

and (where the consent was given by an appropriate person) that written notice had been previously given to that person drawing to his attention the need to consider the welfare of the protected person when deciding whether to give consent.

(6)   The defence provided by subsection (5) is not available if—

(a)   (where the consent was given by an appropriate person) it is proved that written or other notice withdrawing the consent—

(i)   was given to the appropriate recipient by any other appropriate person or by the protected person, and

(ii)   was so given in sufficient time to enable the inclusion in the publication of the matter in question to be prevented; or

(b)   subsection (8) applies.

(7) Where—
(a) a person is charged with an offence under section 49, and
(b) the offence relates to the inclusion of any matter in a publication in contravention of a direction under section 46(2),
it shall be a defence, unless subsection (8) applies, to prove that the person in relation to whom the direction was given had given written consent to the inclusion of that matter in the publication.

(8) Written consent is not a defence if it is proved that any person interfered—
(a) with the peace or comfort of the person giving the consent, or
(b) (where the consent was given by an appropriate person) with the peace or comfort of either that person or the protected person,
with intent to obtain the consent.

(9) In this section—
'an appropriate person' means (subject to subsections (10) to (12))—
(a) in England and Wales or Northern Ireland, a person who is a parent or guardian of the protected person, or
(b) in Scotland, a person who has parental responsibilities (within the meaning of section 1(3) of the Children (Scotland) Act 1995) in relation to the protected person;
'guardian', in relation to the protected person, means any person who is not a parent of the protected person but who has parental responsibility for the protected person within the meaning of—
(a) (in England and Wales) the Children Act 1989, or
(b) (in Northern Ireland) the Children (Northern Ireland) Order 1995.

(10) Where the protected person is (within the meaning of the Children Act 1989) a child who is looked after by a local authority, 'an appropriate person' means a person who is—
(a) a representative of that authority, or
(b) a parent or guardian of the protected person with whom the protected person is allowed to live.

(11) Where the protected person is (within the meaning of the Children (Northern Ireland) Order 1995) a child who is looked after by an authority, 'an appropriate person' means a person who is—
(a) an officer of that authority, or
(b) a parent or guardian of the protected person with whom the protected person is allowed to live.

(12) Where the protected person is (within the meaning of section 17(6) of the Children (Scotland) Act 1995) a child who is looked after by a local authority, 'an appropriate person' means a person who is—
(a) a representative of that authority, or
(b) a person who has parental responsibilities (within the meaning of section 1(3) of that Act) in relation to the protected person and with whom the protected person is allowed to live.

(13) However, no person by whom the offence mentioned in section 44(2) is alleged to have been committed is, by virtue of subsection (9) to (12), an appropriate person for the purposes of this section.

(14) In this section 'the appropriate recipient', in relation to a notice under subsection (6)(a), means—
(a) the person to whom the notice giving consent was given,
(b) (if different) the person by whom the matter in question was published, or
(c) any other person exercising, on behalf of the person mentioned in paragraph (b), any responsibility in relation to the publication of that matter;
and for this purpose 'person' includes a body of persons and a partnership.

51. Offences committed by bodies corporate or Scottish partnerships
(1) If an offence under section 49 committed by a body corporate is proved—
(a) to have been committed with the consent or connivance of, or
(b) to be attributable to any neglect on the part of,
an officer, the officer as well as the body corporate is guilty of the offence and liable to be proceeded against and punished accordingly.
(2) In subsection (1) 'officer' means a director, manager, secretary or other similar officer of the body, or a person purporting to act in any such capacity.
(3) If the affairs of a body corporate are managed by its members, 'director' in subsection (2) means a member of that body.
(4) Where an offence under section 49 is committed by a Scottish partnership and is proved to have been committed with the consent or connivance of a partner, he as well as the partnership shall be guilty of the offence and shall be liable to be proceeded against and punished accordingly.

Supplementary

52. Decisions as to public interest for purposes of Chapter IV
(1) Where for the purposes of any provision of this Chapter it falls to a court to determine whether anything is (or, as the case may be, was) in the public interest, the court must have regard, in particular, to the matters referred to in subsection (2) (so far as relevant).
(2) Those matters are—
(a) the interest in each of the following—
(i) the open reporting of crime,
(ii) the open reporting of matters relating to human health or safety, and
(iii) the prevention and exposure of miscarriages of justice;
(b) the welfare of any person in relation to whom the relevant restrictions imposed by or under this Chapter apply or would apply (or, as the case may be, applied); and
(c) any views expressed—
(i) by an appropriate person on behalf of a person within paragraph (b) who is under the age of 16 ('the protected person'), or
(ii) by a person within that paragraph who has attained that age.
(3) In subsection (2) 'an appropriate person', in relation to the protected person, has the same meaning as it has for the purposes of section 50.

CHAPTER V
COMPETENCE OF WITNESSES AND CAPACITY TO BE SWORN

Competence of witnesses

53. Competence of witnesses to give evidence
(1) At every stage in criminal proceedings all persons are (whatever their age) competent to give evidence.
(2) Subsection (1) has effect subject to subsections (3) and (4).
(3) A person is not competent to give evidence in criminal proceedings if it appears to the court that he is not a person who is able to—
(a) understand questions put to him as a witness, and
(b) give answers to them which can be understood.
(4) A person charged in criminal proceedings is not competent to give evidence in the proceedings for the prosecution (whether he is the only person, or is one of two or more persons, charged in the proceedings).
(5) In subsection (4) the reference to a person charged in criminal proceedings does not include a person who is not, or is no longer, liable to be convicted of any offence in the proceedings (whether as a result of pleading guilty or for any other reason).

54. Determining competence of witnesses

(1) Any question whether a witness in criminal proceedings is competent to give evidence in the proceedings, whether raised—

    (a) by a party to the proceedings, or

    (b) by the court of its own motion,

shall be determined by the court in accordance with this section.

(2) It is for the party calling the witness to satisfy the court that, on a balance of probabilities, the witness is competent to give evidence in the proceedings.

(3) In determining the question mentioned in subsection (1) the court shall treat the witness as having the benefit of any directions under section 19 which the court has given, or proposes to give, in relation to the witness.

(4) Any proceedings held for the determination of the question shall take place in the absence of the jury (if there is one).

(5) Expert evidence may be received on the question.

(6) Any questioning of the witness (where the court considers that necessary) shall be conducted by the court in the presence of the parties.

Giving of sworn or unsworn evidence

55. Determining whether witness to be sworn

(1) Any question whether a witness in criminal proceedings may be sworn for the purpose of giving evidence on oath, whether raised—

    (a) by a party to the proceedings, or

    (b) by the court of its own motion,

shall be determined by the court in accordance with this section.

(2) The witness may not be sworn for that purpose unless—

    (a) he has attained the age of 14, and

    (b) he has a sufficient appreciation of the solemnity of the occasion and of the particular responsibility to tell the truth which is involved in taking an oath.

(3) The witness shall, if he is able to give intelligible testimony, be presumed to have a sufficient appreciation of those matters if no evidence tending to show the contrary is adduced (by any party).

(4) If any such evidence is adduced, it is for the party seeking to have the witness sworn to satisfy the court that, on a balance of probabilities, the witness has attained the age of 14 and has a sufficient appreciation of the matters mentioned in subsection (2)(b).

(5) Any proceedings held for the determination of the question mentioned in subsection (1) shall take place in the absence of the jury (if there is one).

(6) Expert evidence may be received on the question.

(7) Any questioning of the witness (where the court considers that necessary) shall be conducted by the court in the presence of the parties.

(8) For the purposes of this section a person is able to give intelligible testimony if he is able to—

    (a) understand questions put to him as a witness, and

    (b) give answers to them which can be understood.

56. Reception of unsworn evidence

(1) Subsections (2) and (3) apply to a person (of any age) who—

    (a) is competent to give evidence in criminal proceedings, but

    (b) (by virtue of section 55(2)) is not permitted to be sworn for the purpose of giving evidence on oath in such proceedings.

(2) The evidence in criminal proceedings of a person to whom this subsection applies shall be given unsworn.

(3)   A deposition of unsworn evidence given by a person to whom this subsection applies may be taken for the purposes of criminal proceedings as if that evidence had been given on oath.

(4)   A court in criminal proceedings shall accordingly receive in evidence any evidence given unsworn in pursuance of subsection (2) or (3).

(5)   Where a person ('the witness') who is competent to give evidence in criminal proceedings gives evidence in such proceedings unsworn, no conviction, verdict or finding in those proceedings shall be taken to be unsafe for the purposes of any of sections 2(1), 13(1) and 16(1) of the Criminal Appeal Act 1968 (grounds for allowing appeals) by reason only that it appears to the Court of Appeal that the witness was a person falling within section 55(2) (and should accordingly have given his evidence on oath).

57.   Penalty for giving false unsworn evidence

(1)   This section applies where a person gives unsworn evidence in criminal proceedings in pursuance of section 56(2) or (3).

(2)   If such a person wilfully gives false evidence in such circumstances that, had the evidence been given on oath, he would have been guilty of perjury, he shall be guilty of an offence and liable on summary conviction to—

    (a)   imprisonment for a term not exceeding 6 months, or

    (b)   a fine not exceeding £1,000,

or both.

(3)   In relation to a person under the age of 14, subsection (2) shall have effect as if for the words following 'on summary conviction' there were substituted 'to a fine not exceeding £250'.

59.   Restriction on use of answers etc. obtained under compulsion

Schedule 3, which amends enactments providing for the use of answers and statements given under compulsion so as to restrict in criminal proceedings their use in evidence against the persons giving them, shall have effect.

CHAPTER VII

GENERAL

61.   Application of Part II to service courts

(1)   The Secretary of State may by order direct that any provision of—

    (a)   Chapters I to III and V, or

    (b)   sections 62, 63 and 65 so far as having effect for the purposes of any of those Chapters,

shall apply, subject to such modifications as he may specify, to any proceedings before a service court.

(2)   Chapter IV (and sections 62, 63 and 65 so far as having effect for the purposes of that Chapter) shall have effect for the purposes of proceedings before a service court subject to any modifications which the Secretary of State may by order specify.

(3)   The power to make an order under section 39 of the Criminal Justice and Public Order Act 1994 (power to apply sections 34 to 38 to the armed forces) in relation to any provision of sections 34 to 38 of that Act shall be exercisable in relation to any provision of those sections as amended by section 58 above.

62.   Meaning of 'sexual offence' and other references to offences

(1)   In this Part 'sexual offence' means—

    (a)   rape or burglary with intent to rape;

    (b)   an offence under any of sections 2 to 12 and 14 to 17 of the Sexual Offences Act 1956 (unlawful intercourse, indecent assault, forcible abduction etc.);

(c)   an offence under section 128 of the Mental Health Act 1959 (unlawful intercourse with person receiving treatment for mental disorder by member of hospital staff etc.);

(d)   an offence under section 1 of the Indecency with Children Act 1960 (indecent conduct towards child under 14);

(e)   an offence under section 54 of the Criminal Law Act 1977 (incitement of child under 16 to commit incest).

(2)   In this part any reference (including a reference having effect by virtue of this subsection) to an offence of any description ('the substantive offence') is to be taken to include a reference to an offence which consists of attempting or conspiring to commit, or of aiding, abetting, counselling, procuring or inciting the commission of, the substantive offence.

63.   General interpretation etc. of Part II

(1)   In this Part (except where the context otherwise requires)—

'accused', in relation to any criminal proceedings, means any person charged with an offence to which the proceedings relate (whether or not he has been convicted);

'the complainant', in relation to any offence (or alleged offence), means a person against or in relation to whom the offence was (or is alleged to have been) committed;

'court' (except in Chapter IV or V or subsection (2)) means a magistrates' court, the Crown Court or criminal division of the Court of Appeal;

'legal representative' means any authorised advocate or authorised litigator (as defined by section 119(1) of the Courts and Legal Services Act 1990);

'picture' includes a likeness however produced;

'the prosecutor' means any person acting as prosecutor, whether an individual or body;

'publication' includes any speech, writing, relevant programme or other communication in whatever form, which is addressed to the public at large or any section of the public (and for this purpose every relevant programme shall be taken to be so addressed), but does not include an indictment or other document prepared for use in particular legal proceedings;

'relevant programme' means a programme included in a programme service, within the meaning of the Broadcasting Act 1990;

'service court' means—

(a)   a court-martial constituted under the Army Act 1955, the Air Force Act 1955 or the Naval Discipline Act 1957 or a disciplinary court constituted under section 52G of the naval Discipline Act 1957,

(b)   the Courts-Martial Appeal Court, or

(b)   the Courts-Martial Appeal Court, or

(c)   a Standing Civilian Court;

'video recording' means any recording, on any medium, from which a moving image may by any means be produced, and includes the accompanying sound-track;

'witness', in relation to any criminal proceedings, means any person called, or proposed to be called, to give evidence in the proceedings.

(2)   Nothing in this Part shall affect any power of a court to exclude evidence at its discretion (whether by preventing questions being put or otherwise) which is exercisable apart from this Part.

CRIMINAL CASES REVIEW (INSANITY) ACT 1999
(1999, c. 25)

1.   Reference of former verdict of guilty but insane

(1)   Where a verdict was returned in England and Wales or Northern Ireland to the effect that a person was guilty of the act or omission charged against him but was insane

at the time, the Criminal Cases Review Commission may at any time refer the verdict to
the Court of Appeal if subsection (2) below applies.

(2)   This subsection applies if the commission consider that there is a real possibility
that the verdict would not be upheld were the reference to be made and either—

(a)   the Commission so consider because of an argument, or evidence, not raised
in the proceedings which led to the verdict, or

(b)   it appears to the Commission that there are exceptional circumstances which
justify the making of the reference.

(3)   Section 14 of the Criminal Appeal Act 1995 (supplementary provision about the
reference of a verdict) shall apply in relation to a reference under subsection (1) above
as it applies in relation to references under section 9 or 10 of that Act.

2.   Reference treated as appeal: England and Wales

(1)   A reference under section 1(1) above of a verdict returned in England and Wales
in the case of a person shall be treated for all purposes as an appeal by the person under
section 12 of the Criminal Appeal Act 1968.

(2)   In their application to such a reference by virtue of subsection (1) above,
sections 13 and 14 of that Act shall have effect—

(a)   as if references to the verdict of not guilty by reason of insanity were to the
verdict referred under section 1(1) above, and

(b)   as if, in section 14(1)(b), for the words from the beginning to 'that he' there
were substituted 'the accused was under a disability and'.

3.   Reference treated as appeal: Northern Ireland

(1)   A reference under section 1(1) above of a verdict returned in Northern Ireland
in the case of a person shall be treated for all purposes as an appeal by the person under
section 12 of the Criminal Appeal (Northern Ireland) Act 1980

(2)   In their application to such a reference by virtue of subsection (1) above,
sections 12 and 13 of that Act shall have effect—

(a)   as if references to the finding of not guilty on the ground of insanity were to
the verdict referred under section 1(1) above, and

(b)   as if, in section 13(5A), for the words 'there should have been findings that the
accused was unfit to be tried and that he' there were substituted 'the accused was unfit
to be tried and'.

4.   Extent and short title

(1)   Section 1 above and this section extend to England and Wales and Northern
Ireland.

(2)   Section 2 above extends to England and Wales.

(3)   Section 3 above extends to Northern Ireland.

(4)   This Act may be cited as the Criminal Cases Review (Insanity) Act 1999.

SEXUAL OFFENCES (AMENDMENT) ACT 2000
(2000 c. 44)

ARRANGEMENT OF SECTIONS

1. Reduction in age at which certain sexual acts are lawful
    (1) In the Sexual Offences Act 1956—
        (a) in subsection (1A) and (1C) of section 12 (buggery); and
        (b) in sub-paragraphs (a) and (b) of paragraph 16 (indecency between men etc.)
of Schedule 2 (punishments etc.),
for the word 'eighteen' there shall be substituted the word 'sixteen'.
    (2) In the Sexual Offences Act 1967—
        (a) in subsections (1) and (6) of section 1 (amendment of law relating to homosexual
acts in private), for the word 'eighteen' there shall be substituted the word 'sixteen'; and
        (b) in section 8 (restriction on prosecutions), for the word 'twenty-one' there shall
be substituted the word 'sixteen'.
    (3)3 In section 13 of the Criminal Law (Consolidation) (Scotland) Act 1995
(homosexual offences)—
        (a) in subsections (1) and (5)(c), for the word 'eighteen'; and
        (b) in subsection (8), for the word '18',
there shall be substituted the word 'sixteen'.
    (4) In paragraphs (1) and (5) of Article 3 of the Homosexual Offences (Northern
Ireland) Order 1982 (homosexual acts in private), for the word '18' there shall be
substituted the word '17'.
    (5) Section 145 of the Criminal Justice and Public Order Act 1994 (which is
superseded by this section) is hereby repealed.

2. Defences available to persons who are under age
    (1) In section 12 of the Sexual Offences Act 1956—
        (a) in subsection (1), after the words 'subsection (1A)' there shall be inserted the
words 'or (1AA)';
        (b) in subsection (1A), after the word 'circumstances' there shall be inserted the
word 'first'; and
        (c) after that subsection there shall be inserted the following subsection—
    '(1AA) The other circumstances so referred to are that the person is under the age
of sixteen and the other person has attained that age.'
    (2) In section 13 of that Act (indecency between men)—
        (a) after the words 'another man', in the first place where they occur, there shall
be inserted the words 'otherwise than in the circumstances described below'; and
        (b) at the end there shall be inserted the following paragraph—
    'The circumstances referred to above are that the man is under the age of sixteen
and the other man has attained that age.'
    (3) In subsection (1) of section 1 of the Sexual Offences Act 1967—
        (a) the words from 'a homosexual act' to the end shall become paragraph (a); and
        (b) after that paragraph there shall be inserted the words 'and
        (b) a homosexual act by any person shall not be an offence if he is under the
age of sixteen years and the other party has attained that age.'
    (4) In section 13 of the Criminal Law (Consolidation) (Scotland) Act 1995, after
subsection (8) there shall be inserted the following subsection—
    (8A) A person under the age of sixteen years does not commit an offence under
subsection (5)(a) or (c) above if he commits or is party to the commission of a
homosexual act with a person who has attained that age.
    (5) In paragraph (1) of Article 3 of the Homosexual Offences (Northern Ireland)
Order 1982—
        (a) the words from 'a homosexual act' to the end shall become sub-paragraph (a);
and
        (b) after that sub-paragraph there shall be inserted the words 'and (b) a
homosexual act by any person shall not be an offence if he is under the age of seventeen
years and the other party has attained that age'.

3. Abuse of position of trust

(1) Subject to subsections (2) and (3) below, it shall be an offence for a person aged 18 or over—

    (a) to have sexual intercourse (whether vaginal or anal) with a person under that age; or

    (b) to engage in any other sexual activity with or directed towards such a person, if (in either case) he is in a position of trust in relation to that person.

(2) Where a person ('A') is charged with an offence under this section of having sexual intercourse with, or engaging in any other sexual activity with or directed towards, another person ('B'), it shall be a defence for A to prove that, at the time of the intercourse or activity—

    (a) he did not know, and could not reasonably have been expected to know, that B was under 18;

    (b) he did not know, and could not reasonably have been expected to know, that B was a person in relation to whom he was in a position of trust; or

    (c) he was lawfully married to B.

(3) It shall not be an offence under this section for a person ('A') to have sexual intercourse with, or engage in any other sexual activity with or directed towards, another person ('B') if immediately before the commencement of this Act—

    (a) A was in a position of trust in relation to B; and

    (b) a sexual relationship existed between them.

(4) A person guilty of an offence under this section shall be liable—

    (a) on summary conviction, to imprisonment for a term not exceeding six months, or to a fine not exceeding the statutory maximum, or to both;

    (b) on conviction on indictment, to imprisonment for a term not exceeding five years, or to a fine, or to both.

(5) In this section, 'sexual activity'—

    (a) does not include any activity which a reasonable person would regard as sexual only with knowledge of the intentions, motives or feelings of the parties; but

    (b) subject to that, means any activity which such a person would regard as sexual in all the circumstances.

4. Meaning of 'position of trust'

(1) For the purposes of section 3 above, a person aged 18 or over ('A') is in a position of trust in relation to a person under that age ('B') if any of the four conditions set out below, or any condition specified in an order made by the Secretary of State by statutory instrument, is fulfilled.

(2) The first condition is that A looks after persons under 18 who are detained in an institution by virtue of an order of a court or under an enactment, and B is so detained in that institution.

(3) The second condition is that A looks after persons under 18 who are resident in a home or other place in which—

    (a) accommodation and maintenance are provided by an authority under section 23(2) of the Children Act 1989 or Article 27(2) of the Children (Northern Ireland) Order 1995;

    (b) accommodation is provided by a voluntary organisation under section 59(1) of that Act or Article 75(1) of that Order; or

    (c) accommodation is provided by an authority under section 26(1) of the Children (Scotland) Act 1995,

and B is resident, and is so provided with accommodation and maintenance or accommodation, in that place.

(4) The third condition is that A looks after persons under 18 who are accommodated and cared for in an institution which is—

    (a)   a hospital;

    (b)   a residential care home, nursing home, mental nursing home or private hospital;

    (c)   a community home, voluntary home, children's home or residential establishment; or

    (d)   a home provided under section 82(5) of the Children Act 1989,

and B is accommodated and cared for in that institution.

(5)   The fourth condition is that A looks after persons under 18 who are receiving full-time education at an educational institution, and B is receiving such education at that institution.

(6)   No order shall be made under subsection (1) above unless a draft of the order has been laid before and approved by a resolution of each House of Parliament.

(7)   A person looks after persons under 18 for the purposes of this section if he is regularly involved in caring for, training, supervising or being in sole charge of such persons.

(8)   For the purposes of this section a person receives full-time education at an educational institution if—

    (a)   he is registered or otherwise enrolled as a full-time pupil or student at the institution; or

    (b)   he receives education at the institution under arrangements with another educational institution at which he is so registered or otherwise enrolled.

(9)   In this section, except where the context otherwise requires—

'authority' means—

    (a)   in relation to Great Britain, a local authority; and

    (b)   in relation to Northern Ireland, an authority within the meaning given by Article 2(2) of the Children (Northern Ireland) Order 1995;

'children's home' has—

    (a)   in relation to England and Wales, the meaning which would be given by subsection (3) of section 63 of the Children Act 1989 if the reference in paragraph (a) of that subsection to more than three children were a reference to one or more children; and

    (b)   in relation to Northern Ireland, the meaning which would be given by Article 90(1) of the Children (Northern Ireland) Order 1995 if, in Article 91(2) of that Order, paragraphs (f) and (g) and the words after paragraph (h) were omitted;

'community home' has the meaning given by section 53(1) of the Children Act 1989;

'hospital' has—

    (a)   in relation to England and Wales, the meaning given by section 128(1) of the National Health Service Act 1977;

    (b)   in relation to Scotland, the meaning given by section 108(1) of the National Health Service (Scotland) Act 1978; and

    (c)   in relation to Northern Ireland, the meaning given by Article 2(2) of the Health and Personal Social Services (Northern Ireland) Order 1972;

'mental nursing home' has, in relation to England and Wales, the meaning given by section 22(1) of the Registered Homes Act 1984;

'nursing home'—

    (a)   in relation to England and Wales, has the meaning given by section 21(1) of the Registered Homes Act 1984;

    (b)   in relation to Scotland, means a nursing home registered under section 1 of the Nursing Homes Registration (Scotland) Act 1938; and

    (c)   In relation to Northern Ireland, has the meaning given by Article 16(1) of the Registered Homes (Northern Ireland) Order 1992;

'private hospital' has—

    (a)   in relation to Scotland, the meaning given by section 12(2) of the Mental Health (Scotland) Act 1984; and

(b)   in relation to Northern Ireland, the meaning given by Article 90(2) of the Mental Health (Northern Ireland) Order 1986;
'residential care home'—
(a)   in relation to England and Wales, has the meaning given by section 1(2) of the Registered Homes Act 1984;
(b)   in relation to Scotland, means an establishment in respect of which a person is registered under section 62 or 63 of the Social Work (Scotland) Act 1968; and
(c)   in relation to Northern Ireland, has the meaning given by Article 3(1) of the Registered Homes (Northern Ireland) Order 1992;
'residential establishment' has the meaning given by section 93(1) of the Children (Scotland) Act 1995 as the meaning of that expression in relation to a place in Scotland;
'voluntary home' has—
(a)   in relation to England and Wales, the meaning given by section 60(3) of the Children Act 1989; and
(b)   in relation to Northern Ireland, the meaning given by Article 74(1) of the Children (Northern Ireland) Order 1995.

5.   Notification requirements for offenders under section 3

. . .

6.   Meaning of 'sexual offence' for the purposes of certain enactments

(1)   In subsection (1) of section 31 of the Criminal Justice Act 1991 (interpretation of Part I), in the definition of 'sexual offence'—
(a)   after paragraph (f) there shall be inserted—
'(fa)   an offence under section 3 of the Sexual Offences (Amendment) Act 2000;' and
(b)   in paragraph (g), for '(f)' there shall be substituted '(fa)'.

(2)   In subsection (10) of section 210A of the Criminal Procedure (Scotland) Act 1995 (extended sentences for sex and violent offenders), in the definition of 'sexual offence' the word 'and' immediately before paragraph (xix) shall be omitted and after that paragraph there shall be inserted 'and
(xx)   an offence under section 3 of the Sexual Offences (Amendment) Act 2000 (abuse of position of trust).'.

PART B   RULES AND GUIDELINES

PRACTICE DIRECTION (SUBMISSION OF NO CASE)
[1962] 1 WLR 227

LORD PARKER CJ   Those of us who sit in the Divisional Court have the distinct impression that Justices today are being persuaded all too often to uphold a submission of no case. In the result, this court has had on many occasions to send the case back to the Justices for the hearing to be continued with inevitable delay and increased expenditure. Without attempting to lay down any principle of law, we think that as a matter of practice Justices should be guided by the following considerations.

A submission that there is no case to answer may properly be made and upheld: (a) when there has been no evidence to prove an essential element in the alleged offence; (b) when the evidence adduced by the prosecution has been so discredited as a result of cross-examination or is so manifestly unreliable that no reasonable tribunal could safely convict upon it.

Apart from these two situations a tribunal should not in general be called upon to reach a decision as to conviction or acquittal until the whole of the evidence which either side wishes to tender has been placed before it. If however a submission is made that there is no case to answer, the decision should depend not so much on whether the adjudicating tribunal (if compelled to do so) would at that stage convict or acquit but on whether the evidence is such that a reasonable tribunal might convict. If a reasonable tribunal might convict on the evidence so far laid before it, there is a case to answer.

APPENDIX 7   DISCLOSURE:
CRIMINAL PROCEDURE AND INVESTIGATIONS ACT 1996:
CODE OF PRACTICE UNDER PART II

Introduction

1.1   This code of practice is issued under Part II of the Criminal Procedure and Investigations Act 1996 ('the Act'). It applies in respect of criminal investigations conducted by police officers which begin on or after the day on which this code comes into effect. Persons other than police officers who are charged with the duty of conducting an investigation as defined in the Act are to have regard to the relevant provisions of the code, and should take these into account in applying their own operating procedures.

1.2   This code does not apply to persons who are not charged with the duty of conducting an investigation as defined in the Act.

1.3   Nothing in this code applies to material intercepted in obedience to a warrant issued under section 2 of the Interception of Communications Act 1985, or to any copy of that material as defined in section 10 of that Act.

1.4   This code extends only to England and Wales.

Definitions

2.1   In this code:

— a *criminal investigation* is an investigation conducted by police officers with a view to it being ascertained whether a person should be charged with an offence, or whether a person charged with an offence is guilty of it. This will include:

— investigations into crimes that have been committed;

— investigations whose purpose is to ascertain whether a crime has been committed, with a view to the possible institution of criminal proceedings; and

— investigations which begin in the belief that a crime may be committed, for example when the police keep premises or individuals under observation for a period of time, with a view to the possible institution of criminal proceedings;

— charging a person with an offence includes prosecution by way of summons;

— an *investigator* is any police officer involved in the conduct of a criminal investigation. All investigators have a responsibility for carrying out the duties imposed on them under this code, including in particular recording information, and retaining records of information and other material;

— the *officer in charge of an investigation* is the police officer responsible for directing a criminal investigation. He is also responsible for ensuring that proper procedures are in place for recording information, and retaining records of information and other material, in the investigation;

— the *disclosure officer* is the person responsible for examining material retained by the police during the investigation; revealing material to the prosecutor during the investigation and any criminal proceedings resulting from it, and certifying that he has done this; and disclosing material to the accused at the request of the prosecutor;

— the *prosecutor* is the authority responsible for the conduct of criminal proceedings on behalf of the Crown. Particular duties may in practice fall to individuals acting on behalf of the prosecuting authority;

— *material* is material of any kind, including information and objects, which is obtained in the course of a criminal investigation and which may be relevant to the investigation;

— material may be *relevant to an investigation* if it appears to an investigator, or to the officer in charge of an investigation, or to the disclosure officer, that it has some bearing on any offence under investigation or any person being investigated, or on the surrounding circumstances of the case, unless it is incapable of having any impact on the case;

— *sensitive material* is material which the disclosure officer believes, after consulting the officer in charge of the investigation, it is not in the public interest to disclose;

— references to *primary prosecution disclosure* are to the duty of the prosecutor under section 3 of the Act to disclose material which is in his possession or which he has inspected in pursuance of this code, and which in his opinion might undermine the case against the accused;

— references to *secondary prosecution disclosure* are to the duty of the prosecutor under section 7 of the Act to disclose material which is in his possession or which he has inspected in pursuance of this code, and which might reasonably be expected to assist the defence disclosed by the accused in a defence statement given under the Act;

— references to the disclosure of material to a person accused of an offence include references to the disclosure of material to his legal representative;

— references to police officers and to the chief officer of police include those employed in a police force as defined in section 3(3) of the Prosecution of Offences Act 1985.

General responsibilities

3.1   The functions of the investigator, the officer in charge of an investigation and the disclosure officer are separate. Whether they are undertaken by one, two or more persons will depend on the complexity of the case and the administrative arrangements within each police force. Where they are undertaken by more than one person, close consultation between them is essential to the effective performance of the duties imposed by this code.

3.2   The chief officer of police for each police force is responsible for putting in place arrangements to ensure that in every investigation the identity of the officer in charge of an investigation and the disclosure officer is recorded.

3.3   The officer in charge of an investigation may delegate tasks to another investigator or to civilians employed by the police force, but he remains responsible for ensuring that these have been carried out and for accounting for any general policies followed in the investigation. In particular, it is an essential part of his duties to ensure that all material which may be relevant to an investigation is retained, and either made available to the disclosure officer or (in exceptional circumstances) revealed directly to the prosecutor.

3.4   In conducting an investigation, the investigator should pursue all reasonable lines of inquiry, whether these point towards or away from the suspect. What is reasonable in each case will depend on the particular circumstances.

3.5   If the officer in charge of an investigation believes that other persons may be in possession of material that may be relevant to the investigation, and if this has not been obtained under paragraph 3.4 above, he should ask the disclosure officer to inform them of the existence of the investigation and to invite them to retain the material in case they receive a request for its disclosure. The disclosure officer should inform the prosecutor that they may have such material. However, the officer in charge of an investigation is not required to make speculative enquiries of other persons: there must be some reason to believe that they may have relevant material. That reason may come from information provided to the police by the accused or from other inquiries made or from some other source.

3.6   If, during a criminal investigation, the officer in charge of an investigation or disclosure officer for any reason no longer has responsibility for the functions falling to him, either his supervisor or the police officer in charge of criminal investigations for the police force concerned must assign someone else to assume that responsibility. That person's identity must be recorded, as with those initially responsible for these functions in each investigation.

Recording of information

4.1   If material which may be relevant to the investigation consists of information which is not recorded in any form, the officer in charge of an investigation must ensure that it is recorded in a durable or retrieval form (whether in writing, on video or audio tape, or on computer disk).

4.2   Where it is not practicable to retain the initial record of information because it forms part of a larger record which is to be destroyed, its contents should be transferred as a true record to a durable and more easily-stored form before that happens.

4.3   Negative information is often relevant to an investigation. If it may be relevant it must be recorded. An example might be a number of people present in a particular place at a particular time who state that they saw nothing unusual.

4.4   Where information which may be relevant is obtained, it must be recorded at the time it is obtained or as soon as practicable after that time. This includes, for example, information obtained in house-to-house enquiries, although the requirement to record information promptly does not require an investigator to take a statement from a potential witness where it would not otherwise be taken.

Retention of material

(a)   Duty to retain material

5.1   The investigator must retain material obtained in a criminal investigation which may be relevant to the investigation. This includes not only material coming into the possession of the investigator (such as documents seized in the course of searching premises) but also material generated by him (such as interview records). Material may be photographed, or retained in the form of a copy rather than the original, if the original is perishable, or was supplied to the investigator rather than generated by him and is to be returned to its owner.

5.2   Where material has been seized in the exercise of the powers of seizure conferred by the Police and Criminal Evidence Act 1984, the duty to retain it under this code is subject to the provisions on the retention of seized material in section 22 of that Act.

5.3   If the officer in charge of an investigation becomes aware as a result of developments in the case that material previously examined but not retained (because it was not thought to be relevant) may now be relevant to the investigation, he should, wherever practicable, take steps to obtain it or ensure that it is retained for further inspection or for production in court if required.

5.4   The duty to retain material includes in particular the duty to retain material falling into the following categories, where it may be relevant to the investigation:
— crime reports (including crime report forms, relevant parts of incident report books or police officers' notebooks);
— custody records;
— records which are derived from tapes of telephone messages (for example, 999 calls) containing descriptions of an alleged offence or offender;
— final versions of witness statements (and draft versions where their content differs from the final version), including any exhibits mentioned (unless these have been returned to their owner on the understanding that they will be produced in court if required);
— interview records (written records, or audio or video tapes, of interviews with actual or potential witnesses or suspects);
— communications between the police and experts such as forensic scientists, reports of work carried out by experts, and schedules of scientific material prepared by the expert for the investigator, for the purposes of criminal proceedings;
— any material casting doubt on the reliability of a confession;
— any material casting doubt on the reliability of a witness;
— any other material which may fall within the test for primary prosecution disclosure in the Act.

5.5   The duty to retain material falling into these categories does not extend to items which are purely ancillary to such material and possess no independent significance (for example, duplicate copies of records or reports).

(b)   Length of time for which material is to be retained

5.6   All material which may be relevant to the investigation must be retained until a decision is taken whether to institute proceedings against a person for an offence.

5.7   If a criminal investigation results in proceedings being instituted, all material which may be relevant must be retained at least until the accused is acquitted or convicted or the prosecutor decides not to proceed with the case.

5.8   Where the accused is convicted after a not guilty plea, all material which may be relevant must be retained for the following minimum periods after the date of conviction:
— one year, in respect of a conviction at a summary trial;
— three years, in respect of a conviction at a trial on indictment.

5.9   If an appeal against conviction is in progress at the end of the periods specified in paragraph 5.8, all material which may be relevant must be retained until the appeal is determined.

5.10   Material need not be retained by the police for the duration of the periods specified in paragraph 5.8 in these circumstances:
— it was seized and is to be returned to its owner;
— the material is not durable and deteriorates so much that it has no evidential value;
— copies of the material are held by another criminal justice agency, and it is agreed in writing between the police and that agency that the agency will retain these for the minimum periods specified above.

Preparation of material for prosecutor

(a)   Introduction

6.1   The officer in charge of the investigation, the disclosure officer or an investigator may seek advice from the prosecutor about whether any particular item of material may be relevant to the investigation.

6.2   Material which may be relevant to an investigation, which has been retained in accordance with this code, and which the disclosure officer believes will not form part of the prosecution case, must be listed on a schedule.

6.3   Material which the disclosure officer does not believe is sensitive must be listed on a schedule of non-sensitive material. The schedule must include a statement that the disclosure officer does not believe the material is sensitive.

6.4   Any material which is believed to be sensitive must be either listed on a schedule of sensitive material or, in exceptional circumstances, revealed to the prosecutor separately.

6.5   Paragraphs 6.6 to 6.11 below apply to both sensitive and non-sensitive material. Paragraphs 6.12 to 6.14 apply to sensitive material only.

(b)   Circumstances in which a schedule is to be prepared

6.6   The disclosure officer must ensure that a schedule is prepared in the following circumstances:
— the accused is charged with an offence which is triable only on indictment;
— the accused is charged with an offence which is triable either way, and it is considered either that the case is likely to be tried on indictment or that the accused is likely to plead not guilty at a summary trial;
— the accused is charged with a summary offence, and it is considered that he is likely to plead not guilty.

6.7   In respect of either way and summary offences, a schedule may not be needed if a person has admitted the offence, or if a police officer witnessed the offence and that person has not denied it.

6.8   If it is believed that the accused is likely to plead guilty at a summary trial, it is not necessary to prepare a schedule in advance. If, contrary to this belief, the accused pleads not guilty at a summary trial, or the offence is to be tried on indictment, the disclosure officer must ensure that a schedule is prepared as soon as is reasonably practicable after that happens.

(c)   Way in which material is to be listed on schedule

6.9   The disclosure officer should ensure that each item of material is listed separately on the schedule, and is numbered consecutively. The description of each item should make clear the nature of the item and should contain sufficient detail to enable the prosecutor to decide whether he needs to inspect the material before deciding whether or not it should be disclosed.

6.10   In some enquiries it may not be practicable to list each item of material separately. For example, there may be many items of a similar or repetitive nature. These may be listed in a block and described by quantity and generic title.

6.11   Even if some material is listed in a block, the disclosure officer must ensure that any items among that material which might meet the test for primary prosecution disclosure are listed and described individually.

(d)   Treatment of sensitive material

6.12   Subject to paragraph 6.13 below, the disclosure officer must list on a sensitive schedule any material which he believes it is not in the public interest to disclose, and the reason for that belief. The schedule must include a statement that the disclosure officer believes the material is sensitive. Depending on the circumstances, examples of such material may include the following among others:
— material relating to national security;
— material received from the intelligence and security agencies;
— material relating to intelligence from foreign sources which reveals sensitive intelligence gathering methods;
— material given in confidence;
— material which relates to the use of a telephone system and which is supplied to an investigator for intelligence purposes only;
— material relating to the identity or activities of informants, or under-cover police officers, or other persons supplying information to the police who may be in danger if their identities are revealed;
— material revealing the location of any premises or other place used for police surveillance, or the identity of any person allowing a police officer to use them for surveillance;
— material revealing, either directly or indirectly, techniques and methods relied upon by a police officer in the course of a criminal investigation, for example covert surveillance techniques, or other methods of detecting crime;
— material whose disclosure might facilitate the commission of other offences or hinder the prevention and detection of crime;
— internal police communications such as management minutes;
— material upon the strength of which search warrants were obtained;
— material containing details of persons taking part in identification parades;
— material supplied to an investigator during a criminal investigation which has been generated by an official of a body concerned with the regulation or supervision of bodies corporate or of persons engaged in financial activities, or which has been generated by a person retained by such a body;
— material supplied to an investigator during a criminal investigation which relates to a child or young person and which has been generated by a local authority social services

department, an Area Child Protection Committee or other party contacted by an investigator during the investigation.

6.13   In exceptional circumstances, where an investigator considers that material is so sensitive that its revelation to the prosecutor by means of an entry on the sensitive schedule is inappropriate, the existence of the material must be revealed to the prosecutor separately. This will apply where compromising the material would be likely to lead directly to the loss of life, or directly threaten national security.

6.14   In such circumstances, the responsibility for informing the prosecutor lies with the investigator who knows the detail of the sensitive material. The investigator should act as soon as is reasonably practicable after the file containing the prosecution case is sent to the prosecutor. The investigator must also ensure that the prosecutor is able to inspect the material so that he can assess whether it needs to be brought before a court for a ruling on disclosure.

Revelation of material to prosecutor

7.1   The disclosure officer must give the schedules to the prosecutor. Wherever practicable this should be at the same time as he gives him the file containing the material for the prosecution case (or as soon as is reasonably practicable after the decision on mode of trial or the plea, in cases to which paragraph 6.8 applies).

7.2   The disclosure officer should draw the attention of the prosecutor to any material an investigator has retained (whether or not listed on a schedule) which may fall within the test for primary prosecution disclosure in the Act, and should explain why he has come to that view.

7.3   At the same time as complying with the duties in paragraphs 7.1 and 7.2, the disclosure officer must give the prosecutor a copy of any material which falls into the following categories (unless such material has already been given to the prosecutor as part of the file containing the material for the prosecution case):
— records of the first description of a suspect given to the police by a potential witness, whether or not the description differs from that of the alleged offender;
— information provided by an accused person which indicates an explanation for the offence with which he has been charged;
— any material casting doubt on the reliability of a confession;
— any material casting doubt on the reliability of a witness;
— any other material which the investigator believes may fall within the test for primary prosecution disclosure in the Act.

7.4   If the prosecutor asks to inspect material which has not already been copied to him, the disclosure officer must allow him to inspect it. If the prosecutor asks for a copy of material which has not already been copied to him, the disclosure officer must give him a copy. However, this does not apply where the disclosure officer believes, having consulted the officer in charge of the investigation, that the material is too sensitive to be copied and can only be inspected.

7.5   If material consists of information which is recorded other than in writing, whether it should be given to the prosecutor in its original form as a whole, or by way of relevant extracts recorded in the same form, or in the form of a transcript, is a matter for agreement between the disclosure officer and the prosecutor.

Subsequent action by disclosure officer

8.1   At the time a schedule of non-sensitive material is prepared, the disclosure officer may not know exactly what material will form the case against the accused, and the prosecutor may not have given advice about the likely relevance of particular items of

material. Once these matters have been determined, the disclosure officer must give the prosecutor, where necessary, an amended schedule listing any additional material:
— which may be relevant to the investigation,
— which does not form part of the case against the accused,
— which is not already listed on the schedule, and
— which he believes is not sensitive,
unless he is informed in writing by the prosecutor that the prosecutor intends to disclose the material to the defence.

8.2   After a defence statement has been given, the disclosure officer must look again at the material which has been retained and must draw the attention of the prosecutor to any material which might reasonably be expected to assist the defence disclosed by the accused; and he must reveal it to him in accordance with paragraphs 7.4 and 7.5 above.

8.3   Section 9 of the Act imposes a continuing duty on the prosecutor, for the duration of criminal proceedings against the accused, to disclose material which meets the tests for disclosure (subject to public interest considerations). To enable him to do this, any new material coming to light should be treated in the same way as the earlier material.

Certification by disclosure officer

9.1   The disclosure officer must certify to the prosecutor that, to the best of his knowledge and belief, all material which has been retained and made available to him has been revealed to the prosecutor in accordance with this code. He must sign and date the certificate. It will be necessary to certify not only at the time when the schedule and accompanying material is submitted to the prosecutor, but also when material which has been retained is reconsidered after the accused has given a defence statement.

Disclosure of material to accused

10.1   If material has not already been copied to the prosecutor, and he requests its disclosure to the accused on the ground that:
— it falls within the test for primary or secondary prosecution disclosure, or
— the court has ordered its disclosure after considering an application from the accused,
the disclosure officer must disclose it to the accused.

10.2   If material has been copied to the prosecutor, and it is to be disclosed, whether it is disclosed by the prosecutor or the disclosure officer is a matter for agreement between the two of them.

10.3   The disclosure officer must disclose material to the accused either by giving him a copy or by allowing him to inspect it. If the accused person asks for a copy of any material which he has been allowed to inspect, the disclosure officer must give it to him, unless in the opinion of the disclosure officer that is either not practicable (for example because the material consists of an object which cannot be copied, or because the volume of material is so great), or not desirable (for example because the material is a statement by a child witness in relation to a sexual offence).

10.4   If material which the accused has been allowed to inspect consists of information which is recorded other than in writing, whether it should be given to the accused in its original form or in the form of a transcript is a matter for the discretion of the disclosure officer. If the material is transcribed, the disclosure officer must ensure that the transcript is certified to the accused as a true record of the material which has been transcribed.

10.5   If a court concludes that it is in the public interest that an item of sensitive material must be disclosed to the accused, it will be necessary to disclose the material if the case is to proceed. This does not mean that sensitive documents must always be disclosed in their original form: for example, the court may agree that sensitive details still requiring protection should be blocked out, or that documents may be summarised, or that the prosecutor may make an admission about the substance of the material under section 10 of the Criminal Justice Act 1967.

ATTORNEY-GENERAL'S GUIDELINES ON DISCLOSURE OF INFORMATION IN CRIMINAL PROCEEDINGS
Issued 29 November 2000

Introduction

1.   Every accused person has a right to a fair trial, a right long embodied in our law and guaranteed under Article 6 of the European Convention on Human Rights. A fair trial is the proper object and expectation of all participants in the trial process. Fair disclosure to an accused is an inseparable part of a fair trial.

2.   The scheme set out in the Criminal Procedure and Investigations Act 1996 (the Act) is designed to ensure that there is fair disclosure of material which may be relevant to an investigation and which does not form part of the prosecution case. Disclosure under the Act should assist the accused in the timely preparation and presentation of their case and assist the court to focus on all the relevant issues in the trial. Disclosure which does not meet these objectives risks preventing a fair trial taking place.

3.   Fairness does. however. recognise that there are other interests that need to be protected, including those of victims and witnesses who might otherwise be exposed to harm. The scheme of the Act protects those interests. It should also ensure that material is not disclosed which overburdens the participants in the trial process, diverts attention from the relevant issues, leads to unjustifiable delay, and is wasteful of resources.

4.   These guidelines build upon the existing law to help to ensure that the legislation is operated more effectively. In some areas guidance is given which goes beyond the requirements of the legislation, where experience has suggested that such guidance is desirable.

General principles

Investigators and Disclosure Officers

5.   Investigators and disclosure officers must be fair and objective and must work together with prosecutors to ensure that disclosure obligations are met. A failure to take action leading to proper disclosure may result in a wrongful conviction. It may alternatively lead to a successful abuse of process argument or an acquittal against the weight of the evidence.

6.   In discharging their obligations under the statute, code, common law and any operational instructions, investigators should always err on the side of recording and retaining material where they have any doubt as to whether it may be relevant.

7.   An individual must not be appointed as disclosure officer, or continue in that role, if that is likely to result in a conflict of interest, for instance, if the disclosure officer is the victim of the alleged crime which is the subject of criminal proceedings. The advice of a more senior officer must always be sought if there is doubt as to whether a conflict of interest precludes an individual acting as the disclosure officer. If thereafter the doubt remains, the advice of a prosecutor should be sought.

8.   Disclosure officers, or their deputies, must inspect, view or listen to all material that has been retained by the investigator, and the disclosure officer must provide a personal declaration to the effect that this task has been done. The obligation does not apply, however, in the circumstances set out in paragraph 9 below.

9.   In some cases, out of an abundance of caution, investigators seize large volumes of material which may, not, because of its source, general nature or other reasons, seem likely ever to be relevant. In such circumstances, the investigator may consider that it is not an appropriate use of resources to examine such large volumes of material seized on a precautionary basis. If such material is not examined by the investigator or disclosure officer, and it is not intended to examine it, but the material is nevertheless retained, its existence should be made known to the accused in general terms at the primary stage and permission granted for its inspection by him or his legal advisers. A section 9 statement will be completed by the investigating officer or disclosure officer describing the material by general category and justifying it not having been examined. This statement will itself be listed as unused material and automatically disclosed to the defence.

10.   In meeting the obligations in paragraph 6.9 and 8.1 of the Code, it is crucial that descriptions by disclosure officers in non-sensitive schedules are detailed, clear and accurate. The descriptions may require a summary of the contents of the retained material to assist the prosecutor to make an informed decision on disclosure. The same applies to sensitive schedules, to the extent possible without compromising the confidentiality of the information.

11.   Disclosure officers must specifically draw material to the attention of the prosecutor for consideration where they have any doubt as to whether it might undermine the prosecution case or might reasonably be expected to assist the defence disclosed by the accused.

12.   Disclosure officers must seek the advice and assistance of prosecutors when in doubt as to their responsibility, and must deal expeditiously with requests by the prosecutor for further information on material which may lead to disclosure.

Prosecutors generally

13.   Prosecutors must do all that they can to facilitate proper disclosure, as part of their general and personal professional responsibility to act fairly and impartially, in the interests of justice. Prosecutors must also be alert to the need to provide advice to disclosure officers on disclosure issues and to advise on disclosure procedure generally.

14.   Prosecutors must review schedules prepared by disclosure officers thoroughly and must be alert to the possibility that material may exist which has not been revealed to them. If no schedules have been provided, or there are apparent omissions from the schedules, or documents or other items are insufficiently described or are unclear, the prosecutor must at once take action to obtain properly completed schedules. If, following this, prosecutors remain dissatisfied with the quality or content of the schedules they must raise the matter with a senior officer, and if necessary, persist, with a view to resolving the matter satisfactorily.

15.   Where prosecutors have reason to believe that the disclosure officer has not discharged the obligation in paragraph 8 to inspect, view or listen to material. they must at once raise the matter with the disclosure officer and, if it is believed that the officer has not inspected, viewed or listened to the material, request that it be done.

16.   When the prosecutor or disclosure officer believes that material might undermine the prosecution case or assist the defence case, for instance in the case of records of previous statements by witnesses, prosecutors must always inspect, view or listen to the material and satisfy themselves that the prosecution can properly be continued. Their judgement as to what other material to inspect, view or listen to will depend on the circumstances of each case.

17.   Prosecutors should inform the investigator if, in their view, reasonable and relevant lines of further inquiry exist.

18.   Prosecutors should not adduce evidence of the contents of a defence statement other than in the circumstances envisaged by section 11 of the Act or to rebut alibi

evidence. Where evidence may be adduced in these circumstances, this can be done through cross-examination as well as through the introduction of evidence. There may be occasions when a defence statement points the prosecution to other lines of inquiry. Further investigation in these circumstances is possible and evidence obtained as a result of inquiring into a defence statement may be used as part of the prosecution case or to rebut the defence.

19.   Prosecutors must ensure that they record in writing all actions and decisions they make in discharging their disclosure responsibilities, and this information is to be made available to the prosecution advocate if requested or if relevant to an issue.

20.   In deciding what material should be disclosed (at any stage of the proceedings) prosecutors should resolve any doubt they may have in favour of disclosure, unless the material is on the sensitive schedule and will be placed before the court for the issue of disclosure to be determined.

21.   If prosecutors are satisfied that a fair trial cannot take place because of a failure to disclose which cannot or will not be remedied, they must not continue with the case.

Prosecution advocates

22.   Prosecution advocates should use their best endeavours to ensure that all material that ought properly to be made available is either presented by the prosecution or disclosed to the defence. However, the prosecution cannot be expected to disclose material if they are not aware of its existence. As far as is possible, prosecution advocates must place themselves in a fully informed position to enable them to make decisions on disclosure.

23.   Upon receipt of instructions, prosecution advocates should consider as a priority all the information provided regarding disclosure of material. Prosecution advocates should consider, in every case, whether they can be satisfied that they are in possession of all relevant documentation and that they have been instructed fully regarding disclosure matters. Decisions already made regarding disclosure should be reviewed. If as a result the advocate considers that further information or action is required, written advice should be promptly provided setting out the aspects that need clarification or action. If necessary and where appropriate a conference should be held to determine what is required.

24.   The prosecution advocate must continue to keep under review until the conclusion of the trial decisions regarding disclosure. The prosecution advocate must in every case specifically consider whether he or she can satisfactorily discharge the duty of continuing review on the basis of the material supplied already, or whether it is necessary to inspect further material or to reconsider material already inspected.

25.   Prior to the commencement of a trial, the prosecuting advocate should always make decisions on disclosure in consultation with those instructing him and it is desirable that the disclosure officer should also be consulted. After a trial has started, it is recognised that in practice consultation on disclosure issues may not be practicable; it continues to be desirable, however, whenever this can be achieved without affecting unduly the conduct of the trial.

26.   The practice of 'counsel to counsel' disclosure should cease: it is inconsistent with the requirement of transparency in the prosecution process.

Defence practitioners

27.   A defence statement should set out the nature of the defence, the matters on which issue is taken and the reasons for taking issue. A comprehensive defence statement assists the participants in the trial to ensure that it is fair. It provides information that the prosecutor needs to identify any remaining material that fails to be disclosed at the secondary stage. The more detail a defence statement contains the more likely it is that the prosecutor will make a properly informed decision about whether any

remaining material might assist the defence case, or whether to advise the investigator to undertake further inquiries. It also helps in the management of the trial by narrowing down and focussing the issues in dispute. It may result in the prosecution discontinuing the case. Defence practitioners should be aware of these considerations in advising their clients.

28.   Defence solicitors should ensure that statements are agreed by the accused before being served. Wherever possible, the accused should sign the defence statement to evidence his or her agreement.

Involvement of other agencies

(a)   Material held by Government departments or other Crown bodies

29.   Where it appears to an investigator, disclosure officer or prosecutor that a Government department or other Crown body has material that may be relevant to an issue in the case, reasonable steps should be taken to identify and consider such material. Although what is reasonable will vary from case to case, prosecutors should inform the department or other body of the nature of its case and of relevant issues in the case in respect of which the department or body might possess material, and ask whether it has any such material. Departments in England and Wales have established Enquiry Points to deal with issues concerning the disclosure of information in criminal proceedings. Further guidance for prosecutors and investigators seeking information (including documents) from Government departments or other Crown bodies may be found in the pamphlet 'Giving Evidence or Information about suspected crimes: Guidance for Departments and Investigators' (March, 1997, Cabinet Office).

(b)   Material held by other agencies

30.   There may be cases where the investigator, disclosure officer or prosecutor suspects that a non-government agency or other third party (for example, a local authority, a social services department, a hospital, a doctor, a school, providers of forensic services) has material or information which might be disclosable if it were in the possession of the prosecution. In such cases consideration should be given as to whether it is appropriate to seek access to the material or information and if so, steps should be taken by the prosecution to obtain such material or information. It will be important to do so if the material or information is likely to undermine the prosecution case, or assist a known defence.

31.   If the investigator, disclosure officer or prosecutor seeks access to the material or information but the third party declines or refuses to allow access to it, the matter should not be left. If despite any reasons offered by the third party it is still believed that it is reasonable to seek production of the material or information, and the requirements of section 2 of the Criminal Procedure (Attendance of Witnesses) Act 1965 or as appropriate section 97 of the Magistrates Courts Act 1980[1] are satisfied, then the prosecutor or investigator should apply for a witness summons causing a representative of the third party to produce the material to the Court.

---

[1]The equivalent legislation in Northern Ireland is section 51A of the Judicature (Northern Ireland) Act 1978 and Article 118 of the Magistrates' Courts (Northern Ireland) Order 1981.

32.   Information which might be disclosable if it were in the possession of the prosecution which comes to the knowledge of investigators or prosecutors as a result of liaison with third parties should be recorded by the investigator or prosecutor in a durable or retrievable form (for example potentially relevant information revealed in discussions at a child protection conference attended by police officers).

33.   Where information comes into the possession of the prosecution in the circumstances set out in paragraphs 30–32 above, consultation with the other agency

should take place before disclosure is made: there may be public interest reasons which justify witholding disclosure and which would require the issue of disclosure of the information to be placed before the court.

Disclosure prior to primary disclosure under the CPIA 1996

34. Prosecutors must always be alive to the need, in the interests of justice and fairness in the particular circumstances of any case, to make disclosure of material after the commencement of proceedings but before the prosecutor's duty arises under the Act. For instance, disclosure ought to be made of significant information that might affect a bail decision or that might enable the defence to contest the committal proceedings.

35. Where the need for such disclosure is not apparent to the prosecutor, any disclosure will depend on what the defendant chooses to reveal about the defence. Clearly, such disclosure will not normally exceed that which is obtainable after the duties under the 'Act' arise.

Primary disclosure

36. Generally, material can be considered to potentially undermine the prosecution case if it has an adverse effect on the strength of the prosecution case. This will include anything that tends to show a fact inconsistent with the elements of the case that must be proved by the prosecution. Material can have an adverse effect on the strength of the prosecution case:

(a) by the use made of it in cross-examination; and
(b) by its capacity to suggest any potential submissions that could lead to:
(i) the exclusion of evidence;
(ii) a stay of proceedings;
(iii) a court or tribunal finding that any public authority had acted incompatibly with the defendant's rights under the ECHR

37. In deciding what material might undermine the prosecution case, the prosecution should pay particular attention to material that has potential to weaken the prosecution case or is inconsistent with it. Examples are:

(i) Any material casting doubt upon the accuracy of any prosecution evidence.
(ii) Any material which may point to another person, whether charged or not (including a co-accused) having involvement in the commission of the offence.
(iii) Any material which may cast doubt upon the reliability of a confession.
(iv) Any material that might go to the credibility of a prosecution witness.
(v) Any material that might support a defence that is either raised by the defence or apparent from the prosecution papers. If the material might undermine the prosecution case it should be disclosed at this stage even though it suggests a defence inconsistent with or alternative to one already advanced by the accused or his solicitor.
(vi) Any material which may have a bearing on the admissibility of any prosecution evidence.

It should also be borne in mind that while items of material viewed in isolation may not be considered to potentially undermine the prosecution case, several items together can have that effect.

38. Experience suggests that any item which relates to the defendant's mental or physical health, his intellectual capacity, or to any ill-treatment which the defendant may have suffered when in the investigator's custody is likely to have the potential for casting doubt on the reliability of an accused's purported confession, and prosecutors should pay particular attention to any such item in the possession of the prosecution.

Secondary disclosure

39. Prosecutors should be open, alert and promptly responsive to requests for disclosure of material supported by the comprehensive defence statement. Conversely, if no defence statement has been served or if the prosecutor considers that the defence statement is lacking specific and/or clarity, a letter should be sent to the defence indicating that secondary disclosure will not take place or will be limited (as appropriate), and inviting the defence to specify and/or clarify the accused's case. The prosecutor should consider raising the issue at a preliminary hearing if the position is not resolved satisfactorily to enable the court to give directions.

40. Experience suggests that material of the description set out below might reasonably be expected to be disclosed to the defence where it relates to the defence being put forward. Accordingly, following the delivery of a defence statement and on receipt of a request specifically linking the material sought with the defence being put forward, such linked material should be disclosed unless there is good reason not to do so. However, if defences put forward in a defence statement are inconsistent within the meaning of section 11 of the Act, then the preceding guidance set out in this paragraph will not apply. Conversely, if material of the description set out below might undermine the prosecution case, and does not justify an application to the court to withhold disclosure, prosecutors must disclose it at the primary stage. The material is:

(i) Those recorded scientific or scenes of crime findings retained by the investigator which:

— relate to the defendant; and

— are linked to the point at issue; and

— have not previously been disclosed.

(ii) where identification is or may be in issue, all previous descriptions of suspects, however recorded, together with all records of identification procedures in respect of the offence(s) and photographs of the accused taken by the investigator around the time of his arrest;

(iii) Information that any prosecution witness has received, has been promised or has requested any payment or reward in connection with the case;

(iv) Plans of crime scenes or video recordings made by investigators of crime scenes;

(v) Names, within the knowledge of investigators, of individuals who may have relevant information and whom investigators do not intend to interview;

(vi) Records which the investigator has made of information which may be relevant, provided by any individual (such information would include, but not be limited to, records of conversation and interviews with any such person).

Disclosure of video recordings or scientific findings by means of supplying copies may well involve delay or otherwise not be practicable or desirable, in which case the investigator should make reasonable arrangements for the video, recordings or scientific findings to be viewed by the defence.

Applications for non-disclosure in the public interest

41. Before making an application to the court to withhold material which would otherwise fall to be disclosed, on the basis that to disclose would not be in the public interest, a prosecutor should aim to disclose as much of the material as he properly can (by giving the defence redacted or edited copies of summaries).

42. Prior to or at the hearing, the court must be provided with full and accurate information. The prosecution advocate must examine all material which is the subject matter of the application and make any necessary enquiries of the prosecutor and/or investigator. The prosecutor (or representative) and/or investigator should attend such applications.

Summary trial

43.   The prosecutor should, in addition to complying with the obligations under the CPIA, provide to the defence all evidence upon which the Crown proposes to rely in a summary trial. Such provision should allow the accused or their legal advisers sufficient time properly to consider the evidence before it is called. Exceptionally, statements may be withheld for the protection of witnesses or to avoid interference with the course of justice.

Material relevant to sentence

44.   In all cases the prosecutor must consider disclosing in the interests of justice any material which is relevant to sentence (eg. information which might mitigate the seriousness of the offence or assist the accused to lay blame in whole or in part upon a co-accused or another person).

Applicability of these guidelines

45.   These guidelines should be adopted with immediate effect in relation to all cases submitted in future to the prosecuting authorities in receipt of these guidelines. They should also be adopted as regards cases already submitted to which the Act applies, so far as they relate to stages in the proceedings that have not yet been reached.

CROWN COURT RULES 1982

Evidence through television link where witness is a child or is to be cross-examined after admission of a video recording

23A.—(1)   Any party may apply for leave under section 32(1) of the Criminal Justice Act 1988 for evidence to be given through a live television link where—
  (a)   the offence charged is one to which section 32(2) applies; and
  (b)   the evidence is to be given by a witness who is either—
    (i)   in the case of an offence falling within section 32(2)(a) or (b), under the age of 14; or
    (ii)   in the case of an offence falling within section 32(2)(c), under the age of 17; or
    (iii)   a person who is to be cross-examined following the admission under section 32A of that Act of a video recording of testimony from him;
and references in this rule to an offence include references to attempting or conspiring to commit, or aiding, abetting, counselling, procuring or inciting the commission of, that offence,
  (2)   An application under paragraph (1) shall be made by giving notice in writing, which shall be in the form prescribed in Schedule 5 or a form to the like effect.
  (3)   An application under paragraph (1) shall be made within 28 days after the date of the committal of the defendant, or of the consent to the preferment of a bill of indictment in relation to the case, or of the service of notice of transfer under section 53 of the Criminal Justice Act 1991, or of the service of copies of the documents containing the evidence on which the charge or charges are based under paragraph 1 of Schedule 3 to the Crime and Disorder Act 1998, or of the service of Notice of Appeal from a decision of a youth court or magistrates' court, as the case may be.
  (4)   The notice under paragraph (2) shall be sent to the appropriate officer of the Crown Court and at the same time a copy thereof shall be sent by the applicant to every other party to the proceedings.
  (5)   A party who receives a copy of a notice under paragraph (2) and who wishes to oppose the application shall within 14 days notify the applicant and the appropriate officer of the Crown Court, in writing, of his opposition, giving the reasons therefor.

(6)   An application under paragraph (1) shall be determined by a judge of the Crown Court without a hearing, unless the judge otherwise directs, and the appropriate officer of the Crown Court shall notify the parties of the time and place of any such hearing.

(7)   The appropriate officer of the Crown Court shall notify all the parties and any person who is to accompany the witness (if known) of the decision of the Crown Court in relation to an application under paragraph (1). Where leave is granted, the notification shall state—

(a)   where the witness is to give evidence on behalf of the prosecutor, the name of the witness, and, if known, the name, occupation and relationship (if any) to the witness of the person who is to accompany the witness and,

(b)   the location of the Crown Court at which the trial should take place.

(8)   The period specified in paragraph (3) may be extended, either before or after it expires, on an application made in writing, specifying the grounds of the application and sent to the appropriate officer of the Crown Court, and a copy of the application shall be sent by the applicant to every other party to the proceedings. The appropriate officer of the Crown Court shall notify all the parties of the decision of the Crown Court.

(9)   An application for extension of time under paragraph (8) shall be determined by a judge of the Crown Court without a hearing unless the judge otherwise directs.

(10)   A witness giving evidence through a television link pursuant to leave granted under paragraph (7) shall be accompanied by a person acceptable to a judge of the Crown Court and, unless the judge otherwise directs, by no other person.

Evidence through television link where witness is outside United Kingdom

23B.—(1)   Any party may apply for leave under section 32(1) of the Criminal Justice Act 1988 for evidence to be given through a live television link by a witness who is outside the United Kingdom.

(2)   An application under paragraph (1), and any matter relating thereto which, by virtue of the following provisions of this rule, falls to be determined by the Crown Court, may be dealt with in chambers by any Judge of the Crown Court.

(3)   An application under paragraph (1) shall be made by giving notice in writing, which shall be in the form prescribed in Schedule 6 or a form to the like effect.

(4)   An application under paragraph (1) shall be made within 28 days after the date of the committal of the defendant or, as the case may be, of the giving of a notice of transfer under section 4(1)(c) of the Criminal Justice Act 1987, or of the preferral of a bill of indictment in relation to the case.

(5)   The period of 28 days in paragraph (4) may be extended by the Crown Court either before or after it expires, on an application made in writing, specifying the grounds of the application. The appropriate officer of the Crown Court shall notify all the parties of the decision of the Crown Court.

(6)   The notice under paragraph (3) or any application under paragraph (5) shall be sent to the appropriate officer of the Crown Court and at the same time a copy thereof shall be sent by the applicant to every other party to the proceedings.

(7)   A party who receives a copy of a notice under paragraph (3) shall, within 28 days of the notice, notify the applicant and the appropriate officer of the Crown Court, in writing—

(a)   whether or not he opposes the application, giving his reasons for any such opposition, and

(b)   whether or not he wishes to be represented at any hearing of the application.

(8)   After the expiry of the period referred to in paragraph (7), the Crown Court shall determine whether an application under paragraph (1) is to be dealt with—

(a)   without a hearing, or

(b)   at a hearing at which the applicant and such other party or parties as the court may direct may be represented, and the appropriate officer of the Crown Court shall notify the applicant and, where necessary, the other party or parties, of the time and place of any such hearing.

(9)   The appropriate officer of the Crown Court shall notify all the parties of the decision of the Crown Court in relation to an application under paragraph (1) and, where leave is granted, the notification shall state—

(a)   the country in which the witness will give evidence,

(b)   if known, the place where the witness will give evidence,

(c)   where the witness is to give evidence on behalf of the prosecutor, or where disclosure is required by section 11 of the Criminal Justice Act 1967 (alibi) or by rules under section 81 of the Police and Criminal Evidence Act 1984 (expert evidence), the name of the witness,

(d)   the location of the Crown Court at which the trial should take place, and

(e)   any conditions specified by the Crown Court in accordance with paragraph (10).

(10)   The Crown Court dealing with an application under paragraph (1) may specify that as a condition of the grant of leave the witness should give the evidence in the presence of a specified person who is able and willing to answer under oath or affirmation any questions the trial judge may put as to the circumstances in which the evidence is given, including questions about any persons who are present when the evidence is given and any matters which may affect the giving of the evidence.

Video recordings of testimony from child witnesses

23C.—(1)   Any party may apply for leave under section 32A of the Criminal Justice Act 1988 to tender in evidence a video recording of testimony from a witness where—

(a)   the offence charged is one to which section 32(2) of that Act applies;

(b)   in the case of an offence falling within section 32(2)(a) or (b), the proposed witness is under the age of 14 or, if he was under 14 when the video recording was made, is under the age of 15;

(c)   in the case of an offence falling within section 32(2)(c), the proposed witness is under the age of 17 or, if he was under 17 when the video recording was made, is under the age of 18; and

(d)   the video recording is of an interview conducted between an adult and a person coming within sub-paragraph (b) or (c) above (not being the accused or one of the accused) which relates to any matter in issue in the proceedings;

and references in this rule to an offence include references to attempting or conspiring to commit, or aiding, abetting, counselling, procuring or inciting the commission of, that offence.

(2)   An application under paragraph (1) shall be made by giving notice in writing, which shall be in the form prescribed in Schedule 7 or a form to the like effect. The application shall be accompanied by the video recording which it is proposed to tender in evidence and shall include the following, namely—

(a)   the name of the defendant and the offence or offences charged;

(b)   the name and date of birth of the witness in respect of whom the application is made;

(c)   the date on which the video recording was made;

(d)   a statement that in the opinion of the applicant the witness is willing and able to attend the trial for cross-examination;

(e)   a statement of the circumstances in which the video recording was made which complies with paragraph (4) below;

(f)   the date on which the video recording was disclosed to the other party or parties.

(3)   Where it is proposed to tender part only of a video recording of an interview with the witness, an application under paragraph (1) must specify that part and be

accompanied by a video recording of the entire interview, including those parts which it is not proposed to tender in evidence, and by a statement of the circumstances in which the video recording of the entire interview was made which complies with paragraph (4) below.

(4)   The statement of the circumstances in which the video recording was made referred to in paragraph (2)(e) and (3) above shall include the following information, except in so far as it is contained in the recording itself, namely—

(a)   the times at which the recording commenced and finished, including details of any interruptions;

(b)   the location at which the recording was made and the usual function of the premises;

(c)   the name, age and occupation of any person present at any point during the recording; the time for which he was present; his relationship (if any) to the witness and to the defendant;

(d)   a description of the equipment used including the number of cameras used and whether they were fixed or mobile; the number and location of microphones; the video format used and whether there were single or multiple recording facilities;

(e)   the location of the mastertape if the video recording is a copy and details of when and by whom the copy was made.

(5)   An application under paragraph (1) shall be made within 28 days after the date of the committal for trial of the defendant, or of the giving of a notice of transfer under section 53 of the Criminal Justice Act 1991, or of consent to the preferment of a bill of indictment in relation to the case, or of the service of Notice of Appeal from a decision of a youth court or magistrates' court, as the case may be.

(6)   The period of 28 days in paragraph (5) may be extended by a judge of the Crown Court, either before or after it expires, on an application made in writing, specifying the grounds of the application. The appropriate officer of the Crown Court shall notify all the parties of the decision of the Crown Court.

(7)   The notice under paragraph (2) or (6) shall be sent to the appropriate officer of the Crown Court and at the same time, copies thereof shall be sent by the applicant to every other party to the proceedings. Copies of any video recording required by paragraph (2) or (3) to accompany the notice shall at the same time be sent to the court and to any other party who has not already been served with a copy or in the case of a defendant acting in person, shall be made available for viewing by him.

(8)   A party who receives a copy of a notice under paragraph (2) shall, within 14 days of service of the notice, notify the applicant and the appropriate officer of the Crown Court, in writing—

(a)   whether he objects to the admission of any part of the video recording or recordings disclosed, giving his reasons why it would not be in the interests of justice for it to be admitted; and

(b)   whether he would agree to the admission of part of the video recording or recordings disclosed and if so, which part or parts; and

(c)   whether he wishes to be represented at any hearing of the application.

(9)   After the expiry of the period referred to in paragraph (8), a judge of the Crown Court shall determine whether an application under paragraph (1) is to be dealt with—

(a)   without a hearing; or

(b)   where any party notifies the appropriate officer of the Crown Court pursuant to paragraph (8) that he objects to the admission of any part of the video recording and that he wishes to be represented at any hearing, or in any other case where the judge so directs, at a hearing at which the applicant and such other party or parties as the judge may direct may be represented,

and the appropriate officer of the Crown Court shall notify the applicant and, where necessary, the other party or parties, of the time and place of any such hearing.

(10)   The appropriate officer of the Crown Court shall within 3 days of the decision of the Crown Court in relation to an application under paragraph (1) being made, notify all the parties of it in the Form prescribed in Schedule 8 or a form to the like effect, and, where leave is granted, the notification shall state whether the whole or specified parts only of the video recording or recordings disclosed are to be admitted in evidence.

Procedure for applications in proceedings for sexual offences

23D.—(1)   An application for leave under section 41(2) of the 1999 Act must be made in writing to the appropriate officer of the Crown Court and must either—
(a)   be received by that officer within 28 days of—
(i)   the committal of the defendant, or
(ii)   the consent to the preferment of a bill of indictment in relation to the case,
or
(iii)   the service of notice of transfer under section 53 of the Criminal Justice Act 1991, or
(iv)   where a person is sent for trial under section 51 of the Crime and Disorder Act 1998, the service of copies of the documents containing the evidence on which the charge or charges are based under paragraph 1 of Schedule 3 to that Act,
or within such period as the Court may in any particular case determine, or
(b)   be accompanied by a full written explanation specifying the reasons why the application could not have been made within the 28 days mentioned above.
(2)   Such an application must contain the following—
(a)   a summary of the evidence it is proposed to adduce and of the questions it is proposed to put to any witness;
(b)   a full explanation of the reasons why it is considered that the evidence and questions fall within section 41(3) or (5) of the 1999 Act;
(c)   a summary of any document or other evidence to be submitted in support of such evidence and questions;
(d)   where it is proposed that a witness at the trial give evidence as to the complainant's sexual behaviour, the name and date of birth of any such witness.
(3)   A copy of the application must be sent to all the parties to the proceedings at the same time as it is sent to the appropriate officer of the Crown Court.
(4)   Where a copy of the application is received by the prosecutor more than 14 days before the date set for the trial to begin, the prosecutor must, within 14 days of the receipt of the application, notify the other parties to the proceedings and the appropriate officer of the Crown Court in writing whether or not—
(a)   he opposes the application, giving reasons for any such opposition, and
(b)   he wishes to be represented at any hearing of the application.
(5)   Where a copy of the application is received by a party to the proceedings other than the prosecutor more than 14 days before the date set for the trial to begin, that party may make observations in writing on the application to the appropriate officer of the Court, but any such observations must be made within 14 days of the receipt of the application and be copied to the other parties to the proceedings.
(6)   In considering any application under this rule, the Court may request a party to the proceedings to provide the Court with such information as it may specify and which the Court considers would assist it in determining the application.
(7)   Where the Court makes such a request, the person required to provide the information must do so within 14 days of the Court making the request or by such time as the Court considers appropriate in the circumstances of the case.
(8)   An application under paragraph (1) must be determined by a judge of the Crown Court following a hearing if—
(a)   the prosecutor has notified the appropriate officer that he opposes the application; or

(b)   the copy of the application was received by any of the parties to the proceedings less than 14 days before the date set for the trial to begin.

(9)   An application under paragraph (1) must be determined by a judge of the Crown Court following a hearing in any case where he considers such a hearing is appropriate in the circumstances of the particular case.

(10)   The date and time of the hearing must be—

(a)   determined by the Crown Court or the appropriate officer of the Court after taking into consideration—

(i)   any time which a party to the proceedings has been given to respond to a request for information; and

(ii)   the date fixed for any other hearing relevant to the proceedings; and

(b)   notified by the appropriate officer of the Crown Court to all the parties to the proceedings.

(11)   Except where paragraph (8) or (9) applies, an application under paragraph (1) must be determined by a judge of the Crown Court without a hearing.

(12)   The appropriate officer of the Crown Court must, as soon as possible after the determination of an application made in accordance with paragraph (1), give notice of the decision and the reasons for it to all the parties to the proceedings.

(13)   An application under section 41(2) of the 1999 Act may be made orally where the application is made after the trial has begun.

(14)   The person making the application under paragraph (13) must—

(a)   give reasons why the applicant failed to make the application in writing in accordance with paragraph (1); and

(b)   provide the Court with the information set out in paragraph (2)(a) to (d).

(15)   In this rule, 'the 1999 Act' means the Youth Justice and Criminal Evidence Act 1999.

Restrictions on cross-examination of witness

24B.—(1)   This rule and rules 24C and 24D apply where an accused is prevented from cross-examining a witness in person by virtue of section 34 or 35 of the 1999 Act.

(2)   The Court shall explain to the accused as early in the proceedings as is reasonably practicable that he—

(a)   is prevented from cross-examining a witness in person; and

(b)   should arrange for a legal representative to act for him for the purpose of cross-examining the witness.

(3)   The accused shall notify the appropriate officer of the Court within 7 days of the Court giving its explanation, or within such other period as the Court may in any particular case allow, of the action, if any, he has taken.

(4)   Where he has arranged for a legal representative to act for him, the notification shall include details of the name and address of the representative.

(5)   The notification shall be in writing.

(6)   The appropriate officer of the Court shall notify all other parties to the proceedings of the name and address of the person, if any, appointed to act for the accused.

(7)   Where the Court gives its explanation under paragraph (2) to the accused either within 7 days of the day set for the commencement of any hearing at which a witness in respect of whom a prohibition under section 34 or 35 of the 1999 Act applies may be cross-examined or after such a hearing has commenced, the period of 7 days shall be reduced in accordance with any directions issued by the Court.

(8)   Where at the end of the period of 7 days or such other period as the Court has allowed, the Court has received no notification from the accused it may grant the accused an extension of time, whether on its own motion or on the application of the accused.

(9)   Before granting an extension of time, the Court may hold a hearing at which all parties to the proceedings may attend and be heard.

(10)   Any extension of time shall be of such period as the Court considers appropriate in the circumstances of the case.

(11)   The decision of the Court as to whether to grant the accused an extension of time shall be notified to all parties to the proceedings by the appropriate officer of the Court.

Appointment by the Court

24C.—(1)   Where the Court decides, in accordance with section 38(4) of the 1999 Act, to appoint a qualified legal representative, the appropriate officer of the Court shall notify all parties to the proceedings of the name and address of the representative.

(2)   An appointment made by the Court under section 38(4) of the 1999 Act shall, except to such extent as the Court may in any particular case determine, terminate at the conclusion of the cross-examination of the witness or witnesses in respect of whom a prohibition under section 34 or 35 of the 1999 Act applies.

Appointment arranged by the accused

24D.—(1)   The accused may arrange for the qualified legal representative, appointed by the Court under section 38(4) of the 1999 Act, to be appointed to act for him for the purpose of cross-examining any witness in respect of whom a prohibition under section 34 or 35 of the 1999 Act applies.

(2)   Where such an appointment is made—

(a)   both the accused and the qualified legal representative appointed shall notify the Court of the appointment; and

(b)   the qualified legal representative shall, from the time of his appointment, act for the accused as though the arrangement had been made under section 38(2)(a) of the 1999 Act and shall cease to be the representative of the Court under section 38(4) of that Act.

(3)   Where the Court receives notification of the appointment either from the qualified legal representative or from the accused but not from both, the Court shall investigate whether the appointment has been made, and if it concludes that the appointment has not been made, paragraph (2)(b) shall not apply.

(4)   An accused may, notwithstanding an appointment by the Court under section 38(4) of the 1999 Act, arrange for a legal representative to act for him for the purpose of cross-examining any witness in respect of whom a prohibition under section 34 or 35 applies.

(5)   Where the accused arranges for, or informs the Court of his intention to arrange for, a legal representative to act for him, he shall notify the Court, within such period as the Court may allow, of the name and address of any person appointed to act for him.

(6)   Where the Court is notified within the time allowed that such an appointment has been made, any qualified legal representative appointed by the Court in accordance with section 38(4) of the 1999 Act shall be discharged.

(7)   The appropriate officer of the Court shall, as soon as reasonably practicable after the Court receives notification of an appointment under this rule or, where paragraph (3) applies, after the Court is satisfied that the appointment has been made, notify all the parties to the proceedings—

(a)   that the appointment has been made;

(b)   where paragraph (4) applies, of the name and address of the person appointed; and

(c)   that the person appointed by the Crown Court under section 38(4) of the 1999 Act has been discharged or has ceased to act for the Court.

(8)   In rule 24B, 24C and this rule, 'the 1999 Act' means the Youth Justice and Criminal Evidence Act 1999.

PART C EUROPEAN CONVENTION ON HUMAN RIGHTS

CONVENTION FOR THE PROTECTION OF HUMAN RIGHTS AND FUNDAMENTAL FREEDOMS
(Rome, 4.11.1950)[1]

The governments signatory hereto, being members of the Council of Europe,

Considering the Universal Declaration of Human Rights proclaimed by the General Assembly of the United Nations on 10th December 1948;

Considering that this declaration aims at securing the universal and effective recognition and observance of the rights therein declared;

Considering that the aim of the Council of Europe is the achievement of greater unity between its members and that one of the methods by which that aim is to be pursued is the maintenance and further realisation of human rights and fundamental freedoms;

Reaffirming their profound belief in those fundamental freedoms which are the foundation of justice and peace in the world and are best maintained on the one hand by an effective political democracy and on the other by a common understanding and observance of the human rights upon which they depend;

Being resolved, as the governments of European countries which are like-minded and have a common heritage of political traditions, ideals, freedom and the rule of law, to take the first steps for the collective enforcement of certain of the rights stated in the Universal Declaration,

Have agreed as follows:

[1] European Treaty Series, No. 5. Text amended according to the provisions of Protocol No. 3 (ETS No. 45), which entered into force on 21 September 1970, of Protocol No. 5 (ETS No. 55), which entered into force on 20 December 1971, and of Protocol No. 8 (ETS No. 118), which entered into force on 1 January 1990, and comprising also the text of Protocol No. 2 (ETS No. 44) which, in accordance with Article 5, paragraph 3, therefor, has been an integral part of the Convention since its entry into force on 21 September 1970.

Article 1
The High Contracting Parties shall secure to everyone within their jurisdiction the rights and freedoms defined in Section 1 of this Convention.

SECTION I

Article 2
1. Everyone's right to life shall be protected by law. No one shall be deprived of his life intentionally save in the execution of a sentence of a court following his conviction of a crime for which this penalty is provided by law.

2.   Deprivation of life shall not be regarded as inflicted in contravention of this article when it results from the use of force which is no more than absolutely necessary:

(a)   in defence of any person from unlawful violence;

(b)   in order to effect a lawful arrest or to prevent the escape of a person lawfully detained;

(c)   in action lawfully taken for the purpose of quelling a riot or insurrection.

Article 3

No one shall be subjected to torture or to inhuman or degrading treatment or punishment.

Article 4

1.   No one shall be held in slavery or servitude.

2.   No one shall be required to perform forced or compulsory labour.

3.   For the purpose of this article the term 'forced or compulsory labour' shall not include:

(a)   any work required to be done in the ordinary course of detention imposed according to the provisions of Article 5 of this Convention or during conditional release from such detention;

(b)   any service of a military character or, in case of conscientious objectors in countries where they are recognised, service exacted instead of compulsory military service;

(c)   any service exacted in case of an emergency or calamity threatening the life or well-being of the community;

(d)   any work or service which forms part of normal civic obligations.

Article 5

1.   Everyone has the right to liberty and security of person. No one shall be deprived of his liberty save in the following cases and in accordance with a procedure prescribed by law:

(a)   the lawful detention of a person after conviction by a competent court;

(b)   the lawful arrest or detention of a person for non-compliance with the lawful order of a court or in order to secure the fulfilment of any obligation prescribed by law;

(c)   the lawful arrest or detention of a person effected for the purpose of bringing him before the competent legal authority on reasonable suspicion of having committed an offence or when it is reasonably considered necessary to prevent his committing an offence or fleeing after having done so;

(d)   the detention of a minor by lawful order for the purpose of educational supervision or his lawful detention for the purpose of bringing him before the competent legal authority;

(e)   the lawful detention of persons for the prevention of the spreading of infectious diseases, of persons of unsound mind, alcoholics or drug addicts or vagrants;

(f)   the lawful arrest or detention of a person to prevent his effecting an unauthorised entry into the country or of a person against whom action is being taken with a view to deportation or extradition.

2.   Everyone who is arrested shall be informed promptly, in a language which he understands, of the reasons for his arrest and of any charge against him.

3.   Everyone arrested or detained in accordance with the provisions of paragraph 1(c) of this article shall be brought promptly before a judge or other officer authorised by law to exercise judicial power and shall be entitled to trial within a reasonable time or to release pending trial. Release may be conditioned by guarantees to appear for trial.

4.   Everyone who is deprived of his liberty by arrest or detention shall be entitled to take proceedings by which the lawfulness of his detention shall be decided speedily by a court and his release ordered if the detention is not lawful.

5. Everyone who has been the victim of arrest or detention in contravention of the provisions of this article shall have an enforceable right to compensation.

Article 6

1. In the determination of his civil rights and obligations or of any criminal charge against him, everyone is entitled to a fair and public hearing within a reasonable time by an independent and impartial tribunal established by law. Judgment shall be pronounced publicly but the press and public may be excluded from all or part of the trial in the interests of morals, public order or national security in a democratic society, where the interests of juveniles or the protection of the private life of the parties so require, or to the extent strictly necessary in the opinion of the court in special circumstances where publicity would prejudice the interests of justice.

2. Everyone charged with a crminal offence shall be presumed innocent until proved guilty according to law.

3. Everyone charged with a criminal offence has the following minimum rights;

    (a)   to be informed promptly, in a language which he understands and in detail, of the nature and cause of the accusation against him;

    (b)   to have adequate time and facilities for the preparation of his defence;

    (c)   to defend himself in person or through legal assistance of his own choosing or, if he has not sufficient means to pay for legal assistance, to be given it free when the interests of justice so require;

    (d)   to examine or have examined witnesses against him and to obtain the attendance and examination of witnesses on his behalf under the same conditions as witnesses against him;

    (e)   to have the free assistance of an interpreter if he cannot understand or speak the language used in court.

Article 7

1. No one shall be held guilty of any criminal offence on account of any act or omission which did not constitute a criminal offence under national or international law at the time when it was committed. Nor shall a heavier penalty be imposed than the one that was applicable at the time the criminal offence was committed.

2. This article shall not prejudice the trial and punishment of any person for any act or omission which, at the time when it was committed, was criminal according to the general principles of law recognised by civilised nations.

Article 8

1. Everyone has the right to respect for his private and family life, his home and his correspondence.

2. There shall be no interference by a public authority with the exercise of this right except such as is in accordance with the law and is necessary in a democratic society in the interests of national security, public safety or the economic well-being of the country, for the prevention of disorder or crime, for the protection of health or morals, or for the protection of the rights and freedoms of others.

Article 9

1. Everyone has the right to freedom of thought, conscience and religion; this right includes freedom to change his religion or belief and freedom, either alone or in community with others and in public or private, to manifest his religion or belief, in worship, teaching, practice and observance.

2. Freedom to manifest one's religion or beliefs shall be subject only to such limitations as are prescribed by law and are necessary in a democratic society in the interests of public safety, for the protection of public order, health or morals, or for the protection of the rights and freedoms of others.

Article 10
1. Everyone has the right to freedom of expression. This right shall include freedom to hold opinions and to receive and impart information and ideas without interference by public authority and regardless of frontiers. This article shall not prevent States from requiring the licensing of broadcasting, television or cinema enterprises.
2. The exercise of these freedoms, since it carries with it duties and responsibilities, may be subject to such formalities, conditions, restrictions or penalties as are prescribed by law and are necessary in a democratic society, in the interests of national security, territorial integrity or public safety, for the prevention of disorder or crime, for the protection of health or morals, for the protection of the reputation of rights of others, for preventing the disclosure of information received in confidence, or for maintaining the authority and impartiality of the judiciary.

Article 11
1. Everyone has the right to freedom of peaceful assembly and to freedom of association with others, including the right to form and to join trade unions for the protection of his interests.
2. No restrictions shall be placed on the exercise of these rights other than such as are prescribed by law and are necessary in a democratic society in the interests of national security or public safety, for the prevention of disorder or crime, for the protection of health or morals or for the protection of the rights and freedoms of others. This article shall not prevent the imposition of lawful restrictions on the exercise of these rights by members of the armed forces, of the police or of the administration of the state.

Article 12
Men and women of marriageable age have the right to marry and to found a family, according to the national laws governing the exercise of this right.

Article 13
Everyone whose rights and freedoms as set forth in this Convention are violated shall have an effective remedy before a national authority notwithstanding that the violation has been committed by persons acting in an official capacity.

Article 14
The employment of the rights and freedoms set forth in this Convention shall be secured without discrimination on any ground such as sex, race, colour, language, religion, political or other opinion, national or social origin, association with a national minority, property, birth or other status.

Article 15
1. In time of war or other public emergency threatening the life of the nation any High Contracting Party may take measures derogating from its obligations under this Convention to the extent strictly required by the exigencies of the situation, provided that such measures are not inconsistent with its other obligations under international law.
2. No derogation from Article 2, except in respect of deaths resulting from lawful acts of war, or from Articles 3, 4 (paragraph 1) and 7 shall be made under this provision.
3. Any High Contracting Party availing itself of this right of derogation shall keep the Secretary General of the Council of Europe fully informed of the measures which it has taken and the reasons therefor. It shall also inform the Secretary General of the Council of Europe when such measures have ceased to operate and the provisions of the Convention are again being fully executed.

Article 16
Nothing in Articles 10, 11 and 14 shall be regarded as preventing the High Contracting Parties from imposing restrictions on the political activity of aliens.

Article 17

Nothing in this Convention may be interpreted as implying for any State, group or person any right to engage in any activity or perform any act aimed at the destruction of any of the rights and freedoms set forth herein or at their limitation to a greater extent than is provided for in the Convention.

Article 18

The restrictions permitted under this Convention to the said rights and freedoms shall not be applied for any purpose other than those for which they have been prescribed.

PART D CIVIL STATUTES

POLICE (PROPERTY) ACT 1897
(1897, c. 30)

1. (1) Where any property has come into the possession of the police in connexion with their investigation of a suspected offence a court of summary jurisdiction may, on application, either by an officer of police or by a claimant of the property, make an order for the delivery of the property to the person appearing to the magistrate or court to be the owner thereof, or, if the owner cannot be ascertained, make such order with respect to the property as to the magistrate or court may seem meet.

(2) An order under this section shall not affect the right of any person to take within six months from the date of the order legal proceedings against any person in possession of property delivered by virtue of the order for the recovery of the property, but on the expiration of those six months the right shall cease.

2. (1) A Secretary of State may make regulations (limited by subsection (2)) for the disposal of property which has come into the possession of the police under the circumstances mentioned in this Act in cases where the owner of the property has not been ascertained and no order of a competent court has been made with respect thereto.

(2)–(2B) Regulations.

(3) Where property is a perishable article or its custody involves unreasonable expense or inconvenience, it may be sold at any time, but the proceeds of sale shall not be disposed of until they have remained in the possession of the police for a year. In any other case the property shall not be sold until it has remained in the possession of the police for a year.

(4) Regulations may be made by the Secretary of State as to the investment of money and audit of accounts.

CIVIL EVIDENCE ACT 1968
(1968, c. 64)

PART II
MISCELLANEOUS AND GENERAL

Convictions, etc. as evidence in civil proceedings

11. Convictions as evidence in civil proceedings
(1) In any civil proceedings the fact that a person has been convicted of an offence by or before any court in the United Kingdom or by a court-martial there or elsewhere shall (subject to subsection (3) below) be admissible in evidence for the purpose of proving, where to do so is relevant to any issue in those proceedings, that he committed

that offence, whether he was so convicted upon a plea of guilty or otherwise and whether or not he is a party to the civil proceedings; but no conviction other than a subsisting one shall be admissible in evidence by virtue of this section.

(2)   In any civil proceedings in which by virtue of this section a person is proved to have been convicted of an offence by or before any court in the United Kingdom or by a court-martial there or elsewhere—

(a)   he shall be taken to have committed that offence unless the contrary is proved; and

(b)   without prejudice to the reception of any other admissible evidence for the purpose of identifying the facts on which the conviction was based, the contents of any document which is admissible as evidence of the conviction, and the contents of the information, complaint, indictment or charge-sheet on which the person in question was convicted, shall be admissible in evidence for that purpose.

(3)   Nothing in this section shall prejudice the operation of section 13 of this Act or any other enactment whereby a conviction or a finding of fact in any criminal proceedings is for the purposes of any other proceedings made conclusive evidence of any fact.

(4)   Where in any civil proceedings the contents of any document are admissible in evidence by virtue of subsection (2) above, a copy of that document, or of the material part thereof, purporting to be certified or otherwise authenticated by or on behalf of the court or authority having custody of that document shall be admissible in evidence and shall be taken to be a true copy of that document or part unless the contrary is shown.

(5)   Nothing in any of the following enactments, that is to say—

(a)   [section 1C of the Powers of Criminal Courts Act 1973] (under which a conviction leading to discharge is to be disregarded except as therein mentioned);

(b)   section 9 of the Criminal Justice (Scotland) Act 1949 (which makes similar provision in respect of convictions on indictment in Scotland); and

(c)   section 8 of the Probation Act (Northern Ireland) 1950 (which corresponds to the said section 12) or any corresponding enactment of the Parliament of Northern Ireland for the time being in force,

shall affect the operation of this section; and for the purposes of this section any order made by a court of summary jurisdiction in Scotland under section 1 or section 2 of the said Act of 1949 shall be treated as a conviction.

(6)   In this section 'court-martial' means a court-martial constituted under the Army Act 1955, the Air Force Act 1955 or the Naval Discipline Act 1957 or a disciplinary court constituted under section [52G] of the said Act of 1957, and in relation to a court-martial 'conviction', means a finding of guilty which is, or falls to be treated as, the finding of the court, and 'convicted' shall be construed accordingly.

12.   Findings of adultery and paternity as evidence in civil proceedings

(1)   In any civil proceedings—

(a)   the fact that a person has been found guilty of adultery in any matrimonial proceedings; and

(b)   the fact that a person has been found to be the father of a child in relevant proceedings before any court in England and Wales [or Northern Ireland] or has been adjudged to be the father of a child in affiliation proceedings before any court in the United Kingdom shall (subject to subsection (3) below) be admissible in evidence for the purpose of proving, where to do so is relevant to any issue in those civil proceedings, that he committed the adultery to which the finding relates or, as the case may be, is (or was) the father of that child, whether or not he offered any defence to the allegation of adultery or paternity and whether or not he is a party to the civil proceedings; but no finding or adjudication other than a subsisting one shall be admissible in evidence by virtue of this section.

(2)   In any civil proceedings in which by virtue of this section a person is proved to have been found guilty of adultery as mentioned in subsection (1)(a) above or to have been found or adjudged to be the father of a child as mentioned in subsection (1)(b) above—

(a)   he shall be taken to have committed the adultery to which the finding relates or, as the case may be, to be (or have been) the father of that child, unless the contrary is proved; and

(b)   without prejudice to the reception of any other admissible evidence for the purpose of identifying the facts on which the finding or adjudication was based, the contents of any document which was before the court, or which contains any pronouncement of the court, in the other proceedings in question shall be admissible in evidence for that purpose.

(3)   Nothing in this section shall prejudice the operation of any enactment whereby a finding of fact in any matrimonial or affiliation proceedings is for the purposes of any other proceedings made conclusive evidence of any fact.

(4)   Subsection (4) of section 11 of this Act shall apply for the purposes of this section as if the reference to subsection (2) were a reference to subsection (2) of this section.

(5)   In this section—

'matrimonial proceedings' means any matrimonial cause in the High Court or a county court in England and Wales or in the High Court in Northern Ireland, any consistorial action in Scotland, or any appeal arising out of any such cause or action;

'relevant proceedings' means—

(a)   proceedings on a complaint under section 42 of the National Assistance Act 1948 or section 26 of the Social Security Act 1986;

(b)   proceedings under the Children Act 1989;

(c)   proceedings which would have been relevant proceedings for the purposes of this section in the form in which it was in force before the passing of the Children Act 1989;

(d)   proceedings which are relevant proceedings as defined in section 8(5) of the Civil Evidence (Northern Ireland) 1971.

13.   Conclusiveness of convictions for purposes of defamation actions

(1)   In an action for libel or slander in which the question whether a person did or did not commit a criminal offence is relevant to an issue arising in the action, proof that at the time when that issue falls to be determined, that person stands convicted of that offence shall be conclusive evidence that he committed that offence; and his conviction thereof shall be admissible in evidence accordingly.

(2)   In any such action as aforesaid in which by virtue of this section a person is proved to have been convicted of an offence, the contents of any document which is admissible as evidence of the conviction, and the contents of the information, complaint, indictment or charge-sheet on which that person was convicted, shall, without prejudice to the reception of any other admissible evidence for the purpose of identifying the facts on which the conviction was based, be admissible in evidence for the purpose of identifying those facts.

(2A)   In the case of an action for libel or slander in which there is more than one plaintiff—

(a)   the references in subsections (1) and (2) above to the plaintiff shall be construed as references to any of the plaintiffs, and

(b)   proof that any of the plaintiffs stands convicted of an offence shall be conclusive evidence that he committed that offence so far as that fact is relevant to any issue arising in relation to his cause of action or that of any other plaintiff.

(3)   For the purposes of this section a person shall be taken to stand convicted of an offence if but only if there subsists against him a conviction of that offence by or before a court in the United Kingdom or by a court-martial there or elsewhere.

(4)   Subsection (4) to (6) of section 11 of this Act shall apply for the purposes of this section as they apply for the purposes of that section, but as if in the said subsection (4) the reference to subsection (2) were a reference to subsection (2) of this section.

(5)   The foregoing provisions of this section shall apply for the purposes of any action begun after the passing of this Act, whenever the cause of action arose, but shall not apply for the purposes of any action begun before the passing of this Act or any appeal or other proceedings arising out of any such action.

Privilege

14.   Privilege against incrimination of self or spouse

(1)   The right of a person in any legal proceedings other than criminal proceedings to refuse to answer any question or produce any document or thing if to do so would tend to expose that person to proceedings for an offence or for the recovery of a penalty—

(a)   shall apply only as regards criminal offences under the law of any part of the United Kingdom and penalties provided for by such law; and

(b)   shall include a like right to refuse to answer any question or produce any document or thing if to do so would tend to expose the husband or wife of that person to proceedings for any such criminal offence or for the recovery of any such penalty.

(2)   In so far as any existing enactment conferring (in whatever words) powers of inspection or investigation confers on a person (in whatever words) any right otherwise than in criminal proceedings to refuse to answer any question or give any evidence tending to incriminate that person, subsection (1) above shall apply to that right as it applies to the right described in that subsection; and every such existing enactment shall be construed accordingly.

(3)   In so far as any existing enactment provides (in whatever words) that in any proceedings other than criminal proceedings a person shall not be excused from answering any question or giving any evidence on the grounds that to do so may incriminate that person, that enactment shall be construed as providing also that in such proceedings a person shall not be excused from answering any question or giving any evidence on the ground that to do so may incriminate the husband or wife of that person.

(4)   Where any existing enactment (however worded) that—

(a)   confers powers of inspection or investigation; or

(b)   provides as mentioned in subsection (3) above,

further provides (in whatever words) that any answer or evidence given by a person shall not be admissible in evidence against that person in any proceedings or class of proceedings (however described, and whether criminal or not), that enactment shall be construed as providing also that any answer or evidence given by that person shall not be admissible in evidence against the husband or wife of that person in the proceedings or class of proceedings in question.

(5)   In this section 'existing enactment' means any enactment passed before this Act; and the references to giving evidence are references to giving evidence in any manner, whether by furnishing information, making discovery, producing documents or otherwise.

15.   (*Repealed by the Patents Act 1977, s. 132, Sch. 6.*)

16.   Abolition of certain privileges

(1)   The following rules of law are hereby abrogated except in relation to criminal proceedings, that is to say—

(a)   the rule whereby, in any legal proceedings, a person cannot be compelled to answer any question or produce any document or thing if to do so would tend to expose him to a forfeiture; and

(b)   the rule whereby, in any legal proceedings, a person other than a party to the proceedings cannot be compelled to produce any deed or other document relating to his title to any land.

(2)   The rule of law whereby, in any civil proceedings, a party to the proceedings cannot be compelled to produce any document relating solely to his own case and in no way tending to impeach that case or support the case of any opposing party is hereby abrogated.

(3)   Section 3 of the Evidence (Amendment) Act 1853 (which provides that a husband or wife shall not be compellable to disclose any communication made to him or her by his or her spouse during the marriage) shall cease to have effect except in relation to criminal proceedings.

(4)   In section 43(1) of the Matrimonial Causes Act 1965 (under which the evidence of a husband or wife is admissible in any proceedings to prove that marital intercourse did or did not take place between them during any period, but a husband or wife is not compellable in any proceedings to give evidence of the matters aforesaid), the words from 'but a husband or wife' to the end of the subsection shall cease to have effect except in relation to criminal proceedings.

(5)   A witness in any proceedings instituted in consequence of adultery, whether a party to the proceedings or not, shall not be excused from answering any question by reason that it tends to show that he or she has been guilty of adultery; . . .

17.   Consequential amendments relating to privilege

(1)   In relation to England and Wales—

(a)   section 1(3) of the Tribunals of Inquiry (Evidence) Act 1921 (under which a witness before a tribunal to which that Act has been applied is entitled to the same privileges as if he were a witness before the High Court) shall have effect as if after the word 'witness', in the second place where it occurs, there were inserted the words 'in civil proceedings'; and

(b)   section 8(5) of the Parliamentary Commissioner Act 1967 (which provides that, subject as there mentioned, no person shall be compelled for the purposes of an investigation under that Act to give any evidence or produce any document which he could not be compelled to give or produce in proceedings before the High Court) shall have effect as if before the word 'proceedings' there were inserted the word 'civil';

and, so far as it applies to England and Wales, any other existing enactment, however framed or worded, which in relation to any tribunal, investigation or inquiry (however described) confers on persons required to answer questions or give evidence any privilege described by reference to the privileges of witnesses in proceedings before any court shall, unless the contrary intention appears, be construed as referring to the privileges of witnesses in civil proceedings before that court.

(2)   . . .

(3)   Without prejudice to the generality of subsection (2) to (4) of section 14 of this Act, the enactments mentioned in the Schedule to this Act shall have effect subject to the amendments provided for by that Schedule (being verbal amendments to bring those enactments into conformity with the provisions of that section).

(4)   Subsection (5) of section 14 of this Act shall apply for the purposes of this section as it applies for the purposes of that section.

General

18.   General interpretation and savings

(1)   In this Act 'civil proceedings' includes, in addition to civil proceedings in any of the ordinary courts of law—

(a)   civil proceedings before any other tribunal, being proceedings in relation to which the strict rules of evidence apply; and

(b)   an arbitration or reference, whether under an enactment or not,

but does not include civil proceedings in relation to which the strict rules of evidence do not apply.

(2)   In this Act—

'court' does not include a court-martial, and, in relation to an arbitration or reference, means the arbitrator or umpire and, in relation to proceedings before a tribunal (not being one of the ordinary courts of law), means the tribunal;

'legal proceedings' includes an arbitration or reference, whether under an enactment or not;

and for the avoidance of doubt it is hereby declared that in this Act, and in any amendment made by this Act in any other enactment, references to a person's husband or wife do not include references to a person who is no longer married to that person.

(3)   Any reference in this Act to any other enactment is a reference thereto as amended, and includes a reference thereto as applied, by or under any other enactment.

(4)   Nothing in this Act shall prejudice the operation of any enactment which provides (in whatever words) that any answer or evidence given by a person in specified circumstances shall not be admissible in evidence against him or some other person in any proceedings or class of proceedings (however described).

In this subsection the reference to giving evidence is a reference to giving evidence in any manner, whether by furnishing information, making discovery, producing documents or otherwise.

(5)   Nothing in this Act shall prejudice—

(a)   any power of a court, in any legal proceedings, to exclude evidence (whether by preventing questions from being put or otherwise) at its discretion; or

(b)   the operation of any agreement (whenever made) between the parties to any legal proceedings as to the evidence which is to be admissible (whether generally or for any particular purpose) in those proceedings.

(6)   It is hereby declared that where, by reason of any defect of speech or hearing from which he is suffering, a person called as a witness in any legal proceedings gives his evidence in writing or by signs, that evidence is to be treated for the purposes of this Act as being given orally.

19.   (*Repealed by the Northern Ireland Constitution Act 1973, s. 41, Sch. 6, Pt. I.*)

20.   Short title, repeals, extent and commencement

This Act may be cited as the Civil Evidence Act 1968.

(2)   . . .

(3)   This Act shall not extend to Scotland or, . . . to Northern Ireland.

FAMILY LAW REFORM ACT 1969
(1969, c. 46)

PART III
PROVISIONS FOR USE OF SCIENTIFIC TESTS IN DETERMINING PARENTAGE

20.   Power of court to require use of scientific tests

(1)   In any civil proceedings in which the parentage of any person falls to be determined, the court may, either of its own motion or on an application by any party to the proceedings, give a direction —

(a)   for the use of scientific tests to ascertain whether such tests show that a party to the proceedings is or is not the father or mother of that person; and

(b)   for the taking, within a period specified in the direction, of bodily samples from all or any of the following, namely, that person, any party who is alleged to be the father or mother of that person and any other party to the proceedings;
and the court may at any time revoke or vary a direction previously given by it under this subsection.

(1A)   An application for a direction under this section shall specify who is to carry out the tests.

(1B)   A direction under this section shall—

(a)   specify, as the person who is to carry out the tests, the person specified in the application; or

(b)   where the court considers that it would be inappropriate to specify that person (whether because to specify him would be incompatible with any provision made by or under regulations made under section 22 of this Act or for any other reason), decline to give the direction applied for.

(2)   The person responsible for carrying out scientific tests in pursuance of a direction under subsection (1) above shall make to the court a report in which he shall state —

(a)   the results of the tests;

(b)   whether any party to whom the report relates is or is not excluded by the results from being the father or mother of the person whose parentage is to be determined; and

(c)   in relation to any party who is not so excluded, the value, if any, of the results in determining whether that party is the father or mother of that person;
and the report shall be received by the court as evidence in the proceedings of the matters stated in it.

(2A)   Where the proceedings in which the parentage of any person falls to be determined are proceedings on an application under section 56 of the Family Law Act 1986, any reference in subsection (1) or (2) of this section to any party to the proceedings shall include a reference to any person named in the application.

(3)   A report under subsection (2) of this section shall be in the form prescribed by regulations made under section 22 of this Act.

(4)   Where a report has been made to a court under subsection (2) of this section, any party may, with the leave of the court, or shall, if the court so directs, obtain from the person who made the report a written statement explaining or amplifying any statement made in the report, and that statement shall be deemed for the purposes of this section (except subsection (3) thereof) to form part of the report made to the court.

21.   Consents, etc., required for taking of bodily samples

(1)   Subject to the provisions of subsection (3) and (4) of this section, a bodily sample which is required to be taken from any person for the purpose of giving effect to a direction under section 20 of this Act shall not be taken from that person except with his consent.

(2)   The consent of a minor who has attained the age of sixteen years to the taking from himself of a bodily sample shall be as effective as it would be if he were of full age; and where a minor has by virtue of this subsection given an effective consent to the taking of a bodily sample it shall not be necessary to obtain any consent for it from any other person.

(3)   A bodily sample may be taken from a person under the age of sixteen years, not being such a person as is referred to in subsection (4) of this section, if the person who has the care and control of him consents.

(4)   A bodily sample may be taken from a person who is suffering from mental disorder within the meaning of [the Mental Health Act 1983] and is incapable of understanding the nature and purpose of scientific tests if the person who has the care

and control of him consents and the medical practitioner in whose care he is has certified that the taking of a bodily sample from him will not be prejudicial to his proper care and treatment.

(5)   The foregoing provisions of this section are without prejudice to the provisions of section 23 of this Act.

23.   Failure to comply with direction for taking bodily tests

(1)   Where a court gives a direction under section 20 of this Act and any person fails to take any step required of him for the purpose of giving effect to the direction, the court may draw such inferences, if any, for that fact as appear proper in the circumstances.

(2)   Where in any proceedings in which the parentage of any person falls to be determined by the court hearing the proceedings there is a presumption of law that that person is legitimate, then if—

(a)   a direction is given under section 20 of this Act in those proceedings, and

(b)   any party who is claiming any relief in the proceedings and who for the purpose of obtaining that relief is entitled to rely on the presumption fails to take any step required of him for the purpose of giving effect to the direction,

the court may adjourn the hearing for such period as it thinks fit to enable that party to take that step, and if at the end of that period he has failed without reasonable cause to take it the court may, without prejudice to subsection (1) of this section, dismiss his claim for relief notwithstanding the absence of evidence to rebut the presumption.

(3)   Where any person named in a direction under section 20 of this Act fails to consent to the taking of a bodily sample from himself or from any person named in the direction of whom he has the care and control, he shall be deemed for the purposes of this section to have failed to take a step required of him for the purpose of giving effect to the direction.

24.   Penalty for personating another, etc., for purpose of providing bodily sample

If for the purpose of providing a bodily sample for a test required to give effect to a direction under section 20 of this Act any person personates another, or proffers a child knowing that it is not the child named in the direction, he shall be liable—

(a)   on conviction on indictment, to imprisonment for a term not exceeding two years, or

(b)   on summary conviction, to a fine not exceeding [the prescribed sum].

25.   Interpretation of Part III

In this Part of this Act the following expressions have the meanings hereby respectively assigned to them, that is to say—

'bodily sample' means a sample of bodily fluid or bodily tissue taken for the purpose of scientific tests;

'excluded' means excluded subject to the occurrence of mutation. . . .

'scientific tests' means scientific tests carried out under this Part of the Act and made with the object of ascertaining the inheritable characteristics of bodily fluids or bodily tissue.

PART IV
MISCELLANEOUS AND GENERAL

26.   Rebuttal of presumption as to legitimacy and illegitimacy

Any presumption of law as to the legitimacy or illegitimacy of any person may in any civil proceedings be rebutted by evidence which shows that it is more probable than not that that person is illegitimate or legitimate, as the case may be, and it shall not be necessary to prove that fact beyond reasonable doubt in order to rebut the presumption.

CIVIL EVIDENCE ACT 1972
(1972, c. 30)

2.   Rules of court with respect to expert reports and oral expert evidence
    (3)   Notwithstanding any enactment or rule of law by virtue of which documents prepared for the purpose of pending or contemplated civil proceedings or in connection with the obtaining or giving of legal advice or in certain circumstances privileged from disclosure, provision may be made by rules of court—
    (a)   for enabling the court in any civil proceedings to direct, with respect to medical matters or matters of any other class which may be specified in the direction, that the parties or some of them shall each by such date as may be so specified (or such later date as may be permitted or agreed in accordance with the rules) disclose to the other or others in the form of one or more expert reports the expert evidence on matters of that class which he proposes to adduce as part of his case at the trial; and
    (b)   for prohibiting a party who fails to comply with a direction given in any such proceedings under rules of court made by virtue of paragraph (a) above from adducing in evidence, except with the leave of the court, any statement (whether of fact or opinion) contained in any expert report whatsoever in so far as the statement deals with matters of any class specified in the direction.
    (4)   Provision may be made by rules of court as to the conditions subject to which oral expert evidence may be given in civil proceedings.
    (5)   Without prejudice to the generality of subsection (4) above, rules of court made in pursuance of that subsection may make provision for prohibiting a party who fails to comply with a direction given as mentioned in subsection (3)(b) above from adducing, except with the leave of the court, any oral expert evidence whatsoever with respect to matters of any class specified in the direction.
    (6)   Any rules of court made in pursuance of this section may make different provision for different classes of cases, for expert reports dealing with matters of different classes, and for other different circumstances.
    (7)   References in this section to an expert report are references to a written report by a person dealing wholly or mainly with matters on which he is (or would if living be) qualified to give expert evidence.
    (8)   Nothing in the foregoing provisions of this section shall prejudice the generality of … [section 75 of the County Courts Act 1984], [section 144 of the Magistrates' Courts Act 1980] or any other enactment conferring power to make rules of court; and nothing in … [section 75(2) of the County Courts Act 1984] or any other enactment restricting the matters with respect to which rules of court may be made shall prejudice the making of rules of court in pursuance of this section or the operation of any rules of court so made.

3.   Admissibility of expert opinion and certain expressions of non-expert opinion
    (1)   Subject to any rules of court made in pursuance of this Act, where a person is called as a witness in any civil proceedings, his opinion on any relevant matter on which he is qualified to give expert evidence shall be admissible in evidence.
    (2)   It is hereby declared that where a person is called as a witness in any civil proceedings, a statement or opinion by him on any relevant matter on which he is not qualified to give expert evidence, if made as a way of conveying relevant facts personally perceived by him, is admissible as evidence of what he perceived.
    (3)   In this section 'relevant matter' includes an issue in the proceedings in question.

4.   Evidence of foreign law
    (1)   It is hereby declared that in civil proceedings a person who is suitably qualified to do so on account of his knowledge or experience is competent to give expert evidence

as to the law of any country or territory outside the United Kingdom, or of any part of the United Kingdom other than England and Wales, irrespective of whether he has acted or is entitled to act as a legal practitioner there.

(2) Where any question as to the law of any country or territory outside the United Kingdom, or of any part of the United Kingdom other than England and Wales, with respect to any matter has been determined (whether before or after the passing of this Act) in any such proceedings as are mentioned in subsection (4) below, then in any civil proceedings (not being proceedings before a court which can take judicial notice of the law of that country, territory or part with respect to that matter)—

(a) any finding made or decision given on that question in the first-mentioned proceedings shall, if reported or recorded in citable form, be admissible in evidence for the purpose of proving the law of that country, territory or part with respect to that matter; and

(b) if that finding or decision, as so reported or recorded, is adduced for that purpose, the law of that country, territory or part with respect to that matter shall be taken to be in accordance with that finding or decision unless the contrary is proved:

Provided that paragraph (b) above shall not apply in the case of a finding or decision which conflicts with another finding or decision on the same question adduced by virtue of this subsection in the same proceedings.

(3) Except with the leave of the court, a party to any civil proceedings shall not be permitted to adduce any such finding or decision as is mentioned in subsection (2) above by virtue of that subsection unless he has in accordance with rules of court given to every other party to the proceedings notice that he intends to do so.

(4) The proceedings referred to in subsection (2) above are the following, whether civil or criminal, namely—

(a) proceedings at first instance in any of the following courts, namely the High Court, the Crown Court, a court of quarter sessions, the Court of Chancery of the county palatine of Lancaster and the Court of Chancery of the county palatine of Durham;

(b) appeals arising out of any such proceedings as are mentioned in paragraph (a) above;

(c) proceedings before the Judicial Committee of the Privy Council on appeal (whether to Her Majesty in Council or to the Judicial Committee as such) from any decision of any court outside the United Kingdom.

(5) For the purposes of this section a finding or decision on any such question as is mentioned in subsection (2) above shall be taken to be reported or recorded in citable form, if, but only if, it is reported or recorded in writing in a report, transcript or other document which, if that question had been a question as to the law of England and Wales, could be cited as an authority in legal proceedings in England and Wales.

5. Interpretation, application to arbitrations etc. and savings

(3) Nothing in this Act shall prejudice—

(a) any power of a court, in any civil proceedings, to exclude evidence (whether by preventing questions from being put or otherwise) at its discretion; or

(b) the operation of any agreement (whenever made) between the parties to any civil proceedings as to the evidence which is to be admissible (whether generally or for any particular purpose) in those proceedings.

6. Short title, extent and commencement

(1) This Act may be cited as the Civil Evidence Act 1972.

(2) This Act shall not extend to Scotland or Northern Ireland.

MATRIMONIAL CAUSES ACT 1973
(1973, c. 18)

19. (1) Any married person who alleges that reasonable grounds exist for supposing that the other party to the marriage is dead may present a petition to the court to have it presumed that the other party is dead and to have the marriage dissolved, and the court may, if satisfied that such reasonable grounds exist, grant a decree of presumption of death and dissolution of the marriage.

(3) In any proceedings under this section the fact that for a period of seven years or more the other party to the marriage has been continually absent from the petitioner and the petitioner has no reason to believe that the other party has been living within that time shall be evidence that the other party is dead until the contrary is proved.

48. (1) The evidence of a husband or wife shall be admissible in any proceedings to prove that marital intercourse did or did not take place between them during any period.

(2) In any proceedings for nullity of marriage, evidence on the question of sexual capacity shall be heard in camera unless in any case the judge is satisfied that in the interests of justice any such evidence ought to be heard in open court.

SOLICITORS ACT 1974
(1974, c. 47)

18. (1) Any list purporting to be published by authority of the Society and to contain the names of solicitors who have obtained practising certificates for the current year before 2nd January in that year shall, until the contrary is proved, be evidence that the persons so named as solicitors holding practising certificates for the current year are solicitors holding such certificates.

(2) The absence from any such list of the name of any person shall, until the contrary is proved, be evidence that that person is not qualified to practise as a solicitor under a certificate for the current year, but in the case of any such person an extract from the roll certified as correct by the Society shall be evidence of the facts appearing in the extract.

SEX DISCRIMINATION ACT 1975
(1975, c. 65)

74. Help for aggrieved persons in obtaining information etc.

(1) With a view to helping a person ('the person aggrieved') who considers he may have been discriminated against in contravention of this Act to decide whether to institute proceedings and, if he does so, to formulate and present his case in the most effective manner, the Secretary of State shall by order prescribe—

(a) forms by which the person aggrieved may question the respondent on his reasons for doing any relevant act, or on any other matter which is or may be relevant;

(b) forms by which the respondent may if he so wishes reply to any questions.

(2) Where the person aggrieved questions the respondent (whether in accordance with an order under subsection (1) or not)—

(a) the question, and any reply by the respondent (whether in accordance with such an order or not) shall, subject to the following provisions of this section, be admissible as evidence in the proceedings;

(b) if it appears to the court or tribunal that the respondent deliberately, and without reasonable excuse omitted to reply within a reasonable period or that his reply is evasive or equivocal, the court or tribunal may draw any inference from that fact that it considers it just and equitable to draw, including an inference that he committed an unlawful act.

(3)   The Secretary of State may by order—

(a)   prescribe the period within which questions must be duly served in order to be admissible under subsection (2)(a), and

(b)   prescribe the manner in which a question, and any reply by the respondent, may be duly served.

(4)   Rules may enable the court entertaining a claim under section 66 to determine, before the date fixed for the hearing of the claim, whether a question or reply is admissible under this section or not.

(5)   This section is without prejudice to any other enactment or rule of law regulating interlocutory and preliminary matters in proceedings before a county court, sheriff court or industrial tribunal, and has effect subject to any enactment or rule of law regulating the admissibility of evidence in such proceedings.

(6)   In this section 'respondent' includes a prospective respondent and 'rules'—

(a)   in relation to county court proceedings, means county court rules;

(b)   (*applies to Scotland only.*)

SOCIAL SECURITY ACT 1975
(1975, c. 14)

50.   (1)   Subject to the provisions of this Act, where an employed earner suffers personal injury caused after 4th July 1948 by accident arising out of and in the course of his employment, being employed earner's employment, there shall be payable to or in respect of him the industrial injuries benefits specified below in this section.

(2)   The benefits are—

(a)   injury benefit, payable to the earner in accordance with section 56 below if during the period specified in subsection (4) of that section he is, as the result of the injury, incapable of work;

(b)   disablement benefit (by way of gratuity or pension), payable to the earner in accordance with sections 57 to 63 below if he suffers, as the result of the injury, from loss of physical or mental faculty;

(c)   industrial death benefit, payable in accordance with sections 67 to 75 below to the person specified in those sections, if the earner dies as a result of the injury.

(3)   For the purposes of this Chapter, an accident arising in the course of an employed earner's employment shall be deemed, in the absence of evidence to the contrary, also to have arisen out of that employment.

(4)   Regulations may provide for treating an employed earner for the purposes of this Chapter as incapable of work as the result of an accident or injury when he would not be so treated apart from the regulations, and may also make provision—

(a)   as to the days which, in the case of an employed earner who at any time is or is to be treated as incapable of work as the result of an accident or injury, are or are not to be treated for the purposes of industrial injuries benefit as days of incapacity for work; and

(b)   as to the day which, in the case of night workers and other special cases, is to be treated for the purpose of such benefit as the day of the accident.

(5)   Subject to sections 129, 131 and 132 of this Act (Mariners, airmen, continental shelf workers and others), industrial injuries benefit shall not be payable in respect of an accident happening while the earner is outside Great Britain.

PATENTS ACT 1977
(1977, c. 37)

100. (1) If the invention for which a patent is granted is a process for obtaining a new product, the same product produced by a person other than the proprietor of the patent or a licensee of his shall, unless the contrary is proved, be taken in any proceedings to have been obtained by that process.

(2) In considering whether a party has discharged the burden imposed upon him by this section, the court shall not require him to disclose any manufacturing or commercial secrets if it appears to the court that it would be unreasonable to do so.

SUPREME COURT ACT 1981
(1981, c. 54)

69. (5) Where for the purpose of disposing of any action or other matter which is being tried in the High Court by a judge with a jury it is necessary to ascertain the law of any other country which is applicable to the facts of the case, any question as to the effect of the evidence given with respect to that law shall, instead of being submitted to the jury, be decided by the judge alone.

72. (1) In any proceedings to which this subsection applies a person shall not be excused, by reason that to do so would tend to expose that person, or his or her spouse, to proceedings for a related offence or for the recovery of a related penalty—

(a) from answering any question put to that person in the first mentioned proceedings; or

(b) from complying with any order made in those proceedings.

(2) Subsection (1) applies to the following civil proceedings in the High Court, namely—

(a) proceedings for infringement of rights pertaining to any intellectual property or for passing off;

(b) proceedings brought to obtain disclosure of information relating to any infringement of such rights or to any passing off; and

(c) proceedings brought to prevent any apprehended infringement of such rights or any apprehended passing off.

(3) Subject to subsection (4), no statement or admission made by a person—

(a) in answering a question put to him in any proceedings to which subsection (2) applies; or

(b) in complying with any order made in any such proceedings, shall, in proceedings for any related offence or for the recovery of any related penalty, be admissible in evidence against that person or (unless they married after the making of the statement or admission) against the spouse of that person.

(4) Nothing in subsection (3) shall render any statement or admission made by a person as there mentioned inadmissible in evidence against that person in proceedings for perjury or contempt of court.

(5) In this section—

'intellectual property' means any patent, trade mark, copyright, registered design, technical or commercial information or other intellectual property;

'related offence,' in relation to any proceedings to which subsection (1) applies, means—

(a) in the case of proceedings within subsection (2)(a) or (b)—

(i) any offence committed by or in the course of the infringement or passing off to which those proceedings relate; or

(ii)   any offence not within sub-paragraph (i) committed in connection with that infringement or passing off, being an offence involving fraud or dishonesty;

(b)   in the case of proceedings within subsection (2)(c), any offence revealed by the facts on which the plaintiff relies in those proceedings;

'related penalty,' in relation to any proceedings to which subsection (1) applies means—

(a)   in the case of proceedings within subsection (2)(a) or (b), any penalty incurred in respect of anything done or omitted in connection with the infringement or passing of to which those proceedings relate;

(b)   in the case of proceedings within subsection (2)(c), any penalty incurred in respect of any act or omission revealed by the facts on which the plaintiff relies in those proceedings.

(6)   Any reference in this section to civil proceedings in the High Court of any description includes a reference to proceedings on appeal arising out of civil proceedings in the High Court of that description.

CIVIL JURISDICTION AND JUDGMENTS ACT 1982
(1982, c. 27)

32.   Overseas judgments given in proceedings brought in breach of agreement for settlement of dispute

(1)   Subject to the following provisions of this section, a judgment given by a court of an overseas country in any proceedings shall not be recognised or enforced in the United Kingdom if—

(a)   the bringing of those proceedings in that court was contrary to an agreement under which the dispute in question was to be settled otherwise than by proceedings in the courts of that country; and

(b)   those proceedings were not brought in that court by, or with the agreement of, the person against whom the judgment was given; and

(c)   that person did not counterclaim in the proceedings or otherwise submit to the jurisdiction of that court.

(2)   Subsection (1) does not apply where the agreement referred to in paragraph (a) of that subsection was illegal, void or unenforceable or was incapable of being performed for reasons not attributable to the fault of the party bringing the proceedings in which the judgment was given.

(3)   In determining whether a judgment given by a court of an overseas country should be recognised or enforced in the United Kingdom, a court in the United Kingdom shall not be bound by any decision of the overseas court relating to any of the matters mentioned in subsection (1) or (2).

(4)   Nothing in subsection (1) shall affect the recognition or enforcement in the United Kingdom of—

(a)   a judgment which is required to be recognised or enforced there under the 1968 Convention;

(b)   a judgment to which Part I of the Foreign Judgments (Reciprocal Enforcement) Act 1933 applies by virtue of section 4 of the Carriage of Goods by Road Act 1965, section 17(4) of the Nuclear Installations Act 1965, section 13(3) of the Merchant Shipping (Oil Pollution) Act 1971, [section 6 of the International Transport Conventions Act 1983], section 5 of the Carriage of Passengers by Road Act 1974 or section 6(4) of the Merchant Shipping Act 1974.

CIVIL EVIDENCE ACT 1995
(1995, c. 38)

Admissibility of hearsay evidence

1. Admissibility of hearsay evidence

(1) In civil proceedings evidence shall not be excluded on the ground that it is hearsay.

(2) In this Act—

(a) 'hearsay' means a statement made otherwise than by a person while giving oral evidence in the proceedings which is tendered as evidence of the matters stated; and

(b) references to hearsay include hearsay of whatever degree.

(3) Nothing in this Act affects the admissibility of evidence admissible apart from this section.

(4) The provisions of sections 2 to 6 (safeguards and supplementary provisions relating to hearsay evidence) do not apply in relation to hearsay evidence admissible apart from this section, notwithstanding that it may also be admissible by virtue of this section.

Safeguards in relation to hearsay evidence

2. Notice of proposal to adduce hearsay evidence

(1) A party proposing to adduce hearsay evidence in civil proceedings shall, subject to the following provisions of this section, give to the other party or parties to the proceedings—

(a) such notice (if any) of that fact, and

(b) on request, such particulars of or relating to the evidence,

as is reasonable and practicable in the circumstances for the purpose of enabling him or them to deal with any matters arising from its being hearsay.

(2) Provision may be made by rules of court—

(a) specifying classes of proceedings or evidence in relation to which subsection (1) does not apply, and

(b) as to the manner in which (including the time within which) the duties imposed by that subsection are to be complied with in the cases where it does apply.

(3) Subsection (1) may also be excluded by agreement of the parties; and compliance with the duty to give notice may in any case be waived by the person to whom notice is required to be given.

(4) A failure to comply with subsection (1), or with rules under subsection (2)(b), does not affect the admissibility of the evidence but may be taken into account by the court—

(a) in considering the exercise of its powers with respect to the course of proceedings and costs, and

(b) as a matter adversely affecting the weight to be given to the evidence in accordance with section 4.

3. Power to call witness for cross-examination on hearsay statement

Rules of court may provide that where a party to civil proceedings adduces hearsay evidence of a statement made by a person and does not call that person as a witness, any other party to the proceedings may, with the leave of the court, call that person as a witness and cross-examine him on the statement as if he had been called by the first-mentioned party and as if the hearsay statement were his evidence in chief.

4. Considerations relevant to weighing of hearsay evidence

(1) In estimating the weight (if any) to be given to hearsay evidence in civil proceedings the court shall have regard to any circumstances from which any inference can reasonably be drawn as to the reliability or otherwise of the evidence.

(2)   Regard may be had, in particular, to the following—

(a)   whether it would have been reasonable and practicable for the party by whom the evidence was adduced to have produced the maker of the original statement as a witness;

(b)   whether the original statement was made contemporaneously with the occurrence or existence of the matters stated;

(c)   whether the evidence involves multiple hearsay;

(d)   whether any person involved had any motive to conceal or misrepresent matters;

(e)   whether the original statement was an edited account, or was made in collaboration with another or for a particular purpose;

(f)   whether the circumstances in which the evidence is adduced as hearsay are such as to suggest an attempt to prevent proper evaluation of its weight.

Supplementary provisions as to hearsay evidence

5. Competence and credibility

(1)   Hearsay evidence shall not be admitted in civil proceedings if or to the extent that it is shown to consist of, or to be proved by means of, a statement made by a person who at the time he made the statement was not competent as a witness.

For this purpose 'not competent as a witness' means suffering from such mental or physical infirmity, or lack of understanding, as would render a person incompetent as a witness in civil proceedings; but a child shall be treated as competent as a witness if he satisfies the requirements of section 96(2)(a) and (b) of the Children Act 1989 (conditions for reception of unsworn evidence of child).

(2)   Where in civil proceedings hearsay evidence is adduced and the maker of the original statement, or of any statement relied upon to prove another statement, is not called as a witness—

(a)   evidence which if he had been so called would be admissible for the purpose of attacking or supporting his credibility as a witness is admissible for that purpose in the proceedings; and

(b)   evidence tending to prove that, whether before or after he made the statement, he made any other statement inconsistent with it is admissible for the purpose of showing that he had contradicted himself.

Provided that evidence may not be given of any matter of which, if he had been called as a witness and had denied that matter in cross-examination, evidence could not have been adduced by the cross-examining party.

6. Previous statements of witnesses

(1)   Subject as follows, the provisions of this Act as to hearsay evidence in civil proceedings apply equally (but with any necessary modifications) in relation to a previous statement made by a person called as a witness in the proceedings.

(2)   A party who has called or intends to call a person as a witness in civil proceedings may not in those proceedings adduce evidence of a previous statement made by that person, except—

(a)   with the leave of the court, or

(b)   for the purpose of rebutting a suggestion that his evidence has been fabricated.

This shall not be construed as preventing a witness statement (that is, a written statement of oral evidence which a party to the proceedings intends to lead) from being adopted by a witness in giving evidence or treated as his evidence.

(3)   Where in the case of civil proceedings section 3, 4 or 5 of the Criminal Procedure Act 1865 applies, which make provision as to—

(a)   how far a witness may be discredited by the party producing him,

(b)   the proof of contradictory statements made by a witness, and

(c)   cross-examination as to previous statements in writing,
this Act does not authorise the adducing of evidence of a previous inconsistent or
contradictory statement otherwise than in accordance with those sections.

This is without prejudice to any provision made by rules of court under section 3
above (power to call witness for cross-examination on hearsay statement).

(4)   Nothing in this Act affects any of the rules of law as to the circumstances in
which, where a person called as a witness in civil proceedings is cross-examined on a
document used by him to refresh his memory, that document may be made evidence in
the proceedings.

(5)   Nothing in this section shall be construed as preventing a statement of any
description referred to above from being admissible by virtue of section 1 as evidence of
the matters stated.

7.   Evidence formerly admissible at common law

(1)   The common law rule effectively preserved by section 9(1) and (2)(a) of the
Civil Evidence Act 1968 (admissibility of admissions adverse to a party) is superseded
by the provisions of this Act.

(2)   The common law rules effectively preserved by section 9(1) and (2)(b) to (d) of
the Civil Evidence Act 1968, that is, any rule of law whereby in civil proceedings—
(a)   published works dealing with matters of a public nature (for example,
histories, scientific works, dictionaries and maps) are admissible as evidence of facts of
a public nature stated in them,
(b)   public documents (for example, public registers, and returns made under
public authority with respect to matters of public interest) are admissible as evidence of
facts stated in them, or
(c)   records (for example, the records of certain courts, treaties, Crown grants,
pardons and commissions) are admissible as evidence of facts stated in them,
shall continue to have effect.

(3)   The common law rules effectively preserved by section 9(3) and (4) of the Civil
Evidence Act 1968, that is, any rule of law whereby in civil proceedings—
(a)   evidence of a person's reputation is admissible for the purpose of proving his
good or bad character, or
(b)   evidence of reputation or family tradition is admissible—
(i)   for the purpose of proving or disproving pedigree or the existence of a
marriage, or
(ii)   for the purpose of proving or disproving the existence of any public or
general right or of identifying any person or thing,
shall continue to have effect in so far as they authorise the court to treat such evidence
as proving or disproving that matter.

Where any such rule applies, reputation or family tradition shall be treated for the
purposes of this Act as a fact and not as a statement or multiplicity of statements about
the matter in question.

(4)   The words in which a rule of law mentioned in this section is described are
intended only to identify the rule and shall not be construed as altering it in any way.

Other matters

8.   Proof of statements contained in documents

(1)   Where a statement contained in a document is admissible as evidence in civil
proceedings, it may be proved—
(a)   by the production of that document, or
(b)   whether or not that document is still in existence, by the production of a copy
of that document or of the material part of it,
authenticated in such manner as the court may approve.

(2)   It is immaterial for this purpose how many removes there are between a copy and the original.

9.   Proof of records of business or public authority

(1)   A document which is shown to form part of the records of a business or public authority may be received in evidence in civil proceedings without further proof.

(2)   A document shall be taken to form part of the records of a business or public authority if there is produced to the court a certificate to that effect signed by an officer of the business or authority to which the records belong.

For this purpose—

(a)   a document purporting to be a certificate signed by an officer of a business or public authority shall be deemed to have been duly given by such an officer and signed by him; and

(b)   a certificate shall be treated as signed by a person if it purports to bear a facsimile of his signature.

(3)   The absence of an entry in the records of a business or public authority may be proved in civil proceedings by affidavit of an officer of the business or authority to which the records belong.

(4)   In this section—

'records' means records in whatever form;

'business' includes any activity regularly carried on over a period of time, whether for profit or not, by any body (whether corporate or not) or by an individual;

'officer' includes any person occupying a responsible position in relation to the relevant activities of the business or public authority or in relation to its records; and

'public authority' includes any public or statutory undertaking, any government department and any person holding office under Her Majesty.

(5)   The court may, having regard to the circumstances of the case, direct that all or any of the above provisions of this section do not apply in relation to a particular document or record, or description of documents or records.

10.   Admissibility and proof of Ogden Tables

(1)   The actuarial tables (together with explanatory notes) for use in personal injury and fatal accident cases issued from time to time by the Government Actuary's Department are admissible in evidence for the purpose of assessing, in an action for personal injury, the sum to be awarded as general damages for future pecuniary loss.

(2)   They may be proved by the production of a copy published by Her Majesty's Stationery Office.

(3)   For the purposes of this section—

(a)   'personal injury' includes any disease and any impairment of a person's physical or mental condition; and

(b)   'action for personal injury' includes an action brought by virtue of the Law Reform (Miscellaneous Provisions) Act 1934 or the Fatal Accidents Act 1976.

General

11.   Meaning of 'civil proceedings'

In this Act 'civil proceedings' means civil proceedings, before any tribunal, in relation to which the strict rules of evidence apply, whether as a matter of law or by agreement of the parties.

References to 'the court' and 'rules of court' shall be construed accordingly.

12. Provisions as to rules of court

(1) Any power to make rules of court regulating the practice or procedure of the court in relation to civil proceedings includes power to make such provision as may be necessary or expedient for carrying into effect the provisions of this Act.

(2) Any rules of court made for the purposes of this Act as it applies in relation to proceedings in the High Court apply, except in so far as their operation is excluded by agreement, to arbitration proceedings to which this Act applies, subject to such modifications as may be appropriate.

Any question arising as to what modifications are appropriate shall be determined, in default of agreement, by the arbitrator or umpire, as the case may be.

13. Interpretation

In this Act—

'civil proceedings' has the meaning given by section 11 and 'court' and 'rules of court' shall be construed in accordance with that section;

'document' means anything in which information of any description is recorded, and 'copy', in relation to a document, means anything onto which information recorded in the document has been copied, by whatever means and whether directly or indirectly;

'hearsay' shall be construed in accordance with section 1(2);

'oral evidence' includes evidence which, by reason of a defect of speech or hearing, a person called as a witness gives in writing or by signs;

'the original statement', in relation to hearsay evidence, means the underlying statement (if any) by—

(a) in the case of evidence of fact, a person having personal knowledge of the fact, or

(b) in the case of evidence of opinion, the person whose opinion it is; and

'statement' means any representation of fact or opinion, however made.

14. Savings

(1) Nothing in this Act affects the exclusion of evidence on grounds other than that it is hearsay.

This applies whether the evidence falls to be excluded in pursuance of any enactment or rule of law, for failure to comply with rules of court or an order of the court, or otherwise.

(2) Nothing in this Act affects the proof of documents by means other than those specified in section 8 or 9.

(3) Nothing in this Act affects the operation of the following enactments—

(a) section 2 of the Documentary Evidence Act 1868 (mode of proving certain official documents);

(b) section 2 of the Documentary Evidence Act 1882 (documents printed under the superintendence of Stationery Office);

(c) section 1 of the Evidence (Colonial Statutes) Act 1907 (proof of statutes of certain legislatures);

(d) section 1 of the Evidence (Foreign, Dominion and Colonial Documents) Act 1933 (proof and effect of registers and official certificates of certain countries);

(e) section 5 of the Oaths and Evidence (Overseas Authorities and Countries) Act 1963 (provision in respect of public registers of other countries).

16. Short title, commencement and extent

(1) This Act may be cited as the Civil Evidence Act 1995.

(2) The provisions of this Act come into force on such day as the Lord Chancellor may appoint by order made by statutory instrument, and different days may be appointed for different provisions and for different purposes.

(3)   An order under subsection (2) may contain such transitional provisions as appear to the Lord Chancellor to be appropriate; and subject to any such provision, the provisions of this Act shall not apply in relation to proceedings begun before commencement.

(4)   This Act extends to England and Wales.

(5)   Section 10 (admissibility and proof of Ogden Tables) also extends to Northern Ireland.

As it extends to Northern Ireland, the following shall be substituted for subsection (3)(b)—

(b) 'action for personal injury' includes an action brought by virtue of the Law Reform (Miscellaneous Provisions) (Northern Ireland) Act 1937 or the Fatal Accidents (Northern Ireland) Order 1977.

(6)   The provisions of Schedule 1 and 2 (consequential amendments and repeals) have the same extent as the enactments respectively amended or repealed.

CIVIL PROCEDURE RULES 1998

CPR PART 32 EVIDENCE

CONTENTS OF THIS PART

32.1   POWER OF COURT TO CONTROL EVIDENCE

(1)   The court may control the evidence by giving directions as to—

(a)   the issues on which it requires evidence;

(b)   the nature of the evidence which it requires to decide those issues; and

(c)   the way in which the evidence is to be placed before the court.

(2)   The court may use its power under this rule to exclude evidence that would otherwise be admissible.

(3)   The court may limit cross-examination.

32.2 EVIDENCE OF WITNESSES — GENERAL RULE

(1) The general rule is that any fact which needs to be proved by the evidence of witnesses is to be proved—

(a) at trial, by their oral evidence given in public; and

(b) at any other hearing, by their evidence in writing.

(2) This is subject—

(a) to any provision to the contrary contained in these Rules or elsewhere; or

(b) to any order of the court.

32.3 EVIDENCE BY VIDEO LINK OR OTHER MEANS

The court may allow a witness to give evidence through a video link or by other means.

32.4 REQUIREMENT TO SERVE WITNESS STATEMENTS FOR USE AT TRIAL

(1) A witness statement is a written statement signed by a person which contains the evidence which that person would be allowed to give orally.

(2) The court will order a party to serve on the other parties any witness statement of the oral evidence which the party serving the statement intends to rely on in relation to any issues of fact to be decided at the trial.

(3) The court may give directions as to—

(a) the order in which witness statements are to be served; and

(b) whether or not the witness statements are to be filed.

32.5 USE AT TRIAL OF WITNESS STATEMENTS WHICH HAVE BEEN SERVED

(1) If—

(a) a party has served a witness statement; and

(b) he wishes to rely at trial on the evidence of the witness who made the statement,

he must call the witness to give oral evidence unless the court orders otherwise or he puts the statement in as hearsay evidence.

(Part 33 contains provisions about hearsay evidence)

(2) Where a witness is called to give oral evidence under paragraph (1), his witness statement shall stand as his evidence in chief unless the court orders otherwise.

(3) A witness giving oral evidence at trial may with the permission of the court—

(a) amplify his witness statement; and

(b) give evidence in relation to new matters which have arisen since the witness statement was served on the other parties.

(4) The court will give permission under paragraph (3) only if it considers that there is good reason not to confine the evidence of the witness to the contents of his witness statement.

(5) If a party who has served a witness statement does not—

(a) call the witness to give evidence at trial; or

(b) put the witness statement in as hearsay evidence,

any other party may put the witness statement in as hearsay evidence.

32.6 EVIDENCE IN PROCEEDINGS OTHER THAN AT TRIAL

(1) Subject to paragraph (2), the general rule is that evidence at hearings other than the trial is to be by witness statement unless the court, a practice direction or any other enactment requires otherwise.

(2) At hearings other than the trial, a party may rely on the matters set out in—

(a) his statement of case; or

(b) his application notice,

if the statement of case or application notice is verified by a statement of truth.

32.7   ORDER FOR CROSS-EXAMINATION

(1)   Where, at a hearing other than the trial, evidence is given in writing, any party may apply to the court for permission to cross-examine the person giving the evidence.

(2)   If the court gives permission under paragraph (1) but the person in question does not attend as required by the order, his evidence may not be used unless the court gives permission.

32.8   FORM OF WITNESS STATEMENT

A witness statement must comply with the requirements set out in the relevant practice direction.

(Part 22 requires a witness statement to be verified by a statement of truth)

32.9   WITNESS SUMMARIES

(1)   A party who—
    (a)   is required to serve a witness statement for use at trial; but
    (b)   is unable to obtain one,
may apply, without notice, for permission to serve a witness summary instead.

(2)   A witness summary is a summary of—
    (a)   the evidence, if known, which would otherwise be included in a witness statement; or
    (b)   if the evidence is not known, the matters about which the party serving the witness summary proposes to question the witness.

(3)   Unless the court orders otherwise, a witness summary must include the name and address of the intended witness.

(4)   Unless the court orders otherwise, a witness summary must be served within the period in which a witness statement would have had to be served.

(5)   Where a party serves a witness summary, so far as is practicable rules 32.4 (requirement to serve witness statements for use at trial), 32.5(3) (amplifying witness statements), and 32.8 (form of witness statement) shall apply to the summary.

32.10   CONSEQUENCE OF FAILURE TO SERVE WITNESS STATEMENT OR SUMMARY

If a witness statement or a witness summary for use at trial is not served in respect of an intended witness within the time specified by the court, then the witness may not be called to give oral evidence unless the court gives permission.

32.11   CROSS-EXAMINATION ON A WITNESS STATEMENT

Where a witness is called to give evidence at trial, he may be cross-examined on his witness statement whether or not the statement or any part of it was referred to during the witness's evidence in chief.

32.12   USE OF WITNESS STATEMENTS FOR OTHER PURPOSES

(1)   Except as provided by this rule, a witness statement may be used only for the purpose of the proceedings in which it is served.

(2)   Paragraph (1) does not apply if and to the extent that—
    (a)   the witness gives consent in writing to some other use of it;
    (b)   the court gives permission for some other use; or
    (c)   the witness statement has been put in evidence at a hearing held in public.

32.13   AVAILABILITY OF WITNESS STATEMENTS FOR INSPECTION

(1)   A witness statement which stands as evidence in chief is open to inspection unless the court otherwise directs during the course of the trial.

(2)   Any person may ask for a direction that a witness statement is not open to inspection.

(3)   The court will not make a direction under paragraph (2) unless it is satisfied that a witness statement should not be open to inspection because of—
   (a)   the interests of justice;
   (b)   the public interest;
   (c)   the nature of any expert medical evidence in the statement;
   (d)   the nature of any confidential information (including information relating to personal financial matters) in the statement; or
   (e)   the need to protect the interests of any child or patient.
(4)   The court may exclude from inspection words or passages in the statement.

32.14   FALSE STATEMENTS
(1)   Proceedings for contempt of court may be brought against a person if he makes, or causes to be made, a false statement in a document verified by a statement of truth without an honest belief in its truth.
(Part 22 makes provision for a statement of truth)
(2)   Proceedings under this rule may be brought only—
   (a)   by the Attorney General; or
   (b)   with the permission of the court.

32.15   AFFIDAVIT EVIDENCE
(1)   Evidence must be given by affidavit instead of or in addition to a witness statement if this is required by the court, a provision contained in any other rule, a practice direction or any other enactment.
(2)   Nothing in these Rules prevents a witness giving evidence by affidavit at a hearing other than the trial if he chooses to do so in a case where paragraph (1) does not apply, but the party putting forward the affidavit may not recover the additional cost of making it from any other party unless the court orders otherwise.

32.16   FORM OF AFFIDAVIT
An affidavit must comply with the requirements set out in the relevant practice direction.

32.17   AFFIDAVIT MADE OUTSIDE THE JURISDICTION
A person may make an affidavit outside the jurisdiction in accordance with—
   (a)   this Part; or
   (b)   the law of the place where he makes the affidavit.

32.18   NOTICE TO ADMIT FACTS
(1)   A party may serve notice on another party requiring him to admit the facts, or the part of the case of the serving party, specified in the notice.
(2)   A notice to admit facts must be served no later than 21 days before the trial.
(3)   Where the other party makes any admission in response to the notice, the admission may be used against him only—
   (a)   in the proceedings in which the notice to admit is served; and
   (b)   by the party who served the notice.
(4)   The court may allow a party to amend or withdraw any admission made by him on such terms as it thinks just.

32.19   NOTICE TO ADMIT OR PRODUCE DOCUMENTS
(1)   A party shall be deemed to admit the authenticity of a document disclosed to him under Part 31 (disclosure and inspection of documents) unless he serves notice that he wishes the document to be proved at trial.
(2)   A notice to prove a document must be served—
   (a)   by the latest date for serving witness statements; or
   (b)   within 7 days of disclosure of the document,
whichever is later.

PD 32   PRACTICE DIRECTION — WRITTEN EVIDENCE
This practice direction supplements CPR Part 32

EVIDENCE IN GENERAL

1.1   Rule 32.2 sets out how evidence is to be given and facts are to be proved.

1.2   Evidence at a hearing other than the trial should normally be given by witness statement (see paragraph 17 onwards). However a witness may give evidence by affidavit if he wishes to do so (and see paragraph 1.4 below).

1.3   Statements of case (see paragraph 26 onwards) and application notices may also be used as evidence provided that their contents have been verified by a statement of truth.

(For information regarding evidence by deposition see Part 34 and PD 34)

1.4   Affidavits must be used as evidence in the following instances:

(1)   where sworn evidence is required by an enactment, statutory instrument, rule, order or practice direction,

(2)   in any application for a search order, a freezing injunction, or an order requiring an occupier to permit another to enter his land, and

(3)   in any application for an order against anyone for alleged contempt of court.

1.5   If a party believes that sworn evidence is required by a court in another jurisdiction for any purpose connected with the proceedings, he may apply to the court for a direction that evidence shall be given only by affidavit on any pre-trial applications.

1.6   The court may give a direction under rule 32.15 that evidence shall be given by affidavit instead of or in addition to a witness statement or statement of case:

(1)   on its own initiative, or

(2)   after any party has applied to the court for such a direction.

1.7   An affidavit, where referred to in the Civil Procedure Rules or a practice direction, also means an affirmation unless the context requires otherwise.

AFFIDAVITS

Deponent

2   A deponent is a person who gives evidence by affidavit or affirmation.

Heading

3.1   The affidavit should be headed with the title of the proceedings (see paragraph 4 of the practice direction supplementing Part 7 and paragraph 7 of the practice direction supplementing Part 20); where the proceedings are between several parties with the same status it is sufficient to identify the parties as follows:

	Number:
A.B. (and others)	Claimants/Applicants
C.D. (and others)	Defendants/Respondents
	(as appropriate)

3.2   At the top right hand corner of the first page (and on the backsheet) there should be clearly written:

(1)   the party on whose behalf it is made,

(2)   the initials and surname of the deponent,

(3)   the number of the affidavit in relation to that deponent,

(4)   the identifying initials and number of each exhibit referred to, and

(5)   the date sworn.

Body of affidavit

4.1   The affidavit must, if practicable, be in the deponent's own words, the affidavit should be expressed in the first person and the deponent should:

(1)   commence 'I (*full name*) of (*address*) state on oath ......',

(2)   if giving evidence in his professional, business or other occupational capacity, give the address at which he works in (1) above, the position he holds and the name of his firm or employer,

(3)   give his occupation or, if he has none, his description, and

(4)   state if he is a party to the proceedings or employed by a party to the proceedings, if it be the case.

4.2   An affidavit must indicate:

(1)   which of the statements in it are made from the deponent's own knowledge and which are matters of information or belief, and

(2)   the source for any matters of information or belief.

4.3   Where a deponent:

(1)   refers to an exhibit or exhibits, he should state 'there is now shown to me marked ". . ." the (*description of exhibit*)', and

(2)   makes more than one affidavit (to which there are exhibits) in the same proceedings, the numbering of the exhibits should run consecutively throughout and not start again with each affidavit.

Jurat

5.1   The jurat of an affidavit is a statement set out at the end of the document which authenticates the affidavit.

5.2   It must:

(1)   be signed by all deponents,

(2)   be completed and signed by the person before whom the affidavit was sworn whose name and qualification must be printed beneath his signature,

(3)   contain the full address of the person before whom the affidavit was sworn, and

(4)   follow immediately on from the text and not be put on a separate page.

Format of affidavits

6.1   An affidavit should:

(1)   be produced on durable quality A4 paper with a 3.5 cm margin,

(2)   be fully legible and should normally be typed on one side of the paper only,

(3)   where possible, be bound securely in a manner which would not hamper filing, or otherwise each page should be endorsed with the case number and should bear the initials of the deponent and of the person before whom it was sworn,

(4)   have the pages numbered consecutively as a separate document (or as one of several documents contained in a file),

(5)   be divided into numbered paragraphs,

(6)   have all numbers, including dates, expressed in figures, and

(7)   give the reference to any document or documents mentioned either in the margin or in bold text in the body of the affidavit.

6.2   It is usually convenient for an affidavit to follow the chronological sequence of events or matters dealt with; each paragraph of an affidavit should as far as possible be confined to a distinct portion of the subject.

Inability of deponent to read or sign affidavit

7.1   Where an affidavit is sworn by a person who is unable to read or sign it, the person before whom the affidavit is sworn must certify in the jurat that:

(1)   he read the affidavit to the deponent,

(2)   the deponent appeared to understand it, and

(3)   the deponent signed or made his mark, in his presence.

7.2   If that certificate is not included in the jurat, the affidavit may not be used in evidence unless the court is satisfied that it was read to the deponent and that he appeared to understand it. Two versions of the form of jurat with the certificate are set out at Annex 1 to this practice direction.

Alterations to affidavits

8.1   Any alteration to an affidavit must be initialled by both the deponent and the person before whom the affidavit was sworn.

8.2   An affidavit which contains an alteration that has not been initialled may be filed or used in evidence only with the permission of the court.

Who may administer oaths and take affidavits

9.1   Only the following may administer oaths and take affidavits:

(1)   Commissioners for oaths,

(2)   Practising solicitors,

(3)   other persons specified by statute,

(4)   certain officials of the Supreme Court,

(5)   a circuit judge or district judge,

(6)   any justice of the peace, and

(7)   certain officials of any county court appointed by the judge of that court for the purpose.

9.2   An affidavit must be sworn before a person independent of the parties or their representatives.

Filing of Affidavits

10.1   If the court directs that an affidavit is to be filed, it must be filed in the court or Division, or Office or Registry of the court or Division where the action in which it was or is to be used, is proceeding or will proceed.

10.2   Where an affidavit is in a foreign language:

(1)   the party wishing to rely on it—

(a)   must have it translated, and

(b)   must file the foreign language affidavit with the court, and

(2)   the translator must make and file with the court an affidavit verifying the translation and exhibiting both the translation and a copy of the foreign language affidavit.

EXHIBITS

Manner of exhibiting documents

11.1   A document used in conjunction with an affidavit should be:

(1)   produced to and verified by the deponent, and remain separate from the affidavit, and

(2)   identified by a declaration of the person before whom the affidavit was sworn.

11.2   The declaration should be headed with the name of the proceedings in the same way as the affidavit.

11.3   The first page of each exhibit should be marked:

(1)   as in paragraph 3.2 above, and

(2)   with the exhibit mark referred to in the affidavit.

Letters

12.1   Copies of individual letters should be collected together and exhibited in a bundle or bundles. They should be arranged in chronological order with the earliest at the top, and firmly secured.

12.2   When a bundle of correspondence is exhibited, the exhibit should have a front page attached stating that the bundle consists of original letters and copies. They should be arranged and secured as above and numbered consecutively.

Other documents   •

13.1   Photocopies instead of original documents may be exhibited provided the originals are made available for inspection by the other parties before the hearing and by the judge at the hearing.

13.2   Court documents must not be exhibited (official copies of such documents prove themselves).

13.3   Where an exhibit contains more than one document, a front page should be attached setting out a list of the documents contained in the exhibit; the list should contain the dates of the documents.

Exhibits other than documents

14.1   Items other than documents should be clearly marked with an exhibit number or letter in such a manner that the mark cannot become detached from the exhibit.

14.2   Small items may be placed in a container and the container appropriately marked.

General provisions

15.1   Where an exhibit contains more than one document:

(1)   the bundle should not be stapled but should be securely fastened in a way that does not hinder the reading of the documents, and

(2)   the pages should be numbered consecutively at bottom centre.

15.2   Every page of an exhibit should be clearly legible; typed copies of illegible documents should be included, paginated with 'a' numbers.

15.3   Where affidavits and exhibits have become numerous, they should be put into separate bundles and the pages numbered consecutively throughout.

15.4   Where on account of their bulk the service of exhibits or copies of exhibits on the other parties would be difficult or impracticable, the directions of the court should be sought as to arrangements for bringing the exhibits to the attention of the other parties and as to their custody pending trial.

Affirmations

16   All provisions in this or any other practice direction relating to affidavits apply to affirmations with the following exceptions:

(1)   the deponent should commence 'I (*name*) of (*address*) do solemnly and sincerely affirm ....', and

(2)   in the jurat the word 'sworn' is replaced by the word 'affirmed'.

WITNESS STATEMENTS

Heading

17.1   The witness statement should be headed with the title of the proceedings (see paragraph 4 of the practice direction supplementing Part 7 and paragraph 7 of the practice direction supplementing Part 20); where the proceedings are between several parties with the same status it is sufficient to identify the parties as follows:

	Number:
A.B. (and others)	Claimants/Applicants
C.D. (and others)	Defendants/Respondents
	(as appropriate)

17.2   At the top right hand corner of the first page there should be clearly written:

(1)   the party on whose behalf it is made,

(2)   the initials and surname of the witness,

(3)   the number of the statement in relation to that witness,

(4)   the identifying initials and number of each exhibit referred to, and

(5)   the date the statement was made.

Body of witness statement

18.1   The witness statement must, if practicable, be in the intended witness's own words, the statement should be expressed in the first person and should also state:

(1)   the full name of the witness,

(2) his place of residence or, if he is making the statement in his professional, business or other occupational capacity, the address at which he works, the position he holds and the name of his firm or employer,

(3) his occupation, or if he has none, his description, and

(4) the fact that he is a party to the proceedings or is the employee of such a party if it be the case.

18.2 A witness statement must indicate:

(1) which of the statements in it are made from the witness's own knowledge and which are matters of information or belief, and

(2) the source for any matters of information or belief.

18.3 An exhibit used in conjunction with a witness statement should be verified and identified by the witness and remain separate from the witness statement.

18.4 Where a witness refers to an exhibit or exhibits, he should state 'I refer to the (*description of exhibit*) marked ". . .".'.

18.5 The provisions of paragraphs 11.3 to 15.4 (exhibits) apply similarly to witness statements as they do to affidavits.

18.6 Where a witness makes more than one witness statement to which there are exhibits, in the same proceedings, the numbering of the exhibits should run consecutively throughout and not start again with each witness statement.

Format of witness statement

19.1 A witness statement should:

(1) be produced on durable quality A4 paper with a 3.5 cm margin,

(2) be fully legible and should normally be typed on one side of the paper only,

(3) where possible, be bound securely in a manner which would not hamper filing, or otherwise each page should be endorsed with the case number and should bear the initials of the witness,

(4) have the pages numbered consecutively as a separate statement (or as one of several statements contained in a file),

(5) be divided into numbered paragraphs,

(6) have all numbers, including dates, expressed in figures, and

(7) give the reference to any document or documents mentioned either in the margin or in bold text in the body of the statement.

19.2 It is usually convenient for a witness statement to follow the chronological sequence of the events or matters dealt with, each paragraph of a witness statement should as far as possible be confined to a distinct portion of the subject.

Statement of truth

20.1 A witness statement is the equivalent of the oral evidence which that witness would, if called, give in evidence; it must include a statement by the intended witness that he believes the facts in it are true.

20.2 To verify a witness statement the statement of truth is as follows:

'I believe that the facts stated in this witness statement are true'

20.3 Attention is drawn to rule 32.14 which sets out the consequences of verifying a witness statement containing a false statement without an honest belief in its truth.

Inability of witness to read or sign statement

21.1 Where a witness statement is made by a person who is unable to read or sign the witness statement, it must contain a certificate made by an authorised person.

21.2 An authorised person is a person able to administer oaths and take affidavits but need not be independent of the parties or their representatives.

21.3 The authorised person must certify:

(1) that the witness statement has been read to the witness,

(2) that the witness appeared to understand it and approved its content as accurate,

(3)   that the declaration of truth has been read to the witness,

(4) that the witness appeared to understand the declaration and the consequences of making a false witness statement, and

(5)   that the witness signed or made his mark in the presence of the authorised person.

21.4   The form of the certificate is set out at Annex 2 to this practice direction.

Alterations to witness statements

22.1   Any alteration to a witness statement must be initialled by the person making the statement or by the authorised person where appropriate (see paragraph 21).

22.2   A witness statement which contains an alteration that has not been initialled may be used in evidence only with the permission of the court.

Filing of witness statements

23.1   If the court directs that a witness statement is to be filed, it must be filed in the court or Division, or Office or Registry of the court or Division where the action in which it was or is to be used, is proceeding or will proceed.

23.2   Where the court has directed that a witness statement in a foreign language is to be filed:

(1)   the party wishing to rely on it must—

(a)   have it translated, and

(b)   file the foreign language witness statement with the court, and

(2)   the translator must make and file with the court an affidavit verifying the translation and exhibiting both the translation and a copy of the foreign language witness statement.

Certificate of court officer

24.1   Where the court has ordered that a witness statement is not to be open to inspection by the public or that words or passages in the statement are not to be open to inspection the court officer will so certify on the statement and make any deletions directed by the court under rule 32.13(4).

Defects in affidavits, witness statements and exhibits

25.1   Where:

(1)   an affidavit,

(2)   a witness statement, or

(3)   an exhibit to either an affidavit or a witness statement,

does not comply with Part 32 or this practice direction in relation to its form, the court may refuse to admit it as evidence and may refuse to allow the costs arising from its preparation.

25.2   Permission to file a defective affidavit or witness statement or to use a defective exhibit may be obtained from a judge in the court where the case is proceeding.

STATEMENTS OF CASE

26.1   A statement of case may be used as evidence in an interim application provided it is verified by a statement of truth.

26.2   To verify a statement of case the statement of truth should be set out as follows: '[I believe] [the (*party on whose behalf the statement of case is being signed*) believes] that the facts stated in the statement of case are true'.

26.3   Attention is drawn to rule 32.14 which sets out the consequences of verifying a witness statement containing a false statement without an honest belief in its truth.

(For information regarding statements of truth see Part 22 and the practice direction which supplements it.)

(Practice directions supplementing Parts 7, 9 and 17 provide further information concerning statements of case.)

ANNEX 1

CERTIFICATE TO BE USED WHERE A DEPONENT TO AN AFFIDAVIT IS UNABLE TO READ OR SIGN IT

Sworn at ...... this ...... day of ...... Before me, I having first read over the contents of this affidavit to the deponent [*if there are exhibits, add* 'and explained the nature and effect of the exhibits referred to in it'] who appeared to understand it and approved its content as accurate, and made his mark on the affidavit in my presence.

Or, (after, *Before me*) the witness to the mark of the deponent having been first sworn that he had read over etc. (*as above*) and that he saw him make his mark on the affidavit. (*Witness must sign*).

CERTIFICATE TO BE USED WHERE A DEPONENT TO AN AFFIRMATION IS UNABLE TO READ OR SIGN IT

Affirmed at ...... this ...... day of ...... Before me, I having first read over the contents of this affirmation to the deponent [*if there are exhibits, add* 'and explained the nature and effect of the exhibits referred to in it'] who appeared to understand it and approved its content as accurate, and made his mark on the affirmation in my presence.

Or, (after, *Before me*) the witness to the mark of the deponent having been first sworn that he had read over etc. (*as above*) and that he saw him make his mark on the affirmation. (*Witness must sign*).

ANNEX 2

CERTIFICATE TO BE USED WHERE A WITNESS IS UNABLE TO READ OR SIGN A WITNESS STATEMENT

I certify that I [*name and address of authorised person*] have read over the contents of this witness statement and the declaration of truth to the witness [*if there are exhibits, add* 'and explained the nature and effect of the exhibits referred to in it'] who appeared to understand (a) the statement and approved its content as accurate and (b) the declaration of truth and the consequences of making a false witness statement, and made his mark in my presence.

CPR PART 33   MISCELLANEOUS RULES ABOUT EVIDENCE

CONTENTS OF THIS PART

33.1 INTRODUCTORY
In this Part—
(a) 'hearsay' means a statement made, otherwise than by a person while giving oral evidence in proceedings, which is tendered as evidence of the matters stated; and
(b) references to hearsay include hearsay of whatever degree.

33.2 NOTICE OF INTENTION TO RELY ON HEARSAY EVIDENCE
(1) Where a party intends to rely on hearsay evidence at trial and either—
  (a) that evidence is to be given by a witness giving oral evidence; or
  (b) that evidence is contained in a witness statement of a person who is not being called to give oral evidence;
that party complies with section 2(1)(a) of the Civil Evidence Act 1995 by serving a witness statement on the other parties in accordance with the court's order.
(2) Where paragraph (1)(b) applies, the party intending to rely on the hearsay evidence must, when he serves the witness statement—
  (a) inform the other parties that the witness is not being called to give oral evidence; and
  (b) give the reason why the witness will not be called.
(3) In all other cases where a party intends to rely on hearsay evidence at trial, that party complies with section 2(1)(a) of the Civil Evidence Act 1995 by serving a notice on the other parties which—
  (a) identifies the hearsay evidence;
  (b) states that the party serving the notice proposes to rely on the hearsay evidence at trial; and
  (c) gives the reason why the witness will not be called.
(4) The party proposing to rely on the hearsay evidence must—
  (a) serve the notice no later than the latest date for serving witness statements; and
  (b) if the hearsay evidence is to be in a document, supply a copy to any party who requests him to do so.

33.3 CIRCUMSTANCES IN WHICH NOTICE OF INTENTION TO RELY ON HEARSAY EVIDENCE IS NOT REQUIRED
Section 2(1) of the Civil Evidence Act 1995 (duty to give notice of intention to rely on hearsay evidence) does not apply—
  (a) to evidence at hearings other than trials;
  (aa) to an affidavit or witness statement which is to be used at trial but which does not contain hearsay evidence;
  (b) to a statement which a party to a probate action wishes to put in evidence and which is alleged to have been made by the person whose estate is the subject of the proceedings; or
  (c) where the requirement is excluded by a practice direction.

33.4 POWER TO CALL WITNESS FOR CROSS-EXAMINATION ON HEARSAY EVIDENCE
(1) Where a party—
  (a) proposes to rely on hearsay evidence; and
  (b) does not propose to call the person who made the original statement to give oral evidence,
the court may, on the application of any other party, permit that party to call the maker of the statement to be cross-examined on the contents of the statement.
(2) An application for permission to cross-examine under this rule must be made not more than 14 days after the day on which a notice of intention to rely on the hearsay evidence was served on the applicant.

33.5 CREDIBILITY
(1) Where a party—
  (a) proposes to rely on hearsay evidence; but
  (b) does not propose to call the person who made the original statement to give oral evidence; and

(c)   another party wishes to call evidence to attack the credibility of the person who made the statement,
the party who so wishes must give notice of his intention to the party who proposes to give the hearsay statement in evidence.

(2)   A party must give notice under paragraph (1) not more than 14 days after the day on which a hearsay notice relating to the hearsay evidence was served on him.

33.6   USE OF PLANS, PHOTOGRAPHS AND MODELS AS EVIDENCE

(1)   This rule applies to evidence (such as a plan, photograph or model) which is not—

(a)   contained in a witness statement, affidavit or expert's report;
(b)   to be given orally at trial; or
(c)   evidence of which prior notice must be given under rule 33.2.

(2)   This rule includes documents which may be received in evidence without further proof under section 9 of the Civil Evidence Act 1995.

(3)   Unless the court orders otherwise the evidence shall not be receivable at a trial unless the party intending to put it in evidence has given notice to the other parties in accordance with this rule.

(4)   Where the party intends to use the evidence as evidence of any fact then, except where paragraph (6) applies, he must give notice not later than the latest date for serving witness statements.

(5)   He must give notice at least 21 days before the hearing at which he proposes to put in the evidence, if—

(a)   there are not to be witness statements; or
(b)   he intends to put in the evidence solely in order to disprove an allegation made in a witness statement.

(6)   Where the evidence forms part of expert evidence, he must give notice when the expert's report is served on the other party.

(7)   Where the evidence is being produced to the court for any reason other than as part of factual or expert evidence, he must give notice at least 21 days before the hearing at which he proposes to put in the evidence.

(8)   Where a party has given notice that he intends to put in the evidence, he must give every other party an opportunity to inspect it and to agree to its admission without further proof.

33.7   EVIDENCE OF FINDING ON QUESTION OF FOREIGN LAW

(1)   This rule sets out the procedure which must be followed by a party who intends to put in evidence a finding on a question of foreign law by virtue of section 4(2) of the Civil Evidence Act 1972.

(2)   He must give any other party notice of his intention.

(3)   He must give the notice—

(a)   if there are to be witness statements, not later than the latest date for serving them; or
(b)   otherwise, not less than 21 days before the hearing at which he proposes to put the finding in evidence.

(4)   The notice must—

(a)   specify the question on which the finding was made; and
(b)   enclose a copy of a document where it is reported or recorded.

33.8   EVIDENCE OF CONSENT OF TRUSTEE TO ACT

A document purporting to contain the written consent of a person to act as trustee and to bear his signature verified by some other person is evidence of such consent.

CPR PART 34   DEPOSITIONS AND COURT ATTENDANCE BY WITNESSES

CONTENTS OF THIS PART

34.1   SCOPE OF THIS PART

(1)   This Part provides—

(a)   for the circumstances in which a person may be required to attend court to give evidence or to produce a document; and

(b)   for a party to obtain evidence before a hearing to be used at the hearing.

(2)   In this Part, reference to a hearing includes a reference to the trial.

34.2   WITNESS SUMMONSES

(1)   A witness summons is a document issued by the court requiring a witness to—

(a)   attend court to give evidence; or

(b)   produce documents to the court.

(2)   A witness summons must be in the relevant practice form.

(3)   There must be a separate witness summons for each witness.

(4)   A witness summons may require a witness to produce documents to the court either—

(a)   on the date fixed for a hearing; or

(b)   on such date as the court may direct.

(5)   The only documents that a summons under this rule can require a person to produce before a hearing are documents which that person could be required to produce at the hearing.

34.3   ISSUE OF A WITNESS SUMMONS

(1)   A witness summons is issued on the date entered on the summons by the court.

(2)   A party must obtain permission from the court where he wishes to—

(a)   have a summons issued less than 7 days before the date of the trial;

(b)   have a summons issued for a witness to attend court to give evidence or to produce documents on any date except the date fixed for the trial; or

(c)   have a summons issued for a witness to attend court to give evidence or to produce documents at any hearing except the trial.

(3)   A witness summons must be issued by—

(a)   the court where the case is proceeding; or

(b)   the court where the hearing in question will be held.

(4)   The court may set aside$^{(GL)}$ or vary a witness summons issued under this rule.

34.4   WITNESS SUMMONS IN AID OF INFERIOR COURT OR OF TRIBUNAL

(1)   The court may issue a witness summons in aid of an inferior court or of a tribunal.

(2)   The court which issued the witness summons under this rule may set it aside.

(3)   In this rule, 'inferior court or tribunal' means any court or tribunal that does not have power to issue a witness summons in relation to proceedings before it.

34.5   TIME FOR SERVING A WITNESS SUMMONS

(1)   The general rule is that a witness summons is binding if it is served at least 7 days before the date on which the witness is required to attend before the court or tribunal.

(2)   The court may direct that a witness summons shall be binding although it will be served less than 7 days before the date on which the witness is required to attend before the court or tribunal.

(3)   A witness summons which is—
(a)   served in accordance with this rule; and
(b)   requires the witness to attend court to give evidence,
is binding until the conclusion of the hearing at which the attendance of the witness is required.

34.6   WHO IS TO SERVE A WITNESS SUMMONS

(1)   A witness summons is to be served by the court unless the party on whose behalf it is issued indicates in writing, when he asks the court to issue the summons, that he wishes to serve it himself.

(2)   Where the court is to serve the witness summons, the party on whose behalf it is issued must deposit, in the court office, the money to be paid or offered to the witness under rule 34.7.

34.7   RIGHT OF WITNESS TO TRAVELLING EXPENSES AND COMPENSATION FOR LOSS OF TIME

At the time of service of a witness summons the witness must be offered or paid—
(a)   a sum reasonably sufficient to cover his expenses in travelling to and from the court; and
(b)   such sum by way of compensation for loss of time as may be specified in the relevant practice direction.

34.8   EVIDENCE BY DEPOSITION

(1)   A party may apply for an order for a person to be examined before the hearing takes place.

(2)   A person from whom evidence is to be obtained following an order under this rule is referred to as a 'deponent' and the evidence is referred to as a 'deposition'.

(3)   An order under this rule shall be for a deponent to be examined on oath before—
(a)   a judge;
(b)   an examiner of the court; or
(c)   such other person as the court appoints.
(Rule 34.15 makes provision for the appointment of examiners of the court)

(4)   The order may require the production of any document which the court considers is necessary for the purposes of the examination.

(5)   The order must state the date, time and place of the examination.

(6)   At the time of service of the order the deponent must be offered or paid—
(a)   a sum reasonably sufficient to cover his expenses in travelling to and from the place of examination; and

(b)   such sum by way of compensation for loss of time as may be specified in the relevant practice direction.

(7)   Where the court makes an order for a deposition to be taken, it may also order the party who obtained the order to serve a witness statement or witness summary in relation to the evidence to be given by the person to be examined.

(Part 32 contains the general rules about witness statements and witness summaries)

34.9   CONDUCT OF EXAMINATION

(1)   Subject to any directions contained in the order for examination, the examination must be conducted in the same way as if the witness were giving evidence at a trial.

(2)   If all the parties are present, the examiner may conduct the examination of a person not named in the order for examination if all the parties and the person to be examined consent.

(3)   The examiner may conduct the examination in private if he considers it appropriate to do so.

(4)   The examiner must ensure that the evidence given by the witness is recorded in full.

(5)   The examiner must send a copy of the deposition—

(a)   to the person who obtained the order for the examination of the witness; and

(b)   to the court where the case is proceeding.

(6)   The party who obtained the order must send each of the other parties a copy of the deposition which he receives from the examiner.

34.10   ENFORCING ATTENDANCE OF WITNESS

(1)   If a person served with an order to attend before an examiner—

(a)   fails to attend; or

(b)   refuses to be sworn for the purpose of the examination or to answer any lawful question or produce any document at the examination,

a certificate of his failure or refusal, signed by the examiner, must be filed by the party requiring the deposition.

(2)   On the certificate being filed, the party requiring the deposition may apply to the court for an order requiring that person to attend or to be sworn or to answer any question or produce any document, as the case may be.

(3)   An application for an order under this rule may be made without notice.

(4)   The court may order the person against whom an order is made under this rule to pay any costs resulting from his failure or refusal.

34.11   USE OF DEPOSITION AT A HEARING

(1)   A deposition ordered under rule 34.8 may be given in evidence at a hearing unless the court orders otherwise.

(2)   A party intending to put in evidence a deposition at a hearing must serve notice of his intention to do so on every other party.

(3)   He must serve the notice at least 21 days before the day fixed for the hearing.

(4)   The court may require a deponent to attend the hearing and give evidence orally.

(5)   Where a deposition is given in evidence at trial, it shall be treated as if it were a witness statement for the purposes of rule 32.13 (availability of witness statements for inspection).

34.12   RESTRICTIONS ON SUBSEQUENT USE OF DEPOSITION TAKEN FOR THE PURPOSE OF ANY HEARING EXCEPT THE TRIAL

(1)   Where the court orders a party to be examined about his or any other assets for the purpose of any hearing except the trial, the deposition may be used only for the purpose of the proceedings in which the order was made.

(2)   However, it may be used for some other purpose—
    (a)   by the party who was examined;
    (b)   if the party who was examined agrees; or
    (c)   if the court gives permission.

34.13   WHERE A PERSON TO BE EXAMINED IS OUT OF THE JURISDICTION — LETTER OF REQUEST

(1)   Where a party wishes to take a deposition from a person outside the jurisdiction, the High Court may order the issue of a letter of request to the judicial authorities of the country in which the proposed deponent is.

(2)   A letter of request is a request to a judicial authority to take the evidence of that person, or arrange for it to be taken.

(3)   The High Court may make an order under this rule in relation to county court proceedings.

(4)   If the government of a country allows a person appointed by the High Court to examine a person in that country, the High Court may make an order appointing a special examiner for that purpose.

(5)   A person may be examined under this rule on oath or affirmation or in accordance with any procedure permitted in the country in which the examination is to take place.

(6)   If the High Court makes an order for the issue of a letter of request, the party who sought the order must file—
    (a)   the following documents and, except where paragraph (7) applies, a translation of them—
        (i)   a draft letter of request;
        (ii)   a statement of the issues relevant to the proceedings;
        (iii)   a list of questions or the subject matter of questions to be put to the person to be examined; and
    (b)   an undertaking to be responsible for the Secretary of State's expenses.

(7)   There is no need to file a translation if—
    (a)   English is one of the official languages of the country where the examination is to take place; or
    (b)   a practice direction has specified that country as a country where no translation is necessary.

34.14   FEES AND EXPENSES OF EXAMINER OF THE COURT

(1)   An examiner of the court may charge a fee for the examination.

(2)   He need not send the deposition to the court unless the fee is paid.

(3)   The examiner's fees and expenses must be paid by the party who obtained the order for examination.

(4)   If the fees and expenses due to an examiner are not paid within a reasonable time, he may report that fact to the court.

(5)   The court may order the party who obtained the order for examination to deposit in the court office a specified sum in respect of the examiner's fees and, where it does so, the examiner will not be asked to act until the sum has been deposited.

(6)   An order under this rule does not affect any decision as to the party who is ultimately to bear the costs of the examination.

34.15   EXAMINERS OF THE COURT

(1)   The Lord Chancellor shall appoint persons to be examiners of the court.

(2)   The persons appointed shall be barristers or solicitor-advocates who have been practising for a period of not less than three years.

(3)   The Lord Chancellor may revoke an appointment at any time.

PD 34 PRACTICE DIRECTION — DEPOSITIONS AND COURT ATTENDANCE BY WITNESSES
This practice direction supplements CPR Part 34

WITNESS SUMMONSES

Issue of witness summons
1.1   A witness summons may require a witness to:
(1)   attend court to give evidence,
(2)   produce documents to the court, or
(3)   both,
on either a date fixed for the hearing or such date as the court may direct.
1.2   Two copies of the witness summons should be filed with the court for sealing, one of which will be retained on the court file.
1.3   A mistake in the name or address of a person named in a witness summons may be corrected if the summons has not been served.
1.4   The corrected summons must be re-sealed by the court and marked 'Amended and Re-Sealed'.

Witness summons issued in aid of an inferior court or tribunal
2.1   A witness summons may be issued in the High Court or a county court in aid of a court or tribunal which does not have the power to issue a witness summons in relation to the proceedings before it.
2.2   A witness summons referred to in paragraph 2.1 may be set aside by the court which issued it.
2.3   An application to set aside a witness summons referred to in paragraph 2.1 will be heard:
(1)   in the High Court by a Master at the Royal Courts of Justice or by a district judge in a District Registry, and
(2)   in a county court by a district judge.
2.4   Unless the court otherwise directs, the applicant must give at least 2 days' notice to the party who issued the witness summons of the application, which will normally be dealt with at a hearing.

Travelling expenses and compensation for loss of time
3.1   When a witness is served with a witness summons he must be offered a sum to cover his travelling expenses to and from the court and compensation for his loss of time.
3.2   If the witness summons is to be served by the court, the party issuing the summons must deposit with the court:
(1)   a sum sufficient to pay for the witness's expenses in travelling to the court and in returning to his home or place of work, and
(2)   a sum in respect of the period during which earnings or benefit are lost, or such lesser sum as it may be proved that the witness will lose as a result of his attendance at court in answer to the witness summons.
3.3   The sum referred to in 3.2(2) is to be based on the sums payable to witnesses attending the Crown Court.
3.4   Where the party issuing the witness summons wishes to serve it himself, he must:
(1)   notify the court in writing that he wishes to do so, and
(2)   at the time of service offer the witness the sums mentioned in paragraph 3.2 above.

DEPOSITIONS

To be taken in England and Wales for use as evidence in proceedings in courts in England and Wales
4.1   A party may apply for an order for a person to be examined on oath before:
(1)   a judge,
(2)   an examiner of the court, or
(3)   such other person as the court may appoint.
4.2   The party who obtains an order for the examination of a deponent before an examiner of the court must:
(1)   apply to the Foreign Process Section of the Masters' Secretary's Department at the Royal Courts of Justice for the allocation of an examiner,
(2)   when allocated, provide the examiner with copies of all documents in the proceedings necessary to inform the examiner of the issues, and
(3)   pay the deponent a sum to cover his travelling expenses to and from the examination and compensation for his loss of time.
4.3   In ensuring that the deponent's evidence is recorded in full, the court or the examiner may permit it to be recorded on audiotape or videotape, but the deposition must always be recorded in writing by him or by a competent shorthand writer or stenographer.
4.4   If the deposition is not recorded word for word, it must contain, as nearly as may be, the statement of the deponent; the examiner may record word for word any particular questions and answers which appear to him to have special importance.
4.5   If a deponent objects to answering any question or where any objection is taken to any question, the examiner must:
(1)   record in the deposition or a document attached to it—
(a)   the question,
(b)   the nature of and grounds for the objection, and
(c)   any answer given, and
(2)   give his opinion as to the validity of the objection and must record it in the deposition or a document attached to it.
The court will decide as to the validity of the objection and any question of costs arising from it.
4.6   Documents and exhibits must:
(1)   have an identifying number or letter marked on them by the examiner, and
(2)   be preserved by the party or his legal representative who obtained the order for the examination, or as the court or the examiner may direct.
4.7   The examiner may put any question to the deponent as to:
(1)   the meaning of any of his answers, or
(2)   any matter arising in the course of the examination.
4.8   Where a deponent:
(1)   fails to attend the examination, or
(2)   refuses to:
(a)   be sworn, or
(b)   answer any lawful question, or
(c)   produce any document,
the examiner will sign a certificate of such failure or refusal and may include in his certificate any comment as to the conduct of the deponent or of any person attending the examination.
4.9   The party who obtained the order for the examination must file the certificate with the court and may apply for an order that the deponent attend for examination or as may be. The application may be made without notice.

4.10   The court will make such order on the application as it thinks fit including an order for the deponent to pay any costs resulting from his failure or refusal.

4.11   A deponent who wilfully refuses to obey an order made against him under Part 34 may be proceeded against for contempt of court.

4.12   A deposition must:

(1)   be signed by the examiner,

(2)   have any amendments to it initialled by the examiner and the deponent,

(3)   be endorsed by the examiner with—

(a)   a statement of the time occupied by the examination, and

(b)   a record of any refusal by the deponent to sign the deposition and of his reasons for not doing so, and

(4)   be sent by the examiner to the court where the proceedings are taking place for filing on the court file.

4.13   Rule 34.14 deals with the fees and expenses of an examiner.

Depositions to be taken abroad for use as evidence in proceedings before courts in England and Wales

5.1   Where a party wishes to take a deposition from a person outside the jurisdiction, the High Court may order the issue of a letter of request to the judicial authorities of the country in which the proposed deponent is.

5.2   An application for an order referred to in paragraph 5.1 should be made by application notice in accordance with Part 23.

5.3   The documents which a party applying for an order for the issue of a letter of request must file with his application notice are set out in rule 34.13(6). They are as follows:

(1)   a draft letter of request is set out in Annex A to this practice direction,

(2)   a statement of the issues relevant to the proceedings,

(3)   a list of questions or the subject matter of questions to be put to the proposed deponent,

(4)   a translation of the documents in (1), (2) and (3) above unless the proposed deponent is in a country—

(a)   of which English is one of the official languages, or

(b)   listed at Annex B to this practice direction, unless the particular circumstances of the case require a translation,

(5)   an undertaking to be responsible for the expenses of the Secretary of State, and

(6)   a draft order.

5.4   The above documents should be filed with the Masters' Secretary in Room E214, Royal Courts of Justice, Strand, London WC2A 2LL.

5.5   The application will be dealt with by the Senior Master of the Queen's Bench Division of the High Court who will, if appropriate, sign the letter of request.

5.6   Attention is drawn to the provisions of rule 23.10 (application to vary or discharge an order made without notice).

5.7   If parties are in doubt as to whether a translation under paragraph 5.3(4) above is required, they should seek guidance from the Foreign Process Section of the Masters' Secretary's Department.

5.8   A special examiner appointed under rule 34.13(4) may be the British Consul or the Consul-General or his deputy in the country where the evidence is to be taken if:

(1)   there is in respect of that country a Civil Procedure Convention providing for the taking of evidence in that country for the assistance of proceedings in the High Court or other court in this country, or

(2)   with the consent of the Secretary of State.

5.9   The provisions of paragraphs 4.1 to 4.12 above apply to the depositions referred to in this paragraph.

Depositions to be taken in England and Wales for use as evidence in proceedings before courts abroad pursuant to letters of request

6.1   RSC, ord. 70 in CPR, sch. 1, relates to obtaining evidence for foreign courts and should be read in conjunction with this part of the practice direction.

6.2   The Evidence (Proceedings in Other Jurisdictions) Act 1975 applies to these depositions.

6.3   Where a foreign court sends a letter of request under which it is proposed that an application to give effect to the request be made by an agent in England or Wales of a party to the foreign proceedings, the application should be made by an application notice (see CPR, Part 23) and should be supported by a witness statement or affidavit exhibiting:

(1)   the letter of request;
(2)   a statement of the issues relevant to the proceedings;
(3)   a list of questions or the subject matter of questions to be put to the proposed deponent;
(4)   a translation of the documents in (1), (2) and (3) above if necessary; and
(5)   a draft order.

6.4   Where the application to give effect to the request is made by the Treasury Solicitor (see RSC, ord. 70, r. 3 in CPR, sch. 1), he must provide to the court:

(1)   a statement of the issues relevant to the proceedings;
(2)   a list of questions or the subject matter of questions to be put to the proposed deponent;
(3)   a translation of:
   (a)   the documents in (1) and (2) above and
   (b)   the letter of request, if necessary; and
(4)   a draft order.

6.5   The order for the deponent to attend and be examined together with the evidence upon which the order was made must be served on the deponent.

6.6   Attention is drawn to the provisions of r. 23.10 (application to vary or discharge an order made without notice).

6.7   Arrangements for the examination to take place at a specified time and place before an examiner of the court or such other person as the court may appoint shall be made by the applicant for the order (i.e. the agent referred to in para. 6.3 or the Treasury Solicitor) and approved by the Senior Master.

6.8   The provisions of paragraphs 4.2 to 4.12 apply to the depositions referred to in this paragraph, except that the examiner must send the deposition to the Senior Master. (For further information about evidence see Part 32 and the practice direction which supplements it)

ANNEX A

DRAFT LETTER OF REQUEST
To the Competent Judicial Authority of
in the   of
I [*name*] Senior Master of the Queen's Bench Division of the Supreme Court of England and Wales respectfully request the assistance of your court with regard to the following matters.

1.   A claim is now pending in the   Division of the High Court of Justice in England and Wales entitled as follows
[*set out full title and claim number*]
in which [*name*] of [*address*] is the claimant and [*name*] of [*address*] is the defendant.

2. The names and addresses of the representatives or agents of [*set out names and addresses of representatives of the parties*].
3. The claim by the claimant is for:—
    (a) [*set out the nature of the claim*]
    (b) [*the relief sought, and*]
    (c) [*a summary of the facts.*]
4. It is necessary for the purposes of justice and for the due determination of the matters in dispute between the parties that you cause the following witnesses, who are resident within your jurisdiction, to be examined. The names and addresses of the witnesses are as follows:—
5. The witnesses should be examined on oath or if that is not possible within your laws or is impossible of performance by reason of the internal practice and procedure of your court or by reason of practical difficulties, they should be examined in accordance with whatever procedure your laws provide for in these matters.
6. Either/
The witnesses should be examined in accordance with the list of questions annexed hereto.
Or/
The witnesses should be examined regarding [*set out full details of evidence sought*]
N.B. Where the witness is required to produce documents, these should be clearly identified.
7. I would ask that you cause me, or the agents of the parties (if appointed), to be informed of the date and place where the examination is to take place.
8. Finally, I request that you will cause the evidence of the said witnesses to be reduced into writing and all documents produced on such examinations to be duly marked for identification and that you will further be pleased to authenticate such examinations by the seal of your court or in such other way as is in accordance with your procedure and return the written evidence and documents produced to me addressed as follows:—
Senior Master of the Queen's Bench Division
Royal Courts of Justice
Strand
London WC2A 2LL
England

ANNEX B

Countries where the translation referred to in paragraph 5.3(4) above should not be required:
Australia
Canada (other than Quebec)
Holland
New Zealand
The United States of America

INDEX

BLACKSTONE'S STATUTES

TITLES IN THE SERIES